CAPTAIN'S LOGS

THE COMPLETE TREK VOYAGES

By Edward Gross & Mark A. Altman

B◆XTREE

••••
Acknowledgements

For taking the time to be interviewed over the years for this book, we'd like to thank the following people in their "order of appearance": Robert Justman, Joseph Stefano, Jerry Sohl, James Burns, Dorothy Fontana, Oscar Katz, Leonard Nimoy, Robert Butler, Stephen Kandel, William Shatner, James Goldstone, Samuel Peeples, James Doohan, George Takei, DeForest Kelley, Nichelle Nichols, John D.F. Black, Joseph Pevney, Marc Daniels, Harve Bennett, Glen Larson, David Gerrold, Steven Carabatsos, George Clayton Johnson, Gary Lockwood, Adrian Spies, Vincent McEveety, Joseph Sargent, Paul Schneider, Oliver Crawford, Michael O'Herlihy, Carey Wilbur, Ricardo Montalban, Ralph Senensky, Lester Colodny, Walter Koenig, Norman Spinrad, William Campbell, John Meredyth Lucas, Jackie Fernandez, Gilbert Ralston, Jerome Bixby, David P. Harmon, Art Wallace, Margaret Armen, James Komack, Fred Freiberger, Judy Burns, Arthur Heinemann, Richard Colla, Jon Povill, Allan Scott, Robert Goodwin, Harold Livingston, Joseph Jennings, Bob Collins, David Gautreaux, Larry Alexander, Worley Thorne, Robert Wise, Alan Dean Foster, Dennis Clark, Robert Sallin, Mike Minor, Jack Sowards, Nicholas Meyer, Robin Curtis, Steve Meerson, Peter Krikes, David Loughery, Ralph Winter, Mark Rosenthal, Dennis Martin Flinn, Cliff Eidelman, Steven Charles Jaffe, Kim Cattrall, Rick Berman, Michael Dorn, Bob Lewin, Herman Zimmerman, Jonathan Frakes, Herb Wright, Corey Allen, Paul Lynch, Maurice Hurley, Katharyn Powers, Michael Baron, Richard Krzemien, Michael Reaves, Rob Bowman, Cliff Bole, Patrick Stewart, Tracy Torme, Joseph Scanlan, Hannah Louise Shearer, Gates McFadden, Marina Sirtis, Melinda Snodgrass, Dennis Russell Bailey, Winrich Kolbe, Robert Scheerer, Robert Iscove, David Livingston, Les Landau, Michael Piller, Ira Steven Behr, Ron Moore, Peter Alan Fields, David Carson, Timothy Bond, Chip Chalmers, Jennifer Hetrick, Lisa Wilke, David Bischoff, Susan Sackett, Elizabeth Dennehy, Jeri Taylor, Larry Carroll, David Carren, Marc Scott Zicree, Rob Legato, Andreas Katsulas, Colm Meaney, Brannon Braga, Marvin Rush, Brent Spiner, Michelle Forbes, Grant Rosenberg, Patti Yatskue, Avery Brooks, Rene Auberjonois, Siddig El Fadil, Terry Farrell, Armin Shimerman, Nana Visitor and Bob Blackman.

••••
Book design by Paul Nicosia
••••

First published in the UK 1993
by BOXTREE LIMITED, Broadwall House
21 Broadwall, London SE1 9PL

First published in the USA 1993 by Image Publishing

10 9 8 7 6 5

This publication is not licensed by, nor is Boxtree or Image Publishing affiliated with, Paramount Pictures. This is a scholarly work intended to explore the evolution of *Star Trek* over the past 29 years.

No photos appearing in this book are copyright Paramount Pictures.

Cover Photo Credits: Patrick Stewart copyright © Crosby/Shooting Star; William Shatner copyright © Gene Trindl/Shooting Star; Avery Brooks copyright © Berliner/Gamma Liaison.

Some photographs courtesy Foto Fantasies

ISBN: 1 85283 899 X

Printed in Finland by
Werner Söderström Oy

A catalogue record for this book is available from The British Library.

••CONTENTS••

••••

CAPTAIN'S LOGS: AN INTRODUCTION

Captain's Logs is the definitive chronicling of the voyages of the Starship Enterprise, and more than any other book we've collaborated on, this tome is written for us as well as the many readers who will hopefully lie dog eared copies on their shelves for many years to come.

The fact is that there never has been a book like *Captain's Logs*, nor has anything approximating a compendium of this sort ever been assembled. Books have dealt with the *Star Trek* mythos in their separate component parts; *Trek '66* (or *Trek Classic*, as it's fondly, if not reverently, referred to), the so-called Lost Years, the Animated Series, the Movies and, of course, *The Next Generation*.

Our feeling, though, was that *Star Trek* is a single universe with continuity stretching from the original series through its latest incarnation, *Deep Space Nine*, so why hasn't anyone ever conceived a book that would trace *every* mission of the Enterprise? Well, quite frankly, it was a book we were dying to read and since no one else had done it, we've compiled many years worth of research to write that book. Although you won't find any of the comics or novels, this book does feature the animated series, which *Trek* scholars have debated as to whether it is relevant and part of the canon. We have decided to allow our readers to make that determination, without going into too much detail regarding the short-lived cartoon series, but still providing a complete list of credits and episode summaries.

We have compiled reams of interview transcripts and research done over the course of a decade regarding the *Star Trek* phenomenon. Ed Gross has penned a number of books devoted to the subject of the original *Trek*, the lost years, and *TNG* and has been a frequent contributor to *Starlog* Magazine. Mark Altman has also written extensively on the subject, covering both the movies and *The Next Generation*, at length, for *Cinefantastique* in his highly acclaimed year-end retrospectives. *USA Today* called him the leading authority on *Trek* in the 90's.

Both authors have been frustrated by their material turning up edited, abridged or plagiarized in other volumes and magazines dealing with the subject. Rather than paraphrase or read attributed copy, you will find the creators and cast of *Trek* speaking in their own words as taken directly from the authors' taped transcripts, about every trek through the 23rd and 24th century. Brief synopsis are provided, but what lies at the heart of this book is the behind-the-scenes anecdotes and recollections of the makers of *Trek* in producing a television and feature film classic.

Together the authors have assembled the ultimate *Trek* guidebook, following the missions of Kirk & Company for three years on NBC through the most recent adventures of Sisko and the crew of the Deep Space Nine station. We hope you enjoy reading this book as much as we enjoyed writing it. Enjoy!

Mark A. Altman

Edward Gross

April 1993

••••

CHAPTER ONE
The Trek Begins

It's been nearly three decades since the premiere of *Star Trek* on NBC and this show continues to fascinate us today. While many proponents of *The Next Generation* have decried the original show as "hokey" and "irrelevant", they fail to acknowledge that the series has entrenched itself as part of our cultural mythology and that without it there would be *no Star Trek: The Next Generation*..

Kirk, Spock and McCoy are as familiar to most Americans as Washington, Jefferson and Benjamin Franklin. And while the American manned space program has grown mired in entropy and most of today's school-children couldn't name the three astronauts who first set down on the lunar surface, these three fictional pioneers of the cosmos are revered not only by dedicated *Trek* fans, but by casual media watchers as well. *Star Trek* trivia can be found everywhere, ranging from Trivial Pursuit to *Jeopardy*, and more stand-up comedians have tried their hand at parodying William Shatner's gesticulating, staccato recitations of galactic law as Captain Kirk than they have most Presidents.

In fact, *Star Trek* lingo has popped up almost everywhere. The first Space Shuttle was renamed after the show's starship, the Enterprise; William Shatner spoofed his heroic Hornblower image in *Airplane II: The Sequel* and on *Saturday Night Live*; and such terms as "Beam Me Up, Scotty" and "energize" have appeared on T-shirts and become a part of the drug subculture often associated with crack-cocaine. Just say "He's Dead, Jim".

Since the original show's five year mission was abruptly canceled after three seasons on NBC, *Star Trek* has risen like the proverbial phoenix from the ashes throughout the subsequent decades, leaving those reports of its death, like those of its literary antecedent Samuel Clemens, to be greatly exaggerated. Fans' devoted ardor has built upon the foundation of the first 79 cherished

episodes, spawning a diverse array of products, ranging from homemade uniforms and costumes to homoerotic literature featuring liaisons between the original series' Captain Kirk and its alien Vulcan science officer, Mr. Spock.

In fact, although *Star Trek* is slowly disappearing from the airwaves to be replaced by its progeny, *The Next Generation*, in syndication, the show holds up remarkably well today. While some of the special effects and sets may look primitive, the stories are just as relevant and the characters no less compelling than they were in 1966.

Despite the vastly larger budgets of TNG, *Deep Space Nine* and the *Star Trek* features, the original *Star Trek* still plays extraordinarily well today because of the passion that is inherent in the show as instilled by its writers, producers and actors. Remarkably, the successors to the original show have carried on the tradition established by *Star Trek*'s original three year run and expanded upon many of the characters and storylines conveyed in such episodes as "Space Seed" (Khan in *Star Trek II*), "The Doomsday Machine" (Will Decker in *Star Trek: The Motion Picture* was the son of Commodore Matt Decker), "Journey To Babel" (Sarek returned as an aging diplomat in TNG'S "Sarek"), "The Naked Time" (remade as TNG's "Naked Now") and "Amok Time" (*STIII* reflected the seven year Vulcan mating cycle established here). Other mediums have also continued the voyages with novels from Pocket sequelizing "All Our Yesterdays" and "City on the Edge Of Forever" and DC Comics presenting remarkable follow-ups to "Mirror, Mirror" and "The Savage Curtain" / "Errand of Mercy."

For those who would quibble over whether the original show, TNG or *Deep Space Nine* is better, they're missing the point. All three shows are a triumph for televised science-fiction, proving that intelligent, thought provoking, character driven speculative fiction can be brought to the screen without catering to the so-called lowest common denominator.

Few, if any, science-fiction shows have reached the level of critical or popular recognition that *Star Trek* achieved and when one reflects back on

the first five year voyage of the Starship Enterprise, it's hard not to understand why today we refer to those three years of maiden missions as *Trek Classic*.

Yet despite the phenomenal success of *Star Trek*, science-fiction has been unable to find a home on network television, with such rare exceptions as *Beauty and the Beast* and *Quantum Leap*. Things do seem to be on the verge of changing, however, as witnessed by the debut of the Sci-Fi Channel on cable television systems around the country, such current genre fare as *Time Trax* and *Highlander* and forthcoming productions which include William Shatner's *TekWars* and Steven Spielberg's *SeaQuest*. Not to mention, naturally, *The Next Generation* or *Deep Space Nine*.

A distinct possibility for the failure of SF-TV in the past could very well be that the network executives couldn't understand the basic essence of a particular genre show, or they deemed it to be above the heads of the average television viewer.

"Too cerebral, and that's a direct quote," explains veteran producer Robert Justman, regarding the original *Star Trek*'s first—and rejected—pilot, "The Cage." Such a statement seems indicative of network opposition to the genre in those days as well as the present. "NBC's reasoning was that the show seemed to be 'too intellectual' and they wanted something that was more akin to action/adventure."

This hardly seems surprising when considering the time frame being discussed: the early 1960s. Up until that point, and with few exceptions, science fiction on television had consisted primarily of such programming as *Captain Video*, *Sky King* and *Rocky Jones*; entertaining series devoid of intellectual substance. Essentially they were *safe* shows, and that was alright with—indeed, preferred by—the networks. Certainly there were more innovative writer-producers out there who recognized all that the medium could be if given the opportunity to truly create. The executives, however, seemed to believe that those rare individuals could be held down and beaten back, their creativity suppressed. For the most part, they were right, but amidst genre mediocrity arose such visionaries

Rod Serling's The Twilight Zone *was an early forerunner of Star Trek: using allegory to comment on the world of the day.*

as Rod Serling, Leslie Stevens, Joseph Stefano and Gene Roddenberry.

A highly acclaimed writer in television's golden age, Serling had grown frustrated with network censors who would not allow him to deal with the ideas and themes he felt necessary to explore. To counter this opposition, he created *The Twilight Zone*, an anthology with a twist. By couching his stories in a science fiction, horror or fantasy setting, he was able to cover dramatic ground that no one else had been able to.

In the introduction to *The Twilight Zone Companion*, author Marc Scott Zicree writes, "When *The Twilight Zone* debuted in 1959, it was a flower blooming in a television desert, made vacant by an endless number of situation comedies, westerns, and cop shows. To its faithful viewers, *The Twilight Zone* offered far more than empty laughs or a lesson in urban or frontier justice. Instead, at its best, it lived up to the promise of its opening narration, revealing a vista of realities not weighed down by the merely probable. At a time when the rest of television was hammering home the unstated but nonetheless apparent message that the realities and expectations of life were bracketed within very narrow borders, *The Twilight Zone* presented a universe of possibilities and options."

Another series that attempted to present psychological challenges to the audience was Leslie Stevens and Joseph Stefano's *The Outer Limits*, which was, in a sense, the antithesis of *The Twilight Zone.*

"My approach," explains producer/writer Joseph Stefano, "was to do drama and Gothic horror, with some kind of science fiction element, because I was not a science fiction fan. There wasn't much science fiction that I had seen or read that I liked very much. In a way, I was creating a different form. If you look at *my* science fiction as opposed to what other writers did on the show, you'll see the difference.

"They were really much more Gothic horror tales, and much more scary than the others. After *Psycho*, it was expected of me. But I had certain moralistic rules—if you did any damage to the universe, you had to put it back together again by the conclusion because we were on early and we had children watching. I didn't want to overly scare young people, so we always put the world back together with the control voice at the end."

As he explains it, dealing with the television networks is like dealing with "a two-headed monster. On one hand, they want high ratings, and on the other, there are people who want to safeguard the hearts and minds of viewers and they come from the same source. So, one half of the network is telling you to cut this or that out, and the other half tells you to give them more. I don't think it's as big a problem as it was, because they've determined a time when sex and violence should be on TV. We had very little sex in *The Outer Limits*, and very little violence except in the scary sense, not violence as in shooting eight people. If *Outer Limits* should go to series again, I would like to continue in that way. I see no reason to do a cop show."

Robert Justman, who worked on the series as assistant director and had also performed the same function on *The Adventures of Superman*, adds, "In doing *The Outer Limits*, what the network wanted was not necessarily an intelligent science fiction show. What they wanted was a science fiction show that would return a lot of numbers. Their theory was that to do that you had to have a monster in every show. If you're an intelligent person and you like monsters, no, it wasn't a problem keeping science fiction on the air. But if you're an intelligent person and you don't think it should be monsters to do an intelligent show, yes, it was difficult.

"Somewhat of the same attitude was found in the early days of *Star Trek*," he continues, "when the network suggested what they wanted to open the first season with, which was 'Man Trap.' It had a monster. We felt that it wasn't a very good show compared to some of the others we had already made. We lost the battle, they won the battle and 'Man Trap' aired first."

Veteran science fiction author Jerry Sohl, whose teleplay credits include *Twilight Zone, Alfred Hitchcock Presents* and *Star Trek*, says of *Outer Limits*, "The thing that I disliked about it is that you had to see the monster of the week right away, and my feeling was that they should have had some shows where you never knew who the monster was or what it was until near the very end. They don't show the murderer in a crime story right off the bat. You have to figure out who it is and that's half the fun. My story was called 'The Yellow Sand,' and it was in *Imaginative Tales* in 1956. It was a story in which they kept sending spaceships to Mars and they never came back. They would have communications from there, but that would eventually stop. In my story they land and one by one the people disappear and there's nothing there but sand. Where did they go? Obviously, you walk on the sand, and these sharks would come along and eat the people. In the episode, right away, as soon as they land, we see these monstrous sharks. That's just dumb. You should have had these people go out to the other spaceships, like they did in *Alien*. What do you do for suspense?"

From that point of view, Stefano offers no apologies. "In all honesty," he explains, "I cannot say that I was unable to do what I wanted with the show. I pretty much had the exact series that I wanted. There were times when the ABC Standards and Practices Department would ask me to delete something, or, in one case, they pointed to a show which was disturbing to them. There was nothing we could do about it—it was just very disturbing."

Unlike other genre shows, *The Outer Limits* was a hit right from the beginning, but ABC proved that it didn't understand what it had on its hands, as they moved the series to Saturday nights, positioning it directly against the formidable *Jackie Gleason Show*. Needless to say, Gleason ran until 1970. *The Outer Limits* didn't, and it was another nail in the coffin of SF-TV, making it that much more difficult for the next show of its type to come along.

"I left at the first season's end because of the schedule change," Stefano admits. "I said to ABC, 'If you move it like that, the show is *dead*. I will not spend 20-hour days producing and writing a show that's going to be killed because of a pointless schedule change.' The series they put in our slot, *Voyage to the Bottom of the Sea*, ran for four years. If they had left *Outer Limits* where it was, it would have gone on for four or five years. I was in such firm disagreement that I *refused* to be involved with a show that was going down the drain, and that's exactly what happened to it. It went half a season and they canceled it." (Interestingly, history would repeat itself several years later when Gene Roddenberry refused to line produce *Star Trek's* third—and ultimately final—season, citing a similar schedule change. But we transgress.)

Jerry Sohl, feeling frustrated, wanted to do something about the lack of true science-fiction on television.

"Theodore Sturgeon, Richard Matheson, George Clayton Johnson and myself got together and formed what we called The Green Hand," he relates, "and we were really going to know television dead by doing really *responsible* science-fiction. Certainly, the medium could stand better material. We wanted script and quality control. We wanted to breathe something new into the shows; bring the medium up to date and in step with what was happening in SF at the time. We thought that at least half of primetime should be devoted to SF and fantasy."

Their initial attempt at fulfilling this dream upon incorporating met with great success in that Herbert F. Solow, in

"My approach was to do drama, Gothic Horror and some kind of science-fiction element," says Joseph Stefano of The Outer Limits.

charge of television production at Paramount when *Star Trek* was produced, believed in them. Then working at MGM, he gave the group an office on the lot and special parking spaces.

"We had *all* the privileges," Sohl smiles, "including eating in the MGM executives' dining room. To top it off, we had our own refrigerator right there in the office, and our own secretary. It was our opinion that science-fiction had come of age, and we immediately met with the executives at CBS, NBC and ABC, and they seemed genuinely impressed. But we learned it wasn't because we were formidable or heavy with talent and experience, or even angry young men with axes to grind. It was simply because they had *never* seen four science-fiction writers all at once, and four writers in such apparent agreement."

During these meetings, The Green Hand pitched a variety of ideas for TV series, including Richard Matheson's *Hunter*, about a cop who, through an accident, develops ESP which he uses to solve crimes; and Theodore Sturgeon's *E.T.*, which dealt with an extraterrestrial trapped on Earth who has difficulties understanding and adjusting to what he finds on this planet.

"Does he fall in love?" asks Sohl rhetorically. "What kind of super powers does he have? How would people adjust to him when they found out that he was an alien? We had a million storylines ready, but the networks rejected both ideas, believing the average viewer wouldn't understand concepts like ESP and extraterrestrials."

Next offered was *Gestalt Team*, a concept which had three astronauts of the future whose special talents have been blended and meshed, and who are trouble-shooters on the rim worlds, battling aliens and the human floatsam and jetsam who try to survive out there by criminal means.

"The network loved it," says Sohl with a laugh. "Positively loved it! But loving it didn't mean underwriting the two-hour feature production at MGM or saving a slot on the fall primetime schedule. They just loved it. That's all. Period. And that was the end of it."

Gestalt Team was followed by *A Touch of Strange*, which would have been a *Twilight Zone*-like anthology telling only pure fantasy stories; and a series idea about an android.

"He was a male android who

Gene Roddenberry, seen here on the set of Genesis II, *saw* Star Trek *as the only means of expressing his honest point of view on television.*

escaped from a secret army base where he was madeand was being tracked down by assorted government agencies and forces," Sohl explains. "He was always on the run. He didn't want to return to the factory where he was 'born.' As he moves about the country, he learns something about himself and experiences things like emotions, not the least of which is love. Since he can't harm humans, he is always in a predicament, for people want to kill that which they don't understand, since they're afraid of it. A thousand stories came to our minds, but the networks balked. They felt that people would never buy a million dollar man.

"In the end, they didn't buy *any* of the series we offered. It was too bad for the networks, too bad for The Green Hand and too bad for the viewing public. The corporation was dissolved and the four of us went our separate ways. But the ironic thing is that *all* of our series premises eventually became TV shows in one form or another."

Most notably the android series which not only could be linked to *The Six Million Dollar Man* but more directly to *The Questor Tapes,* a TV pilot co-written and produced by a fellow by the name of Gene Roddenberry.

By 1963, Gene Roddenberry, a former police officer and pilot, had proven his writing abilities on such television series as *Dr. Kildare, Naked City, Mr. District Attorney* and *Highway Patrol,* before heading the writing staff of *Have Gun, Will Travel.* He also began to investigate the possibility of creating his own series by writing such original pilots as *333 Montgomery* (starring DeForest Kelley), a World War II adventure entitled APO-923 and a remake of the Kelley pilot called *Defiance Country.* None of them went to series, though they certainly whet Roddenberry's appetite in terms of becoming a producer.

"These pilots were produced by other people," Roddenberry explained, "and none of them sold. I began to see that to create a program idea and write a script simply wasn't enough. The story is not 'told' until it's on celluloid. Telling that final story involved sound, music, casting, costumes, sets and all the things that a producer is responsible for. Therefore it became apparent to me that if you want the film to reflect accurately what you felt when you wrote the script, then you have to produce it, too. This is why television writers tend to become producers.

"Producing in television is like storytelling," he said. "The choice of the actor, picking the right costumes, getting the right flavor, the right pace—these are as much a part of storytelling as writing out that same description of a character in a novel. Although the director plays an important role in this, the director in television comes on a show to prepare for a week, shoots for a week, and then goes on to another show. Unlike the producer, he is neither there at the beginning of the script, nor rarely there for long after you end up with some 25,000 feet of film which now has to be cut and pasted into something unified. There is immense creative challenge and pleasure in taking all of these things and putting them together into something that works."

"Writing for the television audience," he explained in 1988, "does the same thing as the great sculptors and painters and composers also do. What you do is say to the world, 'Hey, these are things as I see it! These are my comments. This is how I see the world.' And you do this with utter selfishness, which is what an artist should always do. All writers should be selfish and say, 'This is the way that I see it,' and under the voice should say, 'Screw you! If you want yours, you can do it too.'"

It was with this attitude that Roddenberry approached his first television producing assignment: 1963's *The Lieutenant,* which starred Gary Lockwood, who would, incidentally, go on to guest star in *Star Trek*'s second pilot, "Where No Man Has Gone Before." In the series, Lockwood portrayed Lt. William Rice, and the essential thrust was an emphasis on the life of a newly commissioned officer in the Marine Corps during peacetime.

The Lieutenant only lasted 29 episodes, but it was significant for several reasons. First off, it created a working relationship between Roddenberry and a great many people who would eventually work on *Star Trek,* including Leonard Nimoy, Nichelle Nichols, director Marc Daniels, Lockwood, Walter Koenig and director Robert Butler. Additionally, it was during the production of this series that he developed his initial concepts for what would eventually become *Star Trek.*

Roddenberry's interest in science fiction can be traced back to his childhood.

"I was 11 years old," he recalled, "and there was a boy in my class who life had treated badly. He limped, he wheezed, I don't know all the things that were wrong with him, but he was a charming, lovely, intelligent person. He, because of being unable to get on the athletic field and do many of the things that others were able to do, had sort of gone into his own world of fantasy and science fiction. He had been collecting the old *Amazing* and *Astounding* magazines from those great old days and he introduced me to science fiction. I started to read them and then discovered, in our neighborhood, living above a garage was an ex-con who had come into science fiction when he was in prison. He introduced me to John Carter and those wonderful Burroughs things. By the time I was 12 or 13, I had been very much into the whole science fiction field."

Which is not to say that when he got into writing, he saw science fiction as the primary creative vehicle to express himself.

"Although I suppose you could have called me a science fiction fan, this certainly was not the Alpha-Omega of my reading," related Roddenberry, whose first script in the genre was *The Secret Defense of 117*, starring Ricardo Montalban. "I think all writers are omnivorous in their reading. I know few writers that I respect that read only science fiction. Isaac Asimov, for example, I know reads broadly on history, economics, sociology, everything. As a result, when I decided to become a writer, I decided to become a *writer*, not just a science fiction writer."

Like Rod Serling before him, Roddenberry did see science fiction (with *Star Trek* as the particular mode of communication), as an opportunity to explore some of life's "larger" themes, while continuing a tradition of literary creativity begun centuries earlier.

"I had been a freelance writer for about a dozen years and was chafing increasingly at the commercial censorship on television, which was very strong in those days," he's said. "You really couldn't talk about anything you cared to

talk about [and] I decided I was going to leave TV unless I could find some way to write what I wanted to. A writer is an artist who's very job is about opening his mind to things. I recalled that when Jonathan Swift was writing *Gulliver's Travels*, he wanted to write satire on his time and went to Lilliput in his story to do just that, [and] then he could talk about insane prime ministers and crooked kings and all of that. It was sort of this wonderful thing. Children could read it as a fairy tale, an adventure, and as they got older they'd recognize it for what it really is. It seemed to me that perhaps if I wanted to talk about sex, religion, politics, make some comments against Vietnam and so on, that if I had similar situations involving these subjects happening on other planets to little green people, indeed it might get by and it did.

"I apparently went right over the censors' heads, but all the fourteen year olds in our audience knew exactly what we were talking about. Also, I had watched science fiction. I was not a science fiction writer, though. I had written all sorts of things. I had said, 'Gee, too much of science fiction is about gadgetry and not about people. And drama is people. If I ever get the chance to write science fiction, I'm going to try to make it scientifically accurate as possible and write them the way we wrote the old *Playhouse 90*s.' And it worked. I thought that [*Star Trek*] might be a way I could infiltrate my ideas, and that's what it's been all the time. It's difficult for people to understand that even in the barren vineyards of television you might do these things. Actually, you can do them better there because you reach more people with more impact. You don't do it by each of your episodes being a fine *Hallmark Hall of Fame*, or those great shows that are meaningful and deep and advertised as such. The power you have is in a show like *Star Trek*, which is considered by many people to be a frothy little action-adventure; unimportant, unbelievable and yet watched by a lot of people. You just slip ideas into it."

Roddenberry's initial ideas for *Star Trek* concerned a starship of the Federation of Planets whose mission would be to—if you'll pardon the cliche—"explore strange new worlds,

seek out new lives and new civilizations...to boldy go where no man has gone before." Interestingly, many people have expressed their feeling that the concept was heavily influenced by the classic science fiction film, *Forbidden Planet*.

"Definitely not," differed Roddenberry to reporter James Burns in the 1970s. "The only time I ever thought of *Forbidden Planet* specifically when I was laying *Star Trek* out was when I said to myself that here were some mistakes they made in the film that I did not want to repeat. I think one of the obvious mistakes, and one that amazed me when I saw the show, although I generally liked [it], was the fact that you had a ship capable of interstellar travel and you had a cook aboard who scrubbed pots and pans by hand, and I said, 'Hey, come on, it just doesn't fit.' At least they would have had a radar range oven or something if they had interstellar capacity! But, no, I cannot remember a single time during the planning of *Star Trek* that I looked at another show and said, 'I will borrow this.' On the other hand, of course, you have this marvelous thing called a brain that all of your life is storing away information and sometimes you pull it out and say, 'This is Heinlein in such and such.' Or even probably what happens more often is your brain, being the marvelous thing it will, will take bits and pieces from three or four things and then meld them together in something you need for a particular show. Most writers who are good writers, or at least *care*, very seldom borrow things specifically. *Hacks* do that. On the other hand, most good writers do write things where people can go to them and say, 'Ah, this is a bit of this from this and this a bit of that from that,' but they don't write it that way."

Wagon Train To The Stars....

In 1991 the world celebrated *Star Trek*'s 25th Anniversary, but in 1963 its basic premise was unlike anything that had been seen on television before. As stated previously, Gene Roddenberry had developed his initial thoughts for the series while producing *The Lieutenant*. His secretary at the time was Dorothy (D.C.) Fontana, who had aspirations to be a professional writer and would eventually play an important role in the *Star Trek* mythos. As Roddenberry's right hand, she was among the first to see the original series premise.

"He asked me to read it in early 1964," she recalls. "This was the very first *Star Trek* proposal; the series presentation. I read it and said, 'I have only one question, who's going to play Mr. Spock?' He pushed a picture of Leonard Nimoy across the table and I, of course, knew Leonard because he had appeared in my first [sale], *The Tall Man*. I thought the proposal had a lot of possibilities and was certainly exciting. Of course you could never tell if it would sell and if somebody else would believe in it, but I certainly did. The captain at the time was Robert April, who eventually became Christopher Pike and the ship was the Yorktown. Mr. Spock was pretty much like the Mr. Spock that appeared in 'The Cage,' and the doctor was Dr. Boyce. The other characters weren't as settled. Nobody was doing anything like it on television."

Roddenberry's original series presentation, dated March 11, 1964, described *Star Trek* as "a one-hour dramatic television series; action-adventure-science fiction; the first such concept with strong central lead characters plus other continuing regulars...; and while maintaining a familiar central location and regular cast, explores an anthology-like range of exciting human experience."

He went on to describe the series premise as one akin to the then enormously popular *Wagon Train*, with regular characters travelling to distant worlds which bore some similarity to ours. Once there, they would encounter whatever circumstances would lead to action, adventure and drama. Their method of travel would be a "cruiser" named the U.S.S. Yorktown, a vessel enroute on a "well-defined and long-range Exploration-Science-Security mission which helps create our format." The time period is described as being some point in the future, which could mean either 1995, 2995 or some other date.

"In other words," Roddenberry wrote, "close enough to our own time for our continuing characters to be fully identifiable as people like us, but far enough

into the future for galaxy travel to be thoroughly established (happily eliminating the need to encumber our stories with tiresome scientific explanation)."

The key to the series, he added, was the concept of the Yorktown encountering numerous parallel worlds. In other words, planets whose conditions, both atmospheric and in terms of lifeforms, would mirror that of Earth. Said Roddenberry, "The 'Parallel Worlds' concept makes production practical by permitting action-adventure science fiction at a practical budget figure via the use of available 'earth' casting, sets, locations and so on. As important (and perhaps even more so in many ways), the 'Parallel Worlds' concept tends to keep even the most imaginative stories within the general audience's frame of reference through such recognizable and identifiable casting, sets and costuming."

There is little doubt that Gene Roddenberry had, at times, wanted to put his head through a wall with frustration as he tried to sell the premise of *Star Trek*. In the past he has discussed in length the long battle it was to convince *anyone* that this show could work. Initially, MGM, the studio behind *The Lieutenant*, had expressed interest in the project, but ultimately declined. Finally, he found someone who would listen: Oscar Katz of Desilu (the company created by Desi Arnaz and Lucille Ball).

By the time Roddenberry and Desilu came to a creative understanding, Lucille Ball was running the studio, having bought out ex-husband Desi Arnaz's share of the business. Oscar Katz, a former CBS executive was brought over as Vice President at Desilu in Charge of Production, and it was his job to develop product for the studio.

"The studio made money two ways," Katz explains. "One, by shows which they owned, such as *I Love Lucy* and *The Untouchables*. The second way was as a rental studio. For instance, Bing Crosby Productions shot all their stuff there as did Danny Thomas and Sheldon Leonard. Desilu owned three lots, and the studio probably made money just by having real estate which was going up in value while they were sitting there.

"The number of shows they owned was declining," he continues.

"Desi, in a sense, was a ballsy guy who at one time had seven or eight series on the air that Desilu owned. But now it had declined and they were down to practically Lucy's show and 14 or 15 rentals."

To change the situation, Desilu signed with talent agent Ted Ashley, proposing that they be represented for sales purposes by his agency. Ashley in turn brought in Oscar Katz who—somewhat reluctantly at first—was brought in as a studio executive.

"I started working for Desilu in April of '64 and began to develop programs," Katz details. "April is a late date to begin developing pilots for the fall, so I had a tough time. I think the first year I did three or four pilots, which means that I might have had 15 or 20 projects in earlier stages of development from which the four were selected. They had to be sold to a network in order to get financing. I think all four sailed, but it was hard to attract creative people. Desilu had a reputation for heavy overhead charges, etc. The second year, I did five pilots and of the five three got sold, which is a pretty good batting average."

While one of the pilots ultimately became "unsold," the other two went into production. The first was a show called *Mission: Impossible* and the other was this little science-fiction thing, *Star Trek*.

Says Katz, "If I had to pick the three people who had the most to do with getting *Star Trek* into a reality, they would be Gene Roddenberry, myself and an agent at Ashley named Augman Schwimmer, who today is a lawyer. I had problems signing creative people, getting them to pitch projects. Schwimmer said, 'Let's get a couple of guys in the long form and the short form, let's make overall deals with them. Let's not say, 'I like this property, I don't like this property.' Let's approach them and say, 'We'd like you to come to Desilu and would like you to make Desilu your home. The way we'd like to do it, don't tell us your properties. We'll make a deal for three properties to be determined.' In the long form, Roddenberry is the guy he recommended. I knew Roddenberry from previous contacts and we made the same sort of deal with one or two guys in the comedy field.

Star Trek was the first project that Katz and Roddenberry decided to collaborate on, and this led to a meeting with CBS.

During that meeting, as Stephen E. Whitfield reported in The Making of Star Trek, "Gene talked for almost two hours, outlining his ideas for the series, explaining ways in which a science-fiction series could be made on budget, and ways it could be made to appeal to a mass audience....They were particularly interested in his ideas on spaceship design, the types of stories to do, how to cut costs, and other technical aspects that Gene had developed. At the end of the two hours, and after having been questioned closely by most of those present, he thought he had sold them. Then they said, 'Thank you very much. We have one of our own that we like better. But we do appreciate your coming in."

In the same book, Roddenberry said, "My attitude was, 'You S.O.B.'s, why didn't you tell me that after the first ten minutes? If you want technical advice and help, hire me and pay me for it!' It's like calling a doctor and having him analyze you for two hours and then telling him, 'Thank you very much for pinpointing what's wrong, and I've decided to go to another doctor for the treatment.'"

Elaborates Oscar Katz, "We were in a dining room with six or seven executives, one of whom questioned us rather closely about what we were going to do on this show. We answered his questions and it turned out that his interest was due to the fact that they were developing a science-fiction show of their own."

That series was Lost in Space, which CBS would debut in the 1965 season. In the meantime, Roddenberry and Katz continued to push forward and finally convinced NBC to take the risk and finance the pilot. In the sales pitch to NBC, Katz explains, the network executives were told that there are four kinds of stories that would represent the Star Trek concept.

"'You have to remember that the space ship is five stories high,'" Katz remembers explaining, "'it has 500 people on it. One of the girls, who's a female yeoman in the crew, it turns out has signed on because she's having trouble back at home in Boston with either a boyfriend or her parents. She's getting away from them and she has an emotional relationship problem. Our two leads, unspecified, are the catalytic agents who help her face her problem and solve it. You never see her again because she's just one of the crew people.' And I said, 'In that respect, what you have is Wagon Train. Wagon Train had two leads, the Wagon Train traveled through the west—although it never got where it was going—and a guest star who was in wagon number 23 had an emotional problem which the two leads had to help solve.

"'The second kind of story is you have to remember that they're out for five years at a clip. They get a message from earth that a planet on which there are earth people doing mining there is claim jumping. They have to go to the planet and do a police action. In that respect, it's Gunsmoke. The third thing that happens is they go to a planet where everything is pretty much like earth, the atmosphere, etc., and subsequently the people on this planet look and have developed very much like us, except that their Chicago, their Al Capone, is in the future, or their Civil War is about to break out. They're either ahead of us or behind us. So it's people that look like us that are going through what we went through or what we will go through. The fourth type is where they go to a planet where the atmospheric conditions are different than on earth. Everything is different. The people don't look like us, they don't behave like us. They're fierce looking animals or whatever.'

"So I said, 'Those are the four types. What we've got is Gunsmoke, Wagon Train and two outer planet type shows. What would you like?' Well, they picked type four and the reason they picked type four was it was the hardest to do. With the Desilu reputation, they wanted to make it as hard as possible so we could prove ourselves. I tried to talk them out of it, because I knew it was going to be expensive and, even more, I felt that it might not be representative of the series. But they couldn't be talked out of it. That's how the first pilot, 'The Cage,' came into being."

"The Cage" was expanded into a teleplay, simultaneously renaming

Prior to commanding the starship Enterprise, actor Jeffrey Hunter portrayed Jesus Christ in King of Kings.

Captain Robert April Christopher Pike, and the Yorktown the Enterprise. What Roddenberry ended up with was a teleplay in which the United Space Ship Enterprise arrives at the planet Talos IV to answer a distress signal. Pike is taken prisoner by the telepathic Talosians who want him to mate with another human being named Vina, so that they can repopulate their nearly lifeless world. To accomplish this goal, they use their abilities to plunge Pike from one fantasy into another, attempting to blur his hold on reality and creating a false sense of security. Number One, Mr. Spock and other crewmembers work together to free him and, together, they end the Talosian plan.

Jeffrey Hunter, who had recently played Jesus Christ in King of Kings and co-starred with John Wayne in The Searchers, was cast as Captain Pike, though other actors had been considered.

"I remember Lloyd Bridges was very much under consideration," Roddenberry recalled, "except when I approached him with it, he said, 'Gene, I like you, I've worked with you before in the past, but I've seen science fiction and I don't want to be within a hundred miles of it....' I understood what he meant then, because science fiction was usually the monster of the week, the ink blot that gobbled up Tokyo. I tried to convince him that I could do it differently, but at the time I wasn't sure that I would treat it dif-

Leonard Nimoy seen here in his first science-fiction film, Zombies of the Stratosphere.

ferently. I wasn't sure I could manage it."

Majel Barrett, who would go on to marry Roddenberry and portray Nurse Christine Chapel in the ensuing television series, was cast as Number One, with John Hoyt as Dr. Boyce. One of the most integral roles to fill was that of Mr. Spock. After considering Martin (*Mission: Impossible*) Landau and Michael (*The Wild, Wild West*) Dunn, Roddenberry decided to go with Leonard Nimoy, whose credits included *Zombies of the Stratosphere* and two episodes of *The Outer Limits*.

Roddenberry reflected on working with Nimoy during an episode of *The Lieutenant*, noting, "He had played a Hollywood producer, of all things, in an episode with a gum-chewing, wise-cracking secretary who later became my wife. I looked at him during those days and I thought that if I ever did this science fiction series, I'd use him because of his Slavic face and his high cheekbones. And so I just cast it with a phone call by asking him to come over."

Elsewhere, Leonard Nimoy recalled the experience. "The first time I heard about *Star Trek*," he mused, "was in 1964. Gene Roddenberry was producing a television series called *The Lieutenant* [and] I was playing a flamboyant Hollywood [producer] who wanted to do a movie about the Marine Corps. When the job was finished, Gene called my agent, my agent called me and they asked for a meeting. I went in to see

Gene at what was then Desilu Studios and he told me that he was preparing a pilot for a science fiction series to be called *Star Trek*, that he had in mind for me to play an alien character. As the talk continued, Gene showed me around the studio, he showed me the sets that were being developed and the wardrobe that had been designed, the prop department and so forth. I began to realize that he was selling me on the idea of being in this series, unusual for an actor. I figured all I had to do was keep my mouth shut and I might end up with a good job here.

"Gene told me that he was determined to have at least one extra-terrestrial prominent on his starship," added Nimoy. "He'd like to have more, but making human actors into other life forms was too expensive for television in those days. Pointed ears, skin color, plus some changes in eyebrows and hair style were all he felt he could afford, but he was certain that his Mr. Spock idea, properly handled and properly acted, could establish that we were in the 23rd Century and that interplanetary travel was an established fact. And with this, our ship would not be the United States Ship Enterprise, it would be the United Space Ship Enterprise, put out there in space by a federation of planets and the crew would be interplanetary in nature. In Spock, we would have a character who reminded us of that constantly.

"The first pilot of *Star Trek* was filmed at Desilu Studios in Hollywood in 1965. It was the most expensive television pilot ever produced up to that time....That first pilot had some great production values and it had some wonderful ideas, but NBC decided that it was too cerebral and it wouldn't sell."

"The Cage" was directed by Robert Butler who had also worked with Roddenberry on *The Lieutenant* and has since gone on to become the "King of the Pilots," having helmed the initial episodes of *Batman, Moonlighting, Remington Steele, Hill Street Blues, Midnight Caller* and many others.

"Gene had finished writing 'The Cage,' and he asked me to read it, which I did," recalls Butler. "I remember thinking it was a terrific yarn, but that it was somewhat obscured because it was such a

showcase script. 'The Cage' showcased such solid, good and fascinating science fiction disciplines, examples and events, that it was, I thought, a little obscure. The story was somewhat remote, and I discussed whether or not people would get it. I could tell at that point that Gene was so consumed with it that he couldn't have heard any objections."

Butler goes on to explain that one of his suggestions was to change the show's name from *Trek* to *Track*, for the simple reason that the former sounded a bit too "tedious."

"It's such old news now, that it sounds totally odd," says the director, "but at that time, without the brainwash of the show becoming a massive hit, I remember *Star Trek* sounded kind of inert and boring to me, whereas *Star Track*, I thought, had a bigger vista to it, but in that discussion, and others regarding the obscurity of the story, Gene was not in the mood to receive any such input.

"Subsequently," he elaborates, "after doing the pilot and executing it in the way we thought it should be done, I'd heard that NBC had said, 'We believe this. We think there's a show here, but we don't understand it. Do it again.' Apparently the network, at its level, was feeling exactly as I did.

"Good ideas were being examined," Butler emphasizes. "Underneath all this I sensed a very honorable and well intentioned group of ideas. By the same token, I also remember that it was somewhat stiff. A street show is very loose in terms of language and characters, but in a science fiction show, or a show where you're creating a new reality, you have to adhere to and honor that new reality. You invent a set of circumstances which translates to a kind of rigidity. After all, they're in the equivalent of an army, and in any kind of service your behavior is more prescribed. Ideally, I don't like that because it's just another constraint. That kind of came with the territory, and wasn't good or bad. But I'm more comfortable with looser behavior."

NBC turned down 'The Cage' as being too cerebral for the television audience. Surprisingly, Roddenberry agreed with them to a certain degree.

At a *Star Trek* 20th Anniversary convention in 1986, Roddenberry discussed what happened with "The Cage," as well as the network's motive for rejecting the pilot.

"The reasons were these: too cerebral, not enough action and adventure," he said. "'The Cage' didn't end with a chase and a right cross to the jaw, the way all manly films were supposed to end. There were no female leads then—women in those days were just set dressing. So, another thing they felt was wrong with our film was that we had Majel as a female second-in-command of the vessel. It's nice now, I'm sure, for the ladies to say, 'Well, the men did it,' but in the test reports, the women in the audience were saying, 'Who does she think she is?' They hated her. It is hard to believe that in 20 years, we have gone from a totally sexist society to where we are today—where all intelligent people certainly accept sexual equality. We've made progress.

"We also had what they called a 'childish concept'—an alien with pointy ears from another planet," he added. "People in those days were not talking about life forms on other worlds. It was generally assumed by most sensible people that this is the place where life occurred and probably nowhere else. It would have been all right if this alien with pointy ears, this 'silly creature,' had the biggest zap gun in existence, or the strength of 100 men, *that* could be exciting. But his only difference from the others was he had an alien perspective on emotion and logic. And that didn't make television executives jump up and yell, 'Yippee!'

"At that time, space travel was considered nonsense. It wasn't until we were off the air three months that man landed on the Moon and minds were changed all over. The Talosian planet's 'ridiculous' premise of mind control annoyed a great many people and the objection, of course, overlooks the fact that the most serious threat we face today in our world is mind control—such as not too long ago exercised by Hitler, and what's now exercised by fanatical religions all over the world and even here in our own country. Mind control is a dangerous subject for TV to discuss, because the yuppies may wake up someday and be discussing it and say, 'Well, wait a minute, television may be the most powerful mind control force of all,' and may begin taking a very close look at television. And so most executives would like to avoid that *possibility.*

"Looking back," he added elsewhere, "they probably felt that I had broken my word. In the series format I had promised to deliver a 'Wagon Train to the Stars'...action/adventure, science-fiction style. But, instead, ['The Cage'] was a beautiful story, in the opinion of many the best science fiction film ever made up to that time. But it wasn't action/adventure. It wasn't what I had promised it would be. Clearly the problem with the first pilot was easily traced back to me. I got too close to it and lost perspective. I had known the only way to tell *Star Trek* was with an action/adventure plot. But I forgot my plan and tried for something proud."

Explains Oscar Katz, "I asked NBC, 'Why are you turning it down?' and I was told, 'We can't sell it from this show, it's too atypical.' I said, 'But you guys picked this one, I gave you four choices.' He said, 'I know we did and because of that, right now we're going to give you an order for a second pilot next season.'"

Where No Man...

Although okaying a second pilot, NBC did make several "suggestions," including the removal of Mr. Spock because, according to Oscar Katz, "they thought Spock's ears would be scary."

"They rejected most of the cast and asked that Spock be dropped too," Roddenberry concurred. "In fact, they particularly asked that Spock be dropped. This is one of those cases where you go home at night and pound your head against a wall and say, 'How come I am the only one in the world that believes in it?' But I said I would not do a second pilot without Spock because I felt we had to have him for many reasons. I felt we couldn't do a space show without at least one person on board who constantly reminded you that you were out in space and in a world of the future. NBC finally agreed to do the second pilot with Spock in it, saying, 'Well, kind of keep him in the background.'"

This was particularly ironic when one considers that Spock would eventually go on to become one of the most popular characters on the show. In fact, the constant struggle between logic and emotion that waged through the half-Vulcan/half-human touched a generation searching for direction.

Adding to the scenario, Nimoy explained, "The network eliminated one character entirely, the role of Number One...They told Gene to also get rid of the guy with the ears, insisting that the audience couldn't identify with an extraterrestrial character. Gene battled this but was finally forced into a compromise. He felt the format badly needed the alien Spock, even if the price was the acceptance of 1960s style sexual inequality. A new pilot was written and Mr. Spock was in Number One's place as second-in-command as well as having some of the woman's computer mind qualities. Vulcan unemotionalism and logic came into being."

In terms of how that second pilot came into being, Stephen Kandel, who would go on to write the popular Harry Mudd episodes of the weekly series, explains that NBC was "of two minds: to forget it and to abandon it. So, after much argument and discussion, Gene got the money to write three additional pilot scripts. 'The Cage' had been a sample of what the series would be like and that frightened the network. They thought the audience wouldn't understand it."

While work began on the three scripts, Roddenberry learned that two key players of "The Cage" did not want to be involved the second time around: director Robert Butler and actor Jeffrey Hunter.

Says Butler, "I told Gene I had been there and done it already, and didn't wish to repeat myself. Another reason I didn't wish to do it is that science fiction, directorially, is a bit of a chore, because you have to share the reigns with graphics, special visual effects and all the other people who supply the tricks. It's very much direction by committee, and I was a little impatient with that. I like working on pilots because you're in on the formulation, and you're handed fewer givens so, equitably, you

William Shatner in his days before assuming the role of Captain James T. Kirk, seen here in The Defenders.

direct more. The more control and freedom I have to direct, the more I enjoy it. I will say that we were all praying and doing our best [on 'The Cage']. The phenomenon was bigger than I expected, not that I really measured it at the time. That wasn't in the equation. You just roll up your sleeves and decide what the hell it is you're trying to do. Then you jump in and never look back."

Of Jeffrey Hunter's departure, Roddenberry said, "I thought highly of him and he would have made a grand captain, except his family convinced him, or his wife or someone, that science fiction was really beneath him."

Adds Oscar Katz, "When you make a pilot deal with an actor, you can't tie him up forever. You usually have a hold on him for approximately six months, but you *don't* have the right to do another pilot with him for the following season, so we had no hold on Jeffrey Hunter. And either he or his wife didn't like 'The Cage' and he didn't want to do the second pilot. I already had the set built—I think it was the largest set in the history of Hollywood, that planet in 'The Cage'—we had the interior of the space ship, the miniature of the outside of the space ship, etc. We had everything and all we had to do was write a new script. But we didn't have a leading man. Business affairs negotiated with Jeffrey Hunter, and we all thought it was the usual actor/network situation. They don't

want to do it for reason XYZ, and it's a device for getting the price up. We kept increasing the price and he kept saying no. One day I said, 'What's with Jeffrey Hunter?' and I was told he just won't do it at any price. Finally I said, 'Tell Jeffrey Hunter to get lost. Tell him we're going to do the pilot without him.' And that's how Shatner got into it, because Hunter wouldn't do it."

Taking over the center seat would be Canadian-born actor William Shatner, whose career had included highly acclaimed roles on stage (*The World of Suzie Wong, A Short in the Dark*T), screen (*The Brothers Karamazov*) and television (*Twilight Zone, The OUter Limits, For the People* and the pilot for an unsold series, *Alexander, the Great*).

"I was offered the part in a rather peculiar fashion," Shatner related to the English press in the 1970s. "They had made a pilot of *Star Trek* with an actor who is now deceased, Jeffrey Hunter, and NBC did not like the pilot but they liked the idea. They said change the cast, change the story but give us another pilot for *Star Trek* and we'll pay a certain amount of money. So they showed me the first pilot and said, 'Would you like to play the part and here are some of the storylines that we plan to go with; you can see the kind of production we have in mind. Would you care to play it?' And I thought it was an interesting gamble for myself as an actor to take, because I've always been fascinated by science fiction. I liked the production; I liked the people involved with the production, and so I decided to do it. But it was under these peculiar circumstances of having a first pilot made that I did it.

"I then talked at great length with Gene Roddenberry about the objectives we hoped to achieve, and one of those objectives was serious drama as well as science fiction. His reputation and ability, which I knew first-hand, was such that I did not think he would do *Lost in Space*. And I was too expensive an actor, with what special or particular abilities I have, to warrant being put in something that somebody else could walk through. So I felt confident that *Star Trek* would keep those serious objectives for the most part, and it did."

Bob Justman, who would go from assistant director on "The Cage" to Associate Producer on "Where No Man's Gone Before," explains, "Gene was very happy that he was able to get Bill Shatner, who was highly thought of in the industry. I had worked with Bill on *Outer Limits* and he had a good reputation in the television and entertainment industries even at that time, well before the second pilot of *Star Trek*. He was someone to be reckoned with and we certainly understood that he was a more accomplished actor than Jeff Hunter was, and he gave us more dimension. The network seemed to feel that Jeff Hunter was rather wooden. He was a nice person, everyone liked him, but he didn't run the gamut of emotions that Bill Shatner could do. Shatner was classically trained. He had enormous technical abilities to do different things and he gave the captain a terrific personality. He embodied what Gene had in mind, which was the flawed hero. Or the hero who considers himself to be flawed. Captain Horatio Hornblower. That was who he was modeled on."

Enthused Leonard Nimoy, "Bill Shatner's broader acting style created a new chemistry between the captain and Spock, and now it was quite different from that of the first pilot."

And the relationship between the two characters and actors—despite whatever ego problems would arise later—positively sparked. David Gerrold, famed science fiction writer, *Star Trek* scholar and author of the episode "The Trouble With Tribbles," notes, "All of the movies and all of the episodes hold together because Shatner holds it together. Spock is only good when he has someone to play off of. The scenes where Spock doesn't have Shatner to play off of are not interesting. If you look at Spock with his mom or dad, it's very ponderous. But Spock working with Kirk has the magic and it plays very well, and people give all of the credit to Nimoy not to Shatner."

Surprisingly, Nimoy himself agrees with this observation. "During the series," he says, "we had a failure-I experienced it as a failure—in an episode called 'The Galileo Seven.' The Spock character had been so successful that somebody said, 'Let's do a show where

Spock takes command of a vessel.' We had this shuttlecraft mission where Spock was in charge. I had a tough time with it. I really appreciated the loss of the Kirk character for me to play against, to comment on. The Bill Shatner Kirk performance was the energetic, driving performance, and Spock could kind of slipstream along and make comments and offer advice, give another point of view. Put into the position of being the driving force, the central character, was very tough for me and I perceived it as a failure."

While Shatner was hired, the three NBC-requested scripts were finished. Roddenberry wrote "The Omega Glory," dealing with a crisis on an Earth-like planet involving Federation colonists; Stephen Kandel wrote "Mudd's Women," which, he says, began with the premise "'What if we start with a character that's not alien or highly technological, but rather somebody whom the audience would identify with easily?' What we came up with was a roofing salesman; a con man."; and Samuel A. Peeples wrote "Where No Man Has Gone Before," which chronicled the metamorphosis of Enterprise crewmember Gary Mitchell into a God-like being.

"My vague memory is that there had been several problems with 'The Cage,'" reflects James Goldstone, who had been signed to direct Star Trek's second pilot. "One of them was that it cost so much money and the other was that it took so long to shoot. NBC was skeptical that a series could be manufactured, so to speak, on a weekly basis. One of the requisites put on the second pilot was to shoot it in, as I recall, eight days, which would then prove to them that a weekly series could be done in six or seven days. We needed the extra day because we were doing the prototype. The other requisite, I would *guess,* it being television, is that NBC very much wanted something that could be 'commercial' against the police shows and all the other action things that were then on television. Things have not changed, I guess. They always want something that will hook the audience and keep them."

In terms of the intention for the second pilot to be faster paced than the original, he says, "I really can't tell you whose idea that was, whether it was

mine or Gene's or the network's. There's also a difference between a two-hour show in an embryonic conceptual form, and something that is going to be a part of a weekly series. The concept of our show was not so much a pilot as it was an example of how we could go on a weekly level."

From the outset, he was enthused about working on the show. "Gene's whole concept," Goldstone details, "was of doing the sort of classic storytelling form in which you can tell the same kind of stories that were told in the Elizabethan Theatre, told in the 19th Century, that were told in classic novels. The convention with westerns is that if you take it out of today, and put it into a western setting, people accept these conventions. We would create conventions which people would accept, and you could therefore tell dramatic stories which people would accept because it was not on the streets they lived on, but were projected forward a little. On the same level, the characters and the dramatic conflicts, albeit space fiction, were really human conflicts. Now I don't know if that applies to all the episodes, and in fact I don't know if that applied to any of the episodes except the one I did,

because I don't know anything about all the other episodes. It would have been miraculous if they could have kept in nonmechanistic.

"A combination of NBC, Gene, perhaps other executives at Desilu and I, read all three [scripts], discussed them in length, decided on what became 'Where No Man Has Gone Before,' and then embarked on a great deal of polishing and rewriting on a conceptual and physical level, so that we could make it in eight days. This one just seemed to have the potential to establish those characters on a human level. The only gimmick is the mutation forward, the silvering of Gary Mitchell's eyes, and it works because it's simple, as opposed to the growing of horns or something. Ours was a human science fiction concept, perhaps cerebral and certainly emotional."

Samuel Peeples, who has written more segments episodic television than anyone could ever keep track of, had actually had some connection with Gene Roddenberry and Star Trek prior to "Where No Man Has Gone Before."

"Gene Roddenberry and I had known each other from writing Have Gun, Will Travel," Peeples recalls. "He was trying to start a science fiction series

Director James Goldstone took audiences "Where No Man Has Gone Before" with the second Star Trek pilot.

and he knew that I had one of the largest science fiction collections in the world. He was researching his show and asked if he could go through my magazines and get some ideas for the Enterprise. Gene went through all the covers, and that's really how the Enterprise was born.

"In the beginning," he continues, "Mr. Spock as we know him now, didn't exist. He was a red-tailed Devil who didn't eat. He absorbed energy through a red plate in his stomach. This is the way he was laid out in the original concept. I argued with Gene that it should be a humanized character because I was adamant that it should be straight science fiction without fantasy. The first pilot he did for NBC, 'The Cage,' was more fantasy than science fiction. NBC was apparently unhappy with it, so they told him they would commission a second pilot, and they wanted a story. Gene asked me to do it, and I did, guessing it would be more of a challenge to me because it's easy to open up your mouth and criticize somebody else's concept. Then if somebody says, 'Okay, let's see you do it your way,' you've got to prove that you know what you're talking about."

In Peeples' script, the starship Enterprise comes across a charred metallic "black box" (similar to what is used today on airplanes) from a long-lost space vessel. Captain James R. Kirk (the middle initial eventually changed to T. once the pilot led to series) has the device beamed aboard. In the meantime strong ties are established between the captain, Lieutenant Gary Mitchell, and first officer Mr. Spock. The Enterprise approaches an energy barrier at the edge of the galaxy and attempts to make its way through, resulting in the ship nearly being destroyed and metamorphosizing Mitchell's natural ESP abilities. Those powers grow to the point where he becomes a god-like being, manipulating everything around him.

Spock listens to the black box and learns that the captain of that vessel was desperate to learn anything he could about ESP, and shortly thereafter ordered that his ship be set for self-destruction. Now Kirk is faced with one decision: kill Mitchell before the Enterprise is crushed by the man's ever-

increasing power.

"We were intrigued with the corruption of power theme manifesting over the ordinary individual," says Peeples. "that was the basic premise, and we had to put in extrapolations of known scientific principles. At that time, the radiation belt had been discovered around the Earth, and my premise was that galaxies themselves might be separated by this type of barrier.

"Gene and I were trying to avoid the space cadet cliche," he elaborates. "We were both very concerned about it being an adult show. One thing, as later episodes proved, was the problem which never should have existed: the bug eyed monsters. We both discouraged the idea, believing that we should keep things as realistic as possible. If a person was different physically, then explain the reason for that difference. In a particular atmosphere, he might have a larger lung. If it was a planet with an extraordinarily bright sun, he would have different eyes. We were actually trying to project reality against an unfamiliar background. In other words, we would deal with reality according to the environmental background we encountered."

"Where No Man Has Gone Before" went into production soon thereafter. Joining Shatner, Nimoy and Gary Lockwood was Paul Fix as Dr. Mark Piper, George Takei as Physicist Sulu, James Doohan as Chief Engineer Montgomery Scott, Lloyd Haynes as Communications Officer Alden and Andrea Dromm as Yeoman Smith, with Sally Kellerman "guest starring" as Dr. Elizabeth Dehner. As fans of the show recognize, the final STAR TREK cast was slowly taking shape.

Doohan was actually brought into *Star Trek* by James Goldstone, with whom he had worked before.

"All he wanted to hear were different accents," related the actor in *The Star Trek Interview Book*, "and that's what he heard. He called my agent and said, 'I want Jimmy down here,' and when I got to the set he asked, 'Well, what sort of an accent shall we do today?' That was kind of fun....I did a bunch of accents, they handed me the pages of the script, I did the accents and they asked, 'Which do you like?' So I told

them. I said I preferred the Scottish, because I think it's traditional that Scotsmen are famous as engineers. They said, 'Well, we rather like that, too,' so I immediately just came right out and named him Montgomery Scott, after my maternal grandfather."

George Takei, who had made a name for himself dubbing Japanese monster films like *Rodan*, and made guest appearances on *Playhouse 90, Hawaiian Eye* and *77 Sunset Strip*, found himself intrigued with the notion of appearing on *Star Trek*, though he thought the show might be a little *too* different.

"Since the pilot was so unlike anything that we had ever seen on television, even under the guise of science fiction," he muses, "I wondered whether or not it would sell. As professional actors, the cast all had worries about the saleability of 'Where No Man Has Gone Before.' We were hoping and praying that it would go, so it was a pleasant surprise when NBC did buy *Star Trek*."

NBC viewed the pilot in early 1966, and gave Roddenberry the green light for his series, much to the delight of everyone, as they were proud of what they had achieved.

"I was very happy with it," enthuses James Goldstone. "From a director's point of view—or this director's point of view—you have certain targets and certain problems which have to be overcome in any picture, whether it's a $20 million feature or a television show. A director measures his success in two ways. Obviously, like everybody else, you measure it by whether or not it's a critical and commercial success, but you also measure it in terms of overcoming obstacles. The obstacles were temporal, budgetary, but they were also conceptual. I was very proud of the work we were able to do. When I say we, I don't mean it in a generous sense. I mean that it was a very collaborative effort, as are all pilots. We, being Gene, especially, Bobby Justman and the main actors who later became the main stars. Everything was planned in detail, and Bobby and I knew if we didn't move from one set to another or one scene to another by a certain hour, we were in trouble."

At a convention appearance, Roddenberry expressed, "The second pilot seemed to have great concepts: humans turning into gods. But they were nice safe gods, gods who go 'Zap! You're punished.' Kind of like the guys you see on those Sunday morning shows...The biggest factor in selling the second pilot was that it ended up in a hell of a fist fight with the villain suffering a painful death. Then, once we got *Star Trek* on the air, we began infiltrating a few of our ideas, the ideas you folks have all celebrated. *Star Trek* fans are people who are ready for the 23rd century dreams now. And I wish to God our leaders could catch up with them."

Elsewhere, he expressed his satisfaction over having been given the opportunity to do a second pilot. "Science fiction pilots are difficult things to do," he said. "You know, if you are going to do a pilot on a police show, let's say mid-town robbery squad, the network can reasonably expect you to get 95% of everything right and it's easy to do because you know what cops wear, you know how to catch a taxi, how to use a telephone and how to work a .38. When you get into SF you're very lucky if 75% of your pilot is believable because you're creating, in space science fiction, everything new. It was very helpful to be able to do one pilot, stand off, take a look at it and then do a second. The second pilot was really better in many ways because we had a chance to look at the costume work, how the gadgets worked and all that."

Oscar Katz left Desilu immediately after *Star Trek* was picked up as a series, but he believes he knows why the show has gone on for nearly three decades in one form or another.

"I think the secret of *Star Trek's* success was its attention to details," opines Katz. "Up until that point, the science-fiction movies on television were all Irwin Allen-type shows, whereas Gene's concept was science-fiction in the true sense of those words. It was like what things might be about in the future, not only in the size of the concept and the ship and they problems they face, but in the smallest details. And Gene was a stickler for details. For instance, do you know why nobody salutes on the ship? That's because Gene decided—after consulting with military people in

Washington—that on a ship that's on duty with several hundred people in a limited space for five years, they are not going to salute each other. Take the scene in sickbay with the instruments on the wall. Y'know, you stick a thermometer in somebody's ass and you read the temperature on the wall. Gene had a meeting with NASA about what that was going to look like. The same thing with the uniforms. I think what made *Star Trek* was its 'truth', its science-fiction truth not only in the big things that were spoken about, but also in the smallest details. I think the fans appreciated that and that's what made them go wild. It's interesting, but I think *Star Trek* is probably the most valuable property ever developed in the history of television. You've got four series, six movies and merchandising you can't believe. It's amazing." And for *Star Trek*, it was only the beginning.

Space...The Final Frontier

The public's first view of *Star Trek* came at the Cleveland, Ohio Tricon on Labor Day weekend in 1966. There, 20th Century Fox screened their upcoming special effects extravaganza, *Fantastic Voyage*, Irwin Allen, the man behind such series as *Lost in Space* and *Voyage to the Bottom of the Sea*, presented the pilot episode of his latest effort, *The Time Tunnel*; and Gene Roddenberry unspooled "Where No Man's Gone Before," later adding "The Cage" due to public demand.

Roddenberry reflected, "I was nervous [at Tricon], particularly when I saw them watching other films that were shown before, and booing, and stomping, and laughing at things. I walked out there thinking, 'They're finally going to show this one.' There was a rather loud gentleman surrounded by other people discussing something at the time my show was starting, and upset already, I turned on him: 'For Christ's sake, could you be quiet? My show is on now.' And Isaac Asimov said, 'Yes, you're perfectly right. We will tone it down.' And someone said, 'You're dead, you just insulted Isaac Asimov.' Well, it turned out that I had not, and over the years we became fast friends. He understood. Then I watched how they accepted this show. I

said to myself, 'Yes, there *are* people, if we go this way and try these things, who are going to appreciate them.' I realized then that we would have fans of some sort and, of course, where that went is insanity."

Also in attendance was author Jerry Sohl, who explains, "There was what felt like 3,000 people watching a new Irwin Allen show, and as soon as they saw his name they started booing. They just booed his name. Then when Gene Roddenberry showed *Star Trek*, they really loved that. I was really surprised. Then when Gene Roddenberry and I sat up at the podium answering questions, I was introduced as the 'head writer of *Star Trek*.' Which I wasn't. I just went along with it because I thought it would be good politics. And it was. It was fun."

While not the head writer, Sohl was one of the first people that Roddenberry had contacted to pen scripts for the forthcoming series.

"Gene Roddenberry knew that I was a science friction writer from people evidently telling him I was," says Sohl. "So he called me up one day and asked me if I would like to go down to the studio. I met him there in like 1965, and he said, 'I have this idea for a science fiction TV show which I think the networks are going to buy, and I wanted to talk to you about the possibilities of stories. Would you be available? I'm meeting with other science fiction writers like A.E. Van Goght, Ray Bradbury, Frederic Brown.' He would meet with them down there and really sort of drained them by one lunch of any ideas. We all did the best that we could, suggesting what to do. We hoped that it wouldn't be like Truman Bradley's *Science Fiction Theatre*. We wanted something more than that. He told us that it would be a good thing, but nobody believed that it would be. I spoke to some writers afterwards and they said, 'Well, what did he do? Gene Roddenberry has only done *The Lieutenant* series and he was a police officer. What the hell does he know about science fiction? It's just going to be a pile of shit.' So we all agreed that, yes, it would be a pile of shit, but we would all work for it anyway. But it didn't turn out to be that way and we wound up

• • • •

being very friendly with him."

As scripts were being written and the series concept honed, Roddenberry turned his attention to casting. William Shatner, Leonard Nimoy, James Doohan and George Takei (with Sulu promoted from physicist to helmsman) would remain, while Paul Fix was out as the ship's doctor and Lloyd Hanes vacated the communications console. In their respective positions were DeForest Kelley as Dr. Leonard "Bones" McCoy and Nichelle Nichols as Lieutenant Uhura, representing one of the first times that a black actress was a network series regular.

Kelley had established himself as a highly qualified actor, usually playing the heavy in any number of television westerns.

"Roddenberry pulled me out of the westerns category," Kelley recalled in the 1970s. "I made a pilot for him in 1960 called *333 Montgomery*, in which I portrayed a famous criminal attorney in San Francisco named Jake Early. This series was before *The Defenders* and it was controversial in nature and ahead of its time. Roddenberry wrote it and produced it, and I starred in it. Unfortunately, it did not sell, but that was really the first pull out of westerns for me, and then later, of course, Gene did *Star Trek*."

The Lieutenant had represented one of Nichelle Nichols' first dramatic roles, and she was thrilled that Roddenberry had contacted her regarding *Star Trek*. In particular, she loved the character devised for her, Uhura.

"I tried to put into Uhura the qualities that I admire and demand of myself," she told *The Official Star Trek Fan Club Magazine*. "Then I tried to develop the kind of person who would be entrusted with that kind of responsibility. She's head of all communications on that ship, so she's not just there pushing buttons. Those buttons are talking to people down in the bowels of the ship. She's responsible for maybe a hundred people. For her or anyone to be entrusted with that kind of responsibility, I felt she had to have a strength and a dignity and a command of authority very much like Spock has."

Of all the characters, it quickly became obvious that the three most

prominent would be Kirk, Spock and McCoy. As Roddenberry explained it, deliberately so.

"The three star billing were the ones that you would see a lot of," he said. "Plus science fiction wasn't 'in' in those days and we were going to do a lot of things we knew people might not understand and I wouldn't have stream of consciousness. In novels, stream of consciousness goes inside the hero's head and you can read what he's thinking. You don't have that in television and so I thought that if I took a perfect person and divided him into three parts, I could have the administrative, courageous part that would be the Captain; the logical part who is the Science Officer and the humanistic part with the doctor. Then, when something comes up, the Captain could say, 'I don't know, fellas. We must do it,' and Spock would say, 'However, the logical thing is...', and the doctor would say, 'Yes, but the humanity of it,' and I could have them talk about it without having stream of consciousness, and it worked!"

A large part of that success was due to the abilities of, and chemistry between, Shatner, Nimoy and Kelley, who managed to sustain a relationship beyond the words written on the printed page.

"They all added to their characters," points out Robert Justman. "For example, as Nimoy added to the character of Mr. Spock, we saw certain things in the portrayal that Gene thought could be taken advantage of and expanded, which we did. You have to learn in making film to deal with the film and not necessarily with what the original conception was. Film has a life of its own and if you try to bend it toward what you originally intended and it didn't turn out that way, it's going to turn out to be quite awkward. You have to learn to take advantage of what's there, to perhaps give it a new shape. It's an interesting problem. You have to have a good concept for a character to begin with to enable the actors to do something with it. Gene has in the past, and with the new show, developed some very interesting characters. Brent Spiner's character [on *The Next Generation*], Data, is basically Pinnochio, but he's learning all the time. He's someone who wants to be human,

not wooden. He wants to be like everyone else, to be better than he thinks he is, not knowing that he's pretty good as he is. We all want to do better, so we can relate to that and the character."

With the proper cast in place, Roddenberry turned his attention back to the show's scripts. He knew that theirs was going to be one of television's first intelligent science fiction series, with realistic characters and extrapolations on today's technology. In other words, every aspect of the Enterprise would be based on items being developed in the present. For example, the diagnostic beds in sickbay, as advanced as they seemed, were studied by one of the U.S. armed forces, who told Roddenberry that they had been developing something along similar lines. Even the weapon system known as phasers was only one step removed from the laser beam.

"We realized that lasers might very well become commonplace by the time the show got on the air," he said, "or at least within the next couple of years. Rather than run the risk of being outdated, we decided to say 'phaser' instead. The reason we picked phaser is the 'phasing' principles in physics by which power can be increased. It was logical and it sounded good, so we used it. We didn't want people saying to us three years from now, 'Oh, come on now, lasers can't do that.'"

The scripts for *Star Trek* had to have a special quality to them, with the original game plan being that top science fiction and television writers would be supplying the show's stories. To ensure this thematic integrity, Gene Roddenberry hired John D.F. Black to serve as associate producer and story editor.

"What *Star Trek* always strived to do, from my perspective, is to take things people can relate to now because it's real in our own lives, and *move* them," explains Black. "What happens if somebody burns down your building? It's the same thing as a monster showing up in your building. So, they used the monster. The parallel was clean."

As Black speaks, he creates the immediate impression he is a man of integrity, caring deeply about his craft and the world around him. It was this integrity that he brought to the original

• • • •

Star Trek TV series.

"I came on about two months before we shot anything," says Black. "I can't remember specifically which writers were on line, but I went in with an ultimate respect for writers. I insisted, as any credible writer would, that I get the opportunity to give shots to young writers who had a great story. I was also talking with Theodore Sturgeon, Ray Bradbury, George Clayton Johnson, Jerry Sohl—that kind of literary heavyweight. It was an awesome thing to confront."

As Black explains it, the *Star Trek* offices at the Desilu Studio were directly below those of *Mission: Impossible*, which was gearing up for production at the same time.

"At the end of the day," he laughs, "we would gather together and talk. Everybody was going crazy. You know, how the hell do you do a science-fiction series? How the hell do you do *Mission: Impossible*? We would bat the day's story problems back and forth, so there's no way to tell who came up with what about what at what time. It was all madness. It was a great deal of work; more work than I had ever done in so compacted a time. It was 12 to 18 hours a day. I can remember many nights wandering around the sets at midnight, trying to figure out story logistics.

"The way television was, there was a hell of a lot that you *couldn't* do, but there was also a hell of a lot that you *could* do then, but nobody was noticing. So, when a show like *Star Trek* came along, it was a marvelous advantage. There was no writer I knew who didn't want to work on that show. We were looking for the most acute science-fiction minds it was possible to acquire, because we were doing something new. But our dilemma was, first of all, that every plant that we showed had to be made. Every weapon or device had to be invented. What the hell did a plant look like on Rigel 9? Dilithium Crystals were a rock which one of my kids brought home. It had a beautiful crystal-like shine, and I really fell in love with the look of it and took it into the office. Somebody asked me what it was and I said, 'It's a Dilithium Crystal.' I didn't know what the hell it was, but it became the power source of the Enterprise. We were creat-

ing *everything*. Conceiving an idea was one thing, getting it on film was another. Cost is relative in doing any series.

"I wasn't that familiar with science fiction," Black admits. "I had read a great deal of it, but science fiction is playing tennis without a net. You could do anything you wanted, and if you look at the one segment I wrote, 'The Naked Time,' you'll see that what I did, purely and simply, was take drunkenness and remove the slurs and staggers from it."

Adding to Black's pleasure was that the realistic qualities of the characters made the series that much more enjoyable to write.

"There was such a natural balance between William Shatner and Leonard Nimoy," Black observes. "There was no way to tell, really, whether they got along or not because they had an easy relationship off camera, and on camera there was an absolute difference that was writeable. You had the advantage in any scene between Shatner and Nimoy where Shatner could take one side and be correct, and Nimoy could take the purely logical side of the situation and also be correct. The scene carried out the conflict which could spark anything along the lines of what was upcoming. I don't mean to sound like a professor of a screenplay class discussing a script's structure, but that's the reality. We know that conflict is the heart of any scene, and the more conflict you have between the characters, the better it is. And it was just built in.

"Uhura was a little more difficult to deal with. Nichelle was breathtakingly gorgeous, a skilled actress and limited to, 'I'm hailing them, Captain.' We could open it up a little, but not much. George Takei, when he came in and became the helmsman, had that marvelous Centurian deep voice that very few people are even aware that he has, although they heard it over and over again. That voice really gave strength to that chair, so that when the captain said whatever to George, and he said, 'Aye, Captain,' the audience knew he was going to do his best and that it was going to be enough. Scotty...if he got an awful lot of repetition because the engines had to go out a number of times, Jimmy

Doohan never lost that characterization that he walked in with on the first day. The dialect stayed in place, as did the amount of smile he permitted. He was a very gifted actor. If we go to our friend Bones, DeForest Kelley, he was as experienced an actor as you could ask for. He had gone from juvenile to character juvenile, to young leading man to leading man and there he was on *Star Trek* with an enormous amount of background and an enormous amount of training. He had his character in hand, although it changed *slightly* during the first five or six episodes where he became a tad more earnest. The conflict built in between he and Spock was electric....Even the extras who would run in and out with their little zap guns were into their characters and into the show. I think that was relevant to the audience. It triggered their emotional responses.

"The show was meaningful for many people. Billy Shatner had just done *Alexander, the Great*. He was good, but it was not a hit. On that night of the first shoot, I left the office and found Bill leaning against my car, and he had a look of enormous innocence on his face. I said, 'How's it going, Billy?' And he said, 'Fine.' I figured there was something going on. And he just looked at me and said, 'It's just so damned important to us.' And I said, 'Yeah, we've got a hit.' That's what you say to everybody when it's in the fan and you don't know what's going to happen next, particularly to actors who are so vulnerable. And he said, 'I hope so,' and walked away. The sense I had was that we were all doing the best we could, and we were giving it everything we had."

"There was a very good team feeling," Dorothy Fontana concurs. "Gene had put together an extremely good team, between the cast, crew and staff, who were united in the feeling that this is a good show, we're doing a fine show and let's keep it up. In fact, I don't think I've ever encountered such a great team spirit on any other show I've ever worked on, although I've had good working relationships with other crews. But that whole unity of everybody, from the top to the least important production person, was right there."

Joseph Pevney, who would play

an extremely important directorial role in the history of *Star Trek*, was as equally enthused about the series. He had begun his career in features, but was eventually convinced to try television where the "real money" was. He began with an episode of *Wagon Train* and moved to other shows, before joining the crew of *Star Trek*. While he directed several episodes of the first season, he would alternate with Marc Daniels during the second.

"I met with Roddenberry," he reflects, "and, wow, what an amazing genius of a man. We had lunch together one day and he told me his background. A very interesting human being. I think he's a half a touch removed from genius. Some of the stuff he did on *Star Trek* is unbelievable. NASA used to come down to the sets to say, 'How did you know about this medical thing...?' They were working on principles he had already thought of. We went down to NASA and watched the development of the 'X' models. Well, we were very big with NASA and all the sci-fi buffs, who dug it the most.

"I'm a high-tech fellow myself," he adds. "I'm very interested in radio, computers, but what I was really interested in was the very creative treatment of the stories. The stories were solid, very well done and the imagination ran rampant. Everything was possible. There was no fantasy in *Star Trek*; it was very real. The people were real, the situations were real, even the episode with the Tribbles was real. It was hi-fi science treated very realistically, socially conscious, good anti-fascist democratic background. All of that stuff was very pleasing to me.

"I also loved the characters. Gene was constantly trying to give it a universal aspect, because that's what's going to be in the theory regarding the future when we go to other worlds. There will be all kinds of things out there. Some will not be completely humanoid, but that was okay. He was quite convincing about that. So he wanted some more nationalities in the show. He had an oriental, a black, eventually a Russian....The '60s were boiling with this out here. At that time we had all kinds of college things going on. The beginnings of the ERA and so on. Civil Rights were tumbling all over the place. Gene was say-ing, 'Let's put a Russian in there.' Wow, what a shockeroo that was."

The late Marc Daniels, who helped pioneer the situation comedy by helming the early episodes of *I Love Lucy* utilizing three cameras and a live studio audience, concurred with the assessment of the characters. "Right from the beginning, it was easy to see that the characters were extremely well drawn. There was some trial and error with the peripheral characters, but the main ones—Kirk, Spock and McCoy—were excellent. With that many characters, it was difficult to give each of them their due. There was a very good contrast between them because you didn't have the same thing going on between any two of them."

While the creative behind the scenes atmosphere was extremely upbeat, things weren't made easier by such obstacles as a weekly budget and directives from the network.

Says Robert Justman, "NBC wanted as many 'planet' shows that they could get. Of course that was very difficult for us to achieve. They, as anybody does, wanted more for their buck. The more things you could cram in a show, the more action you could cram into a show, the happier they were. Their need was to achieve good numbers. In a way, I guess that was our need, too, but we were more concerned with the content of the shows. The network was concerned with content too, but it was their kind of content and the kind that would, in their mind, attract viewers.

"But we were doing the show we were doing. It was all we could do just to do the show. Forget about worrying about anything else. It was a new show, and because of that the network programming department was understandably nervous about what we could show and what we couldn't show, and what subjects we could deal with. Luckily the fact that the show was allegorical in nature, sometimes the content escaped the network's notice. They took the content of the show for what the content *purported* to be. Allegory oftentimes is not about what's there, but what's *not* there. You see, when you're doing a show for a network, you not only have to deal with programming departments and development, but also with what in NBC's case was called the Broadcast Standards Department, which was the censors. Programming might accept a story that Broadcast Standards might find objectionable. It was quite difficult to satisfy three masters, two of them being the network and one of them being ourselves."

While reflecting on those early days, Justman points out that he cannot describe the process of bringing an episode of *Star Trek* to the screen.

"I don't think we have enough time," he smiles. "Just imagine the most incredibly difficult process you can imagine and double it. The gestation is very, very difficult. We had to satisfy many masters. I can't begin to tell you. Add to that the time constraint; you never had enough time to write the episodes properly much less produce them properly. The world of series television is an arcane sort of world; an arcane art. In essence, you really can't do anything in a way that's true. You can only do the best that you can do. You have a finite amount of time and you need to sleep at least a few hours every night, so you accomplish what you can accomplish within those constraints. That's it. It's not easy. The reward every now and then is perhaps turning out a show that affects people, causes them to think and perhaps changes their lives....There was a feeling that we were all together, doing something that was different. Not only different, but worthwhile. *That* was the feeling."

Star Trek premiered on September 8, 1966 and, as Justman states, it quickly proved itself to indeed be different and worthwhile, though the critical reactions were not all that positive. Neither were the show's ratings.

In the early weeks of *Star Trek's* run, audiences were treated to episodes that were completely unlike anything they had seen. "The Man Trap" pit Captain Kirk and company against a "salt vampire" who drained the human body of all its natural salt; "Charlie X" was an adolescent alien with telekinetic abilities who could bend the laws of nature to suit his immature needs; "The Enemy Within" split Kirk in two, resulting in a battle between the good and evil of a man's soul; "Balance of Terror" was a submarine war drama in space between the Enterprise and a war vessel from their enemy, the Romulans; "The Menagerie" was a two-part episode that ingeniously incorporated "The Cage" in a tale of Mr. Spock's apparent mutiny of the Enterprise, forcing it to go to Talos IV, a world deemed off limits by the Federation; and so on. The characters were extremely realistic and the stories plausible no matter what the conflict. Science fiction on television had finally come of age.

"Gene Roddenberry did a good thing in having little moral lessons in most of the shows, and it seemed to be that pointed kids in the right direction," opines writer Jerry Sohl. "Not only that, it made the show entertaining. I don't think it was sugar-coated particularly, because some of those episodes had some pretty racy things in them. On a whole, I think it was, in its time, about the best thing that existed as far as science fiction on screen was concerned. Just the idea of going where no man has gone before is very good."

Behind the scenes, however, in terms of the writing of the scripts themselves, things didn't seem to be going too smoothly after a while, at least as far as John Black was concerned. He was doing whatever he could to bring in top science fiction writers, but they weren't being treated with the respect that he felt they deserved.

Said Roddenberry, "It seems that way, but it wasn't true. I didn't want only science fiction writers, because many of the science fiction writers available to me then talked about objects, about science rather than about people. Over half of them are just good regular writers because I wanted my show to be about people, not objects, and if you think back, the things you remember are the characters. During the first year, I wrote or rewrote everybody, even my best friends, because I had this idea in my mind of something that hadn't been done and I wanted to be really there. Once we had enough episodes, then the writers could see where we were going, but it was really building people to write the way I wanted them to write. I lost a lot of friends, writer friends, because writers don't like to be re-written, but the whole thing was in my head, and I [couldn't] say, 'Mr. Spock, write him like you would

write so-and-so,' because there'd never been anyone like that around. So I rewrote them and lost friendships."

Robert Justman agrees with Roddenberry's feelings. "When we were doing the original show," he explains, "the well known science fiction writers came up with all kinds of marvelous concepts, marvelous premises. Just because you have marvelous premises when you deliver a teleplay, doesn't mean that you've written a proper drama. We had that problem with a number of them, where their premises or concepts were terrific, but they didn't write a drama. They didn't write anything that could actually be photographed or made. The characters didn't necessarily behave in a logical fashion. If you create a character, a character has to be believable and do believable things. If your character doesn't do believable things, your audience is going to get turned off. Whereas you might accept it in the world of prose, you're not necessarily going to accept it in TV drama."

"I guess I'm prejudiced," he says. "I think Gene Roddenberry is a genius. He's an original thinker. Not only in creating *Star Trek*. I *know* him and have known him for years when he has said and done some amazing things," Justman continues. "He's an original thinker. His background was very humble, but he's a man who educated himself and he's found that his mind is fertile ground. It's an astonishing mind. You don't jump into a pool and swim without making waves.

"When you're beginning a series and you have a series premise and you have the methodology and you have a series that has a certain life and logic, your scripts must adhere to that concept. You can't expect a writer to come in and write one episode who is not heavily involved in the series or hasn't been since its inception, and be able to achieve the kind of reality that you the creator have envisioned for the show. Therefore, the show needs rewriting for various reasons. Not only for its content, but for technical reasons and reasons of format. I've done *Star Trek*, I've done a bunch of other series and I've never yet produced a show where the scripts from the writers didn't need revisions in order

to make them as close as possible to what your concept of the show is. It's seldom happened that I've ever shot a show that hasn't been rewritten. Only a few times that I can think of. Generally they're scripts that were turned out by the creator of the show. That's his or her concept, and if the creator happens to be a very good writer, generally there won't be too much need for revisions. Minor revisions, but they're not important."

It's pointed out that the list of complainants over the years have included a variety of highly respected writers, such as George Clayton Johnson, David Gerrold, Dorothy Fontana, Alan Dean Foster, Harold Livingston and Harlan Ellison.

"Bruised ego," Justman says simply. "I can't say I blame them. Nobody wants to be rewritten, because you put a lot of thought and emotion into what you're writing. You believe it's correct or you wouldn't have written it that way. Harry Truman used to say, 'If you can't take the heat, stay out of the kitchen.' No use determining that you're going to work in a certain medium if you're not willing to accept the rules that go with it; the restrictions that apply. This may surprise you, but people don't like to rewrite because it's hard work. You'd much rather get in a script that you can put right to work, but that's not necessarily the way things happen.

"I think Dorothy Fontana knows how to construct a proper drama. So does David Gerrold. You learn this after a while. But people have opinions and sometimes opinions diverge and the guy with the power is the one who prevails. If Dorothy had created a show, she would be doing something very much in the way that Gene has done. Same thing with David. *You* know what your show is supposed to be, and you're going to make it come out that way because that's what you're there for."

John Black offers his view, from the vantage point of *Star Trek*'s story editor and the one dealing directly with the writers.

"Gene was working from the position that he had created the show," says Black, "so it was *his*. G.R.'s approach was that he was in control of the show and he approached the scripts in that way. My deal going in was that if I was going to get really good heavyweight writers, I know that they don't want anybody to screw with their material. They want it to be their concept. The only reason they're going to take television money, which is short, and it was shorter than short story money at that time, and the only way that I will talk to them about it, is if they can rewrite their own material without interference. We could give them all the input we want, but we can't put pencil to paper on their material. Gene said okay, and the head of the studio said yes and that's the way I took the deal.

"This is the reality," he elaborates. "When stories came in on Thursday or Friday, I would read it, make my notes, copies would be made and G.R. would take them home on the weekend. And instead of notes, he would come in on Monday with a rewrite. He would have rewritten everything. God knows how much. And it would never, in my judgement, have been that much for the better. In some cases he got closer to the pattern that the show was becoming, because it was evolving while I was there. But G.R. has never been the writer that Harlan Ellison, Jerry Sohl or Teddy Sturgeon were. He isn't it. That's no knock. Very few people are up to that standing, but Gene couldn't keep his hands off a script. God knows what he would have done with 'To be or not to be, that is the question,' but there's one thing that's absolutely certain: what would have been in the script and what was shot would not have been 'to be or not to be, that is the question.' But it *was* his show. At first it was difficult and then it became impossible. And there was no way to know what would come in the next morning.

"When I did 'The Naked Time,' I delivered my first draft and gave a copy to G.R. I figured, 'Here I am, I'm working on the show and if anybody knows the show it's me, besides G.R. And G.R. brought back a rewritten script. I couldn't cope with it. That was not something I could suck up. The question in my mind, and I put it to G.R., was what the hell am I doing here if I don't know the show? And I asked him what his problem was with it. He told me and I said, 'Okay, I

will rewrite it.' And I rewrote it from my original, then he rewrote my second draft. So nobody got their show on the air...

"You know, you labor over a line...I'll give you an example. This is not an example from 'Naked Time,' but this is the kind of change. If I needed the essence of a cliche someplace, or where the cliche would have been perfect just as it is but it would have been a cliche, as a writer I say, 'How can I state this, where the cliche is clear but it isn't a cliche?' This is the hypothetical line that I would write: 'It's a gift horse. Leave its mouth alone.' Now that's an artfully written line. G.R.'s change would be, 'Don't look a gift horse in the mouth.' There could have been a lot more art in *Star Trek* if G.R. kept his hands off the scripts.

"After Gene would do his rewriting, I'd get the script back, try to satisfy him and get it back to as close a shape to the writer's work as I possibly could. The writer would come in, we would have a story conference, we would discuss changes, the writer would go away and, generally, I would get the writer to do the polish...if there was time. The dilemma with *Star Trek* was that what seemed to a writer to be something that could be done easily inside the context of the starship, became impossible. So alterations were made in a lot of things. They were slight, but necessary. The writers, I think, deserve credit for everything good in everything they did...while I was there, anyway. Any faults you could find in any material can be blamed on me and G.R. The stuff we got was, by and large, brilliant. I cannot remember one instance where I sat across a table from a writer and said, 'Why is this happening?' and they couldn't explain it to me. There was always a reasoning. *Star Trek* was an experience that I'm very glad I had. Talk about a love story. This sounds like a real love story."

Black left *Star Trek* after the first 13 episodes, feeling that he could not compromise himself any longer. "It's always mattered to me that my word was good," he says, "and if I told somebody that they would be permitted to rewrite their own work, that nobody would touch it, and then I would get it back already diddled with, that was not going

to move us into a very happy state of mind. I was there because I could talk to those writers. Those writers respected me and I respected them. Integrity mattered, and I couldn't bear to see quality work changed to the point where the dialogue did not have the sharp edge that it had, and G.R. would use the word 'fast' at least once a page as in, 'We've got to get there...fast.' I was watching too much good material getting screwed up and I couldn't take it. I confronted an executive at the studio and I said, 'I can't really continue if my word does not remain good,' and he said, 'It's G.R.'s show.' So I said, 'Would you like my resignation, or would you like to fire me?' And he said it could be one or the other. There was *no* alternative, so I left the show.

"Please understand, though, it was an experience I wouldn't trade for almost anything. I had never known pressures like the ones on that show, just by its nature. The beautiful demands that the writers made were wonderful. Man, to be sitting across from Ted Sturgeon and talking about a story that was so deeply important to him, and trying to perceive it and become aware...It was the kind of thing where you wanted to exclaim, 'My God, that's incredible!' It was sometimes scary, sometimes emotionally scathing, sometimes great fun, but you had to be there. You had to be present all the time, or you would have missed it. One never knew, particularly with *Star Trek*, what was important. The imagination ran wild. The energy level was just astounding. Looking back at it, I think I'd like to do it again. I can't be certain, but in remembering, I think I would."

While this was going on, both Roddenberry and Justman were working 16 to 20 hour days in an attempt to maintain the show's quality.

"Gene was very fatigued and so was I," says Justman. "We both nearly didn't make it through the first season because of overwork. We were at our wit's end. I was so tired that first season that I came unglued one night at home. My wife called Gene and said, 'That's it, I'm taking him away.' You try working for about six months, seven days a week and averaging three or four hours of sleep a night, with enormous pressure. Eventually something's going to give. It happened to be me that night and Gene was next. We were both basket cases. As a result of that, I think that's how Gene Coon came to be on the show. Gene Roddenberry just couldn't do it by himself. He was excellent, Gene Roddenberry wrote wonderful scenes, but it took its toll."

When Gene L. Coon joined the *Star Trek* staff as line producer, Roddenberry became executive producer.

"I had no choice," said Roddenberry. "The only way I could get people like Gene Coon to come in and produce—and I needed a producer, more helping hands—was to become executive producer, actually a supervising producer. Today, it would be different. No one would object to a very complex show having two, three or even four line producers with a supervising producer over them. In those days, it was unheard of, but I just had to get some extra people in any way I could. I had found myself working 12 or 14 hours a day and I could no longer do it. Everyone on our staff was in the hospital at least once during those three years just from total exhaustion. We were doing a half a science-fiction movie every week. Imagine what a burden that is. Science-fiction movies usually take 20 weeks to do. We were doing one every week!"

Gene Coon is generally considered to be one of *Star Trek*'s greatest strengths, having a natural feel for the kind of story that would be appropriate for the series. Under his sure creative hand came such episodes as "Arena," based on the Frederic Brown story of the same name, which pit Captain Kirk against the lizard-like Gorn creature, and resulted in the crew of the Enterprise being spared by an alien race because Kirk showed the advanced trait of mercy; "A Taste of Armageddon," a powerful Vietnam analogy in which two planets waged a bloodless war via computer, with people living in designated areas voluntarily walking into disintegration chambers; "Space Seed," which introduced Ricardo Montalban as Eugenics superman Khan Noonian Singh and gave the audience a taste of what Earth's future would be like; "The Devil in the Dark," an episode revealing that a creature known as the Horta who was killing Starfleet miners was actually a mother

protecting her young; and "Errand of Mercy," which introduced the Klingons.

"He shaped a lot of the individual shows," says Bob Justman regarding Coon, who passed away in the early 1970s. "But he didn't shape the concept. It was Gene's concept and it was never changed. Gene Coon rewrote the episodes while he was there. He wrote some originals and he was a workaholic. He would push himself to the limit and was marvelous. But the concept of the show had been established early in the first season. It was always Gene's concept. He shaped the show the way he wanted it to be. Then Gene Coon did his best—and his best was really very high—to make the show live up to that concept. Gene Coon was almost totally involved with story and script. He did some casting, but he had nothing really to do with the editing of the show or the scoring. I did all of that, as well as the props, the set dressing and all the other garbage.

"Honestly speaking," he continues, "Gene Roddenberry would have died if he didn't have Gene Coon or someone to do this. Gene Coon was a brilliant find; you couldn't find anyone better. The problem is that we wore him out, which is why he ultimately left in the middle of the second season."

Generally, Gene L. Coon may very well have been the one to define *Star Trek* for future generations. Indeed, his contributions to the series were important enough for William Shatner to mention him at the commemoration of the Gene Roddenberry Building on the Paramount lot several months before Roddenberry's passing.

"In my opinion," offers Shatner, "Gene Coon had more to do with the infusion of life into *Star Trek* than any other single person. Gene Roddenberry's instincts for creating the original package is unparalleled. You can't even discuss it. He put it together, hired the people and the concept was his and set in motion by him. But after 13 shows, other people took over. Gene Coon spent a year and set the tenor of the show. Gene [Roddenberry] was more in the background as other people actively took over."

For producer Harve Bennett, who steered the *Star Trek* feature film series for nearly 10 years, Coon was an

inspiration. "Gene Roddenberry was the Douglas MacArthur of this particular campaign, the George Patton," says Bennett. "And guys like Gene Coon were the Omar Bradleys."

Veteran writer/producer Glen A. Larson, whose credits include *Quincy*, *Knightrider* and *Battlestar: Galactica*, had worked with Coon while the two of them were on the staff of *It Takes a Thief*. During their tenure together, Larson came to look upon Coon as a mentor.

"I used to figuratively sit at his feet and listen to him talk about the business a great deal," reflects Larson. "That was really my whole introduction to television, through Gene. I think Gene Coon was the spirit and soul of the show. I don't think the show would have gone in the direction that it did nor had its enormous credibility of not for Coon. From what I could tell, Gene Coon *was Star Trek*. When he was no longer there, I think the show quickly denegrated to monster of the week, which was always the danger of science fiction in television, because you generally don't have the people around with the intellectual capacity to really explore important themes without making them so obscure that there's no hope of holding an audience. Gene had a good sense of drama in addition to strong concepts."

Gene L. Coon was born in Beatrice, Nebraska and educated within the public school system in both Nebraska and California. Following high school, he attended Glendale College. In 1942 he enlisted in the United States Marine Corp, where he spent four years. From there he wrote scripts for a variety of television series, including *Wagon Train*, *Bonanza*, *Have Gun, Will Travel*, *Rawhide*, *Alcoa Premier*, *Riverboat*, *Suspense*, *General Electric Theatre*, *Mr. Lucky*, *Peter Gunn*, *The Rebel* and *Maverick*. In the early '60s, Coon went to work at Universal Pictures where he co-created *McHale's Navy* and *The Munsters*, the latter of which was originally intended to be a hip satire of *The Donna Reed Show*. From 1964-67, Coon wrote several produced screenplays and penned two novels, *Meanwhile, Back at the Front* and *The Short End of the Stick*. But he seemed to find his true niche in *Star Trek*.

Examining the chronology of *Star Trek*, it becomes obvious that many of the show's more memorable aspects went into effect during Coon's reign.

"If you look at the episodes that Roddenberry was responsible for in the beginning," notes David Gerrold, "which was pretty much like the first 10 episodes, there's not a lot of that noble purpose there. There's a bumbling around trying to find out what the show is about, yet at the same time they did some great episodes. Because no one knew what *Star Trek* was, they wee continually inventing it. You see stuff like 'Charlie X,' 'The Enemy Within,' and they also did a lot of rip-offs—'The Galileo Seven' was *Flight of the Phoenix*, 'Balance of Terror' was *The Enemy Below*—and so they didn't really know what they could do with the show yet. When Gene L. Coon first came on board in the second half of the first season, you start getting things like the Prime Directive and a lot of the stuff that was later identified as the noble parts of *Star Trek*. Gene L. Coon created the noble image that everyone gives Roddenberry the most credit for."

Continues Gerrold, "When Gene L. Coon came in, one of the things that happened is that by then they knew what they could do, and he would concentrate on those areas. The episodes he did were more sure of themselves, but they weren't as adventurous in the same way. The characters by then were more established, so Coon let the characters have the relationships with each other. The advantages were that when Gene L. Coon took over, the characters locked into place very tightly and crisply. And it became Kirk, Spock and McCoy. Before that time, there was a vagueness because Roddenberry didn't know who or what the show was about. After Gene Coon took over, he decided it was about Kirk, Spock and McCoy, and the other characters were ancillary. That became kind of the formula, which was successful."

Coon's scripts contained thinly-veiled social commentary, which became a staple of the series and something that is generally credited to Gene Roddenberry.

"We never sat around talking about that kind of thing," says Dorothy Fontana. "I think that's just the kind of writing that Gene Coon did. It influenced the writers who came in, who were structuring their stories. You could see this kind of flow happening. Another thing that happened is that the humor between the characters began to become more and more developed, particularly the Spock and McCoy relationship became a lot more fun. It evolved into what it ultimately became, which was a basic friendship. It was a friendship conducted with little insults and jabs, but it was always fun. The verbal fencing matches. It was fun to create those conversations once we started getting into them. I think Gene Coon led the way on that."

Notes David Gerrold, "Roddenberry always took the show too seriously and everybody preached. I think Roddenberry wanted to be a preacher and couldn't make it or something. Everybody preached and Gene said, 'No, in the future our people work together,' but what he would write would be sermons. In Gene L. Coon's scripts, people interacted with each other in a whole different way and didn't preach, although it was mandatory to do a little preaching at the end of the script where the captain explains—the captain being the father figure. Gene L. Coon's characters joked with each other. I think that's why the fans loved the show so much. While our people were having an adventure, they were never too busy to snipe at each other, which was the way they showed their affection. I think there was never a question of how much Spock and McCoy loved each other, and that was shown by how vicious they would get when they would start sniping at each other. I think a lot of that was Gene L. Coon."

While Coon "replaced" Roddenberry as the show's hands-on producer, story editor John D.F. Black's role was taken over by a young writer named Steven Carabatsos, who considers himself one of the few people involved in *Star Trek* who has *not* come up with an explanation for the show's enduring success.

"It beats the hell out of me why the show has gone on the way it has," he laughs. "In retrospect, I suppose anyone who talks about the program wants to invest *every* moment with great significance. The honest fact is that when it was first on, to me, at least, and I'm sure to many other people, it was just another show, 79 episodes of employment for most of them. Granted that because of all the famous science fiction writers involved, there was a sense of more going on, but you have to understand, nobody knew what we had there. *Nobody* had any idea. Even when the show came on, it didn't light up the stars."

Carabatsos, not a science fiction fan, was asked by his agent if he would be interested in meeting with the two Genes about the possibility of taking on the position of script consultant. That meeting went well, and Carabatsos entered the realm of the 23rd century.

"The show hadn't been on the air yet," he says. "By the time I came on, there were about six episodes in the can. I'm sure today it's even more frantic because the stakes are higher, but at that time, on the shakedown year of a show, everyone was trying new things and was concerned about it being a success, as well as being the kind of show they wanted it to be. In something as new as *Star Trek*, Roddenberry wanted to do a *legitimate* science fiction program. Not the silly stuff that had been on previously that allegedly passed for science fiction.

"Gene Roddenberry worked very hard. I've got to give the man a lot of credit, he busted his butt. But he had taken on executive producer responsibilities and the line producer was Gene L. Coon, who was actually making sure the scripts got into the right form for shooting and physically produced the show. He's the one I reported to once I came to work.

"In those days, most of the writing was done by freelancers as opposed to today where you've got all these people on staff with commitments for three to six episodes or more. Some of the scripts could have the rough edges rounded off and could be put before the cameras quickly, while others required substantial rewriting, which Gene Coon and I handled. It was an exciting time for me, because I was really just a kid, and this was a big opportunity. I also remember being impressed by the fact that Roddenberry was enlisting a writing corp of experienced science fiction writers. All of them came to their assignments with great enthusiasm and a sense of excitement to do *their* kinds of stories done in the way they wanted them done. My problem is that I didn't share that background; I didn't quite feel that I had the same preparation for it."

He remained with the show for approximately 15 weeks before moving on to other areas. To this day, however, he remains amazed that people are so impressed when they learn he worked on *Star Trek.*

"It was early in the days of one-hour dramatic TV programs," he muses, "and everyone was happy to have a show that lasted more than a year. As it turned out, *much* longer than a year."

When Carabatsos departed, Dorothy Fontana slipped into the position of script consultant, a role she essayed until the end of the second season. Having proved herself to Roddenberry and company, she was a welcome addition to the staff.

"I had dealt with the scripts all the time," Fontana explains, "and had my own opinions about them. I just never put them down on paper, although I spoke to Gene and Gene Coon secretly about the shows they were doing. I got involved with the show first as a writer, so I had my own story conferences with them about it. I felt I could do that same job [of script consultant] and so did Gene, so he let me have it."

Despite an ever changing cre-ative staff, *Star Trek* did manage to maintain its high level of quality. Unfortunately there was another battle being fought, and that was the battle of the Nielsons: once on the air, it became obvious that *Star Trek* was losing the ratings war. In fact, NBC began indicating that the series might be cancelled at the midpoint of the first season. Amazingly, however, as word of this got out, science fiction author Harlan Ellison spear-headed a letter writing campaign to keep the series on the air.

This effort was a success, resulting in a tremendous response that proved there was indeed an audience out there watching *Star Trek* each week and waiting for further adventures aboard the starship Enterprise. The series not only lasted the full season, but was renewed for a second year.

Star Trek had survived a rejected pilot, network opposition and near-cancellation. Unfortunately, this only represented the first round of an interstellar boxing match that would continue over the next two years.

William Shatner and Pat Breslin in the "Nick of Time" episode of The Twilight Zone.

• • • •

CHAPTER TWO
Season 1 Episode Guide

"The Man Trap"

"Charlie X"

"Where No Man Has Gone Before"

"The Naked Time"

"The Enemy Within"

"Mudd's Women"

"What Are Little Girls Made Of?"

"Miri"

"Dagger of the Mind"

"The Corbomite Maneuver"

"The Menagerie" (Pts 1 and 2)

"The Conscience of the King"

"Balance of Terror"

"Shore Leave"

"The Galileo Seven"

"The Squire of Gothos"

"Arena"

"Tomorrow is Yesterday"

"Court Martial"

"The Return of the Archons"

"Space Seed"

"A Taste of Armageddon"

"This Side of Paradise"

"The Devil in the Dark"

"Errand of Mercy"

"The Alternative Factor"

"City on the Edge of Forever"

"Operation Annihilate"

Before becoming the humanist Dr. Leonard "Bones" McCoy, DeForest Kelly had forged a career of playing Western heavies.

Episode #1:
"The Man Trap"
Original Airdate: 9/8/66
Written by George Clayton Johnson
Directed by Marc Daniels
Guest Starring: Jeanny Bal (Nancy Carter), Francine Pyne (Salt Creature), Alfred Ryder (Professor Carter), Michael Zaslow (Darnell)

The Enterprise is assigned the task of proceeding to planet M-113 in order to deliver medical supplies to the planet's only two inhabitants, Doctors Robert and Nancy Crater, the latter of whom had been romantically involved with Dr. McCoy. Rather, he had been involved with *a* Nancy Crater. This one turns out to be a shape-changing salt "vampire" who seduces its victims by appearing as someone they know and then attacking, draining their bodies of natural salt content. The creature gets aboard the Enterprise and must be destroyed, despite the fact it is the last of a species.

••••

Writer George Clayton Johnson explains that his original title for "The Man Trap" was "Damsel With a Dulcimer," but that Gene Roddenberry changed the title as well as some its structure, which the author felt lessened the impact of the episode.

"I'll give you just an example," Johnson reflects. "The initial scene of 'The Man Trap' as initially conceived was that Leonard McCoy and Captain Kirk are entering the transporter on the ship for the purpose of being beamed down to the planet surface to begin the story. We've seen a fly-through of the ship, because that's standard format and we've heard the song and we know what show we're watching now, and we cut to the beginning of the first act and we're not on the bridge, we're approaching this transporter room, walking through hallways, talking and coming into this transporter room.

"Now the character that I wrote for the character of Dr. McCoy, who was a very undefined character, I'd only seen one show of it and was expected as a professional writer to visualize all the surrounding tiles, each tile together would form this huge, colossal thing we know as *Star Trek*. But we just had one of the few of the tiles, one or two or three of the tiles in place, and I had only seen one of them, so on the basis of that one I was expected to dream up *my* version of *Star Trek*. So I had Captain Kirk saying something to Leonard McCoy about, 'What's wrong, Bones?' and Bones saying, 'Look, I just don't like the whole idea of the transporter. I don't care how tight any beam is, there's some scatter and I don't like the idea of atoms of myself being left all over the damn universe. I just don't like that idea. And this thing gives me the creeps.' And that sort of dialogue, whereupon Captain Kirk says, 'Nonsense,' and they show up on the planet surface, whereupon we get some of the underground. In place of that comes a scene written to replace it where McCoy and the Captain are getting into the transporter; they are talking about some flowers that are being carried to give this girl whom McCoy is going to be meeting, who is his old girlfriend, whom he knows is going to be on this planet, this so-called Nancy Crater.

"Now the business about the flowers, for me, is kind of in a certain way very subjectively soft, whereas the business about the transporter is for me very objectively hard, and it also makes a promise of future episodes. It says that one of these days we may see a story about a transporter malfunction. It lets you know that there are limitations on the universe. But it was taken out, so that later on when we see the first transporter malfunction story, we are not prepared for it; if we are regular viewers, it comes out of the blue to us. Now I felt that was damaging to the entire concept. That little mini-story implanted in just a few lines of dialogue, setting the scene, is superior dramaturgy to the business about, 'Oh, I see you need to take along some [flowers] to get girls to like you. Is that your thing?' [It's just] a little bit of familiarity between two pals."

"The idea of the shape changer," he says."I received the go ahead from Gene on the idea, then I went home and worked hard for about 30 days and I came back with a script with which I was very dissatisfied with, and I was reluctant to show the story editor. I told the story editor, John D.F. Black, what my feelings were, and he asked me then what I was doing, and I started telling him and at a certain point he said, 'Oh, you see a problem is that you don't get the creature aboard the ship fast enough. The danger is once the creature gets aboard the ship.' The minute he said that, I could see where my thinking had been wrong, the initial concept of the structure, the very shape which the story took, which suddenly collapsed it into my mind, and I went home and in a matter of just a few days completely rewrote it with his blessing, brought it back and he liked it immediately."

Recalling the experience of George Clayton Johnson, John D.F. Black states, "George Johnson is the best 'soap opera writer' that ever functioned in night-time melodramatic television....Please, God, don't make it sound like I'm saying anything negative, because it isn't. It's a very unique way and it may be George's natural style to write. It's very real, but at the same time there's that kind of theatricalism which is maybe a touch more than what [Richard] Matheson or I would do. It's just a touch more....I say soap opera for wont of another phrase. George worked harder on story with more conscientiousness and more dedication than anybody, because George, of all the writers involved with the show, really wanted *Star Trek* to be a smash. He really wanted science fiction out there, on the tube for people to see. He was dedicated to the media, he was dedicated to the show and there was nothing he wouldn't do. If we had asked him to sneak into the lot at night to build sets, he would have done that."

Shortly before his death, director Marc Daniels opined, "From the point the series began, it was very touchy in terms of how we should deal with these monsters. Did you go for cheap thrills or take the more intelligent approach? What we came up with was the idea that in order to get the audience involved in a very realistic way, you had to treat everything as though it were real."

Episode #2:
"Charlie X"
Original Airdate: 9/15/66
Written by Dorothy Fontana
Story by Gene Roddenberry
Directed by Lawrence Dobkin
Guest Starring: Robert Walker Jr. (Charlie), Abraham Sofaer (Thalasian), Patricia McNulty (Tina Lawton), Charles J. Stewart (Captain Remart), Dallas Mitchell (Tom Nellis)

Shortly after the captain of the Federation ship Antares drops off adolescent Charlie Evans on board the Enterprise, the Antares is mysteriously destroyed. Following other unexplained incidents, the blame falls on Charlie who reveals himself to have incredible telekinetic abilities to alter matter and cause people to "go away," i.e. vanish. Charlie, whose immaturity governs his actions, becomes an even more dangerous threat when he falls in love with Yeoman Janice Rand and will stop at nothing to get her to return his feelings.

• • • •

This episode features a startling moment when Charlie closes in on Janice and the camera fades to black. One gets the impression that he is forcing himself upon her sexually, though this is left entirely to the imagination.

"'Charlie X' was a story that was in the original series presentation," explains Dorothy Fontana, "and I told Gene that if no one else wanted to do it, I would like to do the teleplay. That's precisely what happened. I was in Europe when they shot it, but I did like the way it turned out, and I thought Robert Walker, Jr. was an especially good choice for Charlie."

Several years ago Walker recalled his experience on the episode, particularly the fact that star William Shatner was "very, very helpful. I had only been an actor for about five years and he had always been kind of an idol of mine. I had always thought that he was a terrific actor. I had watched him on different programs for years before I did 'Charlie X.' But he was very helpful and very friendly and the same with Leonard Nimoy. They took the time and were patient with this new, reluctant budding actor.

"That was an interesting, awkward period of my life," he added. "I almost felt like Charlie X. I was 26 when I did the episode but I was a late developer. It was a very difficult time. I didn't have much self-confidence as an actor or as a person. I felt awkward and ineffectual and really kind of lost. I felt at loose ends really. It was a very vulnerable time for me but also a very exciting time for me. You know, at that time, I was very much like Charlie X. We had a lot of similarities."

In the pages of Pocket's *The Star Trek Interview Book*, director Lawrence Dobkin recalled, "Probably my best memory of *Star Trek* is all those people, that young in the series: they did not yet have approval of the crowd. They hadn't any support for what was clearly an attempt to bring the humanities into another time zone, to graph today's relationships in some fashion onto a different time frame, and keep the simplicities and the realities and the human interaction going. My God, what a talented bunch. Wow! It was a very fruitful period in so many ways, fruitful for all of us. It was a fortunate time, and people took chances, people took grave risks....I had played with science fiction in one form or another, and it's very difficult to empathize with something quite strange, quite out of the way. It's difficult for an audience to come to terms with even as human a creature as Captain Nemo in the Jules Verne science fiction...But here, Roddenberry's thrust made very real people and very concerned relationships."

Episode #3:
"Where No Man Has Gone Before"
Original Airdate: 9/22/66
Written by Samuel A. Peeples

Actress Sally Kellerman portrayed Dr. Elizabeth Dehner in "Where No Man Has Gone Before."

Directed by James Goldstone
Guest Starring: Gary Lockwood (Gary Mitchell), Sally Kellerman (Elizabeth Dehner), Paul Carr (Kelso), Paul Fix (Dr. Piper), Andrea Dromm (Yeoman Smith), Lloyd Haynes (Alden)

As the Enterprise attempts to broach an energy barrier at the edge of the galaxy, crewman Gary Mitchell—a close personal friend of Kirk's—is transformed into a god-like being who must be killed before he can inflict his power on the universe.

• • • •

Actor Gary Lockwood, who portrayed Gary Mitchell and who would later go on to portray astronaut Frank Poole in Stanley Kubrick's *2,001*, recalls working on *Star Trek*'s second pilot.

"To tell you the truth," he smiles, "I thought it was a little bizarre and I thought it was kind of embarrassing and I hoped it worked out because everybody was excited about it. It was a very hard job to do. You couldn't see the other actors. I'd rehearse and get everything all ready, but I couldn't see the actors because of the contact lenses that changed my eyes. They didn't blind me for the first few days, but after a few days the eyes swelled up and got sore. Then to have them on for just two or three minutes was agonizing. Scenes were rehearsed without them. The other thing about it, people always thought I was kind of egotistical so when I got to play that part, a lot of people laughed and said, 'He's finally found his niche.' That's been a joke among my friends.

"That character was tough to reach, because there's no prototype character to look at. So you create a mental image and try to fill that slot. All I tried to do was downplay the mechanics and not be too dramatic. It's the same thing I did in *2,001*. Try to play the part very quietly and very realistically, and later on people don't think you're pushing. That's the way to sustain it. There was a natural progression to the character. In order to do that, you have to think it out. Let me say one thing to you that I can say about American actors I don't like and who don't like me. You have to apply a certain amount of intelligence to your role first, and then you can apply the emotion after you've made an intellectual decision. Too many young kids I work with are all trying to figure out how to make the line comfortable. You work in Europe, they're trying to bend to the line. Here they're trying to bend the line to them. It's a different approach. With Gary Mitchell, the idea was trying to go to the character and not make the character comfortable to me. I'm *not* Gary Mitchell."

"I guess 'Where No Man Has Gone Before' is effective because it sold the series. You've got to keep in mind that the *Star Trek* pilot was made in those days on a very, very tight budget. I think there was a big fight between the network and Roddenberry over making the second pilot, so there was a lot of pressure on him. They came up with this idea of two characters getting ESP, which I liked. I think they made up for not having an opportunity to do a lot of effects by just creating a couple of interesting characters, and that helped sell the show. It was a good creative decision on the part of Roddenberry."

Director James Goldstone points out that he most definitely contributed to the creative process of the episode, as emphasized by the notes he wrote on one of his scripts for "Where No Man Has Gone Before."

"A major point," Goldstone wrote, "which applies all the way through the script, and to which there might be specific reference below, concerns the character of Mitchell and the evolution of his mutation toward god status. The purpose is dramatic, to create a subtext. My proposal is that from the time Gary suffers the first realization of what is happening....once he begins to give in to it, to

enjoy it, even, he moves from his human status toward the status of a god within all any any of the criteria we place on such dieties in our Christian-Judaic culture. Specifically, I propose that he become oracular, in the sense of Moses or even Cotton Mather. I propose he do this in his stature, his way of using his hands and arms and eyes, silver or normal, his attitude at it applies to the script, aside from those specific stage directions, perhaps physical actions that pertain to the dialogue. I don't mean to suggest that it become so stylized as to become a symbol rather than a human being. I suggest it happen on a more symbolic level. This can be done by starting him more on the flip, swinging level of articulation so that we don't even notice at one moment that this drops, but it does, on its way to becoming more formal, then more laden with import, more self-declarative, and finally downright miraculous."

Despite this type of contribution, Goldstone emphasizes that he does not believe in the auteur theory. "The director is the person who actually implements the work, but if he doesn't work with the writer, and if he doesn't work with the producer, the technicans in the preparation, then he's being cut off at the knees and so is the film. Television, especially, has just become a producers medium. People would probably rather not have me, because I'm a pain in the ass. I want to do the things that directors, as I understand it, are supposed to do."

Episode #4:
"The Naked Time"
Original Airdate: 9/29/66
Written by John D.F. Black
Directed by Marc Daniels
Guest Starring: Bruce Hyde (Riley),
Stewart Moss (Tormolen),
John Bellah (Dr. Harrison)

While attempting to remove a group of scientists from the doomed planet Psi 2000, an Enterprise landing party is infected with a disease which they bring back aboard the starship and quickly spread. The result is that the crew's inhibitions are stripped away, as though by alcohol, and they start living out their fantasies or confronting their darkest demons. Lieutenant Riley, who establishes himself

as "captain," tampers with the engines and Enterprise is threatened with destruction as it moves closer to the planet's atmosphere. Dr. McCoy labors to find a cure before it's too late.

••••

In John D.F. Black's opinion, "The Naked Now" was a perfect example of just how limitless the *Star Trek* format was.

"There was *no* limit," he enthuses. "We could have villains that you could see and villains you couldn't see, as in my 'The Naked Time.' You could have any character do a complete turnaround simply because there was a difference in oxygen somewhere. We jumped right in there without one single solitary thing in terms of theatricalism that we couldn't do. We could have done Oedipus or anything, although the censors wouldn't allow us to do the Oedipus story. Nor would they allow it anytime you got into those overtly sexually driven stories at that point in time. Except for 'Mudd's Women,' which was basically prostitution at large, which was in the papers every day. We were not promoting it or coming out against it. All we were saying is that it happens here and it happens in outer space, and the censors let it go. We had a lot of support from the censors at NBC. We had some static, but, by and large, they went *with* the show, and that doesn't happen often."

Added director Marc Daniels, "That was the one where I had very little preparation, although I think it turned out all right. The characters were falling into place and we began to get into the workings of Kirk's mind, Spock's powers and things like that. In one of the early episodes, Spock got hurt and bled green blood. I think Gene thought that idea was going too far, but they kept it in later episodes. The green blood was my idea, because if Spock was going to have a yellow complexion, he ought to have green blood. Anyway, in 'The Naked Time' George Takei went a little out of control. We had sharp swords there and he was getting a bit carried away. We had to 'shut him off' so that he wouldn't accidentally hurt anybody."

George Takei recalled, "When I learned that I'd have to fence for 'The Naked Time,' I became panic stricken. I didn't know how to use a sword! I started taking fencing lessons only three weeks before the episode shot."

Interestingly, this show would serve as the springboard for the second episode of *Star Trek: The Next Generation*, "The Naked Now." Unfortunately, it was not as interesting, because the script was more concerned with sexual hijinks among the crew than characterization.

Episode #5:
"The Enemy Within"
Original Airdate: 10/6/66
Written by Richard Matheson
Directed by Leo Penn
Guest Starring: Jim Goodwin (John Farrell), Edward Madden and Garland Thompson (Technicians)

A transporter malfunction splits Kirk into two beings: one pure evil and the other good. What follows is a battle between the two as each battles for supremacy at the expense of the other, though it becomes obvious that they need each other. Spock and Chief Engineer Scott attempt to devise a method of combining the two Kirks into one. Meanwhile, a landing team is trapped on the surface of Alpha 177 and sub-zero temperatures. The Enterprise cannot beam them aboard for fear that what happened to Kirk would happen to them as well.

••••

"Dick Matheson and I knew each other, not well but we had crossed over each other for a long time before I was ever on *Trek*," says John D.F. Black. "In his case what I had to do with the script was miniscule, because he really wanted to make his own fight with G.R., and could do it. He was a professional. I know he had had a conference with G.R. at some point that I was not at, and then we had a talk about the final draft in G.R.'s office and I was there. He understood what the show was. He did not think it was a disguised comedy, he did not think it was the last man on the moon. He knew what we were doing. He tuned in immediately, as he had done on *Twilight Zone* before, so it was difficult for G.R. to make any kind of real arguments about structure. He had some bitches about where the story turned here and where it turned there, but by and large that was one of the easy ones."

In the pages of *Starlog* magazine, director Leo Penn admitted, "It was a challenging show to do. We had to hire a photo double, and it was particularly tough in the scenes where they [the two Kirks] had physical contact. You had to resort to shooting over the double's shoulder, switching them around and so on. It took time, but the results were worth it."

In that same interview with journalist Pat Jankiewicz, Penn noted, "Within certain aspects of American Indian culture, they surmise that evil possesses more energy than good, and Indians believe if they could get to the evil one and comb the snakes out of his hair, he would be cleansed and be able to use that energy for good. One is constantly interested in the struggle between good and evil....In every human being there's good and bad. Hopefully the good is reachable. There are some leaders who bring out the best in people, and Captain Kirk was certainly such a person."

Episode #6:
"Mudd's Women"
Original Airdate 10/13/66
Written by Stephen Kandel
Story by Gene Roddenberry
Directed by Harvey Hart
Guest Starring: Roger C. Carmel (Harry Mudd), Karen Steele (Eve), Susan Denberg (Magda), Maggie Three (Ruth), Gene Dynarski (Ben Childress), Jim Goodwin (Farrell), Jon Kowal (Gossett), Seamon Glass (Benton)

The Enterprise beams aboard interstellar conman Harry Mudd and the three incredibly beautiful women he has along with him as cargo. Kirk regrets saving them from their doomed vessel when he cripples the Enterprise in the process, and the only way for the ship to continue on its way is to make it to a mining world to replenish their dilithium crystal supplies. Harry manages to contact the miners first and manipulates them with the women, thus hoping to achieve his freedom from the authorities. As time goes on, it becomes obvious that the women's beauty has been achieved artificially.

••••

"Gene had the idea of using a personal enhancer-allure drug," says writer Stephen Kandel of the script's

origins, "and I provided the idea of the character of Harry Mudd. We spent an afternoon talking about it and out of the conversation evolved the story idea and then, of course, I wrote the story. Gene went over it in great and meticulous and obsessive detail, and then I wrote the script.

"I thought Harry was a marvelous character of the highly recognizable human quality set against the alien in time or alien in space activity that evolved," he enthuses. "That's what made it amusing, and it's also hard to do because you had stern-jawed Kirk who would meet an eight foot intelligent reptile and deal with him as any astronaut would. Then the reptile would meet Harry Mudd, whose first impulse would be to run and hide, and second impulse would be to sell it scale enhancer."

John D.F. Black says, "The basic problem we had with 'Mudd's Women' was not the script so much as the wardrobe as designed and getting it past the censors. It was a very overtly sex oriented piece."

Episode #7:
"What Are Little Girls Made Of?"
Original Airdate: 10/20/66
Written by Robert Bloch
Directed by James Goldstone
Guest Starring: Michael Strong (Dr. Korby), Sherry Jackson (Andrea), Ted Cassidy (Ruk), Harry Basch (Brown), Vince Deadrick (Matthews), Budd Albright (Rayburn)

Nurse Christine Chapel is to be reunited with her fiance, Dr. Roger Korby, who is on the planet Exo III. When she and Kirk beam down to the planet's surface, they learn that Korby has discovered an ancient technology that allows him to create androids which are an exact duplicate of people. He uses this technology to make an android of Kirk, with the intention of using the Enterprise to spread this new race throughout the galaxy.

••••

"Robert Bloch is one of those venerables," opines John D.F. Black. "He's a writer with a phenomenal and enormous stature among science fiction writers. I respected him and when he

••••

The late Ted Cassidy, forever known as The Addam's Family's Lurch, portrayed Ruk in "What Are Little Girls Made Of?"

came in the story was already on line; the deal had already been made when I signed on to the show. It was a story that I wanted to see what the hell he would do with in the translation from story to teleplay. I don't think I would have touched it. G.R. did. I don't know what went wrong with it. I think it was one of those things that on paper was one thing, and translating it through actors and through a director was another. But the script, by and large, worked as I perceived it. I know that there was a long stretch between the first draft and the second, and I can't remember if it was because it was difficult to execute what had been told to Bloch or whether in fact he had some hang-up and he was pissed at the comments. You've got to remember that stories were affected by cost factors all over the place. I think there was a cost factor involved in the Bloch piece, but I'm not sure."

Director James Goldstone is more succinct with his memories. "There were problems," he says simply. "I got a panic call from Bobby Justman that whatever plans they had for the episode had turned into a big problem. Would I please help them out? I happened to be free that week. Largely out of affection for Gene and other people involved, I read the script. It was not like anything else I'd done, and it was not like the pilot in any way. My memory of it is that I was not at all emotionally involved, nor did I think it was the kind of story we had

originally conceived of. It was done as a favor to Gene and others, rather than something I wanted to do."

Episode #8:
"Miri"
Original Airdate: 10/27/66
Written by Adrian Spies
Directed by Vincent McEveety
Guest Starring: Kim Darby (Miri), Michael J. Pollard (Jahn), Jim Goodwin (Farrell)

Upon Enterprise discovering an Earth-like planet , a landing team that includes Kirk, Spock, McCoy and Rand beams down and discovers a group of 300 year old children. They learn that a disease prolongs youth, but upon reaching adolescence—no matter how long it takes—it triggers madness and then death. Infected, the landing party is trapped there unless McCoy can devise a cure. In the meantime, a young woman named Miri develops a strong crush on Kirk, and is extremely jealous of the captain's affection for Rand.

••••

"I had no idea *Star Trek* was going to be such a big deal. I wrote 'Miri' to the best of my ability and it was a good script, I thought, but it was *just another script,*" admits writer Adrian Spies. "I had already won big awards, including the Edgar [the Mystery Writers of America award], and had been nomi-

nated for an Emmy. I didn't think this was going to fit into that kind of category for me. *Star Trek* just didn't sound like my schtick. But to this day, people say, 'Oh my God, you wrote "Miri!"', and I get chagrined. In those days, Gene told the writers he called that this was 'really an anthology. This is a chance to write about anything you want.' I didn't know what he was talking about. But we were two professionals and we worked out the story together. He had good ideas and good contributions. In the final analysis, it was a good experience. I just wasn't into very much science fiction at that point.

"I have a feeling that [with 'Miri'] I was trying to develop an idea for a film," he adds, "and when I went to see Gene I offered him the idea of a bunch of kids in this place where they are permanently young, but are really very old. If he was to tell you that he came up with the idea, I wouldn't say no, but it's not my memory. I do remember that he said, 'You have to develop a language for these people.' I said, 'What the hell are you talking about?' He said, 'The kids would talk differently.' In that conversation, he made up the word 'grups' for grownups. I immediately liked it. That's an example of a creative producer at work."

"The idea of 'Miri' was absolutely intriguing and fascinating, and it felt wonderful right from the get go," smiles John D.F. Black. "The stresses that

"Miri" stars Kim Darby and William Shatner were reunited in ABC's 1972 TV movie, The People.

• • • •

were built in had a natural energy in the concept. It was there from the first draft and Adrian kept it there throughout. He was easy to work with because he was a consummate professional and experienced at the time. What it would take you 10 minutes to say to somebody else, you could say to him in 30 seconds and he would have a clamp on it and know exactly what you meant. We were lucky to have him."

Director Vincent McEveety had gotten his big break on *The Untouchables* and had moved on to Gene Roddenberry's *The Lieutenant* before helming six episodes of *Star Trek*.

"'Miri' was a great love story with beautiful performances," he continues, "and it's definitely my favorite episode. I think if we have one obligation as so-called 'creative people' in this business in the function of writing, producing and directing, it's to entertain. By entertaining, I mean moving the audience. If you can move somebody, change somebody, give somebody a change of heart, have them look at something different than they may have in the past, provide some kind of introspection to themselves and have them walk away saying, 'Wow,' then I think you've done what you set out to do. If you're just putting out some joke or a kaleidoscope of scenes, that might be enough for Saturday morning, but it isn't enough for a show with the caliber of *Star Trek*. I think 'Miri' fit in perfectly."

Episode #9:
"Dagger of the Mind"
Original Airdate: 11/3/66
Written by Shimon Wincelberg
Directed by Vincent McEveety
Guest Starring: James Gregory (Dr. Tristan Adams), Morgan Woodward (Dr. Van Gelder), Marianna Hill (Dr. Helen Noel), Suzanne Wilson (Lethe)

While delivering supplies to penal colony Tantalus Five, Kirk happens upon the madness of Dr. Tristan Adams, who is using a revolutionary neural neutralizer to control and manipulate his patients. Fearful of exposure, he uses the device on the captain.

••••

John D.F. Black smiles sheepishly at the memories of working with writer Shimon Wincelberg. "When I did story notes, I never did the first draft for the writer. My notes were expressions of what I thought, i.e. 'What is this piece of shit?' and things like that. Well, I wrote scathing notes about Shimon's story: 'It doesn't look like something he's written, it looks like he's taken it out of his trunk...an ancient piece that really doesn't deserve to see the light of day,' and so on. In my notes to myself, from which I would write courteous notes in which I would offer proper criticisms, I pulled no punches. Then, I wasn't in my office and Shimon showed up for his story conference. G.R. sent Dorothy Fontana into my office to pick up my notes. She xeroxed my notes and gave them to Shimon, and then he came into my office later on and thanked me for being that frank and that honest. He told me I was right and went home to rewrite the story. Now that's not only a gentleman, but that's an honest and dedicated writer. I thought his title was one of the more artful and the concept was absolutely clean. If you think about it, it's really an intelligent concept and I wasn't even sure if it would work as *Trek*. But it got a little more 'commercial' as it went from first to second draft and finally to filmed episode."

Episode #10:
"The Corbomite Maneuver"
Original Airdate: 11/10/66
Written by Jerry Sohl
Directed by Joseph Sargent
Guest Starring: Anthony Hall (Dave Bailey), Clint Howard (Balok)

The Enterprise destroys a dangerous alien probe while exploring an uncharted region in space. Moments later, they are locked in the tractor beam of a ship identifying itself as the Fesarius, which has threatened them with destruction. All attempts at escape fail, and Kirk develops an ingenious plan to trick his opponent. What's even more ingenious is the episode's denouement, in which the *true* identity of the Fesarius' captain is revealed.

••••

Writer Jerry Sohl explains, "I was thinking suppose you ran across a cube in space. A cube is so damn finitive and so square and so unlike nature, and so un-asteroidish, that you know right away that it represents intelligent life, unless of course it could be some salt cubes or something like that. Anyway, a thing like that in space, whirling around all by itself, has to be a great mystery. Immediately I thought, 'What is it doing there?' Then I thought, 'It's like an electronic warning system at the frontier, and Kirk and his group are so arrogant that they just destroy it,' which, of course, is the point where this ship appears and says, 'Okay, you guys stepped too far and it's tough shit.' That's where my thinking went.

"You go in with a half a dozen ideas," he adds, "and that was one of them and they liked it. I had it entirely different in my mind to begin with, but in talking it out they knew what they wanted. I wanted Kirk to be on a mission wherein he was being observed by a person from the Federation who is sitting there watching and making a report on him. They occasionally have people who go on airplanes and sit with the pilot or co-pilot, and make a report on them. Why shouldn't they do that on space ships? But the truth of the matter is that they thought, and rightly so, that that would clutter up the story. I went through it, and it would have been too much to get into one hour. I thought it turned out very well with considerable drama and incident. How the hell were they going to get out of this one? And then they added the fellow at the end, which was so much like the end of many of my novels, where a little kid is behind the whole thing. That tickled Gene Roddenberry, and Robert Justman was quite taken by the whole thing. It worked out very well, and I was highly pleased with it. It was probably the best *Star Trek* that I did anyway."

John D.F. Black notes, "The thing about 'The Corbomite Maneuver' is that it was such a simple story. When you think about it, structurally, in terms of most science fiction, and I can think of three or four others that we had that would be the exact antithesis; that were so much more complicated naturally that it was something to watch. Here the situation was to watch that the story was not expressed as simply as it really was. Television and any entertainment medium is magic. We are all in the magic business. Well, here it was like close-up magic, which is what Jerry was doing. It was like he has five cards in his hand and he wipes his hand and he's got four, he wipes it again and he's got three, and you're only a foot and a half away and you don't know what he did with them."

Director Joseph Sargent, whose other foray into the world of science fiction was the 1970 cult classic, *Colossus: The Forbin Project*, recalls, "They chose mine as to open up the series [though it aired as the tenth episode]. The comforting thing is that I had a hand in shaping the characters. For instance, they had an Asian, a Scotsman and an alien. I suggested that they have a black communications officer. Gene Roddenberry instantly jumped on the idea because it provided an interesting balance."

Sargent, however, had a differing view of that logical "alien," Mr. Spock.

"Leonard Nimoy was unhappy because his character was without emotion," Sargent laughs. "He said, 'How can I play a character *without* emotion? I don't know how to do that. I'm going to be on one note throughout the entire series.' I agreed with him and we worked like hell to give him some emotional context, but Gene said, 'No way, the very nature of this character's contribution is that he isn't an earthling. As a Vulcan, he is intellect over emotion.' Leonard was ready to quit because he didn't know how he was going to do it. Humorously enough, after I saw *Star Trek IV*, I called him and we discussed the ironies of life. If he had quit, he wouldn't be anywhere near where he is now. Not only is he a household symbol, but he's also a very high-priced director."

Despite only directing one episode, Sargent's feelings about *Star Trek* and what it was trying to do are very succinct.

"I'm *not* a science-fiction fan because after a while, it gets into a sameness," he states. "But *Star Trek* was filled with imagination and substance. Each episode had that distinctive added dimension to it. It's science fiction with something to say, along the lines of Ray Bradbury, who I think was a big influence on Gene Roddenberry in terms of making the stories say something as well as provide entertainment. That's why *Star*

Trek has been so enduring. It's not just because the characters are fun and appealing, which they are, and not just because somebody's beaming somebody else up, but also because they're beaming up something a little more important than action and adventure."

Episode #11:
"The Menagerie"
Original Airdates: 11/17 and 11/24/66
Written by Gene Roddenberry
Directed by Marc Daniels
Guest Starring: Jeffrey Hunter (Captain Pike), Susan Oliver (Vina), Malachi Throne (Jose Mendez), Julie Parrish (Miss Piper), Hagan Beggs (Lt. Hanson), Peter Duryea (Tyler), Meg Wylie (The Keeper), John Hoyt (Dr. Boyce), Majel Barrett (Number One)

When a crippled and paralyzed Christopher Pike is beamed aboard the Enterprise, Spock commandeers the vessel to Talos IV, a world deemed off-limits by the Federation. As a result, the Vulcan is placed on court martial for mutiny, and during the trial the ship's viewscreen flashes back to footage from "The Cage," which details Pike's connection with the Talosians. It is Spock's hope that Pike will find some happiness amongst the illusionary abilities of that alien race.

••••

This two-part episode represented one of the most ingenious uses of old footage ever devised, effortlessly maintaining the audience's attention while utilizing *Star Trek*'s rejected pilot. The concept was Gene Roddenberry's, and it was a brilliant stroke on his part.

"'The Menagerie' presented a difficult technical problem," observed Marc Daniels. "I had to work around what was there. The script did it, of course, and it was certainly an interesting episode to do. Most of it took place in this room where they watched the flashbacks. We handled the unavailability of Jeffrey Hunter by taking another actor, Sean Kenney, [and] putting disfiguring make-up on him in a wheelchair, which was a neat way out of it. It took a considerable amount of preparation and work to get it done properly, but we were all satisfied by the results."

Robert Butler, who had shot "The Cage" several years earlier, recalls

that he would have liked a different look for the Enterprise and her crew than the one audiences eventually would see. "I remember to some extent begging Gene and company not to do a new show, a new world, a new bunch of costumes, a new craft. I begged him to do a timeworn craft that had been up there for twenty years, a captain who had been out there for seven, etc., and it all fell on deaf ears. I really like that much, much better. Not long ago, I got into heavy discussions with Harve Bennett about doing the second feature. The first movie was very expensive, and was run through the feature department at Paramount. Then Harve was hired to run the subsequent movies through the television department with greater economy applied. And though Harve didn't offer me the job, we talked about my doing the thing, and I've known him forever, so it was easy to say, 'Harve, let's save time for both of us and don't hire me if you want to do it clean, because I want to do it dirty. I wanted to do weathered uniforms and all the rest of it.' And he said, 'Well, it's good we're having this conversation because in my view the fans are going to expect what they've seen, which is to say a clean show,' and I said, 'Well, it doesn't sound like I'm your best guy.' So we just agreed to have dessert and forget it. But I still like that idea, and it was certainly proven in *Star Wars*. It brings a great reality and a great frailty and humanity to what is potentially sterile stuff. Anyway, I'm satisfied that I was right and they were wrong at that point, but it didn't have much to do with the success of the show."

Episode #12:
"The Conscience of the King"
Original Airdate: 12/8/66
Written by Barry Trivers
Directed by Gerd Oswald
Guest Starring: Arnold Moss (Anton Karidian), Barbara Anderson (Lenore), Bruce Hyde (Kevin Riley), Eddie Paskey (Lt. Leslie)

A travelling Shakespearean troupe led by Anton Karidian is being transported to their next performance by the Enterprise. Prior to this, Kirk has been contacted by Dr. Thomas Leighton, who tells him that Karidian is actually Kodos the Executioner, former governor of

••••

Arnold Moss (Anton Karidian in "Conscience of the King") portrayed an alien in **The 27th Day.**

Tarsus IV who masterminded the deaths of many of his people when it seemed that they were threatened with starvation. No sooner had these deaths (which included members of both Kirk and Leighton's families) been carried out than the Federation supply ships arrived. Kodos disappeared and Karidian's career began at roughly the same time. The captain has agreed to provide transportation for the actors on the sheer *chance* that Karidian and Kordos are one and the same. The noose tightens around the man's neck when a series of deaths begin to occur on the Enterprise.

••••

In the pages of *Starlog* magazine, guest star Arnold Moss explained to journalist Diane Butler, "They tell me ['Conscience of the King'] was one of the three best episodes they ever did. The character was called Anton Karidian or Kodos, either one or the other. You never knew which because he was either a man from some other planet who had killed 8,000 people or an actor—a Shakespearean actor who traveled from planet to planet to entertain....My episode was well-written, it was beautifully directed. Then, it was credible, and

in a thing like *Star Trek,* where the whole premise is incredible, you must have something that's believable. Everything there was quite believable."

Episode #13:
"Balance of Terror"
Original Airdate: 12/13/66
Written by Paul Schneider
Directed by Vincent McEveety
Guest Starring: Mark Lenard (Romulan Commander), Paul Comi (Andrew Stiles), Lawrence Montaigne (Decius), John Warburton (Centurion), Stephen Mines (Robert Tomlinson), Barbara Baldwin (Angela Martine), Gary Walberg (Hanson)

In a game of interstellar cat and mouse, the Enterprise comes up against a flagship of their unseen enemy, the Romulans, which has the ability to cloak itself. The episode takes on the feel of a submarine war film as the two commanders try to outthink each other and achieve victory.

••••

"Balance of Terror" finally introduces us to an enemy of the Federation, and a longtime one at that. It's established that it's been 75 years since the last military contact between the the Federation and the Romulans, and that neither race has ever seen the other. What they do know is that the Romulans are an off-shoot of the Vulcan race, which provides some wonderful moments as Lieutenant Andrew Stiles, who lost family members in the Federation's last battle with the Romulans, turns his prejudice on Spock, accusing him of being a spy.

Writer Paul Schneider admits that it was he who created the Romulans. "It was a matter of developing a good Romanesque set of admirable antagonists that were worthy of Kirk. I came up with the concept of the Romulans which was an extension of the Roman civilization to the point of space travel, and it turned out quite well. It holds up remarkably well.

"I had the concept of this battle in space and this battle over a neutral zone," he continues, "and I sat there with Gene and developed it with him. Gene said, 'Take it this way, that way,' I added my bit and a story came out of it. I've forgotten how many times I revised the

story, but I think a couple of times before it went into teleplay."

Director Vincent McEveety recalls, "They were very heroic characters pitted one against the other, and it dealt with the length to which people would go for their honor. It was a morality fantasy play, but terribly gripping. I thought that Mark Lenard's performance was brilliant, as was Bill Shatner's. It was a two-people show that I felt was real strong. I had, incidentally, seen *The Enemy Below,* but I didn't notice the similarity until later, when somebody told me about it. Obviously it's the same story."

"I remember that that one was tough," says John D.F. Black, "but I can't remember why or what steps we took. I can presume why. We were dealing with the Romulans and the Spock relationship to them, and that was something that needed very special handling, as was the case any time Spock met with aliens. It was important not to blow the Spock character and not to equate him to somebody who sucks salt out of somebody else's body. We had to keep him Spock. Then it became a habit and subsequently when I saw the episodes I wasn't involved with, Leonard, by the time I was gone, already had a lock on what he wanted to play as Spock and he was right. He made Spock his own character and so he survived that way. I don't think he ever said an out of character line on the show. At the very beginning it was because of care on our side, and then it became Leonard protecting the character. If you notice the takeoffs, the comics are never able to pull off a spoof of him. They can use what became the cliches of the character, but they can't catch Spock. Leonard had him, and the character just somehow survived from script to script."

Episode #14:
"Shore Leave"
Original Airdate: 12/29/66
Written by Theodore Sturgeon
Directed by Robert Sparr
Guest Starring: Emily Banks (Tonia), Oliver McGowan (Caretaker), Perry Lopez (Rodriguez), Bruce Mars (Finnegan), James Gruzaf (Don Juan), Shirley Bonne (Ruth), Sebastian Tom (Samurai)

Captain Kirk grants shore leave

for the crew on an idyllic Earth-like plan-et, and it turns out to be one of the most incredible leaves anyone has ever had. Those Enterprise people who are among the first are amazed to discover that their every wish is coming true; they are meet-ing people from their past and living out fantasies. Things turn dangerous, howev-er, when these apparitions turn deadly.

• • • •

Writer Theodore Sturgeon enthused, "Gene believes—'In the begin-ning was the word.' One reason *Star Trek* worked is that it was a writer-oriented show. I was all over that lot. Wherever I wanted to go, I was free to go. I studied the actors. I wrote Kirk just exactly the way Bill spoke. Leonard spoke Leonard's own language. There was a fiendish design in my doing that. My lines weren't changed very often."

As to the character of Kirk he added, "I didn't see a tremendous origi-nality in the *concept* of Kirk. I don't mean that we had done this before, but that kind of protagonist, as conceived, had been around before. But then Shatner did it as well asit could possibly be done. He was just right for it. He was awfully good at what he did. And *then* he began to put more into it. There were things like the emotional quality, and the humor, and the relationship with Spock, the protectiveness of each other, say. *That* came out of Bill's character."

Episode #15:
"The Galileo Seven"
Original Airdate: 1/5/67
Written by Oliver Crawford and S. Bar David
Directed by Robert Gist
Guest Starring: Don Marshall (Boma), Peter Marko (Gaetano), Rees Vaughn (Latimer), Grant Woods (Kelowitz), Phyllis Douglas (Mears),
John Crawford (Commissioner Ferris)

While enroute to deliver med-ical supplies to Makus III, the Enterprise pauses to examine a quasar formation. Kirk tries to quell the objections of Galactic High Commissioner Ferris by pointing out that such examinations are as much a part of the starship's mission as delivering medical supplies are, and that the delay will be a short one. Disaster strikes, however, when Spock

leads a team aboard the shuttle Galileo and crashes on the surface of Taurus II. The quasar phenomenon disrupts Enterprise sensors so they are unable to locate the shuttle or the survivors.

Meanwhile, on the planet's sur-face, Spock uses his purely logical mind to deal with their situation in a hostile environment, and comes across as a cold-blooded monster. With McCoy's encouragement he is ultimately forced to take a very human chance to ensure that they survive and are found by the Enterprise.

• • • •

Writer Oliver Crawford details, "I did the story and teleplay for that one, and then, as often happens, someone else was called in. They proba-bly felt that I had run dry on the idea and came as far as I could, and they got Shimon Wincelberg [a.k.a. S. Bar David] to do a polish, just as I had done for other *Star Trek*s and other shows. Most of my approach as a writer had been to look to old movies and say, 'Gee, this would make a good *Star Trek* or a good western or a good detective story.' The foundation for 'The Galileo Seven' was actually an old [1939] motion picture called *Five Came Back*. That was about a plane crash in the Andes and the sur-vivors who have to deal with head-hunters over the next hill. I remembered it because it was such a dramatic gim-mick, a very tight one."

Episode #16:
"The Squire of Gothos"
Original Airdate: 1/12/67
Written by Paul Schneider
Directed by Don McDougall
Guest Starring: William Campbell (Trelane), Richard Carlyle (Jaeger), Michael Barrier (De Salle),
Venita Wolf (Ross)

The Enterprise is captured by an alien being named Trelene who is equipped with a wide variety of powers that enable him to manipulate the world around him. Having grown bored with loneliness, he has chosen Kirk and his crew to stay on his world to provide him with entertainment. Coming across as an impudent child (and turning out to be just that), Trelene grows furious when Kirk disrupts his plans, and he puts

humanity on trial.

• • • •

Trelene and "The Squire of Gothos" would be reincarnated some twenty years later as the premiere episode of *Star Trek: The Next Generation*, "Encounter at Farpoint," in which the new Enterprise encounters the all-powerful (and very Trelene-like) Q, who forces Captain Picard to stand trial on charges against humanity.

Says Paul Schneider, "'The Squire of Gothos' flowed through the process with less changes than 'Balance of Terror.' It just worked very well. I do remember that I was very excited that they built a whole special set for it; a totally round set which was then kind of a new concept in itself. If you look at the episode, you'll see that the camera goes all the way around.

"My inspiration was an anti-war message," Schneider continues. "The fierce toy soldier loving child insisting on getting humanity involved in further war-fare. The biggest problem was coming up with a climax. How do you end some-thing like that? So we used the climax of *The Most Dangerous Game*."

Guest star William Campbell's strongest memory of working on this episode was meeting producer Gene L. Coon.

"Gene Coon and I became very dear friends," he says. "I found him to be a guy you could not dislike. He was awfully fair. I remember there was much ado when I was getting the wrig for 'Squire', and I was building my part around the particular wig that I was going to wear. On the day we were supposed to do that scene, the wig was wrong. I looked like Shirley Temple, and we went through a long thing. Remember, you don't give a television script historic intent. When you do a series, after a while you're doing it by rote and you want to finish your day and get back to normal. When I help up the production by saying I refused to use that wig, Bill Shatner was disturbed. He said, 'Bill, what the hell difference does it make? Who's going to notice that?' I said, 'I know it, don't you understand?' The next thing you know, there was a call for the director, who did not want to get in to the debate, although I had the feeling the director was on my side. We called Gene Coon and Gene didn't take two seconds to say, 'Campbell's right. Get another wig. Go to another sequence.' Which is exactly what we did, and it didn't hold up anything. That's the kind of guy he was. He was very sensitive about the quality of the show, how it was done."

Episode #17:
"Arena"
Original Airdate: 1/19/67
Written by Gene L. Coon
From a Story by Fredric Brown
Directed by Joseph Pevney
Guest Starring: Carole Shelyne (The Metron), Jerry Ayers (O'Herlihy), Grant Woods (Kelowitz), Tom Troupe (Lt. Harold), James Farley (Lang),
Sean Kenney (DePaul)

When a Federation starbase is destroyed, the Enterprise sets off in pursuit of the attackers. Enroute they enter an uncharted sector of space where Kirk and the commander of the other vessel, the lizard-like Gorn, are transported to a planet's surface where they are forced to carry out their barbarism against each other in a battle to the death, with the loser's ship and all those aboard being destroyed. What follows is a savage struggle, with Kirk's ultimate humanity sparing both him and the Enterprise.

••••

"A tough show to do for the actor in the Gorn suit," says director Joseph Pevney. "It was designed by a fellow who has since died, and the suit was very hot. The guy I found for that was a fellow named Gary Cooms, a stuntman, and he worked out just fine. I talked Roddenberry into using a stuntman, because the Gorn was a heavy rubber suit. An actor would have been worn out in nothing flat, and I would not have been able to get enough footage without building a fan into the suit. I said, 'We'd better get a guy accustomed to roughing it out there,' somebody who would be able to go for that length of time in order to get enough footage or we'd be stopping all the time to allow someone to put the suit on and take it off again and again. They didn't realize that stunt people are very talented. Now they're beginning to realize it because all of TV is stunts."

According to the on-air credits, the script for "Arena" was based on the Frederic Brown short story of the same name. "What happened," says Dorothy Fontana, "is that Gene Coon wrote the story as an original. When it was read by research, they said, 'Oh, this is very much like the Frederic Brown story.' Gene said, 'Yes, you're right. I must have read it and didn't realize it.' So he instantly gave credit to Frederic Brown and Mr. Brown was properly paid. The way the development came about, the relationship between the antagonists—Kirk and the Gorn—had a lot of nice stuff to it. It could have been just a brute contest, but it wasn't. It turned out not to be that way."

Episode #18:
"Tomorrow is Yesterday"
Original Airdate: 1/26/67
Written by D.C. Fontana
Directed by Michael O'Herlihy
Guest Starring: Roger Perry (Captain Christopher), Ed Peck (Colonel Fellini), Hal Lynch (Police Sergeant), Richard Merrifield (Technician Webb), John Winston (Transporter Chief Kyle)

After an encounter with a black hole (here referred to as a black star), the Enterprise is hurled backwards in time to the 20th Century and in Earth orbit. There they are photographed by the Air Force's Captain Christopher, who is flying by in his jet when the starship enters the atmosphere momentarily. Kirk has the craft placed in the ship's tractor beam, but it proves too frail and breaks up. Christopher is brought aboard before the fatal moment, and is the world's first man to see the future. Kirk's dilemma: how to return Christopher without threatening the course of history.

••••

"'Tomorrow is Yesterday' was kicked off by 'The Naked Time,' which ended with the Enterprise spinning off of a collapsed star," says Dorothy Fontana. "Originally, it was supposed to be a two-parter, but John D.F. Black had a movie deal and couldn't be involved with the second part. I said that I would develop the idea of being thrown back into space. They were going back in time at the end of 'The Naked Time,' so I took the idea and played with it.

"Then, I had everything Kirk does, though it's the right thing to do, land him deeper and deeper into trouble. Once he begins to get his footing in this strange and different time, he starts putting his feet right again. The human interest aspect is the pilot who wanted to go into space and didn't make the cut, as it were. But the irony of history is that his son, who wasn't born yet, gets to make a space flight which is vital to the space program's development. All of that, I felt, made for a fun and an interestingly human show. The sequel idea was dropped, and we actually wound up putting a new front end on it so that it would sit alone without being linked to 'The Naked Time.'"

Episode director Michael O'Herlihy, who had a long directorial history with the Walt Disney Company, notes, "I rather liked the script. The one thing I did like about *Star Trek* is that Gene Roddenberry went into the realm of science fiction, but he didn't go too far too often. Take the one I did, which was rather nice with the time warp thing. I'm not a science fiction fan, but even I could relate to it and understand it. I wasn't interested in funny things with ears coming out of them. But playing around with psychic forces and time, I understood. I enjoyed it very much."

And despite his modern-day sensibilities, he didn't find it difficult to deal with *Star Trek*'s future reality.

"I can only speak as a director and a storyteller," he explains. "You have the story to tell and you must tell it with as much honesty as you possibly can, that this *did* in fact happen. You can't say, 'This only happened because we're making science fiction.' This is the story, fellows, so it has to be told to the best of our abilities. That has always been my attitude on every show I've done. Once you begin to edit the veracity of the reality or unreality, you're wrong. Then, you're turning into a preacher instead of a director. I've always tried to do my best from that point-of-view.

"On *Star Trek* you can suspend your disbelief and just tell the story as if people at this time and at this space are dressed in these funny clothes, although you must not consider them funny clothes. You must consider that this is the

••••

way people live. It's like going back to the 12th Century. We know that has happened, so we can just tell the story. In this other material dealing with the future, we don't know whether it would happen or if it could, but I don't think people are going to change anyway.

In studying the *Star Trek* phenomenon, O'Herlihy is quick to point out that he has *not* devised his own theory as to why the show has remained so popular.

"I know very well that in retrospect we can all come up with something we did to make the show a success," he confides, "but it was just an accident that became a fashion."

The method of time travel as established in "The Naked Time" and "Tomorrow is Yesterday" was utilized again to great effect in the 1986 feature film, *Star Trek IV: The Voyage Home*.

Episode #19:
"Court Martial"
Original Airdate: 2/2/67
Written by Don M. Mankiewicz and Stephen Carabatsos
Directed by Marc Daniels
Guest Starring: Percy Rodriguez (Commodore Stone), Joan Marshall (Areel Shaw), Elisha Cook, Jr. (Samuel Cogley), Richard Webb (Finney), Alice Rawlings (Jamie Finney), Hagan Beggs (Hanson), Winston DeLugo (Timothy)

A computer malfunction implicates Kirk in the death of crewman Ben Finney, and he stands trial for negligence. It is up to Spock and Kirk's lawyer, Samuel Cogley, to prove his innocence as well as the truth about Finney.

••••

"I thought that wasn't a very good one," said Marc Daniels. "I didn't like it because the actor who was playing the prosecutor, Elisha Cook, Jr., wasn't very good with his lines. When you're on a six-day schedule, trying to make time, and you've got to keep stopping and going back, it drives everyone absolutely crazy. You've got a courtroom scene and you're shooting him a line at a time because he can't remember two. When you put it in the editing room, you don't see that because you cut to someone else and then come back to him. Cook is a fine actor, but he had a terrible time with that....See, these

are the kind of things I remember."

Episode #20:
"The Return of the Archons"
Original Airdate: 2/9/67
Written by Boris Sobelman
Story by Gene Roddenberry
Directed by Joseph Pevney
Guest Starring: Harry Townes (Reger), Torin Thatcher (Marplon), Charles McCauley (Landru), Christopher Heid (Lindstrom), Brioni Farrell (Tula), Sid Haig (First Lawgiver), Jon Lormer (Tamar), Morgan Farley (Hacom), Ralph Maurer (Bilar), Eddie Paskey (Leslie), David L. Ross (Guard)

While checking up on the crew of the Archon, who transported down to Beta III, the Enterprise learns that the people there are being controlled by a computer named Landru who takes over their minds to make them all a part of the body. Kirk takes it upon himself to destroy the mechanism and bring freedom back to that world's people.

Episode #21
"Space Seed"
Original Airdate: 2/16/67
Written by Gene L. Coon
and Carey Wilbur
Directed by Marc Daniels
Guest Starring: Richard Montalban (Khan), Madlyn Rhue (Marla McGivers), Blasidell Makee (Spinelli), Mark Tobin (Joaqin)

The Enterprise comes across a derelict "sleeper ship" named the Botony Bay, which contains a crew of approximately 70 men and women in suspended animation. Led by Khan Noonian Singh, these people turn out to be the result of genetic experimentation on Earth in the 1990s. Basically a race of supermen, with strength and intelligence nearly ten times that of an average person, they had attempted to take over the Earth and triggered World War III, the Eugenics War. They managed to flee in the Botony Bay, and are now revived in the 23rd Century.

Khan seizes the moment and, using historian Marla McGivers, nearly takes over the Enterprise. Kirk and company manage to gain the upper hand (barely) and sentence Khan and his people to the somewhat savage Ceti Alpha V. At least it will give Khan, McGivers

and the others a chance to tame a world, rather than waste their lives in a Federation penal colony.

••••

Surprisingly, Khan Noonian Singh may never have come into existence at all if it hadn't been for Captain Video.

"Hell," laughs writer Carey Wilbur, "the plot for 'Space Seed' came from an old *Captain Video* I did some 30-odd years ago. Of course we did some very far out things on that show, including the popular idea of people being transported in space while in suspended animation."

Allan Asherman's *The Star Trek Compendium* states that "Carey Wilbur began his outline for 'Space Seed' by explaining how out of place in today's world a man from Renaissance times would be."

"That sounds a little grand to me," Wilbur smiles. "I was just thinking of an adventure story, although there was some of that element there. I had this idea, which I revived from Captain Video because I thought it was time to do it again. It was a crazy story where we did the legend of men being turned into beasts, and our villainess had been transported from the days of Greek mythology to the future. So in doing 'Space Seed,' we took away the mythological powers and replaced them with a genetically altered human being.

"To be honest, I don't remember a heck of a lot about Khan. He was a

Ricardo Montalban, the quintessential Khan, seen here in the TV movie version of The Mark of Zoro

criminal who had been deported in a seed ship who tried to take over the Enterprise after he was more or less accidentally revived."

As a writer for hire, Wilbur had been asked to supply a script for the show, which eventually became "Space Seed." Gene Coon did a rewrite on it and the author had no further contact with *Star Trek* as he went off to other assignments.

"I had no qualms about Gene rewriting me," he points out. "He was an excellent writer and certainly knew the show better than just about anyone. I'm sure he rewrote the script to conform to the series, but I've never seen it. I think I've only seen three or four things I've written, for the simple reason that I know what's in them. The only exception has been *Lost in Space*, which I wrote numerous scripts for. We were doing fairy tales and I used to watch them all the time. Hell, I used to watch other people's episodes as well, simply because it was such a fun show.

"People want to believe that there's going to be that glorious period of space flight. We want to believe that there's something out there. *Star Trek* offered the human race a future, and God knows we need the promise of the future."

Stated director Marc Daniels, "There's not much I remember about the episode except that we used those capsules which carried people in suspended animation. Ricardo Montalban was a very capable and good actor, and the episode, of course, led to *Star Trek II: The Wrath of Khan*. Part of the problem in 'Space Seed' was trying to visualize Khan's tremendous power—where he could turn out a finger and turn somebody upside down. That was difficult, but we got away with it thanks to stunt people and judicious editing."

Recalls actor Ricardo Montalban, who had previously starred in Gene Roddenberry's *The Secret Defense of 117*, "I thought the character of Khan was wonderful. I thought it was well-written, it had an interesting concept and I was delighted it was offered to me. I still get fan mail from it. Not just from the United States, but from other countries. People remembered this Khan character whenever I talk about having done a *Star Trek*."

Episode #22:
"A Taste of Armageddon"
Original Airdate: 2/23/67
Written by Robert Hamner
and Gene L. Coon
Directed by Joseph Pevney
Guest Starring: Gene Lyons (Ambassador Fox), David Opatoshu (Anan 879), Robert Sampson (Sar 627), Barbara Babcock (Mea 349),
Miko Mayama (Tamura)

Ambassador Robert Fox is on board the Enterprise to negotiate a peace treaty with the planet Eminiar VII, despite that world's obvious lack of interest in such a treaty. Kirk himself points out, "It *is* their planet, Mr. Ambassador," but Fox arrogantly forces the starship forward. It is a short matter of time before they find themselves immersed in an interplanetary war between Eminiar and Vendikar which is being fought by computers. Said computers pinpoint the location of theoretical bombings, and people living in those areas voluntarily march into disintegration chambers so that their respective societies will live on.

Enterprise unwittingly becomes a target and Eminiar's leader, Anan 7, expects Kirk to have his crew enter the disintegration chambers to keep the peace. Kirk, naturally, has his own ideas and sets about carrying them out.

••••

Perhaps the reason "A Taste of Armageddon" is so powerful is that it seems a perfect allegory to the soldiers in Vietnam at the time, and the body counts of those killed in action which were revealed over nightly newscasts. As those numbers grew, it seems that they, too, were walking into disintegration chambers of a sort.

"The original story was by Robert Hamner," recalls Dorothy Fontana. "Gene did a rewrite on that. I think some of the things he added really had a lot to do with the character of Kirk. To the best of my recollection, it was Gene Coon who wrote the speech at the end that man has a reputation as a killer, but you get up every morning and say, 'I'm not going to kill today.' It seems to me that Gene Coon added that speech in particular. It was one of those things that began to identify Kirk far more solidly than we had before."

"The final speech from Bill," muses Joseph Pevney, "the demand for peace and not giving up human lives to a computer, was rewritten several times until we got it the way we wanted. Gene Coon rewrote the script and it was quite powerful."

Episode #23:
"This Side of Paradise"
Original Airdate: 3/2/67
Written by D.C. Fontana
Story by Nathan Butler and
D.C. Fontana
Directed by Ralph Senensky
Guest Starring: Jill Ireland (Leila), Frank Overton (Sandoval), Grant Woods (Kelowitz), Dick Scotter (Painter)

The Enterprise investigates the status of a group of Federation colonists on Omicron Ceti III, who are presumed dead after being exposed to the deadly radiation of Berthold rays over the past three years. Instead, what they find are the colonists in absolutely perfect health, and in a peaceful bliss. Both are chalked up to spores on the planet which strip away the more negative feelings, resulting in an idyllic state of mind.

Kirk's problems begin quickly as the influence of the spores spreads through the ship, with everyone wanting to remain on the planet. Even Spock is affected, as he lets down his veneer of logic and expresses the love he feels for colonist Leila Kalomi, with whom he had had a relationship. Kirk, who is alone on the Enterprise, must snap his first officer out of the state he's in, before the starship burns up in the planet's atmosphere.

••••

The script for "This Side of Paradise" was begun by Jerry Sohl, but rewritten by story editor Dorothy Fontana to the point where Sohl decided to put his pen-name on it.

"I have a whole draw full of ideas," says Sohl on the story's genesis, "and I had the idea that.spores, as you kow, are inanimate up until the point when they are mixed with water or with anything else, then they come alive. Like yeast. So I had the idea that these things could be consumed by someone and as a result the whole character chemistry of that person could change to a nice, peaceful and loving person. In other

As Leila, the late Jill Ireland allowed audiences a glimpse into the past of Mr. Spock in "This Side of Paradise."

words, it was a psychedelic kind of thing. A lot of that was going on at the time. The premise of the thing was that everyone on the Enterprise takes LSD. What would happen? In effect, that's what this was. They go down to the planet and they all get the spores in them and turn into different people. That was the basis of the whole thing, and I thought it was an interesting premise. It was the only time that Spock was allowed to be a loving, caring, cherishing human being. That was my idea. Worked out just swell, I think. I've forgotten what the payoff was. I think they had to be made angry. The adrenaline going into your system is what defeats the spores."

Dorothy Fontana adds, "That was actually the rewrite that got me the job of story editor. Originally that story and script featured Sulu as the love interest, and the spores were contained in a cave, so, therefore, they weren't much of a threat unless you went into the cave. My idea, that I stressed to Gene, was that it could be made a better story if we have the spores all over the place, so that you can't avoid them, and that Spock is the love interest. Everybody kind of said, 'Spock?' And I said, 'Trust me.' And Gene did. It was an enjoyable episode to write, because there are so many things you can get into which, under normal circumstances, you wouldn't dare,

because it would not work. But under these circumstances, it did. It also had wonderful actors. Leonard's always good, but Jill Ireland was exquisite. Bill was good also. We always played Bill, at least back then, as the man whose real love affair was with his ship. He was a dedicated officer and a man who really did want to go down to the sea in ships. In this case it was a sea of stars. That ship was truly his love."

In tracing his involvement with the series, director Ralph Senensky admits, "I don't even know how it happened. There's an agency that books you and I guess I must have been pitched. All of a sudden the agent called and said, 'Do you want to do *Star Trek*?' They sent me the script for 'The Devil in the Dark,' and I was kind of excited about it. I was not a science fiction buff, so I went out and bought a lot of Arthur Clarke and read practically everything I could. I took the script back to Iowa, where I was visiting my family, and while I was ther another script arrived in the mail with another note saying that they had switched and I would be doing 'This Side of Paradise.' I was kind of disappointed, because I liked 'Devil in the Dark' better. But 'This Side of Paradise' was a very good show and it's developed its own reputation.

"I didn't know it at the time, but it's probably because it was such a major personal story for Spock. He did things in that story that he never got to do, like hang from a tree. As a freelance director in television, you just bounce from show to show and that was one of the bounces. As you bounce around, you find little niches, places where it's comfortable. You like them, they like you and you stay on. *Star Trek* was such a place."

Episode #24:
"The Devil in the Dark"
Original Airdate: 3/9/67
Written by Gene L. Coon
Directed by Joseph Pevney
Guest Starring: Ken Lynch (Vandenberg), Barry Russo (Giotto), Brad Weston (Appel), Biff Elliot (Schmitter), Janos Prohaska (Horta)

When miners on Janus VI are being murdered by a creature that can move through solid rock, chief engineer Vanderberg contacts the Enterprise and

asks for assistance in hunting it down and putting an end to the threat. The starship arrives with Kirk and Spock leading a landing party to investigate the situation. What they discover is that this so-called creature is actually an intelligent creature known as the Horta and that it has only killed to protect its young, which are encased in silicone shells that the miners mistook for worthless rocks.

••••

In *The Making of Star Trek*, Gene Roddenberry explained, "What's been wrong with science fiction in television and in motion pictures for years is that whenever the monster was used, the tendency was to say, 'Ah, ha! Let's have a big one that comes out, attacks and kills everyone.' Nobody ever asked, 'Why?' In any other story, if something attacks (a bear, a man or whatever), the author is expected to explain, 'Here is why it is the way it is, here are the things that led it to do this, here is what it wants.'

"A classic example of doing this right was one of our most popular episodes, written by Gene Coon, entitled 'The Devil in the Dark.' The 'Horta' was an underground creature which attacked a group of miners. In the end they find out that it attacked because—surprise—it was a mother! It was protecting its eggs because the miners were destroying them in the belief that they were just strange-looking mineral formations. With this understood, the Horta suddenly became understandable, too. It wasn't just a monster—it was *someone*. And the audience could put themselves in the place of the Horta...identify....feel! That's what drama is all about. And that's its importance, too....If you can learn to feel for a Horta, you may also be learning to understand and feel for other humans of different colors, ways and beliefs."

"From my point of view," says Joseph Pevney, "the primary problem was photographing the Horta. We had to put glisten on them, a kind of sheen to make them stand away from the walls because everything was the same color. We then exaggerated the motion of the way it moved so we would be sure to see them.

"It was a tough show to do, because William Shatner's father died during the filming of it. They were very close, but he managed....He was very shaken then and Leonard was very good to him. They were together all the time and Leonard was able to provide him with a great deal of comfort."

David Gerrold opines, "I would have to point to 'Devil in the Dark' as being the best episode Gene L. Coon ever wrote, because it really gets to the heart of what *Star Trek* was. Here you had this menace, but once you understood what the creature is and why it's doing what it's doing, it's not really a menace at all. We end up learning more about appropriate behavior for ourselves out of learning to be compassionate, tolerant, understanding. To me, in many ways Gene L. Coon was the heart and soul of *Star Trek*. He was the guy who had to roll up his sleeves and make it work. He was the guy who would do a rewrite if a script needed a rewrite and try to stay true to the original concept. He actually, of all the people who worked there at the time, had the clearest story sense, both in terms of story structure and dialogue. I think that shows in the scripts that he did. 'Devil in the Dark' he wrote over a weekend."

Laughs Coon's friend Lester Colodny, "Not only did he write it in a weekend, but he probably read two books, made dinner for 14, redid the entire front lawn, helped me with 30 pages of my book, rewrote four other pieces for the studio, went to visit two friends....he was incredible.

In terms of the development of the script idea, Dorothy Fontana recalls, "The costume guy who did a lot of creatures for us came to the studio and said, 'I have to show you this new creature,' and it was this kind of lumpy thing that was orange and misshapen and it was real low to the ground. He put a rubber chicken out in front of the thing. He climbed inside this suit and on his hands and knees he brought this creature over the chicken and the chicken disappeared. After he passed over it, some bones appeared out the back. Gene said, 'I've got to find a way to use that,' and he came up with the Horta. Of course it's a wonderful story, because it's really all about other love. It was a great story."

John Colicos, the Klingon Kor in "Errand of Mercy," seen here as Baltar in Battlestar: Galactica.

Episode #25:
"Errand of Mercy"
Original Airdate: 3/23/67
Written by Gene L. Coon
Directed by John Newland
Guest Starring: John Abbott (Ayleborne), John Colicos (Kor), Peter Brocco (Claymare), Victor Lundin (Lingon), David Hillary Huge (Trefayne)

Tensions between the Federation and one of their arch enemies, the Klingon Empire, are growing more intense, and Kirk is told to secure an alliance with the people of the strategically located Organia. No sooner have Kirk and Spock beamed down than the Klingons arrive, with their military commander, Kor, commandeering the world as the latest possession of the Empire.

Kirk is frustrated by the absolute complacency of the Organians, and his frustration turns to anger when he learns that things have grown worse between the Federation and the Klingons. It appears that an intergalactic war is about to begin, when the Organians reveal themselves to be something far removed from human, with the power to stop both sides from warring....permanently (though this fact was later forgotten in the *Star Trek* feature films).

••••

A highlight of "Errand of Mercy" is when the Organians stops the conflict between the Federation and the Klingons, and Kirk protests their interference. "You have no right to interfere," snaps Kirk. We have the right...."

"To wage war, Captain?" asks an Organian.

As David Gerrold notes in his book *The World of Star Trek*, "And then [Kirk] realizes that the whole purpose of his mission was to *prevent* a war."

"Gene came up with the Klingons though we never liked the name," explains Dorothy Fontana. "We said, 'Gene, can't you come up with a different name than Klingon? We hate it.' But we never come up with anything better, so we left it. Then the Klingons kind of became a stock villain, because they were easier to do in make-up than the Romulans. We wound up doing the Klingons quite a bit and they became a very good adversary, because once you established them, you had to find out ways to explore them."

Actor John Colicos, in reflecting on his role as Kor, told *Starlog* magazine that when he got the role, make-up maestro Fred Phillips said, "'What do *you* want to look like?' I saw the script as a futuristic Russia and America at loggerheads over this peaceful little planet, so I said, 'Let's go back in the past and think of Genghis Khan, because Kor is a military commander, ready to take over the entire universe with his hordes.' My hair happened to be very short and combed forward, so I said, 'Spray my hair black, kink it up a bit and give me a vaguely Asian, Tartar appearance. Let's go for a brown-green makeup so I'm slightly not of this world,' and within two hours, this thing emerged and that was it."

••••

Episode #26
"The Alternative Factor"
Original Airdate: 3/30/67
Written by Don Ingalls
Directed by Gerd Oswald
Guest Starring: Robert Brown (Lazarus),
Janet MacLachlen (Charlene Masters),
Richard Derr (Barstow),
Eddie Paskey (Lt. Leslie)

Easily one of Star Trek's most convoluted and least appealing episodes, "The Alternative Factor" was the 20th episode shot but was held up to air as the 26th. The Enterprise encounters two versions of a man named Lazarus, one of them seeming perfectly rationale and the other a snarling madman from an anti-matter universe. The latter is planning on opening a rift between the two dimensions, damning both to a form of Armageddon. It is up to Kirk and the rational Lazarus to set things straight before its too late.

••••

"I had in mind parallel universes, in which there are positive and negative forces," writer Don Ingalls relayed to Lee Goldberg, "and you have to keep the two universes separate, because if they're drawn together, you have annihilation. You have the bright side, the positive world we know and the negative world, whee everyone's a villain. My idea was that one person from the negative world tries to break through—and if he succeeds, he destroys everything."

Episode #27:
"City on the Edge of Forever"
Original Airdate: 4/6/67
Written by Harlan Ellison
Directed by Joseph Pevney
Guest Starring: Joan Collins (Edith Keeler), John Harmon (Rodent), Bartell LaRue (Voice of the Guardian)

The Enterprise is in the midst of studying time disturbances in the area of a particular world, when McCoy accidentally injects himself with an overdose of cordrazine. As a result, he becomes a paranoid madman and beams down to the planet's surface to avoid everyone's attempts to sedate him.

Kirk and Spock lead a landing party in pursuit, and there they find an ancient stone structure which identifies itself as the Guardian of Forever, a time

portal into the past. When the moment presents itself, McCoy leaps through its center and does something in the past that causes history to be changed: the Enterprise is no longer in orbit. To try and counter this, Kirk and Spock pursue him to Earth in the year 1930, where they meet the focal point in time: Edith Keeler, social worker.

Keeler, we learn, was meant to die in a traffic accident but something McCoy does alters that. As a result, all of history is changed and in the altered history she leads a pacifist movement that delays America's entry into the second world war, thus giving Nazi Germany the chance to capture the world. Kirk's decision is simple: he must allow Edith Keeler to die as she was intended to. The one thing he had not counted on, however, was falling in love with her.

••••

"City on the Edge of Forever" is generally considered the best episode of Star Trek ever produced. At the same time, it is perhaps the most controversial due to the fact that Gene Roddenberry supposedly rewrote Harlan Ellison's original teleplay and Ellison was not happy about the rewrite.

"How can I do this without be a creep?" Ellison rhetorically asked a journalist. "Gene Roddenberry and I had a falling out in terms of creativity, about what would be done with my show. I thought that the rewrite that was expected of me, and that I did several times, and the couple [of] other writers [put] on to follow me up, cut the guts out of my show. I thought that, at the time, Gene had lied to me, and I will not work with anyone who lies to me. Life is too short. So Gene and I didn't talk for many years as a result of it, and it was strictly on an artistic basis. Gene has always been a very kind and decent man, but I think he was under pressure from the network at that time as the budget was being cut, and I think he wanted to satisfy the network so he did things to my show which I was not happy about and which he had promised me would not be done to my show. Subsequently, Gene and I buried the hatchet as it were, we reached reproachment, and he has done a number of very kind things for me and so I'd kind of like to not bad mouth him at this

point because this is many years later.

"There's two ways of looking at it," he continued. "First of all, the one that won the Writer's Guild award was my original version of the script, it was not what was shot. The Writer's Guild awards are the most honest awards in this industry, not like the Oscars which are Mickey Mouse. They're nothing but popularity awards. The Writer's Guild awards are given on the basis of the written material. And so it was in fact my original script that won the award. The one that won the Hugo was the televised version and of course I would like to be arrogant enough to think that the script was just so damn good that even butchering it couldn't hurt it, but in comparison to most of the other segments that were on Star Trek, which I wasn't wildly enthusiastic about, it was a pretty good show. But having done the show myself, having written it, and I know how good the quality of the script was, I can only say that what people see was one twentieth of what was there originally."

At a 1988 presentation at the Museum of Broadcasting, Roddenberry was asked if Star Trek: The Next Generation would use writers like Harlan Ellison.

"Most of those I wouldn't want in the same room with me," he replied. "I've given all of them a chance. Harlan got a chance on the first show and wrote a $350,000 estimated budget show when I only had, in those days, $186,000. And when I told him to cut the budget, he sent me back the script, saying in parenthesis to do it with special effects. He then submitted it to the Writer's Guild, which gave him the Writer's Guild prize which he deserved for the script, except that many people would get prizes if they wrote scripts that budgeted out to three times the show's cost. I rewrote that script for Harlan and it won the Nebula Award, which he rushed up on stage and took credit for, too!"

For over two decades fans have accepted the fact that Roddenberry did the rewrite of Ellison's script, however Glen Larson disputes this point, stating that it was actually Gene L. Coon who was responsible. This startling revelation came to Larson's attention during a Writer's Guild Award ceremony in which the script was a

••••

nominated entry.

"That night," Larson reflects, "I knew that something was troubling Gene and I asked him what was wrong. And he said, 'There are two scripts up tonight for the Writer's Guild Award, and I wrote them both.' One of them was by Harlan Ellison ['City on the Edge of Forever'], and he said, 'If Harlan wins, I'm going to die.' Harlan was just an amazingly stubborn person. That night he also told me a story about Harlan. Harlan would write a script that said, 'Five thousand people accosted him on the city streets.' Gene said, 'Harlan, why do you bother writing this into a script that you know is for television? You know we can't have 5,000 extras.' So Harlan would go home, do the rewrite and say, 'Four thousand extras.' And that was his rewrite. Gene would have to sit down and make a television show out of it. Obviously he kept all of the theoretical things, but he would have to write a script that was a script that could be shot on the stage with a rock.

"But Gene made his contributions in an unheralded way," continues Larson. "His name wasn't on the Ellison script. It is unique in the business these days, it wasn't so much then, for someone to do the kind of work he did and not submit for an arbitration or a credit. It's that simple. An awful lot of guys today will put their name on it and let the Guild fight it. Coon had a great respect for writers. Therefore, even if he had to do a massive amount of work, he would not take away the guy's credit, which, by the way, is linked to residuals. Nevertheless, if you knew a guy was going to stand up and accept an award for what you did, that was more painful than the money. The mere fact that somebody was going to get credit for his thoughts and actual words, because they were so important to him, was almost too much to bear. He shared that with me. He didn't make that a public announcement, but he was feeling great pain. Harlan would stand up and bow from the floor."

As far as Roddenberry's taking credit for the rewrite, Larson offers, "Gene [Coon] was there. Gene made the show work. Gene was the guy and later on, when *Star Trek* gained prominence, I was always surprised at what I heard Roddenberry say, because there are people who create something who don't know how to make it work on a week to week basis, a show to show basis. I suspect that's kind of the way Roddenberry was. I'm not an expert on that. I'm giving you this directly from the horse's mouth, because [Gene Coon and I] used to sit there and talk about things every day."

Director Joseph Pevney is someone who doesn't agree with Ellison's view of his own script.. "This was the end of the first season," he says. "Harlan was very happy to get his story on *Star Trek*. He was down on the set thanking me. It's great that Gene rewrote it, though, because Harlan had no sense of theatre. He had a great sense of truth, which was very nicely placed in there, all of the 1930's stuff was well documented. It was a well conceived and written show. But in the original script's dramatic moments, it missed badly.

"It was a motion picture," he continues. "I treated it as a movie, as I did all television. It was a very honest episode and the doctor was so good for the first time. I think he's kind of dull, but he came to life magnificently. It was a pleasure working with the actors. They realized their full potential in that one."

It's noted that Captain Kirk's final line, "Let's get the hell out of here," probably represented one of the first times that the word "hell" had been used on television.

"That was a problem," he points out. "Bill said it and there were objections from the network. Roddenberry had a meeting with them and said, 'There's no word that has the same connotation as hell in this particular moment.' Of course Bill fought for it too. We all wanted it, because it sounded so great. I think finally the network said, 'What the hell, who's watching the show anyway? Leave it in.'"

Although "City" aired at the end of the season, its development had begun at the beginning and John D.F. Black has strong memories of working with Harlan Ellison.

"Harlan always had 40 things going," Black smiles. "He was doing a book and he had this short story he had to get in, or whatever. Now Harlan didn't

Joan Collins, Kirk's love interest in "City on the Edge of Forever," seen here in less bitchy, pre-Dynasty days.

know anything about the production side. He knew half of what I knew, and I didn't know anything. I knew what a travelling matte was, and I think Harlan knew that too, and we knew what the difference between a fade and a dissolve was, and those kinds of things. But production...can you build a 40-foot tall pyramid on a stage? We didn't know what height you could build it. That's technical and certainly outside our expertise.

"At one point," he elaborates, the memories washing over him, "Harlan was supposed to deliver, was supposed to deliver, was supposed to deliver...and he was ill or he was this or he was that. The story just wasn't finished. We all lie. After a while it came down to, 'For Christ's sake, Harlan, when are we going to get the story?' And Harlan said, 'Maybe it would just be better if I came in and had an office on the lot.' Which, at that juncture, was terrific because we wanted the story. And I loved Harlan, although I don't know what G.R.'s feeling for him was. So Harlan shows up with a phonograph, his typewriter and about 12 records of the Rolling Stones, among other things. We put him in an office at the very end of the corridor. At first Harlan would be there with this rock and roll playing very loud, with the casting people trying to have readings and saying, 'Turn it down, Harlan.' Or I couldn't hear people in my office on the telephone and I'd tell him to turn it down. At one point, I guess the second or third day that he was there, I walked down the hall because the Stones were playing very loud, knocked on the door and there wasn't any answer. I opened the door and Harlan wasn't there. The machine was just playing.

"I had to go over to the set. I had to go there three or four times a day, and there he was sitting there talking to Leonard and Billy, having his picture taken. I said, 'Harlan, you're supposed to be writing. What are you doing over here?' He said, 'I came over here for lunch with the comapny.' 'Harlan, it's 3:30 in the afternoon. The company has lunch at 2.' 'Well, I wanted to see what they were doing.' I said, 'Harlan, please go back to the office and finish the story.' So Harlan walked back with me, went into his office and the record goes on again, because I had taken the arm off earlier, and I figured that I would leave my office door open so that I could see him if he went down the hall. And I never saw him.

"When I went down the hall in the middle of the next day to see how he was doing. I got there, the record was playing and Harlan wasn't in his office again. What he had done was gone out the window, and Bobby Justman was of the mind that we should nail the door and the window shut. In any case, Harlan ultimately finished the story. I read it, made my notes and gave it to G.R. and he made his notes on it. If I recall correctly, and this I'm not certain of at all, Harlan did not continue to occupy that office. He either went home to continue the teleplay or he had some other thing that he had to finish first, and the story stayed on the shelf until Harlan got back to it. I remember conferences on the story with Harlan, and it was enormously interesting. I thought it was a little corny conceptually. I didn't think it was the best thing that Harlan could have done.

"I remember the hassles about the expense inherent in it, and what had to be adjusted. Sequences that had to come out because they were impossible to do, and things like that. I remember he had come in with a script in which all of the *Star Trek* people were on a merry-go-round which came out of the side of a mountain. Justman said, 'My God, that effect would cost us a half a million dollars just to try it. There's no guarantee it would work. Where the hell would we get a merry-go-round that moves from inside a mountain to outside a mountain?' And Harlan was explaining how we could do this out of cardboard, and got so pissed at Bobby because he couldn't budget it."

Episode #28:
"Operation Annihilate"
Original Airdate: 4/13/67
Written by Stephen W. Carabatsos
Directed by Herschel Daugherty
Guest Starring: Dave Armstrong (Kartan), Craig Hundley (Peter Kirk), Joan Swift (Aurelan), Maurishka Taliferro (Yeoman Zara Jamal)

Responding to a report of mass insanity on Deneva, the Enterprise arrives and Kirk is stunned to learn that his brother, George, is dead as a result of the disease. Further investigation leads them to amoeba-like creatures about the size of large rodents, which become one with a "host's" nervous system. Our heroes must discover a way to rid Deneva of this, and the answer comes from their apparent sensitivity to intense light. McCoy begins experimenting and Spock volunteers as a test subject, but things backfire when the Vulcan is blinded in the tests. Bones is devastated to later learn that the creatures can be destroyed by ultra-violet light, so Spock was blinded for no reason.

Needless to say, Spock's blindness is temporary, as he was protected by an additional eyelid that all Vulcans have to cope with the sunlight of their home world.

••••

"'Operation Annihilate' was not really my original idea," admits Steven Carabatsos. "Somebody gave me the idea—Roddenberry, I believe. He had wanted to do an episode involving Captain Kirk's brother. Kind of a family connection. More than that, I don't know what he suggested. We were just looking for basic jeopardy, character involvement and the uniqueness of the arena. Each planet was an opportunity to create a brand new world, a brand new society. As we approached each episode, that was one of the things that we had to address. I do know that it was eventually revised, which is normal for TV."

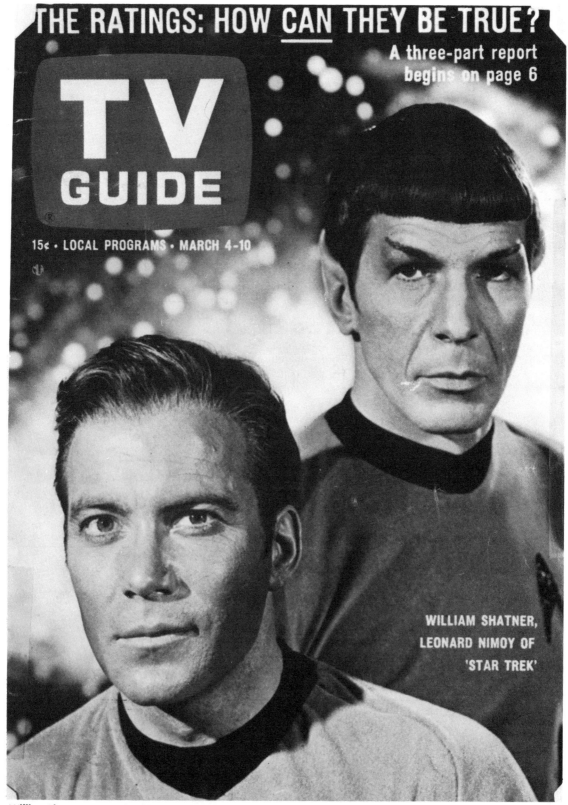

William Shatner as Captain Kirk and Leonard Nimoy as Mr. Spock graced the cover of TV Guide in the 1960s.

CHAPTER THREE
Trekking to Season 2

Star Trek's second season introduced several changes to the series, among them the addition of actor Walter Koenig as Russian navigator Pavel Chekov. This character made the bridge of the Enterprise a true United Nations-like ensemble in space.

"The Russians were responsible," said Gene Roddenberry. "They put on the Pravda youth paper that, 'Ah, the ugly Americans are at it again. They do a space show, and they forget to include the people who were in space first.' And I said, 'My God, they're right.' Walter Koenig and I had worked together on a show I did earlier, and he's great and I brought him in. And then I wrote the Russians and told them, 'I'm sorry we did it, and here's the information.' I never heard back from them. But not 'cause they're bad guys. The Air Force announced they had succeeded in phasing a thing and they were gonna call it a 'phaser.' And I wrote them and I said, 'I hope you use it with the respect for life as we did.' They didn't answer that either."

Both director Joseph Pevney and Walter Koenig himself remember the actor's hiring somewhat differently.

"When Roddenberry said he wanted to put a Russian on the show," recalls Pevney, "I said, 'I just used a kid in a television show at Universal named Walter Koenig, who I think I heard do a little Russian. Why don't we have him in and have him read?' Gene saw him and fell in love with him. He looks Russian; his face has a Slavic look to it. He looked right and was not a typical Russian cliche."

Added Walter Koenig in the pages of The Star Trek Interview Book, "Well, the facts are that they were looking for somebody who would appeal to the bubble gum set. They had somebody in mind like Davey Jones of The Monkees, and originally it was supposed to be an English character to kind of break off that segment of the audience;

however, in acknowledgement of the Russians' contribution to space they made the decision to go that way. All that stuff about Pravda—you know, the complaining—that's all nonsense. That was all just publicity. But it was a very practical decision. They wanted somebody who would appeal to eight-to-fourteen year olds and they decided to make him Russian."

"On the other hand," says Koenig today, "I had no idea how momentous this casting was in my career. I was told that the character might recur, but there was no guarantee. It was a matter that one of the things that happened, fortuitously, was that George Takei was shooting The Green Berets and was late reporting for the second season. They brought me back mainly to fill that seat for some sense of continuity, because at that point we had not had an audiece reaction. I guess I was lucky that George was unavailable."

By the time Star Trek had entered its second season, there was also a shift in attitude, both creatively and behind the scenes. In terms of the scripts, there had been a gradual shift toward featuring Kirk and Spock, and, to a somewhat lesser degree, McCoy as the primary focus of the stories, while Sulu, Scotty, Uhura and, now, Chekov, were delegated to background duty and such lines as "Hailing frequencies open, Captain," "The engines canna take any more, Captain," "Warp factor three, Captain," and "Aye, Captain."

In 1990, Nichelle Nichols related to Starlog magazine, "Initially, Star Trek the series and Star Trek the films were designed for an ensemble of stars who would each be given equal time. But at some point, the decision was made to separate Bill and Leonard Nimoy from the rest of us. And I'm not happy with that situation. I don't mind Bill and Leonard being the stars. But, in light of the fact that we were totally typecast through Star Trek, I felt the least they could have done was not totally defuse our characters."

The other actors (James Doohan, Walter Koenig, George Takei) have expressed similar concerns over the years, highlighted each time a new Star Trek feature film is being produced and

the press chronicles their efforts to get their characters more to do.

Director Joseph Pevney most definitely felt the change in attitude during the second year, and he didn't like it.

"In the beginning, there was the word and the word was cooperation," he states emphatically. "But then they started reading the fan mail. This was the first year and they were on tenter hooks. Everytime the phone would ring it was like, 'Are we cancelled? Are we cancelled?'

"Everybody was lovely in the beginning," he continues. "The relationships were exciting and good and then Gene Roddenberry let things get out of hand. I have to blame the producer on this, because the director is a lover and a father image and all that, and he's in love with his people and must treat them very carefully so as not to offend or hurt. But the producer's function is to be the stern father who punishes for misbehavior and so on. Gene could never play that role. Gene Coon could a little, but they didn't pay too much attention to him because Roddenberry was the top boss. So they would give lip service to Gene Coon, and then Roddenberry would come down and love everything he saw.

"Right after the pick up, things started to occur. The actors wanted to make a bigger contribution in the writing, so they wanted a rehearsal table thrown on the stage. The motivator of all this was, I think, Bill Shatner. Leonard could make his contributions in a quiet way by going into the office and talking to Coon or Roddenberry, and they were all very receptive. But all of a sudden things started to move away from the producer and director and to the actors. So, like a producer himself, Bill would arrange the table and seats and he would talk to the property man to move the thing over to the side. Well, when you're doing television in five or six days, or whatever the schedule was back then, there's no time for this constant rehearsal, a reading rehearsal, off-stage, with pencils in hand and making changes. Because once you start making changes on the set, they have to be approved by the producer."

Robert Justman adds, "Bill was the instigator of the rehearsal table. He wanted to be able to rehearse and I said,

'Okay, I'll tell you what. In between takes we'll set up a table, we'll grab everyone and go over the next scene.' Bill had wanted to do that and we made it possible. It was useful. It certainly helped an awful lot."

"It's time consuming," Pevney differs. "It destroys the most important thing of all, the disciplinary control of the director on the set. It's a very critical and tentative thing, which the television industry has gone away from completely. The director on a television set is nothing anymore. He doesn't mean a goddamned thing. He's an errand boy, which is one of the reasons I don't work anymore. I'm an angry guy when it comes to this kind of shit. I come from a disciplined school where everything is in the script. Nothing else counts. What is the story? And *that* is your function. Your responsibility is to tell the story as the writer intended it. That is my definition of a director. Once that's interfered with, he loses all control. So, anyway, everytime you would have a 'Cut. Print,' you'd have these guys rushing over under Bill's command to the table to work on the next scene."

Robert Justman responds, "I don't think Leonard or Bill ever gave up wanting to make the show better. Especially Leonard. He always wanted to make it better, make his character more believable and not take the easy way out. The problem is, of course, that the actors get the script a few days before they start the shooting, and then it's a little late to try and effect changes. We did try to accommodate them as much as we possibly could, even though it made our lives hell. There wasn't any time."

It's pointed out to him that Pevney believed that the directors were losing control of the series. Justman considers this for a moment.

"I initiated a policy in the second season that may have had something to do with that feeling," he admits. "We alternated directors rather than in the first season where we had scatter-gunned. [For the most part] we had Marc Daniels and Joe Pevney alternate, because they knew the show, they seemed to know what to do with the show first season very well and the film was generally

very, very good. So I said, speaking from a cost factor, we'd be able to get as many shows as we could possibly get with the time and money we had to spend. These two guys were very, very good, but at the same time we found out—I found out—familiarity breeds contempt. I shouldn't say that. It tends to relax a little bit too much when it's the same guy every time and you lose a little bit of that excitement you wanted to maintain. You should understand that Joe was extremely well liked on the set. The cast really liked him, the crew really liked him. He was very likable and motivated. Marc on the other hand was a different kettle of fish.

"Marc, in my opinion, turned out better shows, but he was a more difficult personality. He was truly well-versed in all forms of drama and comedy. His experience was unlimited, because he had been a successful movie director, stage director, television director and he had a good eye for compositions. He was a very all around kind of director, but he was more demanding than most. He ran a tougher set."

Pevney particularly noticed the problems when he and Marc Daniels would go off to do other shows and directors such as Ralph Senensky and Vincent McEveety would step in to helm episodes.

"While Marc and I went off to other shows, they brought in new directors and the new directors had ideas," he explains. "But the actors were already ingrained in behavior patterns which did not permit new inventiveness which was, as they felt, opposed to their character. That was the real beginning of the problem. Bill would not do certain things because Kirk wouldn't do that. Leonard certainly felt that way, very strongly, because his character was so deeply ingrained that he knew precisely how Spock would behave in a certain setting.

"It was right in certain respects," he allows, "with the actors protecting themselves, and it was wrong in the fact that their minds were closed to new inventiveness. There were good and bad things involved, but then when we would come back, there would be a whole different attitude by the actor. Now the actor had become co-producer, co-director and co-writer. A whole different attitude toward

me, Joe Pevney, or toward Marc Daniels. Now my attitude toward that is a very strong one. I don't bend with that kind of stuff. The director is the director. You want to be a director, God bless you. Go and be a director. But when I'm the director, I'm the director and you are the actor and you make the greatest contributions that you can, and I make the choices."

To a certain extent, director Vincent McEveety agrees with Pevney's observations.

"I think it's true of many series," he states. "Look at how locked in *Gunsmoke* was. Take Jim Arness, for example. How much did he vary from his basic portrayal? Any time there was a stretch, they'd pull back. The traditional words on *Star Trek* were, 'Well, Spock wouldn't do this, Kirk wouldn't do that.' All of a sudden, they're entities in and of themselves, when they were nothing two years prior when no one knew what they would do in a situation. By saying this, I'm not necessarily being critical, but, as Joe Pevney said, it is extremely limiting and that's all. I have worked on too many series where the attitude from the actor has been similar, if not more vocal, and they've been extremely successful.

"They call it protecting the character," elaborates McEveety. "The character first, before story, before stretch, before anything, because they claim in their vision that that is the key to the success of the series, and I think in many instances they're right. What you have to do is write *for* the character. Sometimes writers get very lazy and just write a script, but these actors are very concerned about being put in a weak position. That's okay in acting class, but they're depreciating their character. If anything was lacking in the later years on the show, even more than not accepting growth of the characters or even more conflict, it was lack of writing. I think it became more cliche writing, if you will. They came up with a story, went in there and put the actors in that story. They bring in writers that aren't terribly familiar with the series who say, 'Wouldn't it be fun if Spock did this?' Then you get on the stage and find out that Spock just doesn't do those kinds of things, so it isn't much fun. It's not writing with total intelligence."

• • • •

Director Ralph Senensky remains philosophical about the whole situation. "Doing episodic television is like jumping on a freight train that's in movement," he says. "As a director, what you have to do is jump on it and not break your legs. Once you've boarded it, you have to climb on top of the train, run across and get in the engine and take over running it. What happens is that before you can bring anything personal to the story, you have to get acquainted with who the people are. Not in terms of who you want them to be, but in terms of who they really are already. These are already-established characters. You do that, and *then* you can start to find the warts and things to do, outlets to extend and expand. As a result, what would happen is that you have to kind of rely on the cast to help you out. You'd say, 'Would your character do this?'

"I just accepted it," he continues. "A major area where they would get into that tact with was not so much in the acting, but in the scripting. The script might not fulfill their character or would go off on tangents. Sometimes actors come in the first season and get a job that they're thrilled to get, but by the second season they know more about writing, directing, producing...whatever else, than anyone. There is a taking advantage of that position too. There's a very fine line that I certainly appreciate, because actors do help. Through the years I've found myself many times using the actor as a way to get a script changed when we've both agreed that it should be. I would go through the actor, because the producer will be more apt to relent if the actor goes to him than if a new director comes in and says, 'I don't like your script.'

"I remember on the third season episode 'Is There in Truth No Beauty?', it was the first day of shooting and the cast literally refused to shoot it. Gene Roddenberry, who wasn't very involved in the third year, came down, they had a meeting and we lost half a day. We literally sat around talking and then I went off to shoot something with the guest stars. I shot a scene with them in the afternoon, while Gene was rewriting the other sequence to try and mollify the objections. That's not only *Star Trek*, that's an ongoing battle. That doesn't mean that

I'm more lenient about it than Joe or Marc, but I've had it in so many other places too, that people shouldn't think that it only happened on *Star Trek*."

Star Feud...?

The rumors of behind the scenes conflicts between lead actors on a weekly series have probably been around for as long as the medium has existed. As is the case in most rumors there is one side, the other side and the truth. Did Jack Klugman and Tony Randall love each other on *The Odd Couple*? Yes, there's no doubt. Just look to the recent slew of Eagle Snack commercials featuring the two actors as proof that their friendship has spanned over two decades. Did Penny Marshall and Cindy Williams have difficulties on the set of *Laverne & Shirley*? Considering the fact that the last season featured Laverne (Marshall) without Shirley, one can assume that they did.

And what of William Shatner and Leonard Nimoy on *Star Trek*? Since the days of the series to the making of the feature films, there have been reports of a strained relationship, due mostly to the whirlwind they found themselves caught up in and, some say, the unleashing of their egos. To an extent this is understandable. When you've got millions of fans elevating to you a level above humanity, it has got to have an effect. Still, both actors have stated over the years that there was never a feud.

"I really love Leonard," Shatner explained in the 1970s. "I really care for him a great deal. He's a very fine human being. He stands behind what he says with his total character. When he says something, he really means it. You can take him at his word. He is slyly humorous and very affectionate in his own way, which is remarkable. And to address myself to the elements of friction on the stage, I would put it in a way that two children [from] the same family might squabble over something. Loving each other, but squabbling. Any member of a family would know what I mean, and that means all of us. You can say, 'No, I don't think that's right' in that quarrelous tone and be angry at the moment, and

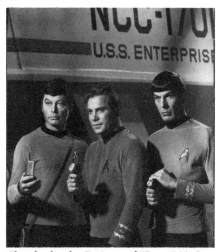

The classic trio: Dr Leonard "Bones" McCoy, Captain James T. Kirk and Mr. Spock. (Photo copyright © Globe Photos)

then forget it the following moment because you care about that person."

In *The World of Star Trek*, Nimoy said, "Bill and I are both very committed to and concerned with the work that we do, and we both tend to have strong personalities...and we both have strong feelings about what's right and what's wrong. So, yes, there were times when we had differences of opinion about how a thing should be done or whether it should be done at all. But, we are very good friends, we're very close."

World of Star Trek and "Trouble With Tribbles" author David Gerrold relates, "During the first season, *Saturday Review* did this article about *Trek* that Spock was much more interesting than Kirk, and that Spock should be captain. Well, *nobody* was near Shatner for days. He was furious. You've got to look at it from his point of view. He had been hired to be the star of the show. It was 'Starring William Shatner, *with* DeForest Kelley and Leonard Nimoy.' All of a sudden, all the writers are writing all this great stuff for Spock, and Spock, who's supposed to be a subordinate character, suddenly starts becoming the equal of Kirk. The show that started out about Kirk is now about Kirk and Spock. Bill definitely feels that he was lessened by that. On the other hand, Leonard is a very shrewd businessman, a very smart actor, and recognized that this Spock business was a way to be more important than an 'also ran,' and he pushed."

Science fiction author Norman

Spinrad wrote season two's "The Doomsday Machine." In that episode, the Enterprise encounters a device that has the capability of wiping out entire star systems. Guest starring is Commodore Decker (William Windom), who commanded a starship recently destroyed by the weapon. Spinrad was surprised by some of the ways that he *had* to approach the characters and his on-set observations.

"I had had a long unpublished novella that took place entirely on a space ship which was kind of a variation on *Moby Dick*, so that became 'The Doomsday Machine,'" reflects Spinrad. "I was also told to write a part for Robert Ryan, who they wanted to give a good role to. So I developed the idea of Robert Ryan playing an Ahab-type character. And then when they didn't get Ryan and they got William Windom, things had to be adjusted. I had to make him a little softer, and I think it might have taken some of the edge off of the story.

"In the original version, Commodore Decker was much stronger," he continues. "They don't find him slumped over in the ruined ship. Instead, they find him staring out the viewscreen and in a *very* bad mood. There was also the feeling that a guest star with that kind of presence would overshadow Captain Kirk, and therefore his character had to be toned down and his lines reduced. Also, some of Spock's lines had to be given to Kirk.

"Yes, he [Shatner] counted lines. I was on the set during the making of that episode. Marc Daniels was directing and they couldn't get it to work. The reason for this is that it was a dialogue sequence set up as Kirk, Spock, Kirk, but the intervening Spock line had been taken out in the line count, so there was no reaction line for the next line to work. I took Marc aside and said, 'Have him grunt or something,' and I explained that there was a missing line there. But things like that did happen. Observing it depended on how close you were to the production. Here I was watching the director struggle. But not too many people were able to hang around the set. The point is that they have to give their lead characters prominence."

Spinrad notes that he was impressed with the series itself, and to a degree could understand the difficulties between the actors.

"I thought that it was a genius thing that Roddenberry did," he muses. "The anthology series was dead on television as a doornail, and he devised a format in which you could do a self-contained anthology story every week. All you had were these people on a spaceship who could go to any damned planet they felt like. It was a genius concept because it literally left them open to do anything at all. As far as the characters, Spock was a really interesting and good character. The rest were fairly typical 'type' characters, without strong or weird characteristics.

"That was always Bill Shatner's problem. He just wasn't given as interesting a character to play as Nimoy was. He was the lead character—supposedly the most important—but he couldn't be most interesting. It was not a reflection on him as an actor, because I remember him as a very good actor before that, but he didn't have the part even though the contract said he did. That led to all the line stealing and all that kind of crazy lunatic stuff in any number of scripts where the captain went crazy because somebody was trying to take away his ship. In a funny kind of way, this gave the character of Kirk more depth. It gave Kirk a little edge somewhere that was really Shatner, which is a good way to use it. Another thing to consider is that if this cast has been together for this long, then the actors have got to become a part of the character which can give them more depth...if people know what they're doing."

Joseph Pevney considers the notion of the feud, and nods his head in understanding.

"If there are rumors about a rivalry," he begins, "they're probably true. Now Leonard and Bill are both good actors. They enjoy working with each other. If the script is equally as good to both characters, there's no problem. It's when one became a straight man for the other that you have rivalry. That they resent and probably for good reason. Sometimes, storywise, it's impossible to have both people answer the question, but a good writer can solve that in two seconds. All he's got to have is a straight man who's a third character, and let both of the heroes be heroes. It's not *too* difficult to do. Roddenberry was always conscious of it, but he lost control of the show because of Bill and Leonard. I'm sure of that.

"I left the show long before it folded, because I couldn't enjoy working with those two anymore. The whole character of the show had changed for me. The quality of the writing deteriorated, I think primarily because they were scared that whatever they submitted would be torn to shreds by Bill and Leonard. There was loss of confidence from the top in the material, and if you do that, you're shaking up something awful. If I had come in with the script for 'The Trouble With Tribbles' during the third season, I would have been laughed off the set. They'd say, 'You can't do this piece of shit,' and that would be the end of it. The hero of the show was a little fuzzy animal, and they don't want that. They want to constantly be the heroes and this is the mark of a spoiled actor. This is a guy who reads his mail and is no longer aware of the need for teamwork.

"When we started the show, teamwork was the key word. Nobody was more important than anybody else. The captain was the captain of the ship, but the actor was no more important than anybody. When Gene Coon left the show, a lot of the discipline had gone out of it. From the time I made 'Arena' to the time I did my last show, there was a hell of a difference. If you run both of them, there was a difference in performance quality, changes which give you a sense of the overbearing captain and Spock. And a kind of challenging between the two of them on screen, which is okay in life and rehearsal, but shouldn't be there on screen. Then Leonard would say, 'I'm the second in command, when can I do a story where I'm commanding the ship?' Well, those stories came to be and, after a while, Bill would say, 'Wait a second, I'm the captain!' There you've got problems, originating from, I would say, actor to producer, because when they were through with their shows, Leonard, primarily, and Bill would be up in Gene's fanny, making suggestions as to how the show should go, some good and some

• • • •

48

horrible. All of them, I think, very selfishly instigated. Now I wasn't witness to this, I only heard it from Gene Coon and Gene Roddenberry, who was coming to the studio less and less. The whole atmosphere, the feeling of teamwork and whole *Star Trek* quality disintegrated."

The Changing Season

Despite whatever controversies were brewing behind the scenes, *Star Trek*'s second season presented some of the show's finest episodes.

"Metamorphosis" was a different kind of love story, between an energy being and the human it rescued a century earlier; "Who Mourns For Adonais?" actually pit Kirk and company against the Greek god Apollo, and managed to pull it off believably; "Amok Time" delved into the nature of the Vulcan mating cycle; "Mirror, Mirror" was a fascinating look at the dark side of the universe as Kirk, McCoy, Scotty and Uhura are transported to a mirror dimension in which the Federation serves the place held by the Klingon Empire in "our" universe, and members of the crew move up in rank through assassination; "The Deadly Years," in which Kirk, Spock, McCoy and Scotty are victims of advanced aging; "The Trouble With Tribbles," *Star Trek*'s first comedy about a fuzzy critter that multiplies like crazy and actually threatens everyone aboard the Enterprise and the space station K-7; "Journey to Babel," which had the Enterprise serve as transport for various races enroute to a peace conference, and a show that introduced us to Spock's parents, Sarek and Amanda; "The Ultimate Computer," in which the Enterprise becomes the toy of the M-5 and is used in war games exercises that become horrifying reality; and "Assignment: Earth," a pilot for a series that never happened in which the Enterprise travels back in time to Earth in the 1960s, where they encounter a man from the future who has been trained to help mankind save itself from the threat of nuclear destruction. All of these were examples of *Star Trek* at its best.

Story Editor Dorothy Fontana reflects, "In the first and second season I think we went from strength to strength, because, basically, we knew our direction

by the sixth show in terms of the actors who filled out the characters. We had begun to know them as the characters and began writing for their strengths. I think the stories just got better, although you always have a klinker or two. On the whole, I think our batting average was awfully good during the first two seasons."

While there was great success in terms of the stories utilized on the show, there was also a disturbing sense of repetition in the use of the "parallel worlds" theory. Season one had used Earth-like settings three times, one of them ("Miri") being an alien world, while both "Tomorrow is Yesterday" and "The City on the Edge of Forever" took place on Earth in the past (respectively the 1960s and 1930s). During season two, however, "Bread and Circuses" gave us a modernized twist on Old Rome; "A Piece of the Action" was a light-hearted variation of Chicago in the Roaring 20s; "Patterns of Force" represented a world being run by a Nazi regime; "The Omega Glory," was a frontier story involving a Federation captain who "infected" an alien society, resulting in the development of a Constitution quite similar to America's; "A Private Little War," another frontier tale this time serving as a Vietnam analogy in which the Federation and the Klingons each arm different sides of an alien world to maintain a balance of power; and the aforementioned "Assignment: Earth."

Although some of these shows were quite good, it nonetheless seemed to point to *Star Trek* losing a bit of its edge.

"Once you solve the mystery in anything, the thrill is gone," says Robert Justman. "The thing that's motivated me in working in the television business was getting the challenge of a new show and finding out if you could do it. My feeling was once you knew you could do it, I wanted to try something new. So, yes, the original magic, the original excitement, tends to pass on once you solve the mysteries of it. But there was still the comraderie.

"We had another problem in the second season that was highly intensified during the third," he adds. "In the second season we were cut down on how much we could spend per show by

a sizeable amount of money. Despite the fact that there had been cast escalations, so our cast costs were higher. This in turn had an effect on the kind of shows we could do. It was even worse the third season when we got cut down again despite even more cast escalations."

Corroborates director Ralph Senensky, "There wasn't any money. If you saw the soundstage we shot on, you'd be amazed. One of them was the starship interiors, which filled the entire stage and it wasn't that big a stage to begin with. The other one was the stage where we built everything else we needed. For example, in 'Metamorphosis' we had the Enterprise shuttle, the Galileo, on the sound stage. We were supposed to have a spacecraft and sell the idea of a huge, huge planet. I don't know if you remember the wide shots we did, but the spacecraft looks so small that you would think it was a model. This was achieved by our cinematographer, Jerry Finnerman. We literally had the spacecraft at one end of the stage and the camera as far back as it could go on the other end of the stage. Jerry shot it with a 9mm lense just to give it that scope. You see it today, I think it's marvelous. But you couldn't use the 9mm with actors because it distorts. That's an example of the budgetary limitations. Rather than fight it, you try and find a way to use the imagination and rise above it."

For Senensky, a major change in atmosphere came when Paramount Pictures took over Desilu.

"Desilu was like a family," he smiles. "Herb Solow, who was the head of the studio, used to come down and talk with you on the sound stage. He didn't seem like the other studio heads who never seemed to talk to you. Herb went out of his way to help you. Can you imagine a studio working like that?

"I think when Paramount bought the company, it had a lot to do with the demise of the series. Gene Coon had told me that the shows were originally scheduled for six day shoots, though they averaged six and a half days or seven. It was pretty remarkable when you consider the kind of quality they were delivering. When Paramount bought it, a kind of corporate mentality took over. In a way I think that's why I resent Paramount having such a hit in *Star Trek*, because if they had their way, they would have killed it off. It survived in spite of them and now they have this bonanza making all of this money. With them there was a six-day schedule, *period*. They would not allow for any overruns at all. You would have a 7:30 crew call in the morning, you'd start shooting at 8:00 and you'd go until about 7:00, 7:30 at night. We're talking a six-day schedule and you had to absolutely pull the plug at midnight on the sixth day. In terms of actual hours, it really pulled us down to about a five and a half day schedule. It was a big cut. The other schedule hadn't given you that much grace, but all of a sudden you felt like you were shooting schlock because you were shooting so quickly."

As noted, Gene Coon decided to leave *Star Trek* in the middle of the second season due to the fact that he had simply burned himself out. Twelve to 16 hour days for months at a time had proved too much, and he departed.

Glen Larson, based on conversations he had with Coon, believes that the producer had simply had enough of *Star Trek*, and could not work on the series any longer.

"Gene had two scripts on his desk in front of him which he had to rewrite," Larson relates. "He suddenly put his pencil down and finally said, 'This is it,' and he got up and walked out. It had been an around the clock, very draining experience."

Part of the problem, according to actor William Campbell (who had portrayed Trelene in season one's "Squire of Gothos"), was that high-quality writers were no longer attempting to write for the show. Opines the actor, "I think it was starting to become a tremendous chore to come up with anything new. Don't forget, they were using writers from the outside and it was becoming more difficult to get them. You've got to remember that we're talking about a period when the great writers no longer were doing anything. When television was making its first inroads, you had some of these great people doing television shows."

Coon left and eventually went to work for Universal Pictures and *It Takes a Thief*, though he nonetheless continued to write for *Star Trek* under the

pen name Lee Cronin. This, according to Glen Larson, was not by choice.

"At first, Gene Roddenberry wouldn't let him leave because he had a contract," Larson offers. "The only way they'd let Gene out is if he continued to write for the show, and he continued under a psuedonym. He would be in there typing away while were were supposed to be doing *It Takes a Thief*, but that was great because more and more of it fell on me and I became an instant producer. Roddenberry knew they needed Gene, and didn't feel they could function without him, so he had to promise to make script commitments."

To replace Coon, Gene Roddenberry chose writer/director/producer John Meredyth Lucas.

"I was on the lot shooting *Mannix*," recalls Lucas, "and I wrote a script for Gene Coon. Gene was going to retire and suggested that I take over because I had produced *Ben Casey*. He asked if we could get together, I went over his house, we talked for a while and that was it. At that time, Bob Justman was handling the production end of things. When I came in, I got into production too, and was also directing. Gene had said, 'When they hired me, they knew I was writing and that was it.' That was *not* the way that I produced.

"When I joined the show, they had a very complex system of memoranda to everybody. Everyone involved would send incredibly long memorandums, almost equivalent to the old Hollywood technique. I abandoned that pretty quickly because it took so much goddamned time. I also remember that there was a great deal of tension with the actors. Not civil war but a great deal of tension among the cast and the company. As a matter of fact, Gene took me out to location to introduce me as producer. We came up to the company. When they'd gotten a particular shot, we walked over and Shatner walked away from us. He would not speak to Gene or to me. They were feuding over something, though I've no idea what the problem was.

"There was tension among Shatner and Nimoy and Gene. Just a great deal of tension that had built up. In happens on every show, but it was particular-

ly noticeable on *Star Trek* when I first came in. I won't say I solved it, but I simply ignored it, went on and was on the set a great deal. I tend to be hands-on with everything. It was just a different kind of approach. Whatever had caused the tension, I'm not quite sure. Actors tend to feel that if you're not there all the time and petting them a little bit, or at least there to hear their screams of anguish, that they're abandoned. Eventually we all became very friendly. That doesn't mean there weren't complaints about someone's part not being meaningful, but we developed a mechanism to talk them out."

Actor William Campbell offers this view: "I don't know anything about the relationship with the two guys, but I can tell you this. What happens to actors when they've acquired a position on a television show, after a short period of time—they can't help it—they become precious. And recognize that in some ways they can tell producers off, can make their presence felt. They all have ideas.

"I don't remember a situation where Gene Coon would tell either of those actors how to act, nor did he suggest that he was a director, but he did have an inner sense and he might have held the line on certain things that they would have changed. Or areas where they would have liked another direction be taken, and Gene Coon perhaps debated them on occasion and they didn't like it. But I never heard him say word one bad against anybody."

Jackie Fernandez, the woman who married Coon shortly after his tenure on *Star Trek*, recalls, "Basically Gene wasn't crazy about actors. They were just too needful and too egocentric. He wasn't. He didn't get along with Robert Wagner either when he went over to *It Takes a Thief*. I would take his feelings about these actors he didn't get along with with a grain of salt, because he didn't care for actors in general."

When John Meredyth Lucas took over the writing reigns, he was determined to get back to what he felt *Star Trek* had been in its original concept.

"If there was one element that I brought back to the show when I was producer, because it had been a little bit lost, it was Gene Roddenberry's inspiration for the series: Horatio Hornblower. *That's* the thing that I kept trying to bring back. The constant warfare—frontier warfare—to make Kirk Captain Hornblower again. A lot of that stuff had gotten lost into the areas of fantasy, which is fine. But as the season progressed, there'd been less and less of the Hornblower elements, which appealed to me as exemplified in 'The Ultimate Computer' and things like that.

"A creative problem on the show was that we loved doing pieces which had some kind of concept. That's a terrible word to use when you're talking to the network. You would think that high concept would mean a lofty purpose, but to them it simply means something you can tell in one word. The network tended to want green space monsters that ate the ship each week, and we tended to want to do shows which had,

what seemed to us, some kind of concept, saying something and being different. But God knows we did our share of the green monsters eating the ship."

In between all of these elements being worked out, and while the show continued to touch its primary audience—the youth of America—NBC made the announcement: STAR TREK would be cancelled at the end of the season. Fortunately, a second letter-writing campaign kept the show alive. Barely.

••••

CHAPTER FOUR
Season 2 Episode Guide

"Amok Time"

"Who Mourns For Adonais?"

"The Changeling"

"Mirror, Mirror"

"The Apple"

"The Doomsday Machine"

"Catspaw"

"I, Mudd"

"Metamorphosis"

"Journey to Babel"

"Friday's Child"

"The Deadly Years"

"Obsession"

"Wolf in the Fold"

"The Trouble With Tribbles"

"The Gamesters of Triskellion"

"A Piece of the Action"

"The Immunity Syndrome"

"A Private Little War"

"Return to Tomorrow"

"Patterns of Force"

"By Any Other Name"

"The Omega Glory"

"The Ultimate Computer"

"Bread and Circuses"

"Assignment Earth"

••••

"Amok Time" co-stars Leonard Nimoy and Arlene Martel reunited at an early Star Trek *convention.*

Episode #29:
"Amok Time"
Original Airdate: 9/15/67
Written by Theodore Sturgeon
Directed by Joseph Pevney
Guest Starring: Arlene Martel (T'Pring),
Celia Lovsky (T'Pau),
Lawrence Montaigne (Stonn),
Byron Morrow (Komack)

Spock begins to lose control of himself as he is overtaken by pon farr, the Vulcan mating cycle that occurs every seven years in which the affected male must return to the homeworld to mate or die. It's a cycle much like the salmon on Earth, which must return to its birthplace to spawn eggs or die trying.

As Enterprise is in the midst of a mission, Kirk—who believes that Spock merely needs shore leave—is unable to divert to Vulcan for several days. Spock, in the midst of his madness, countermands the captain's orders and has a course laid in for his homeworld. Eventually Kirk comes to understand what is going on and disobeys Starfleet orders to go to Vulcan.

There, the madness takes its full control on Spock and through the manipulations of his of his supposed betrothed, he is pitted against Kirk in a battle to the death.

●●●●

Then Story Editor Dorothy Fontana recalls the conferences regarding the specifics of Vulcan mating.

"I don't remember whether it was Gene Roddenberry, Gene Coon or Ted [who came up with the Vulcan seven-year mating cycle], but the way we have established it, most people don't stop and understand this," says Fontana. "Vulcans mate normally anytime they want to. However, every seven years you do the ritual, the ceremony, the whole thing. The biological urge. You must, but any other time is any other emotion—humanoid emotion—when you're in love. When you want to, you know, when the sex urge is there, you do it. This every seven years business was taken too literally by too many people who aren't stopping and understanding. We didn't mean *only* every seven years. I mean, every seven years would be a little bad, and it would not explain the Vulcans of many different ages which are not seven years apart."

The late writer Theodore Sturgeon once recalled, "Do you know that [the actors] got so far into their characters that they would *speak their own lines*? In 'Amok Time', for example, in the last scene where the doctor was so pleased to see the sudden flash of humanity in Spock, where Spock suddenly came up with this brilliant smile and said, 'Jim!' when he saw Kirk alive and had thought he was dead—and then was still denying having any emotional reaction, at all, and Dr. McCoy said, 'In a pig's eye!'—that was De. That wasn't me. De put that in his very own self. They all did that from time to time. Bill certainly did. And when it worked, they let it stand, because that was one of the things the show had going for it."

Adds director Joseph Pevney, "'Amok Time' was a good one. I brought in the actress who played T'Pau. The fight was absolutely excellent, and one of the most exciting we ever did. What made it dramatically interesting is that it took place between Kirk and Spock. During this episode, Leonard Nimoy and I worked out the Vulcan salute and the 'Live long and prosper' together. He dis-

cussed this finally in an interview and he never mentioned my name. He said the director, but never me by name. Well, Leonard is now a big director, and I hope he doesn't change as a human being. He was a nice Yiddish boy with a nice mastery of the language. I just hope he doesn't believe all the bullshit, because it's so easy to believe. I don't care who you are, you can get captured by it."

Elsewhere, Leonard Nimoy recalled, "We arrived on the planet, the three key figures—Captain Kirk, Mr. Spock and Dr. McCoy—were greeted by a procession coming out from the city. When the procession arrived, we discover that Vulcan is a matriarchy, the head of the planet being brought out, carried in a sedan chair by some bearers. The character was named T'Pau, played by Cecilia Lovsky, a wonderful actress, and she was to be seated and I was to approach her and we were to say some nice things to each other. I thought, 'Here's a special opportunity to create something special in the way of a Vulcan greeting; some kind of signal that they have between each other.

"And I said to the director, 'Humans shake hands when they meet and military people salute each other.' He asked me what I had in mind. I was raised in an orthodox Jewish family, and during the high holidays I'd go to the temple with my parents and sit with my father and my brother, and at a particular point in the service, the kohanim, who are the priests of the Hebrew tribes, would bless the congregation with a blessing that is familiar to all of us from the old and new testament, 'May the Lord bless you and keep you,' and so forth. When that time comes during this ritual, the congregation turned their back and does not look at these men. I'm not sure of the reason for that, but in any case, children are taught not to look at the kohanim while they are performing this blessing. My father would say, 'Don't look, turn away.' Of course, I being a curious eight or nine year old child, I peeked. What I saw was.....". Nimoy demonstrated the gesture. "...These gentlemen were holding their hands in this position while they were giving this benediction to the congregation...I was fascinated. I thought I've got to learn how to do that, and I worked long and hard to accomplish it."

●●●●

Carolyn Palamas, impregnated by Apollo in an early draft of "Who Mourns for Adonais?", was played by Julie Parrish, seen here in The Wild Wild West.

Episode #30:
"Who Mourns For Adonais?"
Original Airdate: 9/22/67
Written by Gilbert Ralston and
Gene L. Coon
Story by Gilbert Ralston
Directed by Marc Daniels
Guest Starring: Michael Forest (Apollo),
Leslie Parrish (Carolyn Palamas),
John Winston (Kyle)

The Enterprise is literally snared by the hand of the Greek god Apollo, who has decided that the time has come for mankind to worship him again. Kirk must use the force of the starship as well as crew woman Carolyn Palamas, who is in love with Apollo, to combat his awesome powers and gain their freedom. Finally realizing that the species cannot be forced to worship anything, Apollo moves to a spiritual plane, joining the other gods who had long ago realized that their time had come and gone.

••••

There is a startling moment in this episode where Carolyn Palamas rejects Apollo's love (despite her feelings to do otherwise) and she is ravaged by a storm of Apollo's making. If you watch this scene, you can't help but get the feeling that he is raping her. Indeed, an earlier draft of the teleplay had her pregnant with his child.

Of this script, Dorothy Fontana notes, "I think Gene Coon basically enhanced the relationships, the fact that

the god wanted this woman to not only be his consort, but his foremost among his worshippers. And then the antagonistic relationship between Kirk and Adonais. Kirk wasn't going to fall on his knees and worship a god. No way. Again, it was a matter of character development."

"Immodestly," writer Gilbert Ralston begins, "I'm an expert in Grecian history, and I got interested in some of the characters tucked away in my various textbooks. Using Apollo just seemed like a good idea, and Gene Coon liked it very much.

"I liked *Star Trek* because of Gene and some of the people who originally worked on it. Their conception was highly intellectual and very sophisticated, and it was fun to write because they were apparently very demanding in so far as literary quality was concerned. Shows like that were always a pleasure. It was a *people* show, without an emphasis on stunts and special effects. It was about people, and the fact that one had funny ears didn't make any difference. They were not afraid to emotionalize what they did and, in its own peculiar way, it had a kind of reality which I think was very important. I think *Star Trek* will continue as a kind of quasi-classic for a long time to come."

Episode #31:
"The Changeling"
Original Airdate: 9/29/67
Written by John Meredyth Lucas
Directed by Marc Daniels
Guest Starring: Blaisdell Makee (Singh),
Arnold Lessing (Lt. Carlisle),
Vic Perrin (The Voice of Nomad)

Over four billion people are obliterated in the Malurian star system, and the perpetrator is a combination probe and computer identifying itself as Nomad, which has more power than the Enterprise or the entire fleet.

Nomad is brought aboard the Enterprise. Mistakenly it believes that Captain Kirk is actually its creator, Jackson Roykirk, and for that reason, he obeys Kirk's commands. In a Vulcan mind-meld, Spock learns that the machine was actually an Earth probe lost in space centuries earlier. Captured by a machine planet, it was given intelligence and the ability to purify all things impure.

Kirk must trick the machine into destroying itself.

••••

Writer/producer John Meredyth Lucas says, "I was always fascinated by the concept of the machine as God. That was really the spark for it; the selling point. Although 'The Changeling' does comment on worshipping the machine, I was not trying to make any particular statement. It was simply a fascinating concept that a machine could become—in a very real sense—alive. In the story it was accidental, but it became a very real, judgmental being and a threat."

It's pointed out that *Star Trek: The Motion Picture* was quite similar to this episode. "If anything," he replies, "it's a little hard to sustain that plot for a full movie. God knows the effects and everything else that had been done are effects which were pretty damn good in their day, but are primitive today. The plot, of course, I recognized."

"'The Changeling' required a great deal of ingenuity," recalled Marc Daniels. "We had to have three different Nomads mounted in three different ways. One on a wire, to hover in a room; one on a dolly, to be moved through corridors and onto the bridge; and one on the floor. You just couldn't take one on a wire through the door, hence the dolly system. If you wanted to see Nomad in all its authority, you would put it on a wire."

Episode #32:
"Mirror, Mirror"
Original Airdate: 10/6/67
Written by Jerome Bixby
Directed by Marc Daniels
Guest Starring: Barbara Luna (Marlena),
Vic Perrin (Tharn)

During an ion storm, Kirk, McCoy, Scotty and Uhura are transported to a parallel dimension on an alternate, savage Enterprise. In this universe, the Federation is as feared as the Klingons and crewmen move up in rank by assassination. Spock (with a beard!) is still first officer, but his logic is coupled with a shocking ruthlessness.

Kirk and company try to fit in until they figure out a way home, barely avoiding discovery by those around them. Simultaneously, Kirk tries to con-

••••

vince Spock to see the logic in changing the order; that the Federation will ultimately be defeated by rebel forces and he, Spock, can be the man who can lead the revolution.

Scotty ultimately devises a plan by which they will attempt the conditions present during the ion storm and transport to their own universe, but if they miss the window of opportunity they will be trapped there forever.

••••

Veteran science fiction author Jerome Bixby, whose script credits include Rod Serling's *The Twilight Zone* and 20th Century Fox's motion picture *Fantastic Voyage* was a real coup to the series.

"Mirror, Mirror" came about because "I wanted to do a parallel universe story. I had already done a fiction story called 'One Way Street' which was a parallel universe story, and I thought that would make a good *Star Trek*. The universe I created was a very savage counterpart, virtually a pirate ship, into which I could transpose a landing party. I submitted the outline, they loved it and I did the script."

"That was a good one," commented Marc Daniels. "I'm not sure if it was 'Mirror, Mirror,' but I remember a big fight scene which resulted in several bodies lying on the floor for quite some time. After a while there was a considerable amount of snoring from these people who were supposed to be unconscious. I also remember that Nichelle Nichols was furious because I used a stunt woman in the fight. She said, 'I want to do that. That woman doesn't look anything like me!' I said, 'You've got to be out of your mind. This is a complicated stunt. You could get badly hurt unless you know what you're doing, and the production couldn't afford to have you knocked out.'"

Episode #33:
"The Apple"
Original Airdate: 10/13/67
Written by Max Ehrlich and Gene L. Coon
Story by Max Ehrlich
Directed by Joseph Pevney
Guest Starring: Keith Andes (Akuta), Celeste Yarnall (Martha Landon), Jay Jones (Mallory), Shari Nims (Sayana), David Soul (Makora)
Captain Kirk does the computer

shuffle again as the Enterprise goes to a world run by Vaal, an ancient computer that controls the laws of nature as well as the inhabitants.

While this is an idyllic world, the people are exactly like children. No cares and no concerns, allowing Vaal to take care of them and, in turn, making offerings to "him" in appeasement. Kirk and company must make them see that this is wrong; that they have a right to govern themselves.

••••

Actor and Gene Coon friend William Campbell points out, "Gene recognized some of the shortcomings of *Star Trek*. He saw the cult atmosphere and felt that no American would go along with that concept—being policeman of the universe. It was a little L. Ron Hubbardish. Here you've got a leader who's omnipotent, this rocketship is a city traveling around spanking people who are getting out of line. You don't tell Captain Kirk what to do, because he's boss. There's no sitting down and saying, 'We're having a meeting of the council to find out if we're going to let you do this.' He knew the impossible parts of it, but he said, 'We can take young people—because they're going to be the leaders of the future—and show them that right should be right, because today we don't know who the good guy is.'"

Episode #34:
"The Doomsday Machine"
Original Airdate: 10/20/67
Written by Norman Spinrad
Directed by Marc Daniels
Guest Starring: William Windom (Commodore Decker), Elizabeth Rogers (Lt. Palmer), John Copage (Elliot), Richard Compton (Washburn), John Winston (Sgt. Kyle), Tim Burns (Russ)
After several star systems have been destroyed, the Enterprise investigates the situation and discovers what's left of the U.S.S. Constellation, with her commander, Commodore Matt Decker, the only person on board. He relates a terrifying tale, detailing how a virtual tunnel in space emitted energy waves that sliced up whole planets which it devoured. He beamed his crew down to one of the local worlds in the hopes of protecting them, but that particular

Veteran character actor William Windom played Commodore Matt Decker, commander of ruined starship, in "The Doomsday Machine."

planet was the next target.

Kirk and Spock come to the conclusion that this thing is actually a doomsday machine—an ultimate weapon—created by a long dead race, that has been destroying planets for centuries. Now the hope is that the Enterprise and whatever can be salvaged of the Constellation will be able to defeat it before it continues on its way.

••••

"The Doomsday Machine" was famed science fiction author Norman Spinrad's first television script.

"I had seen both *Star Trek* pilots at conventions, met Gene Roddenberry a couple of times and wrote a review of *2,001* in *Cinema* magazine, in which I mentioned *Star Trek* favorably," Spinrad recalls. "Gene asked me to come in and pitch something. Then he said, 'These things are really expensive. We're over budget on a lot of them, so can you think of anything that takes place entirely on the ship in terms of sets?' I had had a long unpublished novella that took place entirely on a space ship which was kind of a variation on *Moby Dick*. So that became 'The Doomsday Machine,' which is how it came to be known.

"I just rewatched the episode again for the first time in a long time," he elaborates, "and I was more pleased with it than I remember being, especially in

••••

comparison to the crap that has been on television since. I didn't think it was all that hot when I first saw it, because what I saw was the unaltered version that was in my head, and I thought it could have been done a lot better. And that godawful Doomsday Machine itself! Originally Gene Roddenberry asked me to design the thing. The concept was actually made less complex because there was a limit to what they could do. In my original concept, it is neither a machine nor an organism. It's a combination of both; a tailored weapon/organism."

Episode #35:
"Catspaw"
Original Airdate: 10/27/67
Written by Robert Bloch and
D.C. Fontana
Directed by Joseph Pevney
Guest Starring: Antoinette Bowers (Sylvia), Theo Marcus (Korob), Michael Barrier (DeSalle), Jimmy Jones (Jackson)

Star Trek does Halloween! Beaming down to Pyris VII, Kirk, Spock and McCoy confront Sulu and Scotty, who have been transformed into zombies. At the same time, they battle aliens who are out to conquer the universe and go about it through some traditional all hallows eve methods, right down to black cats and witches.

••••

Robert Bloch told *Starlog* magazine, "They wanted a Halloween story. I wanted to do something that would involve changes in appearances. So I decided that instead of having the usual Jekyll and Hyde transformation, I'll have a female who was capable of chameleon-like adaptations, and the rest just fell into place. I do have quibbles about the way in which things were done. It wasn't their fault, but they just didn't have the budget. 'Catspaw' cried out for the use of opticals in post-production effects. Shooting a cat's face in tight close-up is not exactly any substitute for having a giant cat. Running down a few feet of cardboard corridor isn't the same thing as having your characters trapped in a labyrinth of frightening proportions! Otherwise, 'Catspaw' was shot pretty much as I had written it."

Director Joseph Pevney dismisses the episode with, "That's not a very

good one. I hated the actors in that one."

Episode #36:
"I, Mudd"
Original Airdate: 11/3/67
Written by Stephen Kandel
Directed by Marc Daniels
Guest Starring: Roger C. Carmel (Harry Mudd), Richard Tatro (Norman), Mike Howden (St. Rowe), Michael Zaslow (Ensign Jordan), Kay Elliot (The "Stella" series), Rhae and Alyce Andrece (The "Alice" series), Tom and Ted LeGarde (The "Herman" series)

The Enterprise is forced to an uncharted planet by an android minion of Harry Mudd. Harry, it seems, has been elevated to the level of Emperor by the population of androids existing on a world he accidentally crashed on. Desperate for human company, he has brought the starship there. Unfortunately, the androids have another idea in mind. They are determined to stop mankind from destroying itself and, to do so, wish to spread their kind throughout the race as sort of intergalactic watchdogs. Captain James T. Kirk—licensed machine killer—does his stuff again.

••••

Marc Daniels noted, "Probably the biggest problem had completely to do with all the twins we had to present. It required a lot of trick photography, and it was necessary for us to be absolutely precise or else the story wouldn't have worked."

"Roger C. Carmel was wonderful as Harry," exclaims writer Stephen Kandel. "He inhabited the character and expanded it. He developed the character physically as an actor."

Gene Coon had given "I, Mudd" to David Gerrold, who performed an uncredited rewrite on the teleplay. "Gene Coon," Gerrold says, "could recognize a doable story and had a good sense of how to translate it to television. He asked me to do a rewrite of 'I, Mudd.' He said, 'We want to get to the planet faster at the end of act one, and Kandel gets us there at the end of act two.' I read the first draft Stephen Kandel script, and it was good. I thought it was shootable. But I understood it when Gene Coon said, 'Structurally we want to do this instead.' I understood exactly what he

Intergalactic con-man Harry Mudd was portrayed by Roger C. Carmel in the episodes "Mudds Women" and "I, Mudd."

wanted. First of all, he was testing me to see if I could rewrite, I'm sure of that, but secondly, much more important, he was teaching me something about story structure. When you're going to a planet with an interesting problem, you want to get there quickly. He said, 'How can you cut two acts down to one, and how can you fill the extra act?' He gave me some suggestions and instructions and let me go home. I bought it back over the weekend and he said, 'That's it, you've got it.' I put in the idea that there are 500 girl robots, and he said, 'That's a funny idea, let's go with it.' My feeling is that Coon's strengths were that he was receptive, he listened, he understood what would make a good television story, he had a great sense of structure and great sense of dialogue. I think he was just an all around good producer."

"I thought Harry Mudd was a good character," the late Roger C. Carmel told *The Official Star Trek Fan Club Magazine*, "but when the show developed such an emotional attachment with a large audience then I certainly thought that the character I played would also persist. I think it was very well written. When I did the shows, I never thought it would evolve into this. I don't think any of us thought of it in terms of the immortality it seems to have achieved."

••••

Episode #37:
"Metamorphosis"
Original Airdate: 11/10/67
Written by Gene L. Coon
Directed by Ralph Senensky
Guest Starring: Glenn Corbett (Zephram Cochrane), Elinor Donahue (Nancy Hedford)

Kirk, Spock and McCoy are transporting Federation Commissioner Nancy Hedford to the Enterprise via the Galileo, when they are captured by an energy cloud that brings them to Gamma Canaris N. There, they meet Zefram Cochrane, a famous scientist who disappeared over a century earlier.

Cochrane, it's revealed, told the energy cloud—an intelligent creature he refers to as "The Companion"—that he was lonely; that he needed companionship. Instead of freeing him, the Companion brought the Galileo there.

Ultimately, this turns into a cosmic love story between Cochrane, the Companion and Nancy Hedford and, as such, becomes one of Star Trek's most touching episodes.

••••

"We had the problem to cope with of the Companion," relates director Ralph Senensky. "We didn't know what it was going to look like, and they didn't know what it was going to look like. What they wanted me to do was shoot it in such a way so that they wouldn't have to do any travelling mattes. In other words, in the scene where you see the Companion and Cochrane in a long shot and then his point of view of Kirk and Spock watching, and then when the Companion engulfs him...if I had just shot a wide shot with Cochrane to the right of the frame and blank space at the left of the frame for the Companion, and just stayed with that shot so that they would have had to move whatever the optical was across the screen, that becomes very expensive. I worked it out where I would move the camera. They would just be able to do the optical in the middle of the shot and the camera would carry it where they wanted it to go."

"This was a very delicate and touching love story," enthuses Dorothy Fontana. "The idea that a man could accept a relationship with this alien, and

the young woman, to save her life, accepted the alien into her body. It was really a lovely story and a very touching one. I think Gene Coon did it with great deftness and delicacy."

Episode #38:
"Journey to Babel"
Original Airdate: 11/17/67
Written by D.C. Fontana
Directed by Joseph Pevney
Guest Starring: Jane Wyatt (Amanda), Mark Lenard (Sarek), William O'Connell (Thelev), Reggie Nalder (Sharas), John Wheeler (Gav), James X. Mitchell (Josephs)

The Enterprise serves as a transport for various alien races who are enroute to the planet Babel and the signing of an important peace treaty. Murder and intrigue ensue, as well as a glimpse into the relationship between Spock and his parents, Sarek and Amanda.

••••

"'Journey to Babel' came about because of the mention a couple of times of Spock's parents," explains Dorothy Fontana. "I said to Gene, 'We've talked about them, let's show them.' He told me to go and do it and I came up with 'Journey to Babel.'

"John D.F. Black had mentioned Spock's mother without being specific in 'The Naked Time,' and I mentioned the mother and the father, without giving them names, in 'This Side of Paradise.' I sat down then and created two characters, especially the relationship with Sarek and the rift between he and Spock, and Amanda positioned in the middle. She was a thoroughly human woman with an all Vulcan husband and a half-cast son, which is bound to create a lot of character problems. It was wonderful casting."

Interestingly, more money could be spent on the show's makeup effects due to the fact that it took place entirely on board the Enterprise.

"You always did trade-offs in that sense," she says. "If you went on location, you had to give away your costume and makeup. If you stayed on the ship you could do more. I did ship shows so we would have more money to go on location and make more elaborate planet sets."

Joseph Pevney elaborates, "That

was a good show in certain areas. I thought the greatest contributor to it was the makeup artist. He did a fabulous job of bringing alien humanoids on board. Remember Star Wars? The entire sequence in the bar looks like it came from this episode."

Episode #39:
"Friday's Child"
Original Airdate: 12/1/67
Written by D.C. Fontana
Directed by Joseph Pevney
Guest Starring: Tige Andrews (Kras), Michael Dante (Maab), Julie Newmar (Eleen), Cal Bolder (Keel), Kirk Raymone (Duur), Ben Gage (Teer Akaar), Robert Bralver (Grant)

Both the Federation and the Klingons vie for an alliance with the people of Capella IV, which is no easy task for Kirk and the Enterprise as the Klingon commander, Kras, backstabs them and attempts to manipulate the Capellans at every turn.

Added into the mix is the pregnant Eleen, wife of a former ruler who becomes a pawn in the negotiations and nearly costs Kirk and McCoy their lives when the latter delivers her child.

••••

"Basically an adventure," Dorothy Fontana relates, "but I felt the story that a woman was a pawn, and that she and her baby were the most important pawns in the game, was an interesting story. What happened was that they learned that they were no longer pawns.

Julie Newmar, decked out here as Catwoman, portrayed Eleen in "Friday's Child."

••••

She felt that she was no longer a pawn, that she had the power to make decisions for herself. In a way it was sort of a women's lib story, but I didn't mean it that way. I just meant it as a character development kind of thing in the sense of a person finding themself."

"This was the first time that I had been given the opportunity to wear a costume in a film role," recalls Tige Andrews, who portrayed Kras, "and I was very much into the role. I particularly remember feeling more like 'someone else' during the filmmaking. It was a fun part."

Episode #40:
"The Deadly Years"
Original Airdate: 12/8/67
Written by David P. Harmon
Directed by Joseph Pevney
Guest Starring: Charles Drake (Commodore Stocker), Sarah Marshall (Janet Wallace), Beverly Washburn (Arlene Galway), Felix Locker (Johnson), Carolyn Nelson (Atkins), Laura Wood (Mrs. Johnson)

While on the surface of Gamma Hydra IV, Kirk, Spock, McCoy and Scotty are infected with a disease that causes premature aging. Chekov, who is also there but separated from the others for a short time, is not affected.

As the landing party beams back aboard the Enterprise, the aging becomes more pronounced, threatening their lives. McCoy labors to find a cure, using Chekov as his guinea pig. In the meantime, Kirk's memory is starting to slip, and Commodore Stocker, who was being transported by the vessel, eventually realizes that he's got to take command. He orders the Enterprise to proceed to Starbase 10, which lies in the midst of the Neutral Zone. This is all the provocation that the Romulans need to launch an attack.

••••

Details writer David P. Harmon, "I was inspired to write the script by examining the American syndrome versus the Oriental reverence of old age. The concept of youth and beauty is such a shallow one, simply because it doesn't last very long. That's the inch of truth I was looking for. How important is it in the overall scheme of things in a person's life, if at all? But *we*

make it important."

For Joseph Pevney, "The Deadly Years" was a show filled with behind the scenes conflict. "I had a run in with DeForest Kelley during the making of this episode when he thought he was fantastic. We had quite a thing on the stage after the makeup was applied when he said, 'Bill can't do that, that should be me.' I tried to explain to him the situation. He was playing this old man and doing it quite well, incidentally, and Bill, I think, was maybe copying some of the things DeForest did to give him an aged look, because Bill was not very good as the old man. DeForest was beautiful in the role. The big problem there, of course, was time and two or three hours later I would get my first take. It was just ridiculous. It was just a gimmick on the show. Who in the hell cared if the wig wasn't precisely wrinkled in the right place? Nobody's going to know. Alright, if you're in motion pictures, spend a day. But you can't do that in television. But the actors no longer cared about schedules. I never shot a show off schedule, but I *heard* about them going over schedule and, after a while, the show became too costly."

Episode #41:
"Obsession"
Original Airdate: 12/15/67
Written by Art Wallace
Directed by Ralph Senensky
Guest Starring: Stephen Brooks (Garrovick), Jerry Ayres (Rizzo)

Kirk becomes obsessed when he has the opportunity to battle a gaseous creature that feeds on human blood cells, and one which he faced as a lieutenant. Half the crew of the USS Farragut perished during that earlier battle, and Kirk has blamed himself ever since because he had hesitated in firing his phaser at the creature.

••••

"Gene Roddenberry and I were having dinner one night," writer Art Wallace explains, "and then it came to me that it wouldn't be a bad idea to do a version of *Moby Dick*, which became 'Obsession.' I just substituted the cloud for the great white whale."

Jack the Ripper reincarnated himself in the persona of actor John Fiedler in Robert Bloch's "Wolf in the Fold."

Episode #42:
"Wolf in the Fold"
Original Airdate: 12/22/67
Written by Robert Bloch
Directed by Joseph Pevney
Guest Starring: John Fiedler (Hengist), Charles Macauley (Janis), Peter Seurat (Sybo), Joseph Bernard (Tark), Charles Dierkop (Morla), Judy McConnell (Tankris), Virginia Ladridge (Karen Tracy), Judy Sherven (Nurse), Tania Lemani (Kara)

Kirk, McCoy and Scotty are visiting Argelius Two for shore leave, following an accident in which Scotty injured his head. No sooner have they arrived then a serial murderer strikes, and all evidence points to the chief engineer.

A mystery follows, in which the crew of the Enterprise discovers that an alien force of pure evil that had appeared on Earth in the form of Jack the Ripper, has unleashed itself on Argelius.

••••

Doing a variation of Jack the Ripper was suggested to Robert Bloch by the *Star Trek* production team. "They wanted me to do a Jack the Ripper story in the future," he once explained. "So, I said, 'All right, let's put him into a computer or something instead of having him skulking around with a knife on shipboard.' There were a number of changes made to that script because I knew very little about computers. I still do."

••••

Episode #43:
"The Trouble With Tribbles"
Original Airdate: 12/29/67
Written by David Gerrold
Directed by Joseph Pevney
Guest Starring: William Schallert (Nilz Barris), William Campbell (Koloth), Stanley Adams (Cyrano Jones), Whit Bissell (Lurry), Michael Pataki (Korax), Charlie Brill (Arne Darvin), Ed Reiners (Fitzpatrick), Guy Raymond (Trader), Paul Bradley (Freeman),
David Ross (Guard)

An emergency distress signal brings the Enterprise to space station K-7. There, the Undersecretary of Agricultural Affairs, Nilz Barris, is panicking because the Klingons are in the quadrant and he wants the grain (quadrotriticale) in the station's storage compartments protected, due to the fact that it is the only grain that will take root on Sherman's Planet.

Kirk is *not* amused, believing that Barris misused the emergency signal and he can barely be bothered to post two guards near the storage compartments. Things get out of hand, however, when Uhura is given a furry tribble by space trader Cyrano Jones, and the creature multiplies like crazy. In a short matter of time, they are all over the station and the Enterprise. Add into the mix a Klingon conspiracy and you've got a real roller coaster ride of an episode.

••••

"The Trouble With Tribbles" was significant in *Star Trek*'s history because it proved that the show could do comedy with the characters remaining true to themselves. This episode more than any other probably influenced the decision to go with the lighter tone of the feature film *Star Trek IV: The Voyage Home*; and it was the show that the writers and producers kept returning to in terms of best using the characters in a humorous situation.

And how does it feel for David Gerrold to have written one of *Star Trek*'s most popular episodes?

"I have to be real honest here," he says. "It feels great. I remember when I wrote 'The Trouble With Tribbles,' I looked at it as an honor and a responsibility, and I set out to write the very best *Star Trek* episode ever made."

"A delightful show from beginning to end," enthuses Joseph Pevney. "I had a lot of fun with it, went out and shopped for the tribbles, and made some contributions to that show. It was the first effort of a writer named David Gerrold and I thought he made a hell of a contribution to the show. *My* biggest contribution was getting the show produced, because there was a feeling amongst the people involved that we shouldn't do it. It was a comedy and we had no business doing outright comedy. I certainly wanted to treat it as such, because that's the way it was intended. It was a lovely, warm show and I put Stanley Adams in it. 'Tribbles' was a highly successful episode in terms of audience appeal, and the network was happy with it. It turned out fine, with Bill doing bits he loved to do. The premise was humorous as hell."

Episode #44:
"The Gamesters of Triskelion"
Original Airdate: 1/5/68
Written by Margaret Armen
Directed by Gene Nelson
Guest Starring: John Ruskin (Galt), Angelique Pettyjohn (Shana), Steve Sandor (Lars), James Ross (Tamoon), Victoria George (Jana),
Mickey Horton (Kloog)

Kirk, Chekov and Uhura are spacenapped by the beings of Triskelion, and forced to partake in gladiator games they have designed to amuse themselves. Kirk turns the tables by making a wager which will either provide many more participants in the "sport," or the aliens will have to free those already in slavery. One guess as to who wins the bet.

••••

"The idea for 'Gamesters' was a science fiction premise I'd had in mind for a long time, before there was ever a *Star Trek*," explains writer Margaret Armen. "I thought that one of these days I might do it as a science fiction short story or a story about a planet where people are used as gaming animals. So when *Star Trek* came on the air, I thought, 'Oh, wouldn't I love to do this story as a television show.' It was there, jotted down among a couple of other ideas I had to present to Gene if and when I got in to see him. *Star Trek* seemed the perfect vehicle for the nucleus of this story, and when I went in to Gene with it, it was

very roughly developed since I had never written for the show before. But Gene immediately saw the potential in it, and talked it through with me until it had been tailored to the *Star Trek* format.

"I was happy with the results," she continues. "I wasn't completely happy with some of the fight action toward the end, but it was very effective. I don't know if the fight action that I had suggested would have been more effective or not. I felt it would have been more unique, but you never know because the writer is never on the set or anything. There may have been some reason why they had to use the old net that was used during Roman games."

Episode #45:
"A Piece of the Action"
Original Airdate: 1/12/68
Written by David P. Harmon
Directed by James Komack
Guest Starring: Anthony Caruso (Oxmyx), Vic Tayback (Krako), Lee Delano (Kalo), John Harmon (Tepo), Steve Arnold (Zabo), Sheldon Collins (Boy), Dyanne Thorne,
Sharyn Hillyer (Girls)

A century after the crew of the USS Horizon visited Iotia, the Enterprise arrives to examine the level of "contamination." What they find is a society based entirely on a book detailing the mob wars of Chicago in the 1920s. After initially approaching the inhabitants—mob bosses and all—on an intellectual level, Kirk realizes that he's got to do as the Romans do and it's only a short matter of time before he and Spock come on like mobsters, slang and all.

••••

"A Piece of the Action" was obviously influenced by "The Trouble With Tribbles," and while the results are quite humorous, this episode is a little more uneven.

Writer David P. Harmon believes that the very best episodes of *Star Trek*, and indeed all drama, featured what he calls "an inch of truth."

"As long as you had that, you could easily put it into a science-fiction setting," he explains. "Gene Roddenberry and Gene Coon didn't want a '20s or '30s type pulp. They wanted an inch of truth and from there you could expand.

••••

They knew exactly what they were looking for, and although it was hard work, you didn't mind rewriting until it was exactly right.

"I had read an article in *The New Yorker*," Harmon says of the episode's origins, "not about *Star Trek*, but about an idea. I pitched it as a possible show. Again, the story had what they were looking for, which was that honesty. I felt that our western civilization is based on a Judeo-Christian ethic, so what I did in 'A Piece of the Action' was say that suppose a ship crashed, and the people on the planet salvaged a book called *The Life of Al Capone*, which they treated as their version of *The Bible*, and from which they built their own society."

Although uncredited, Gene Coon had done a rewrite on this particular teleplay. Points out Dorothy Fontana, "I think one of the main things Gene added was Kirk and Spock really getting into the gangster stuff, and the whole business with Kirk trying to drive the car. That was certainly Gene Coon, which added so much to their characters. Again, you get another look at the relationship between these two men, and also the fact that they had a sense of humor."

James Komack, a journeyman director in television whose credits include episodes of *77 Sunset Strip, Dr. Kildare, Hennesey, My Favorite Martian* and *The Dick Van Dyke Show*, was approached to helm an episode of *Star Trek* by Gene Roddenberry, because the show's creator wanted to take on a humorous episode.

"I was a natural contender," says Komack, "because I had done long forms and was a comedy director. He called me in, I loved the show, read the script, made some adjustments and said, 'I would love to do this,' and I found myself on the starship Enterprise.

"Usually when you're a director working on episodic television, the actors mostly know their part, who they are and what they do and all you're doing is trying to find new ways for them to move around. The acting was already locked in because they'd done it. This was fun because it was [one of the first times] they did a comedy and Bill Shatner loves to do comedy. Leonard Nimoy I knew

from *Combat*, and I populated it with funny comedy gangsters and then set about doing it."

One interesting dramatic dilemma was sustaining the reality of the future while combining it with the past.

"Absolutely," Komack concurs. "That was tough, remembering that these guys were from another time and we're trying to make a picture about the '20s. You constantly have to say that it's got to be the '20s from everyone else's point of view, but it's got to be future-time for Leonard Nimoy and Bill Shatner, and that gets a little bizarre. The joke going on around them was that they had never seen a machine gun before, they never saw pool tables or cars. We'd have to work out the jokes right then and there. You'd say, 'Wait a minute, you've never seen that before. I've got to shoot something that shows you've never seen this before.' Spock and Kirk came down with this great intellect and great intelligence that they possess, and they were dealing with monkeys. These guys had an I.Q. of about room temperature, and it was funny to watch Kirk and Spock stare at them, because they were just ludicrous. They had a book, they were mobs, they were taking over cities. Their brains just weren't working that well. That was great fun."

But did he have to handle attitudes made up of, "Well, Kirk wouldn't do this and Spock wouldn't do that?"

"That's where they formulate their own characters," he replies. "When you come on a show they say, 'I've been doing this show for three years. I would never say that.' You can't argue with the guy. But in this episode I could say, 'Hold it. You're down in the 20th Century, pal. You're dealing with morons. You've never done this before, so therefore you could say this.' And they would buy it that way. But not in the spaceship. In the Enterprise they had it down."

Episode #46:
"The Immunity Syndrome"
Original Airdate: 1/19/68
Written by Robert Sabaroff
Directed by Joseph Pevney
Guest Starring: None

A giant, one-celled amoeba-like creature has destroyed the Gamma 7A

star system as well as the USS Intrepid, a starship with a full complement of Vulcans. The Enterprise computers determine that the cell is about to reproduce, and a plan is devised in which the starship itself will be used as an "anti-body" that will infect it before reproduction can take place.

••••

Interestingly, there is a moment in this episode that would be repeated almost verbatim in George Lucas' *Star Wars*. When the Intrepid is destroyed, Spock jerks his head up, feeling the pain of all those lost souls. In *Star Wars*, Obi Wan Kenobi has a similar reaction when a planet is destroyed by Darth Vader's Death Star.

Episode #47:
"A Private Little War"
Original Airdate: 2/2/68
Written by Gene Roddenberry
Story by Judd Crucis
Directed by Marc Daniels
Guest Starring: Nancy Kovack (Nona), Michael Witney (Tyree), Booker Marshak (Mbenga), Arthur Bernard (Apella), Joe Romeo (Krell)

Put simply, this analogy of the Vietnam War deals with a balance of power established on a frontier planet between the Klingons, first, and then the Federation. As the Klingons have interfered with the natural progression of the inhabitants, one part of the race is more advanced than the other. Kirk sees no choice but to bring the other part up to speed so that there will be a level of equality.

"A balance of power," Kirk says. "The oldest, dirtiest trick in the book but the only one that preserves both sides."

••••

"I like the science fiction aspects of *Star Trek*," said Marc Daniels, "but I also like the fact that in the first two seasons there was some genuine dramatic appeal and social feeling about them, and they weren't gimmicky in terms of just being space operas. 'A Private Little War' is an example. I remember that episode also provided a problem in terms of wardrobe. The people on this planet were supposed to be dressed in prehistoric clothing, and we

••••

discovered that costuming them would cost a fortune. Bill Theiss, who was always adept at handling such crises, bought a bunch of cheap sheepskin jackets, cut off the sleeves and turned them inside out. We were always trying to work around things like that because of budgetary limitations."

Writer Don Ingalls, who used the pen name Judd Crucis, wrote the first draft of the teleplay. As he explained to *Starlog*, "Mine was more of an adventure in a vacuum; Gene's [Roddenberry] was more a political statement. His story was more tilted to parallel Vietnam than did."

Offers Walter Koenig, "That was the one episode that I thought digressed from a rather liberal, political posture. I had a very strong feeling about it. I thought that in maintaining this balance of power we were justifying the building of armaments. It was just like the Cold War to a point."

Episode #48:
"Return to Tomorrow"
Original 2/9/68
Written by John Kingsbridge
Directed by Ralph Senensky
Guest Starring: Diana Muldaur (Ann Mulhall)

Three aliens who have been without bodies for centuries—having lived in a purely mental state—ask Kirk, Spock and McCoy to "loan" them their bodies so that the trio can construct androids that will house their minds. After some reluctance they agree to do so, although the being that takes over Spock decides that he likes being flesh and blood, and he will stop at nothing to keep his host, even at the expense of his two companions or the crew of the Enterprise.

• • • •

Guest star Diana Muldaur, as most *Star Trek* fans know, would go on to portray Dr. Kate Pulaski in the second season of *Star Trek: The Next Generation.*

"It's funny, but when we get into 'Obsession,' 'Bread and Circuses' and 'Return to Tomorrow,'" says Ralph Senensky, "which were all shot on that crazy, fast schedule, it's like I shot them on fast forward and my primary memory of them is just trying to get them done; done by midnight on the sixth day. The

pressure was there to try and give the actor the chance to give a performance, which wasn't always easy."

Episode #49:
"Patterns of Force"
Original Airdate: 2/16/88
Written by John Meredyth Lucas
Directed by Vincent McEveety
Guest Starring: David Brian (John Gill), Skip Homier (Melakon), Richard Evans (Isak), Valora Norand (Daras), William Wintersole (Abrom), Patrick Horgan (Eneg), Bart LaRue (Newscaster), Ralph Mauer (SS Lieutenant)

Parallel Earth time again, as the Enterprise goes to Ekos, a planet controlled by a Nazi movement. The Nazis are led by Federation historian John Gill, who believed that the efficiency of Hitler's regime, if handled with a conscience, would theoretically work. Unfortunately, history merely repeats itself and it is into this nightmare that Kirk and Spock find themselves thrust.

• • • •

"The totalitarian, particularly the Nazi, society had always fascinated me," explains John Meredyth Lucas. "How could this come about? I know the history, but how in the minds of people could this come about? I started off with the premise that I would try to explain it. The explanation is that it was a system that worked because it was told to work. I have a story that I'm playing with; a story—a true story—that takes place in China and deals with the eradication of disease in an area, and American doctors visiting can't find any cases of disease. It's wonderful, but when you have the resources of a nation totally and completely behind you, and you're given to do such and such which you cannot do in a democratic society, you can accomplish an end like that. I was trying to explain in my head, which is not to say that I was looking for a true explanation, how this could happen, and the premise was that it was an efficient society for accomplishing specific ends. But I wanted to explore how it could have come about and how an entire country could get swept up in it. It's still difficult to comprehend. Thankfully there was very little problems in terms of covering such dramatic material. Gene tended to do no censorship on that basis. He would come in and, if

anything, would encourage wilder statements. He was a very adventurous guy, so there was no opposition in terms of 'My God, what are you writing about?'"

"That was the most forgettable one I've done," counters director Vincent McEveety. "It's so forgettable that I can't remember anything, except where I shot it. As you know, you get 'em in every series and you can't say, 'Look, I'm sorry, but I don't want to do this one.' They say, 'Tough, buddy. It's yours.' The story seemed awfully forced and hokey to me. I can't put it any other way."

Episode #50:
"By Any Other Name"
Original Airdate: 2/23/68
Written by D.C. Fontana and Jerome Bixby
Story by Jerome Bixby
Directed by Marc Daniels
Guest Starring: Warren Stevens (Rojan), Barbara Bouchet (Kelinda), Stewart Moss (Hanar), Robert Fortier (Tomar), Carol Byrd (Lt. Shea), Leslie Dalton (Drea), Julie Cobb (Thompson)

Members of the Kelvan race take human form and assume control of the Enterprise by turning the majority of the crew into tetrahedron blocks. The goal is to report to their people that Federation territory is ripe for colonization. Kirk, Spock, McCoy and Scotty come up with a plan to use the Kelvans' newly acquired human emotions against them.

• • • •

"I made the mistake of not paying attention to the format, the poop sheet saying 'this is what we want, this is what we don't want, avoid these, these are the staples,'" admits Jerome Bixby. "'New writers tend to be, particularly when writing stories about the cosmos at large, overwhelmed by the immensity of it all, and don't fall into this trap.' Well, I fell into it head over heels. I was doing a story about the Enterprise being hijacked to the Andromeda Nebula. At best—at hyper-c velocities—a 300 year voyage, so Kirk and the others are facing the end of their existence as they had known it. They are totally the prisoners of these great, powerful entities. Creatures from Andromeda want to take over our galaxy, because radiation levels there are making existence impossible for them. And I went off into a, I guess,

• • • •

60 page essay on how lonely it is to be in that boat. I was told that it was very good, but it wouldn't make a *Star Trek*. And so I didn't know how far I was off the beam until I began to see revised pages. I didn't work with Dorothy; she rewrote my script. Primarily, she interjected the humor and the conflict into the episode."

Dorothy Fontana says, "I don't even recall what my contribution to it was, but it was enough to get me a split credit. I seem to recall that it was an effort to involve the characters—the *Star Trek* characters—more. The initial concept was good, but there wasn't enough involvement of our people. The one thing I definitely put in was Scotty's drinking contest. I love that. It's one of my favorite scenes that I've written."

Episode #51:
"The Omega Glory"
Original Airdate: 3/1/68
Written by Gene Roddenberry
Directed by Vincent McEveety
Guest Starring: Morgan Woodward (Captain Tracey), Roy Jensen (Cloud William), Irene Kelley (Sirah), David L. Ross (Galloway), Eddie Paskey (Leslie), Ed McReady (Carter), Lloyd Kino (Wu), Morgan Farley (Scholar)

Yet another renegade Federation captain, this time Ronald Tracey, interferes with a frontier society and alters its progression. When Enterprise arrives, Kirk, Spock and McCoy discover that Tracey has sided with the Kohms, utilizing advanced technology against the Yangs. Our heroes must set things right, with Kirk using a somewhat parallel version of the U.S. Constitution to convince both sides that they must be united as one.

••••

"I know it was a way out show," laughs Vincent McEveety, "but I thought Bill brought it off tremendously well. In lesser hands, and I'm talking about acting, it could have been terrible. He made it extremely powerful. I had empathy for the character and, as an audience, realized the importance of that particular document to me as an American citizen; seeing what they were faced with in a rather primitive state. I thought it was extremely powerful in making a statement."

William Marshall, Dr. Daystrom in "The Ultimate Computer," seen here as Blacula in the film of the same name.

Morgan Woodward (Captain Tracey) told *The Official Star Trek Fan Club Magazine,* "'Omega Glory' was simply a good man gone bad, perhaps because of some ego-induced insanity. Captain Tracey didn't become a starship captain by being a jerk or a bad guy. It was just a good man gone bad. That's the way I tried to play him."

Episode #52:
"The Ultimate Computer"
Original Airdate: 3/8/68
Written by D.C. Fontana
Story by Lawrence N. Wolfe
Directed by John Meredyth Lucas
Guest Starring: William Marshall (Daystrom), Barney Russo (Wesley), Sean Morgan (Harper)

Dr. Richard Daystrom is given permission by the Federation to hook his state-of-the-art computer, the M-5, to the Enterprise to prove that a starship can be run more efficiently by a machine than by humans.

For a time, things go perfectly and Kirk begins to feel useless, but eventually the M-5, whose memory patterns are based on Daystrom's, acts without logic, destroying another starship for no reason. Kirk, rising to the occasion, talks a machine to death.....again.

••••

Dorothy Fontana details, "The other writer involved was Lawrence Wolfe. Unfortunately this was a script that didn't want to work, or the writer didn't want to make the changes that we recommended and they were rather strong changes. As I recall, and I may not be right on this, it was because the *Star Trek* characters were not deeply involved in this story about the M-5 and Dr. Daystrom. *Star Trek* isn't about technology. *Star Trek* is about the characters. And how this machine acts on them, or how they act on it, is the story. The writer just did not want to make the changes. He kept bringing back the same script, until finally there was a rewrite that Gene assigned to me, and I did the best I could with it."

Episode #53:
"Bread and Circuses"
Original Airdate: 3/15/68
Written by Gene Roddenberry and Gene L. Coon
Story by John Kneubuhl
Directed by Ralph Senensky
Guest Starring: William Smithers (Merik), Logan Ramsey (Claudius Marcus), Ian Wolfe (Septimus), Rhodes Reason (Flavius Maximus), Lois Jewell (Drusilla), Bart LaRue (Announcer), Jack Perkins (Master of Game)

••••

On planet 892 IV, the Enterprise discovers a society that resembles Earth in the 20th Century, though there is an ancient Rome slant to it in that gladiator battles are televised as a sport for the public. Captain Merik, Kirk and his boys learn, had some time earlier gotten sucked into the politics surrounding "the game," eventually having his crew beamed down one by one so that they, too, could participate.

Mixed in with this is the struggle of what everyone assumes are "sun" worshippers, but who turn out to be servants of the "son" of God, Jesus Christ.

••••

"Certainly there was a nice philosophy going on there with the worshipping of the son," says Dorothy Fontana, "and then the indication that it was the son of God; that Jesus or the concept had appeared on other planets. I thought that was a nice touch. There have been other stories written with the same theme as the main point, but just adding it at the end really seems quite nice."

Director Ralph Senensky notes, "Gene Roddenberry is a very creative man. When we did 'Bread and Circuses,' I remember having a meeting with Gene about it and he was going to do some writing. I went there the next morning at 6:00 to get the new material, because there were things about that script which weren't working. Both Gene Roddenberry and Gene Coon were writing on that show as we were shooting. I don't remember what the problem was, except that we were doing the Roman arena in modern times with television. I do remember that my concern was that the whole thing about the 'sun,' which they talked about from early on, might not be a mystery when we got to the end. We didn't want to tip that we were doing a Christ story from the word go. That

took some doing because it wasn't really in the script, but they did it. They were sealing up the loose ends, because originally when they were talking about the sun you knew right away that they were talking about the son of God."

Episode #54:
"Assignment Earth"
Original Airdate: 3/29/68
Written by Art Wallace
Story by Gene Roddenberry and
Art Wallace
Directed by Marc Daniels
Guest Starring: Robert Lansing (Gary Seven), Terri Garr (Roberta Lincoln), Jim Keefer (Cromwell), Morgan Jones (Nesvig), Lincoln Demyan (Rawlings)

In this pilot for a separate series, the Enterprise is doing some Earth research in the 20th Century, when they encounter Gary Seven, a man who had been captured by alien beings and trained to save mankind from destroying itself.

Seven teams up with secretary Roberta Lincoln and tries to carry out his assignment. Kirk's dilemma is that he isn't sure of Seven's true intentions: will he help mankind or destroy it?

••••

"'Assignment Earth' is interesting in a sense," points out writer Art Wallace, "because I had gone to Paramount and pitched a series idea to them. They had said that Gene Roddenberry had come up with a very similar idea. So I saw Gene and we decided to pool the idea, which was about a man from tomorrow who takes care of the present on Earth. That was intended to be the pilot, although it was never made into a series. It was a very good pilot and it's a shame, because I think if they had done it as a series with just Gary Seven, it would have been a very successful show. I believe Gene and I split the credit on that one."

"Assignment Earth" was a pilot for a proposed series which would have starred Robert Lansing.

Guest star Robert Lansing told *Starlog* magazine, "What Gene had done was go to futurists and scientists and ask them what advanced societies out in space might do towards more primitive societies like ours. One of the futurists said that they would probably kidnap children from various planets, take them to their superior civilization, raise them, teach and enlighten them and then put them back as adults to lead their worlds in more peaceful ways. That was the idea behind Gary Seven."

"It was interesting trying to balance the episode between the regular crew and Robert Lansing," said Marc Daniels. "It was also difficult because we came back to the present and it's always a dangerous idea to take the *Star Trek* characters into the present. Suddenly you're in a very tangible situation. The show's reality becomes that much harder to sustain."

••••

CHAPTER FIVE
Voyages Interruptus

"As you know, we had a good fight," Gene Roddenberry told a gathered Berkeley audience in 1968 regarding the letter writing campaign to save *Star Trek*. "NBC was certain I was behind every fan, paying them off. And there was a group from MIT picketing the building and a group in New York and...bless MIT, bless Cal Tech, bless them all. They [the network] had a coterie of junior executives down there buttonholing all of the people saying, 'Listen, did Gene Roddenberry send you?' And they finally call me up. They say, 'Listen, we know you're behind it.' And I said, 'That's very flattering, because if I could start demonstrations around the country from this desk, I'd get the hell out of science fiction and into politics.' From what I've seen of politics lately, they could use a few good science fiction fans.

"At any rate," he continued, "you all know we won the fight and at that time I told them that if they would put us on the air as they were promising—on a weeknight at a decent timeslot, 7:30 or 8:00, I would commit myself to produce *Star Trek* for the third year. Personally produce the show as I had done at the beginning. This was my effort to use what muscle I had. In fighting a network, you must use what muscle you have. They are monolithic, multibillion dollar corporations whose interests are not necessarily in the quality of the drama. Basically, the hard facts of life in television and the one you must understand is that a show is bought or sold on how much toothpaste or underarm deodorant will that show sell. Basically, that is why a show is bought and why and how it is kept on the air.

"But at any rate, about ten days to two weeks later I received a phone call at breakfast and the network executive said, 'Hello, Gene Baby...' Well, I knew I was in trouble right then. Said, 'We have had a group of statistical experts researching your audience, researching youth and youth-oriented people, and we don't want you on a weeknight at an early time. We have picked the *best* youth spot that there is. All of our research confirms this and it's great for the kids and that time is 10:00 on Friday nights.' I said, 'No doubt this is why you had the great kiddie show, *The Bell Telephone Hour* on there last year.'

"Well, I want you to understand some of the politicking, some of the pressures they dropped on me. The only gun I then had was to stand by my original commitment, that I would not personally produce the show unless they returned us to the weeknight time they promised. As a matter of fact, I threatened for a time to walk with the whole show because this was the only possible muscle to say—I don't own any General Motors or anything like that, so I had to threaten them with the one thing I do on the show, which is what I might be able to bring to the show on a line producership level. I wasn't particularly anxious to put in a third year of 14 hours a day, six days a week, but *Star Trek* was my baby and I was willing to risk it if I could have a reasonable shot at a reasonable time. And we talked it over and held fast. We almost swayed them and ultimately they said, 'No, we will not do it.' And then I had no option, I could not then say, 'Well, I'll produce it anyway,' because from then on with the network any threat or promise or anything I made, once you back down you become the coward and your muscle from then on in any subsequent projects will never mean anything.

"So I had no option but to then drop back and become executive producer of the show, and I did find a producer, Fred Freiberger, who has produced *Slattery's People* and *Ben Casey*, and has impeccable credits and an honest love of science fiction since boyhood. He is backed up, of course, by our regular staff of Bob Justman and the directors, the cameramen, Bill Theiss, costumer; Matt Jeffries, art; so backed up by the regular staff they are now producing *Star Trek* while my function in it is judiciary, is policy administration. I limit myself to reading the scripts, commenting on them and the runs. I forsee a good season if we have a lucky break on the weekend, the shows that come before us, and with your help we ought to be able to maintain our audience and go for a successful year and then to others.

"But I felt I owed it to the fans who did so much for the show to give them the inside story of what happened from the time we won the campaign till I received the 'Gene Baby' call."

Despite his attempts to provide a proper explanation for why he stepped away from the series, there is a widely-held feeling that his doing so was a veritable slap in the face to the people who labored to keep *Star Trek* on the air. In a sense, it was as though their efforts meant nothing.

Actor George Takei has noted, "Gene was aware that even if he had stayed with *Star Trek*, NBC intended to cancel the show after its third year. From another vantage point, maybe it should have been a matter of personal integrity on Roddenberry's part. *Star Trek* was Gene's creation and the third season would be identified with him whether he liked it or not. If the quality of the show was in some way to erode, it couldn't help but reflect on Roddenberry. Inevitably, it would be Gene's reputation that was at stake. Now, Gene Roddenberry's a human being, so I can certainly understand his position. At the same time, giving myself distance and perspective, I can't help but wish that Gene had looked at the entire picture and realized how *Star Trek*'s third season might finally affect his professionalism and artistic integrity."

Over the years, Roddenberry added to the comments he had made at Berkeley, stating, "I think there was a little rationalization in [my decision]. I think also what was affecting me at that time was enormous fatigue; I think maybe I was looking for an excuse to get out from under the fight that I had not just been having for two years, but really for four....I think the fatigue just caught up with me....I think I would come back and produce it the third year myself if I had it to do over. I'm not taking a back-handed slap at the people who did produce it, line produced it. Obviously when you bring a producer in and you're going to let him produce it, you've got to let him do it his way. I think his way, or their way, was somewhat different than our way

••••

the first two, so it did look different....As long as the original creator stays with the show, it gives it a certain unity. When other minds become involved, it's not that they are lesser minds or not as clever writers, but you lose the unity of that one driving force."

There is a feeling amongst some people that *Star Trek* was on a downward cycle anyway due to the departure of Gene L. Coon.

"I'm going to tell you a blasphemy," says one writer, who doesn't wish to give his name. "The real brain behind *Star Trek* was not Gene Roddenberry. It was Gene Coon. Everybody who has ever worked on that show knows that. And let me give you a prime example. Gene Coon left during the second season, and everybody has always said that the reason the show went downhill in the middle of the second season is because they lowered the budget on them in order to keep it on the air. That *is* a factor. The main factor is that the guy with the writing talent was no longer there."

"I'll say it and I won't even threaten you if you attribute it to me," adds David Gerrold. "Gene L. Coon came in early in the first season and pulled it together, and he stayed there until more than halfway through the second season. If you look at the episodes in sequence, you can see that the best episodes are the ones where Gene Coon's hands were at the tiller. Gene Coon made the show work, very, very strongly. What I think you see happening is that in the first 13 with Roddenberry, there's a bumbling around trying to find out what the show is about, yet at the same time they did some great episodes.

"Where the show really lost its creativity was third season, in which it became Kirk, Spock and McCoy have an adventure and everything works alright in the end. The stories were bad science and bad fiction. It was pure television crap. It was the worst stuff of the '60s when we point to it and say, 'Television is not doing drama, it's just doing television. It's automated daydreaming. There's nothing there for the mind to fasten on to.'"

There's no denying that *Star Trek* had its share of creative problems as the third season approached. John Meredyth Lucas moved on to *The Fugitive* when word came down that *Trek* had been cancelled and before the letter writing campaign proved fruitful; director Joseph Pevney had departed the fold and Dorothy Fontana, who had been there before there actually was a *Star Trek*, was ready to move on.

"I felt that I was becoming perhaps too associated with *Star Trek*," she explains, "and wanted to prove that I was able to write other shows. In fact, when I left I did several westerns, dramatic contemporary shows and so on. I had to prove to other producers that *Star Trek* wasn't all I could do."

To make matters worse, the budget for the series was lowered yet again, as it had been at the outset of season two, while cast salaries increased.

"The third season we were reduced to what I call a radio show," reflects Robert Justman. "We couldn't go on location any longer because we couldn't afford it. We had to do shows that we could afford to do. It was quite difficult and that did affect what the concept was. Certain concepts just couldn't be handled. We didn't have the money. Forget about what the actual numbers are, but in those days, in the first season, each show cost $193,500. That was good money for those days. The second season was $187,500. The third season was $178,500. So that was an enormous drop. The studio had deficit financing situations and every time you shot a show you lost more money. In those days, they didn't think they had a chance of syndication, especially since everybody knew that third season was it. They just cut it down to the bone to cut their losses.

"It was very simple," he continues. "When you get moved in a timeslot to a night when your audience isn't home, you know that the handwriting is on the wall. Remember, they tried to cancel us at the end of the second season. By the time the third season rolled along, it was no longer Thursdays at 8:00. It wasn't Fridays at 8:00. It was Friday at 10:00. If your audience is high school kids and college-age people and young married people, they're not home Friday nights. They're out, and the old folks weren't watching. So our audience was gone."

This was the less than auspicious conditions that greeted Fred Freiberger as he assumed the reigns of *Star Trek's* producer.

Freiberger Steps In

Fred Freiberger's long list of credits include co-writing *The Beast From 20,000 Fathoms* and *The Beginning of the End*, as well as producing stints on *The Wild Wild West*, *Ben Casey*, *Space: 1999*, *Superboy* and, of course, *Star Trek*.

"I was familiar with *Star Trek* only in that I had seen the first pilot they had done," says Freiberger. "I had seen Gene Roddenberry at the beginning to talk to him about producing the show at the start, but I was going to Europe on a vacation that I had planned. I mentioned to Gene—not that it was offered to me, but I was up there as one of the candidates—that the pilot was terrific, and if the job was still available when I got back, I was interested. I thought the pilot was pure science fiction and very intriguing. By the time I came back, he had gotten Gene Coon and I was off doing other shows. Then, when third season came along, my agent brought me into Gene's office and he said he would like me to produce the show. Gene Coon had done the first season, John Meredyth Lucas did the second and I assumed he wanted to change producers every year."

Obviously *Star Trek* had changed quite a bit between "The Cage" and the third season, and one must question whether a new producer coming in felt the series to be a daunting challenge.

"It wasn't a question of daunting," replies Freiberger, "it was a question of going in on a show that was being successfully produced with a lot of people involved who were very loyal to the show. You can walk into *Family Affair* and it can be daunting for you. You get into a situation where everybody knows each other and they've been together for some time. I was more concerned with improving the ratings, because the show had about a 20 or 24 share. Today that would be a hit. In those days, even if you had a 30 share, you were very iffy. It was the loyalty of the fans that kept it on when NBC threatened to cancel it. They did keep it on, and it was impressive that

NBC succumbed to the campaign. But in all three years, the ratings remained the same no matter what went on. It kept the same fans. Our hope was to improve the ratings, and we tried different kinds of stories. But the ratings always stayed the same....always.

"The cutting of the budget hurt us badly," he adds. "Then the salaries of the actors were raised and we were hit with a lot of restrictions. We had to do at least four of the shows completely on the Enterprise. There were a lot of restrictions, but that's no excuse if the stories aren't very good or aren't executed properly. It's a question of judgement and you have to go with what you think. That's the way television works. I think, on balance, we did some pretty nice stories and some that didn't come out so good. Some shows you're happy with, some you're disappointed with and others you're ashamed of. That's the way it goes, but if you're a pro, you accept those things, you understand them and all you can do is make sure that everybody does their best."

Unfortunately, a great many of the creative people involved with the third season were disappointed with the direction the show took. Marc Daniels—who had played so integral a role in the course of the series—directed "Spock's Brain," and decided that one episode under the new regime was enough.

"Fred Freiberger and I didn't agree on what the director's role was," Daniels said. "There are many writer/producers who don't consider the director a partner. They consider him, shall we say, an employee. This is particularly true in episodic TV. They just want you to do the work, get the shots and forget the rest of it. I didn't particularly care for that kind of thinking."

Margaret Armen, who had written for both Gene Roddenberry and Fred Freiberger, explains, "I suppose they were looking for two different types of stories. Fred was looking for all action pieces. That's why he wasn't crazy about 'The Paradise Syndrome.' He didn't think that there was enough violent and terrifying action in it. He didn't realize that the suspense would come from the characters, their relationships and so forth. There was some action in it, but there was no monsters and that sort of thing.

So Fred was looking primarily for action pieces, whereas Gene was looking for that subtlety that is *Star Trek*. Action, but with people carrying the story."

Writer David Gerrold, who has had "sparring" matches with Freiberger in the press before, admits, "I understand Freddy Freiberger's problems a lot better today than I did 24 years ago. Oddly enough, I have a respect for the man that I don't think he realizes. He's able to do something that not a lot of people can do: he can bring in a show on time, under budget. He can do the job. There are people who crumble under that kind of pressure....As a producer, I'm sure his opinions are correct for what he's doing. As a writer, I think his biggest weakness is that he doesn't have a sense of humor. He doesn't allow the show he's working on to have fun."

A major blow was the departure—about two thirds through the season—of Robert Justman, who had been involved with *Star Trek* since production of "The Cage."

"I felt I was in prison and I had to get out," he exclaims. "I just didn't want to take it anymore, because I was so unhappy with what was happening with the show. We couldn't make the kind of shows that we wanted to make because we couldn't afford them, and I felt that the content of the shows was going downhill. I finally asked for my release and left. I left a lot of bruised feelings behind at Paramount. They pleaded with me not to go, and I said, 'Fine, I won't go. Just take me off the show and I won't take any other jobs and I'll come back to you on anything else you want me to do in the spring.' They didn't want that and I said, 'I'm leaving. I just don't want to stay anymore.' I went to work at MGM.

"It was my feeling that the show wasn't what it ought to be. There was also the feeling of disappointment over the fact that I was made co-producer instead of producer. I know that doesn't mean anything to people not in the industry, but in effect I had been line producing the show since the beginning, even though my title was associate producer. When the third season came around, instead of producing the show, Freddy was brought in with the title of producer and I was made co-pro-

ducer to him. The studio felt, as all studios do and I can't blame them, that they wanted a writer to be there to do the work of story and script. On the other hand, I felt that I could produce the show with someone there to do the writing.

"Of course there's a lot of ego in that. I was much, much younger and ambitious. I can't blame the studio, but in the meantime I was unhappy about that and I didn't like the way the scripts were turning out. There was no excitement, or there wasn't enough excitement. And when they had good concepts, they kind of got whittled down and weren't as magical as they ought to be."

Strangely enough, he found that the atmosphere behind the scenes remained fairly positive.

"As far as I could see, the atmosphere was still much the same," Justman reflects. "I got on fine with everyone, as always. I got on fine with Freddy Freiberger, as always. He was a nice man. I think he did what he did as best he could do it. I never had any harsh words. I don't think I ever had an argument the whole three seasons with anyone. I would disagree with Gene Roddenberry at times and fight him on certain things that I thought we ought to do or should not be doing, but in the end if Gene said it was yes, it was yes. If he said no, it was no. Whether I felt he was right or wrong, if that's what he wanted to do, that's what I would do. After all, it was his show. I had wonderful feelings working with those people. It just wasn't the same without Gene in a hands-on position that third season."

Freiberger believes that the morale on *Star Trek* was fine until the last few shows when the end was approaching. "When they cut the budget down, you know that's not a good sign. The last couple of shows the morale went down a little, but prior to that I hadn't noticed. Despite that, if you're a pro, you do the best that you can right up until the last minute. Listen, three years for a show—any show—isn't bad, especially when the ratings are so low.

"Our problem was to broaden the viewer base. To do a science fiction show but get enough additional viewers to keep the series on the air. I decided to do what I would hope was a broad canvas of shows, but I tried to make them more dramatic and to do stories that had a more conventional storyline within the science fiction frame."

While it's true that that the third season lagged seriously behind the first two in terms of production and script value, it nonetheless produced a number of effective episodes. "Spectre of the Gun" was a surrealistic western written by Gene Coon; "The Tholian Web" dealt with the disappearance of Captain Kirk and provided some wonderful moments of characterization between Bones and Spock; "The Day of the Dove" pit Enterprise crewmen and Klingons against each other in armed combat; "Plato's Stepchildren" featured the first interracial kiss on television and examined the abuse of power; "Let That Be Your Last Battlefield," while heavy-handed, demonstrated the idiocy behind preju-

dice; and "All Our Yesterdays" was a time-travel adventure that further developed the McCoy-Spock relationship, while allowing Spock to do things no one had ever seen him do before.

And thus, at the end of its third season, *Star Trek* was cancelled by NBC with no hope of a reprieve. Cliched as it may be, however, nearly twenty seven years later we realize that the end was merely the beginning.

••••

CHAPTER SIX
Season 3 Episode Guide

"Spock's Brain"

"The Enterprise Incident"

"The Paradise Syndrome"

"And the Children Shall Lead"

"Is There No Truth in Beauty"

"Spectre of the Gun"

"Day of the Dove"

"For the World is Hollow,
And I Have Touched the Sky"

"The Tholian Web"

"Plato's Stepchildren"

"Wink of an Eye"

"The Empath"

"Elaan of Troyius"

"Whom Gods Destroy"

"Let That Be Your Last Battlefield"

"The Mark of Gideon"

"That Which Survives"

"The Lights of Zetar"

"Requiem for Methuslah"

"The Way to Eden"

"The Cloud Minder"

"The Savage Curtain"

"All Our Yesterdays"

"Turnabout Intruder"

••••

Episode #55
"Spock's Brain"
Original Airdate: 9/20/68
Written by Lee Cronin
Directed by Marc Daniels
Guest Starring: Marj Dusay (Kara),
Sheila Leighton (Luma),
James Daris (Primitive Man)

The Eymorgs steal Spock's brain to use as a power source on their planet, and the race is on for the Enterprise to retrieve it before his body dies. The less said about this one the better, though it's surprising that Gene Coon, under the name Lee Cronin, is credited with the teleplay.

••••

"In the original version of the script," recalled Marc Daniels, "Spock didn't go along, staying, instead, on the Enterprise. I thought that was dull, so I decided to bring him along. Then the concern was whether or not he would look like a zombie walking around. Thankfully Leonard was able to pull it off."

Producer Fred Freiberger says, "A hell of a concept, but how do you get drama into it? We had a lot of problems making that work."

"I suspect," muses David Gerrold, "that 'Spock's Brain' was Gene L. Coon's way of thumbing his nose at Roddenberry or something. If not Roddenberry, he was thumbing his nose at how seriously the show was taking itself. I suspect what had happened is that they were a little panic-stricken because there weren't a lot of scripts to shoot. The history of *Star Trek* is management by crisis. I think somebody called up Gene L. Con and said, 'We need a script in a hurry, can you do it?' And he did it under a pen name, and I don't think he deliberately set out to write that show seriously. I don't think there's any way you can take that episode seriously. You've got to take it as a joke. What's the stupidest science fiction idea to do? What if somebody stole Spock's brain? I think Gene L. Coon had that kind of sense of humor to do that kind of impish stuff. He had an irreverent sense of humor, and I think he wanted to poke *Star Trek* because someone was taking it too seriously. Maybe it was his way of not buying into it."

Episode #56
"The Enterprise Incident"
Original Airdate: 9/27/68
Written by D.C. Fontana
Directed by John Meredyth Lucas
Guest Starring: Joanne Linville (Commander), Jac Donner (Tal)

Star Trek meets *Mission: Impossible* as the Enterprise is sent on a secret mission to penetrate the Romulan Neutral Zone and steal a cloaking device from one of their vessels. Enroute, there is a romantic relationship between Spock and the Romulan commander and Kirk is given the opportunity to put on the pointed ears as he has himself surgically altered to resemble a Romulan.

••••

"There were errors in that episode that I protested against, and I believe David Gerrold's *The World of Star Trek* covers those in a memo I wrote in regards to my protests about it," details Dorothy Fontana. "Overall it was not a bad episode, but I did have a lot of complaints about it and things that weren't approached or handled right. It was really based on the Pueblo Incident, in the sense that here's this ship caught spying and they have to find a justification for their being there. Kirk's sanity is put on the line in terms of why they're there. Then, of course, they have to get out safely, preferably with the information they came for. Now that's not what happened with the Pueblo, but the Pueblo Incident kicked off this line of thinking in my mind.

"[But] let's face it, the romantic scene between the Romulan Commander and Spock was totally out of context. Any Romulan worth her salt would have instantly suspected Spock because they are related races. That was wrong. Kirk's attitudes were wrong. A simple thing—the cloaking device was supposed to be a very small thing, about the size of a watch, for instance, and it could be easily hidden. Here's Kirk running around with this thing that looks like a lamp. You know, highly visible. This is stupidity as well as illogical thinking. Visually it was stupid, conceptually it was very bad. There were a lot of things, little things, that were changed, but my biggest objection is the scene between Spock and the woman, because I really did not believe

it. And I did not believe that the Romulan did not suspect Spock of something underhanded. She does know enough about Vulcan and Vulcans to know that something's afoot."

Episode #57
"The Paradise Syndrome"
Original Airdate: 10/4/68
Written by Margaret Armen
Directed by Jud Taylor
Guest Starring: Sabrina Scharf (Miramanee), Rudy Lolari (Salish), Richard Hale (Goro)

When a planet is threatened by an asteroid, a landing party beams down to try and evacuate the population. An accident gives Kirk amnesia and he is eventually found by a tribe of Indians, who look upon him as a god. Referring to himself as Kirok, he takes a bride in Miramanee and is ultimately the victim of the changing mood of the crowd, who realize that he is actually human and not someone to be revered. This episode is marked by a particularly tragic ending in which Miramanee is killed, along with her and Kirk's unborn child.

••••

"My thinking," says writer Margaret Armen, "is that these people on a space ship for years and years have to get awfully sour, and have a special longing for their home planet and the simplicity of an Earth-type nature. So I wondered what would happen if they were just hungry for R&R on an Earth-like planet, and they suddenly and unexpectedly came upon a planet which has a primitive Earth sort of idyllic civilization. Kind of like the Garden of Eden, with primitive and friendly natives and so on. From there I worked out the story as it was shown on the screen. It's supposed to be an uninhabited planet, but when they beam down it turns out to be a primitive Indian civilization, and Kirk, who is extremely strung out and tired at the time....we had to cut some of the build-up to that because of time....was really taken by this idyllic situation.

"There just wasn't enough time to show it," Armen elaborates. "One of the reasons he is at the obelisk alone is that he wandered away from the group, enjoying the flora and the fauna. I liked 'The Paradise Syndrome,' but I thought it

••••

was too bad that we couldn't get a little bit of Kirk's longing for, well, the paradise syndrome, before he beamed down. But Freddy wanted more action and less *approach* to action. There again, some of the action which he wanted....I would have preferred action which I had suggested, and I wouldn't have made such a big thing of it. I think action is inherent in it, as well as danger and suspense. I had a little bit more character building in the situation."

"Quite frankly, I wasn't happy with that show," concurs Fred Freiberger. "It didn't come out as well as I had expected. To me, it lacked a certain element. That was one of the shows I was disappointed with. The good thing was that we shot it on location, which was very rare indeed in the third season. That's probably one of the reasons I wanted to do it; I wanted to get away from a bare planet set."

Episode #58
"And the Children Shall Lead"
Original Airdate: 10/11/68
Written by Edward J. Lasko
Directed by Marvin Chomsky
Guest Starring: Melvin Belli (Gorgon), James Wellman (Professor Starnes), Craig Hundley (Tommy), Pamela Ferdin (Mary), Mark Robert Brown (Don), Brian Tochi (Ray), Caesar Belli (Steve)

The Enterprise retrieves a group of orphaned children on Triacus. A short matter of time later, it becomes obvious that they are being manipulated by "Gorgon, the Friendly Angel," who turns out to be something far more sinister. Kirk and company must make the children see him for what he truly is.

• • • •

"To boost the ratings," explains Fred Freiberger, "we tried to get something unusual in there and in this case unusual in terms of casting. So we brought in attorney Melvin Belli. It could have been a better show. I thought the idea was good, but it just wasn't as strong as it could have been. Besides, I don't think it boosted the ratings."

Melvin Belli told *Starlog's* Eric Niderost, "I enjoyed myelf *immensely*, and I was struck by the professionalism of William Shatner and Leonard Nimoy and all the rest. They were very profes-

sional—yet imbued with a great sense of fun. The most fun for me personally was my 'melting' death scene. Even though they had taken casts of my face much earlier, the makeup required for the scene still took the better part of the morning. They would shoot for a time, pause, then take me back to makeup to make me look more hideous. I remember they built up my nose with putty and made my jowls sag with each successive stage. Then it was back to the soundstage to shoot some more."

Walter Koenig admits that he was not comfortable with the casting of Belli. "Freiberger had a reputation as someone who comes in and takes an ailing show and forces it into the ground. I don't know if that's true or not, but that's the reputation that he had. I think it [*Star Trek*] really requires someone with a knowledge or background in science-fiction, in the genre itself because the stories start to be extrapolations, a more prosaic kind of storytelling. To me, the most heinous violation he [Freiberger] perpetrated was casting Melvin Belli in 'And the Children Shall Lead.' That infuriated me because Marvin was a friend of his, evidently, and it's one thing to cast friends who are actors, and another to cast friends who are not actors. Not only did it dilute the impact, whatever there was to begin with, but it took an acting job away from an actor. I was really upset about that. It was very unfair."

Episode #59
"Is There in Truth No Beauty?"
Original Airdate: 10/18/68
Written by Jean Lisette Aroeste
Directed by Ralph Senensky
Guest Starring: Diana Muldaur (Miranda), David Frankham (Marvick)

The Medusans are a race of energy patterns deemed so horrifying to look at that they have a tendency to drive humans insane. One of their kind is taken aboard the Enterprise by Dr. Miranda Jones for transport, and amidst insanity and attempted murders, we learn that all things are not as they are initially perceived.

• • • •

"We did a lot of morality shows, and I thought this was a hell of an example of one," enthuses Fred

Diana Muldaur, later to portray Dr. Pulaski on Star Trek: The Next Generation, appeared in two classic Star Trek adventures.

Freiberger. "The basic concept is that on the outside what is reputed to be ugly and horrible, is really something lovely and beautiful. Hopefully it will teach the viewer to be more tolerant."

Director Ralph Sensensky states, "My problem with the episode is that it felt like they were trying to turn it into a monster movie. All of those shots which kept cutting back to the box and those light effects.....they kept trying to build menace in an artificial manner. To me those kinds of cuts were insulting to an audience, like it was telling them that it was time to be nervous. It just curtailed the imagination. An audience is smarter than that. It was just a different mentality, treating it as a monster show rather than a sublte picture."

Episode #60
"Spectre of the Gun"
Original Airdate: 10/25/68
Written by Lee Cronin
Directed by Vincent McEveety
Guest Starring: Ron Soble (Wyatt Earp), Rex Holman (Morgan Earp), Bonnie Beecher (Sylvia), Charles Maxwell (Virgil Earp), Sam Gilman (Doc Holiday), Bill Zuckert (Sheriff Behan), Ed McReady (Barber), Abraham Sofaer (Melkotian Voice), James Doohan (Voice of Melkotian buoy)

Upon ignoring warnings not to proceed into Melkotian space, Kirk, Spock, McCoy and Chekov find them-

• • • •

selves on a world surrealistically mirroring the old west, where they are to take part in the famous gunfight at O.K. Corral. They are the Clantons, and if history proceeds the way it's supposed to, they will be killed by the Earps.

••••

"When Gene Coon wrote the original script, it was set in an actual western town," states Fred Freiberger. "Bobby Justman and I thought about how we could help it some and therefore we did this surrealistic kind of town to try and give it an other-worldly approach. Vincent McEveety was a hell of a creative director. I thought he did some wonderful things with it. I thought the show came out well, and that was satisfying considering that was my first episode on *Star Trek*, though it aired later in the season. "

Recalls Walter Koenig, "One day during the second season I asked Gene Roddenberry to have a meeting between seasons wen it looked like we were going to be on 8:00 Mondays. I asked him abøut how my character would evolve based on its popularity. I went to his house and he proceeded to show me some memos he had written, and memos from Schlosser and Werner, the guys at NBC, through Paramount. All the memos were very positive, saying let's involve Chekov more, he has appeal. Let's bring him down to the planets more, involve him with members of the opposite sex. And it looked enormously promising. 'Spectre of the Gun' was the first episode written with that in mind for third season, and it reflected what my participation was going to be. Immediately thereafter we were switched and everybody sort of threw up their hands and gave up on the show. They brought in Freiberger who had no particular style as far as I could tell, or empathy for the character. I don't think he had any antipathy either. I just don't think he saw it as being important."

"That was an episode which was fun, a comic strip and certainly not significant," Vincent McEveety muses. "I thought it was reaching a bit, and not one of my favorites. Even though it was hokey, it was more enjoyable to me than 'Patterns of Force,' because I thought it was far more stylized. It was saying,

'Okay, we're going to do a fantasy, and here we are.' There was too much realism in the Nazi story. I didn't like the treatment of it or anything about it. I don't know if they were running out of material or if they thought it would be wonderful to put these guys in a Nazi occupied city, or put them back in the West or Old Rome. Some of it worked, some of it didn't.

"Even though 'Spectre of the Gun' is not one of my favorites by a long shot, the effects, the wind, the stylized sets—the fragmented sets—all make it feel like a stage play. It was the kind of thing that takes a lot of imagination to relate to. You may have ended up empty from it all, but it was certainly an arresting story. Whereas at the end you're not saying, 'What a brilliant piece of work; a great show,' you might say, 'Hey, that was interesting.' If even that. However, it's interesting that what little fanmail I get in my life usually pertains to that show. People love it, which I can't believe, because I don't."

Episode #61
"Day of the Dove"
Original Airdate: 11/1/68
Written by Jerome Bixby
Directed by Marvin Chomsky
Guest Starring: Michael Ansara (Kang), Susan Howard (Mara)

An energy force that feeds on anger, hatred and hostility arms both the Klingons and Kirk's people with swords and sets them at each other's throats on board the Enterprise. Kirk and his opponent, Kang, must come to grips with what exactly is putting them through this, and combat it before both sides are slaughtered.

••••

"'Day of the Dove' was kind of my response to the Vietnam thing at that time," says Jerome Bixby. "Throw down the swords. I wanted to write a peace story. My original story was very late sixties, and I ended it with a peace march which, thank God, also came out."

In the pages of *The Star Trek Interview Book* he added, "I originally wrote 'Day of the Dove' for Kor, the Klingon from 'Errand of Mercy,' but John Colicos was unavailable. He was abroad doing a film, and he said that when he first read the script he wept and threw

"Day of the Dove" featured actor Michael Ansara in the role of the Klingon named Kang.

himself at walls and nearly jumped off a balcony because he wanted to play the part so bad, but he was committed to that other production and he couldn't play Kor. So they changed it to Kang. They were looking around for a Klingon and they almost hit on Joe Campanella, but they didn't think he could draw quite enough fire. So they hit on Michael Ansara, who just ate up the part."

"A shipboard show," Fred Freiberger points out. "Considering our restrictions, I thought it came out well. It was more of a derring-do kind of show, and Michael Ansara was wonderful."

"What a *magnificent* character to play!" Michael Ansara enthused to journalist Mark Phillips. "Immediately, just from reading the script, I knew how special the role was and how rare it was to find a character like this in either television or film. Kang had nobility and that's a quality that I have always been fascinated by."

Episode #62
"For the World is Hollow, And I Have Touched the Sky
Original Airdate: 11/8/68
Written by Rik Vollaerts
Directed by Tony Leader
Guest Starring: Kate Woodville (Natira), Byron Morrow (Admiral Westervelt), John Lormer (Old Man)

What appears to be an asteroid is actually a cleverly disguised vessel that is on a direct course for a Federation planet. Kirk and Spock must unlock the secrets of the ship's computers to alter its course and save countless lives. In the meantime, McCoy discovers that he has an incurable disease and, as he falls in love with one of the ship's inhabitants (Yonada), he elects to stay with her until the end. Naturally, they find a cure.

• • • •

"That was a love affair for Doctor McCoy," reflects Fred Freiberger. "I was trying to spread the material to the other actors, and I wanted to give DeForest Kelley something because he was always just kind of hanging around without a lot to do. I wanted him to have something a little more solid, and I liked the idea of the planet being a spaceship in transit. I thought it was an okay show."

He does admit that it was somewhat difficult to service the entire cast.

"They wouldn't be actors if they didn't want more to do," laughs Freiberger. "You're doing an ensemble show and what's selling the show, hopefully, is the personality of the stars and the relationship between the three most prominent ones, Shatner, Nimoy and Kelley. You would try to give all the others something, but it's very difficult because you have so many format characters and you've only got about 50 minutes to tell your story. I certainly sympathize with any of them who wanted more to do. They would legitimately fight me, and I would do my best to do what I had to do to give them something more meaningful than, 'Ahead, warp three,' and the rest of the usual material."

Episode #63
"The Tholian Web"
Original Airdate: 11/15/68
Written by Judy Burns and Chet Richards
Directed by Ralph Senensky
Guest Starring: No one.

While exploring the remnants of the USS Defiant, Kirk is accidentally trapped in another dimension. Most of the crew believe him to be dead, though they continue to see his apparition. Meanwhile, Spock works on trying to retrieve him when the Defiant enters our dimension again for a brief period of time. Add the Tholians, who don't want the Enterprise in their territory, to the mix and you've got

some genuine suspense in terms of whether or not Spock will succeed.

• • • •

"I met a student who was a physicst and told him that I wanted to write a *Star Trek* script which would be a ghost story based on fact," says writer Judy Burns. "He said, 'Why don't you use the theory of infinite dimensions?' What came out was 'In Essence Nothing,' which became 'The Tholian Web.' At the time, if I remember correctly, the very first draft of the story had Spock as the one who disappeared.

"Eventually I received a classic memo from Bob Justman, who summed up by saying, 'I think we can use it, but it should be Kirk out there. He would be schmuckishly heroic to stay behind on this other ship.' Besides that, there was another episode called 'Spock's Brain' in which Spock was out of it for a period of time and they didn't want to have him incapacitated for two scripts. So, I got a phone call that said, 'We have some interest in the piece, could you come up and talk about it?' They provided a lot of commentary and suggestions and said, 'Go off and do this.' I think it turned out very nicely, and Fred and Bob had much to do with it. Many of the suggestions Bob made in his memo caused it to become what it became.

"Some of the things I was a little disappointed in were caused by technical problems. Originally there were no space suits when Kirk and the others beamed over to the other ship. There were force field belts which kept them encapsulated in a kind of mini-force field, which included an oxygen bank. It kept them secure as long as the batteries held, but if the batteries ran out—which was the greatest threat to Kirk—then they die. They didn't have an infinite amount of time within the force field. Therefore, Kirk would have wandered around the ship looking like he looks, except for a little force field belt. I think it would have made a better ghost story. He looks silly constantly appearing in that space suit. I really had a lot of qualms about that. Not from poor designing or anything, but from a story point-of-view, it would have been better. They felt strongly that if they started something like a force field belt, it might have ramifications down the line

on other stories. I was a novice in those days, but today I probably would have countered that it was a prototype model that had been given to us this one time. In 25 years, we would get it back again."

Episode #64
"Plato's Stepchildren"
Original Airdate: 11/22/68
Written by Meyer Dolinsky
Directed by David Alexander
Guest Starring: Michael Dunn (Alexander), Liam Sullivan (Parmen), Barbara Babcock (Philana), Ted Scott (Eraclitus), Derek Partridge (Donyd)

The Enterprise proceeds to Platonius in response to a distress signal, and what they find are a race of people who have based their society somewhat on ancient Rome. The difference is that they have developed extraordinary telekinetic abilities which they use to control their jester, a dwarf named Alexander.

What the Platonians eventually detail is that they want Dr. McCoy to remain behind to tend to them should they get ill. When Kirk refuses to allow this, these self-acclaimed gods start trying to control them, forcing Kirk, Spock, Uhura and Nurse Chapel into somewhat humiliating positions. Additionally, they were basically the catalyst behind television's first inter-racial kiss.

• • • •

"The big thing," says Fred

Michael Dunn, Alexander of "Plato's Stepchildren," is perhaps more recognized for his role as Dr. Lovelace in The Wild Wild West.

Freiberger, "was who was going to kiss Uhura, a black girl. We had quite a few conversations on that one, because someone said, 'Let's have Spock do it,' and I said, 'No, if we have Spock do it, we're going to have all these people screaming that we didn't have the guts to have a white man kiss her. We went through a whole thing, but it all worked out and Shatner said to her, 'It's not that I don't want to, but I don't want to humiliate you.' That's a show I'm very proud of."

In his autobiography *Shatner: Where No Man*, the actor remarked, "I remember now that they had mentioned [that this was the first interracial kiss] earlier and said, 'Would you mind?' and I said, 'Mind? No, I don't mind.' And then they kind of backed off on it, in that I was being forced to do it. It wasn't Kirk actually kissing Uhura. It was Kirk being forced by some power beyond there—to kiss her. So the edge was taken off the first interracial kiss on television by the fact that this guy was going, '...uh, argh, not me—no—kiss.

"I'm well aware that there could have been different ways to write the scene or play it," Shatner continued. "We did try some variations. There could have been a whole different story, if anybody had wanted to emphasize an interracial love story. But in fact, that wouldn't have made the point as effectively. Kirk and Uhura wouldn't even think of a kiss or a love story as interracial. That would be the *last* thing they would think about. If we did any good with that kiss or anything we did on *Star Trek*, it was to push in the direction of not having to think about that."

Episode #65
"Wink of An Eye"
Original Airdate: 11/29/68
Written by Arthur Heinemann
Story by Lee Cronin
Directed by Jud Taylor
Guest Starring: Kathie Browne (Deela), Jason Evers (Rael), Eric Holland (Ekor), Geoffrey Binney (Compton)

After drinking Scalosian water, Kirk's metabolism accelerates to a different plane of existence on a par with the Scalosians themselves. Their race is nearly dead, and they want to use the crew of the Enterprise to repopulate their species.

While Kirk does what he can to foil these plans, Spock, on the slower level, works with McCoy on a cure for the effects of the water.

••••

"'Wink of an Eye' was my favorite of the three episodes I did," explained the late Arthur Heinemann a week before his death. "Director Jud Taylor asked a lot of questions about the people in the script. What they felt, what they thought, what they were like. He and I had a thorough discussion about the people and he got his actors to project exactly what I had in mind."

The story credited to Lee Cronin, actually Gene L. Coon, was perceived as being somewhat disappointing from the man who gave audiences "Devil in the Dark" and the Klingons. Dorothy Fontana believes that the seeming drop in writing quality was due to the fact that Coon was under enormous time pressure and forced to write scripts between his other assignments. "It wasn't like being on a series where you could devote all your time to that series," she suggests. "I think the writing suffers because of that."

"If you're not producing," Glen Larson says, "somebody else takes it and does the rewriting. Knowing his attention to detail and his work ethic, I would imagine that somebody rewrote him. It would be interesting to be able to see his first draft scripts."

Episode #66
"The Empath"
Original Airdate: 12/6/68
Written by Joyce Muskat
Directed by John Erman
Guest Starring: Kathryn Hays (Gem), Alan Berman (Lal), Willard Sage (Thann), Jason Wingreen (Dr. Linke), Davis Roberts (Dr. Ozaba)

A pair of aliens named Lal and Thann (who look like they're related to the Talosians of "The Cage") capture Kirk, Spock and McCoy, and involve them in a series of experiments that include a mute woman named Gem, who has empathic abilities which allow her to absorb the pain and suffering of others. The aliens are doing so in order to determine whether or not Gem's race is worthy of being saved from a forthcoming super nova, or if a neighboring planet is worthier to survive.

Episode #67
"Elaan of Troyius"
Original Airdate: 12/20/68
Written and Directed by
John Meredyth Lucas
Guest Starring: France Nuyen (Elaan), Jay Robinson (Petri), Tony Young (Kryton), Lee Duncan (Evans), Victor Brandt (Watson), K.L. Smith (Klingon)

Enterprise is told to transport Elaan of Elas to her marriage ceremony at the planet Troyius, which will result in an alliance between the two hostile worlds. It sounds like a simple enough assignment, until one takes into account the fact that the woman has no interest in the marriage, the Klingons want to see the alliance fall apart and are doing what they can to make this happen, the Troyius ambassador is murdered and Kirk falls madly in love with Elaan due to the chemical reaction of her tears on his skin.

••••

"That was an original premise of Gene Roddenberry's," says writer/director John Meredyth Lucas. "I enjoyed the love story aspect of the show and thought it was an interesting change of pace. You didn't get to do too many of those. Basically we were doing *Taming of the Shrew*."

Recalls Fred Freiberger, "Part of the reason we did that one was because the network had told us they had done a survey in which they discovered that women, generally, were terrified of space. They needed stability, they needed surroundings. They'd rather be in valleys than on top of mountains. So we tried to get the women, which is why we did a romantic story. We tried to reach a segment of the audience we couldn't otherwise reach, and didn't succeed."

Probably the most enduring aspect of this episode is Scotty's brief mention of the Elaan during his 24th century visit to *The Next Generation* in sixth season's "Relics."

Episode #68
"Whom Gods Destroy"
Original Airdate: 1/3/69
Written by Lee Erwin
Directed by Herb Wallerstein
Guest Starring: Yvonne Craig (Marta), Steve Ihnat (Garth), Key Luke (Cory)

The inmates have taken over the Elba II asylum, and it is in that situa-

••••

Yvonne Craig, Batgirl of the Batman *television series, was a resident of the Elba II asylum in "Whom Gods Destroy."*

tion which Kirk and Spock are captured by former Starfleet captain Garth, who has acquired the power to change his shape at will. Our heroes do what they must to turn the tables. Basically, that's it.

Episode #69
"Let That Be Your Last Battlefield"
Original Airdate: 1/10/69
Written by Oliver Crawford
Story by Lee Cronin
Directed by Jud Taylor
Guest Starring: Frank Gorshin (Bele),
Lou Antonio (Lokai)

The Enterprise finds itself in the midst of a chase between an alien law enforcement officer named Bele and his prey, Lokai. Half the face of each man is white while the other half is black. The only difference is the side on which the particular color is. Bele reveals that, on their world, Lokai is a criminal and lower life form because his colors are on the wrong side. Ultimately Kirk makes the discovery that the aliens are sole survivors of their homeworld, the population having killed itself.

••••

"That was originally a Gene Coon story that was brought to me," relates writer Oliver Crawford. "It dealt with racial intolerance, and I thought it was a marvelous visual and cinematic effect. The whole point of the story was that color is only skin deep. How could

any writer not respond to that? That fit right into today's scene, and I was very pleased with the episode."

Recalls Fred Freiberger, "Gene originally had a devil with a tail chasing an angel. We used actor Frank Gorshin and thought, 'What an idea it would be to do black on one side and white on the other, and the other guy has it the opposite way.' *That's* the stupidity of prejudice. There's a wonderful moment when Kirk says, 'What's different about him?' And he says, 'He's white on the other side.' That was a big morality show and I liked the idea of it. As a side note, we ran a little short on that show which is why it ended with a chase that went on forever. I thought it was a hell of a creative situation."

It also marked Gene Coon's final effort for *Star Trek*, though Freiberger was grateful for the contributions made to the series.

"Gene Coon was a lovely, talented guy," says Freiberger, "who came up with certain stories and said do what you want with them. He worked as much as he could with us and he was a complete gentleman and completely professional about the whole thing."

Episode #70
"The Mark of Gideon"
Original Airdate: 1/17/69
Written by George F. Slavin and
* Stanley Adams*
Directed by Jud Taylor
Guest Starring: Sharon Acker (Odona),
David Hurst (Hodin), Gene Kynarski
(Krodack), Richard Derr (Admiral
Fitzgerald)

Kirk attempts to beam himself down to the planet Gideon, but is shocked to find himself back on the Enterprise, with the difference being that he is the only person on board. This turns out to be the work of the inhabitants, who have created an exact duplicate of the starship (how they pulled this off is anyone's guess] to trick Kirk. It seems that the planet is suffering from overpopulation because the citizens are disease-free. Kirk, though, carries the remnants of a disease that nearly killed him. They want the captain to infect one of their people so that disease, and then death, will spread across the planet.

••••

The plot of this episode could very well have inspired the feature film *Zardoz*, whose story is quite similar.

"One of my pet themes is over population," relates Fred Freiberger, "and I thought this was a good idea. We were taking a shot at something fresh and gutsy, and it worked out pretty well. That one was also shot entirely on the Enterprise. I felt that if we had to do the show under those restrictions, we had to come up with good stories and that one worked."

Actress Sharon Acker, as related in the *Official Star Trek Fan Club Magazine*, enjoyed playing Princess Odona. "I thought she was fun," said Acker. "I was really looking forward to playing her. Odona was a little out of my field. I mean, I never thought of myself as a princess, I never thought of myself as particularly exotic, so to play the role of somebody who was both of those things and who also came from another planet was a real exciting challenge for me. But I didn't necessarily see her as different from me emotionally, except, I guess, from the point of view of her commitment to be willing to give her life for the people of her planet. She was willing to die to bring death and dignity back to the people of her planet. From that point of view I don't know if Sharon Acker could ever take such a step. So I think she was heroic and grand and very special and rather beautiful and quite a bit beyond the Sharon Acker that was playing the part."

Episode #71
"That Which Survives"
Original Airdate: 1/24/69
Written by John Meredyth Lucas
Story by D.C. Fontana
Directed by Herb Wallerstein
Guest Starring: Lee Meriwether (Losira),
Arthur Batanides (D'Amato), Naomi
Pollack (Lt. Rahada)

While exploring unique geological conditions on an unnamed planet, Kirk, Spock and McCoy confront the holographic image of a woman named Losira. She is actually a warning device left behind by an ancient civilization to repel their enemies, the Kalandans. Her "touch" is death, and it is up to the crew of the Enterprise to shut down the com-

Lee Meriwether, decked out here in Catwoman's traditional leather outfit, was the lethal Losira in "That Which Survives."

puters that continue to generate her lethal image.

Episode #72
"The Lights of Zetar"
Original Airdate: 1/31/69
Written by Jeremy Tarcher and Shari Lewis
Directed by Herb Kenwith
Guest Starring: Jan Shutan (Lt. Mira Romaine), John Winston (Lt. Kyle), Libby Erwin (Rindonian)

Lieutenant Mira Romaine, who Scotty has fallen in love with, is possessed by the lights of Zetar, a cloud-like being that is actually the collective existence of a now-dead race. Enjoying physical existence again, they decide to keep their human host at the expense of her own life.

••••

"I haven't seen [the episode] since the first time it aired," said director Herb Kenwith in *Starlog* #179. "I remember going to the first cut, and at the time, directors didn't have that much say about it, and I was disappointed. It wasn't telling the story the way I had hoped it would be told. You get 10 people in a room who read a script, and you get 10 versions. It's like *Hamlet*. There are so many ways to play it. Since *I* was directing it, I wanted *my* version told. I felt there was a lot of distortion to it upon seeing ht efirst cut.....I was so dismayed and hurt by it. I

didn't have the kind of shell you need to observe your work when it's done for the efforts of someone else.

"I liked the script," Kenwith added. "I though it was interesting and so far removed from anything I had done, because I had done theater and plays. While doing *Star Trek* we all laughed at a lot of it. We throught, 'Oh, this is silly, but let's do it.' Of course, it turns out to be a classic. It wasn't so silly after all."

Episode #73
"Requiem for Methuslah"
Original Airdate: 2/14/69
Written by Jerome Bixby
Directed by Murray Golden
Guest Starring: James Daly (Flint), Louise Sorel (Reena)

While searching for a cure to a rare disease, Kirk, Spock and McCoy beam down to the surface of Holberg 917-G. There they are surprised to find a man named Flint, who turns out to be an immortal. Kirk falls in love with Flint's daughter, Rayna, and is horrified to learn that she is actually an android, as are all the "people" living there.

••••

"I always wanted to do a story about a Neanderthal who found himself gifted with immortality," reflects Jerome Bixby, "who lived up to the present day. Learning, learning, learning throughout this enormous lifetime, mastering the arts

and sciences through philosophy. I wanted him to have been Beethoven, because Beethoven has kind of a Neanderthal cast to his face. And so I had that story kicking around that I had never done. Why not do a story about a virtually immortal man for *Star Trek?* So I came up with Mr. Flint, which by the way was the name of my Neanderthal. It pleased me very much when I wrote it, [and] there is a story behind that. I have a habit, and I can make this work very well in prose, and that is alliteration. I can make prose jump through hoops, and when you start uttering these things aloud, they often sound somewhat contrived and sometimes ludicrous unless you are deliberately writing poetry.

"Some of my dialogue near the end between Spock and McCoy where McCoy is really coming down on Spock and saying, 'You poor schmuck. You have no emotions. You can't live. You'll never know what love is like. That hope doesn't exist for you,' etc. I pulled out all the stops and wrote about 15 pages of dialogue that De Kelley absolutely refused to utter. He said, 'This sounds like poetry!' 'We are the hollow men, we are the stunted men,' like T.S. Eliot. So whoever was directing that—Murray Golden—wanted to do the tag. He wanted to do that ending. But he said, 'We can't do that without dialogue. It just won't play.' So I said, 'Give me three minutes,' and I went over and sat down in Captain Kirk's chair on the Enterprise set and rewrote the speech right there, because I didn't want to lose that ending either. Five minutes later they had a draft."

"Some good emotion there," says Fred Freiberger, "and the reveal of her being an android was well handled. I liked the idea of walking into a factory and seeing the woman you love being replicated."

Episode #74
"The Way to Eden"
Original Airdate: 2/21/69
Written by Arthur Heinemann
Story by Michael Richards and Arthur Heinemann
Directed by David Alexander
Guest Starring: Skip Homeier (Dr. Severin), Charles Napier (Adam), Mary Linda Rapelye (Irina, Victor Brandt (Tongo Rad), Deborah Downey and

••••

Phyllis Douglas (Hippies)

A group of space-hippies attempt to take over the Enterprise so that they can be transported to the mythical world of Eden, a realm supposedly of paradise. You haven't lived until you've seen Mr. Spock in a jam session.

••••

As originally conceived, "The Way to Eden" was entitled "Joanna" and dealt with Dr. McCoy's daughter, who was among the "space hippies."

"The producers didn't care for that idea," says Dorothy Fontana, who removed her name from the story, "so they made it Chekov's Russian girlfriend. And then they shifted the focus of the story. I've never seen the episode."

Fred Freiberger sheepishly admits, "I didn't like it at all and I don't blame Dorothy's original story. We probably did it all wrong. I'm unhappy to take the blame for that one, but there's no one else to blame."

Arthur Heinemann, who wrote the teleplay based on Fontana's story, added, "It was my idea to inject the element of deadliness in Eden. The original story did not have any deadly aspects. It just dealt with space-age hippies who wanted to find a romantic place to live. I wanted to make a comment that underneath all that beauty was a deadliness. I enjoyed that too, because I wrote some lyrics for some songs that the hippies sang. As a matter of fact, I get a royalty from EMI for it. About once a year a check comes for $3.47.

"I wasn't particularly pleased with the episode itself, though. It was directed in kind of a one, two, three manner. Over simplistic, if I remember."

Episode #75
"The Cloud Minders"
Original Airdate: 2/28/69
Written by Margaret Armen
Story by David Gerrold and
Oliver Crawford
Directed by Jud Taylor

The Enterprise arrives at Ardana to obtain zienite, cure for a plague on Merak II. What they find is a divided race, with the elite living in a city in the clouds while the "have-nots" mine the zienite mineral, and they seem quite insane. Kirk realizes that the gas of the mines is causing this madness and he sets about getting both sides to talk out their differences.

••••

Writer David Gerrold recalls, "I submit a story later on called 'Castles in the Sky,' and the point of the story is that there are people living in the sky cities and it's like Beverly Hills. Then there are people working in the cotton fields down below and it's Watts. They're working the mines for the dilithium crystals. The point of the story is that McCoy in the shuttlecraft crashes on the surface of the planet and he ends up helping the children of the people on the surface who are suffering from high pressure disease. When the rebels come to kill McCoy [because] they represent the sky people, the parents of the children stand in front of him, like the scene in *The Ugly American*. Meanwhile, in the sky city, there's Kirk and Spock, and the official representative arguing about the shape of the table, just like the Paris Peace Talks. Finally we run the action in the story appropriately, and it's a lot of moving around and finally a confrontation.

"It wasn't a bad story. It really was a story that addressed the issue of 'haves' and 'have nots.' The problem was that at the end we get into the starship and we head away. Kirk says, 'Well, another good job. We didn't solve the problem totally, but we got them talking to each other and that's a lasting solution, because they will solve their problems.' And McCoy says, 'Right. But how many children are going to die in the meantime?' And nobody has an answer. In other words, you're expecting a happy ending, and McCoy gives you a little nudge. I felt that *Trek* had established that it was capable of doing that kind of story.

"What happens is Freddy Freiberger saw this as a polemic, and it annoyed the hell out of him. He wanted to do a nice, safe story where everything was wrapped up in the end. I said, 'It doesn't quite work that way in real life. Let's do a story with a little grit to it,' and he said, 'Alright, you've had your one shot on the outline. I want you to take on a co-writer.' I talked to my agent and he said, 'Take the co-writer, otherwise he'll cut you off.' So suddenly I'm working with

Ollie Crawford on the next draft of the outline. He forced him on me. I thought that since Ollie was the story editor on the last show he produced, maybe he'll know what Freddy will buy. 'Ollie will keep me from making mistakes. I'll learn from him and we'll definitely go the distance on this one.' Ollie's a good guy."

Oliver Crawford adds, "I recall Freddy calling me up and saying, 'I want to put an old pro together with a young writer.' Writers are constantly wounded, but television is very much a collaborative medium. To get the happy circumstance where everything gels and everybody's talent enhances everybody else's is tough to achieve, but worth it when you do. When people go off on tangents, you find that you don't have much of anything. I know very few writers who are happy with all of their work as produced, unless they're in a position of power and not too many of us are. I thought 'The Cloud Minders' was right in line with the good work and thrust of the series. It was almost like a *Brave New World*. The key thing there was exploitation, and that's something we must deal with all the time."

Margaret Armen explains, "The reason that I ultimately did the teleplay is that Freddy Freiberger called me in and said that he had two writers, he didn't tell me who, that he had gotten this story from. He said, 'I don't want you to look at the teleplay, Margaret, because it doesn't work. It's all philosophizing and talk. We need something with action. It's a good basic theme and a good basic story, and we're going to tell you the basic story. From that we want you to start from scratch and do a scene breakdown and, hopefully, a teleplay.' All they told me was that part of the society was living on the surface of the planet in great luxury, and the larger part of the society was down in the caves working like slaves and kept that way. As I say, I never saw David Gerrold's screenplay nor did I see Oliver Crawford's rewrite, so I don't know that it was static and didn't work. So I wondered how in the world I could build action into this philosophical notion, and that's why I added the gas in the caves which numbed the minds of the people so that they appear to be stupid. I told the story against the background of rebellion, in which Kirk and Spock become involved and it worked that way. For all I know, the first draft of the story and teleplay may have been even more acceptable than mine, but mine happened to be what the producer wanted."

Says Gerrold, "I hinted in one of those meetings with Fred Freiberger that I didn't want to sell out to television, and he said, 'I've been in television for 20 years and I've never sold out.' In television it's not whether or not you sell out, but how badly you sell out. The giveaway is when they say they've never sold out. Obviously you've never challenged anyone. You've sold out before you got there. You look at 'The Cloud Minders' now and it's kind of harmless, but at the time it was suddenly a story that said 'We're right to be in Vietnam, we're right to send the troops into the ghettos, and we're right to do whatever we want. Yes, they have some valid concerns, but if we give them gas masks, they'll stay in the ghettos.' That pissed me off, because it ignored the fundamental issue that these are human beings and there is an unfairness in who is living in the sky cities and who is living down below. And the issue was never resolved in the story. I was very upset about the way that turned out. I didn't like the episode. So it was an unhappy experience, particularly for a new writer, who needs reassurance that he can succeed in the industry."

Today, Fred Freiberger keeps his thoughts on the whole situation rather succinct. "I liked the story when David came in with it, but nobody was thrilled with the script," he says. "We fought to save Gerrold's credit on that to which, I'm sure, we got no gratitude. There was no appreciation on his part in that we told every writer that came in that we wanted to save his credit."

Episode #76
"The Savage Curtain"
Original Airdate: 3/7/69
Written by Arthur Heinemann and Gene Roddenberry
Story by Gene Roddenberry
Directed by Herschel Daugherty
Guest Starring: Lee Bergere (Abraham Lincoln), Barry Atwater (Surak), Phillip Pine (Colonel Green), Nathan Jung

(Genghis Kahn), Carol Daniels Dement (Zora), Robert Herron (Kahless)
The ultimate battle between good and evil as Kirk, Spock, President Lincoln and Vulcan pioneer Surak go up against mad scientist Zora, Genghis Khan, murderer Colonel Green and the Klingon that inspired the Empire, Kahless. The mediator is a rock creature named Yarnek, who is curious as to which side will prove victorious.

••••

"Gene Roddenberry wrote half a script," explained Arthur Heinemann, "and I don't know if he couldn't figure out how to end it or got tired and had other things to do. He was in and out of the show at the time. His script was handed to me and I wrote the last two acts, and rewrote some of the first two acts. I guess I must have liked it, otherwise I wouldn't have taken it. Although at that time I found myself capable of making myself like anything that they gave me. It wasn't hard to sell. If somebody says, 'I love you,' you just have to believe them.

"The story was interesting because the four greatest heroes in the history of man, or the universe, were pit against the four worst. How could you end that thing except by having them fight? I tried to inject some sort of moral underpinnings to it by saying that the good guys were fighting for the safety of other people, whereas the bad guys were just fighting for the sake of fighting; for the game. But I wasn't happy with the final execution of that episode. It was written toward the end of the season. The final fight scene was supposed to take place in a huge canyon, but they figured the daylight hours at the time weren't long enough to shoot on location, so they had to build rocks out of canvas and paint, and nobody could climb on them because you'd fall through. Maybe it was the only way. Who knows?"

Episode #77
"All Our Yesterdays"
Original Airdate: 3/14/69
Written by Jean Lisette Aroeste
Directed by Marvin Chomsky
Guest Starring: Mariette Hartley (Zarabeth), Ian Wolfe (Atoz), Kermit Murdock (Prosecutor), Johnny Haymer

Mariette Hartley was Mr. Spock's third love interest in the annals of StarTrek. The actress is seen here in Gene Roddenberry's Genesis II.

(Constable), Stan Barrett (Jailor), Ed Bakey and Al Cavens (Fops), Anna Karen (Woman)
A landing party beams down to Sarpeidon to remove the inhabitants from a forthcoming explosion of their sun. What they find is a massive library, and a librarian named Mr. Atoz (A to Z). Quite by accident, Kirk, Spock and McCoy step through a portal and are transported back in time. Kirk appears at the time of witch-hunts in a Salem-like setting, while Spock and Bones go back much farther to a more savage time where Spock actually falls in love with a woman trapped there, Zarabeth. The trio must make it back to their own time before the sun explodes and they are trapped forever.

••••

"I love that episode," smiles Fred Freiberger. "The woman who wrote it was a librarian at UCLA. I remember that when Leonard Nimoy read that script he came to me and said, 'I'm a Vulcan, how can I be passionately in love with a woman with emotion involved?' So I said, 'This is way back in time, before the Vulcans had evolved into a nonemotional society.' He accepted that, for which I was very grateful. One of my favorites.

Episode #78
"Turnabout Intruder"
Original Airdate: 6/3/69
Written by Arthur Singer
Story by Gene Roddenberry
Directed by Herb Wallerstein

••••

Guest Starring: Sandra Smith (Dr. Janice Lester), Harry Landers (Dr. Coleman)

Kirk finds himself the victim of Dr. Janice Lester's hatred. She was once romantically involved with the captain, and has been unable to assume a command of her own. Now she wants revenge and has found it in an alien device which is able to transfer her mind to Kirk's body and vice-versa.

••••

"I have to tell you, Shatner is a very creative guy," enthuses Fred Freiberger. "When I say creative, I mean he's willing to try *anything*. He loved 'Turnabout Intruder.' I was, frankly, a little concerned when Gene Roddenberry came up with a story where Kirk changes places with a woman. When I originally read it, I had said to Gene, 'I wonder what Shatner is going to say about this,' and Gene said he wouldn't have any problem with it. He was right. When I mentioned it to Shatner, he just loved the idea."

William Shatner (Captain James T. Kirk) and Leonard Nimoy (Mr. Spock) together at the Academy Awards.

••••

CHAPTER SEVEN
The Remaking of Star Trek 1970-1978

Reunited on stage for an early Star Trek *convention: Walter Koenig, George Takei, William Shatner, DeForest Kelley, Nichelle Nichols, Leonard Nimoy and Arlene Martel.*

Network cancellation was the best thing that could have ever happened to *Star Trek*. Had NBC renewed the show for a fourth or even a fifth year, the series would have undoubtedly continued to chug along. But, with considerable budget cuts each season, there would have a diminishing quality about the whole project and it would have undoubtedly faded into the annals of television history.

Star Trek had been such a ratings disappointment for NBC, that the final episode, "Turnabout Intruder," was not aired until summer reruns of 1970. In the fall of that year, Paramount began offering the show to independents, hoping that they would be able to recoup a few lost dollars on this "dog." Despite a slow beginning, the number of stations interested in carrying the series gradually increased, with the audience, in turn, growing as well.

Shortly thereafter, it had become obvious that there was something brewing. With Neil Armstrong's boot gracing the lunar surface the previous July, outer space suddenly became vogue. Space was the place, and *Star Trek* was the ticket to get there.

"*Star Trek* probably came along too early," explained Gene Roddenberry in *The Making of Star Trek: The Motion Picture* [1980, Wallaby Books]. "Had man landed on the moon during our first or second year, the idea of space flight wouldn't have seemed so ludicrous to the mass audience. *Star Trek* probably would have stayed on the air. The eye of the world did not turn to space seriously as a future possibility until we were in our third year, and by then it was too late.

With the continually mounting interest in *Star Trek* came the idea of a convention dedicated to the show, which would be held in New York during January of 1972. Episodes would be shown, merchandise pertaining to the series sold, and fans given the opportunity to meet and listen to the creative talents behind the series. The promoters of the con were expecting, with a little luck, maybe two or three hundred people. They were not prepared for the two thousand that actually showed up.

A year later, a second convention was held, with guests including James Doohan, George Takei, and *Star Trek* and science fiction writer David Gerrold. Again, the promoters took what they thought would be adequate precautions, and again they were wrong. This time between six and seven thousand fans showed up. The same thing happened in 1974 when what is estimated to be between ten and fourteen thousand people attended. A firmer grip was placed on crowd control for the 1975 convention when registration was closed at approximately eight thousand, and those people lucky enough to get in experienced William Shatner's first (and now all too rare) con appearance. The next year's convention was limited to six thousand people, and guests included DeForest Kelley, Gene Roddenberry, Majel Barrett, James Doohan, Nichelle Nichols and George Takei.

Throughout the "convention years," the syndicated episodes were breaking all kinds of records, easily equating itself with the most popular shows in reruns. Paramount noted this with interest, and was somewhat more than intrigued when the public began to demand a revival of the show. Rumors abounded, with the general feeling being that *Star Trek* would either come back as a new television series or perhaps even a feature film.

Still, Paramount made no official move. It's likely that they viewed the phenomenon as little more than a fad; that any such revival would, in effect, "miss the boat," and they would stand to lose even more money. They were wrong. *Star Trek* was no fad.

While fandom flourished, as did the merchandising of the show, animation production companies began to approach Gene Roddenberry and Paramount Pictures with the idea of doing an animated version. Many of these suggestions were turned down, but Filmation came to them with a package that they liked. Most important to Roddenberry was that he would have complete creative control, thus being able to insure that the series did not resemble any other kid vid on the air at the time.

"That was one of the reasons I wanted creative control," said Roddenberry

••••

The animated William Shatner/Captain James T. Kirk as seen in this publication that covered Star Trek-Animated.

at the time. "There are enough limitations just being on Saturday mornings. We have to eliminate some of the violence we might have had on in the evening shows. There will probably be no sex element to talk of either, but it will be *Star Trek* and not a stereotype kids cartoon show."

The idea was to do a series that would air on Saturday mornings, but would also feature the basic ideals of the original show. Both Roddenberry and Paramount agreed that this would be a good idea, and to that end the original cast was signed to provide the vocals to their animated counter-parts. Additionally, many of the writers involved with the live-action series to pen scripts. Former *Star Trek* story editor Dorothy Fontana was signed to repeat her duties here, and take on the new ones of associate producer.

"When Gene approached me to do the show," she explains, "he asked me if I would like to come on as story editor and producer. Since I wasn't a part of another regular staff at the time, I decided to do it. I had not worked in animation, which I do enjoy, so I had a good time on the show. I left after the first season, because I wanted to move on to something else and not get stuck in animation. The business is funny. If you stay too long in one thing, people start to buttonhole you there and say, 'You can't do anything else,' regardless of all your other credits."

Roddenberry believed that the animated series would be the first step in getting a *Star Trek* feature film made, but DeForest Kelley wasn't so sure. "I questioned it at the time," he explained back in the '70s, "and he said he was going to do it. I thought it was the death blow. Gene said, 'No, I don't feel that way at all. I think it's important to keep some form of *Star Trek* alive and in the minds of people." It's not the network, it's Paramount. The network wants the show again, and would love to have it back. But Paramount, the studio that owns *Star Trek*, doesn't want to make *Star Trek* prime time because they're making so much money in syndication with it. They feel they would be competing with themselves."

Opines James Doohan, "[The animated series] is forgotten. I think it was ordinary. It was ordinarily drawn. It was fun doing it because I did three characters and in ten of the episodes I did four. I pushed for that, because once you did more than three they had to double your pay. Strangely enough, I didn't use any accents. I just changed the tone of my voice. It's kind of like being back in radio again. Also the very fact we did it and made a little money. We certainly hadn't made any on the series because the residuals ran out in April 1971. The unions remedied that situation because of *Star Trek*, absolutely. They never thought any show would run like *Star Trek* has run."

One person not included in the animated series was Walter Koenig. "I was upset about the way I found out about the series," admits the actor. "It was at a convention. Everybody thought someone else had told me apparently. Dorothy thought Gene had, Gene thought Dorothy had. Apparently to save money, Filmation wanted to have Majel do Uhura's voice and Jimmy do Sulu's voice—this because in cartoons at the time you got paid one check to do two character voices. To Leonard's credit, he said he would not do the series unless they hired George and Nichelle since they had been there from the beginning. I wrote a script for it and in fact they asked me to write another one, but I wasn't interested since I was still upset over not being part of the series."

Twenty two episodes were produced in all, and, for the most part, Fontana's efforts in securing the finest possible talent paid off. Those scripts, penned by Fontana herself as well as veterans from the old show and the genre, proved themselves to be quite literate, and certainly a bright spot on the Saturday morning schedule. Unfortunately, like its predecessor, *Star Trek: Animated* was cancelled prematurely, with Roddenberry and the original cast once again going their separate ways, apparently forever.

The Cast

Prior to *Star Trek*, William Shatner had carved an impressive niche for himself as an actor, having scored quite successfully on stage, screen and television. Incredibly, his most difficult time came immediately after his three year-stint on *Star Trek*, following a divorce which left him in a precarious financial position.

"There was a time, before *Star Trek*, when I wouldn't accept a role that I didn't think worthwhile enough to play. Then, because things are so cyclical in show business, I needed to take those roles," Shatner explained in his autobiography, *Where No Man*. "There even came a point when I thought—I don't know whether I'm ever going to break through—

*William Shatner in one of his early post-*Star Trek *films,* The Devil's Rain.

• • • •

Leonard Nimoy co-starred with Donald Sutherland and Brooke Adams in the remake of Invasion of the Body Snatchers

to get those roles that I think I should be playing. That was just before *Star Trek. Star Trek* hit. And after *Star Trek* I've had the opportunity to play a few of those things that I thought should be coming my way. But, I was in a financial bind and had to accept a lot of things that I wouldn't have done in an earlier day."

Following the release of *Star Trek: The Motion Picture*, Shatner's fortune would take a definite upswing, leaving the tumultuous '70s behind him.

Leonard Nimoy, who would have seemingly been the most typecast from *Star Trek*, had actually gone on to the most successful career of all the cast members during the ten year period between cancellation and revival. He immediately shifted from *Star Trek* to a co-starring role in the hit series *Mission: Impossible*, on which he played make-up genius Paris. "I thought it was an opportunity to do a wide variety of characters so that I would, perhaps, become better known as a character actor rather than a Spock actor," he said in *The Star Trek Interview Book*. "It didn't really work out that way, in fact, but that was one of the reasons for doing that show."

Nimoy quit the series after three seasons to pursue other roles. "Quitting the show was kind of a dangerous thing to do, but I felt confident," he admitted. "But '71 was the first year out of six years of TV series and it

turned out to be a perfect year with a mix of all the things I wanted to do." Among them was the film *Catlow* and the lead in the national touring company of *Fiddler on the Roof*. Eventually his career led him to tackle another "logical" character, that of Sherlock Holmes on stage.

In addition, he began directing episodic television, narrated the syndicated series *In Search of....* and received acclaim for his one-man-show *Vincent*, based on the life of Vincent van Gogh, as well as for the books of poetry he wrote (including one called *I Am Not Spock*) and his Broadway role in *Equus*. Prior to the filming of *Star Trek: The Motion Picture*, he starred in Phil Kaufman's remake of *Invasion of the Body Snatchers*, which he described as "a frightening aspect of image-making modeled on preferred roles that people play as dictated by the media." Naturally it would be his return as Spock that would garner the most attention, and ultimately lead to a fruitful directing career.

DeForest Kelley has the most easy to summarize post-*Star Trek* career of anyone: he did a feature film entitled *Night of the Lepus*, about giant killer bunnies, and retired, with the exception of the animated *Trek* spinoff and feature films.

James Doohan made a comfortable living for himself throughout the '70s via the *Star Trek* convention circuit, as well as roles in such films as *Pretty Maids All in a Row* (produced by Roddenberry) and as a regular on the CBS Saturday morning series *Jason of Star Command`*, which he left after one season. "They really didn't give me anything to do so I said, 'Goodbye.'"

George Takei certainly diversified following *Star Trek*. Not only did he make appearances on a variety of television series, but he wrote a pair of science-fiction/swashbuckler novels and threw his hat into the Los Angeles political arena.

Nichelle Nichols parlayed her *Star Trek* success as Lieutenant Uhura into a singing career, and a position with NASA and its astronaut recruitment drive. "When I began," she pointed out, "NASA had 1,500 applications. Six months later, they had 8,000. I like to think some of those were encouraged by me. I did a

lot of traveling, speaking to universities, to professional and minority and women's groups, sometimes just to one person I found to be a particularly good prospect. The aim was to find qualified people among women and minorities, then to convince them that the opportunity was real and that it also was a duty, because this was historic. I really had this sense of purpose about it myself."

Walter Koenig, like his costars, did his fair share of episodic television work following his two seasons as Chekov, and even co-starred in the Gene Roddenberry television pilot, *The Questor Tapes*. Additionally, he served as an acting teacher, directed plays, wrote novels and penned the scripts for such primetime television fare as *Family* and *The Class of '65*.

It's unlikely that the ensemble could have known in 1969 that their lives would continue to be drawn together over the next two and a half decades, fueling a phenomenon that has just celebrated its 25th anniversary.

Gene Roddenberry

For the fans of the little science fiction show that refused to die, it probably seemed as though Gene Roddenberry came out of nowhere when *Star Trek* premiered, and had done nothing from the show's cancellation in 1969 until the release of *Star Trek: The Motion Picture* a decade later. Nobody can say the guy didn't try.

Roddenberry, who prior to *Star Trek* had worked on westerns, police

James Doohan spent one season co-starring in the Saturday morning series, Jason of Star Command

shows and even produced a show about the Marines called *The Lieutenant*, did his best to equal the ultimate success of *Trek*. His feature film *Pretty Maids All in a Row* was a disappointment, and his efforts to create a realistic version of *Tarzan* never got beyond the scripting stages. His supernatural television pilot *Spectre* went nowhere, and a proposed film project with Paul McCartney fell to the wayside when the revival of *Star Trek* seemed to be becoming a reality.He did, however, manage to create a pair of television pilots that came *this* close to becoming weekly series: *Genesis II* and *The Questor Tapes*.

Shortly after these tentative series were cancelled, the word from Paramount was that there might indeed be some kind of revival of *Star Trek*.

The Trek Begins Anew

Roddenberry was given his old office at the studio and told to write a movie script for a low-budget feature film.

"They turned me down a couple of times," Roddenberry said, "then finally they said, 'Write a script and we'll give you an office on the lot and think about it.' They were not that serious about [it] when we first started. I think they had in mind a $2-$3 million picture. We debated a long time whether it would be a two-hour TV film or a movie for theatrical release. I didn't want to do it for television. When the original *Star Trek* ended, Paramount thought it had a real loser on its hands, a stinker. Oh, they'd make a couple of bucks on reruns but they *knew* the show would never amount to much. They destroyed all the sets. Everything. Even Spock's ears. I felt that for TV, the limited budget allowed just would not suffice for the rebuilding of the sets and of the Enterprise. It would be the same quality as on the old show and, after all these years, I felt that they wouldn't be good enough. They said, 'Okay, we'll do a theatrical release. Go write a script.'"

Although little is known about the resulting script, entitled *The God Thing*, reports have stated that the premise questioned the very nature of God and the universe around us.

Paramount was apparently not interested in a script which, essentially, pit Captain Kirk against God.

Director Richard Colla, who had helmed *The Questor Tapes* TV movie pilot, was very familiar with that particular screenplay, and recalls it fondly.

"That script was much more daring," he says. "They went off in search of that thing from outer space that was affecting everything. By the time they got on to the spaceship and got into its [the alien's] presence, it manifested itself and said, 'Do you know me?' Kirk said, 'No, I don't know who you are.' It said, 'Strange, how could you not know who I am?' So it shift-changed and became another image and said, 'Do you know me?' Kirk said, 'No, who are you?' It replied, 'The time has passed, and you should know me by now.' It shifts shapes again, and comes up in the form of Christ the Carpenter, and says, 'Do you know me?' And Kirk said, 'Oh, now I know who you are.' And he says, 'How strange you didn't know these other forms of me.' Really, what Gene had written was that this 'thing' was sent forth to lay down the law; to communicate the law of the universe, and that as time goes on the law needs to be reinterpreted. And at that time 2,000 years ago, the law was interpreted by this Carpenter image. As time went on, the law was meant to be reinterpreted, and the Christ figure was meant to reappear in different forms. But this machine malfunctioned, and it was like a phonograph record that got caught in a groove, and kept grooving back, grooving back, grooving back. It's important to understand the essence of all this and reinterpret it as time goes on. That was a little heavy for Paramount. It was meant to be strong and moving, and I'm sorry it never got made."

"I handed them a script and they turned it down," Roddenberry stated matter of factly in 1980. "It was too controversial. It talked about concepts like, 'Who is God?' [In it] the Enterprise meets God in space; God is a life form, and I wanted to suggest that there may have been, at one time in the human beginning, an alien entity that early man believed was God, and kept those legends. But I also wanted to suggest that that might have been as much the Devil

as it was God. After all, what kind of god would throw humans out of Paradise for eating the fruit of the Tree of Knowledge? One of the Vulcans on board, in a very logical way, says, 'If this is your God, he's not very impressive. He's got so many psychological problems, he's so insecure. He demands worship every seven days. He goes out and creates faulty humans and then blames them for his own mistakes. He's a pretty poor excuse for a Supreme Being.' Not surprisingly, that didn't send the Paramount executives off crying with glee. But I think good science fiction, historically, has been used that way—to question *everything*.

"[Anyway,] the movie then sagged for quite some time," he continued. "It really got bogged down. I didn't hear anything for over three months. Meanwhile, unknown to me, the executives then in charge were interviewing writers, accepting outlines. I found out about all this quite by accident. None of the outlines were accepted. I think the main reason for all the problems with those scripts rested in the fact that most of the people making decisions concerning the film knew little or nothing about *Star Trek*. As it turned out later on, several of the principals had never even seen the show."

Despite this statement to the contrary, according to *The Making of Star Trek: The Motion Picture*, some script activity took place between Paramount's rejection of *The God Thing* and their soliciting story ideas from other writers.

Jon Povill, who would eventually go on to be story editor of the proposed *Star Trek II* television series and associate producer of the first film, had worked with Gene Roddenberry as a researcher for what was then planned to be a novelization of *The God Thing*.

"Gene went to work on that script in May of 1975," details Povill, "and it was his first attempt at a *Star Trek* feature. By August it was shitcanned by [Paramount President] Barry Diller. Gene, who had gotten to know me pretty well by then, suggested that I take a crack at writing a treatment, which I did."

The resulting treatment dealt with the people of planet Vulcan going mad, and the Enterprise's mad-dash

• • • •

through time to set things right by combatting a psychic-cloud that is affecting the population. It, too, was rejected.

The studio's search for the proper vehicle to launch the first *Star Trek* film began around this time, with those writers approached including John D.F. Black, who has served as story editor of the original show's first season and penned "The Naked Time," and then wrote the story for the "Justice" episode of *The Next Generation*; famed author Harlan Ellison, whose sole contribution to the show had been its most popular episode, "City on the Edge of Forever;" and science fiction veteran Robert Silverberg.

John D.F. Black describes the storyline he pitched with a good-natured shrug. Something in his voice conveys the feeling that he still can't believe the way the studio handled the proposed film.

"I came up with a story concept involving a black hole," recounts Black, "and this was *before* Disney's film. The black hole had been used by several planets in a given constellation as a garbage dump. But with a black hole there's a point of equality. In other words, when enough positive matter comes into contact with an equal amount of negative matter, the damn thing blows up. Well, if that ever occurs with a black hole, it's the end of the universe—it'll swallow everything. The Enterprise discovered what's happened with this particular black hole and they try to stop these planets from unloading into it. The planets won't do it. It comes to war in some areas and, as a result, the black hole comes to balance and blows up. At that point, it would continue to chew up matter. In one hundred and six years Earth would be swallowed by this black hole, and the Enterprise is trying to beat the end of the world. There were at least twenty sequels in that story because the jeopardy keeps growing more intense."

Paramount rejected the idea. "They said it wasn't big enough," Black notes wryly.

In his excellent nonfiction assessment of horror and science fiction, *Danse Macabre*, Stephen King reported the rumor that Harlan Ellison went to Paramount with the idea of the Enterprise breaking through the end of the universe and confronting God himself. And that wasn't big enough either.

Ellison gave Stephen King a little more information on his story meeting with Paramount.

"It involved going to the end of the known universe to slip back through time to the Pleistocene period when man first emerged," he said. "I postulated an alien intelligence from a far galaxy where the snakes had become the dominant life form, and a snake-creature who had come to Earth in the *Star Trek* future, had seen its ancestors wiped out, and who had gone back into the far past of Earth to set up distortions in the time-flow so the reptiles could beat the humans. The Enterprise goes back to set time right, finds the snake-alien, and the human crew is confronted with the moral dilemma of whether it had the right to wipe out an entire life form just to insure its own territorial imperative in our present and future. The story, in short, spanned all of time and all of space, with a moral and ethical problem."

Paramount executive Barry Trabulus "listened to all this and sat silently for a few minutes," Ellison elaborated. "Then he said, 'You know, I was reading this book by a guy named Von Daniken and he proved that the Mayan calendar was exactly like ours, so it must have come from aliens. Could you put in some Mayans?'"

The writer pointed out that there were no Mayans at the dawn of time, but the executive brushed this off, pointing out that no one would know the difference.

"'I'm to know the difference,'" he exploded. "'It's a dumb suggestion.' So Trabulus got very uptight and said he liked Mayans a lot and why didn't I do it if I wanted to write this picture. So I said, 'I'm a writer. I don't know what the fuck you are!' And I got up and walked out. And that was the end of my association with the *Star Trek* movie."

The Robert Silverberg story, entitled *The Billion Year Voyage*, was more of an intellectual foray as the Enterprise crew discovered the ruins of an ancient, but far more advanced, civilization, and must battle other aliens in order to take possession of the wondrous gifts left behind; gifts which would surely benefit mankind some day in the future when he is ready to accept that responsibility.

This trio of stories were fascinating attempts at reviving the show, and it seems unimaginable that all of them were turned down. The revival game was destined to continue for some time to come.

Ten Years And Counting

By 1976, *Star Trek* was celebrating its ten year anniversary, and the show's fan following was continuously growing larger, with the demand for a new film or television series growing more vehement. It had been seven years since the last new episode, and the only difference was that the idea of reviving the show, in one format or another, was actually being considered by Paramount.

If any attempt to do so seemed likely to happen, it would probably be the one initiated in July of 1976. Jerry Eisenberg was hired as producer, with Phil (*Invasion of the Body Snatchers, The Right Stuff*) Kaufman directing. Scripting were a pair of English writers named Allan Scott and Chris Bryant, whose credits included *Don't Look Now* and *Joseph Andrews*. Their experience in science fiction was non-existent, but what they lacked in knowledge, they made up for in enthusiasm, and a willingness to learn.

Kaufman, in particular, was thrilled with the prospect of being involved. "George Lucas is a good friend of mine," he had told one reporter. "He told me before he made *Star Wars* he'd made inquiries as to whether *Star Trek* was available to be bought. I thought George had a great thing going. When I was asked if I would be interested in doing *Star Trek*, well...I felt I could go through the roof."

In addition to all of this, the original cast had essentially been signed to reprise their original roles, with the exception of Leonard Nimoy, who, at the time, had refused all interviews pertaining to *Star Trek*. William Shatner, however, had no problem in discussing the situation.

"Leonard Nimoy has a beef, and it's a legitimate one," Shatner said in 1976. "It's about the merchandising and it's something that irks me as well. Our faces appear on products all over the country, all over the world, and we've not really been compensated fairly for it. Leonard was walking in London, England. He stopped to look at a billboard. The billboard's divided into three sections. The first section is Leonard's face with the ears—Spock—the ears are drooping. The second section of the billboard has Leonard, with the drooping ears, holding a tankard of ale. The third section has an empty tankard of ale, and Leonard's face, with pointed ears straight up in the air. So Leonard and I have had this battle, with whoever licenses *Star Trek*, for a long time. I mean, kids are walking around with my face on their shirts. Occasionally I see a postcard with my face on it. People are exploiting us. So anyway, Leonard goes back to the studio and says, 'There's a demeaning billboard of me out there. Did you guys okay it?' So he goes to his lawyer and tries to sue. Right now Paramount wants Leonard, and Leonard wants fair recompense. It's only reasonable that Paramount meet his demands. Something has happened here. Someone has made a lot of money from the show, and the people who were the show have seen very little of it. I think Leonard is totally in the right."

While Nimoy would eventually agree to do this attempt to resurrect *Star Trek*, the format would again be changed and he would, again, drop out.

The Scott/Bryant screenplay opens with the Enterprise investigating a distress signal sent from the USS DaVinci. By the time they arrive in that quadrant of space, the other starship is gone. Suddenly, Kirk's brain is struck by electromagnetic waves, which results in erratic behavior and his commandeering a shuttlecraft. He pilots it towards an invisible planet and disappears. Three years later, Spock leads an expedition back to that area of space, and they discover what they believe to be the planet of the Titans, an ancient, but highly advanced race which had been thought extinct. Problem is that the planet is being drawn towards a black hole, and it becomes a race against time between the Federation and the Klingons, who are both interested in that particular world. The one who saves the planet will receive the fruits of their knowledge.

On the planet's surface, Spock discovers Kirk, who has been living there as a wild man. However, the captain is

ILLOGICAL

Heineken. Refreshes the parts other beers cannot reach.

This advertisement raised the ire of Leonard Nimoy, who launched a lawsuit against Paramount Pictures for using his likeness without paying a royalty.

restored to normal in short order, and together they discover that the planet is actually populated by the evil Cygnans, a race which had destroyed the Titans. The story concluded with Kirk, in an effort to destroy the hostile Cygnans, ordering the Enterprise *into* the black hole. As Susan Sackett noted in *The Making of Star Trek: The Motion Picture*, "During the trip through the black hole, the Cygnans are destroyed and the Enterprise emerges in orbit around Earth. But it is Earth at the time of the Cro-Magnan man, the dawn of humanity. The ancient Titans, it would seem, were the men of the Enterprise."

Jon Povill, who had shifted into the background as Gene Roddenberry's assistant, noted the project with interest, though he wasn't convinced it was right for *Star Trek*'s debut on the movie screen.

"It was an interesting script in a certain sort of way," Povill explains. "It was not Star Trek. People would have gone to see it, and it would have done as well as we did with *Star Trek: The Motion Picture*, but it's just as well that it didn't get made. Chris and Alan even felt that it was something that wasn't quite successful. They didn't feel they had brought off a script that was just right. They didn't feel confident about it. Then Phil Kaufman decided that he wanted to take a run at the script. His treatment was, I think, worse than the script. Then the whole thing kind of fell apart."

Reflects Allan Scott, "The difficulty for us was trying to make, as it

were, an exploded episode of *Star Trek* that had its own justifications in terms of the new scale that was available to it, because much of the show's charm was the fact that it dealt with big and bold ideas on a small budget, and of course the first thing that a movie would do, potentially, was match the budget and scale of the production to the boldness and vigor of the ideas. Of course we spent weeks looking at every episode of *Star Trek*, and I would guess that more or less every member of the cast came by and met us.

"We were surprised that it didn't go, because it seemed that it would. It was absolutely a 'go' picture. But it was a very exciting project to be involved with. I'm sorry it didn't work, because we would have enjoyed it even more if it had. We had a lot of fun and it was really an enjoyable time. I don't feel unhappy about it at all. It was just one of those deals that happens at studios from time to time that fell down the middle."

Phil Kaufman's reaction to the cancellation of the film was not quite so idealistic. "We were dealing with important things," he said. "Things that George [Lucas] has a smattering of in *Star Wars*. We were dealing a lot with Olaf Stapledon. There were chapters in *Last and First Men* that I was basing *Star Trek* on. That was my key thing. Gene and I disagreed on what the nature of a feature film really is. He was still bound by the things that he had been forced into by lack of money and by the fact that those times were not into science fiction the way they are now. Gene has a very set way of looking at things. My feeling always was that he was anchored in a 10-year-old TV show which would not translate for a feature audience ten years later with all that had been done and could potentially be done in a feature scope. For years I had walked around San Francisco with George Lucas talking about what *he* was doing. I knew what the potential of this kind of stuff was."

Perhaps most shocking to him was the feeling that Paramount canceled the film because of the success of *Star Wars*, which was released in May of 1977, and the belief that they had blown their opportunity at the box office. "They didn't even wait to see what STAR WARS would do," Kaufman said incredulously. "I don't think they tried to understand what the phenomenon of *Star Trek* was."

"We considered the project for years," summed up then Paramount president Barry Diller. "We've done a number of treatments, scripts, and everytime we'd say, 'This isn't good enough.' If we had just gone forward and *done* it, we might have done it quite well. In this case [the Scott/Bryant/Kaufman version], it was the script. We felt, frankly, that it was a little pretentious. We went to Gene Roddenberry and said: 'Look, you're the person who really understands *Star Trek*. We don't. But what we should probably do is return to the original context, a television series.' If you force it as a big 75 millimeter widescreen movie, you go directly against the concept. If you rip *Star Trek* off, you'll fail, because the people who like *Star Trek* don't just like it. They love it."

So, once again, the Enterprise's destiny was being charted towards the television screen, although no one had any idea—though they should have suspected—that she would never complete the voyage.

TV Trek-Take 2

And the Earth shook. If it didn't, then it must have been a movement of damn near equal proportion to the fans of a little television series they had had

refused to let die. They had taken "control" of the show's destiny by generating an unprecedented amount of enthusiasm, resulting in a phenomenon whose closest relative was probably Beatlemania circa 1964. They gathered together at conventions, met their idols, penned original fiction dedicated to the characters and ideals of the show and never stopped hoping for the day when it would be resurrected on either television or the movie screen. In the middle of 1977, it seemed as though their efforts had finally borne fruit: *Star Trek* was returning to television.

After numerous attempts to bring the show back as either a feature film, television movie or weekly series, it finally seemed that a revival would come to pass. The original cast, with the exception of Leonard Nimoy, who for career and litigation reasons did not wish to play the role of Spock on a weekly basis, had actually been signed to reprise their most famous roles, scripts were being developed and sets constructed for the brand new starship Enterprise. Everything was coming together, allowing *Star Trek* to touch a new generation in the same way as it had the previous one.

For some time, Paramount Pictures had dreamed of starting a fourth network to compete with the three majors, much as the Dumont Network did during television's Golden Age. To this end, they contacted independent stations all over the United States and began offering product to fill one night a week with new programming, cornerstoned by the series entitled *Star Trek II*.

Robert Goodwin had been with Paramount Pictures for two years. Originally he was assistant to Arthur Fellows, who, in turn, was the Senior Vice President in charge of television production and had taken over Playboy Enterprises, whose name had been changed to Playboy-Paramount. Goodwin spent approximately one year as the Director of Development.

"Then a guy named Gary Nardino came in and took over as President of Paramount Television, and made the decision to start a fourth network," Goodwin details. "The plan was that every Saturday night they were going to do one hour of *Star Trek* and then a two hour movie. My interest had always

been more in the long form rather than the series side of television. Nardino decided that he was going to put me in charge of all these two hour movies, which was great for me."

At that point, forces were at work which would pull Goodwin away from this choice assignment and bring him over to Roddenberry's team. Meanwhile, Roddenberry himself grew more vibrant with each passing day, as a seven year battle to bring *StarTrek* back seemed at an end, and he was essentially being given the opportunity to top himself, although he never really looked at it that way.

"Those [original] episodes will always be there for what people want to make out of them," he told *Starlog* at the time. "We're making a new set of them ten years later under very different circumstances. I think neither takes away from the other. The worst that can happen is someone would say that Roddenberry couldn't do it a second time. That doesn't bother me, as long as I did my damndest to do it a second time."

What was truly exciting to him was the opportunity to deal with different social issues in a new and fresh style, as television had been altered considerably by such series as *M*A*S*H* and *All in the Family*. Gone were the days when you *had* to hide your ideas within entertainment, for fear that network censors would not allow the show on the air. Things had changed to such a degree, that television was actually *challenged* to express itself in new and different ways.

"Dialogue is more naturalistic on television today," Roddenberry explained. "Direction is more sophisticated. There are better methods of optical effects. There are better methods for special effects. The audience is certainly more sophisticated and able to reach their minds out further. The audience is ready for statements on sex, religion, politics and so on, which we never would have dared to make before."

Star Trek II was envisioned as a dream come true, and efforts were made to secure the proper creative team. First choice was the aforementioned Robert Goodwin as producer.

"They were looking for someone to come on as producer," says

Goodwin, "and Gene Roddenberry had heard about me. To be perfectly honest, I wasn't anxious to do it. My real interest, as I said, was the long form, and I was supposed to supervise all those two hour movies. I was pretty much strong-armed to do it, and not given too much of a choice. Paramount said, 'Forget the two hour movies, you're doing *Star Trek*.' So I went over to see Gene and initially I got kicked out of his office. His assistant, Susan Sackett, thought I was an agent or something, and she didn't know that I had an appointment to see him. She wouldn't let me in, and I said, 'Fine,' and walked out. I was about a half a mile away at the other side of the studio, when Gene Roddenberry came running after me. To make a long story short, he wanted me to go in as one of the two producers. They were going to hire a writing producer and a production producer. It was kind of a strange situation."

Roddenberry found his "writing producer" in Harold Livingston, novelist and television writer.

"I had never met Roddenberry," admits Livingston, "but I think I was working at Paramount at the time. Bob Goodwin and I were both going to work under Gene. If I remember correctly, there were a lot of interviews and bullshit that went on, but Gene and I kind of hit it off. We had similar backgrounds. We had both been in the Air Force during the war and we both worked for civilian airlines after the war, so I think that's one of the reasons that Gene, in the beginning, liked me.

"I had never paid much attention to *Star Trek*," he smiles sheepishly. "I'd always considered it something of a media event. I was totally unwashed. Anyway, the object of the new series was very vague. All they knew was that the studio had some kind of arrangement with what was then going to be a fourth network. I suppose it would take the form of some kind of syndicated program. So thirteen episodes plus a pilot were ordered, and it was then my job to develop these stories, which I set upon doing."

To this end, he began to utilize Jon Povill, Gene Roddenberry's assistant.

"I wanted Jon Povill to be my story editor," Livingston explains, "and Gene wanted him to continue cleaning his

garage or something, so we had a big thing about that. I eventually got my way."

"Harold was primarily responsible for getting me the story editor job," concurs Povill. "Gene was reluctant to move me 'that far, that fast,' to use his words. Harold was adamant that I was doing the job of a story editor and, by God, I should be getting paid as one."

"Harold had not been very familiar with the old series at all," he continues, "and kind of relied on me to be the monitor of whether something fit with *Star Trek* or not. Once everything got rolling, and we were in a lot of writer's meetings, I sort of took over as the person who pointed out where there were holes in the stories, and where they did not conform to what *Star Trek* was supposed to be."

Rounding out the early cast of behind the scenes characters, was Jim Rugg, a veteran from the original series who was to handle the special effects, and production designer Joe Jennings. Matt Jeffries, who had designed the original Enterprise, but was, at the moment, tied up on *Little House on the Prairie*, would serve as technical consultant.

On July 15, 1977, Gene Roddenberry issued a memo telling the production crew that they needed to come up with a new bible for potential writers. Bob Goodwin, Harold Livingston, Jon Povill and several others began making contributions to this item, which had proved a successful tool during the course of the original series. The "bible" which eventually evolved, stated that the series would chronicle the second five year mission of the Enterprise. While in drydock following its initial mission, the vessel had been completely refurbished.

James T. Kirk, we learn, has refused a promotion to admiral so that he can command the starship on its newest voyage. All of his original crew have been reassigned to him, with the exception of Mr. Spock, who has "returned in high honor to Vulcan to head the Science Academy there." In updating the series and attempting to fill the void created by Spock's absence, three new characters were added and hopes were high that actor Leonard Nimoy would frequently reprise his role of Spock for guest appearances.

The guide detailed the intricacies

of the Enterprise's weapon and defense abilities, followed by a character breakdown, focusing on the new additions.

Lt. Xon, a full Vulcan, has taken the place of Mr. Spock as ship science officer. This twenty year old, who is "a genius even by Vulcan standards," was destined to prove himself as capable as his predecessor. The primary difference between the two is that Xon has virtually no knowledge of the human equation, and realizes that the only way he will be able to equal Spock is by making an effort to touch his repressed emotions, thus allowing him to more fully relate to the crew. Roddenberry wrote that "we'll get some humor out of Xon trying to simulate laughter, anger, fear and other human feelings." Interesting to note is that the Spock-McCoy feud would have been carried over to Xon and the doctor, with the difference being that McCoy believes their "feud is a very private affair...and McCoy has been known to severely chastise (in private) those crewmen who have been unfair to the Vulcan in comparing his efforts to Spock's."

The second new character mentioned is Commander Will Decker, Enterprise first officer who is something of a young Captain Kirk. The son of Commodore Matt Decker, who met his demise tackling "The Doomsday Machine," he comes quite close to worshipping the captain, and would "literally rather die than fail him." This is in direct contrast to the somewhat antagonistic Kirk-Decker relationship demonstrated in *Star Trek: The Motion Picture*. Essentially Decker is a captain in training, and the idea was that the audience would watch his gradual growth during the five year mission. In many instances, he would lead landing parties, thus alleviating the perpetual logistical flaw of the initial *Star Trek* TV series: a ship's captain would never beam into potential danger as often as Kirk did, and it's a format change which would eventually be incorporated into *The Next Generation*.

The final new addition to the crew would have been Lieutenant Ilia, the bald Deltan, whose race is marked by a heightened sexuality that pervades every aspect of their society. Additionally, Ilia, as is common among her people, is abnormally intelligent, second, perhaps, only to Xon, and gifted with some rather unique esper abilities. As noted, "unlike the mind-meld of Vulcans, it simply is the ability to sense images in other minds. Never words or emotions, only images.shapes, sizes, textures. On her planet, sexual foreplay consists largely of lovers placing images in each other's minds." Like Decker, Ilia made it into the first feature film, and remained, essentially, as the guide depicted her.

These character profiles were followed by a breakdown of the original crew, an explanation of the standing sets, description of equipment and an explanation of terminology.

With the guide having been written, Harold Livingston began contacting writers and agents in an effort to get the first thirteen scripts in motion.

"I wanted to make *Star Trek* more universal," explains Livingston matter of factly. "I felt that success not withstanding, the show had a restrictive audience. There was a greater audience for this. I felt that almost all of the stories seemed to be allegorical, and I wanted to make them a little harder and a little more realistic. My broad intention was to create a series that would attract a larger audience by offering more. We would still offer the same elements that *Star Trek* did, i.e. science fiction and hope for the future, and do realistic stories.

"I just thought they had reached a certain barrier with it," he continues. "How much could you do before it becomes totally redundant, and then where do you go? I wanted to bring it down to Earth...figuratively. They had so many stories which, to manipulate or move the plot, this goofy thing appeared out of nowhere. I'm thinking specifically of some Greek with an echoing voice that came on and saved them. That was done too often. And I simply also wanted scripts that were interesting and made sense and moved from a literary standpoint. I felt that too much of that was neglected or overlooked, because they had their science fiction themes. I wanted to do both, although I don't know if it would have worked. I have a great fear of these cultist series-films, because they're really self defeating in the end. You're going to have a limited audience. That

was my feeling, right or wrong."

Famed science fiction author Norman Spinrad wrote to Harold Livingston regarding a story the two men had discussed, that essentially dealt with the search for ultimate knowledge as well as personality changes in some of our crewmembers, some of which pick up traits of the others

On August 4, Gene Roddenberry referred to the story by saying, "We could use any ideas [which] might make this story work. Spinrad is brilliant and he is onto the right thing." Negatively speaking, he noted that the production probably couldn't afford the maze as described in the story. "Also," he explained, "it is largely a two-man story with them interacting with a 'hidden power.' It is hardly action adventure. The jeopardy is mostly intellectual."

The entire *Star Trek II* company was very excited by Spinrad's full treatment which came later on. Roddenberry in particular was extremely positive, suggesting that perhaps the alien power could sway the Enterprise crew over by offering to give the individual whatever it was they desired most. This, he pointed out, was similar, but different to the premise of the original show's first season episode, "The Naked Now." Interestingly enough, the idea of trying to sway the crew by offering them whatever they desire, was picked up in the "Hide and Q" episode of the new series.

"I don't remember where the idea came from," Spinrad admits, "except that I've always been fascinated with the high-mind concept, which I have dealt with in books. It would have made a great TV piece, because it's all in the acting. They all take on each other's characteristics, which .is something really weird and strange, that wouldn't be as interesting in a novel, but would as a film or play. Something oral. Something with acting."

Several sub-standard script ideas caused Roddenberry to note, "Apparently the past has a way of repeating itself. During our first three years, a principal problem in most story ideas received was that they usually presented our captain and crew with no particular *jeopardy* or *need*. In other words, it is not sufficient for a story idea merely to have

our people in starship running into something interesting while out in space. In fact, it is not even sufficient to have them run into merely something fascinating!

"The above is why the typical story of 'two interesting civilizations' rarely works out," added Roddenberry. "Too often a writer thinks he has brought in enough if there are needs created for other characters in the story. This simply doesn't work. Yes, we want our *Star Trek* story to involve fascinating things we meet out there, but those fascinating things *must* create an important need for one or more of our characters. That need can be for something to happen—or something *not* to happen. That need should grow steadily more and more important so story moves toward climax. Also, the resolution of that need must grow more and more impossible. Admittedly, all this is fairly elemental and stuff every writer knows. But I think that *all* of us (including yours truly) often tend to forget it when doing science fiction."

One of the writers contacted was Alan Dean Foster, author of numerous genre novels, including the *Star Trek Log* series for Ballantine Books.

Foster adapted a Roddenberry *Genesis II* story idea to the *Star Trek* format."Robot's Return" dealt with a space probe returning to Earth after hundreds of years, and in search of its creator NASA. "In Thy Image" took this basic premise and placed it in the *Star Trek* universe, enlarging the overall threat along the way as Kirk and company must save the entire planet from this deadly machine.

"At that point," interjects Bob Goodwin, "they had spent about four years trying to get a script for a feature, but they couldn't come up with anything that Michael Eisner liked. We had various options on the two hour premiere [which would be released theatrically in Europe], and I suggested to Gene that since it had never been done in the series before, we should come up with a story in which Earth was threatened. In all the *Star Trek* episodes before, they never came close to Earth. 'In Thy Image' fit that criteria perfectly. I remember that one day we went into the administration building. In there was Michael Eisner, Jeff Katzenberg, Gary Nardino, me, Gene and a bunch of other people. In the course of that meeting, I got up and pitched this two-hour story. Michael Eisner slammed his hands on the table and said, 'We've spent four years looking for a feature script. This is it. Now let's make the movie.'"

The plan still called for a two hour television film, but no one in that room realized that the groundwork had just been laid down for *Star Trek: The Motion Picture.*

The Meeting

The atmosphere of that meeting, held on August 3, 1977, was a combination of joy and sobriety. On the one hand it was proof that *Star Trek* was very much alive in Paramount's eyes, and on the other it revealed how problematic resurrecting the show actually was.

Meeting with Michael Eisner, Jeff Katzenberg and other key executives, Gene Roddenberry stated at the outset that he expected to have up to ten scripts in development within a two week time period. Michael Eisner felt that their primary concern must be the two hour opening episode for the simple reason that it would kick off the new series and tap into the "enormous amount of worldwide potential in the first return of *Star Trek.* A February 1st answer print is vital, and the film must be superb."

While Roddenberry agreed with this, his general feeling was that the more stories they get into development, the wider their choice of an opening story. "The intention," he said, "is to give the best material to top established writers."

Michael Eisner, without hesitation, pointed out that he had no problems with paying whatever writing cost was necessary to insure the best possible script. He even went so far as to state a willingness to pay up to two hundred thousand dollars. Another concern was the lack of director, although Gary [*The Black Hole*] Nelson was being talked to, with Bob Collins as a backup.

Eisner continued to emphasize how important it was for them to meet the February 1st date, and for the story to be finalized so preproduction could begin.

"We'd be kidding you if I didn't say we have some problems on the February 1st date, but we're hoping to overcome them," Roddenberry explained.

"Look," Eisner responded, "I'm willing to go with a three million dollar budget, if the script is good enough. I'm not encouraging extravagance, but I am concerned that we meet the target date and the film be visually fabulous. We need a writer who can make the characters come alive, with a terrific director and a terrific story."

Changing the subject for a moment, Gene Roddenberry admitted that he was bothered by the idea of tailoring the opening script to both William Shatner and Leonard Nimoy, as the latter would not be a part of the regular series. "I'd prefer to eliminate Nimoy completely," he said.

Eisner disagreed, stating that it was absolutely necessary for them to have both actors reprising their original roles, and that they must be signed even at unreasonable figures.

"I don't agree," countered Roddenberry. "I can almost promise us that the excitement generated by the return of *Star Trek* with most of the original crew, aided by a publicity campaign to hype excitement over the new, different type of Vulcan, would cancel out any disappointment over Nimoy's absence."

The Paramount chieftain would not accept this. The actor, he insisted again, must appear in the film, even if only briefly during the opening scenes. Both Roddenberry and Goodwin agreed, feeling that it would be a preferable way of handling the situation, because it would satisfy audience demand while at the same time allowing them the freedom to work with the new story and characters.

As stated earlier, one of the reasons that Nimoy did not wish to appear on the series stemmed back to a lawsuit launched because the actor felt he should be compensated for the money Paramount was making from his likeness on *Star Trek* merchandise. Gary Nardino explained that a deal had been offered to the actor which would include the opening film, select episodes and a settlement of his lawsuit against them. In response, Eisner said that he would be willing to pay the actor up to $100,000 for three days work, but the deal with Shatner should be closed first so as to keep his cost down.

"It's understood," he added, "that there's no interest in him for the series, although we may have to make a pay-or-play PTS [Paramount Television Service] commitment as incentive for the two hour film."

Roddenberry again stated that he was concerned about making the February 1st date, and Eisner explained that he was attempting to generate money abroad on the property before it went to television. Approval was given to put thirteen scripts into work for series delivery in March 1978, but no series problems/deadlines should affect the two hour film.

"There is only one priority at Paramount," Eisner stated emphatically. "*Star Trek.*"

Bringing New Life To An Old Show

In attempting to bring *Star Trek* back to audiences of the 1970s, the show found itself saddled with one particular problem that had to be overcome in order for the series to work effectively.

"The original series had seventy nine episodes," points out Jon Povill, "and therefore a lot of things had already been done. I think the biggest challenge was coming up with things that weren't repeats of ideas which had already been explored. What we were definitely striving for on the show was doing things that were different, and I think by and large we were successful. That was the biggest challenge, coming up with things that were fresh, and were *Star Trek* as well.

"I think we were helped out tremendously by the new characters. It's something that the features really need at this point. Someone has to start taking over. I think it's absolutely essential. They're all good people and they're just right for their parts, but if you don't start setting something up here, they're going to start...no offense to anybody...dying off. The characters of Xon, Decker and Ilia would have helped in this area. We wanted characters that could go in new directions, as well as the old crew.

"I particularly liked Xon," says Povill. "I thought there was something very fresh in having a nice young Vulcan to deal with; somebody who was trying to live up to a previous image. That, to me, was a very nice gimmick for a TV show that was missing Spock. But we *never* wanted Xon to be a Spock retread. We wanted him to be somebody who definitely had his own direction to go in, and he had different failings than Spock. Also, he didn't have Spock's neurosis regarding his human half. As far as Xon was concerned, Spock had a distinct *advantage* in being half-Vulcan and half-human in the context of where he was, what he was doing and where he was working. If he was on Vulcan, it wouldn't have been an advantage, but to be living with humans, it really helped. Xon's youth was also very important and he would have brought a freshness that people would have appreciated.

"Ilia was sort of an embodiment of warmth, sensuality, sensitivity and a nice Yin to Xon's Yang. Decker, of course, was a young Kirk. I think he would have been the least distinct. He would have had to grow, and the performance probably would have done that, bringing something to Decker that the writers would have ultimately latched on to for material. He's the one who would have had to develop more through the acting and performance than the other two. Xon and Ilia were concept characters. They would have developed too, I'm sure, because characters grow when they're performed much more than they do from just the writing. In the early writing, you don't realize the full potential. You don't know who's going to play the character, how they're going to play it and what the characteristics of their performance are going to be. If you look at 'The Menagerie,' for example, Spock laughs."

On August 9th, Roddenberry responded to Alan Dean Foster's one hour treatment of "In Thy Image."

"The principal problem in your *Star Trek* story outline is certainly not lack of imagination," he pointed out. "Rather, I believe, most of my comments will bear upon control and selective use of that imagination. *Believability* of characters, incidents and scenes is much more critical in picture/sound science fiction than in printed. Most of our story problem seems to boil down simply to getting to know our alien machine character better. Its abilities, limitations, motivations, needs, and so on. With all that

established, it should then be much easier to build a tale which rises steadily in excitement and jeopardies (to the starship *and* to Earth) to a very exciting and satisfying climax."

Ironically, this problem would plague the script even after it had metamorphosized into *Star Trek: The Motion Picture*, and it was a thematic trap that no one could extricate themselves from.

While Alan Dean Foster took Roddenberry's comments to heart and began to expand his outline, *Star Trek II* was coming to life on the Paramount soundstages. On August 9, Bob Goodwin filed his first production report.

"Work is continuing on stage 9," he explained, "with construction of the Enterprise set. All frames and platforms have been built for the bridge...By tomorrow we will have a lay-out on the stage floor for the corridor and by the beginning of next week we will start framing and constructing the corridor walls. Joe Jennings has worked out most of the design problems of the engineering room and has started working on drawings which will be ready for you to see by the end of the week. The plan now for stage 8, which will be used as the planet set is to put in the ground row and the backing, but to leave the dirt out until we see if we need that stage space for any extra sets that might needed for our first show."

As all this was developing, production designer Joseph Jennings was in the midst of creating the interior of a starship which would be completely unlike the rather primitive looking sets of the original *Star Trek*.

"I had been working at Paramount," explains Jennings, "and the Production Manager of Television called me in and said, 'How would you like the assignment?' We started preparing and that was about it. It was as simple as that."

In attempting to upgrade the ship from the original series, he says that the idea was to make the mechanics of the starship much more sophisticated. "The bridge of the Enterprise was designed to go into series, so we were designing it to be all things to all people. As a result, all of the devices were practical and they worked off proximity switches. You didn't have to touch the

board, but simply had to reach toward it and whatever effect you were tripping would show up. This was not for one specific show. What you're being asked to do is design a set that will function for at least three years of shows, so we were being a great deal more sophisticated than perhaps we would have been were it laid out to begin with as a feature film in which there were a certain given set of actions that had to be performed on that set. Then you only build those things that operate properly.

"When you talk about series," Jennings elaborates, "you don't know down the line what you're going to need. As a result, I wrote an operations manual for the bridge, which was intended to be given to guest directors who would come in and would not be familiar with the set, but in a matter of several days would have to come up with a working knowledge of it. So all of the stations and every switch, button and light flash was all spelt out as to what it did and what it was supposed to be. It was an attempt on my part to make the operation of the ship consistent from show to show. As I say, all of that effort and energy when it became a picture was superfluous. To be specific, directors walk in on the bridge of a spaceship and want every damn light winking and blinking, and now you get your spaceship in trouble and the meteor is coming. What do you add to it that's going to look dramatic? Besides, if you look on the instrument panel of any comparable vehicle we know, all of those lights aren't blinking all the time. So I thought perhaps by being very specific in making the thing operable, we could get a little more believability into it from that point of view."

On August 16th Harold Livingston filed a "writers status report," noting that those assigned included Arthur Heinemann, Alan Dean Foster, James Menzies, Margaret Armen, John Meredyth Lucas, Worley Thorne, Shimon Wincelberg and Theodore Sturgeon. Of them, only Sturgeon would not ultimately deliver a story.

In addition, Livingston met with a total of seventeen other writers, of which only Bill Lansford had a story which fit *Star Trek* requirements. Entitled "Devil's Due," the producer noted that he and Roddenberry had met with the author "concerning a story with Faustian overtones, a Devil and Daniel Webster conflict and we expect to assign Lansford after a final meeting."

While these meetings did not bear much fruit, Livingston was still quite pleased at the way things were progressing. "We find that these initial meetings are beneficial to writers," he said, "because despite the writer's guide and the two scripts we usually give as representative *Star Trek* scripts, it is always helpful when the writers discuss face to face and we explain our problems, requirements, standards and specifications. With almost no exception, writers have recontacted us and/or have reacted enthusiastically."

He added that the search had begun for a writer to flesh "In Thy Image" out to script form. His first choice, Steven Bochco (*Hill Street Blues, L.A. Law*) was unavailable and would be for several months. Two other names being considered were British author David Ambrose (who would ultimately pen the "Deadlock" script for the proposed series) and science fiction veteran William Norton. An attempt to interest Michael Cimino was unfruitful, which is probably just as well. Imagine *Heaven's Trek*.

"The problem with many name writers," Livingston opined, "is that we do not want to involve ourselves in a situation where we will sign a writer who will be tempted to 'write down' to the story. We must have someone who is actively into science fiction, namely *Star Trek*, and will be so enthusiastic he will give us the very best he has.

"After four weeks of developing stories," he closed, "talking to writers, word has come back to us now and it is very interesting to note that *Star Trek* is considered the 'hardest sell in town.' It is also considered perhaps the most prestigious credit a writer can receive. This, needless to say, we consider very encouraging. The result has been that we are very selective in our story material, and we feel that the stories we now have in work are the best possible stories we could find. Our status now is that we have eleven hours assigned. This includes two 2-hour versions. This would leave us with two one hour openings. We have request-

ed the purchase of an additional five back-up hours, and are anxiously awaiting approval on this request."

Bob Collins, in the meantime, had been signed to direct the opening episode, and began to help in the screen-test process to determine who would be most suited to portray the pair of alien characters, Xon and Ilia. He elected to begin with the Vulcan, and tested hundreds of actors in pointed ears before he spotted the one he felt most comfortable with to take over the science station from Mr. Spock.

"I found an actor named David Gautreaux to play Xon," Collins recalls. "He was a nice young man and a terrific actor, and all of that would have worked, although there was some concern over how people would react to the fact that there was no Spock."

That was a question which crossed quite a few minds.

The Man Who Would Be Xon

Although the general public may not be aware of it, actor David Gautreaux was a part of the *Star Trek II* company for over a year. In fact, plans still called for him to play the role even when the TV series metamorphosized into the first feature film. But then Leonard Nimoy was signed on as Spock, and Xon was dropped at Gautreaux's request.

"I was doing a play at the time," he reflects, "trying not to think that I was going to be playing an alien for the rest of my life. Then I spoke to Gene Roddenberry and said, 'What's the story? Did you see that Leonard Nimoy is coming back to play his character? What's going to happen to Xon?' He said, 'Oh, Xon is very much a part of the family and you're very much a part of our family.' I responded, 'Gene, don't allow a character of this magnitude to simply carry Mr. Spock's suitcases on board the ship and then say, "I'll be in my quarters if anybody needs me." Give him what I've put into him and what you've put into him. If he's not going to be more a part of it and more noble than that, let's eliminate him.' They continued with the idea of Xon for quite a while."

Gautreaux's involvement began

Actor David Gautreaux as Xon, the character designed to take over the science officer position from Spock in the Star Trek II *television series.*

when he screentested for the role with hundreds of others and was chosen for the part. This occurred several months before preproduction on *Star Trek II* had begun, thus scripts for the series had been written and preparations made for the two hour premiere movie.

Upon being announced as *Star Trek*'s newest Vulcan, he felt that there were two things that had to be done. The first was for Paramount to downplay his signing aboard, with a bare minimum of publicity. The second was that he purchase a television and learn what the phenomenon was all about. The actor explains his views on both points.

"I remember when I was first cast as Xon," Gautreaux reflects. "A fair amount of the fans reacted very strangely. Somebody recently told me that actors in soap operas place themselves in serious jeopardy if they antagonize the favorite character of the show. They, the actor on the street, can be the object of the fans' wrath. That does happen in this business. When *Star Trek II* was announced and I was essentially the replacement for Spock, I received some really strange letters from people saying, 'Don't drink the water,' or somebody was going to drop LSD in my Coca-Cola. It was like poison pen letters, because Spock was God to these people.

"I personally was never a fan," explains Gautreaux. "I never watched the show. I bought a television two weeks after I was actually signed for the role, because I was given an advance large enough to actually do something like that. I was a hard working, but not making money, kind of actor. I just thought I had better start watching the show and catching up with this incredible history. Much of the time I would watch the show and say, 'I don't get it,' not thinking of what it would have looked like if I had seen it in '67 or '68, and compared to it television of the time. It was so revolutionary, but to be looking at it in 1978 or 1979, I didn't think that much of it, although it did carry a large philosophical leap of faith that was wonderful for television."

Studying episodes very carefully, Gautreaux got a firm grasp of just what makes a proper Vulcan and began intensive preparations for the role of Xon, attempting to make him the quintessential representation of that particular race. One of his greatest motivations was the initial description of the character in the screenplay of "In Thy Image," where the Vulcan, smelling rather strongly, has just beamed aboard from a meditative monastery in the Gobi Desert.

"I actually went off on a meditative trek and fasted for ten days," Gautreaux says. "I allowed my hair to grow long, I started researching to be a Vulcan with no emotion. For an actor, that's death. I was looking at it from an actor's point of view, which is how do you appear as having no emotion without looking like a piece of wood? That was my acting objective, and I went to several acting coaches. Jeff Corey is the one who gave me the key of how I could actively play the pure pursuit of logic as being my primary action. Then I felt I needed a physical equivalent, and I followed the teachings of Bruce Lee, who taught about dealing with emotions and a freedom from emotions that allowed you to live in a non-violent world. That's really what he was all about, despite the impression his films gave. His methods, his trainings and his students existed in a nonviolent life. The way to do that was to not let anything 'stick.' If somebody hits you, it doesn't stick; it just flies through you. So with a Vulcan dealing with 'lame brain' human beings....if they said something particularly stupid, or, in the case of Doctor McCoy, something particularly

antagonistic, because of the training I had gone through, it would not have the stick effect. It would not attach itself. The idea is that a Vulcan is pursuing something much larger than what is around him at that moment.

"In all honesty, I was looking forward to playing Xon. His actions were tremendous. His strength without size, and the aspect of playing a full Vulcan. When I say that, I mean somebody who had a larger presence than, say, Spock's father, who was a full Vulcan. By presence I mean a more involved presence on the show and the running of the ship. It was a very exciting premise to be playing. To me, it was a potentially good gig that didn't work out."

Gautreaux, who, as stated earlier, requested that his character be eliminated rather than diminished, ended up playing Commander Branch of the Epsilon 9 space station in two scenes of *Star Trek: The Motion Picture*. Apart from that, he left the show behind, but has managed to retain the most positive aspects of Xon and his preparation for the role.

"I have found ways to put that training to use," he says. "I was an avid bowler at the time and a pretty consistent 160 or 170 kind of bowler. Using the principles of an actor working to become a Vulcan, increased my bowling to a consistent 220. The primary goal of a Vulcan is to always be removing his energy away from himself and onto the task, the pursuit of logic or the need of the other person who needs what you have to give them. So you're constantly removing the energy from yourself, thus freeing yourself from obstacles. This is what I learned from fasting. When we remove three meals a day plus snacking, get past the third or fourth day, which is the real hump stage, the next ten days are gravy. You can go on forever as long as you have some water and some freshly squeezed juices for necessary proteins now and again. But you are so clear. You ask for something, you know exactly what you're asking for. What you find is that human beings are not very good at dealing with straightforward requests. They always want to know about the grey area and the pink area; they don't want to just give you the black and white. That's what makes life very silly and full of jokes and

shenanigans and why things don't get done as well. Vulcans are like *Zen and the Art of Archery*. There's no such thing as a target. There's no such thing as an arrow. There's no such thing as a bow. Everything is one motion, and there's no such thing as hitting the target or not hitting the target, because the bow, the arrow and the target are all one. So in bowling, you remove at least fifty percent of the effort, which is to do things correctly, and concentrate on the game itself. That kind of concentration can be done on anything you do. I use it all the time."

David Gautreaux pauses for a moment, as though trying to make sure he's expressed the enduring influence of the Xon character throughout his professional and personal life.

"I have never personally felt badly, upset or any of those things for not playing Xon," he concludes sincerely. "I've always felt that it was too bad the public didn't get the chance to see this character, given the preparation I had given to it. But for how it enhanced my own life, they paid me a hundred fold. Xon took me from a state of physical to a state of metaphysical, which is something that I've never lost."

"In Thy Image"

On August 29, Harold Livingston presented a new writers status report, and noted that they had met some twenty odd writers.

"We have also received a large number of submissions from various writers, either in one or two page outlines, and in some cases full scripts," he said. "We have investigated most of these, none have really met *Star Trek* standards. They keep coming in and the response from writers is totally overwhelming. I have recently received a submission from Thomas Ardies, who has published a best selling novel, is a well known novelist and short story writer, and also extremely desirous of doing a *Star Trek*.

"Richard Bach," the producer continued, "the author of *Jonathan Livingston Seagull*, and the current best selling novel *Illusions*, is a *Star Trek* fan. He has submitted two stories, both of which were so eminently desirable, we purchased them. One story is a tale of a society whose people are, for the most part, repressed and annually release these emotions by viewing their star ships in combat with other star ships. It is a very entertaining and provocative story, and Bach had submitted a five page outline. Almost simultaneously, Art Lewis, a very accomplished writer, came in with a similar idea. It was decided to graft both of these stories and assign Lewis to develop the story and teleplay. At the same time, Bach's second story is, what we consider a truly representative *Star Trek* vehicle, about a kind of dream world where our crew members become actively and dangerously involved in the dreams of a lady who had been in suspended animation for 200 years, kept alive throughout that time with periodic dreams. Bach is now writing the outline and actually has requested we allow him to do the script first, and if we do not like the script we can drop the project. I encouraged him to write the traditional outline and we would proceed from that point.

"Alan Dean Foster delivered the final draft of the two-hour movie. We met with him extensively, discussed the story, made numerous revisions and I am now in the process of rewriting the first act which we all, in concert, consider too slow. We should have the story ready to show a screen-writer some time this week."

In early September, several treatments arrived at the *Star Trek II* offices, including Shimon Wincelberg's "Lord Bobby," William Lansford's "Devil's Due," the Margaret Armen/Alf Harris collaboration, "The Savage Syndrome" and John Meredyth Lucas' "Kitumba."

"Lord Bobby," which would eventually be retitled "Lord Bobby's Obsession," was a good attempt which incorporated an alien being, again something like Trelene in "Squire of Gothos," as well as the Romulans.

"Kitumba" had Enterprise travelling to the Klingon home world in an effort to avert a potential intergalactic war. This story would have made a wonderful "prequel" to the sixth *Star Trek* film, *The Undiscovered Country*.

"The Savage Syndrome" had Decker, McCoy and Ilia investigate a derelict vessel in orbit around a lifeless planet. On board, they find that the crew had been driven mad and killed each other

in particularly brutal and savage ways. In the meantime, a space mine detonates in the vicinity of the Enterprise, unleashing energy that affects the crew's neural impulses. Instantly, they, including Kirk, are transformed into savages, and it's up to the trio to set things straight again.

From a production standpoint, this episode would have been quite important for the simple reason that it was primarily a ship-board story, and therefore more cost effective than the average episode. This had been a problem that occurred during the run of the original series, and has been a constant one on *The Next Generation*.

On September 2, 1977, producer Bob Goodwin wrote, "...in order to do an effective job on our stories that take place in settings other than the Enterprise, and still remain within our financial and production limitations, it is absolutely vital that we have an equal number of ship-board stories....If we don't have some good Enterprise stories in our back pockets, we could find ourselves with very serious production problems comes December."

The memo specifically cited "The Savage Syndrome" as a perfect example. For instance, the first draft of the outline had Decker, McCoy and Ilia actually land the shuttlecraft on the surface of a planet, where they studied ancient ruins as well as "several other things they encounter." Goodwin made the suggestion that the shuttle be investigating an object in space; this way it "would confine our story, for the most part, to the Enterprise." The second draft of the outline made this adjustment.

Harold Livingston came up with the idea of using 23rd Century technology to fight back against the savages. "Wouldn't it be more exciting and interesting if either Decker or McCoy—or both—used their brains to outwit [them]?" he asked. "For example, they might use the viewing screens and other instruments to completely enthrall the savages, perhaps on a level of the old 'B' movies, where the white explorer, knowing the moon was due to eclipse, filled the natives with awe and dread when he promised to make the sky dark and (as the eclipse occurred) did!" Livingston was right, and the scene would have

played most effectively. In fact, a later draft had a scene in the rec room, where McCoy threatens to bring the wrath of the gods upon the primitives. On cue, Decker activates the proper controls and "the walls become a crashing ocean, the air filled with the thunder of the waves and wind. An instant later the ocean becomes a World War II battlefield— shells bursting, cannon fire, and the deafening shrieks of the wounded." From there, the image becomes a raging fire, earthquakes and so on.

These illusionary walls were probably inspired by Ray Bradbury's *The Illustrated Man*, and would eventually make it to *The Next Generation* in the form of the Enterprise's holodeck.

Writer Margaret Armen explains the genesis of the episode from her point of view: "Alf and I started with the *what if?* motif. There's an old saying, 'Scratch the man and the savage bleeds.' So, what if these people from this futuristic, very scientific civilization have something happen to them which strips them down to the basic emotions and drives of the cave? That was the line of thought we pursued."

"Devil's Due," which was rewritten as an episode of *The Next Generation*, essentially put Captain Kirk in the form of a defense attorney, vieing for the freedom of a planet in a struggle against what appears to be the devil. Jon Povill felt that this story worked very well and that it had "all the elements necessary for a very exciting, involving episode."

While things were shaping up nicely with the various stories coming in, the opening two hour episode was proving to be something of a problem.

"William Norton was engaged to write it," said Livingston, "but on September 5th he contacted me to say that after considerable agonizing he had reached a conclusion that he could not write a proper *Star Trek* script. Although this set us back considerably in time, I think that in the end his honesty and candor and professionalism will prove beneficial. I personally feel this supports my theory that most writers find it extremely difficult writing a *Star Trek* script unless they have been completely immersed in it for some time. *Star Trek* stories require special treatment,

• • • •

special handling; the writers really should be well acquainted with the nuance, characterization and various other colorations that make *Star Trek* stories the unique things that they are. This situation, needless to say, leaves us in a serious state, bordering on crisis. If we are to meet the November 1st production date it is essential we receive a script no later than October 1st. We have examined and re-examined and re-examined again the names of writers considered qualified to write this initial episode."

None seemed suited for the job, so as a solution to the problem, the plan called for Livingston to work on the script himself over the next few weeks. "It is a step not taken lightly," he added, "but as something we feel we cannot avoid and leaves us no choice other than to proceed in this manner."

As he dove into the first draft script of "In Thy Image," he managed to issue yet another writer's status report in which he explained that there were only three remaining stories to be filled, and that they were being very selective as to which ones they went with.

"All of the stories," he said, "that have come in present no great problems, but all seem to need some work to get them into second draft and subsequently into script. The 'emergency' situation we are faced with slows us up somewhat now in that I am involved writing the script and am unable to devote full time to story development. However, Jon Povill has been very helpful in this area and is keeping things balanced until I can get back to devoting full attention to this."

Regarding the development of "In Thy Image," he felt that the script was turning out "extremely promising," and that the visuals would be spectacular and easily achieve the "big screen" effect that each of them had been looking for.

"The hour episode situation," Livingston concluded, "is, as I have stated above, somewhat uncertain because of this 'emergency.' Although we would prefer some time on the back, I think with some diligent efforts on all our parts, we'll be able to overcome the time problem and when the two hour episode is in production, we fully anticipate having enough

hour scripts to go forward immediately.

"In essence, then, everything is under control."

Not exactly.

Script Wars

By the time Harold Livingston had taken to writing "In Thy Image," the working relationship between he and Gene Roddenberry had begun to disintegrate...badly.

"I don't remember when I began to pierce the Roddenberry myth," Livingston says, "but he and I suddenly started to have creative differences. I resented his interference and he, apparently, wanted someone to carry his lunch around, and that wasn't me. We became socially friendly for a while, but in any case we started to have various difficulties. Out here they're called 'creative differences.' I just didn't think he was a good writer, and I didn't like the way he was doing some of the material. We developed these stories and somewhere along the line I began to get tired of having to go to him for approval of a story, because this wasn't my understanding of my function there. It's one of those things that no one wants to touch, because it could be a very serious problem. All you can do is ignore it and hope that the problem doesn't arise. Well, it did, and I began to commission stories without his approval."

Both creative talents weathered this rapidly intensifying storm for the next two months while plans were rapidly being laid out to bring "In Thy Image" to the television screen, with much attention going to the scripts which would fill up the rest of the first thirteen put into work.

As Livingston was wrapping up his first draft, talk began that the character of Decker would somehow be done away with in the next draft, as the general consensus was: "Who needs two Captain Kirks?" What had started out as a solid addition to the crew, was turning out to be something of a headache.

"I think it would be very beneficial for us to determine as soon as possible whether or not the character of Will Decker will continue or be eliminated," said Livingston just before handing in his script. "Every story in work and those also in script contain

Decker as a very integral character. If we're going to eliminate him, I think we had better move on it now to further save ourselves much unnecessary work re-writing, and writing around the elimination of that particular character."

Later, Arthur Fellows, head of television production, issued a memo to Gene Roddenberry in which he discussed his and Michael Eisner's feelings regarding the first draft script.

"The return of *Star Trek* is an event in itself," wrote Fellows, "and we believe that this script really incorporates the elements that will be an extraordinary send off for the next 'five' years. The action and basic story are well conceived. However, at this rough draft stage a problem exists throughout in the arena of character and relationships."

Fellows believed that through the course of the script we never really felt the enormous pressure that had been placed on Xon's shoulders, nor were we given the opportunity to see him win the respect of the crew. This situation, he felt, should be rectified in order for the public to accept this new and different Vulcan. In addition, the feud between McCoy and Xon (ergo, humanitarianism versus logic) should be dealt with more fully, filling the viewer with warm recollections of the McCoy-Spock relationship.

"In many ways we face a similar task with Decker," he wrote. "[If he's] going to be around for a long time, any intensifying of the emotions surrounding his existence and purpose on the ship will only aid in endearing him to all involved."

While feelings were strong regarding Ilia, it was generally believed that the character should not be bald. "Her baldness," pointed out the executive, "may really get in the way of the audience buying the intense relationship between Kirk and the woman. We would prefer to have Ilia with hair, keeping the bald girl but giving her some other function on the show." It seems that Gene Roddenberry had a somewhat similar struggle over twenty years ago, when network executives pleaded with him to get rid of "the guy with the ears."

"The storyline presented is quite special and extraordinary," he enthused, "but somehow the ending seems to be too 'small' when we consider what led up to it. The slow, steady build-up of excitement and tension as this story unfolds is so effective that the ending deserves to soar. Right now, it is a bit anti-climactic. The final dialogue and moment when Ilia has convinced Vejur to save the servo-units is too convenient."

"Robert Goodwin's theory about the ending," muses Livingston, "is that I just pissed it away because I was so disgusted with the situation. I think the truth is that I couldn't come up with an ending. I just couldn't do it. The problem was that we had an antagonist so omnipotent that to defeat it, or even communicate with it, or have any kind of relationship with it, made the concept of the story false. How the hell do we deal with this? On what level? Everything pretty much worked in the story until we got to the ending. We tried all kinds of approaches, including aesthetic, theological and philosophical. We didn't know what to do with the ending."

Jon Povill, on the other hand, did. "We knew we had to have a big special effects ending," he says. "The problem of what was going to happen at the end and why it was going to happen, was one that plagued the script from the very start. The original treatment had a showdown between Vejur (although it wasn't called Vejur at the time) and Captain Kirk in which he draws a droopy daisy. Vejur recognizes that there is great power and value in this droopy daisy and flies off. Real deep. Then Gene came up with the idea of the machine dumping its data into Decker, with a lightshow of all the information it had accumulated. We were going to get all this amazing, incomprehensible stuff that Vejur had accumulated in its travels across the universe, and, of course, nobody could come up with these images. So that didn't work.

"It was pretty much my contribution," Povill goes on, "to say that the reason for what was happening was that this thing needed to go on to the next plane of existence; that it was transcending this dimension and going on to the next. It then became logical that the machine would need that human element to combine with. It was the only thing that could have made sense."

As Povill notes, Gene Roddenberry's rewrite of "In Thy Image" featured Vejur unloading its information into Decker, and then using the commander to transcend this dimension to enter another.

By the time early November 1977 came along, production of "In Thy Image" was scheduled to begin in just a matter of weeks. It seemed that nothing was going to interfere with Star Trek's return.

The Motion Picture

"Gene Roddenberry's values lay in his knowledge and experience. Now if he had imparted that and allowed the professionals to do their job, they might have had a picture. Rewriting was compulsive with him; he simply could not live with himself knowing that someone else was writing Star Trek," states Harold Livingston matter of factly. "In December of '77, Roddenberry and I were really at each other's throats. My contract was up around that time and I quit before they could fire me. I knew there were too many problems. The film was in preproduction, and they had gone back to basically what I wrote, with Collins as a writer, restoring much of what he had left out, but little of Gene's."

Interestingly, Livingston would ultimately quit the Star Trek project three times—and would eventually have to fight it out with Roddenberry concerning the screenplay credit on the film—but was always coaxed back by the Paramount brass. For the moment, however, he believed that he was leaving the realm of the 23rd Century behind him forever.

As the new year came in, so did the decision—though not an absolute one—to turn the Star Trek II television series into a feature film. Jon Povill, who had taken over the writers status reports after Livingston's departure, pointed out that "all the scripts that we have in hand are in very good shape, and should Paramount at some point decide to proceed with the series, I feel that we have here the nucleus of an excellent first season."

On January 19th, Jeff Katzenberg stated that "We are currently analyzing all of the aspects necessary to move forward with Star Trek II as a theatrical motion picture. Unfortunately, much information—premature and potentially destructive to our long-range planning—already has leaked out to the media and the public. This has become most alarming, even though we are appreciative of such wide-spread interest in the project and aware of its future value to us [a classic case of understatement, considering that Star Trek has become a billion dollar industry for Paramount]. It therefore becomes imperative that no information regarding the film be given out at this time. I must emphasize how essential it is that information concerning this show not now be given out by those associated with it in any capacity. The project at its present stage can suffer seriously. And the success of a properly timed, well-coordinated future public relations campaign can be jeopardized."

The decision to produce Star Trek: The Motion Picture came about for a number of reasons. First of all, the three networks, fearful of any new competition, reportedly lowered their advertising rates, thus making it less viable for Paramount to begin their fourth network.

Second, not only had Star Wars been released and become an unprecedented phenomenon, which had convinced Paramount to do the new series as opposed to a film in the first place (believing that their opportunity had come and gone); but Steven Spielberg's Close Encounters of the Third Kind found box office life as well, thus proving that science fiction most definitely could appeal to movie audiences of the 1970s and '80s.

"It was a combination of things," said Gene Roddenberry in regards to the decision to make a feature film as opposed to a new series. "Five years ago, Paramount began looking at the remarkable rerun of the Star Trek series—and they began to say, 'Well, gee, maybe we do have something here.' And it resulted in, four years ago, my checking into the studio with the idea of putting together a Star Wars feature. At the time, the plan was just to do a modest-budget feature; and they were convinced they had a sufficient audience. But we couldn't come up with a script that Paramount really liked. Paramount wasn't that much into science fiction at the time. I think a lot of studios at the time had a rather simplistic view of science fiction—rocket ships and blasters and high adventure—the kinds of things that, really, you saw in *Star Wars*, though probably with a few more half-nude women. I just wasn't interested in doing a space pirate type of show—a film is just too great an exertion of time and energy. The concepts I was working in and trying to get by at the same time had some fairly complex and, I thought, daring thematic material. And that just kind of shook them up, because they weren't thinking of science fiction as being a really heavy thematic thing. We finally ended up starting to do it as a spectacular for television to open up a new series. But about that time, *Star Wars* did come along and showed that there was, indeed, not only the audience that they thought might be there, but a rather unusual-sized one at that. They have been moving toward it for a number of years. Not fast enough to suit me, nor with a large-enough budget, but they were moving."

"When 'In Thy Image' became a feature," adds director Bob Collins, "we were given a budget of about eight million dollars. Somewhere around that time we were talking about special effects. Roddenberry and I went down to the Pacific Theatre and sat down for what I think was a noon performance of *Close Encounters*. We came out and were both pretty blown away by the film. I turned to him and said, 'Well, there goes our low budget special effects.' After *Star Wars* and *Close Encounters* you couldn't do those kind of special effects anymore. That meant a whole new thinking and a whole reorganization of the production and concepts. They needed a great deal more money and time, and there were only a few people who could do it. We spoke to John Dykstra and Robert Abel, and they chose Abel. So he came on board and decided that he would make it into a Robert Abel production. His budget, which had originally been one or two million dollars, suddenly jumped to seven and ten million dollars. The budget kept rising, and Paramount was getting more and more nervous as it kept pumping more and more money into it."

As the budget on the film rose, Collins began to suspect that his time with the project was limited. What he did not know, or expect, was a political back-stabbing by some of those involved.

"We were preparing to make this picture," he says, "but the writing was on the wall. I was a television director who had not done a feature film at that time. It was kind of evident that they were going to hire somebody who was used to working with big budget special effects. Paramount wasn't brave about such things, so I called up Jeff Katzenberg and said, 'You're going to replace me, right?' He said, 'No, Bob, never. Take my word for it, Bob. Trust me.' Then my agent, who at that time handled Robert Wise, called up and said, 'Look, we've got an offer for Robert Wise to replace you on the picture.' Apparently Paramount couldn't remember that we both had the same agent, so I called up Jeff again and said, 'Look, are you going to replace me?' He said, 'Absolutely not. Never. You're absolutely staying with the project.' I pointed out that Robert Wise and I had the same agent, so he said, 'If Robert Wise doesn't do it, then you are absolutely going to do it. ' I kind of laughed about that for a while. I knew it would happen sooner or later. They wanted to get somebody in place before they fired me. So they got Wise, and the first step was to redecorate my office.

"I was more angry about the way it happened. I could understand them wanting someone else when the budget escalated to twenty million dollars, but I wish they would have been nicer about it and said, 'Look, these are the facts of the situation.' But Paramount's not the only place in town that works that way either. I was angry at Katzenberg. Anyway, and this isn't sour grapes, but I never really thought the film did all that it could do. It wasn't as good as it could have been. This is not against Robert Wise, because given the circumstances, I don't know how anybody could have done. But I didn't think the script was very good in any case."

He's quick to add that any anger he felt was not really directed at Gene Roddenberry.

"Gene would often say about the script, 'This isn't *Star Trek*,'" Collins reflects. "One could argue that it may not be *Star Trek*, but it's good. At the same time, you had to realize that on a human

level, on a personal level, that he was wrapped up in it. His whole way of defining himself was involved with the series and with this project. I don't think any of us ever felt very angry at him. We all wanted to help him realize his ambition, and we wanted to make a good picture too. Paramount was kind of holding a gun to his head, saying that they were going to do it, and then they weren't going to do it. That tension, I think, flowed through all of us. I'm not sorry about calling somebody an asshole if that's what I think they are, but I liked Roddenberry and I always felt sympathetic towards him and the project."

So Bob Collins left the film, with actor David Gautreaux (as detailed earlier) soon to follow. At that time, casting had been going on for someone to portray Decker, but this was put on hold for a time.

"They went with Robert Wise as director," offers Bob Goodwin as an explanation for why he never cast the role. "Gene and I were never really informed of what the steps of the deal were. It turns out that Robert Wise is used to getting producing and directing credit. Apparently he would not accept a producer, so Gene Roddenberry was moved to executive producer and I was asked by Gene and the studio if I would stay on as associate producer. I didn't want to spend a minute of my life doing that. I was an associate producer ten years earlier, and it was like taking a step backwards, especially facing two years of production. So I left.

"What really upset me about all this," he seems to be punctuating each word, "is that at the same time I had a pilot that had gotten a go ahead. I had developed it under the Playboy job. It was a wonderful script, but I was having severe problems with the director, who was shooting down in New Orleans. I was the executive producer and had hired a producer, but no one was watching the store down there. The dailies were coming in and they were just terrible. So I wanted to go down there and try to pull it together, because I saw the handwriting on the wall, but the guys at the feature department threatened that if I went down to New Orleans, they would take me off the picture. At the same time, they were negotiating a deal that would

• • • •

have me off the picture anyway. So what ended up happening was that by the time I finally got word on the Robert Wise deal, I immediately got on a plane and went to New Orleans, but by that time it was just too late. So not only did I end up not doing the *Star Trek* film, but I ended up with a terrible pilot that did not sell. So there I was, literally out on the street. I came to work one day and they had taken my name off the door. My stuff was packed in boxes in the hall and the janitor told me I had to be off the lot in twenty minutes.

"That's the way they handled it," Goodwin concludes. "That's the kind of thing that can destroy you. I began to wonder, 'What did I do wrong?' Luckily, someone I knew with money had been waiting for me to leave Paramount, because he wanted to start a company with me. Thank God for small miracles."

Leonard Nimoy and Director Robert Wise at the press conference announcing *Star Trek: The Motion Picture.*

••••

CHAPTER EIGHT
Star Trek in the 1970's
An Episode Guide

Star Trek: The Animated Series

SEASON ONE
Episode #1:
"Yesteryear"
Written by Dorothy Fontana
Original Airdate: 9/15/73

Spock must travel backwards in time through the Guardian of Forever to discover why he no longer exists in the eyes of those in the present time frame. Arriving on Vulcan, he meets himself as a child and helps the young Spock through a rite of passage. The child is saved by his pet sehlat, but the beast is wounded in the struggle and, by young Spock's decision, must be put to sleep.

••••

"'Yesteryear' resulted from my looking back at the things we had done on the series and remembering the time portal from 'City on the Edge of Forever,'" states Dorothy Fontana. "I thought we could use that for a legitimate trip, but then have something happen so that Spock has to return to Vulcan to his childhood. We could probe into these characters and see the beginning of some of the trouble with Spock and Sarek, Amanda's problems back and then and part of what made Spock Spock. I also felt strongly about dealing with the death of a pet. It was a very serious thing for kids. We were trying to put across a lesson to children, that when it comes time for an animal to die, if he must go, it should be with dignity."

Episode #2:
"One of Our Planets is Missing"
Written by Marc Daniels
Original Airdate: 9/23/73

An energy cloud that consumes planets that lie in its wake is threatening the population of Mantilles, and the Enterprise must devise a way to combat this threat before it's too late. Only after the starship is pulled within the cloud

does Spock come to the conclusion that it is actually an intelligent creature that can be reasoned with.

Episode #3:
"The Lorelei Signal"
Written by Margaret Armen
Original Airdate: 9/29/73

In this variation of "The Deadly Years," Kirk, Spock and McCoy beam down to a planet within the Taurean star system, where they are captured by a race of female aliens. These women are immortals who gain their life force from others by utilizing a special headband. The trio must find a way to counteract the effect of these headbands before they die of old age.

Episode #4:
"More Tribbles, More Troubles"
Written by David Gerrold
Original Airdate: 10/6/73

All of the elements of "The Trouble With Tribbles" are back, with Kirk and company running into and rescuing Cyrano Jones. Accompanying Jones, naturally, are tribbles, but supposedly a variation of the one that appeared in the live-action episode. These tribbles, he explains, have been genetically engineered *not* to reproduce. What the con man fails to mention is that the more quadrotriticale the tribbles eat, the *larger* they get. Added to this is Captain Koloth and his Klingon soldiers.

••••

This episode was originally to appear as a live-action *Star Trek*, but never did due to third season producer Fred Freiberger's reaction to "The Trouble With Tribbles."

"I went in there with the attitude of having to prove myself to the new producer," says David Gerrold. "I said, 'I know how well "Tribbles" turned out, I know I can do it, I've got my credential, and everyone who saw "Tribbles" loved it, the episode turned out well, I don't have anything to be embarrassed about, I don't have to prove myself.' I walk in, Freddy Freiberger is looking at me and his first words are: 'I saw "Tribbles" this morning,' because he was having episode screened for him. The polite thing to say is, 'Not bad,' or 'Well done,' or 'Good job.' His words were, 'I don't

like it. *Star Trek* is not a comedy.' From that point on, our relationship never recovered. I said, 'Well, Gene said he wanted a sequel,' and he said that he had no interest in it."

When contacted by Dorothy Fontana for the animated series, Gerrold resurrected the idea.

Episode #5:
"The Survivor"
Written by James Schmerer
Original Airdate: 10/13/73

A shape shifter dupes the Enterprise crew into believing its philanthropist Carter Winston, who has been missing for five years. Once on board, it transforms itself into Captain Kirk and takes the Enterprise into the Romulan neutral zone, where the vessel is quickly surrounded by enemy vessels. The shifter, we learn, is actually a Romulan spy.

Episode #6:
"The Infinite Vulcan"
Written by Walter Koenig
Original Airdate: 10/20/73

Arriving at the planet Phylos, the Enterprise discovers a giant being who is actually a clone of Dr. Starros Keniclius, a scientist who had existed during the earth's Eugenics Wars (discussed in the live-action episode "Space Seed"). It is Keniclius' intentions to clone Spock so that the duplicate of the Vulcan can serve as a peacemaker for different worlds. Kirk's arguments that the universe is basically at peace falls on deaf ears, and the captain must use all of his resources to convince the Spock clone that he is merely a copy, and that the original might be dying.

Episode #7:
"The Magicks of Megas-Tu"
Written by Larry Brody
Original Airdate: 10/27/73

When the Enterprise is brought into another dimension, the ship and her crew is rescued by a pan-like being named Lucien who, like all his people, is in possession of a variety of extraordinary, even magical, abilities. To use these powers is forbidden, and the people of Lucien's realm, the Megans, detect what he is doing, they put him on trial. As Captain Kirk defends Lucien during a trial, it becomes apparent that Lucien had once visited earth long ago in the past and may have been the inspiration for the legend of Satan.

Episode #8:
"Once Upon a Planet"
Written by Len Jenson and Chuck Menville
Original Airdate: 11/3/73

This sequel, in many ways a retread, of live action's "Shore Leave," has the Enterprise crew return to the planet where any wish can come true. Once again things go terribly wrong as the Keeper has died and no one is left in charge of the equipment.

Episode #9:
"Mudd's Passion"
Written by Stephen Kandel
Original Airdate: 11/10/93

Kirk, despite his better judgement, rescues Harry Mudd from a group of miners that he has attempted to con. No sooner has Harry beamed on board the Enterprise than all hell breaks loose when he lets Nurse Christine Chapel know about a love potion he has in his possession, which she proceeds to use on Spock. At first her attempt fails, but following a delayed reaction Spock falls madly in love with her and the potion's influence is felt all over the ship.

••••

Stephen Kandel, who had the distinction of writing the two Harry Mudd live action adventures, penned this animated spin-off as well. "Dorothy Fontana just called me for a script. It was as simple as that," he says. "Animation is great because you direct as well as write. You could go anywhere and do anything."

Episode #10:
"The Terratin Incident"
Written by Paul Schneider
Original Airdate: 11/17/73

When the Enterprise investigates a mysterious distress signal, the starship is struck by a lightning bolt. As a result, all organic matter on the vessel begins to shrink in size. Needing to do *something* before it's too late, Kirk and a landing party beam down to the source of the distress signal and discover a miniature city which is threatened with

destruction when their planet explodes. The only way they could elicit help was to infect the crew of the Enterprise with the same "disease" that affected them. The true hero of the day turns out to be the Enterprise transporters, which are able to restore everyone to their natural size.

••••

"The 'Terratin Incident' was based on a one-paragraph story idea that Gene Roddenberry had," explains writer Paul Schneider. "I took it from there with Dorothy Fontana, the show's associate producer. I just loved the concept of doing something related to *Gulliver's Travels*. I enjoyed that, as well as watching the process of the animation develop. Overall, I thought the episode turned out rather well."

Episode #11:
"Time Trap"
Written by Joyce Perry
Original Airdate: 11/24/73

The Enterprise gets trapped in the Delta Triangle, an intergalactic version of the Bermuda Triangle, which has become something of a graveyard for vessels which have disappeared, representing such diverse races as the Klingons, Gorns, Romulans, Kzin and Vulcans. What Kirk and the crew are shocked to discover is that the descendants of the crews of these various vessels are still alive, and have formed something of a government under the umbrella title "The Elysian Council." Escape from the triangle is deemed impossible until Kirk and Klingon captain Kor (who went up against Kirk in the live-action "Errand of Mercy") realize that they have to work together to discover the key to this elusive puzzle.

Episode #12:
"The Ambergris Element":
Written by Margaret Armen
Original Airdate: 12/1/73

While underwater exploring the world of Argo, Kirk and Spock are rendered unconscious. When they come to they discover that they are now water-breathers, as they've been surgically altered by the race that exists here, the Aquans. These beings believe that Kirk and Spock have come in peace, which is why they have bestowed this "gift" upon them. But when Scotty leads a rescue

team, the Aquans suddenly believe they're under attack and their benevolence takes a dark turn.

••••

Admits writer Margaret Armen, "I didn't really see how an animated series could work, but they have marvelous artists at Filmation. Dorothy Fontana was the story editor and she approached me. I thought it would be fun. She said the main difference is that for the artists' sake, you must describe every scene and every action in great detail so that the artists will know what to draw. Both of my episodes were fun to write, and I enjoyed doing them."

Episode #13:
"Slaver Weapon"
Written by Larry Niven
Original Airdate: 1215/73

While transporting a Slaver stasis box (created by a race that once ruled the galaxy), Spock, Sulu and Uhura are attacked by the cat-like Kzin race who wish to possess the device. Intrigue piles upon intrigue as the box passes from hand to hand, until the Kzin results in the destruction of their own people.

Episode #14:
"Beyond the Farthest Star"
Written by Samuel A. Peeples
Original Airdate: 12/22/73

Enterprise is captured by the gravity of a black hole known as Questar M-17. There they discover a starship whose sole occupant is a evil, and formless, creature that had been stranded there by those who had built the ship. It manages to take control of the Enterprise and only after Kirk and Spock convince it that they intend to destroy the vessel and everyone on board does it release its grip.

••••

Samuel A. Peeples, who also wrote the second live-action *Star Trek* pilot, "Where No Man Has Gone Before," notes, "Dorothy Fontana used to be my secretary when I was at Universal. She was nineteen or twenty years old. I think I bought her her first legal drink on her twenty first birthday. She was hired as the Associate Producer. She called and said, 'Gene suggested that since you had done the pilot for the original *Star Trek*, maybe you'd like to do the pilot for the

••••

animated *Star Trek.*' And that's what I did. I did the pilot and it was aired later on. The *Variety* review was absolutely incredible. As far as the inspiration for the story, I don't have the vaguest idea. It seems to me that I was trying to say that it would be interesting if there was a space ship which was actually a living creature. It's alive, but it is used to going from one planet to another. They did great animated stories, and they didn't write down to children, by and large. There were a couple that were, obviously, designed for the younger market, but most of them were quite mature."

Episode #15:
"The Eye of the Beholder"
Written by David Harmon
Original Airdate: 1/5/74

While searching for the survivors of a missing starship, Kirk, Spock, McCoy and Scotty are captured by the slug-like race of Lactra VII and put into cages as exhibits in a zoo. It is only after Spock mind melds with a child Lactran that the race realizes they have captured an intelligent species.

Episode #16:
"Jihad"
Written by Stephen Kandel
Original Airdate: 1/13/74

Kirk and Spock are among the beings contacted by the Vendala, supposedly the first race ever to venture into outer space, to take part in a mission to recover the stolen brainwave pattern of Alar. This being (Alar) is the one who transformed the Skorr from a war-like race to one of peaceful benevolence. If the brainwave pattern is not restored, then a holy war (jihad) will take place throughout the galaxy.

••••

"'Jihad' was an idea I'd had for a long time," explains Stephen Kandel. "It was a message story and difficult to sell on network television. Network executives would have said, 'My God, what are you doing? That's a message story!' I jumped at the opportunity to drop it into a *Star Trek* format, which we did, and it worked very well. In fact, I won a humanitarian award for it."

SEASON TWO

Episode #17:
"The Pirates of Orion"
Written by Howard Weinstein
Original Airdate: 9/7/74

When Spock contracts a strain of choriocytosis, Kirk has three days to rendezvous with the S.S. Huron, a vessel equipped with the antidote for this disease. Enroute, however, the Huron is boarded by an Orion pirate ship which steals its cargo. Kirk must recover the cure before time runs out.

Episode #18:
"Bem"
Written by David Gerrold
Original Airdate: 9/14/74

Bem, an observer from the planet Pandros, is on board the Enterprise. Unbeknownst to Kirk, Bem is trying to determine whether or not the Federation is an alliance worthwhile for his world to be a part of. To learn the truth, he manipulates a series of circumstances which leads a landing party down to Delta Theta III, where a female voice—claiming to be a god—warns Kirk and company away. When Bem disappears, Kirk must live up to his responsibility to find the being despite the risk to himself and his ship.

Episode #19:
"Practical Joker"
Written by Chuck Menville
Original Airdate: 9/21/74

When the Enterprise inadvertently enters Romulan territory, Kirk tries to elude Romulan warships by entering an energy field. This field turns out to be alive as it proves by taking over the ship's computer and begins launching one practical joke after another.

Episode #20:
"Albatross"
Written by Dario Finelli
Original Airdate: 9/28/74

When the Enterprise delivers medical supplies to Dramia II, Dr. McCoy is arrested and charged with the murders of millions of inhabitants. It seems that nearly twenty years earlier the doctor had been part of a medical team chosen to vaccinate the populace against

a Saurian virus. Shortly after that team left a plague broke out that wiped out most of the population. Now McCoy will stand trial for the crime he is accused of. Complicating Kirk's attempts to free him from prison is the spread of the virus onboard the Enterprise.

Episode #21:
"How Sharper Than a Serpent's Tooth"
Written by Russell Bates and David Wise
Original Airdate: 10/5/74

In this storyline, which is extremely similar to the live-action "Who Mourns for Adonais?", the Indian god Kulkukan captures members of the Enterprise as it has done other species from around the galaxy with the intent that they worship him as a god just as the people of earth did thousands of years earlier. He has about as much success as Apollo did in the earlier version.

Episode #22:
"The Counter-Clock Incident"
Written by John Culver
Original Airdate: 10/12/74

Enterprise first captain, Robert April, is being transported by the starship to his retirement ceremony. The ship is accidentally plunged into a nova where everything works in a counter-clockwise way, resulting in the people aboard the Enterprise growing younger to the point where they are children. April, now a 30 year old man, takes command and must get the starship out of this dimension before it's too late.

STAR TREK II
(The Television Series)

Episode #1:
"In Thy Image"
Written by Harold Livingston

In many ways, this is *Star Trek: The Motion Picture* sans Spock. The newly refitted starship Enterprise sets out to combat the mysterious energy cloud that has been destroying vessels and is on a direct heading for earth. Captain James T. Kirk, Dr. McCoy, Scotty, Sulu, Uhura and Chekov are joined by first officer Commander Decker, science officer Lieutenant Xon and navigator Lieutenant

Ilia as the discover the truth behind this enemy: it is actually an ancient earth space probe enroute to its home world in search of its creator.

Episode #2:
"The Child"
Written by Jon Povill
and Jaron Summers

The Enterprise passes through a mysterious cloud. As it does so, an energy form penetrates the starship's hull and proceeds to Lieutenant Ilia's quarters. A glow envelops her entire body and she begins to moan with pleasure. When she awakens the next morning, she informs Dr. McCoy that she's pregnant.

Within three days Ilia gives birth to a beautiful girl, who begins to age rapidly. In a matter of hours she is ten years old and growing older. While McCoy tries to discover what's happening, the Enterprise is afflicted with one near-disaster after another, every one of which is averted at the last possible moment by the child (named Irska, which, in Deltan, means "bright light"). Kirk learns that the molecular structure of the Enterprise's hull is breaking down and will turn to dust in a matter of hours.

Xon performs a Vulcan mind-meld on Irska and learns that she must be transported directly into a bright light which has been following the ship. This is done and the hull's breakdown is instantly reversed.

Kirk and company conclude that in some strange way Ilia served as Irska's first womb, while the Enterprise served as the second. The aliens had arranged it so that the child would learn all about human emotions, wants, needs and the ability to make sacrifices for loved ones, before it metamorphosized into a higher life form.

••••

This script, which was eventually rewritten as an episode of *Star Trek: The Next Generation*, holds a special place in writer Jon Povill's heart.

"One of the keys to me becoming story editor on *Star Trek II* was that 'The Child' had to be written in a week," Povill recalls with a laugh. "I had Jaron Summers do a first draft and then I had to do a pretty complete rewrite. It had to get into shape for shooting, and the way that

script came out would determine whether or not I could be the story editor."

He got the job.

Episode #3:
"The Savage Syndrome"
Written by Margaret Armen
and Alf Harris

Decker, McCoy and Ilia investigate a derelict vessel in orbit around a lifeless planet. On board, they find that the crew had killed each other in brutal and savage ways. But why?

Meanwhile, a space mine detonates near the Enterprise, unleashing an energy which attacks the neural impulses of the crew and transforms them into savages. Primitive forces drive their every move. Decker, McCoy and Ilia return to the Enterprise to try and reverse the mine's effects before the starship and her crew are destroyed.

••••

Notes writer Margaret Armen, "Gene Roddenberry was very close to the show. Alf and I went in with three stories, and in the end it was 'The Savage Syndrome' that he liked, because he was looking for *Star Trek* stories that were really different."

Episode #4:
"Practice in Waking"
Written by Richard Bach

The Enterprise comes upon a sleeper ship with only a single passenger. Scotty, Decker and Sulu beam over to investigate and discover a woman in suspended animation. Scotty accidentally touches a control panel and the three collapse to the deck, only to reawaken in ancient Scotland without memory of their lives aboard the starship. In the past, they meet with the same woman and protect her from the mobs who claim that she is a witch.

On the Enterprise, McCoy discovers that Scotty, Sulu and Decker's life signs are growing steadily weaker. His prognosis is that the longer they remain in this dreaming-state, the closer they come to actually dying. Kirk and crew must somehow awaken them before they drift off into final sleep.

••••

Producer Harold Livingston noted at the time, "Getting Richard Bach

to work on *Star Trek* is a real score for the show. His story should make one hell of an episode."

Livingston's assessment was common among the staff. Despite never making it to script form, "Practice in Waking" was one of the most popular story ideas among the *Star Trek II* crew. They felt that Richard Bach would add a certain amount of class to the series and pave the way for new directions.

Episode #5:
"To Attain the All"
Written by Norman Spinrad

While trapped in another dimension, the Enterprise is boarded by a blue-skinned alien who refers to himself as The Prince. He tells Kirk and the others that if they prove worthy, mankind will be the recipient of the ultimate gift: the attaining of the "All."

Kirk reluctantly accepts the demand that Decker and Xon, representative of their respective species, be the ones who'll attempt to unlock the Prince's secret. If Kirk refused, the starship would never be allowed to return home. The duo appear in a maze-like structure within a planetoid and are told that their goal awaits them at the other end. They proceed, and at mid-journey take note of a bizarre switch in personality traits: Xon utilizes human intuition while Decker applies Vulcan-like logic to problems.

They ultimately reach the other end of the maze and the glowing spheres that await them. Xon reaches out to touch it and his mind is assaulted by an energy unlike any encountered before. Then, with the Vulcan serving as a conduit, the alien intelligence within the sphere begins spreading its influence through the Enterprise. It rapidly possesses the majority of the ship's crew and engineers a permanent switch of personality traits. It's soon obvious that they're all becoming part of a single mind.

The intelligence inside the sphere plans to force the humans to merge with the All. The All, after acquiring physical bodies, could go deep into space and merge with all intelligent beings in the galaxy. The Prince believes this is fair, for even though humanity will lose its individuality, it will gain immortality. The price, naturally, is too high and it's up to Kirk (and eventually Decker) to save them.

Episode #6:
"The Prisoner"
Written by James Menzies

The bridge crew is understandably shocked when the image of Albert Einstein appears on the main viewscreen, requesting that the starship help him. Einstein explains that he and many other earth scientists were kidnapped and kept alive by a "storage battery" on an alien planet. While Kirk doesn't believe that he is truly speaking to Einstein, the captain's curiosity is aroused. He orders the ship to that world.

While the Enterprise is in orbit, six scientists from earth's past (circa the early 20th century) appear in the transporter room. Xon is quick to discern that they aren't living beings, but rather highly realistic illusions. Now aware of the trap they've been caught in, Kirk orders the Enterprise to break orbit. The ship cannot. Beaming down to the planet, the captain comes face-to-face with Logos, the alien behind the charade. His goal is to assume the identity of all human life, beginning with Kirk and his crew. This, Logos feels, is only fair considering that humanity is such a savage race, constantly living under the threat of nuclear annihilation. Kirk counters that the earth Logos speaks of is ancient history. The alien refuses to believe this, insisting that man will never change.

A battle of wills between the Enterprise crew and Logos follows, with the destiny of humanity hanging in the balance.

Episode #7:
"Tomorrow and the Stars"
Written by Larry Alexander

Due to a transporter malfunction, Kirk is sent back in time to Pearl Harbor in 1941—mere days before the Japanese attack. At first he materializes in a ghost-like state, unable to touch or be touched by anything.

Kirk meets Elsa Kelley, a woman unhappy with her marriage to career-Army husband Richard. Initially frightened by Kirk's appearance, she ultimately tries to accept his story.

Meanwhile, Xon and Scotty attempt to "yank" Kirk back to the Enterprise. That fails but does have the effect of making him solid again. This in turn leads to Kirk and Elsa falling deeply in love. The dilemma arises of whether or not Kirk should alter history by warning her of the imminent Pearl Harbor attack, or merely depart with Decker and Xon when they locate him.

●●●●

An interesting moment in "Tomorrow and the Stars" occurs shortly after the transporter malfunction, when the ghost-like Kirk screams out, "Xon, what have you done to me?" This line seems to indicate Kirk's bitterness that Xon isn't Spock.

"Oh yeah," laughs writer Larry Alexander, "but that's only because I was able to take it one step further. In other words, Xon is not Spock even though I considered him Spock from a character point-of-view. So there is a little resentment there. It seemed the 'logical' thing to do."

This script began when Gene Roddenberry gave Alexander "The Apartment," a story he had written for the aborted *Genesis II* series. Alexander came up with "Ghost Story," in which Kirk and the landing team arrive on a planet that lies in ruin. There they discover highly advanced technology but no sign of a living civilization. Kirk enters a science lab and is projected backwards in time. He encounters a pair of scientists who have developed a device to scan the mind. ON a human, however, it operates quite differently.

Hooked up to Kirk's brain, the machine causes him great agony. The demons from within his mind, the Id, materializes and destroys all life on the planet (resulting in the destruction the crew finds in the beginning).

Alexander freely acknowledges the debt that "Ghost Story" owes to *Forbidden Planet*, but points out that it goes beyond that film.

"I thought it was a wonderful story idea to have Captain Kirk responsible for the death of a planet," he enthuses, "and it's the one step beyond *Forbidden Planet* that had never been dealt with. It makes it much more human

and, to me, much more of an interesting irony. That's the kind of material I think is interesting and I was shocked when Gene Roddenberry said he didn't want to go with it."

It's suggested that saddling Kirk with a planet's death wasn't the right thing to do to such a heroic series character.

"In effect it wasn't his doing," Alexander differs. "He asked them not to do it. I was very strict about that. He didn't volunteer to do this, and when he realized what was going on, he did everything possible to stop it. All of that, I think, holds up on that basis. I was thinking very strictly about what happened to Kirk in many episodes where things didn't turn out the way he hoped. That's what makes *Star Trek* so wonderful. As heroic as Kirk was, through no fault of his own, hard choices had to be made. In Harlan Ellison's story ['City on the Edge of Forever'], Kirk has to allow Edith Keeper to die. It's a gulp at the end of the show, and it's like that when the people of this planet find that it's his demons which have destroyed their world, not theirs. It makes it that much more ironic."

Roddenberry preferred instead that Kirk go back to earth's past and chose Pearl Harbor as the time and place.

"It seemed a very obvious choice," muses Alexander. "Pearl Harbor is good, though, because you can use footage from various war films, which would work. But I didn't want to have the responsibility, because the story works as a story. It's like sending somebody back in time to kill Hitler in the crib, and he does it. The only irony you can have is his coming back and them saying, 'Why didn't you kill Kowalski like we asked you to?' History would be the same, but somebody else would do the job."

Episode #8:
"Devil's Due"
Written by William Lansford

Responding to a distress signal from a solar system "that shouldn't exist," the Enterprise arrives at Neuterra. Kirk, Xon, McCoy, Sulu, Ilia and Chekov beam down to the surface. They find a paradise, and a profound sadness amongst its people.

Meeting with the world's most blessed member, Zxoler, Kirk comments

●●●●

on the planet's beauty. The elderly man announces that all life on Neuterra will be destroyed in 20 days, which is the reason for the distress signal. One thousand years earlier (when Zxoler was a young man), the people had reached a point where their science outreached their wisdom to control it. As a result, the planet was ecologically raped and their civilization on the verge of extinction. Then, a being identifying itself as Komether appeared in answer to their prayers. It promised them 10 centuries of prosperity in exchange for their planet at the end of that time.

Unfortunately the prosperity of the planet extinguished the civilization's desire to develop. They never came up with a way to leave their world, choosing instead to enjoy paradise. Now their time is almost up.

While Kirk feels sympathy for their plight, he points out that the Enterprise is not equipped to transport more than a handful of extra passengers; any additional aid would arrive too late. Kirk then finds himself, as a representative of the Federation, defending the planet in a trial against Komether, who just might be the Devil himself. The captain suspects this demon may have been created from the Neuterrans' mind.

• • • •

In Jon Povill's opinion, "Devil's Due" could "work very well. It had all the elements necessary for a very exciting, involving episode."

"This was essentially 'The Devil and Daniel Webster'," said Harold Livingston. "The story has been developed to a point where we all feel it will be a most exciting *Star Trek*."

"Devil's Due" was later rewritten as an episode of *Star Trek: The Next Generation*.

Episode #9:
"Deadlock"
Written by David Ambrose

Commodore Hunter informs Kirk that the Enterprise will partake in war game activities. The captain is to take orders from Starfleet Science Advisor Lang Caradon. Knowing the man's reputation, McCoy points out that the tests will likely be an experiment in behavior control. This does not please Kirk.

Continuing games of manipulation ensue, culminating in a very real near battle-to-the-death between the starship and Starbase 7. Kirk, Decker, McCoy and Xon beam over to the base to see what they can do to prevent the imminent destruction. They ultimately discover that key Starfleet personnel, including Hunter and Caradon, have been replaced by alien beings. They reveal that the Federation is approaching their territory, which concerns them deeply. It's their intention to create hostilities among humans so that they'll eventually destroy themselves and never infect the aliens' part of the galaxy. Kirk must defeat this scheme while convincing the aliens that the Federation poses no threat.

• • • •

"David Ambrose is a British writer whom we had at one time considered for the two-hour premiere," explained Harold Livingston "His story, 'Deadlock,' concerns the Enterprise and a starbase involved in war games which turn out to be much more serious and which truly test the mettle of all our characters, our procedures and the bravery of our Enterprise crew. This should also be an extremely exciting story."

The concept of "gods" striking against man—an old standby used by Gene Roddenberry—may have been added to the story at the request of others. Ambrose's earlier treatment, "All Done With Mirrors," offered the same story with a different resolution. In this scenario, Caradon belongs to an underground organization which plans to overthrow the Federation. The struggle between a flagship and a starbase was just one of many accidents triggered by "dedicated fanatics" in key Starfleet positions, all pledged to sacrifice their lives for the cause.

Episode #10:
"Lord Bobby's Obsession"
Written by Shimon Wincelberg

Starfleet sensors detect a possible penetration of the Neutral Zone by a Romulan vessel. The Enterprise is ordered to investigate. At the Zone, they encounter a smaller ship and a humanoid who identifies himself as Lord Bobby, actually Lord Robert Standish, the Earl of

Lancashire, kidnapped from earth by aliens at the beginning of the 20th century. Somehow, these vanished aliens made him immortal. Bobby is thrilled to be among humans again.

As soon as the visitor boards the starship, five Romulan vessels surround and fire upon the Enterprise. They disable the warp drive. Kirk must convince the Romulans that the Enterprise isn't on a hostile mission, while at the same time dealing with the potential threat of Lord Bobby. An examination by Dr. McCoy reveals Bobby as an alien whose real purpose is unknown.

Episode #11:
"Are Unheard Melodies Sweet"
Written by Worley Thorne

A landing party arrives on the surface of a planet within the Haydes star cluster. It searches for the remains of the USS St. Louis, which reportedly crashed there. Xon locates the ship's log and, via tricorder, learns that the crew had been afflicted by a strange delirium from the planet and had piloted the ship into the atmosphere.

Decker mysteriously disappears while the Enterprise crew contracts the disease. Kirk must return to the ship while still attempting to locate Decker. The commander is held prisoner by an alien race with illusionary abilities, who force him to live out one sexual fantasy after another. Their lives exist only within illusions, which has resulted in their world falling into ruin. They face extinction and that's where the Enterprise personnel come in. The aliens plan to "manufacture" hormones to enhance their dream worlds and prolong their race. The earthlings serve as suppliers.

Kirk and his crew eventually learn that this race had once been extremely savage, but by focusing on the unreal they suppressed their true nature. Fantasy sex fills a void in their lives, but they no longer produce the necessary hormones. As a result, their old aggressions are returning.

Kirk must resist temptation and rescue Decker while McCoy (again) searches for a cure to the rapidly spreading disease.

• • • •

"Working on *Star Trek* was

something I very much wanted to do," says writer Worley Thorne, who would ultimately pen the "Justice" episode of *The Next Generation*. "I began my career the year that the original show started and I felt as though I missed out because I wasn't established enough to write for it. This was an opportunity to do something I had always wanted to do."

Episode #12:
"Kitumba"
Written by John Meredyth Lucas

The Enterprise embarks on a potential suicide mission to the Klingon homeworld to prevent an intergalactic war. Aided by a warrior named Ksia, who doesn't believe either side could survive such a conflict, they pass safely to the planet's surface. There they encounter the leader of the Klingon people, the Kitumba, a child destined for greatness.

Kirk does his best to convince the Kitumba that an invasion of Federation space would be disastrous for both sides. The captain seems to be winning the youth's confidence, but realize that there's no clear-cut way to end the potential war. The Enterprise crew falls into the midst of a power struggle between the ruler and his most trusted aides. That struggle will determine whether the ultimate war begins.

••••

"Kitumba" could easily served as a prequel to the feature film *Star Trek VI: The Undiscovered Country* in which the Federation and Klingon Empire begin the peace-making process.

Producer Harold Livingston had said at the time, "I think 'Kitumba' is very exciting, visually interesting and dramatic. It should be one hell of a show. [My notes] on it are really very minor, which illustrates the excellent flow of the story."

John Meredyth Lucas is justifiably proud of this particular effort. "I wanted something that we had never seen before on the series, and that's a penetration deep into enemy space. I then started to think of how the Klingons lived. Obviously for the Romulans we had Romans, and we've had different cultures modeled on those of ancient earth, but I tried to think of what the Klingon society would be like. The Japanese came to mind, so basically that what it was, with the Sacred Emperor, the Warlord and so on."

••••

••••

CHAPTER NINE

Star Trek:
The Movies

Paramount had never ceased to vacillate about the future of *Star Trek*, always fearful the phenomenon would abruptly end and leave them to foot the bill for an ill-advised "reunion" film or series. It wasn't until the back-to-back sucess of *Star Wars* and *Close Encounters of the Third Kind* that the studio realized there was an insatiable appetite for genre fare, thus the scuttling of the *Star Trek II* series one week before production was to commence.

When *Star Trek: The Motion Picture* was announced, Paramount Pictures envisioned it as a modestly-budgeted $15 million film. At a cost of about $5 million more than George Lucas had spent on *Star Wars*, it was imagined that the film could compete with that special effects extravaganza and win the battle hands down. Wrong! Conflicting visions, a special effects debacle that had the production begin with one F/X house then changing to others in mid-stream, and a scripting nightmare that resulted in much of the movie being shot without a completed third act, all combined to bloat the budget to $44 million, a budget only surpassed (at that time) by Twentieth Century Fox's *Cleopatra* and a Soviet screen version of *War and Peace*. Ironically, *Star Trek: The Motion Picture* reached theatres screens on December 7, 1979—Pear Harbor day. Based on the universal criticism it received, it appeared the film's release date was prophetic.

Star Trek: The Motion Picture was savaged by just about everyone, from reviewers to moviegoers drawn in by ten years worth of hype. The fans themselves were disappointed, though they were so desperate for *any Star Trek* that they turned the movie into a $175 million success and labored to have over an hour of truncated footage restored to a re-release in the hopes it would buoy the film. Although Paramount rejected the notion of a re-release in 70mm (the original hadn't been released in 70mm since

the final answer print had only been completed several days before the release date), they did include some deleted footage in the film's video release—another unprecedented sucess which helped launch the fledgling home video market.

David Gerrold, an integral part of the creation of the *Star Trek* spin-off *The Next Generation*, notes, "The fans had come off this two year high with *Star Wars* and the audience wanted more *Star Wars*, but there wasn't any more. So they went to see *Star Trek* and they were hungering for more, so *Star Trek* benefitted from the *Star Wars* phenomenon. They went and they saw it over and over again, but it was embarrassing to watch the fans because they were all apologists for this picture: 'Well, it's not that bad. It's a different kind of *Star Trek*.' Instead of really just acknowledging that it was a bad movie, they tried to explain that it was wonderful and you were an idiot for not understanding it. It was wonderful to watch them fuck their minds over to explain away a bad movie. The truth was that there was this movie that they wanted to love and they were so disappointed, but they wouldn't dare say that they were disappointed."

In fact, even *Star Trek*'s creator Gene Roddenberry, who had shepherded the film through production and been responsible for the endless rewrites that typified the shoot, couldn't defend the film from its detractors. Sitting next to Roddenberry on a plane heading towards the film's glamorous premiere in Washington D.C., Walter Koenig, who hadn't seen the movie, recalls querying the producer about the final product.

"Gene had just seen the cut and it was literally still wet," says Koenig. "I said 'What do you think of the picture?' He answered, 'It's a good picture.' It was a death knell, as soon as he said that I knew it wasn't going to work. He didn't put it down. He didn't denigrate it, but I heard it in his voice. I absolutely knew. Then you hope against hope that it's going to be good and you see the limousines and the red carpets and the spotlights. Then you see those first five minutes of the film with the music and you see V'ger and the destruction it causes. I got very excited but shortly thereafter I

began to become aware of time; that time was passing. That I wasn't involved in the picture. I was sitting in the audience and my heart sank and sank and sank, and I knew, ultimately, it was not a good film. I had no way of knowing what the critics would do. It was devastating, particularly *The Washington Post*, the first one that we saw the next day. It was the only time in my life that I thanked God for the relative anonymity that I had on *Star Trek*, because I was not mentioned in any way, shape or form."

The auteur theory notwithstanding, the individual who was saddled with the blame for *Star Trek: The Motion Picture*'s critical savaging was not its director, but producer/writer Gene Roddenberry who, although allowed to keep an office on the Paramount lot following the film's release, was considered a pariah and the prime reason that the film had spiralled overbudget and resulted in an aesthetically abysmal enterprise.

Yet when the film was originally announced, there was a great deal of enthusiasm and belief that the filmmakers would be creating a modern *2,001*.

The Press Conference

"The fans have supported us and consistently written us to pull our act together," announced former Paramount President Michael Eisner to the press on March 28, 1978.

Apparently the studio had, for on that day Eisner made the announcement that production would soon begin on the long-awaited *Star Trek: The Motion Picture*, featuring the entire original cast, with series creator Gene Roddenberry serving as executive producer and Robert Wise handling the directorial chores. After 10 long years, the dream was about to become reality.

Highlights of the press conference, reportedly the largest since Cecil B. DeMille announced production of *The Ten Commandments*, included:

William Shatner on returning to the role of Captain James T. Kirk: "I somehow always felt that we would be back together. Regardless of what I was doing, or where my career was taking me at the moment, I knew Captain Kirk was *not* behind me. He still would be very

••••

Leonard Nimoy, DeForest Kelley, Stephen Collins, Persis Khambatta and William Shatner co-starred in the $44 million "epic", Star Trek: The Motion Picture. (copyright © Globe Photos)

important in my future life—and work....I think Spencer Tracy said it best—'You take a deep breath and say the words.' Of course you have to have some years of experience to know how to say the words and suck in your breath. An actor brings to a role not only the concept of the character but his own basic personality, things that he is, and both Leonard and myself have changed over the years, to a degree at any rate, and we will bring that degree of change inadvertently to the role we recreate."

One question on the mind of the press was why Leonard Nimoy had seemed so reluctant to return to the fold.

"We've had a long and complicated relationship, Paramount and myself, for the last couple of years," Nimoy explained, "and probably the thing that took the most time was the fact that the mail service between here and Vulcan is still pretty slow. It's not really a matter of reluctance. We had a lot of details to work out. There have been periods of time when the Star Trek project was moving forward and I was not available. For example, last summer we had come to what I felt was an understanding about doing the movie. I went off to do Equus on Broadway. During that period of time, the concept changed to a TV series. It was difficult then to get together because there was a question of availability. When the project turned around and I was available again, we started talking immediately. It has been complicated; it has been time consuming. But there was never a question of reluctance to be involved in Star Trek on my part. I've always felt totally comfortable about being identified with Star Trek, and being identified with the Spock character. It has exploded my life in a very positive way. The Spock character has always been part of my life. I have never tried in any way to reject that. I'm very proud of the fact that I'm associated with the character. And I look forward to playing the character because I certainly wouldn't want either one of two things—anybody else playing it, or Star Trek happening without it."

One thing that Gene Roddenberry emphasized at the time was that the storyline of the film, like so many of the episodes, would bring with it a powerful message.

"It definitely will," he emphasized, "and this is one reason I was so pleased that Bob Wise joined us in the production, because he feels the same way about this motion picture. I think all good stories have something to say, and without anyone getting on a soapbox at any time in this film, we will be talking about something that we think is very important."

A Wise Move

"I thought it was time," explains Robert Wise in terms of his reason for accepting the directorial reins of Star Trek: The Motion Picture. "I have always been intrigued by science fiction, even though I have only done two other films in the genre, and I thought it was time that I did a science fiction picture that took place in space. Both my my other ones were earth-bound. In The Day the Earth Stood Still we had a visitor from outer space, coming in a spaceship....that really intrigued me more than anything else. So I was glad to have a chance to explore this further. I liked the idea of doing Star Trek from the beginning, the quality of it....It was really the fascination and the desire to do a film which dealt with the experience of being in space."

Wise admits that he was not familiar with the Star Trek universe before he accepted the picture. "Of course I knew of it," he clarifies, "but I had not become a Trekkie when the TV series had first come out and I had only seen one or two segments, which I thought were alright—but I didn't get hooked on it. After the President of Paramount asked me if I would be interested in considering directing the movie, I said, 'Well, I just don't know. I'll have to read the script, of course, and I would have to see several more of the TV segments.' I had to get familiar with what it was and what had caused it to become so immensely popular. So that's what happened: I read the script and I saw about a dozen episodes of the series so I could become familiar with it, and make my own judgement."

Given his track record, it's not surprising that Robert Wise is used to autonomy on his films, yet in the case of

Star Trek he was in the position of working closely with the concept's creator, Gene Roddenberry, which, he notes, "was comparatively easy. Of course, as much as producers and directors are separate entities, you always have little conflicts at times but, by and large, it was fine. When I came on after being asked to do the film, I said, 'What about Mr. Roddenberry? Because it's his baby,' and they said, 'Well, you'll have to work it up.' So Gene and I talked at some length about how we could work together, how he and I saw the whole thing. We came to reach a working agreement about halfway in our positions and I think we functioned pretty well on that level."

For his part, Roddenberry told journalist Tom Rogers that in terms of having control, he had "as much as I have the personality to take over. But more is not always more in making a movie. Making movies is quite different than making a television show. In television, I had directors that came and went, different directors every week. Naturally I had to assume a lot of control over the initial show because it was my idea, and I wanted all of the directors to be directing the same Mr. Spock next week as they directed last week. In a movie, however, which is a director's medium, I can hardly get a director of the quality and ability of a Robert Wise and then walk in and say, 'Listen, I want you to do everything exactly as I tell you.' When you bring in Robert Wise, you're bringing in his talent, his ability of wide-screen movies. There's a wonderful partnership between he and I, rather than one or the other trying to seize more control.

"There are a lot of places we disagree," he continued, "but in a friendly, professional way. My taste for costumes was a little different than his, but in the end I went with his taste because he was the man responsible for creating the whole visual image. If it had been more than just a question of taste, if I had thought the costumes violated Star Trek format, then we would have probably had a very serious fight. But we didn't, because it was just a question of taste. There are some places where he wanted to do some things, I can't remember an example right now, and I would say, 'Bob, the Star Trek format has always

• • • •

been this. I don't want to lock you into format, but let's not change unless we have some value that makes the change worthwhile.'"

In this respect, Robert Wise was in the unusual position of not only working in a format familiar to the audience but with a cast that had better knowledge of the characters and film than even he had.

"I should tell you a story first," laughs Wise. "After Paramount finally signed everybody, they had a big publicity party for the press and they set up a large table with Roddenberry, all the cast, etc. When my turn came to speak, I said, 'You know, I'm the alien here,' because I was the only one who hardly knew anything of *Star Trek*. They all knew more than I did. But it worked out very well. They're all very good actors, very professional. There were some very pleasant moments with all the actors on the set because I found that they really loved their characters and always looked for ways of improving their roles, like 'So and so wouldn't say it like that.' At the same time, they were never pushy or overly tempted to be demanding—to take the whole thing. I found all of them, and particularly Bill and Leonard, to be professional and very good actors."

Unlike his other genre efforts, *The Day the Earth Stood Still* and *The Andromeda Strain, Star Trek: The Motion Picture* represented an extremely complex shoot due to the elaborate special effects.

"Control was much simpler [back] then," sighs Wise. "In *Star Trek* all of this was very elaborate; very, very difficult because I had so much to deal with which was not even done yet. Scenes in which my actor had to play and react to that screen and I had nothing to show them on the screen. All that came in months later. The best I ever had for them to react to was a projection of a sketch or a picture of what the effects men were planning to achieve. That's all I had for them. I had to remind them of what was going on in terms of the action, to describe the best I could from the script and from my own ideas of the sketch and what they were supposed to be looking at. It takes some very professional actors to respond to something like that, and that made it very difficult—in fact, it was perhaps the most difficult part

of the film. And then we had, of course, the big problem of having to change the special effects people after a year."

One of the strongest criticisms levelled against the film was the fact that the interpersonal relationships—which were so integral to the success of the original *Star Trek*—were given a back seat to the F/X.

"It [wasn't as] if somebody say down at the beginning and said, 'Listen, we want to get a lot more special effects.' It was not a deliberate move to shift the emphasis from one area to another," Wise emphasises. "That was really because of the story. That was the script, or the story we had to tell, and we didn't try to put more special effects in it. I didn't try. None of us tried. We had people reacting to things that were happening on the screen, so we had to show these things. If there is a valid criticism coming from those Trekkies who really love these characters with all their heart, there still wasn't anything we could do about it. We would have had to have a totally different story."

One would imagine that Wise wishes that they had.

The Script's The Thing

Star Trek creator Gene Roddenberry often attributed the success of the series to the fact that it showed man transcending his intolerance for his fellow man; that we as a species had moved beyond our petty differences which have, for so long, separated us, and achieved a peace amongst ourselves and the stars.

Unfortunately, what was true for a network television series and the motion picture it inspired, was not true for the real-life behind the scenes relationships which brought the magic to life. This has never been more true than in the writing of *Star Trek: The Motion Picture.*

As detailed earlier in this volume, the film began as a two-hour episode of the abandoned *Star Trek II* television series. The plot of "In Thy Image" had been derived from a Roddenberry-written premise for *Genesis II* entitled "Robot's Return," in which a NASA space probe returns to Earth seekings its creator.

Famed science fiction writer

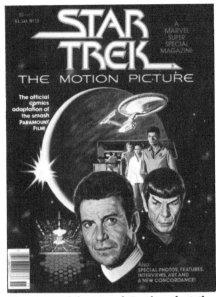

The cover of the Marvel Comics adaptation of Star Trek: The Motion Picture.

Alan Dean Foster explains, "When they were thinking of the *Star Trek II* TV series, a number of writers were called in to submit treatments for hour-long episodes. Roddenberry got in touch with me based on the *Star Trek Log* series I had done for Ballantine Books, and he said that he felt I was comfortable with the *Star Trek* universe and comfortable and familiar with the characters. So I submitted three story ideas. One of them was based on a page and a half of his notes on something called 'Robot's Return.' He thought that could be developed and wanted to see what I could do with it.

"After my treatment based on Roddenberry's page was handed in," he continues, "it was decided to open the new series with a two-hour movie for TV, which is fairly standard procedure when they can manage it for dramatic series, and it was decided that my treatment of the ones they had at hand would be the best suited to carry two hours. At least that's what I heard. I went home and developed a 32-page outline."

That outline, like "Robot's Return," dealt with an old space probe that had achieved consciousness and was now returning to Earth to join with its creator. While the story worked quite well as far as the show's production team was concerned, there was no intention of having Foster write the actual teleplay.

Harold Livingston, co-producer of the series, says, "Alan Dean Foster was a protege of Gene's and he was brought in to me to write something. So I wanted to see something he had written, and he brought me two screenplays which I thought were terrible, and I didn't want him to write. I just didn't think he was right for the job. This was obviously a very subjective judgement, but that's what they're paying me for. They either rely on my judgement or they get some-one else.

"I made a deal with Alan's agent that he would write a story and agree *not* to do the script. So he wrote a story which was this business of the old machine coming back to Earth and assuming a kind of life form. I didn't know that this had also been an episode of the original *Star Trek* ['The Changeling']. By the way, at this point we're starting to come to a production date as well. I then began to look for writers to turn the story into a script. I went through two or three weeks of talking to people and I couldn't find anybody that I liked. With five weeks to go, I decided I'd write it myself.

"So I sat down and for five weeks I wrote this script of 'In Thy Image.' I finished the first draft, delivered it to Gene and Gene said, 'God, it's good. You've done your job. Now just relax and I'll write the second draft.' He writes it in a week. Then he brought it in, gave it to us proudly in a bright orange cover, and there it is, 'In Thy Image,' by Gene Roddenberry and Harold Livingston. He took first position. We all read it and I was appalled, and so was everyone else. There was [story editor] Jon Povill, [pro-ducer] Bob Goodwin, myself and Bob Collins, who was the director."

Adds Collins, "Harold and I sat there and we asked each other which one of us was going to tell him that it wasn't quite right. Finally, I said 'Hell, I'm the director,' and walked out of the room."

Harold Livingston continues the scenario, "I said, 'I'll tell him.' I went in and I said, 'Gene, this doesn't work.' Well, his face dropped to his ankles. Then I got myself wound up and I told him why it didn't work, and I said, 'Why'd you do it? When something

works, you don't piss in it to make it bet-ter!' In any case, he was pretty stubborn about this. He thought it was good and said, 'We'll give it to the front office.' Well, about three days later, we have a meeting in Michael Eisner's gigantic white office. We sat around this huge table. There was Roddenberry, myself, Eisner, Jeffrey Katzenberg, the head of television, Arthur Fellows; and a couple of other guys. Michael had the two scripts. 'In Thy Image' by me was in a brown cover, and Gene's version was in an orange cover. Michael had one script in one hand and one in the other, bal-ancing them in his palms. And he said, 'Listen, this is the problem. This,' Gene's orange script, 'is television. This,' the brown script, 'is a movie. Frankly, it's a lot better.' Well, holy shit! Everybody was clearing their throats. The great man had had his feathers ruffled. Anyway, after some heated discussion, it was decided to let Collins write a third ver-sion using the best elements of both. So Collins did this after two or three weeks, and his was a total disaster.

"Along that time, Roddenberry and I really began to get at each other's throats. December came along and my contract was coming up. Before they could fire me, I quit. We had too many problems there. I just didn't think that Gene was a good writer. He, for his part I'm sure, considered me a total interlop-er. Who the hell am I to come in? I understand that, in fact I understood it, but I wanted to instill some literary value into these science fiction myths. He had his own formula which worked. He was obviously saturated with science fiction. I think he knew a lot about a lot of things, generally, and he had a great following. Here I was getting on his nerves."

One undeniable contribution to the script that came from the rewrite, how-ever, was Roddenberry's idea of having the probe, eventually called V'Ger (short for Voyager 6) release all its data into Will Decker. Livingston's conclusion, on the other hand, merely had the probe recog-nizing the positive qualities of man as a species and departing the galaxy.

"Robert Goodwin theorized that I just pissed away the ending because I was so disgusted with the situation," muses Livingston. "I think the truth is that I

couldn't come up with an ending. I just couldn't do it. The problem was that we had an antagonist so omnipotent that to defeat it, or even communicate with it, or have any kind of relationship with it, made the concept of the story false. How the hell do we deal with this? On what level? Everything pretty much worked in the story until we got to the ending. We tried all kinds of approaches, including aesthetic, theological and philosophical. We didn't know what to do with the ending."

Jon Povill, on the other hand, did. "We knew we had to have a big spe-cial effects ending," he says. "The prob-lem of what was going to happen at the end and why it was going to happen, was one that plagued the script from the very start. Then Gene came up with the idea of the machine dumping its data into Decker, with a light show of all the infor-mation it had accumulated. We were going to get all this amazing, incompre-hensible stuff that V'Ger had accumulat-ed in its travels across the universe, and, of course, nobody could come up with these images, so that didn't work. It was pretty much my contribution to say that the reason for what was happening was that this thing needed to go on to the next plane of existence; that it was tran-scending this dimension and going on to the next. It then became logical that the machine would need that human ele-ment to combine with. It was the only thing that could have made sense."

Upon quitting *Star Trek*, Livingston went to work at Aaron Spelling Productions, believing he was leaving the 23rd Century behind him. Under the guise of wanting to infuse the production with "fresh writer blood," Dennis Clark was hired just as the TV-movie became a theatrical film. From the writer's point of view, it was *not* a happy experience.

Clark explains, "I try never to bum-rap people. The problem with Gene is that his heart was never in the right place at the right time. It's a good heart, but he puts it aside at the wrong times. I was the subject of a practical joke from him. An awful one, and it was right at the beginning of the relationship and it set things off badly. Gene's a nice man, unless you give him some power. That practical joke was the beginning of the

• • • •

end. I got pissed off, Gene got pissed off and the only mediator was Bob Wise who looked at me and said, 'I'm going to have to fire you, aren't I?' And I said, 'Yes.'"

Clark's involvement with the film lasted approximately three months, two of which "I spent hiding from Nimoy and Shatner because they didn't want me to talk to them. I'd have to leave my office when they were on the lot, because actors want to tell you, 'This is how I perceive the character,' and Gene didn't want their input. He didn't want me to have their input. He didn't even like Bob Wise's input....I wish I could tell you more, but my point of view is very biased and it's a part of my life I don't even like to think about."

Paramount's Jeffrey Katzenberg, Robert Wise and Gene Roddenberry all asked that Livingston return to the film. Reluctantly, he did so.

"I had an understanding with young Mr. Katzenberg and Mr. Wise and Gene that I would do it as long as Gene didn't write," explains Livingston. "'I don't want Gene to put pen to paper. You want me to write it, I will write it. I'll do all the rewriting you want, but *I* will do it.' I had a certain style I wanted to do the script in and I had directions I wanted the characters to explore. The first thing that happened is that I rewrote 'x' number of pages and they were to be pouched to Eisner and Katzenberg in Paris. Somehow, Roddenberry got a hold of it, rewrote it and sent that to Paris. Eisner called up from Paris and said, 'What kind of shit is this?' Then Wise and I had to explain what happened. This kind of thing continued and Gene would be very remorseful and contrite, 'I was just trying to help.' I said, 'Listen, Gene, I'm not going to do this if you're going to keep this up.' Well, I quit three times. I resigned. I'm talking about $10,000 a week."

Each time he quit, Livingston was cajoled to come back to work by either Robert Wise or Jeffrey Katzenberg. Needless to say, the same problems would begin anew.

"As we began shooting," recalls Livingston, "we would get to a point where I would send in pages and then Gene would send in different pages and Wise would get two different versions. Sometimes I would write it and put my initials on them, and Gene would put 'G.R., 4PM' under mine, as though that's what should count and my pages should be ignored. This was the way the picture was made. For the third time I quit, I said, 'Screw it, nothing is worth this.' Now we weren't talking to each other. Gene has a brilliant story mind for this kind of thing, but he's a bad writer. He's clumsy. Anyway, the third time they really went behind Gene's back. I said I wouldn't have anything to do with it, and Eisner called me himself from New York and said I had to fix the script. I said I would do it if Gene promised he wouldn't do anymore writing, which of course was broken immediately. Finally, the picture was somehow filmed."

Which is not to say that the problems were over. The writing credits proposed to the Writer's Guild by Paramount was screenplay by Harold Livingston and story by Alan Dean Foster.

"They left Roddenberry out," Livingston says, "so he protested. He's the one who launched the protest. I knew he couldn't win an arbitration, because it wasn't his script. Anything he'd done was tossed out, or most of it. In any case, I blackjacked Foster into splitting the story credit with Gene. He agreed to do it and Gene wouldn't accept it. On that basis, I said, 'Okay, Gene, screw you. We'll go to arbitration.' When I said that, he withdrew, and he withdrew in a funk; he was mad. I said to him, 'If you felt you deserved credit, then you have a system for determining this. Why didn't you use it?' He said, 'I don't want to lower myself to that.' At that point, I guess, he decided to withdraw and assume this injured pose. But he would have lost this arbitration because he didn't write any script. All he did was rewrite, patch up, fool around and screw up everything."

At the time, Roddenberry explained, "It [the script] started off a bit simpler because it had been written as a two-hour television program. It got more and more complex as it got to be a bigger and bigger movie, and we started adding things on to make use of the wide-screen, big-vision, like the wing-walk, where they go out on top of the Enterprise saucer section. I put that in. I put the climax of the show inside V'ger, where the original script did not. I'm not taking screen credit because we had a writer who worked very hard on it. He felt he deserved the credit and my policy is to never get into a credit dispute. That was my policy all through *Star Trek*. If a writer felt he wanted it and wanted it badly enough to have a Guild action on it, I'd withdraw."

Of the situation, Alan Dean Foster recalls, "The first thing they did was try to deny me screen credit. When the credits came out to be filed with the Guild, the credits read, 'Screenplay by Gene Roddenberry and Harold Livingston, Story by Gene Roddenberry.' I'm a very low-key guy. I'm an old handshake-is-my-bond kind of guy. Once it became a big budget movie, I became the non-existent man as soon as the budget increased, because it became serious money. Trying to keep my blood pressure down I called my agent and said, 'What's going on?' And she said, 'Oh, that's nothing.' 'What do you mean that's nothing?' 'Nobody's mad at you or anything, that's just the business.' I said, 'Well, it's not my business and we picked up and moved to Arizona.

"My agent suggested I file for solo credit. I said, 'Sure,' because I did 98% of the writing on the treatment. Then Harold Livingston called me and said, 'Just because Roddenberry is being a son of a bitch, doesn't mean that you have to be one too.' I thought about it and I said, 'You're right.' So I called and said, 'Look, all I'm interested in here is having it read the way that it read on the script, which is 'Story by Alan Dean Foster and Gene Roddenberry,' because it was, as I freely admit, based on his one page idea. I then get this very strange letter back saying that Gene Roddenberry is off in La Costa someplace recuperating, he's very tired, very busy and he really doesn't have time for this. I just laughed. Is this real life or kindergarten? I just threw up my hands and said, 'Fine, whatever,' and that's why I have sole story credit on the movie.

"I had only worked with people like George Lucas, who is one of the nicest people in the movie business, and Ronald Shusett, who produced *Alien*. But *Star Trek* was my worst experience. Nobody had ever tried to do that to me before. That's just the way it is, apparent-

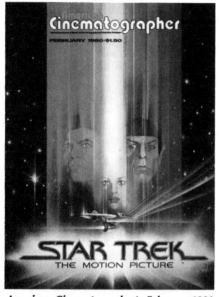

American Cinematographer's February 1980 issue examined the making of Star Trek: The Motion Picture.

ly. They put you in the shark cage, you learn how to fight with the other sharks or you go back in the goldfish bowl. I belonged in the goldfish bowl."

Although not bitter, Foster does recall Roddenberry hugging his shoulder and saying, "You remind me of me when I was getting started. I'm going to teach you everything I know about the business."

"He *did* teach me quite a lot about the business," Foster laughs with-out humor, "although I don't think that's what he originally had in mind."

Considering the critical scorning that *Star Trek: The Motion Picture* received, it hardly seems to have been worth all the battles, though Harold Livingston remains philosophical.

"I was upset with the film," he states. "It just wasn't what I wanted. I can't honestly say this wasn't my fault, because in the end I took the rap for it anyway. But if I do a poor job, I'll tell you it's bad. I know it's bad and I'll welcome help. I'm certainly not infallible. Gene would never admit that he wrote a bad line or couldn't write. He made an industry of *Star Trek* and he's really done nothing else. Gene's values lay in his knowledge, his experience. If he had imparted that and let the professionals do their job, you'd have had a picture."

• • • •

CHAPTER TEN

Star Trek II:
The Wrath of Khan

Star Trek: The Motion Picture was nothing like *Star Trek*: The TV series. It was as if the powers that be decided to remake *Star Trek* by violating every principal the series' popularity was based on. Couched-in subdued, generally unpleasant hints of their former personalities, the characters wandered through an aimless and irritating plot which seemed primarily an excuse for a self-conscious special effects extravaganza. The plot was unabashedly drawn from several episodes of the series, most notably "The Changeling," and the climactic "revelation" was expounded with such numbing heavy-handedness that even the most dedicated Trekkie must have suppressed a shudder before jumping up to praise the Emperor's new clothes.

"We had no idea that the first film would be a disaster," actor William Shatner admitted in 1982. "We never knew it was falling apart while we were shooting. We didn't have an ending to the script when we started, but we had months to play around with solving it. With all the high-priced talent around, we were sure that someone would come up with a corker of a finale. Somebody would certainly create something which made *sense*. [But] we never got it together. Nobody connected with the film ever sat in a theatre and saw the movie with an audience *before* it opened. After you've spent nearly two years on a project, that's essential. By that point, you're just too close to a movie to judge it objectively. The finished *Star Trek: The Motion Picture* was really two movies: one about *Star Trek*, one about special effects. Had 15 minutes been trimmed out of the released version, I think it would have been a different, stronger film. I also felt that the characters weren't as fully realized as they could have been. We certainly were dwarfed by the special effects. It was a very confusing time for me. One felt helpless. I remember having lunch with the studio head who asked me, 'What made *Star Trek* so successful?'

I couldn't tell him anything. What was I going to say? 'Character development and story?' If I had told him that, he would have said, 'Yeah, but we need big effects to compete with *Star Wars*.' As a result, you wound up with a weak movie."

That "weak" movie cost $45 million "that Paramount will admit to," according to one film industry figure. But like the TV show, extensive merchandising saved the first movie. The myriad products created in conjunction with the movie sold very well. And when the movie finally earned back its nut—a film must gross about three times its production costs to start showing a profit—it was plain that even severe maltreatment had not killed the golden goose.

Word of a Gene Roddenberry-produced sequel began making the rounds shortly after the premiere of *Star Trek: The Motion Picture*. One proposed plotline, according to *Starlog* magazine, had the Enterprise travel backwards in time to save the life of President Kennedy. As a result, all history would have been changed. Reportedly, this tired retread of "City on the Edge of Forever" would have concluded with Spock firing a deadly phaser blast at the president to set things straight. Nothing more was heard of this premise.

"We know a little bit more about how to use *Trek* in motion pictures," Roddenberry said in 1980. "The second run in anything is easier. If you've ever played golf, the second try you can always sink the putt. It's that first shot at the hole...The sequel story is much more intra-crew, intra-character. It has many more of the difficult decisions that Kirk always had in the TV episodes; decisions about morality and ideals—but I'm not going to say anything more. It's good *Star Trek*. It would have made a good three-parter on the TV show—if I'd had the money to do it."

Many of Roddenberry's views of the *Star Trek II* script would ultimately prove themselves correct, but, ironically, he would have nothing to do with the final film.

Project Genesis

Paramount began to think once more about bringing out the sets it had

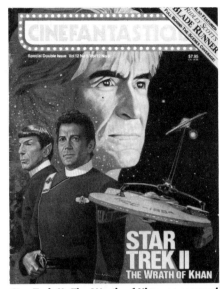

Star Trek II: The Wrath of Khan *as covered in the pages Cinefantastique's July-August 1982 edition.*

carefully stored away after the first film wrapped. This time, things would be done differently, they decided sensibly enough. This time the television arm of the studio would produce the motion picture. This time its budget would be strictly controlled and kept to about a quarter of the final cost of the first film. This time it would be *Star Trek* as it had been in the much-loved TV series: a story about people, not technology or special effects.

Gene Roddenberry, creator and executive producer of the series and producer of the first movie, became "executive consultant."

"My contract gives me the total right to produce and write all motion pictures," Roddenberry told *The Official Star Trek Fan Club Magazine*. "But I did *Star Trek* 79 times. I just can't be a creature of *Star Trek* all my life. I wanted to see bright, new people come in and put a good stamp on it and add certain differences. As the consultant, they send me everything from the first story idea to the final draft of the motion picture. I also see the dailies and rough-cuts and all of that. I make my comments to them. I have told them the only time I would say, 'no, stop, I refuse to put my name on it,' is if they should break any of the very basic things about *Star Trek*. If you're going to have good people, you've got to give good people some latitude to do it their way."

• • • •

Harve Bennett was chosen to serve as executive producer. Bennett has been respected for his intelligence, his articulateness and his fund of general knowledge since the days when, as Harvey Fischman, he was one of the original radio show "Quiz Kids" in the '40s. Since then, he has worked for the Sun Times in Chicago, CBS-TV, ABC-TV (where he was executive producer for *The Six Million Dollar Man*) and as an executive producer/writer for Universal. Bennett was executive producer of the *Rich Man, Poor Man* and *From Here to Eternity* mini-series.

"I came to Paramount with no anticipation of doing feature pictures at all," Bennett has told journalists. "I was here to do television. But the second week I was here I got a call from [studio president] Barry Diller. Now you have to remember that running the studio at the time was Barry Diller, who used to be my assistant at ABC, Michael Eisner, who used to be a counterpart of mine at ABC New York, and running the entire operation was the great immigrant, the last of the moguls, Charlie Bludhorn, who built Gulf and Western, and bought Paramount. Barry calls me in and says, 'Will you come to a meeting in my office?'"

At that meeting were the aforementioned executives, including Charles Bludhorn, who asked Bennett what he thought of *Star Trek: The Motion Picture*. "I....decided that the truth was the only thing I could say. So I said, 'I thought it was boring.' He suddenly turned on Michael Eisner and said, 'See, by you, bald is sexy.'"

With the script for *Star Trek II* still to be settled upon, Bennett began gathering his production staff. He selected Robert Sallin, a director and producer of television commercials and an old college chum, to produce the movie. Bennett and Sallin both attended UCLA's Film School "in the early fifties," joked Sallin, "before it was fashionable." Sallin has made over 1600 commercials and won virtually every top national and international award, including the 1978 Clio for Most Humorous Commercial of the Year and the 1970 Grand Prix of the Venice Film Festival for outstanding commercial worldwide. It fell upon Sallin, who joined the production in February

1981, to bring in STAR TREK II quickly and cheaply. The film's budget is officially $12 million.

Sallin says, "Before I joined Harve on the project, I sent him a lengthy memo. I had studied *Star Trek I* and I pinpointed a lot of the fundamental weaknesses of the first film. First and foremost, I felt it was too much a special effects picture and that the humanity of *Star Trek* just wasn't there. I felt that the focus of our picture should be humanity. Let the special effects support it as any effect should support basic storytelling, not be driven by the effects which so many science fiction films are. I felt that the look of the picture from a design point of view had been all wrong, the lighting was too flat and uninteresting. I made a very strong point about one thing. I said, 'Let's not attack this as though it's another film project or another television project. I want to interview every member of the crew. I want to make sure that these guys are not only mentally competent, but I want an attitude here. I want an attitude that we're all in this together. As corny as it sounds, I wanted to make sure we had a great time making this film."

Bennett also hired Michael Minor as art director and it was Minor who suggested the direction the script would eventually take. At that time the story was called *The Omega Project* and it revolved around a destructive weapon.

"Harve wanted something uplifting, something that would be as fundamental in the 23rd Century as the discovery of recombinant DNA is in our time," said the late Minor, who suggested an idea to Bennett during a casual phone call. "Then something just came to me and I said, 'Terraforming.' Harve asked, 'What's that?' and I told him it was the altering of existing planets to conditions which are compatible to human life.

"I suggested a plot, just making it up in my head while talking on the phone," he continued. "The Federation had developed a way of engineering the planetary evolution of a body in space on such a rapid scale that instead of eons you have events taking place in months or years. You pick a dead world or an inhospitable gas planet, and you change its genetic matrix or code, thereby speed-

ing up time. This, of course, is also a terrible weapon. Suppose you trained it on a planet filled with people and speeded up its evolution. You could destroy the planet and every lifeform on it. The Federation is involved with playing God, but at the same time, trying to take barren dead planets and convert them into lovely worlds. Harve liked the idea a lot. At the story conference the next day, he came over, hugged me and said, 'You saved *Star Trek!'*"

In other ways than the re-encounter with his old nemesis, Khan, the past is catching up with Kirk. The script realizes that these people are no longer the same people we met 15 years ago. They've grown older. They're surrounded by a bevy of cadets who make them feel their age. Kirk, in particular, is feeling the cold breath of mortality on the back of his neck. He has just turned another year older as the story begins, and is starting to realize that he has not been exactly building an emotional nest.

"Throughout the story," explains Sallin, "Kirk goes through a great deal of introspection and reflection on his life. In a sense, he's having a mid-life crisis. Throughout the film we exposed and plumbed the interpersonal relationships, which were established back on the series, to a level I don't think you've seen before."

In the script, Kirk meets his son, someone he was never particularly interested in becoming involved with, and he doesn't even recognize him. David Kirk (actually David Marcus, having taken his mother's name) is not a little boy, not a teenager, but a grown man, a scientist on an advanced project, indicating years of education and experience behind him. "I stayed away because you asked me to," Kirk tells his son's mother, but staying away and staying totally out of touch are two different things, and they both know it. Kirk has always worked hard at being emotionally superficial, and it has come home to haunt him in many ways.

Stated Harve Bennett to journalist Marc Shapiro, "The main thing that rang false about the first film was that the characters had gone 20 years and hadn't aged which, to my way of thinking, was totally unbelievable. I felt a major element in future films would be to have the characters age and to focus on what they were going through as people as they did so. At one point, I even sat down with Shatner and told him point blank that there was a real danger in having a middle-aged Kirk running around like a 30-year-old."

As the script developed, Sallin began preproduction and was determined not to let the film's special effects get out of hand, a factor which drove up the budget on the first film.

"I just applied some old commercial production techniques," he details. "I storyboarded everything. I had a chart made which listed, by scene, every special effect and optical effect, and I timed each one. I designed and supervised all the special effects. Mike Minor, our art director, sat up here in my office and did the storyboards. Then I held meetings with four or five optical effects companies, and some of those meetings ran over three hours.

"I gave them thorough information, so that when the movie was finished, the amount of deviation from the plan was very slight. As you recall, in the first movie there were quite a few problems with special effects. Because I knew how to handle and manage production, I was left very much alone by the studio. I think they were all a little intimidated by what had gone on previously, and the idea of of special effects escalating the way they did on *Star Trek I* was a major fear and concern. This time we came in so close to budget that you couldn't go out for a decent lunch on the difference."

The storyboarding process began in June, before the script had been finalized. As different scripts came in, art director Mike Minor redrew the boards. "I laid out four different features in storyboard," said Minor. "Literally different. Different plots, different characters, different events, different effects. I put in maybe 400 man-hours before we settled on what we used to get bids for the effects."

The Search For Nimoy

Harve Bennett began the process of selecting the storyline for the film by screening numerous episodes of the original television series. While quite a few of them appealed to him, the one that absolutely captured his imagination was "Space Seed," which introduced Khan Noonian Singh.

At the time, Bennett had asked himself, "'Who is the heavy? Who is the black hat? We won't make this picture unless there *is* a black-hat heavy.' You know the solution the writers and producers came with with for [*Star Trek*] *II*: Khan. I had been watching the *Star Trek* episodes, and I said, 'Okay, where's my heavy?' Montalban, especially now that he's become 'Mr. White Suit,' is the best heavy there ever was. It's great! Great reverse casting, and it works."

Initially, Bennett wrote a one-page outline entitled *Star Trek: The War of the Generations*, in which a new generation is planning on overthrowing the United Federation of Planets. Their leader, it turns out, is Khan, who sees this as a chance for revenge against Kirk and all that the Federation stands for.

Next, Bennett had to find someone to collaborate with to expand the premise into a screenplay. "After considering other writers," said Bennett, "I found out that Jack Sowards, a great 'movie of the week' writer, was a great *Star Trek* fan. We talked and he clearly knew more about *Star Trek* than I did, so I hired him. Jack and I went to work, and I say *we* went to work because the process is like this: you talk, and you rap and the responsibility is that the writer records, in whatever fashion he chooses the fruits of the give and take of this process. His task is then to go and make it become a script. Jack made an enormous contribution to this picture."

Most notable among them was the idea of killing the Spock character as a means of enticing Leonard Nimoy to star in the film, after the star had stated he had no interest in *Star Trek II.*

"There have been times when I've been concerned about the future of my career, because of the identification with the character," explained Leonard Nimoy. But I never had a confrontation with the studio in which I've said I would never play the part again. My only concern with *Star Trek* has been that if we're going to do it, we do it well. I don't want to just do a rip-off *Star Trek* title just because people will pay to see it. If it's

going to be good, I wanted to be there. I'd hate like hell to see a great *Star Trek* movie hit the screen and not be in it. I'd feel very jealous. [At the time] I really was adamant that I would not work on *Star Trek II* because I had been so frustrated with the other and I was feeling very negative about the whole thing."

Jack Sowards continues the scenario: "When Harve and I had our first meeting, Harve said, 'Look, Nimoy has refused to do it.' I said, 'You want Nimoy to do it?' He said, 'Yeah,' and I told him to dial Nimoy's number. He picked up the phone, dialed the number and said, 'What do I say?' I said, 'You say, 'Leonard, how would you like to play your death scene?' Leonard came on the phone, Harve said, 'Leonard, how would you like to play your death scene?' And Leonard's comeback was, 'Where does it come in the picture?' Harve looked at me and said, 'Where does it come in the picture?' And I said, 'Right up front. Right in the very beginning.' Harve said, 'Right in the very beginning.' A minute or two later Harve hung up and said, 'Leonard will do it.' Of course when we wrote it, it came in the very beginning. But everytime we wrote a little bit more, we moved it back and we moved it back and we moved it back, until it came at the end."

"[Harve] caught me completely by surprise with that one," Nimoy related. "The more I thought about it, the more I thought, 'Well, maybe that's the honest thing to do. Finish it properly rather than turn your back on it.' So, eventually, we agreed that Spock would die. There was a lot of controversy over whose idea it was and why. It was even said that it was the only way I would do it and that it was in my contract that Spock would die! It got to be a messy situation.

"The only thing I can tell you is that when Harve and I started to explore the idea, I thought back to the first season of *Star Trek*, when the Spock character had taken root and been widely accepted. The whole concept of his lack of emotionality, his control of emotions, was a very interesting and important part of the character. Dorothy Fontana, who was a writer on the series, came to me on the set one day and said, 'I'm going to write a love story for Spock.' I told her she couldn't do it because it would destroy the character, destroy the whole mystique about whether or not he's emotional. The whole story we'd been telling was that he was completely in control of his emotions. She said, 'I have an idea that might work, and I'm going to try it.' She did, and wrote 'This Side of Paradise,' a beautiful episode in which Spock fell in love. At the end of it, there was a bittersweet parting and it was all over. And he had gone through this fantastic experience!"

The Scripts Of Wrath

With the Nimoy matter settled, Jack Sowards and Harve Bennett got down to business in their approach to the screenplay for *Star Trek II*.

Relates Soward, "We sat down and watched 'Space Seed' and the original motion picture. Actually, we sat through the original picture and talked. It was beautifully done, but the effects overwhelmed it. You can't have five minutes of dialogue and 15 minutes of effects, but that's what they did. We looked at it from the point of view that we wanted to take bits and snatches of those effects—the ships, spacedock, etc.—and use them in the picture. Of course we thought that nobody has really seen this. When you've got a character scene going and you cut outside, cut somewhere else, you don't linger on it for five minutes, it works. That's one of the reasons we watched the original picture, to see how many of the effects we could use without making it look like we were just cannibalizing an old picture. We both knew that it had to be told in a totally different way, and that was in terms of the characters. Fortunately, the big upside is that we eventually got Nicholas Meyer to direct, who has a talent for bringing a scene to life. With him, the characters are living their lives. That's what a director is supposed to do. A director is supposed to make these scenes a part of a person's life. Some directors point the camera a certain way and shoot the scene. They don't realize that that person has to be living a life, and the scene happens within that life. If the life doesn't exist, the scenes loses its meaning."

While watching "Space Seed,"

Sowards found himself delighting in Ricardo Montalban's performance as Khan and knew that Bennett's instincts regarding the use of the character were correct.

"I thought 'Space Seed' was wonderful," he enthuses. "Ricardo Montalban is a classically trained actor. Anybody who can deliver those lines has got to be. Most actors in town would mumble them, but the man knows just how far to go. If you've watched *Fantasy Island* or his movies, there's a smoothness. In this, he was something totally different and he knew just where to go with it without going over the edge. He *is* Khan. He brings that sort of macho arrogance to it and you believe this is a genetically engineered man who is stronger, smarter and brighter. A hero is nothing without a villain. If you overcome a slug and a snail, you haven't done anything. If you overcome something like Khan, a hero is defined."

Sowards explains that he didn't feel there was any problem in adapting the characters to changing times. "I think they're timeless," he says. "The only thing we had to do with the characters was let them age. I think they're a good set of characters you can move anywhere, and these actors are so good. They're so used to working with each other and they have such a rapport. It's almost as if they can read each other's mind. They know when the cue's coming and how to play it, and it's a pleasure to work with people like that."

The first result from the Bennett/Sowards collaboration was the December 1980 "*Star Trek* Outline," which expanded upon the elements of Bennett's one-page story idea. Added was a romantic relationship between Kirk and a bridge personnel member named O'Rourke, the death of Spock early on and a face-to-face confrontation with Khan, in which the Eugenic survivor used acquired mind control powers to try and defeat his opponent. Many of these elements, including the last one, made it to the screenplay entitled *Star Trek: The Omega Syndrome*. By the time the script was written, Khan's goals had grown considerably. He now planned on using the technology of "the Omega system" to set himself up as ultimate ruler, with the Romulans, Klingons and Federation all

under his control. In between, he wanted revenge against Kirk.

Next was a screenplay called *Star Trek: The Genesis Project*, which introduced the concept of Genesis and moved the story closer to that of the finished film. Again, Khan and Kirk had a hands on confrontation.

"Kirk and Khan may not have met in the film, but they did in my script. You bet your ass," Sowards laughs. "In my script, Khan was more of a mystic than Attila the Hun. I invested Khan with certain powers. He could make you see things which didn't actually exist. It was a battle of wills, which Kirk ultimately wins when Khan realizes he cannot control his mind. Nobody wins the fight and it ends up as a fight in space with the ships. But they do have this confrontation. It was a 12-page fight that they simply took out and threw away. The fight *would* have required a lot of special effects, because it was really a mind attack by Khan on Kirk and Kirk's being able to resist it. He would take it to different places. They would be on a shore somewhere, fighting with whips. They would be in a stone room of a castle. When you got into the whole thing, it was a very expensive process, so I can understand their dropping it. But not the face to face confrontation. I could never understand that."

Shortly after this script was handed in, Harve Bennett decided to go with another writer to develop it further. Although David Gerrold and Theodore Sturgeon were in the running, he ultimately chose Samuel Peeples, who wrote, among other things, the second *Star Trek* pilot (and the one which sold the series), "Where No Man Has Gone Before."

"Sam Peeples had done outstanding work in other areas when I was at ABC," related Bennett. "He had done two pilots that I had been involved with, and I thought he could write robustly. So I brought him in, he read the script and I said, 'Sam, you know more about *Star Trek* than I do. I want you to fix this.' He said, 'I know just what to do.' The result was his script."

Interestingly, the Samuel Peeples draft of *Star Trek II* incorporated many of the elements of Jack Sowards' version, with the *exception* of Khan.

Added were a pair of aliens named Sojin and Moray, beings from another dimension who want to use their powers to take command of ours.

Notes Robert Sallin, "Neither the Jack Sowards or Samuel Peeples script worked. It felt like television. It felt like a long television episode, and I didn't believe that the underlying humanity and the relationships between the people were very strong. There was a lot of intergalactic weirdness in the scripts which I felt were defeating."

Bennett "went right back to Jack's script and did a quick rewrite of my own, just to get everything together," he said in *The Star Trek Interview Book*. "Enter Nick Meyer. When I saw *The Seven Percent Solution*, I was so impressed with the screenplay that I went out and read the book, and I was even more impressed with the book....Nick read my rewrite of Sowards and Peeples and said, 'This has promise. What if...' He signed on and said, 'You write it, and I'll rewrite you.'..."

Robert Sallin remembers things a bit differently. "I was preparing a list of all the directors I thought might be acceptable for this film," he said. "I must have had somewhere in the area of 30 or 40 names, but I kept striking out because either they didn't want to do *Star Trek*, they didn't want to do a sequel to *Star Trek*, they didn't want to do science fiction, they didn't want to do any kind of special effects material or they weren't available. A lot of people simply didn't want to do it after what happened with the first one. Because the film was being done under the aegis of the television division, I wanted to find a director who was on his way; who hadn't hit it yet but whose heart and soul was in to it, and who would bring a certain passion to the project.

"Then," he continues, "Nick Meyer's name came up. I saw *Time After Time* and I thought it was inventive, and I very much liked the writing of the *Seven Percent Solution*. I thought that was a very fine and inventive piece of work. He seemed to come up with things with a fresh point of view. So I suggested it to Harve. We sent the script over to Nick and had a meeting with him. I remember standing in the alley, saying to Harve, 'I think the guy's dynamite. I think he has a

great vision of what can be done here.' Time moved on, the studio seemed to respond to Nick and so we went with him. It is, in all candor, Nick's uncredited rewrite that is on the screen. Contrary to what the critics may say, Harve made contributions, Sowards made contributions, I made contributions, but I think it was Nick's final version that we used. Nick never took credit for it and he told me his agent said he was crazy. But he said it was just something he wanted to do."

The Meyer Connection

Not only had Nicholas Meyer written the book and screenplay of *The Seven Percent Solution*, but he was the director behind the sensational *Time After Time*, which transported Jack the Ripper and H.G. Wells from Victorian England to the modern world. His talents were highly respected, and the attachment of his name to *Star Trek* was a major coup.

Said Meyer, "They sent me the script, which I loved. I met Harve and Bob [Sallin] and I thought they were wonderful, and I haven't changed my views since. As far as the film was concerned, I could not have been better partnered to not look like a fool because of the expertise and support I was given. The miracle of it was that we were all making the same movie. Everything really could have come unstuck if we had started going off in different directions. But there was never a substantive disagreement about the tone or the action. Details, yes."

Meyer admitted to not have ever seen an episode of the original series, noting that he didn't particularly like the science fiction genre.

"I'm interested in good stories first," he stated. "I loved *Star Wars* and *The Empire Strikes Back*, which I thought were very exciting and a lot of fun. I saw some *Star Trek* stuff after the film was offered to me, and they also ran the first movie for me. I didn't like that very much. I thought that it was spectacular in some ways, but I didn't like the way the people looked or what I considered the lamentable absence of story and human interaction. There are really two reasons to do remakes and sequels, aside from

financial considerations. One is because, for whatever reason, it's been so long and people really didn't see the original, except on late-night television. The other reason is that there was something wrong with the original. It didn't fulfill what it was supposed to, or could be improved upon. I looked at the first film and thought that there was no way that we were going to make a movie as filled with ennui as that one. I also knew we could do it for a quarter of the cost, so we would probably look like heroes!

"[Adding dimension to the characters] was definitely the aim. I have always thought, to the extent that I've had any clear thoughts about *Star Trek*, that it was something that for one reason or another never quite fulfilled its promise. Either because in terms of a TV show, they couldn't afford the sets or the effects, or because in the first movie they dropped the ball somewhere. This was an opportunity to make something right that had never quite been on the nose before. The more specific you get, the better. It was not necessary for me to see Admiral Kirk go to the bathroom, but I said why couldn't he read a book? At which point, I grabbed the first book off my shelf, which was *A Tale of Two Cities*, and for some reason or another, I just stuck with that, which was interesting because it's the one book that everybody knows the first line and the last line to. That became the bracket of the movie and it also somehow became the theme of the movie. Leonard and Shatner got excited because they always felt in some way that they had the Sidney Carlton-Charles Darnay relationship going on between them. That's very specific, and from the book we got the glasses, which was specific too, and real! From all of that came age! Interestingly enough, *Star Trek II* is not very much about science fiction, the Genesis Planet aside. Its themes are entirely earthbound—death, aging, friendship."

One of the issues Meyer was pressed with was deciding what elements of the *Star Trek* formula he should keep in the film and what should be discarded.

"Very simple," he mused. "I kept what was good and changed what was bad! I decided that I owed allegiance to what was good in either the first movie or, more importantly, the television series and that I owed no allegiance and no respect to things that were bad. What that really boiled down to was the characters. I had to keep the characters as they were but at the same time I had to redesign everything that I could—the uniforms, the sets, etc. Again, it was in the context of what they were, the overall shapes, I couldn't do anything about. But I could add twinkling lights whenever possible, I tried to get away from that grey look. Philosophically, I said that I was simply going to take these characters more seriously and more literally than anyone has ever taken them before."

Meyer was faced with his own share of problems regarding the cast itself. Nimoy had been convinced to come back, but there were near defections by George Takei and DeForest Kelley, who were not satisfied with the script.

Noted George Takei, "When I first got the script and saw the kind of participation Sulu had, I saw that he wasn't much more than a talking prop. There was no character there, and I decided that I just couldn't go back under those conditions. My heart just wouldn't be in it. I told this to Harve Bennett and Nick Meyer, and they understood, but the script was already written and there wasn't much that they could do with it at that point....Harve understood the problems and had a few scenes added that bolstered my part a little, but I was still unhappy. Filming was due to begin soon and a decision had to be made. So they made me certain promises and I was on the set the first day of filming without even a contract. The first shots included me on the simulation bridge, so I was locked in. Unfortunately, when the film came out, some of the little scenes which would have added to my character ended up on the cutting room floor."

Explained DeForest Kelley, "At first I turned it down. I strongly disliked the first script handed to me. I felt it was a busy story and didn't work, so I had a big conversation with Harve Bennett. He was upset. I said I would rather *not* be in it, because the role was not meaningful, and the script just was *not* a good *Star Trek* script. He said, 'Well, what do you think we should do?' 'I think you should hire a writer who has written for *Star Trek*

and rewrite it!' He looked at me funny and said, 'Well, who would you hire?' I said, 'Gee, Harve, I don't know, I'm not in that line of work." Meyer, as stated above, was brought in and did a rewrite. "I feel that Meyer brought it to life and really made it a kind of *Star Trek* script. When he sent me that draft, I said, 'That's more like it,' and I went with it."

Sharing Kelley's view of working with Meyer was William Shatner. "Nick Meyer had written a script and we were in love with the script and impressed by his creative ability," he enthused. "So even though it was only the second picture he had directed, we felt that his imagination should be given full flower. And so here he was. He had written the script but he hadn't directed very much. Whatever help we could give him was offered and he would accept it or not accept it, depending on whether he thought we were correct. But he had written the script and had therefore brought to it another unquestionable aspect."

He's Dead, Jim

Principal photography with the main actors began on November 9, 1981 at the Paramount Studios in Hollywood. Production ended January 29, 1982, a few days over schedule and slightly over budget, a rather remarkable feat for a production of *Star Trek II*'s scope.

From the beginning, the film was marked by keen interest from fans, seemingly fed by rumors that Spock had been killed off in a script. There was considerable speculation that publicity "leaks" about Spock's death were deliberately planted to stir up Trekkies and media attention for the film. Such suspicions were exacerbated when the TV news magazine *Entertainment Tonight* (also produced by Paramount) ran a call-in viewer poll on the subject of whether Spock should perish or be spared, and then it conducted three-days worth of interviews on the bridge set of the Enterprise.

"The studio did not generate any of the rumors about Spock's death," says producer Robert Sallin. "People have assumed that when this movie was conceived the first thing the studio did was to run out and create the rumors that

Spock was going to die, to get the Trekkies excited and generate publicity. That is contrary to my knowledge. I know that the position of the studio brass is that they would just as soon nobody said anything. Early drafts of the script were stolen and made their way into the hands of fans, and that fueled the furor."

However the rumors were promulgated, in the final analysis Spock *did* die, so at least the concern on the part of the fans was not completely wasted on cynical manipulation. What constitutes Death is a matter of semantics and debate even now, let alone in the 23rd Century. "In science fiction there are many kinds of life, and many kinds of death," Sallin pointed out.

Ironically, this was one death that Leonard Nimoy himself had tried to avoid as filming of that scene grew closer. "I found myself being moved by the scene early, very early, at about the point where Kirk says to Scott something about you have to get us out of here in three minutes or we're all dead," related Nimoy to *Starlog* magazine. "You see Spock hear that and react. I'm already feeling emotional about what's coming. [I] really came within a hair's breath of walking off the lot rather than playing the scene. The day we were going to shoot it, I was very edgy about it and scared of it—scared of playing it, almost looking for an excuse not to, finding something to pick an argument about. It was a very tense time. And I *still* feel that way seeing it. It's a moving scene and I'm pleased with it in the context of the film. I'm glad we did it. I think we did it well. I think we did it honestly and sincerely."

According to Nicholas Meyer, it was the filming of that scene which finally made him comprehend the true power of *Star Trek*.

"The scenes which were the most difficult, or at least the most wrenching to do, were the death of Spock [sequences]," he said. "Everybody stood around on the stage in tears, which was very surprising to me because I'm not that experienced as a movie director and I was amazed at how moved they were. The next day at the dailies, same thing. Everybody cried. I come from the 'less is more' school of thinking. You can have somebody point to something and say, 'Look at that' and you don't have to cut to what he is pointing to. In fact, you can raise considerable tension by not showing the audience what the character sees. For example, once Spock enters the reactor room I deliberately didn't cut back to him for a long time. After hearing, 'You can't go in there, you can't go...', you gotta be wondering, 'What's happening to him?' You want to see what's going on there. It's a matter of choice, of taste. I would rather underplay and let the audience imagination rise to meet something halfway. From what I've seen of the series, I tend to think they overacted or showed too much.

"My attitude has changed perceptively. I don't know whether it was the actors themselves or the characters, but I finally thought, when I was watching the death scene and I realized that *I* was choked up, I thought, well, we have now transcended the subject matter. This is no longer simply about a man with pointy ears, which is how I felt because I didn't know it that well."

While George Lucas' Industrial Light and Magic (ILM) finished the special effects work on *The Wrath of Khan*, Paramount began to lift the film's veil of secrecy in an effort to publicize the forthcoming release. Public statements by director Nicholas Meyer led to some friction on the production, however. Robert Sallin took exception to off-hand remarks made by Meyer which characterized the ongoing effects work as being disorganized.

"I don't believe in taking credit for other people's work and I don't believe in making myself seem more important at other people's expense," says Sallin. "Nick did not supervise the creation of the effects storyboards, and Nick did not supervise the execution of the shots. He attended one meeting with me at ILM, at which time I ran through every frame of every shot, and that was it. He was overwhelmed with the special effects and just backed away from them."

Director Nicholas Meyer was pleased with his cut of *Star Trek II*. Traditionally, the first editing of a film is done at the director's order, but may be amended or recut later, at the discretion of producers or studio. Meyer's cut was tightened somewhat, according to Robert Sallin. "We had too much plot, essential-

ly," he explained. "Nick's background is that of a writer, and in his version there was an extraordinary amount of exposition that we didn't feel was totally necessary; so Harve Bennett and I made some changes, in response to notes from the studio. It had to do with the tempo of the film. What we have is essentially the same picture as the director's cut."

Meyer has disputed the idea that fans had any influence on the ultimate ending of the film. After a screening at a science fiction convention in Kansas on May 8, a high-placed Paramount official indicated that other endings had been considered, perhaps filmed, and that the one used would depend on fan reaction. Meyer has firmly denied this.

"The question in my mind was not whether he died, but whether he died well. His death needed some organic relationship to the rest of the movie, and a plausible connection to whatever else was going on. If we did that, I don't think anyone would question it. On the other hand, if the movie suddenly turned around a corner on two wheels and we 'fulfill Leonard Nimoy's contract by bumping off his character which he has grown tired of playing,' if indeed that was the scenario, which I have never heard, that wouldn't be so good. That stuff that we were going to have more than one ending, that we were going to let the audience decide...that was all bullshit. Art is not made by committee and it's not made by voting."

As far as can be determined, Spock always died, in every version of the script and every cut of the film. Additional scenes involving Spock's death were shot by an ILM crew, with Robert Sallin, at San Francisco's Golden Gate Park in late April, more than two months after principal photography wrapped, when the movie was, for all intents and purposes, complete. The scenes show Spock's casket, a photon torpedo casing, drifting after his burial in space, finally coming to rest on the planet created by the explosion of the Genesis device aboard Khan's ship. Originally, Spock's casket was simply set adrift in space. These extra scenes were filmed after the results of opinion screenings before carefully-selected, demographically-balanced audiences.

"One of the major conflicts Nick and I had in the making of the picture was the whole idea of reminding people, of planting the seed that Spock might come back," explains Robert Sallin. "It was not in the original script, that idea of going back to the planet. Nick hated the idea, but I think the studio wanted it because they were getting so much flack about killing Spock."

Commenting On Khan

Star Trek II: The Wrath of Khan was a critical success, with the majority of reviewers noting that this is the way the first film should have been done.

The cast, as related to various journalists, had nothing but unanimous praise regarding the film, believing it to be far superior to *Star Trek: The Motion Picture* and a much more satisfying experience.

William Shatner: "I was nervous about it. Especially after the first film. The success of your performance, essentially, rests in the words. Everything rises and falls on the script. When a script is good, it takes a heroic effort to ruin it. As this script developed, I swung wildly from awful lows to exalted highs. I began to realize that the movie might be good. By the time we were ready to shoot, I knew *Wrath of Khan* would be great. I knew we had ILM for the effects, so the movie couldn't *look* bad. We also had a very human, *Star Trek*ian script. It was a wonderful working experience. It was as if the years between this film and the old show never existed."

Leonard Nimoy: "In doing [*Star Trek: The Motion Picture*], somebody, somewhere, decided that if we're going to do a motion picture, it must be different than what we did on TV, so we must now start to work out the differences. We'll change the color of the bridge, the wardrobe, the attitudes of the characters. It seemed to me that somebody was watching *2,001* a lot, and getting into a cerebral, futuristic trip rather than an adventure romp, which is what *Star Trek* is built on. Maybe it's because they felt that people would not pay to see in the theatre what they had seen on TV, that they would want something different. My opinion is that if we can do the best *Star*

Trek episode ever done, well-produced and well-acted, and put it on the big screen, it will work. I think that's what we've got this time. It's great! There's nothing wrong with success. It's terrific and I'm relieved because Bill, Dee, myself and other people who have talked about this picture before its release, felt strongly that it would be successful and that we were on the right track. What has happened here is that our perspective of what *Star Trek* is really supposed to be has been verified. The audience has said, 'Yes, that's right.'"

DeForest Kelley: "In my mind, there's no comparison [between the first two films]. This is the kind of film that in fact we had all hoped for the first time. It's not easy to convince the studio that, as successful as *Star Trek* was, the fans nevertheless have a deep feeling about the characters, and that you can't ignore it. In my opinion, that was the mistake that was made with the first film, ignoring the relationships that were so popular in the TV series."

James Doohan: "To me, this movie is *Star Trek* the way it should be. The first one was just some grandiose idea that somebody had. There is gorgeous action going on at all times. The characters all have some great things to say. It's just a beautiful blend of all of the good things that were in all of the good shows that we had in the series."

George Takei: "I think in *The Wrath of Khan* we have genuine drama because of the confrontation of two strong, cunning, inventive adversaries that are driven to an inevitable collision. You know that they are not going to avoid each other, that there is going to be some dramatic confrontation. Ricardo Montalban is an awesomely well-suited adversary for Kirk."

Nichelle Nichols: "I was both pleased and surprised [with *Star Trek II*]. I felt that, this time, they did it right. I think this is the definitive *Star Trek*. They've captured the essence of what made the show wonderful."

Walter Koenig: "I think that if you can point to one single element that makes this film successful, it is the presence of a formidable, worthy antagonist. You can't have conflict unless you have something to butt up against. V'ger was more like something you were in awe of. I think Ricardo Montalban, on the other hand, has done a wonderful job with the character of Khan. Not only is he a presence in terms of villainy, but he's also a character of depth. Even when you hate him, you feel a certain sympathy toward him. That, to me, is extraordinary. Nick Meyer was quoted as saying that he would like to direct Montalban in *King Lear*, and I can believe it. I think that is what makes this story work—-the fact that he's not only against Kirk but against the whole crew. We're all heroes to varying degrees, and our opponent has to not only be the equal of Kirk but also, in effect, the equal of all of us. I think Montalban embodies that very well."

One person not overly impressed with the film was *Star Trek* creator Gene Roddenberry. "I think it was an exciting picture," he explained. "I had many problems with it, though. I thought they were very lucky they had the actor they did in Ricardo Montalban to play Khan, since it was not a well-written part. 'I will chase you through the moons of Jupiter' and so on, in the hands of almost any other actor would have gotten snickers from the audience. Montalban saved their ass. Khan was not written as that exciting a character, he was rather flimsy. The Khan in the TV episode was a much deeper and better character than the movie Khan, except that Montalban pulled it off.

"I also objected to other little things. Remember when the eel came out of Chekov's ear? What did Kirk do? He had a look of disgust on his face and grabbed his phaser and went 'zap.' Now, how dare he destroy a life form that had never been seen before! It needs studying. They had him act like an old woman trampling on a tarantula. Now that's not the Kirk we built up for three years. So many of those fine little things in the episodes, hundreds of them, are what gave *Star Trek* its quality. Unfortunately, they began doing those things incorrectly in that movie. There was also a great deal of violence. But yet, it was exciting—exciting photographically. I'm grateful that it did what it did."

At this juncture in time, the results of "what it did" are obvious. *Star Trek II: The Wrath of Khan* was quite successful, grossing a little more than half of *Star Trek: The Motion Picture*'s take, but proving itself to be considerably more profitable due to its much lower budget. Additionally, the hoopla surrounding Spock's death ultimately became little more than a moot point, as evidenced by the next film in the series, *Star Trek III: The Search for Spock.*.

The saga of *Star Trek* would most definitely continue.

•••

CHAPTER ELEVEN

Star Trek III: The Search for Spock

Beginning The Search

Leonard Nimoy's desire to involve himself with aspects of filmmaking other than acting seems to be one of the major forces which have ultimately propelled the direction of the *Star Trek* films, particularly concerning the death and resurrection of Spock.

What he never expected, and what made his career move to temporarily get away from Spock all the more successful, was that he would end up being the director of *Star Trek III: The Search for Spock*.

Getting the job was, to some degree, an accident. Prior to *Trek III*, Nimoy still wanted his contract with Paramount to include projects other than *Star Trek*, but they did not have anything specific for him to do in the future. "For many years," Nimoy explained, "my concern has been to try to build a career outside of *Star Trek* so that it wasn't that single straight line of only *Trek*-oriented work. So there was nothing for us to discuss. I said to Gary Nardino—I was being arrogant—with all due respect to Bob Wise, who directed the first picture, a top notch filmmaker; and all due respect to Nick Meyer, an extremely talented writer/director who directed *Trek II*; I know more about *Star Trek* than either of them and I said I could direct *Star Trek III* successfully. When I first presented the idea of my directing to Paramount, the response was very good—but there were certain trepidations. We had to talk them through. My position during those discussions was 'I don't want you to perceive me as a problem. I don't want you to think I'm an actor trying to build a directing career on the strength of my leverage. I want you to see me as the *solution* to your problem. You need a director, and I know this material. I will bring you a movie that will satisfy the *Star Trek* audience.' I didn't want to take the posture with the studio of, 'You want me to act in

Star Trek III ? Then *I'm* the director, period.' Instead, we worked out what I felt was a constructive approach. Basically, I told them, 'Promote from within.'

"Michael Eisner [then Paramount president] got very excited about it and said, 'Great idea! Leonard Nimoy directs *The Search for Spock*!' It went downhill from there. At one point they said, 'No, we're not going to do it.' Harve [Bennett] and I kept operating on the assumption that it was going to work out and kept talking story ideas. In April of '83, I started my prep on the picture, reported on the lot and immediately went to work with Harve."

It may be hard to believe, coming from someone who has been a part of the industry since the 1950's, but Leonard Nimoy insists he honestly felt that moving out of the cast and taking over the film would not be a major concern to his fellow cast members. It was only a matter of time before he discovered that he was wrong.

Said Nimoy, "I must be really naive about this. I really must. I was surprised that there was so much interest and so much concern about that. The interests and concerns are valid. I just didn't perceive the potential problems or friction that other people perceive. My fellow actors were concerned about it before we started doing the picture. I simply took it as fact that I had their best interests at heart. That I would know their characters well, and I certainly knew their potential well and would try to explore it. That was one of the things I argued in that period of time when I was asking for the job."

One interesting thing that happened, possibly as a test to Nimoy's intentions and loyalty, was when he and producer Harve Bennett first discussed the script with friend and co-worker William Shatner. Naturally, since Nimoy was now in the position of authority, Shatner might feel a bit threatened, if not downright insecure about the situation. Before, he and Nimoy were a team. What if that changed?

"Leonard and I are the dearest of old friends," Shatner told writer James Van Hise. "We had shared a mutual struggle with the management in various stages, whether it was a script, a thought, a con-

The cover of Starlog Press' official **Star Trek III: The Search for Spock** *movie tie-in.*

cept or a dressing room and ask each other what we thought. We'd have a plan! Whenever we were to deal with management, we'd plan it out together. Now, suddenly, my 'brother' was saying, 'Well, you should do this and I think you should do that.' There was an awkward period of time for me, although I don't think for Leonard, where I felt alone in anything I might have objected to. From my point of view, it was more awkward in the beginning than with either of the other two directors [Robert Wise and Nicholas Meyer]. But that slowly erased itself."

In writing the script, Bennett did 12 outlines in all. It took six months. He says the last scene in the movie is the first one he wrote. "Somewhere along the line I read a fan poem in one of the hundreds of fan magazines about *Star Trek*. It was first person Kirk. It said, 'I left you there. Why did I do that? I must come back to you, my friend.' I thought, 'That's it!' I suddenly had a thrust. It got a lot easier from that point. A great motion picture has a very similar last scene. It was almost, beat for beat, the last scene in *The Miracle Worker* by William Gibson. It is the moment in which, after the entire play, little Helen Keller is at the well with her teacher and she begins to get some understanding, and finally with her hand on his face she says, 'Water.' And the teacher says, 'Yes!'

••••

"On *Star Trek III*, I said, 'Look, it's got to be faster and more efficient [than the writing of *The Wrath of Khan*]. So I was the sole writer on *Star Trek III*, [which] was the easiest writing job I ever had. The reason for that it, since it was so direct a continuation of *Star Trek II*, the outline was already in place. I knew exactly what I had to do and I did it in six weeks.

"I had to make a story out of the following 'givens': One, there is a casket on a planet that has been created by the reformation of life forces and life has been created from death. Two, 'There are always possibilities.' Three, before he died, Spock said, 'Remember.' Remember what? The puzzle was solved so easily that I think 17 other people could have written the script to *Star Trek III*. If you end a film with a Genesis device that can, in one 'poof,' create life where there was lifelessness, you have created an enormous story device that can not be ignored. Now the fans would be justified in saying, 'Well, why not just create a planet as a plot solution?' Or, 'What would happen if the Klingons got hold of this? They wouldn't use it to make a planet, they would destroy a planet.' Therefore, the final puzzle solving was the denial of the validity of the Genesis device. That was—as 'The Lord giveth, the Lord taketh away—necessary, or we would have expanded the borders of *Star Trek*, even subliminally, that it would have had the same impact the A-bomb had on the 20th Century, so as to make conventional things no longer viable. That's fine, but who needs to restructure *Star Trek* on that basis?"

Writing the script, Bennett ran into other problems that were set up in *The Wrath of Khan*. First, there was Saavik. The original character, played by Kirstie Alley, did not want to come back to do the movie. "We didn't want to cut [her] scenes," Bennett said, "so we decided to recast the character and keep the part. How did we fare putting Robin Curtis in where Kirstie Alley had gone before? About even."

Kirstie Alley, who has achieved incredible fame since *Star Trek II* thanks to her varied movie roles as well as her continuing stint on *Cheers*, told *Starlog* magazine, "They offered me less money than they did for *Star Trek II*, so I figured

they weren't very interested in me for Saavik. I thought [Robin Curtis] was at a real disadvantage playing a role someone else established, especially with *Star Trek*, which has an enormous following. I think she did a fine job. I have no problem with what she was doing except that, when I saw the film, I said, 'She isn't Saavik, *I* am.'"

Said Robin Curtis, "I did want to keep things fairly separate between myself and Kirstie Alley and as it turned out, each and every one of the people involved in *Star Trek III* were wonderful. I think Leonard set an example that everyone followed and that is to say I was never made to feel like I had to fill someone else's shoes. Never for a moment was I made to feel like that and I think that was really Leonard's kind of healthy approach to the whole thing."

Two other major script decisions, killing David and destroying the Enterprise, were rather easy for Bennett. He believes in a balance. If you get something, you have to pay for it. Kirk gets Spock back, but at what cost? He loses two very major things along the way. Is it worth it? That makes for a good script, and lots of emotion and tension.

"I confess to being old fashioned," Bennett continued. "There is in my vision such a thing as ultimate retribution. The reason David dies, structurally, is because he's messed with mother nature. He allowed himself to bend the rules at the wrong time, in the wrong place. He's there on that planet for only that reason. The whole story dates back to David putting protomatter in the matrix. The death of Spock, everything rests on his shoulders if you want to blame him for it."

One of the secondary themes of *Trek III* is don't mess with mother nature. The concept fo the Genesis device was too massive to deal with in the TREK universe for future stories. It had to be destroyed. "Gene Roddenberry said, 'Let's try protomatter.' It became a tool for me to solve the problem,' " Bennett explained, "which is the interjection of a human value system in an otherwise antiseptic, impossible box—the perfect scientist. The value system is ambition. That interested me. It all snapped together. Kirk changed the computer on the Kobayashi

Maru scenario before *Star Trek II*. His son says to him, 'You've cheated.' His father says, 'I changed the rules.' Well, it turns out that the kettle was calling the pot black. David says it at a time when he knows he's changed the rules."

The loss of the Enterprise was the big risk in the script, the big surprise, though word of it leaked to the fans and campaigns, not unlike the ones to save Spock, were begun to save the Enterprise from its demise.

Bennett admitted, "The death of the Enterprise caused serious ripples. The death of David did not. That's....backwards for me. How could you destroy the Enterprise is a burden I take full responsibility for. I will justify it to the end and once again I think I have been playing fair. My choice was a humanistic choice. It began as a writer's problem. Usually it happens when you reach a sticky point. I had a whole justification for it. Oliver Hazard Perry of the U.S. Navy scuttled the Niagara at the battle of Lake Erie and won the battle as a result. He was rowed on a rowboat to another ship and took command. Perry happens to be one of James T. Kirk's great heroes. Actually, there is a model of the Niagara in Kirk's quarters for those who love *Star Trek* trivia. So, the scuttling of the ship to achieve the greater good is a tactic. Also, with the death of his son and the hopelessness of the situation, it seemed like the right solution, and also because in the series there had been one notable, false countdown."

Star Trek creator Gene Roddenberry made no secret of the fact that he disliked the idea of the Enterprise being destroyed.

"I'm upset about it," he said at the time. "I felt it wasn't really that necessary. I would rather have seen the saucer blow up. As all the old-time fans will know, our ship is supposed to come apart. The star-drive part is the nacelles and the underneath, and the saucer is not star-driven. If the saucer had been blown up, at the end of the picture we couldn't had a new saucer come down and reunite the two. Symbolic of the end of the story. They preferred to do it the other way."

Actor William Shatner saw the death of both David Marcus and the

Enterprise in a different light. "I thought the loss of the Enterprise and David's death were very clever devices used to create drama in a situation. The problem is that, in a continuing series of movies where the characters appear through all the films, we have to raise some jeopardy. But everybody knows the characters are not going to die. So, two elements that were expendable, David and the Enterprise, were killed off because nothing else could be killed off. In fact, the real problem is, what else can we kill? We're looking around for people to die! It's like the court-martials where you come into the room and if the knife is pointing towards you, you're dead."

Joked DeForest Kelley, "When I read that in the script, I couldn't believe it! You know, I thought, 'My God, the Enterprise is a bigger star than any of us! If they're shooting this guy out of the script, they can shoot anybody out!'"

"There are two elements in the making of a story whether it's on film or not," Bennett stated. "Suspense and surprise. You're either hoping a character will do something or he does something that you didn't expect. The sure knowledge of the audience saying, 'Oh, no, they're not going to do that,' and the sheer surprise of saying, 'Oh, yes we are.' There are many other moments in the film which were intended to be one or the other. The death of David is one clear example of surprise, because you're playing off the cliches of the expected. One of the joys of motion picture writing as opposed to television is that you have full use of those two ranges. In television the surprise is limited, and suspense is limited to the fact that the episode must end with the hero surviving."

One obvious aspect of the film was that Kirk and company would ultimately locate Spock, alive and, relatively speaking, well. The return of Spock at the climax, which is something Leonard Nimoy was not at all nervous about.

"I had confidence in the way the story was structured that it would work," he told The Official Star Trek Fan Club Magazine. "I certainly didn't want to do a ghostly Spock like Alec Guiness in Star Wars. I felt there was obviously a tremendous amount of interest from the fans as to whether or not he was coming back. By the time the picture opened, I think the feeling really was, 'OK, he's probably coming back, but let's find out how.' And if it's done interestingly, then it works."

Since Leonard Nimoy's directorial credits were limited to such episodic television fare as The Powers of Matthew Star, Night Gallery and T.J. Hooker, the challenge of getting Bennett's script on film was a difficult yet exhilarating experience, from the filming of scenes to the actual editing of the movie. His love for Star Trek and his obsession for perfection is what made the movie work. However, that kind of dedication has a price.

"The shooting began on August 15, 1983," Nimoy stated, revealing what his workload as director was like. "It was 49 days of shooting during which the biggest problem I had was lack of sleep. I went to bed at 9:00 or 9:30, set the alarm for 5:00 or 5:30 and would be up at 3:00, the head going with ideas. I was just so super-charged and wired. It was a constant tiredness of the best kind."

There were many things he learned, too, on this project, such as how frustrating it can be to direct oneself.

"There is no question in directing yourself that you need help," Nimoy explained. He relied quite heavily on Harve Bennett, William Shatner, director of photography Charles Correll and others for that help. They are "People off-camera I've come to trust. I cannot emphasize enough that you don't make these pictures alone. You sure need an awful lot of talented support. In some cases, there is simply the fact that there are things going on behind you that you cannot see as an actor. The biggest problem I had, and this is really silly, but it happens that it was the scene in the sick bay of the Bird of Prey. Spock is unconscious and McCoy is talking to him. Now, not only am I in the scene, but I have to play the scene with my eyes closed. So I can't even look to see if the actor I am playing the scene with is looking anything like I think he should look. It drove De Kelley crazy. He swears that I was trying to direct him with the movement and flutter of my eyelids. It was very difficult. In a sense, I was very pleased and relieved that the design of the story allowed me to do a minimal amount of performing."

Said Bennett about one moment of Nimoy's directing, "I'll tell you what was a great directorial achievement by Leonard was getting emotion over David's death out of Shatner because he wanted to play it more stylistically. It's the only scene I remember where Leonard said, 'Clear the bridge.' Literally, he said, 'Will everyone please leave. I want to talk to Bill.' I never asked him what he said to Bill. It was very personal. It was director talk to actors."

That scene was a very crucial part of the script. It was the moment where Kirk realizes he has lost a good portion of the fight with the Klingons because they have in their hands everything he loves or cares about. It called for a riveting, emotional and yet not overdone performance. Nimoy explained:

"On the day of the shooting of that scene, he and I got ourselves off into a corner and discussed it slowly in a relaxed atmosphere, and privately. What I said to him was this: 'You have to decide how far you want to go with this. How far you want to take this reaction. My opinion is that you can go pretty far and get away with it, maybe strip off some of the veneer of the admiral, the hero, always in charge, always on top of the situation, and show us a vulnerable person.' He took it further, frankly than I expected him to. And it was scary. I mean, how many space epics do you see where your hero, on receiving personal news, stumbles back and falls on the person's own ship? You don't see that a lot. It was a scary thing for all of us hoping that it would be perceived as a very touching moment. Some little kid breaks in laughter in the audience and you're dead. We did several takes and used the one where we really thought Bill lost control and stumbled and fell. It looked accidental, not a performance. I'm very moved by it. In my opinion, it is some of the best work he has ever done. It looked as though he had received a physical jolt, as if somebody had hit him with the information. He looks deeply hurt. Some of the most personal and vulnerable work I've ever seen done in the role of Kirk."

An intriguing part of the directing for Nimoy involved editing. "In the editing process, specifically, the most interesting challenge was how to tell the story and in what sequence. Having seen it on the screen in its rough cut form, we all came to the conclusion that there was something about the juxtaposition, scene to scene, idea to idea, character to character; it wasn't quite in its proper order. The jigsaw puzzle hadn't quite fallen into place. Gradually we worked our way towards it and discovered what the picture turned out to be.

"The flow just didn't want to come to life until we repositioned certain of the opening scenes. For example, what we came to call the caper, which was the gathering of the Samurai to steal the Enterprise. In its original form, it was scattered in pieces throughout the first third of the film and they were all wonderful, fun pieces. But somehow, when you cut away from each of the happenings, it was always as though the fun was being interrupted. When you came back to it, you had to get geared up to have fun again. And suddenly that little piece would be over and you were being interrupted and taken away from the story again.

"The one major reconstruction that took place in editing was to put much, if not all, that caper together as a piece so that once we start with the idea of Bill Shatner walking up and saying, 'The answer is no, I am therefore going anyway,' it starts. So that piece became a trump within itself whereas it had been originally constructed as several pieces. I think 14 minutes from the time we first started looking at cuts of the film were cut down to its present condition. Perhaps two or three minutes were cut after the picture went to preview audiences. So we were pretty close to what we had planned to put on the screen. I think that's due in great part to very successful writing and producing for the film."

Star Trek III: The Search for Spock completed production on schedule and under budget. For both Nimoy and Bennett, it was a job well done.

"For me," Bennett said, "this movie is about honor and friendship and decency and values higher than the complex value system we have inherited since the atomic age. It's a return to innocence."

Noted Nimoy, "I wasn't making a personal statement. The major theme in this film is about friendship. What should

a person do to help a friend? How deeply should a friendship commitment go? What price should people be willing to pay? And what sacrifices, what obstacles, will these people endure? That's the emotion line of the film. For me, that's its reason for existence."

A Fruitful Search

The "texture" of *Star Trek III: The Search for Spock* came together beautifully as far as fans were concerned. The film was released in June 1984 to generally positive reviews, though the critics weren't quite as enthusiastic as they had been about *The Wrath of Khan*. As *The New York Daily News* noted, "Installment three falls somewhere ahead of the first feature and way behind the highwater mark of [*Star Trek*] *II*. Enough exciting sparks are struck—rest assured—and now that the gang's all here, 'the adventure continues.'"

Despite the fact that the climax of the film was a foregone conclusion (there was simply no way that they weren't going to find Spock), *Star Trek III* does make a terrific episode, giving each of the characters a moment to shine and examines the depth of the Kirk-Spock-McCoy triangle.

Additionally, Nimoy's co-stars had nothing but raves for him as well.

William Shatner: "Leonard had a point of view and knew what he was doing. [He's] very organized and methodical. He's very creative. I'm looking forward to working with him on *Star Trek IV*. I thought *Star Trek III* was very good. I think it could have been a little more complicated in storyline, but very good."

DeForest Kelley: "I enjoyed watching *Star Trek III* more than I did *Star Trek II*. This one comes closer to the TV series than the others. I, for years, have

had full confidence that Leonard could direct *Star Trek*, or for that matter, anything he wanted to had he been given the opportunity. Leonard is the kind of director who will accept input from you because he knows that we know and feel certain things about our characters."

George Takei: "Leonard brings with him an intrinsic understanding of the show, the characters and the relationships. That was a great advantage. He also is a guy that is very intelligent and a fine artist, so he brought those qualities."

Walter Koenig: "*Star Trek III* is obviously a very successful film. I think it, perhaps more than either of the first two features, promotes a sense of family and congeniality and warmth. I think there's a feeling of affection generated by the members of the Enterprise crew, much more a sense of simpatico."

On his feature directorial debut, Leonard Nimoy hit the proverbial home run both critically and financially, as *Star Trek III* matched the gross of its predecessor. Things were, however, amiss in the *Star Trek* universe itself, given the death of David Marcus, the destruction of the Enterprise and the fact that her former crew were now renegades who had disobeyed Federation orders to go after Spock.

The groundwork had been laid for a fourth film, which would ultimately prove to be the most popular of all.

••••

CHAPTER TWELVE

Star Trek IV:
The Voyage Home

The Voyage Begins

Considering the resounding success of *The Search for Spock*, it came as no surprise to anyone that Paramount Pictures was interested in dipping back into the well at least one more time with a fourth film. The trek got off to a less than smooth start when William Shatner made it plainly clear to the studio that he would not return as James T. Kirk unless the good admiral was given a considerable pay increase.

Six months passed while returning director Leonard Nimoy and executive producer Harve Bennett awaited word. As negotiations continued, a variation of the *Star Trek* formula was developed.

"A proposal was made by me that we didn't have to have Bill," said Bennett, "that we could do *Star Trek* in the beginning, which was Ralph Winter's idea. Let's do them at the academy. That picture seems to have worked in a variety of incarnations including *Top Gun*. It's a very workable picture. But the franchise wasn't the same without the stars and there is merit in that argument."

Interestingly, the story, entitled *Starfleet Academy*, would come up again shortly after the production of *Star Trek V*, a fact which will be discussed in depth further on in this volume.

Finally, after a total of eight months had passed (and this delay would ultimately have repercussions on Shatner himself when he took the helm of the fifth film adventure), Shatner signed on the dotted line for $2 million and *Star Trek IV* was back on track. By this time, however, quite a bit had happened behind the scenes, the least of which was the development of the film's tone and storyline, as well as the idea that this would be the concluding chapter of a trilogy; a trilogy which had not been intended when Bennett took over the series' production reigns.

"In moving through the trilogy,"

Bennett has stated, "I confess that every one of the major tricks I learned in television, I used. I'm out of tricks now....I've gotta find another one because we have now completed a trilogy and we have to go where no man has gone before. When you go where no man has gone before, you have to build things and then it starts getting expensive. Here are the three tricks of the trilogy: *Star Trek II*, in television we call that the 'bottle show.' The 'bottle show' in television takes place in an elevator that's hopefully trapped between two floors. Or it takes place in a mine shaft where people are desperately coming to try to save you and you have to stay down there and talk a lot. Sixty-five percent of the film was on the Enterprise bridge in one incarnation or another. It was also the Reliant bridge. And it was also part of the science station. We used that set for 65 percent of the movie and that is an incomparable savings in terms of time, dollars and moves. We'd shoot a scene, move the people out, repaint it and it would now be the Reliant.

"*Star Trek III*," he continued, "was the classic television 'the leading actor loses his memory' show. I did that on *Mod Squad*, *Six Million Dollar Man*, *Bionic Woman*, and you usually do it when your leading actor is exhausted or needs a rest. He's in a coma-like state. In *Star Trek III*, we had a man who was directing the movie, and who had never directed a feature before, and we felt that to act and so forth would kill him. We had our choice of how to utilize that asset, and what we did was we spent most of our money building one great set, the Genesis planet, and the story became let's find him while he directs. [For *Star Trek IV* we decided to use] local location. We've gotta add some size to this picture, so what do we do? We go out. How do you go out in the 23rd Century? You come to the *20th Century*."

Said Leonard Nimoy, "We decided early on that we wanted to do a time travel story. When I say we, I'm talking about Harve Bennett and I. We were asked by the studio to come up with a story, and our very first conversation was about doing time travel, which we both agreed was a good idea. We also felt that we should lighten up. The

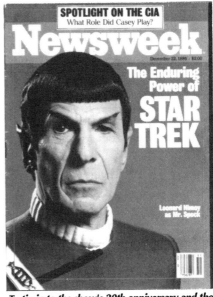

To tie-in to the show's 20th anniversary and the release of The Voyage Home, Newsweek devoted its December 22, 1986 issue to the show.

picture should be fun in comparison to the previous three. The first movie had no comedy at all. That was intentional. It was intended to be a serious study of a problem. The second film had a little. The third film had a little. But there we were dealing with a lot of serious drama. There was a lot of life and death going on. In [*Star Trek*] *II* Spock died. In [*Star Trek*] *III* Kirk's son died, the Enterprise was blown up and people were being killed and planets were disintegrating. I just felt it was time to lighten up and have some fun. That meant that if we were going to do time travel, the best thing we could do was come back to contemporary Earth, where we could have some fun with our people. They would more or less be a fish out of water on the streets."

Shortly thereafter, Nimoy had numerous conversations with members of M.I.T. regarding communication with other species.

"We were talking about the idea that if alien intelligence was trying to contact us, it would probably take quite a long time for us to know what it is saying, and for us to communicate with it," Nimoy stated. "I became intrigued with the idea that there was some lack of communication that was causing the problem. [I was] aware that humpback

••••

whales sing this unusual kind of song, which we don't understand but which obviously means something to them. They communicate it to each other, they pass it on one to the other, they repeat it. It has a form, lasting anywhere from six to 30 minutes in cycles, and they sing it again and again. Then they cease periodically, and they change the song. It's quite a complex structure, and that's very interesting. We don't know, and we may never know, what the communication is all about, so supposing that something in the 23rd Century is trying to communicate with them and they're gone. That's how it all happened, and it's a hell of a lot more interesting and challenging, cinematically, to come back to the 20th Century to pick up a pair of whales than it is to pick up a plant or insect."

The search for a writer began, while the film was struck with an interesting....dilemma. Eddie Murphy, a golden boy at Paramount at the time, had been pretty vocal in the fact that he loved Star Trek and would be very interested in co-starring in the new film.

"Now the meeting with Eddie Murphy was a little bizarre," said Bennett. "He had a separate meeting with Leonard. Leonard said, 'He's a little strange in a room.' So he came in with two thugs, good looking thugs, and they were all in black leather. [We] told Eddie this story and the thought about it for awhile and he said, 'It's good. Let me see a script,' and he walked out. We sat there and thought, 'Wouldn't it be terrific to have Eddie in this movie?' Later, the studio started getting very anxious for a very good reason. Here you have a franchise called Star Trek and it performs in a certain wonderful way. Here you have a franchise called Eddie Murphy and it performs in an even bigger way. Why not take them together and form one franchise? Bad economics because you are probably diminishing by compositing. So the studio was resistant to it, but Eddie has a certain amount of clout and he said that he hadn't decided whether he wanted to do it or not and so much of the development of the story was with the very distinct possibility that Eddie Murphy was in it."

As is the norm for Star Trek films, word of this little news item reached fandom, and memories of Richard Pryor's guest starring in Superman III sent a shudder through them. Naturally, a letter writing campaign was quickly initiated.

Said Harve Bennett, "The Star Trek fans who are our greatest asset, are also gigantic pains-in-the-ass. They know I love them and they know I can say that. They do have a propriety interest and to some extent they do pay for it. The fans found out about this and they got the word out."

"Star Trek is a lot of different things to a lot of different people," related Leonard Nimoy. "Some people watch it because they love the Enterprise, some people because they love the space battles, others because of the characters or the aliens. There are a lot of different reasons that you enjoy Star Trek. There have been people who have said to me, 'How could you destroy the Enterprise? What's Star Trek without the Enterprise?' We're doing drama. We're doing entertainment. We're doing fiction. If there's an individual who can't handle that and who steps over into a personal fantasy, that's his personal problem. I think the handling of the death and resurrection of Spock was tastefully done, dramatically done and was good science fiction. We're doing an entertainment piece. It shouldn't be taken too seriously."

Penning The Voyage Home

Based on their screenplay The Long Way Home, a black comedy about the plight of the Indian in America today, Steve Meerson and Peter Krikes were chosen to write the screenplay for Star Trek IV.

Said Meerson, "We sat in a room with Leonard and Harve, and Leonard told us that he wanted to do a departure, although they weren't sure what they wanted to do."

Added Krikes, "They wanted to do a film sort of based on 'The City on the Edge of Forever'...."

"Leonard started talking about plankton, cells, that cells become plankton, that things eat plankton and then whales entered the conversation."

"And we said, 'Why not make it as simple as the whale and the whale song?' That was our idea, though that's not to say that Leonard hadn't done research on whales, because he had."

"Leonard has mountains of information on various things," pointed out Meerson. "I guess we were hired in February of 1985 and between that time and May or June, Peter and I did several outlines of what eventually became the story. Before we could start writing the script, we had to get the studio to approve the outline. We registered all the outlines with the Writer's Guild, and after we came up with the story for the movie, Harve and Leonard took our outline and went through it step by step with the studio executives, and we got the go-ahead to start writing."

The duo were given two instructions: keep Eddie Murphy in mind for the guest star, and make sure that the character of Admiral Kirk is the driving force behind every aspect of the story.

"The approach we were told to take is that Kirk really had to be the one to lead everyone," explained Meerson. "Not necessarily that he had to actually have the idea to do something, but it had to appear as if he has the idea. I think the perfect example in the movie is when Spock goes into the belly of the Bird of Prey to use the computers and learns that the sound is whale songs. It's Kirk who has the idea to go back through time, although Spock is the one who plants the suggestion in Kirk's mind. Kirk verbalizes it, and that's the way it had to be played. We were told Bill had to be the leader at all times. In that scene, if you're reading it, you say, 'It's Spock's idea,' but on film Spock's discovery that it's humpback whales is not as important as Kirk's idea of going to get them."

"Visually," added Krikes, "the scene between Spock and his father at the end is another example. You kind of ask, 'Why is Captain Kirk standing there listening to this?' He has to be a part of everything."

Naturally word reached them of the controversy surrounding Murphy's possible appearance, and the fact that the cast was not happy about the idea.

"I think all of those guys became terrified that Eddie would blow them off the screen," mused Meerson.

"They also got a lot of negative mail from the fans."

All of the "noise" ultimately came to nothing, as Murphy decided to bow out.

"I'm a Trekkie," claimed Murphy. "I've always loved *Star Trek* and *have* wanted to do one of the films. I wanted to be in *Star Trek* and that's where they got the idea of coming back in time to Earth in 1987. The script was developed, but we eventually dropped the idea. *Golden Child* came along and I decided to do that film instead, because I thought it would be better for my career. In retrospect, I might have been better off doing *Star Trek IV*."

Explained Harve Bennett, "We went through every writer we could think of. We finally found Steve Meerson and Peter Krikes, whose work was highly regarded. Nothing came of it. Some of that, in fairness to them, was because we had saddled them with what appeared to be a male character that we thought was going to be Eddie Murphy at one time. Then when Eddie Murphy fell out, we had to readjust the script. But, by then, it had turned to paste, it just didn't work. Frankly, there are two scenes in the picture that they wrote that stayed pretty much the same. One of them is outstanding, which is the hospital scene that had minor modifications by Nick Meyer and me. They had also laid down the outline for the plexiglass factory scene. But, essentially, we didn't have a script we felt good about or even submittable to the studio."

As one would suspect, Meerson and Krikes *did not* take kindly to such comments.

"Actually," stated Meerson, "every beat of the film's first, second and third acts is *exactly the same* as our script. The *only* thing that changed slightly was that our Eddie Murphy character and the marine biologist were combined. Eddie Murphy was going to play a college professor who taught English, but a professor who we probably all had in the '60s or '70s, who's a little bit wacky and believes in extraterrestrials. Every Wednesday, he would open up his class to a discussion and the room would light up with conversation."

Krikes said, "He would play

whale songs, and it was the whale songs he played in the classroom that the ship locked on to."

"That was in the first draft we wrote, but the second draft was different. After you write a first draft of anything, once the director, the cast and the producers come aboard, *everything* changes, and not necessarily for the better. But the tone was pretty much a reflection of what was in the movie. For example, there was a scene where the Eddie Murphy character was trying to convince the Catherine Hicks character that aliens do exist on Earth. In the first draft, Hicks was a newswoman and there was a marine biologist as well. Gillian Taylor was ultimately a marriage of about three characters."

"Murphy believed in aliens and saw them beam into the classroom."

"It was the boy who cried wolf," Meerson noted. "No one would ever believe him, so he took it upon himself to follow the crew, and in one scene, he lifted a phaser from Kirk, took it back to the newswoman and said, 'See, they really *do* exist.' And she says, 'What's this?' and casts the gun aside, accidentally activating it. The phaser lands on the floor and her cat jumps off the couch. We follow her to her bedroom and she goes to sleep. The cat keeps phasing things out of the apartment by hitting the phaser, and when she wakes up, she sees that all the furniture is gone."

"That's just the side stuff," Krikes remarked. "If you look at our script and the movie you saw, basically everything is still there, like Eddie Murphy going to meet the aliens in the park to bring them gifts, and he runs into the invisible ship...."

"....Which is what Catherine Hicks did when she ran into the park to find Kirk. The structure really is exactly the same. Also, she grabbed Kirk's waist, Eddie Murphy grabbed his ankles. Murphy says goodbye to Kirk who starts to beam out, then he grabs him by the ankles and is transported aboard. He goes back to the 23rd Century, and he salutes Kirk when they get the Enterprise II. You know when Spock nerve pinches the guy on the bus? In our draft that took place in an underground subway system....You can't imagine the frustration of watching them take all the credit for

something that was completely blocked out for them."

"Plus they removed a lot of the emotional qualities that we thought it would have," Krikes mused. "It's interesting how they downplayed certain things. We spent months trying to figure out how you could get dilithium on Earth, sincere there was none. We had put in a sequence with a linear accelerator, where they break into the linear accelerator at Stamford University and have to take whatever element we have and charge it. And Spock had to work on rearranging the elements."

"They simplified the sequence, essentially, and said, 'Let's just stick this little machine on top and it'll change it into something.' I think it was actually a good idea, because it wouldn't have fit into the movie."

That's not to say that there weren't some significant differences as well, including the idea that Lieutenant Saavik was pregnant due to her *pon farr* sequence with young Spock in *Star Trek III*.

"There was a scene with Kirk on the Bridge of the Bird of Prey," recalled Krikes. "They cut out five lines where Kirk says to Saavik, 'Have you told him yet?' And she says, 'No. I'm taking a maternity leave.'"

"That's why she's standing with Amanda when the Bird of Prey leaves," Meerson revealed. "Because Amanda *knows* Saavik is carrying Spock's kid."

"All they did was cut out five lines of dialogue, and you lost that whole thing, which, I believe, will turn up in a Harve Bennett script in a couple of years."

Stated Meerson, "You'll have a story meeting with Harve Bennett for about eight hours and you'll say something in the first hour, and in the eighth hour he'll say, 'What does everybody think of this?' And it's exactly what you said eight hours ago. But that's really what Saavik's involvement was."

Krikes recalled another change. "One of the things we had in our earlier drafts that they took out was what happened when they first went through time. Instead of that horrible time sequence that looks like Russian science fiction, we had them using the sling-shot effect around Jupiter and Mars. Also, when they first appeared in the 20th Century, they were in a fog, and as they lowered, the monitors picked up all of this cheering and applause. As they come out of the fog, they find themselves over a Super Bowl game and everyone thinks it's a halftime show. Then, they cloak and disappear."

Meerson explained, "That's how we introduced the Eddie Murphy character, because he's at the Super Bowl and he's the only one who believes he just saw what he saw. I thought that would have been a wonderful moment. Also, I love our ending better. Our sequence of events were similar. After the shuttle has picked them up and Earth is saved, we cut to this little chamber where they're waiting to stand trial."

"They discuss whether or not they would do everything the same if they could...."

"....And they say they would. We cut away to Spock and Sarek, who have that same chat that they had in the movie. It was originally much more bonding, but they removed about half-a-page of dialogue, which changed things quite a bit."

Commented Krikes, "Basically, Sarek was saying, 'You're half-human and I'll never understand that, but I accept you.'"

"So we cut from that to someone knocking on the door and saying, 'It's time to go on trial,' and they put them in a pool. They go through this endless black tunnel and come out into the docking area for the trial...."

"....And everyone is gathered by the windows of the dock, cheering them on."

Meerson smiled at the memory. "Everyone is confused, saying to the pilot, 'Where are you taking us?' That's when the pod rises and you see the new Enterprise II. It would have been much more emotional, instead of saying, 'You've been exonerated for this, this and this,' you could have done it in three sentences, and with everyone cheering, screaming and yelling, it would have been an emotional high. Harve likes bookends, which is why the film begins with a trial and ends with a trial. That was always a point of contention between the three of us, that you didn't need to do that sequence again because it would be understood why. You could

just take them to the ship so that everyone would be on a high, rather than waiting for it to happen. Structurally, I think they made a mistake."

Meerson and Krikes emphasize that they were excited when they were contacted about the film, but found that the road to the screen wasn't exactly easy. Part of it was the difficulty in giving *all* of the characters something to do, as well as what happened to their script after they handed it in.

"We were told to *only* worry about Kirk, Spock and Bones," said Meerson. "In their minds, those are the only people that matter."

Added Krikes, "They also took out a scene we wrote which dealt with the people's mortality and age."

"My favorite scene we wrote was between Bones and Scotty, where they talk about the fact that they're getting too old to be doing this. I personally they they [DeForest Kelley and James Doohan] would have loved to play it. It was two guys sitting on a park bench in Union Square, completely out of time and space, saying, 'We're really getting too old. If we ever do make it back, maybe we ought to give it all up and retire.' Then, they both decided that they'll *never* retire, because there's more to life than sitting on your duff."

As stated earlier, once Eddie Murphy left the project, Bennett turned his attention to other writers. One of his first creative decisions was to alter the Murphy character into a female marine biologist, who would also serve as Kirk's love interest.

Recalled Bennett, "I remember saying, 'Well, I know it's corny, but it would be better if it was a woman. Kirk hasn't had a woman to play to, which he does so wonderfully. The whole series is the woman of the week. Remember that whale special we saw where the girl was bidding adieu to the whales who had to leave Marineland because the female was pregnant and they could not keep them and they had to send them back to the sea and she was bereft? Remember that character? That's the lady,' and Leonard thought that was great.

"So, now we're getting down to where we've got a movie to make and a whole new script to write. That's when

we were fortunate enough to find that Nicholas Meyer was available."

In the pages of *Cinefantastique*, Meyer told journalist Dennis Fischer, "I got involved in number IV because they had another script they were not happy with. Dawn Steele, who [was] the head of Paramount and has been a friend of mine for many years, called me and said, 'Would you do us an enormous favor?' And I said, 'For Harve and Leonard? Yeah, absolutely.' They had a script written. The script, I guess, was for Eddie Murphy as a guest star. I never read it, so I don't know. But they weren't happy with it. They wanted to go back to their original story and write another script. Harve said, 'This is what I want to do. I write the first 20-25% of it, and when they get to Earth or when they're about to get to Earth, then you take it, finish the Earth stuff, and I'll do the ending.' We went over each other's stuff. My contribution begins with Spock's crack about 'Judging by the pollution content of the atmosphere, I believe we have arrived at the late 20th Century,' and goes from there to someplace after they get the whales and leave. I didn't read the other script because I just thought it would confuse me and since they didn't like it, why bother?"

Reflected Bennett, "Nick and I had written the final script of *Star Trek II* in 10 days. This one we wrote in about 20, and it was very simple to do it that way because I took act one and act three and Nick took act two. Now if you think about that in structural terms, I got us into the dilemma and into time travel, he carried us through San Francisco, and I got us back. That was like breathing for me because it's pure *Star Trek* and it was like breathing for him because his irreverence is what really makes the fun. Then we swapped pages and I rewrote him a little bit and he rewrote me a little bit and we put it all together and had a script. Nick always said, 'You know the problem with this script is you've got five endings.' And he was right, we did have five endings. He said, 'Why don't you have the whales save the Earth? That's the end of the picture!' No, I said, that's the end of the picture for the hoped for extended audience who's never seen *Star Trek* before. But for people who have seen *Star Trek* before, we have a trilogy to complete. So we've gotta get them back, get them off the hook and give them the Enterprise back. We've got to do that, so that when we finish this picture, we have brought the franchise back to square one and it can go anywhere it wants to go. That's only fair. Besides, that's what the fans want. So that's what we did. We kept every ending."

As finally rewritten, *Star Trek IV: The Voyage Home* opens with an alien probe that is threatening to destroy planet Earth. Kirk, Spock, McCoy and the rest, on board the Bird of Prey and heading home to turn themselves over to the proper authorities, discover that the alien signal is actually being transmitted in the language of humpback whales, a species extinct in the 23rd Century. They take the Klingon vessel back to Earth circa 1987, get involved with marine biologist Gillian Taylor, who plays an integral role in their obtaining the necessary whales and then joins them on the return to the future. There, and once Earth has been saved by the whales singing to the probe, she joins the crew of a science vessel, and our people have the charges against them dismissed, with their being sent aboard a brand new starship Enterprise.

As vehemently as Meyer opposed the suggestion at the close of *Star Trek II* that Spock would come back, he was against Gillian's sojourn through time.

"In my version of the script," he said, "originally, when they all leave to go back, she didn't leave. She said if anyone's going to make sure this kind of disaster doesn't happen, somebody's going to have to stay behind, which I still think is the 'righter' ending. The end in the movie detracts from the importance of people in the present taking responsibility for the ecology and preventing problems of the future by doing something about them today, rather than catering to the fantasy desires of being able to be transported ahead in time to the near-utopian future society of the *Star Trek* era."

While it's common knowledge that rewrites are a part of every produced screenplay, writers Steve Meerson and Peter Krikes were nevertheless shocked to discover that Harve Bennett and Nicholas Meyer had been nominated for lead writing credits on *Trek IV*. This led to Writer's Guild arbitration.

Steve Meerson said, "Harve wanted to sort of roll up his sleeves and, as he called it, *Trek* it up, claiming that we weren't that familiar with *Star Trek*, which was a lie. Unbeknownst to us, he was telling the studio things like, 'They're going to deliver the first act today,' which he never told us and of course the studio got upset with us and said, 'Where's the first act?' and then Harve would say, 'I didn't say that.' Basically, you're talking to two people who did not leave this office for seven months. I'm talking we were working seven days a week, with food being slipped under the door. Our arbitration statement on the movie said, 'If a story had previously existed, what were we doing between February and May and June coming up with like seven outlines to write the script from?'"

Noted Krikes, "I don't know if you're aware how arbitration works, but within three days from the end of filming, the producer entities must turn in all the written materials to the Writer's Guild. In this case, it took two months to turn them in. They were trying to get our names off the script."

"There's actually a rule you can go by," stated Meerson. "When a script goes to arbitration at the Guild, the people that get first position—it goes to follow—did the lion's share of the work. We got first position on the script. I don't really want to get into the arbitration, *per se*, only to say that it was very political. Peter and I were lucky that we ended up with any credit at all. They have a very high-powered machine which is not very kind to outsiders, and we aren't the first people to experience that. It was a difficult pill to swallow. The reason it hasn't affected us that much is that everyone in town *knows* we did the story. They know our work, and it's such a departure from the other movies. *Star Trek IV* was so different, and we were the only new element."

Both men found their experience to be enlightening and—despite everything—something to be proud of.

"We can sum it up by saying we learned to sit with our backs to the wall, and to make sure what's on the other side of the wall first," said Peter Krikes. "It was a real roller coaster experience and, so far, it's the most successful in the series. *That's* a wonderful feeling."

Noted Steve Meerson, "When you go into story meetings with people who are constantly claiming that your ideas are theirs, what you need to do is take notes, write memos, confirm memos about what transpired, make sure all materials are registered and make sure you're aware of the arbitration process, which is supposed to function on your behalf, but doesn't. It's very political. You learn the avenues that are open to you, and basically you grow up. You learn that you can't trust anyone.

"By the same token, I think we were both delighted that we were a part of something that will go on forever, and I also think it said some things that needed to be said. There are some important messages there, and being allowed to have that forum was very exciting. It's hard for me to say this, but it was worth all the aggravation."

Bringing The Voyage Home

Although the set of *Star Trek IV* was generally very upbeat, there was a severe falling out between Leonard Nimoy and Harve Bennett, reportedly resulting in Bennett's actually being thrown off the set.

In the pages of *Captain's Log*, Bennett explained, "I had been emotionally beat up by Leonard Nimoy. I respect him for what he has done, but in the transition between *III* and *IV*, Leonard had come to regard me as in his way, with regards to the auteurship of the film. I was not only the man who said 'No,' but the man who was conspiring to....you know. So that on one occasion, it got really mean on the stage—mean from him to me. I was smarting—'Who needs this shit?'—was foremost on my mind."

A production source wishing to remain anonymous added, "Harve, actually, was barred from the set. He and Leonard weren't speaking on literally half of the filming. They had a major argument on the set and Harve was thrown off."

While Nimoy did not discuss this issue with the press, he did detail the challenge of not only directing the film, but co-starring in it as well.

"It was hard physically," he

said. "But I had a good time doing it because I really enjoyed playing the Spock character in this picture. He's a very different Spock. A Spock who's evolving, who's confused. He's trying to figure out who he's supposed to be and how he's supposed to function. It was great fun to play, but, physically, very tough because it's a long day. If you just direct the picture, it's a tough job. If you act in it as well, it's tougher. Then you have to add on a two hour make-up job every day, which means that you have to be in at 5:00 every morning. [But] this is a funny Spock. He's also very touching. I think it's a very touching moment when Spock discovers his identity. It happens at the moment when Kirk and McCoy are talking about what to do about Chekov in the hospital, and Spock says, 'We must help Chekov.' Kirk says, 'Is that the logical thing to do, Spock?' Spock replies, 'No, but it is the human thing to do.' I hope audiences [were] touched by that. It's the kind of moment when you say, 'Ah, Spock is there. He found his way.'"

As a director, Nimoy felt that *Star Trek IV* was much more ambitious and exciting than the previous films.

"We were off the soundstages for the first time," he enthused. "The first three pictures were almost exclusively on the soundstages. In *Star Trek I*, we were off the soundstage for a couple of days; on *Star Trek III* we were off for a couple of nights for the Vulcan exterior scenes. To get off the soundstages on this one was very invigorating. It gave a lot more energy to me and the cast of the picture, and I had a little bit more time. I shot *Star Trek III* in 49 days and on this one I had 53. Actually, I had 57, and I came in four days early."

To put it mildly, *Star Trek IV: The Voyage Home* was a great success, pulling in some $126 million and quickly establishing itself as the favorite of the series among many people, including the vast majority of film critics and some of the cast members.

William Shatner: "We discovered something in *Star Trek IV* that we hadn't pinpointed in any of the other movies—and it just shows how the obvious can escape you—that there is a texture to the best *Star Trek* hours that verges on tongue-in-cheek but isn't.

There's a line that we all have to walk that is reality. It's as though the characters within the play have a great deal of joy about themselves, a joy of living. That energy, that 'joie de vivre' about the characters seems to be tongue-in-cheek but isn't, because you play it with the reality [that] you would in a kitchen-sink drama written for today's life."

DeForest Kelley: "I have always felt from the very beginning that the core of *Star Trek* was the family. It was always this group of people that were working in this bizarre-type world together. That's what made the show successful. One of the greatest mistakes in the first motion picture was that they neglected the people and went around us. It's taken some time but now it's back to normal thaniks to Leonard Nimoy."

James Doohan: "*Star Trek IV* was absolutely delightful. It was a delight to do, and a delight to watch. Our best, dramatically speaking, mostly on account of Ricardo Montalban, was *Star Trek II: The Wrath of Khan*. But *Star Trek IV* was cute and funny, and everybody loved it just for that. Also, there was the great comraderie between the characters. The fans just absolutely love the banter that goes back and forth."

George Takei: "I thought *Star Trek IV* was perhaps the most successful *Star Trek* movie we've done. It brought together the various elements that made *Star Trek* as a television series so sucessful. It certainly had the interrelationships of all the characters that the series such an accessible show....In terms of commentary on a pertinent contemporary issue, we explored the fact that there is a price to be paid when we play with our ecology."

Nichelle Nichols: "The first film was good science fiction if you don't think of it as being *Star Trek*. Unfortunately, that's what everybody thought they were getting which is why it seems to be people's least favorite film. The second film was centered around Spock dying and the third, around bringing Spock back to life so there wasn't enough time to introduce the things that made *Star Trek* on TV so great. Those elements finally came together with *Star Trek IV*. The humor and action were there. The idea of the

whales was wonderful. It was definitely a step in the direction of what the old series was all about."

Walter Koenig: "I thought *Star Trek IV* was a delightful picture. The biggest surprise was seeing Leonard's performance, because I'd never seen him work in the picture, except for the scenes in which he was behind us on the bridge, but those individual scenes....those scenes with Bill, I'd never actually seen. That was the most effective performance he'd given as Spock because he maintained the sense of emotional distance and at the same time there was a wonderful underpinning of compassion to the character. I'm pleased for him, for his success, for the picture's success, and I'm very pleased to have been part of that."

Leonard Nimoy summarized his own feelings regarding the film, by noting, "[The feeling on the first film] was that we had to do a 'motion picture.' Nick Meyer brought a jauntiness back to it. I tried in *Star Trek III* to do a dignified job of resurrection, and do it with a sense of mysticism, a sense of wonder and, above all, to really capture the loyalty of these people for each other; their willingness to sacrifice themselves and their careers for the purpose of helping Spock. Having done that, I really wanted to have a good time on this one. Somebody had been constantly dying in the films, and this time I said, 'Nobody's going to die. I don't want anybody hitting anybody, I don't want anybody shooting anybody,' or any of that stuff. If anybody was going to be injured, it was going to be accidental.

"I insisted that there be no bad guy," Nimoy closed. "We had done two pictures in a row with black-hat heavies, and I didn't want a bad guy anywhere. Circumstances would be the problem. Lack of awareness, lack of concern. Ignorance would be the problem. Not a person. I hope with this one we've really gone full circle and come home, which is why, in a sense, we're calling it *The Voyage Home*. We're saying, 'Enjoy yourself, have a good time, and don't mind us as we drop off a few ideas along the way.'"

• • • •

••••

CHAPTER THIRTEEN

Star Trek V: The Final Frontier

Captain's Log

Star Trek IV: The Voyage Home was both a critical and commercial success that achieved its goal of being the much sought after "crossover film;" a *Trek* film that appealed to the mainstream audience. As such, it was a hard act to follow, a fact that no one could deny, let alone William Shatner. The actor had, as stated previously, made a point in his contract for the fourth film in the series of being given the opportunity to direct number five. After all, Leonard Nimoy had twice been given that chance and Shatner knew that he was contractually entitled to the same thing.

In the pages of *Captain's Log*, Shatner stated, "Somewhere along the line, Leonard's lawyers and my lawyers had gotten together and drawn up a favored nations clause, which meant everything he got, I got and vice versa. Well, in the beginning, I was commanding more money, so that any raises I was getting, Leonard would get also. So I made Leonard a great deal of money on my lawyers by bringing him up to the salary I was getting. We used to joke about that, how that clause had benefitted him so much. But in the end, the fact that Leonard directed a picture, which meant that I would get to direct one, was by far the most important consequence of that clause."

"Directing has been a lifelong dream," Shatner enthused elsewhere. "My business is to entertain people, and to communicate my feelings to them, so I find the best way is to direct. Directing is the pinnacle of our business. A really good director has a point of view on his film and all his other skills emanate from that spine. I've always wanted to entertain, and I think I can do that with my point of view, so I'm under the impression that I can gather all my skills around me to make people laugh and cry. I wanted to do more. I haven't done it to the extent that I wanted to. I think the movies have matured beyond the series and we have to give our audience that maturity. I'd like to think that's what I've done."

No sooner had production been completed on *Star Trek IV*, then Shatner began thinking of the next chapter in the ongoing saga. He definitely had his storyline in mind, beginning with the fascination he had always held for television evangelists who claim that God is speaking through them, rather than someone else. "I took the TV evangelist persona and created a holy man who thought God had spoken to him," said Shatner. "He believed God had told him, 'I need many followers, and I need a vehicle to spread my word throughout the universe.' That vehicle he needed became a starship [the Enterprise] which the holy man would capture when it came to rescuing some hostages he had taken....Finally the Enterprise arrives at the planet where God supposedly resides, in the center of the universe....Kirk, Spock, McCoy and the holy man are beamed down to the planet. It's like the drawings of Dante's *Inferno*, like a flaming hell. When God appears, he seems like God....but gradually, in a conversation between God and the holy man, Kirk perceives that something is wrong and begins to challenge God. God gets angrier and angrier, and begins to show his true colors, which are those of the devil....So essentially that was my story: that man conceives of God in his own image, but those images change from generation to generation, therefore he appears in all these different guises as man-made Gods. But in essence, if the devil exists, God exists by inference. This is the lesson that the *Star Trek* group learns. The lesson being that God is within our hearts, not something we conjure up, invent and then worship."

"The real problem with *V*," returning producer Harve Bennett told *Cinefantastique*, "was that the premise was faulty. You pick up a *TV Guide* and you read the log line which says, 'Tonight on *Trek*, the crew goes to find God.' Automatically, and unconsciously, you know we're not going to find God because no one has and no one will, and

The making of Star Trek V *as seen through the eyes of Starlog Press' official publication.*

no one would be so arrogant to say what they're depicting on screen is actually God, because others will say, 'No it's not.' So we know we're going to face an anticlimax, a trick. The nature of the trick is the only suspense in the story. But you'd say this to Bill and he's say, 'No, no, it's the greatest adventure of all time,' and I'd say, 'No, it's not an adventure because everyone is ahead of you. So what we have to do is make getting there as interesting as possible."

The Final Screenplay...?

"I would say that the trilogy probably stands because of its centering on the life, death, resurrection of Spock and his refulfillment," stated Harve Bennett to *The Official Star Trek Fan Club Magazine* (#64). "This film is continuous only in the sense of time. What we are trying to do in each picture is explore other angles and other undiscovered depths of these very legendary and familiar characters. And that's not too easy because you reach a point where you say, 'How much more can we explore these people?' But remember, these people are also aging, which they did not do in the series. So as they age, they are revealing more and more of their back and foreground stories. That's where the challenge is for me: to try to keep mining these relationships. [*Star*

••••

Trek V also] has with it an imperative of going back to deep space. Star Trek II, III and IV were all, to some extent, manageable in terms of budget, shooting time and scope. With Star Trek V, we have now come to the space imperative and we have some very, very difficult appetites: planetary and construction appetites—things you have to show and places you have to go, and an alien here and there. All these things make the cost and complexity of the film more difficult."

To make things a bit easier, both Bennett and Shatner began an intensive search for the proper screenwriter to bring this vision to the screen. Who they found was David Loughery, the writer behind Dreamscape.

"I sold an original screenplay to Paramount called Flashback," says Loughery. "Based on the merits of that script, Paramount offered me an overall deal, which I accepted, and one of the executives at that time asked me if I had any interest in working on Star Trek V. I said, 'Sure,' thinking that would be the last I ever heard of it. A couple of weeks later, they put me together with Harve Bennett. We talked and got along real well, and then we met Bill Shatner, who had already written an outline which he had turned into Paramount."

That outline, subtitled "An Act of Love," dealt with the Enterprise being commandeered by a rogue Vulcan named Sybok (as is the case in the final film), and being led to a world beyond the Great Barrier where they encounter God, who turns out to be the Devil.

"Paramount liked Bill's outline," says Loughery, "but they thought that it was a little too dark. After the success of Star Trek IV, they wanted to make sure that we retained as much humor and fun as possible, because they felt that was one of the reasons for the big success of that film. They wanted us to inject a spirit of fun and adventure into the story. I think they just wanted a balance between the darker elements and some of the lighter stuff. One particular change was in the character of Sybok. Originally, he was a very messianic, possessed kind of figure who was willing to trample anyone who got in his way, but he began to remind us too much of Khan and we had to take him in a different direction. It

would have been easy to write Sybok as a black-hat or a crazed Mohammed, but that was too much Khan.

"The idea of God and the Devil was reflected in the script's earlier drafts. Those drafts were much cleaner and more comprehensible in terms of the idea that you think you're going to Heaven, but you turn out to have found Hell. We weren't literally saying Heaven and Hell, but we were suggesting the idea that it was like, 'Wait a minute, is this God or the Devil?', without saying specifically that it's either, but instead is an alien entity that has tapped into our perceptions about where they're going. We did, however, run into some problems, one with Gene Roddenberry."

Roddenberry rejected the notion of the Enterprise encountering God, believing that Star Trek should avoid such specific religious themes.

"I didn't object to it being an alien claiming to be God," Roddenberry said in Captain's Log, "but there was too much in it that an audience could have thought was really God or really the devil, and I very strongly resist believing in either. I do not perceive this as a universe that's divided between good and evil. I see it as a universe that is divided between many ideas of what is."

Admits Shatner, "[Gene] did come down strongly against the story and set up circumstances that were negative and unfortunate. There's nothing wrong with a good story about the search for the meaning of life. That's basic to any great storytelling, no matter what form it takes whether it's The Bible or a myth or a fairy tale. I was hoping to be able to accomplish that with Star Trek V."

Loughery quickly adds that as fascinating as the theme of "meeting God" may be, it was the exploration of the relationship between Kirk, Spock and McCoy that appealed to him the most.

"To me, God was never the most important part of the script," he explains. "Yes, it was part of the story, but my focus and concentration was on the relationships. The whole God idea was almost a subplot. We had to tread a fine line, because we could really become very pretentious and pretend that we're saying something infinitely important. What I think we're really say-

ing is something that's very simple, which is that if there is a God, he's not a place you go to in terms of outer space. He's a place you go to inside yourself. We also wanted to challenge the audience's imagination and expectations when they realized that this is what Sybok's divine mission was. We really wanted the audience to stir around, look at each other and say, 'Are they serious? Can they possibly mean that we're going to see God?' Because, for me, Star Trek is probably the only arena in which you might actually try to do that. Star Trek has always been big enough to encompass almost any kind of concept, so we thought when we dropped the bomb and said, 'Oh, by the way, we're going to see God,' it would be something the audience would be excited about and say, 'Gee, maybe they will....who knows?'

"In terms of the Kirk, Spock and McCoy relationship, one of the things that occurred to me," he states, "is that if you look at Star Trek, you see these three men who are in middle age, and their lives have been spent in space. They're not married, they don't have families, so their relationship is with each other. They represent a family to each other, maybe without always acknowledging it. That, to me, was the most attractive thing, saying, 'What is family?' If it's not three people who care about each other, I don't know what it is."

Nobody Said It Was Gonna Be Easy

There was a point in the development of Star Trek V in which William Shatner had to go off to act in Ted Turner's Voice of the Planet, while David Loughery and Harve Bennett wrote yet another draft of the screenplay. This version was so different from the original concept, that Shatner felt betrayed upon his return.

"In truth," explains David Loughery, "we had gone too far, but sometimes you need to go too far in order to really see where you need to be. We found a median that was satisfying to all of us. We had some interesting ups and downs. I did lots of drafts over two years, and each one was a little different from the one before. What Harve and I had written—where we had really gone off from the original concept—was where we began to deal more with the idea of this legendary planet, this mythic place called Sha Ka Ree, being Sybok's goal and thinking of it more in terms of Shangri-La. It's a kind of Eden that existed, and a place one could reach by passing through this ordeal called the Barrier. We were leaning in the direction of it being more a mythic and heaven-like place, and dealing less with the idea that a physical God existed there. We were shying away from the idea of going to see God, and thinking more in terms of achieving Heaven. What we ended up with, as you can see in the film, is a balance between those two things."

The resulting screenplay chronicled Sybok's abduction of representatives from the Federation, Klingon and Romulan Empires, and using them as bait to lure a starship in. Naturally that starship is the Enterprise, which Sybok (who improbably turns out to be Spock's half-brother), utilizing great prowess in Vulcan mind control, gains command of. By freeing crewmembers from their greatest personal pain, he is able to enlarge his army of God-seeking followers. Even Spock and McCoy are swayed to his side, leaving Kirk to take on Sybok alone.

Both Leonard Nimoy and DeForest Kelley were unhappy with the way their characters were portrayed. In Kelley's case, it was a flashback sequence where Dr. McCoy performs euthanasia on his father. For Nimoy, Spock had been written in such a way that Sybok revealed to him his greatest pain, which was coming to grips with his human half, resulting in his betraying Kirk and the Enterprise to partake in Sybok's divine mission.

William Shatner explained, "After De read the script, he didn't want to do the scene. So I took him to lunch and tried to convince him it would work. I said, 'De, this is the best scene you've had to play in a long time.' He's such a wonderful actor, and I really felt he hadn't had a chance recently to show what he was capable of doing. Finally, after much talking, I convinced him to do it. His one stipulation was that we add an explanation of why McCoy committed the euthanasia. We added a short bit of

dialogue where Sybok asks, 'Why did you do it?' and McCoy answers, 'To preserve his dignity.' With these new lines, De felt that McCoy's motivations were clearer and more understandable. Once we solved De's objections, we were then closer to getting the scene I had envisioned."

In #71 of The Official Star Trek Fan Club Magazine, Kelley explained, "When the scene was first presented to me, it was a little harsher. Once we smoothed it out, I still knew it was going to be a difficult scene to do and I felt if that scene didn't come off absolutely right, we would be in trouble....I don't know whether the public realizes it or not, but a character that people have watched for over 20 years was being stripped in front of them of a very private and secretive situation that took place in his life....That moment of McCoy's privacy in Star Trek V would have been divulged to Kirk before anyone. His opening line in the scene was, 'Oh my God, don't do this to me!' And that meant many things: he knew that it was happening to him there, in front of these people, plus the fact he had to relive it again was tough.....The more I looked at it and studied the scene, the more important it became to me because it's a topic that goes on today. I thought it would be interesting to lay it out in the presence of a motion picture audience and let them decide within themselves what is right or wrong."

Leonard Nimoy wasn't at all happy with the flashback Sybok takes Spock on, nor his betrayal of Kirk.

Explains David Loughery, "Leonard had some problems with the earlier drafts, feeling that there were things that Spock would not do. His suggestions were very helpful, and along those lines we made the change that Spock had previously come to understand his human self, and does not betray Kirk. The way it turned out, I think is interesting because it really shows that the bond between these guys is strong and can't be broken. Rather than have Sybok walk off in a snit, he kind of admires this. His reaction is not really one of disappointment when it turns out that Spock won't go with him. He really kind of understands that Spock couldn't go with him. I think he sort of admires

that in a way. I was surprised, actually, when I eventually watched it with an audience. When Spock told Sybok he couldn't go with him, the audience let out a cheer. I wasn't anticipating that. And when McCoy sheepishly says, 'I guess you better count me out too,' they went for that. Then you go to Bill, who has this look on his face that says, 'Eat it, Sybok!' And they loved that too.

"One of the smart things we did early one was bring Leonard and De in to go over the script, because we wanted their input. These guys have lived with these characters for more than 20 years, and have very strong opinions on what their characters would and wouldn't do. There were problems with this too, however. As originally conceived, only Kirk held out against Sybok, which gives you more of a one man stands alone kind of thing, betrayed by his best friends. Leonard and De objected and it was changed. Suddenly there were three guys against Sybok. When you start doing that kind of stuff, bit by bit you remove and dilute the real strength of the original vision and finally you end up with a bit of a mish-mash. It would have been great for Kirk to have squared off against Spock in some way. But you find the script beginning to accommodate the needs of the actors who know their characters and say, 'Spock wouldn't do that.' It's kind of indefensible. You don't really have an argument that can turn them around on something like that."

The script—which had been finished shortly before the 1988 Writer's Guild strike that lasted some six months—was only part of William Shatner's problems. During its long development, Leonard Nimoy accepted the assignment of helming The Good Mother, thus delaying production by several months. Rumor had it that Shatner threatened to shoot the film without Nimoy, but everyone knew that this was a threat without meaning. One can't help but wonder if, in some way, Shatner was being paid back for prolonging negotiations on Star Trek IV, thus delaying production on that film.

To make matters worse, Paramount announced that Star Trek V was overbudget and that cuts would have to be made. The natural place to cut was special effects, the majority of which occurred toward the end of the film. A frustrated Shatner related, "My original concept for the movie had the characters descending into the equivalent of hell. The angels surrounding 'God' turned into horrible gargoyle-type figures and chase Kirk, Spock and McCoy into a burning chasm. I was quickly told that my idea was much too expensive. So we changed the gargoyles into Rockmen. That is, as Kirk, Spock and McCoy are running away, these huge, twisted shapes break free from the rocks surrounding them and pursue the characters. I had in mind six Rockmen, six hulking, strange creatures—terrifying! But each of those Rockmen were incredibly expensive....so the first thing I was told was that I could only have one Rockman. So here I had gone from this fantastic image of floating cherubim turned into flying gargoyles, then to six hulking Rockmen, now down to one Rockman. It was one of the first lessons I had in the realization that the movie in my head was going to be different from the one in reality."

Ultimately production snafus would cost the actor-director even his one Rockman, and much of his original vision. There were times when the production was in chaos, and it was all that everyone could do to stay as close to schedule and budget as possible.

Noticing what was happening, Leonard Nimoy on *The Tonight Show* said, "I gave him one piece of advice the first couple of days of shooting. I said stop talking so fast. It's the sign of a first-time director. You come on a stage the first day on the set and you're excited and you've got the adrenaline going and you're nervous and if you want to spot a first-time director, you look for the guy with the sweaty palms and he's hyperventilating and he's talking too fast. He thought that by talking fast it would speed up the schedule but you couldn't understand a word he was saying."

Assessing The Final Frontier

Kirk stands alone. As he races back towards the shuttlecraft, a horde of unspeakably evil gargoyles are unleashed by the malevolent god-creature intent on

devouring him. They pursue Kirk relentlessly while Scotty desperately tries to repair the damaged transporter—disabled by a phaser blast when the chief engineer accidentally beamed a gargoyle on board the ship and vaporized it.

For Shatner, the loss of his grand vision for *The Final Frontier*'s ending was a major disappointment. His substitute idea also went unrealized in which a Rockman, the god-thing's creature formed out of solid rock, attacks the Shuttlecraft Copernicus. The footage, first shot on location in the desert and later on a soundstage at Paramount, was deemed unsuitable and considered a major disappointment to both the crew and its director.

"I was required to reduce the budget and I kept slicing away at the ending," says Shatner. "I didn't realize until we got there how much of the ending I had lost and what a disservice I had done to the film. That was lesson number one."

Explained screenwriter David Loughery, "When the torpedo came down and explodes the hole, it's like the bottle is uncapped and all the imps spill out, free, and chase our characters back to the shuttle. That was our original concept. A movie, especially a movie like this one, goes through so many transformations from original story to final film. Because of all the hands involved in the making of these movies, it sometimes starts to take on a committee atomosphere to moviemaking. Things don't turn out exactly the way you originally wanted them to, but there are reasons for that. We certainly wish we could have hung on to some of that concept. The area of the movie that has always been in flux is *how* we represent the god-being. That sequence got lost when it became financially impossible for us to create the gargoyle creatures. You're always sorry to see those things go, because your imagination is one thing and the budget is something else. In various places, we had to make certain cuts and rearrangements based on how much we could afford."

"What the final result was, was the final result," says Shatner. "I have certain regrets but I feel in total that a lot of the vision was there. I made one major compromise at the beginning which was mitigating the original idea of the

Enterprise searching for God and instead finding an alien pretending to be God. The enormous thrust of the idea was eviscerated and that was my first compromise. It seemed that was a necessary one due to the fact that everybody was very apprehensive about the obvious problem. I thought [the film] was flawed. I didn't manage my resources as well as I could have, and I didn't get the help in managing my resources I could have. I thought it was a meaningful *attempt* at a story and I thought it was a meaningful play. It carried a sense of importance about it. Technically it went well, I thought. We hired a lot of different people. We went to New York and got other special effects people. So we experimented and I had to learn a great deal, not only about film but the politics of film. I don't think I'll make those same errors again. The experience has made me froth with ambition."

"In retrospect," offers David Loughery, "you always look back from the distance of a couple of years and I've always felt—it was always in the back of my head—that one of the problems is that it's a reactive story rather than an active one. What I mean by that is that our guys are kind of required to stand by and be dragged along on somebody else's quest. In this case, Sybok's. It's sort of *his* quest and *his* passion, and Kirk, Spock, McCoy and the rest of the crew are dragged along almost as though they were a supporting cast to this guy. If it had been Kirk who suddenly had this vision of God and hijacked his own ship and turned against the Federation, *then* you've got this much more active, passionate kind of story."

Co-star Leonard Nimoy diplomatically offers, "Bill worked very, very hard and he directed it as well and as capably as any of our other films. He was not riding on a good script. If you're not riding on a good script, you're the person people point fingers at. And he was responsible, it was his story. I've had that experience. I did a movie for Paramount [*Funny About Love*] that didn't work at all. I wasn't successful with the script."

Of the screenplay for *Star Trek V*, Nimoy points out, "I complained. I said, 'I think you've got some problems here,' and the message I got back is, 'We know what we've got and we know what we want to do.' Having sent in my notes, once they got them it's not my place to say, 'You must do the following.' Once the tank starts rolling, it's tough to stop it. It's very interesting. You cannot draw a rule and say, 'It must be done this way.' Sometimes things bubble together and sometimes they don't, even though you've got very well paid and professional people doing the job. Sometimes it works and sometimes it doesn't, and that's why some pictures succeed and some pictures fail."

To criticisms levelled against Shatner's sometimes unorthodox approach to direction, he has an immediate response.

"It's like youth," defends Shatner. "I wish I were able to say it was because of my youth. A first time director knows no boundaries and it's not knowing them that you shatter them. Rather than accepting the status quo, I tried to break the boundaries and make the camera do things that it wasn't supposed to, not because I didn't know how, but I thought that by standing firm and being as adamant as possible it would happen. But there came a point where I had to compromise. I was rushing around trying to save what I thought was my movie, but I had spent days and weeks with Harve telling him the story and him telling me his version of the story and going over and over and over as we built the story and the script and we worked in a very close and intimate way. It got to the point where we were talking about the death and birth of people close to us and there were times where tears passed between us in the intimacy of his office. These moments are part of the making of *Star Trek V* for me. If anybody else is doing another trip, that's their problem."

Another problem that helped torpedo the acceptance of Shatner's installment in the *Star Trek* mythos were the widely criticized special effects of Bran Ferren and Associates, which was hired to replace the more expensive *Trek* veteran effects teams of Industrial Light & Magic.

"I took a lot of personal hits about that and I feel a tremendous sense of responsibility and it hurts," says *Star Trek V* Executive Producer Ralph Winter. "At the time I made the decision on what

I felt would be best for the picture. It was not a capricious decision. It was based on testing we all did. There were a number of people involved in that decision, but I was leading the process. I felt like we were going to get something better and, in the beginning, we did...but it didn't work out that way."

Shatner shared Winter's regrets about the film's visual effects. "We had problems that we might not have had if we had different personnel," he admits. "I followed other people's leads because I did not have first-hand knowledge of these things, but I was in on the decision so I make no excuse for that, but it is an instance where my lack of experience showed."

Trek V Producer Harve Bennett disagrees that choosing Ferren to provide the film's visual effects was a mistake. "I think that's peripheral," says Bennett. "You should have seen ILM's test for God, they were silly. We went with the creative judgement that Bran had a more vigorous attack to help us sell the illusions and it was a picture that needed fancy footwork. In addition, it's important to note that when were ready to start ILM was overcrowded, we would have been the fourth or fifth major picture at ILM and we would have received their D team instead of their A team, which was a very important consideration. All the people we had worked with in the past were booked."

Bennett holds the success of *Star Trek: The Next Generation* partially accountable for the failure of *Star Trek V* to meet financial expectations. "In my opinion, and marketing never agreed with me, there are only so many hours in a *Star Trek* fan's life," says Bennett. "You've given the cult, where they were used to having turkey dinner every two years and old turkey sandwiches in between, a fresh turkey sandwich every Saturday and Sunday, big moviegoing nights. I know from a lot of mail I've received that people felt about *Star Trek V* that maybe they'd see it next week because they didn't want to miss *The Next Generation*. After all, turkey is turkey. I think the appetite for *Star Trek* movies was seriously impacted by the success of the series, not destroyed, just kind of subdivided and the feeding frenzy

we experienced on *Star Trek II, III* and *IV* did not exist on *V,* even if it had been a better movie."

In addition, Bennett feels that the growing popularity of *The Next Generation* ultimately hurt the success of *Star Trek VI* as well. "There has been an erosion and a conversion in the *Star Trek* cult," he says. "At first they tended to be resistive of *The Next Generation* and then, as the show improved and the habit accrued [and] they were getting fresh material as opposed to reruns and the inevitable wait for movies, I think they became very interested. You can see in all the publications where the letter ratio is shifting where the minority opinion is that the original characters were more interesting and the majority opinion is, 'Hey, let's get on with it.' Sitting in a theatre and watching the trailer for *Star Trek VI* you didn't get the electric shock that you did watching the promos for the other movies, that we've got to be there. On the contrary, you got some titters, talk back to the screen and I was startled to find the audience restless. That may mean nothing, but it may mean I don't want to go see a funeral."

David Loughery has his own theories as to why the film warped out of theatres almost as quickly as it warped in.

"That was the summer of *Batman,*" he reflects. "I don't know how many movie-spending bucks there are out there, but I think that everybody had a weekend that summer. We had an opening weekend where we made $17 million, and everybody thought we were all right, but it just didn't continue that way. Frankly, it was the kind of summer where the money was divided among a handful of films, and *Star Trek V* didn't turn out to be one of them. We were all taken by surprise.

Regardless of the film's reception, for Shatner exploring *The Final Frontier* was one of the most rewarding experiences of his career, one from which he learned many lessons he hopes to benefit by in future directing endeavors—which may or may not include *Star Trek VII*.

"Directing film is a wild adventure for anyone equipped to do it," says Shatner. "I made compromises on *Star Trek V* thinking I had to do that, that's the

The jacket adorning the Star Trek V: The Final Frontier CD, music composed by Jerry Goldsmith.

nature of the business and it is the nature of the business to compromise. But the line where you do not compromise I couldn't tread because of a number of factors, not the least of which is my own nature. I got to learn when it's time to stand and when it's time to turn and that, really, for a knowledgeable person in the business is a more important lesson than where the camera is and how to play a scene and what your establishing shot is. Those mechanics of making a film no longer become a point of discussion, it's automatic, it's there creatively. The political point of a director is a constant learning process because of the interpersonal relationships between the director and the rest of the people; the cast, the crew, the management and that is con-stantly changing from day to day and moment to moment, depending on how confident you feel and how confidently you express that feeling. It changes from job to job. I had the most joyful time of my life directing *Star Trek V* and whether it's *Star Trek VII*, another film or one of the several books I have out now that lend themselves to filmic adaptation, I intend to direct again."

Favored nations clause not withstanding, the subject of Shatner's possibly directing STAR TREK VI never came up.

••••

CHAPTER FOURTEEN
Star Trek VI: The Academy Years

After the chilly box-office reception of *Star Trek V* and the continuing chorus of naysayers criticizing the cast as being too old to continue, many suspected the silver screen voyages of the starship Enterprise had truly passed into the final frontier. But Producer Harve Bennett, in conjunction with *Star Trek V* screenwriter David Loughery, was hard at work creating a new vehicle to continue the *Star Trek* movie missions.

"Every time they go to make one of these *Star Trek* movies," notes Loughery, "the producers and the studio always run into the same problem in getting the original cast together. The reasons for that are money, power, creative differences, ego, health, unavailability....all of those things. Harve always had this ace up his sleeve, which was if we can't get everybody together for one of these *Star Trek* movies, we should do a prequel."

Called *Starfleet Academy*, the proposed film would have chronicled a young Kirk, Spock and McCoy's days at the Academy, as part of *Trek*'s 25th anniversary celebration. Instead, a sixth and final film featuring the original "classic" cast was put into production by Paramount, resulting in Harve Bennett's departure from the series.

"We had a better movie and we had a film that would have allowed them to make the same *Star Trek VI* eighteen months later," says Bennett of *Starfleet Academy*, which was aborted after objections from fans made the project untenable.

"I think there was a fat chance of that happening," comments Walter Koenig. "I can't read Harve's mind, but if *Starfleet Academy* had done well, they would have gone on with that group. If it hadn't, they probably would have abandoned the whole project."

"Because of the way *Star Trek VI* is being sold, don't miss your chance to

say good-bye, it's unlikely that *Starfleet Academy*, which asks 'Would you like to know how it all happened?' will be made," continues Bennett, whose previous producing chores included work on *The Mod Squad*, *The Six Million Dollar Man*, the Emmy Award winning miniseries *A Woman Called Golda* and *The Jesse Owens Story*.

Starfleet Academy chronicled the story of a young James T. Kirk, a Spock who is estranged from his parents and becomes the first Vulcan to attend Starfleet Academy, and Leonard McCoy, a 30 year old doctor who attends the Academy after having pulled the plug on his terminally ill father and is searching for meaning in his life. Michael Curtiz's 1940 film, *The Santa Fe Trail*, served as an inspiration for what Bennett envisioned as the classic triumvirate's first trek. The film which could have been made, according to Bennett, for $27 million would also have avoided the hefty multi-million dollar salaries of its leads—Shatner and Nimoy—as well as Kelley's take-home of nearly a half a million dollars and the $125,000 paychecks the supporting players pocketed.

"I pitched the idea to Harve at his daughter's Bat Mitzvah," recalls *Trek VI* producer Ralph Winter. "We had already locked in the *Star Trek IV* storyline with the whales and I said, 'You know, I have a great idea, let's do a prequel' in the middle of this reception for his daughter. I suggested we develop a series of films to be another franchise, another tent pole that we could open. We could do a prequel and find out how Kirk and Spock met at the Starfleet Academy. When we were doing *Star Trek V*, we got the studio to approve work on the script. It is an excellent story, but it has been misperceived. It's a great story finding out about this young cocky character on a farm who goes to flight school and meets up with the first alien that comes from Vulcan and how they meet the other characters. It would have been a gift for the fans on the 25th anniversary."

David Loughery notes, "When I heard about the idea, I thought it was terrific. Not from the point of view of recasting, but from the point of view of storytelling, because I worked so closely with these characters on *Star Trek V*, that the idea of doing an origin story—where you show

them as young cadets and kids—was tremendously exciting. What it was, was a real coming of age story. In outline form, it was the story of Kirk and Spock meeting for the first time as cadets here on Earth. We've got a young Jim Kirk, who's kind of cocky and wild. He's not exactly what you might think starship captain material might be. He's like one of these kids who would rather fly hot planes and chase girls. Spock is this brilliant, arrogant, aloof to the point of obnoxiousness, genius. It's this mask he's hiding behind to cover his own conflicting human emotions. He's an outcast, he left Vulcan in shame against his father's wishes and, like all adolescents, he's trying to find a place to fit in, but he keeps screwing it up.

"Over the course of this story," he continues, "which is one year at Starfleet Academy, Kirk and Spock are sort of put to the test and they begin as rivals and end up as friends and comrades who learn that they have to combine their talents for the first time to defeat a deadly enemy. In the final scene, where they say goodbye at graduation and go their separate ways, we're able to see the legends that these two boys are going to grow up to become."

But for Bennett, who had spent a decade living with *Star Trek*, *Starfleet Academy* was not to be. The rejection of the project was a big disappointment for the veteran producer who planned the film as his freshman directorial effort.

"It meant a lot to me because I came out of UCLA film school wanting to be a director and other winds blew me to to other ports," says Bennett. "It was a desire of mine to direct and it was accepted by the studio and, the fact is, part of the deal was for us to do a *Star Trek VI*, with the original cast after *Starfleet Academy*."

But once word leaked out about the project, support was marshalled against the film and vociferously denounced on the convention circuit by members of the supporting cast, as well as *Star Trek* creator Gene Roddenberry.

Said Roddenberry in the pages of *Cinefantastique*, "I didn't like it. Who was going to cast the new Kirk and Spock? No one has ever cast a *Trek* character besides me that's worked. Braggadocio or whatever, that is the history of *Trek*. It wasn't good. Some of it was like *Police*

Academy. You could hardly do this without the magic of a group of characters tailored for *Star Trek*, which this was not."

Letters began to pour into Paramount decrying the planned feature as heresy.

"We were really caught off guard and surprised by the fans who reacted so negatively to the idea of this movie," admits David Loughery. "Somehow they conceived it as sort of a spoof or a takeoff. That's where we got off on the wrong foot. The fans had misinformation, which may have been put out there by people for their own reasons. Certainly if we were going to make a movie like that, it meant that Walter and whoever wouldn't get that job a year or two down the line that they had come to expect. I don't know if that's the case, but I do know that the misinformation released had people convinced that we were going to do a cross between *Police Academy* and *The Jetsons*. It was never that kind of story. I think it's traditional that the fans have objected to different things. Harve's always been smart enough to double-cross them; give them what they've objected to, but surprise them with something that makes it good and worthwhile. We felt that there was a powerful story there, one that the audience would be interested in. We're always interested in young Indiana Jones and young Sherlock Holmes, and how they started and came to be who they are. This was sort of the way to explain Kirk and Spock and where they came from."

"There *was* pressure from a lot of people not to do this," Bennett emphasizes. "I don't think there was any question that the self-interest of the supporting cast was not served by it and if I was George Takei, I would do exactly what he did and if I were Jimmy Doohan, I would be a really unhappy man. The only one I'm really furious at though is Jimmy Doohan. He said I was fired and I can't abide lies. My term was up and I was offered $1.5 million to do *Star Trek VI* and I said, 'Thanks, I don't wish to do that. I want to do the Academy.'"

Responds Doohan, "I was impressed with Harve when he first came in and did *Star Trek II* and *III*, but I think he got a little greedy. He wanted things his own way. He wanted to take over *Star Trek* for himself. What the heck, you don't

do that sort of thing, trying to destroy instead of building. He obviously did not realize the strength of the old cast. The whole thing would have been starting out as if from scratch. I think it was [Frank] Mancuso who didn't realize we were not going to be in it. When he found out, [he] said good-bye Harve."

"My last words to Mancuso before he was asked to leave [by the then recently installed head of Paramount, Stanley Jaffe] was if it was a question of anyone's concerns about my directing, I'd back off on that," says Bennett. "They then offered me *Star Trek VI* and gave me a pay or play commitment to direct and produce *Starfleet Academy* afterwards. My position was, and I think it was correct, that they would pay me to do *VI* and make the movie which would have been a real big, fat check for me and never made *Starfleet Academy*. To be paid off because the movie I might have done, which is being done by others, would close the franchise was not my intention. I had a life, it's not like I hadn't done anything else before *Star Trek*. The *Star Trek* curse is something that the poor supporting cast has to live with, but I don't."

Opines William Shatner, "Harve was striving to find an answer for the studio's question 'Are these guys too old to continue?' So he tried to find a solution as a storywriter and he must of said here's a way of going. Apparently everybody agreed, but at some point they shut him down after preparing this production for a year and he got very upset about it and left. I wasn't too clued in on the politics of what was happening. I had heard about the prequel and was considering my options, but it was never approved and we didn't know whether or not there would be another *Star Trek* until the last second."

For Ralph Winter, *Starfleet Academy* would have ushered in a new approach to the *Star Trek* franchise for the studio in which a coherent plan would be created for producing the *Trek* films on a semi-regular basis as opposed to the sporadic, fitful stop and go start-up on a new film every three years with the arduous contract negotiations that initiating each new chapter entailed.

"*Starfleet Academy* may have looked like a mistake," says Winter, "but look at the franchise as a whole. We have

a successful series of feature films, then a new television series and with the film series ending it made sense to start a new series of films. You could have opened a whole new frontier. When *Star Trek: The Next Generation* came out, the people said this will never work, how can we have a new Captain? It will never equal Kirk and Spock. But they've achieved their own success. It could have been the same with a prequel cast, now you would have three different fronts. Make the successful features with the original cast, features with a prequel cast and the television series with the new cast. That's what could have happened. You look at the long term and you develop two or three scripts at a time and you maximize production. The unfortunate part about today's economy and the thinking of these big companies is let's see how this one does and then we'll decide on the next one. There was never a plan after any of these films to do another one. *Star Trek II* was the last picture, Spock was dead. That was it. It's just getting too expensive to drag out all the wardrobe, sets, models. With a long term plan you could milk this forever and the fans would be thrilled, but if you go one step at a time and don't know where you're going, then the films are expensive and maybe it does make sense to the do the sixth film with the original cast."

As for the *Star Trek VI* that did materialize on the screen, Bennett has mixed feelings, having hoped that Nimoy and his confederates would meet with success, but is dubious. "I'm sure glad that it's not my movie," mused Bennett. "I was presented with the choice of doing *Star Trek VI* in 11 months and I didn't want to do a conventional film and I didn't believe I could do it in that time. The fact that they have done it is a tribute to all my buddies, and they are good buddies. Nicholas Meyer is the fastest writer in the world, Ralph Winter is the most ethical and perfect producer of special effects movies anywhere and one of the nicest men I've ever know. It wasn't easy to walk away from that, but if your heart is not in something and you've earned the right not to have do things that cause you pain, then you don't do them."

In terms of the future of *Starfleet Academy*, as the saying goes in the *Star Trek* universe: "There are always possibilities."

• • • •

●●●●

CHAPTER FIFTEEN

Star Trek VI: The Undiscovered Country

"On the Beach"

During the Christmas 1991 movie season, while Oliver Stone was pinning the murder of President John F. Kennedy on the CIA and the military-industrial complex, simultaneously grabbing the covers of every major magazine from *Esquire* to *Life* to *GQ* to *Newsweek*, *Star Trek* was not only attributing the assassination of its architect of the new frontier to these familiar and conveniently nebulous 20th century arms merchants, but perhaps the very fabric of galactic peace to their nefarious machinations.

But, of course, no cover stories here. It's only sci-fi, right?

The genesis of *Star Trek VI* began when Leonard Nimoy, at the behest of then Paramount studio chief Frank Mancuso, set about to revive the floundering film series for its 25th anniversary. In essence, he became the newest in a long line of perennial great birds of the *Star Trek* galaxy.

"Frank Mancuso had called Leonard into his office and said, 'Leonard, help me make this film,'" recalls *Trek VI* co-writer and novelist Dennis Martin Flinn, author of a number of well regarded detective novels including *San Francisco Kills, Killer Finish* and *Lady Killer*. "At that point, Leonard was the producer, writer, the director, the star and it was up to him to discharge those duties or pass them onto other people. Mancuso apparently knew he could trust him to get the whole thing going and to get it going quickly, and I think that had something to do with *Star Trek V*. Let's face it, nobody wanted to have anything to do with anybody who had anything to do with *V*, except as necessary. I don't think *Star Trek V* was entirely Shatner's fault by any means. Moviemaking is a very collaborative business, but no one was happy with it."

In total agreement with Flinn is screenwriter Mark Rosenthal, who, along with partner Lawrence Konner, are the unsung heroes of *Star Trek VI*. It was this team that came up with the original storyline for the film, a fact that did not become apparent to the public until about a week prior to the film's opening when newspapers heralded, "Story by Leonard Nimoy, Lawrence Konner and Mark Rosenthal." Even the paperback adaptation does not feature their names amongst the credits.

"We were under contract at Paramount and the feeling was that they were not going to do another *Star Trek* movie," reflects Rosenthal, whose credits include *Jewel of the Nile* and *Superman IV*. "The guys were getting old and *Star Trek V* was a disappointment. Everybody was disenchanted with Shatner's direction. There was a bad taste in everyone's mouth and no one wanted to go out like that. They knew the 25th anniversary was coming up, and we were approached by the vice president of production, Teddy Zee, who's now at Columbia. Teddy called us up and said, 'Frank Mancuso has spoken to Leonard, Leonard was still upset because of the last one and he was floating out the idea of one last adventure.' He asked us what we thought about it. The reality was that I am a Trekkie and my partner is incredibly non-science fiction oriented. We were kind of a Yin-Yang but we liked that idea, because Larry would provide a good balance.

States actor-writer-executive producer Leonard Nimoy,"The Berlin Wall had come down. The Russian government was in severe distress. Communism was falling apart. These changes were creating a new order in our world. I thought there would be a new kind of dialogue, a new thinking of these relationships. And a whole new military vision and a whole new vision of hardware. Realizing that over the 25 year history of *Star Trek*, the Klingons have been the constant foe of the Federation, much like the Russians and Communists were to democracy, I wondered how we could translate these contemporary world affairs into an adventure with the Klingons. I thought it was an ideal way for us to have our closure too, because the Klingons for us have always been the

The official Star Trek *fan club provided indepth coverage on the making of* Star Trek VI: The Undiscovered Country.

Communist Block, the Evil Empire. It just made sense to do that story."

"The main thing we were concerned with," Rosenthal says, "was that we had never really gotten details about the Klingon Empire. There was a whole question of whether we should go to the actual home planet. What happened was that they felt in terms of budget, recreating the entire planet would be impossible, so it became this prison concept. The original idea was to go to the actual capital city. I still think it was a better idea, but you can see how this process happens. The first *Star Trek* had a horrendous budget and it was a bad movie. Paramount began to realize that the Europeans did not grow up with *Star Trek*, so there's a very small market for it. The studio always feels that they have to make their money in a domestic situation, which for a big-budget special effects movie is tough. When you write, you try to come up with stories that take place in one ship, because that's pretty cheap to do. When you start talking about sets and locations, the budget gets very high.

"At one point we had a discussion about using Chernobyl, and that really opened the floodgates," he enthuses. "Then we began to look at specific events and, of course, recent Soviet histo-

●●●●

ry serves as some kind of basis for the movie. Once you get on that track of thinking, we said, 'What's really going on?' Everyone is paranoid that someone is going to try and sabotage peace between the Soviet Union and the United States. Why not have the same thing occur between the Klingons and the Federation? It all kind of led to the idea of assassination. What if Gorbachev was assassinated and the blame fell on Kirk? That was really the key. We were also trying to see what else had happened in *Star Trek IV*, what kind of threads could be picked up. Everybody remembered that a Bird of Prey had crashed into San Francisco Bay at the end of the movie, and the Bird of Prey was equipped with a cloaking device. That led us to thinking. One of the rules about the Bird of Prey was that they had to decloak when they fired. What if, given the Stealth Bomber, they could fire while cloaked? That became an important element."

Nimoy returned to the studio and pitched the idea: a peace overture between the Federation and the Klingon Empire triggers a hostile reaction from those on both sides who had invested the most in the existing state of belligerence. The studio was hooked. This time there was no hokey science-fiction concept, no search for God, just Klingon battle cruisers and starships slugging it out in the stars...for peace.

The man who had once declared "I Am Not Spock," and whose character had been killed off in hopes of luring him back into the fold for one final film in *The Wrath of Khan*, had now assumed a paternal, nurturing role over the series. Nimoy had shepherded *Trek* for half a decade and now recruited *Star Trek II* savior Nicholas Meyer to co-write and direct the film. Hiring Meyer was an inspired choice. Not only did the veteran *Trek* helmer work and write fast, but bringing him onboard would help avoid any problems with Nimoy's co-star and fellow director, William Shatner, who was itching to get behind the camera again and whose ire would surely been raised had Nimoy attempted to direct his third *Trek* film.

Shatner admits to a degree of disappointment over not captaining from the director's chair of what could

be the Enterprise's final voyage. "I felt a sense of loss that I couldn't be the problem solver," he says. "I would have loved to have been immersed in those very same problems and bring to bear what I had learned on the previous film. But on the other hand there was a sense of tremendous relief, as I was only too aware of the pressures on Nick Meyer both from a production point of view and a political view from the studio and, as time would get short, the anxiety that was involved in trying to get it done on time. I was very sensitized to the things he needed to accomplish."

Shatner is quick to point out that he was very pleased with the film's storyline. "It's a really good idea," he says. "It's a classic *Star Trek* idea in that the important issue of the day is incorporated into the story of *Star Trek*, and by doing so—and because we put it into the future—we're able to comment on it as though it has nothing to do with today, yet it makes a commentary."

Going to the beach in Cape Cod, Leonard Nimoy shared the premise credited to him, Rosenthal and Konner. with the vacationing Meyer, who had co-written *Star Trek IV*, but rejected overtures to helm *Star Trek III* and *V* in years past. This time Meyer was hooked, partially because the film he was in post-production on, MGM's *Company Business*, shared a similar glasnot-inspired theme, but had been "butchered" by the studio, according to Meyer.

"Leonard said to me, 'Let's make a movie about the wall coming down in outer space.' His statement just spoke to me," Meyer admits. "What I wanted to do with it, was to widen the world of *Star Trek* before closing out the series, if that's indeed what's happening. The thing I've learned from these movies is that your only chance of succeeding is not to repeat yourself, not to try the same exact thing. I didn't want to go mano-a-mano because I had done that with *II*; I didn't want to make a comedy because I felt *IV* was the most broadly comedic of any of them. So I thought, 'I want to make an ensemble piece and I want it to be a political thriller.' Like everybody else, I was fascinated by the events of the last two years from 1989 on. I had been

in Berlin working on another film and I had seen the wall coming down. God, what are the possibilities? What are the potentials for greatness or disaster? Who would have thought it? It's a bright spot, but it's filled with the potential for real disaster, and this is the theme of the movie, because change is *real* scary. In this film, the intention is certainly to deal with what people do when they are confronted with the prospect of radical change. There are some people who are capable of embracing it, and some who have a lot of trouble with it."

It was in May of 1990 that Mancuso had first called Nimoy to his office to recruit him to have a new *Star Trek* film featuring the "classic" cast ready for the show's 25th anniversary. By October of that year, Flinn and Meyer were completing their first draft script based on the Konner and Rosenthal story.

"Nick was involved with *Company Business* in London and wasn't going to be able to write the screenplay in time to get the film into production for the release date that would coincide with the 25th anniversary," recalls Flinn. "So he told Paramount that the only way he could do it is if he could co-write the script with me, and that's how it came about. He was kind enough to trust me, and while he was in London we communicated via computer. When we turned in our first draft in December of last year, the studio greenlighted it."

The screenplay evolved constantly, not least of all to reflect the myriad of comments from Nimoy, Shatner and Gene Roddenberry who, according to Nimoy, was very much involved in a creative consultant capacity.

"I'm a Roddenberry disciple," says Nimoy, who was reportedly one of the stumbling blocks in the release of Roddenberry's book celebrating 25 years of *Star Trek*. "He was very much involved. I went to him for regular meetings on this script. Everytime we had a draft, I met with him and we discussed it. He was very intrigued with the idea that we would be exploring the relationship with the Klingons. He was concerned in this particular story about the prejudice question, because it's an interesting issue. Sometimes when you show people showing a prejudice, even though your

• • • •

intention is to show that they're wrong, there are going to be people who identify with them. Here you've got a couple of guys saying, 'What do you think of the smell? Only the top of the line models can talk.' Gene was concerned about that stuff. He said, 'I don't feel good about Enterprise crew talking that way.' We pointed out, 'These are bad people who are racists and who turn out to be assassins.' 'I'm just uncomfortable with a couple of guys walking around in Federation uniforms talking that way about another race.' And I understood it. It's a danger. By and large, he was quite taken with the idea of a Klingon detente. It was his idea to put a Klingon in the Federation on *The Next Generation*, and this was the beginning of that link."

Co-writer Dennis Martin Flinn notes, "When *Star Trek* relies on science-fiction, it's a big failure. Maybe that's part of why nobody likes *Star Trek I* and *V* very much. Gene Roddenberry originally called *Star Trek* "Wagon Train to the stars" because westerns served the purpose in our society of being morality tales about good guys versus bad guys and, in many cases, in those thousands of westerns it was irrelevant that the setting was the Old West. What was important and great in a movie like *Shane*, for instance, was the story of the individual in society, and *Star Trek* is best when it's a morality play. That's what Gene called the original episodes, so when Leonard came up with the idea that the Klingons could stand in for the Russians and we could deal with the end of the Cold War, we were home free in terms of fundamentals that we knew worked."

Distilling the action/adventure plot was even more attractive to Flinn, who relied on familiar cinematic conventions to drive his metaphoric storyline.

"The idea sprung up from what would happen if someone attempted to assassinate Gorbachev," says Flinn. "In our story, Kirk might be blamed for that. Then comes something that I grew up on in movies, which is 'I've got to get out of here so I can clear my name.' I thought that's a good way to go and it worked for forty years in westerns and detective stories."

Flinn offers that had *Star Trek VI*'s story been pitched as a contemporary allegory, the studio would never have greenlighted the production. "Science-fiction allows you to do that," he says. "You can hide it from the executives; they don't get it. Nobody would touch it. The studios would say the military industrial complex goes to see movies and they would come up with a reason not to make a movie that exposes this. That's the kind of advantage science-fiction offers. Issues have gone to television, but they're the exception and not the rule. Our advertisers don't want you to insult anyone, they don't want you to insult serial killers. They may be watching."

Both Meyer and Flinn were not afraid to wield their pen to take the 25 year old characters in new directions. In addition to Spock's attachment to his Vulcan counterpart, Valeris, Kirk, who had always represented the best qualities of 1960's America in the finest Kennedy-esque tradition, was set-up as a bigoted right wing zealot, prejudiced against a very evil empire for having slain his son in *Star Trek III*.

"In the script there's a wonderful line," says William Shatner. "'In space, all warriors are cold warriors.' Both sides have come to define themselves by their antagonism. 'What will I be without my enemy?' The best *Star Trek* stories have their genesis in real life. For this story, you just have to pick up the daily newspaper."

"There are three kinds of people in the universe of *Star Trek VI*," Flinn points out. "The people who wanted peace, the people who did not want peace for their own self interest, and then there were the people, like Kirk, who had lived a certain way for 25 years vis a vis with the Klingons, but were intelligent enough to say what does the future have to offer? Maybe this isn't wrong. I think we were lucky to be able to see Kirk as a man who, if he was rigid at all, at least recognized his own rigidity. That in itself was flexible and not rigid. And of course it allowed us to create a character that, in essence, was a spokesman for the uncertainties and the whole idea of the undiscovered country. The future, being scary, got nailed down because we had a character that could say that."

Nicholas Meyer opines, "I think the heroic thing about Kirk and the rest of the crew is their effort to acknowledge, to confront and ultimately try to overcome their prejudice. If a man leaps into a raging torrent to save a drowning child, he performs a heroic act. If the same man leaps into the same pond to save the same child, and does so with a ball and chain attached to his leg, he must be accounted not less heroic, but more heroic still because he overcomes a handicap. And that's what heroism and drama is about. I think Kirk is more of a hero for being a human being and not less because he's super human, which I never believed."

"The portrayal of Kirk," adds William Shatner, "attempts to show a man who has spent a lifetime imbued with the idea that his mission in life is to subdue, subvert and make the enemy submit to his nation's or his Federation's view. That's his whole training and that is the military training. He learns differently and that is the classic dilemma that *Star Trek* has sought to present in its most successful shows."

It was the central dichotomy in Kirk's character, and in the film, that Cliff Eidelman attempted to capture in his score for the movie. "It gave me a theme for the opening," says Eidelman. "It's Kirk taking control one last time and as he looks out into the stars, he has that spark again.one last time. It's his one last spark into space, but there's an unresolved note, because it's very important that he doesn't trust the Klingons and he doesn't want to go on this trip even though the spark is there that overtook him."

Nimoy, too, felt that the script's underlying theme was effective. "Spock experienced prejudice growing up half-Vulcan and half-human," stated Nimoy. "In *Star Trek VI*, Spock becomes an emissary against prejudice and discovers, during the course of the story, his own prejudices."

Despite the strength of its script, *Trek VI* was far from a sure thing. Once the word got out that *Star Trek VI* was indeed underway, while the fans rejoiced the cast became the butt of a many jokes. "The talk shows were making fun of us for weeks," remembered Flinn. "David Letterman was doing the search for geritol—so it was risky already. Two of the actors are 71 years old, but, hell, they're healthy."

With the realization that the previous film had been a commercial and critical disappointment, the producers of *Star Trek VI* sought to make the new film as different from its predecessor as possible.

Ralph Winter elaborates, "*Star Trek IV* reached out to an audience that had never seen a *Star Trek* picture before. We increased our audience 30-40% and *Star Trek V* didn't do that. Everybody started out to make a good movie, a lot of people read that script and thought it was going to be great, but we stumbled. Has that affected our thinking about this picture? Yes, it has. We have a different composer, a different look. We're doing everything we can to give this film a fresh look."

According to a member of the new film's production team, "They got ILM on the project very fast because they didn't want the problem that they had the last time and Lucas can deliver fast."

"We went away from the visual effects on *Star Trek V* because we thought we were going to get something new and different from another guy, which didn't happen," Winter says. "We went back to what we know is proven and the stuff that ILM did is spectacular. We were the benefactors of technology from *T2*. The look of the picture, the cameraman, the set dresser, the designer, everything about this film is trying to stretch and be something the other films haven't. I was a key member of *Star Trek V*, and when someone talks about it, it hurts. You didn't like it? Fine. We're trying to fix it. We wanted to make a film that the fans are going to like for the 25th anniversary. We looked at the areas of the picture where we could make it distinctive and different and not just the fifth sequel to a motion picture. Where we could do it and not spend a tremendous amount of money, we did."

Adds director Nicholas Meyer, "A lot of people said *Star Trek II* was such a terrific movie and had a lot of unkind things to say about *Star Trek I*, but I don't think they realize that *Star Trek II* wouldn't have been so good if someone hadn't gone boldly where no one had gone before and showed us, in effect, what not to do when it was really impor-

tant. It's damn hard work to make those movies and I'm not going to look down my nose at any of them."

However, even with a suitable script, having a major feature film ready in less than a year was a difficult challenge. With the studio vacillating for months over the future of *Star Trek*, now it was up to the assembled team of director Meyer, executive producer Nimoy, and producers Winter and Steven Charles Jaffe to have a film ready by the end of 1991.

"We got a go on February 13th and we had to have it in theatres by December 13th," says Winter. "That's really a short amount of time and money for the expectation level. The fans don't think about how much the budget was, they just want to know why the picture wasn't good, if it wasn't good."

Problems resulting from the tight shooting schedule typified the production from its inception. Recalls Nicholas Meyer, "I told them it would take 55 days. They said you have 51 and I yelled and screamed and they finally gave me 53...and I came in at 55."

But the tight production schedule was not the only daunting obstacle. With the recession cutting into box-office receipts and the failure of a crop of big-budget action movies in the summer of 1990, all the major film studios were preaching fiscal prudence when it came to their pictures. *Star Trek* was no exception. With box-office for most of the films in the series averaging in the $70-80 million range, Paramount balked when they were handed the budget for the latest Enterprise mission. The studio halted pre-production in order to cut its inflated budget, threatening to discontinue work on the film unless extensive production costs could be severely curtailed.

"This picture almost didn't get made," Winter explains. "It almost died a number of times. It's being made for less money than the last one and it's quite a feat. The above the line [cast and other non-technical related expenses] is substantial with the number of stars we have, so the money I have available to make this picture is a lot less than you have to make *Alien 3* or *Terminator 2*."

Rejecting the nearly $40 million price-tag for the film, Paramount had put *Star Trek VI* into turnaround in early

1991, hitting the brakes on a project which was screeching toward production at warp speed. "Bill and Leonard made concessions to get this picture made because they wanted to make it, we all did," Winter details. "Everyone made concessions and, frankly, Nick and Steven and I deferred a significant portion of our salaries to get this picture made, because we believed the story was worthwhile."

Says co-producer Steven Jaffe, "One of the ways that Nick and I have worked together as producer and director in the past is that I have directed second unit on every movie we've done together from *Time After Time* to *The Day After*, where I was hired exclusively as a second unit director. On *Star Trek* the pressures we were under to do this project were greater and for less money than the others. It's a sensitive subject to me because it's something that comes up every single movie, and we've prided ourselves in the past on bringing in all of our movies on budget and on schedule or under, beginning with *Time After Time*. It's kind of disturbing when you have an enormous amount of pressure put on you as though you weren't going to try and do it that way."

Scrambling to reduce the film's inflated budget, set-pieces were cut from the film and instead of building all-new Enterprise interiors, it was decided that redressed sets from *Star Trek: The Next Generation* would stand-in for the Enterprise 1701-A. "Those sets were built for *Star Trek: The Motion Picture* in 1978 and I've used them on every one of these pictures," says Winter. "We were fortunate to schedule the sets as soon as they wrapped for the season and we were in there ripping out walls and changing lights. As soon as we were done, we had to repaint, slap it back together and recarpet them. They were used for hallways, transporter rooms and stuff like that."

With the budget trimmed to a manageable $26 million, Paramount greenlit the picture on February 13th, 1991 with a mandate that the film be ready for release by the end of the year. The cameras starting rolling on April 16, 1991 but before then, the production team had to round out the supporting cast.

"Wanted: Master Thespians"

Once Flinn and Meyer fulfilled their first qualification for good *Star Trek*, creating a solid action/adventure story with a message, the second hurdle awaited and that was finding a strong guest cast. With the assist of casting director Mary Jo Slater, they loaded the last *Trek* with a cast of all the Hollywood heavyweights they could afford.

"Nick wanted an all-star ensemble cast and in addition to the seven stars that have been in *Star Trek*, he wanted to populate it with stars on every player that wasn't a regular, even if you couldn't recognize them," says producer Steven Jaffe. "What's important to Nick, especially with the aliens, is that he wanted them to be very articulate and great actors that could project through the make-up. I think that's a very smart way of making it not just a really good *Star Trek* movie, but a good movie in general. It's very hard for an actor with a couple of pounds of make-up on his face to project through there. A great actor like Chris Plummer has the range and power to blast through it. You feel a personality and not just like you're looking at a guy with a mask on. To that degree, we achieved our goals. There were some people that we wanted that we couldn't afford. In the long run it may have worked out for the best, because I think David Warner is extraordinary in the movie, which would have been totally different from Jack Palance. I was also happy to work with him again, [as] the last time we worked together was on *Time After Time*. Kim Cattrall is extraordinary. We were very happy she wanted to be in the movie."

On being able to achieve the casting for the film he did, Meyer says, "I hunted them down and twisted arms and I said, 'Read the script.' When people read the script, then they wanted to do it. That was a good sign. Christopher Plummer's last day of the movie I felt myself going into a deep depression, and going over to have a cry in the corner of the soundstage. I was so upset when he left. First of all, he's great. Secondly, he's a really terrific guy. We were having fun and it was such a thrill to work with him.

David Warner's an old friend of mine. I'd use him everytime I make a movie if I had my way. I think Kim Cattrall is the most underrated actress of her generation. I'm always surprised to find out that she was in this movie or that movie, and then I realize she's so good that she sort of disappears into the role. I loved working with her. I think she's a great actress and a real beauty too."

For Cattrall, who was initially wary of taking the role of Valeris, *Star Trek VI* was an exciting experience made even more intriguing by the constantly evolving script. Time pressures forced the film into production before Meyer could finish his revisions.

"Things changed dramatically," says the actress. "The final scene Leonard and I had together on the page was written as one thing, but [in] he and I doing it, it took on a life of it's own. It's an exciting scene to experience because not until the last moment did either of us know what was going to happen. You've never really seen Vulcans mind meld. The only other instance that Leonard could recall was when he was brought back to life and there was a mind meld. There is such an infusion of two people's chemistry and energy caught between incredible pain and pleasure. It's the closest thing to a sexually heightened experienced that you would get in a *Star Trek* movie."

Says Flinn, "*Star Trek* is known for great guest stars. I think [having] a regular cast helps enormously, because what people want more than anything in movies, and maybe in all art, is something old and something new. When the audience is comfortable they're happy, but at the same time that doesn't allow for any originality. So in *Star Trek II* you have Ricardo Montalban. Here we have Christopher Plummer, and you have the best of both worlds. Even in the episodes, whether it was Joan Collins or Teri Garr, they would always meet some alien out there who, on a pure entertainment level, would provide something new so that you could tune in not just for your favorite characters, but the weekly surprise as well. We definitely have that with Christopher Plummer, who is such a marvelous actor."

"The thing that I can say *Star*

Trek VI has going for it that none of the other films had, is the preponderance of quality guest performers," admits Walter Koenig. "We have some really strong people. Kim was wonderful. There's a mind meld scene that the first time a mind meld is really sexy. It's very sensual. Rosanna DeSoto, Chris Plummer, Brock Peters, David Warner are all great."

"I've worked with Christopher Plummer and he's just a fabulous actor," adds Jimmy Doohan. "I saw him at Stratford doing Cyrano in Canada, and he just wiped the floor with every other Cyrano in the business. He's just sensational. Thank God, we had a great supporting cast because that's what this movie called for."

Decades before, Shatner had understudied for Plummer in *Henry V* in Canada, and now the two were squaring off among the stars in *Star Trek VI*. Unlike *Star Trek II* where Khan and Kirk never met, Kirk got to spar Shakespeare with General Chang face to face. "Mary, Queen of Scotts and Elizabeth the First never met and playwrights have been putting them together ever since," reflects Meyer. "Did they [Kirk and Khan] really never meet? They should have met."

Flinn was at first worried that Meyer's propensity for injecting classical quotations may have been overdone until he saw what Plummer was able to do with the polished prose. "Once we got this guy, Nick said, 'This guy can really do this stuff,' and kept adding more and more," says Flinn. "Whether it's pretentious or not, I think it depends on how it's used. It's a case of writing for the actor or getting the right actor for the role, which is a very grey line sometimes. Nick did polishes and rewrites right up until the night the scenes were shot. I don't quite agree with using too much of that sort of thing, but once you get Chris Plummer, suddenly it's working. In *Star Trek II*, he put the book in Shatner's hands and the bifocals and he made a marvelous statement that, no matter how information is delivered to us in the 23rd century, great literature will still exist and I thought that was a marvelous statement. In terms of literary allusions, I can only say to you that Nick is very, very well read with an education that is certainly classically oriented. I happen to have appreciated that for some time, and kind of went with the flow when I began working on the script myself."

One of the surprises that the film's casting offered was Christian Slater as a member of the Excelsior crew, serving under Captain Sulu. Notes George Takei, "I have a new puppy and it's the cutest thing. Its tail wags, it just bounces up and down. Well, that was Christian Slater. He was so happy. He lobbied to get on the set because he was a *Trek* fan from a child. My childhood dream was to swashbuckle in Sherwood Forest. He did that, but his dream was to wear a Starfleet uniform. He was like   my puppy, bouncing up and down, dashing down the corridor, climbing up a ladder and saying, 'This is where Scotty did so and so.' He was literally a 21-year-old kid in his fantasy land."

Offers producer Ralph Winter about the film's casting, "Nick wanted to go for a classy approach. He wanted to go with actors who were going to make a contribution and really wanted to work with us. Despite not having the budget of some of the enormous pictures, we didn't want to be deterred by that. We wanted to find people who liked the material and would treat it as if it was the biggest picture ever made. We went for the best actors in each role. We were not looking for someone to say, 'Okay, I'll do it,' but people who got excited about the material, who were *Star Trek* fans and would love to be in the picture. That's what attracted us to Kim Cattrall, Christopher Plummer, Rosanna DeSoto and Kurtwood Smith. In other places, we went for a specific look, and also a good actor—Iman."

As for the comely chameloid, writer Flinn envisioned a somewhat different approach to the last woman to stir Kirk's loins. "The person I had in mind was as different as night and day from Iman," says Flinn. "I had Sigourney Weaver in mind, but I'm not sure we didn't come up with a better choice. I didn't imagine that we could ever afford her, but I just saw the character as a big, ballsy space pirate; a female version of the dark side of Han Solo. She turns out to be rather villainous, but a kind of swashbuckling female space pirate, and I thought of Sigourney."

Equally taxing was finding a place for each of the supporting players who demanded their share of screen time. Not surprisingly, in a cast that has been lauded and extolled for nearly 25 years with a nearly religious fervor, tempers and egos have periodically flared and often festered. One of the unique challenges of crafting a *Star Trek* film is providing the ensemble with their share of the action to appease both the actors and their respective cheering sections.

"You've got a picture with seven stars and you want to give everybody a meaningful role," notes Ralph Winter. "That is the challenge of doing something like this as opposed to doing James Bond or Indiana Jones, where it's clear there's only one hero with a lot of supporting characters. You've got a team of seven people that have to be given something meaningful to do. Nick [Meyer] has done a great job of weaving that together. We know who the core audience is and we've got to satisfy them, but beyond that it's got to be fun, it's got to be entertaining and capture your imagination."

One could hardly imagine Bernard Lee clamoring for a larger role as M in the James Bond film series, just as one would have found it equally outrageous if Denholm Elliot had held out for expanding the role of Marcus Brody in the Indiana Jones trilogy. But when George Takei expresses dissatisfaction with his navigating chores as Sulu, people take notice.

"Accommodating them is part of the assignment," Dennis Martin Flinn states. "If you hate it, don't take the assignment. We had to make sure both Leonard and Shatner were satisfied and they both had notes from the first draft. In this one circumstance, the actors probably have a leg to stand on. In any original film or work of art, the play's the thing and if somebody says my part isn't big enough, that's just ego talking. What a writer or a director tries to do is tell the story as effectively as possible, but maybe in *Star Trek* part of it is the story and you're adding to the 25 years of lore of these people. The audience wants to know what happened to Uhura and Sulu and we made a conscious effort to promote Sulu, maybe partially because he's

been complaining about being a navigator all his life and certain things fell into place.and maybe others didn't."

"It's a terrific picture for everybody," Jimmy Doohan remarks. "George finally got to be somebody on his own ship and Leonard had a lot to do with that."

In *Star Trek II*, Chekov was given a larger role as a member of Captain Terrell's crew. In *Star Trek V* it was Uhura whose nude dance captured the attention of a desert scouting party. Spoiled by *Star Trek IV*, the entire cast got into the action as the reconnaissance parties looked for whales in '80s America. For Koenig, these opportunities to work away from his William Shatner were a godsend.

"*Star Trek II* was a delight from start to finish and one of the greatest delights was working with Ricardo Montalban and Paul Winfield, and not being on the Enterprise having to be judged by our leading man," says Koenig. "It was great not having scenes reblocked by our leading man, which I found very oppressive. I was working with actors who give as well as take. Totally professional. There's no question Ricardo has a strong ego and that's great. He's very colorful. He's really very flamboyant. Working with him was a pure delight. He was always there for your close-up and always very giving. I remember Nick [Meyer] saying something to him about his performance needing fine tuning, and I thought, 'Oh shit, here it comes,' and he said, 'Ah, you're right.' It was beautiful. That's the way every theatrical experience should be. With us, unfortunately it wasn't. The two weeks I worked with Bill as the leading actor wasn't as much fun."

Shatner, who along with co-star Nimoy, has been the principal beneficiary of *Trek*'s success, having segued into other roles successfully as well as that of a popular science fiction writer, is not surprised to be the butt of criticism and is diplomatic in responding to the criticism. "If the original concept of the show was still in effect and the series was still going today, the situation would be exactly the same," he says. "There are people whose names and parts are above the title and people who aren't. That's the nature of the business and that's the way these stories are told."

• • • •

As for the criticism he has received on the convention circuit and in the press from not only Doohan and Koenig but other members of the ensemble, Shatner is puzzled. "It's coming from a couple of people," he says. "I don't understand that. I'm not even aware of it, quite frankly. Occasionally I'll hear something from an ardent fan of mine who'll say so and so said this about you, and it bewilders me because I have had no trouble with them.   Nothing certainly bad, nothing particularly good either. We have done our job and gone on and I have never had bad words with anyone. I don't know what vitriol is spilling out. The people who I see a lot of—Leonard, DeForest and the people in management and the directors—I've heard nothing bad from."

Ralph Winter, who had initially expressed trepidation over working with Shatner on *Star Trek V*, has nothing but praise for the actor turned director. "It went a lot smoother than I thought. I had a great time with Bill. He was terrific and he was a lot of fun."

Kim Cattrall also was positive about her dealings with Shatner. "He's sort of a technical shark," she says. "He can technically do almost anything as an actor. He was a gentleman with me and it doesn't matter how I feel about him personally. We're both Canadians and I had a professional relationship. I never told him that when I was first starting out as an actress I was a day-player in a series of commercials he was doing. I don't think anybody does better what he does. He *is* Captain Kirk and he's amazing in what he does. I can't say I'm the same kind of actor he is. His technical expertise is like somebody doing a skill extremely well and you know that's what he's going to do. I never had any problems with him or his outcrys. I found him respectful, he runs his lines a lot, over and over and over again, which is kind of annoying, but everybody has their own way of working."

"Bridging the Generations"

When *Star Trek V* went into production four years ago, it was easy to ignore the upstart interloper, *Star Trek:*

The Next Generation, but with *Star Trek VI*, it was executive producer Leonard Nimoy who gave impetus to bridging the generations and establishing continuity between the series.

According to *Next Generation* producer Rick Berman, "They're interested in getting right what we have defined so there are no contradictions. We have a wonderful relationship with Nicholas Meyer and Leonard Nimoy, and they have been terrific in coming to talk to us. There's much more of a family-like atmosphere than there was with *Star Trek V*. They want the movie and our show to have a symbiotic relationship."

Perhaps realizing the surging popularity of *The Next Generation*, Nimoy agreed to guest star in an episode ("I thought it was time," he said), giving his tacit approval to the venture by acknowledging its success and possibly hoping to bolster interest in the flagging feature film series by starring in a story linked to the events of *Star Trek VI*.

"I had a number of conversations with Gene Roddenberry over the years about appearing in a *Next Generation* story," he relates. "We both had agreed that it was a good idea and that all we needed was to come up with the right idea. The idea of doing it never really went away. Frank Mancuso brought the subject up when we sat down to discuss *Star Trek VI*, I went to *Next Generation* executive producers Rick Berman and Michael Piller. I said, 'This is Frank Mancuso's idea. Do you have any thoughts?' Their response was whether I would do the show. I told them that if they got the right story, I would do it. They came up with this terrific story and I said, 'Let's do it.'"

Star Trek VI is peppered with references to its syndicated offspring. Not only in its storyline, which paves the way for eventual peace between the Klingon Empire and the Federation, but references to the Khitomer Outpost and, of course, Michael Dorn playing his great, great grandfather, a Klingon defense counselor named—what else?—Worf.

For Dorn, who downplays his affinity for the old show, appearing in the film was a treat. "It was a lot of fun," he says. "It was an honor. I liked the show when I was growing up and I like doing

our show very much, but you don't think about it till it happens and then you realize how important it is. The best thing about being in this business is working with really good actors. It gets the old creative juices going."

Says Denny Martin Flinn, who co-wrote the script and had even considered having the classic crew turning over the Enterprise at the end of *The Undiscovered Country* to Picard and company until he realized the difference in timelines, "The genesis was really Nick saying 'How about if we get Michael Dorn to play the part of Worf?' and everybody said 'Nick, *The Next Generation* is 75 years later!' and Nick said, 'Okay, we'll make it his great, grandfather' and that was it. Nick had not created the part of Worf for a particular actor, but we got Michael Dorn and they explained to him he couldn't play himself."

For Dorn, playing one of his ancestors meant subtly altering his performance in the role. "I felt Worf was more at peace with himself in *Star Trek VI* than Worf on the television show, because he's a Klingon, all Klingon," the actor explains. "He is a Klingon and he's from Klingon, he's never been taken away from his family. He's spent all his time with Klingons and was more in touch with himself. He was more even-keeled and not quite as racked with inner turmoil."

For special effects make-up artist Richard Snell, approaching the challenge of creating Worf's great grandfather required some thought. "Originally they thought they were going to possibly use his old prosthetics from the series. It was decided not to because it was too much of a tie-in," says Snell. "My Klingons are different than the series TV Klingons, and I have a different idea about it. Like all art, it's subjective and so it was decided there should be some tie-in in design, but for the subtlety of motion we were going to sculpt it very thin over the eyebrows so you could get in very close with a camera. We definitely felt there should be some tie-in, a genealogy and blood line involved. We refined it for film work, but I'm not the type of person who would throw out someone else's designs and say this is going to be mine."

Originally it had been intended

that *Star Trek VI* and *The Next Generation* would be even more closely linked with *The Undiscovered Country* being the Enterprise's "classic" cast's final mission. In the last Captain's Log as originally scripted, Kirk stated, "...This ship and her history will shortly became the care of a new generation. To them and their posterity will we commit our future. They will continue the voyages we have begun and journey to *all* the undiscovered countries, boldly going where no man...where no *one* has gone before."

However, reportedly after Michael Dorn gave an interview stating that *Star Trek VII* would definitely feature the *Next Generation* cast, Leonard Nimoy, irked over Dorn's comments, had the ending changed. Instead, when the Enterprise is called back to spacedock, Spock joins Kirk in disobeying orders and continuing on their mission. The final log now is changed to simply refer to *The Next Generation* as "another crew."

Ironically, despite *Trek VI's* myriad references to *Next Generation*, no one involved with the production claims to follow the show except for Nicholas Meyer, who labels himself a fan. Even he insists that he was not concerned with developing a continuity. Members of the "classic" cast are still less than effusive in their praise for their 24th century counterpart.

"I originally thought it would be detrimental to the feature films," says Walter Koenig, who plays Chekov. "I had this propriety feeling based on my own insecurities and neuroses. I looked askance at the show, hoped it would fail and was comforted by the fact that a couple of the episodes first season were trading on stories we had done, which reassured me that they weren't as good. I am aware that my reactions weren't objective and perhaps to this day they are not. I still like the best of our show better than theirs, but their show has definitely shown enormous progress and has considerably more merit than I ever attributed to them, and the actors are all very strong performers. I would love to have the resume of Patrick Stewart. These are very talented people. What I sense is missing, and maybe it's because of my territorial feelings, is the dimensionality of characters and the sense of fun that

Kirk, Spock and McCoy had. Their interchanges, their human weaknesses, the way they reacted, the fears exposed by Bill Shatner in his character. I don't see those things in *The Next Generation*. They seem more straightforward, more in control and in command. Kirk, for all his heroics, what made him appealing to me were his anxieties, his concerns, his fears, his amorous interludes. All of that made him very human to me."

In a *TV Guide* poll celebrating the original *Star Trek's* 25th anniversary, the magazine asked readers to vote on who they would feel more comfortable captaining the Enterprise if earth was in peril. Readers came down firmly on the side of James Tiberius Kirk. Responding to the poll, William Shatner says, "It's unfortunate that they perceive it as a competition, which it isn't because it's two different shows and two different characters. But, on the other hand, wouldn't it have been awful if I had lost?"

And for Shatner, who professes not to have had the opportunity to watch *The Next Generation* at any great length, he finds "classic" *Trek* far more appealing. "My perception is that it's more interesting storytelling to have passion and have one person in a dilemma. It's a more personally effective way of telling a story to my way of thinking. A story told by committee is not as exciting. There's more distance between you and the audience."

Koenig would be hard-pressed to disagree with Shatner. "I do recognize that my initial feelings about *The Next Generation* were fairly mean spirited," he acknowledges. "I had propriety feelings and didn't like the idea of somebody else taking over. I still feel a twinge when I realize that if there is a *Star Trek VII*, it would probably be with the *Next Generation* and even though I'm not anxious to do anymore *Star Trek*, I still have those vestigial feelings about not giving it up."

"I think they're doing a darn good job," says Jimmy Doohan, *Trek's* Chief Engineer Montgomery Scott who reprised the character in the sixth season *Next Generation* episode "Relics". "They're good stories, but there's no messages. I think maybe the messages are what make the older ones so great. When I talk to people about *The Next Generation*,

they tell me they always wonder what the message is. The original always had a message and there's no message. To me, this movie has one of the greatest messages that we can possibly imagine, particularly in light of our present day situation and this brilliant story talks about where we are going today."

Doohan's optimistic appraisal of *Trek VI's* message and *TNG's* moralistic failings is a philosophy that is not shared by Michael Dorn. "I have a tendency to talk about reality and there are a lot of things going on in the real world that are compelling and inspirational," says Dorn. "There's also a lot of things that *Star Trek* is trying to say which is the same thing. If you want to get a message out of *Star Trek*, then I think that's good. But the whole purpose of the thing is good, exciting entertainment. I think the more that Gene was involved with it, the more we were trying to exploit things and bring across messages and show there's something out there. The same with Nick and the movies. Our show has that message, but it's more like good television. No matter what I think, it's highly rated and doing very well. I would say it's basically good television, we don't show anything that isn't known. Maybe it brings to light some things, but we're just a mirror of society."

Dorn rejects the notion that the original series could be more progressive in addressing social issues because of the preponderance of socio-political concerns which America grappled with in the '60s, and that the '80s offer less of an opportunity for *Star Trek* to deal with topical issues as has been suggested by many involved with the series. "That's wrong," says Dorn. "*Star Trek* is the perfect forum for those types of things to deal with new, fresh, untried ideas. How can you say everything has been done? The fall of Eastern Europe, famine, these are contemporary issues. What about a society that is the richest in the world where people are starving and dying on the streets with nothing, or a society that puts so much emphasis on arms and protecting our country that our schools are going bankrupt? I think our show is the perfect forum for entertainment and to deal with social issues. We've just scratched the surface and it's good televi-

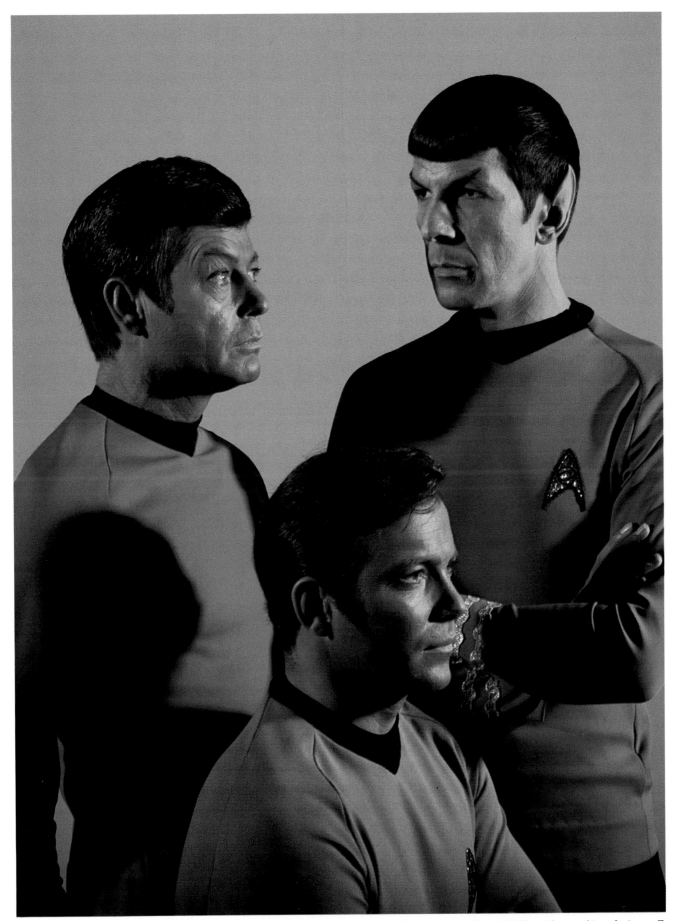

The original generation: DeForest Kelley (Dr Leonard "Bones" McCoy), Leonard Nimoy (Mr. Spock) and William Shatner (Captain James T. Kirk) as seen on Star Trek. (Photo copyright © G. Trindl/Shooting Star)

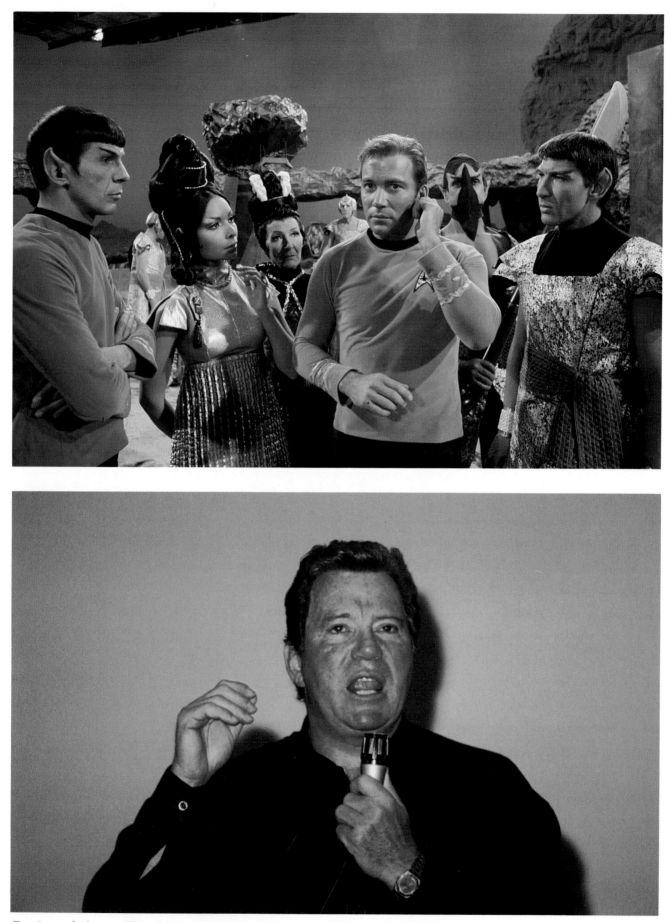

Top: Leonard Nimoy, William Shatner and assorted Vulcans in a behind-the-scenes shot from season two's "Amok Time". (Photo copyright © Trindl/Shooting Star)   Bottom: William Shatner in an all-too-rare convention appearance. (Photo copyright © Karen Witkowski)

William Shatner, DeForest Kelley and Leonard Nimoy reunited as Kirk, McCoy and Spock on the set of the first feature film, Star Trek: The Motion Picture. (Photo copyright © Trindl/Shooting Star)

Top: William Shatner as Admiral James T. Kirk and Leonard Nimoy as Mr. Spock visit modern day earth in Star Trek IV: The Voyage Home. (Photo copyright © Bruce Birmelin/Onyx)   Bottom: Leonard Nimoy delivers the Vulcan salute to gathered fans. (Photo copyright © Karen Witkowski)

From Top Left: James Doohan (Scotty), Nichelle Nichols (Uhura), Walter Koenig (Chekov) and George Takei (Sulu).
(Photos copyright © Karen Witkowski)

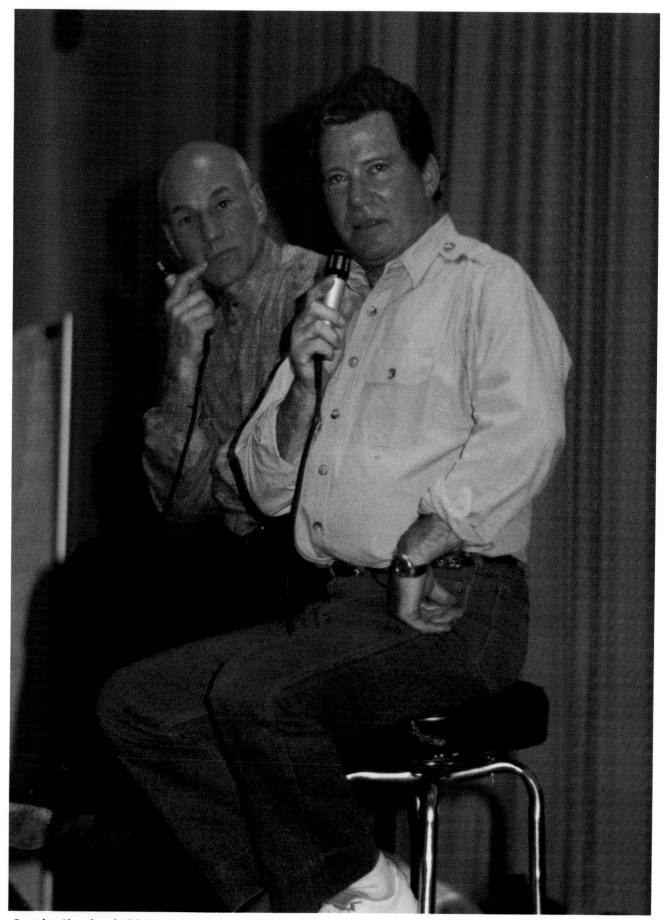

Captains Picard and Kirk (Patrick Stewart and William Shatner) are brought together at a New York Star Trek convention. (Photo copyright © Karen Witkowski)

Top: The first season cast of Star Trek: The Next Generation, including Denise Crosby as Security Chief Tasha Yar and Wil Wheaton as Wesley Crusher. (Photo copyright © G Trindl/Shooting Star) Bottom: Wil Wheaton, Denise Crosby, Gene Roddenberry and Marina Sirtis answer questions from fans. (Photo copyright © Karen Witkowski)

Top: Patrick Stewart (Captain Picard) awaits the beginning of another take while (bottom) Michael Dorn takes a Worf's-eye view of the bridge through the camera lens. (Photos copyright © David Strick/Onyx)

Top: Patrick Stewart, LeVar Burton and Brent Spiner (Picard, LaForge and Data) block out a scene during rehearsal.   Bottom: A grumpy looking Worf awaits the director's call for action. (Photos copyright © David Strick/Onyx)

From Top Left: Patrick Stewart (Picard), Jonathan Frakes (Riker), LeVar Burton (La Forge) and Brent Spiner (Data).
(Photos copyright © Karen Witkowski)

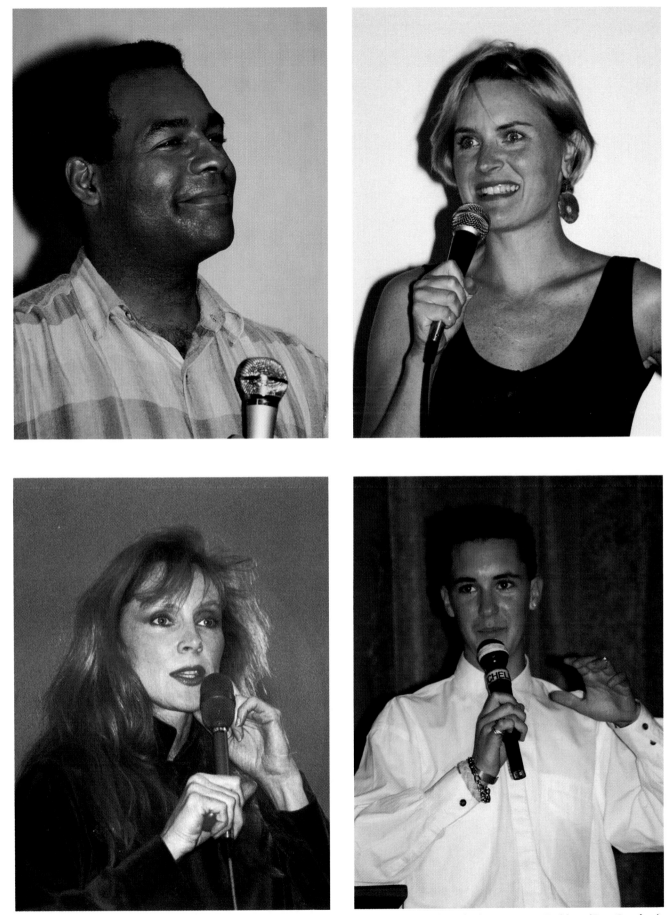

From Top Left: Michael Dorn (Worf), Denise Crosby (Yar), Wil Wheaton (Wesley), Gates McFadden (Dr. Crusher).
(Photos copyright © Karen Witkowski)

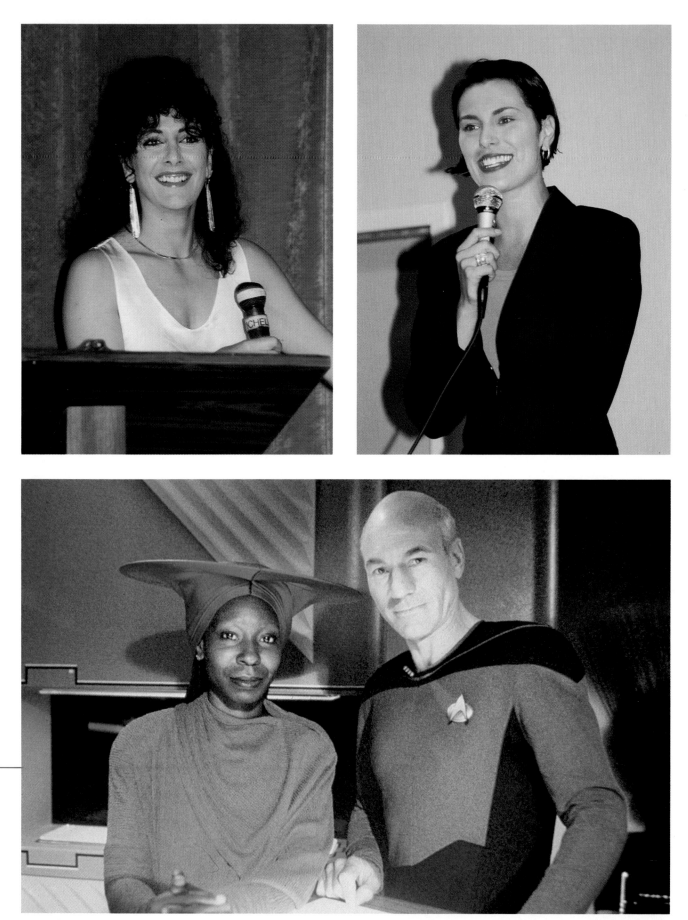

Top Left-Right: Marina Sirtis (Deanna Troi) and Michelle Forbes (Ensign Ro) take questions from the audience. (Photos copyright © Karen Witkowski)   Bottom: Whoopi Goldberg (Guinan) joined Patrick Stewart (Picard) on the set of Ten-Forward beginning in season two. (Photo copyright © Fred Sabine/Shooting Star)

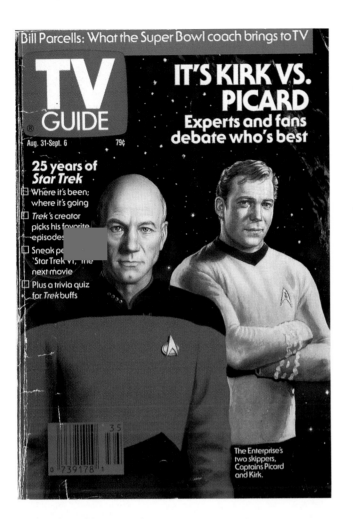

TV GUIDE

Aug. 31-Sept. 6   79¢

IT'S KIRK VS. PICARD
Experts and fans debate who's best

25 years of Star Trek

- Where it's been; where it's going
- Trek's creator picks his favorite episodes
- Sneak peek 'Star Trek VI', the next movie
- Plus a trivia quiz for Trek buffs

The Enterprise's two skippers, Captains Picard and Kirk.

0 739178 1

Jan. 2-8

TV GUIDE

89¢

SCI-FI ISSUE

STAR TREK'S
NEWEST FRONTIER
DEEP SPACE NINE

Bill Bixby fights for his life

Long Island Lolita
One crime, three TV movies

Charles & Di
Sneak peek at the movie

0 864415 2

EXCLUSIVE PHOTOS
1ST EPISODE PLOT SECRETS

SPECIAL TO TVG:
CAPT. PICARD BRIDGES THE NEXT GENERATION GAP

PLUS Babylon 5 and TV's Sci-Fi Boom

Avery Brooks and Patrick Stewart

entertainment
WEEKLY

NO. 85 • FROM FRIDAY, SEPT. 27, 1991

'STAR TREK' AT 25

A SLIGHTLY WARPED LOOK BACK AT THE FUTURE

LEONARD NIMOY AND WILLIAM SHATNER IN 1966

$1.95 (CAN. $2.50)

0 72440 10210

From Bottom Left: Leonard Nimoy and William Shatner grace the cover of Entertainment Weekly to celebrate Star Trek's 25th anniversary; TV Guide features Patrick Stewart and William Shatner on the cover in a battle of the captains (Kirk won the poll hands down); Avery Brooks and Patrick Stewart are pictured together in order to launch Star Trek: Deep Space Nine.

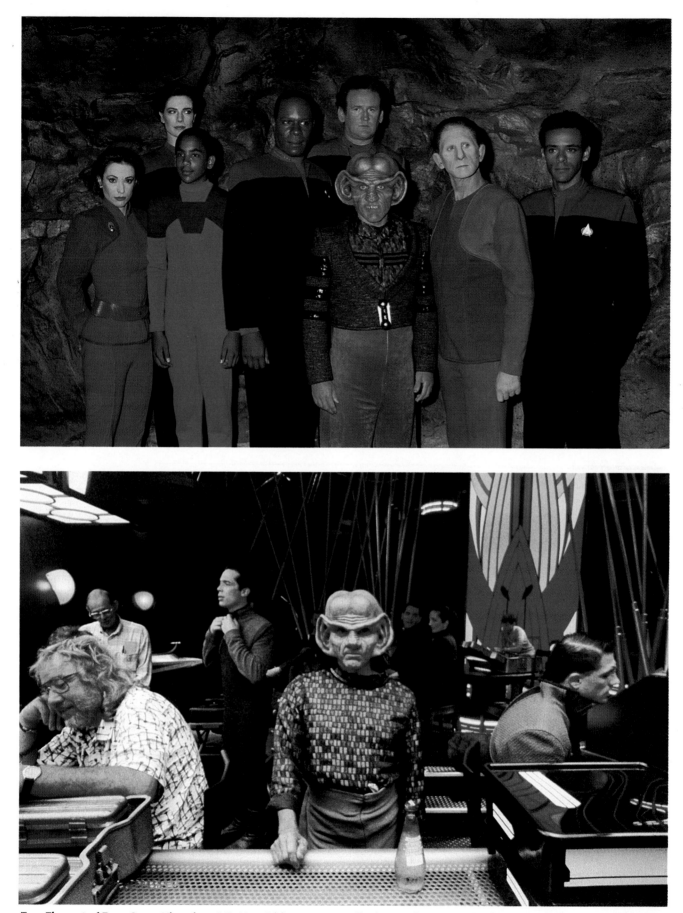

Top: The cast of Deep Space Nine, from L-R: Nana Visitor, Terry Farrell, Cirroc Lofton, Avery Brooks, Colm Meaney, Armin Shimerman, Rene Auberjonois and Siddig El Fadil. (Photo copyright © Celebrity Photo Agency) Bottom: A behind-the-scenes moment at Quark's. (Photo copyright © David Strick/Onyx)

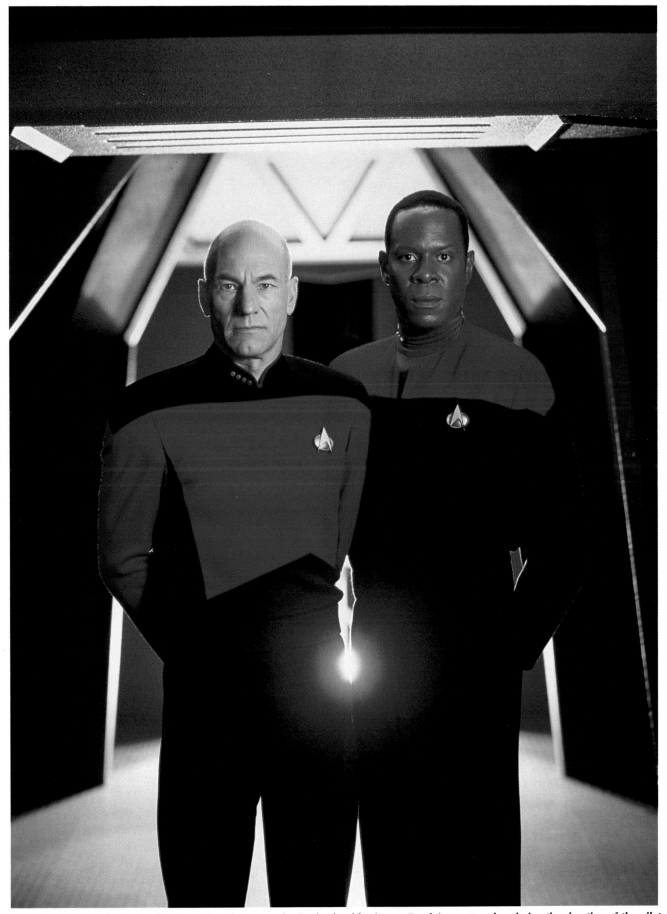

Captain Jean Luc Picard (Patrick Stewart) and Commander Benjamin Sisko (Avery Brooks) seen together during the shooting of the pilot episode of Star Trek: Deep Space Nine, "Emissary" . (Photo copyright © Timothy White/Onyx)

Gene Roddenberry, creator of both Star Trek *and* The Next Generation, *relaxing in the transporter room of the starship Enterprise.*
(Photo copyright © David Strick/Onyx)

sion, but we're not really trying to break any ground."

For Dorn, *The Next Generation* and his two week stint on *Star Trek VI* have afforded him some of his most cherished acting experiences. "*Star Trek* really is wonderful," he says. "It's a dream come true, but it's still acting. How do you act in front of a blue screen? How do you act as a doctor if you've never been a doctor before? It's [pure] acting."

As for the future of *Star Trek*, both generations, Dorn can only cautiously speculate. "There's several avenues it can take," he says. "The one I'd like to see happen is the show goes six or seven years and we'll start doing movies, but there are other possibilities. We could go six or seven years and that's it, but I don't think that'll happen."

"This is the End.... Or Is It?"

With the idea in mind that *Star Trek VI* would be the classic cast's swan song, co-writer Dennis Martin Flinn devised an ending for the film in which the characters would sign their names to their final log aboard the starship Enterprise, which not only ended the series with an emotional flourish but passed the baton to the next generation, both literally and figuratively. And although the signatures remain in the final cut, several changes were made.

"They reversed the order of the names so Shatner's is last, like an opera," says composer Cliff Eidelman. "It's a minute of signing off, which is real emotional music."

However, the only emotion writer Flinn experiences when he sees the signatures is anger. "They are different than how I conceived them originally," says Flinn. "My original script read the signatures were James T. Kirk, Mr. Spock, etc. What we were doing is offering them a chance to sign the final log. I thought that would be rather touching, especially since it's the last film and all, but it got changed to the actors instead of the characters and I personally dislike it very, very much. One of the actors who's executive producer, who shall go unnamed, likes it since I suppose he'd rather see his own name than his charac-

ter's name up on the screen. A lot of people have argued both sides and I guess we lost. Frankly, I think no one gives a fuck about Leonard Nimoy and William Shatner and those people in any substantive *Star Trek* sense. Those people are Mr. Spock and Kirk and Dr. McCoy, and I don't see any point of the actors signing their name to the log of the U.S.S. Enterprise. I'm upset that other people on the production haven't spoken up more who carry more weight than I do, like the producers who I know damn well agree with me but just did not fight it strongly enough. We're certainly in the majority, but the situation was not easy because I think the director and Leonard are the only two people who wanted that, but nobody wanted to argue except me."

And with the final flourish of Cliff Eidelman's score as the house lights came on in theatres, *Trek* fans were left to wonder if what they had just watched was truly the final mission of the original crew of the starship Enterprise. That question had become an equally hot topic among the members of the *Trek VI* production team prior to the film's release, with rumors running rampant that the ending was changed to be left more open-ended.

"I heard the same thing with *Star Trek II*," says director Nicholas Meyer. "I had nothing to do with bringing Spock back to life and if it had been up to me, my picture would not have ended ambiguously. This movie has only had one ending from the very beginning and that ending has never changed. I remember all the rumors that we filmed multiple endings for *II*. We never did that either. This film was written from the first draft the way it ended. There has never been any studio pressure or suggestion to change that, and I suppose that's because the ending doesn't preclude anything."

Flinn recalls a somewhat different coda for *Trek VI*'s climactic moments. "In rewrites and polishes Nick did the night before shooting, the final, final scene was rewritten. I honestly don't believe this came out of any desire on Nick's part to leave the door open, but out of the story and the metaphorical way that he writes. The nice thing that he wanted to do was a Peter Pan line—I

guess he was in an optimistic mood that night—and the way the scene is structured there's no door being slammed, but, of course, you could always finesse that. It's up to the studio—and probably Leonard and Shatner as well."

Like most people both on and off the crew, Flinn, had been under the impression that Paramount had officially sanctioned *Star Trek VI* as the final chapter of the "classic" cast's voyages, so he was surprised to find the recently installed studio head Brandon Tartikoff mulling *Trek*'s future after an early screening of the film for executives.

"I had always heard that this was the last film," recalls Flinn. "We had a very early screening for the executives [and] they liked it very much. They were all just standing around afterwards and Brandon Tartikoff, who had just literally taken over the studio, and who had virtually nothing to do with the film until that day, said 'Why is this the last film?' Everybody looked at each other saying 'Gee, didn't you tell me this was it?' and then everybody looked at Leonard, who really is the key, and he did not say 'No more from me.' I sort of thought he was saying, 'Well, it's your studio. Make me an offer.'"

"Brandon was very happy with the picture. He said 'You guys have given me an unexpected Christmas present'," agrees Ralph Winter, who adds, "I had watched *Star Trek* as a kid and thought it was fun. It was a thrill to be involved with the picture. If you had asked me ten years ago that I would be producing the sixth *Star Trek* film, I'd think you were crazy. It's fun to think that this is really a part of American culture and to become a part of that and to make a contribution to that is fun and rewarding. But the biggest reward is to go to opening night at 8 o'clock and to sit down with an audience that has waited for months, avoided reading the script, wears a costume, brings a phaser and sits there and laughs, cries and has a good time. We do it for ourselves as much as everyone else and if we're entertained, we think everyone else will be. That's the reward.

"For 10 years I've been working on these pictures," continues Winter. "They've always said it's the last one. I'm tired of saying that and being wrong. This is the picture for the 25th anniversary and my feeling is the fans are going to be very pleased. It's a good story and good entertainment and a good mystery of unravelling the story with familiar characters."

Notes George Takei, Captain Sulu of the Excelsior in *Star Trek VI*, "Maybe I need to recite you the history of the *Star Trek* movies. The first film was titled *Star Trek: The Motion Picture,* suggesting that's it, that's the movie. That was released, did mega business and they started talking about the only sequel, because sequels only do a certain percentage of their predecessors. They killed off Spock and you can't imagine doing *Star Trek* without Spock. That was released and made a ton of money and they started talking about a trilogy, which was kind of trendy at that time. But that means three, right? In *Star Trek III* you saw the Enterprise go down in flames, so that was the end. That made two tons of money. Then you start hearing about the last *Star Trek*, number four. Now we've done six and that's what they're telling you again, that this is the last one. Stick around. You'll start hearing about the ultimate, *very* final last movie."

Like Doohan and Takei, Nichelle Nichols is open-minded regarding the reprisal of her role as Commander Uhura in any future films. "This could be the end, but then again, who knows?" she states rhetorically. "This is a wonderful one to end the series of films with and it wouldn't bother me one way or the other. I loved doing all of the films, each one of them being a miracle to me." Nichols pointed out that there was no great sense of loss on the last day of shooting because, "We never had a last day of shooting. On the supposed last day we went right to a *Good Morning America* interview on stage, we had all of the champagne and food and so forth, then we had a big photographic 'opportunity,' then the next day we had to get back into makeup and have a photo session. So it sort of kept going. I guess the most poignant feeling, for me anyway, was the first day, because going in to *VI* with the understanding that it was definitely the last *Star Trek* film, we were adjusted to that. Then the brass started coming in, the shinier brass from New York started flying in, they heard about the dailies being so

good, they started to get excited and whispering began."

Walter "Chekov" Koenig would probably like to ignore those whispers, and leave the 23rd century behind him. "Maybe it's because I feel a certain satisfaction with the way this picture works," he suggests. "There is a sense of closure here. There are certain pragmatic aspects as to why this should be the last film. There are many people, certainly in the media, who feel we've overstayed our welcome to begin with. Each picture seems to emphasize more and more that we're at retirement age—we certainly look like we're at retirement age. When the media brings all that up, it really bothers me. It bothers me because that seems to be the springboard for every comment that comes afterward. To condemn the project or the performers because of their age is very unfair. I see that again and again. Once the statement is made that they all look like the over-the-hill-mob, it seems like there's no room to say anything good or positive. We no longer have Bill thrusting his tongue down some young lady's throat, because that wouldn't work. We've made that concession. We don't get involved in hand-to-hand fighting, because that would perhaps be stretching credibility. But in terms of reflexes, in terms of functioning on the ship, in terms of ideas, I don't think we should be condemned as a group and summarily dismissed as a consequence of the age factor.

"I [also] think the studio feels they have an up-and-coming contender waiting in the wings, *The Next Generation*," he adds. "I think they think this is the last picture, not that that stands irrevocable, but their thinking now is along those terms. 'For 25 years you've done a bang-up job. We've made a whole thing about this being the last voyage, let's leave it at that.' There's a certain amount of wish-fulfillment on my part. I'm ready to let go. I'm not fed up, not oversaturated with *Star Trek*, I'm just ready to let go and see if there's anything else out there. I'd like to be hungry again. With that apprehension, with that need, comes hopefully some inspiration and some creativity."

DeForest Kelley, who is finally taking in Dr. Leonard "Bones" McCoy's medical shingle, considers what he'll miss most. "Just knowing it's not there," he

begins. "It's been such a big part of my life for 25 years. Nothing has hit me yet. I will think more about it when somebody says, 'This is it.' Then you kind of take a breath and say, 'It's not going to be there.' *Star Trek* felt like something that was always going to be there, and it isn't. But I think after the finality of it really hits, then I'll reflect on it and get on with my life."

"The last day of the old series," states Leonard Nimoy, "when we found out we had been cancelled, I carefully took off my ears, put them in a box and mounted them on a wall in my home. I really thought that was the last time I would wear them. I never thought we would do this again. It looks like I've got another pair of ears to mount on the wall, but this time I'm sure it's the last time. I'm very grateful that it happened. I feel a great sense of accomplishment. Overall, we've done some sincere work. I hope that the general fallout is positive; I think it is. I'm very pleased when I hear that people's lives have been affected positively in one way or the other because of *Star Trek*. In general, I've had very good, positive feelings about it."

Notes William Shatner, who has apparently concluded his portrayal of Captain James T. Kirk, "This is definitely the last one, no question about it. The studio says it's the last one, it's written as the last one, the cast accepts it as the last one and it is definitely the last one. I suppose that in its wisdom the studio thinks it's time to call a halt to it and give it a sense of finality. [I'm feeling] great nostalgia, great sadness. I feel a sense of loss. It's a wonderful character and another setting in which to place the character. I love action films with some kind of conflict, so the human conflict is told in action-adventure rather than a sedate tone. A picture should move, and *Star Trek* lends itself to that genre. There are lots of stories to be told and lots of things to be done in the film still, but unfortunately, for one reason or another—and don't ask me what those reasons are—it's been decided that this is the last film. I leave it with great reluctance and great sorrow."

December 1991

$5.50
CAN $6.50
UK £3.75

STAR TREK
THE 25TH ANNIVERSARY

Gene Roddenberry,
the visionary behind
the final frontier.

HOOK
The scoop on Steven
Spielberg's Peter Pan.

Volume 22 Number 3

THE ADDAMS FAMILIES
The TV show, the movie, the genius of Charles Addams.

Cinefantastique's December 1991 issue celebrating Star Trek's 25th anniversary, highlighted one of Gene Roddenberry's last interviews.

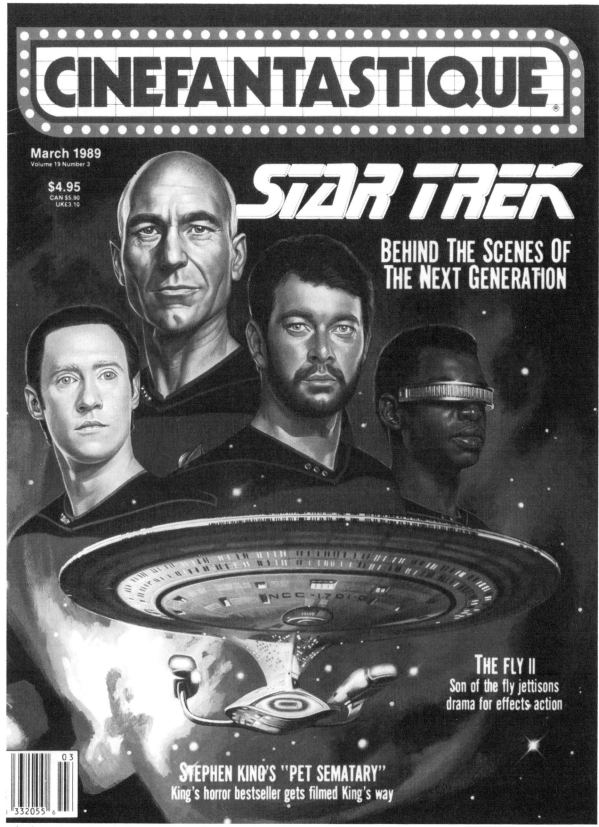

March 1989
Volume 19 Number 3

$4.95
CAN $5.90
UK£3.10

CINEFANTASTIQUE

STAR TREK

BEHIND THE SCENES OF THE NEXT GENERATION

NCC-1701-D

THE FLY II
Son of the fly jettisons
drama for effects action

STEPHEN KING'S "PET SEMATARY"
King's horror bestseller gets filmed King's way

Cinefantastique magazine begins their yearly visits to the set of Star Trek: The Next Generation

●●●●
CHAPTER SIXTEEN
These Are
the New Voyages....

"While the original *Star Trek* looks primitive now, it still has a lot of content. The idea for *The Next Generation* was to provide the same content in a 1987 capsule; with 1987 parameters. The difficulty has been that the public is extremely sophisticated, and the ideas that seemed new and revolutionary in the early show are no longer revolutionary...The whole experience has been very stimulating, because we're trying to cover new ground"
　　　　—Bob Lewin, former producer of
　　　　Star Trek: The Next Generation

In 1988, the *Trek* flame was once again rekindled with the return of *Star Trek* to the small screen. The year was 1986 and Paramount Pictures feared there would indeed be a final frontier in their future. The franchise which they had at first ignored, then exploited and finally cultivated into a monetary bonanza seemed to be heading toward permanent space drydock.

Despite the fact that it was the 20th anniversary of *Star Trek* and the studio was anxiously awaiting the word on their forthcoming *Star Trek IV: The Voyage Home* feature film, which would eventually become the most successful of the movies, there was deep concern over the fact that *Star Trek* was losing ground in syndication as well as beginning to look extremely dated as television had became bigger and more sophisticated. The future was starting to look old. After all, regardless of the fans' devotion, how many times could they watch the same 79 episodes before their fervor began to dissipate?

In fact, the television series that had put the phrase "off network syndication" in the dictionary, was getting tired. Independent stations were running it less, and the studio's prize goose of the past decade and a half looked as though it was nearly deplete of golden eggs. Some of the blame can be shifted to the December 1979 release of *Star Trek: The Motion Picture*. Although a financial

success, the film was a milestone in an important respect. It was the last time fans would lop up whatever they were force-fed by the Paramount machine. If *Trek* was new but not improved, the windfall might turn to a trickle.

The thinking in 1986 was that even if *Star Trek IV* went on to great success (which it did), a hit every two years was not the same as cash pouring into the coffers on a weekly basis from the syndication of a series. It was clear that a new *Trek* was necessary, and with a near-geriatric and exorbitantly priced ensemble of talent in the form of the original cast out of Paramount's reach on a weekly basis, it was decided that it was time to build a better starship.

During the hoopla of the shows' 20th anniversary, Paramount Pictures announced the anticipated means of pumping artificial life into the waning phenomenon.

"The speculation is over," said Mel Harris, then President of Paramount Television. "The answer is yes. *Star Trek* lives. Starting next fall, beginning with a two hour telefilm followed by 24 one-hour episodes, *Star Trek* will return to television in the form of a new series, *Star Trek: The Next Generation*. Although this is a new starship Enterprise, a new cast and new stories, the man at the helm is still the same: the creator of *Star Trek*, Gene Roddenberry. And we're proud to have him once again supervising all aspects of production."

What Harris had failed to mention was that Roddenberry was third on their A-list of producing choices for the series. First they had gone to father and son team of Sam and Greg Strangis (who went on to produce Paramount's syndicated *War of the Worlds*), whose take on the show—which dealt with Starfleet Academy and space cadets—was not what the studio was looking for. Leonard Nimoy, whose evolution from *Star Trek* actor to director and fiscal frugality had earned him critical kudos and respect among the Paramount hierarchy, was approached next. He rejected the offer because he did not want to get tied down to the rigors of producing a weekly series when his directorial career was first taking off. With nowhere else to go, Paramount reluctantly turned to

The late Gene Roddenberry at one of his generally infrequent convention appearances. (photo copyright © Karen Witkowski)

Roddenberry. Their reluctance was quite understandable, considering the image that Gene had painted of the studio's executives throughout the 70's, blaming them for the aborted attempts at reviving the show.

David Gerrold points out, "Roddenberry would go out to various speaking engagements and would say 'It's difficult. How do you convince the studio executives that what you're talking about is changing the world?' And he'd do it very sly. Studio executives are maligned by everyone who works for them. If a studio makes fifteen hit pictures a year, who gets the credit? The directors, the actors, the executive producers of the picture, but the studio executive who said, 'I'll buy this picture, I'll finance it', he's just lucky enough to be sitting there when they brought the project into him. They can tell the difference between a good story and a bad story. They get excited when they work with exciting people. You don't get to be the head of a studio by accident. Admittedly there have been stupid men as studio executives who do make mistakes, but twenty years at Paramount? Paramount is the most successful studio in the industry. Down the line they're doing all these great pictures like *The Godfathers, Saturday Night Fever*...and

●●●●

Patrick Stewart in the persona of a knight in shining armor in John Boorman's Excalibur.

they can't get *Star Trek* on the boards? Give me a break. Finally, they get *Star Trek* going and what does Gene do? He spends their money like there's no tomorrow. He makes a $40 million epic. An awful movie."

Paramount hoped that Roddenberry could be contained this time out, despite the fact that they had been forced to cede full creative control to obtain his cooperation. Eventually the studio's saving grace would be a young producer named Rick Berman who would ultimately become the real winner in the power struggle that was to ensue involving the studio, Roddenberry and a cadre of writers. Berman would be the one responsible for shaping the series and turning it into a bonafide sensation in its own right. Ironically, Berman who has become the prime force behind the success of Next Generation hadn't sought to run the series and was only handed the producing reigns when the division of Paramount he presided over, longform and miniseries production, was phased out by the studio, leaving the executive nowhere to go. When he was offered the chance to steer the new *Star Trek*, he took it despite being advised against it by his peers.

"I had a lot of people who told me I was nuts," recalls Berman. "But I had a feeling it was going to work and I

decided it was worth the risk of leaving a well paying job at a movie studio to work on a science-fiction sequel syndicated television series."

Berman's most recognizable production credit prior to *Star Trek* was his years spent on PBS' children's educational show *Big Blue Marble*, which hardly prepared him for the rigors of riding herd over a technologically complex and expensive one hour dramatic series pioneering the first-run syndicated television market.

But by the time the first script for the pilot episode was finished, the conceptual template for the new show had been firmly embedded. Whether this template could make for riveting drama was beside the point. The show's two-hour pilot, for instance, was widely considered a disappointment and derivative of episodes of the old series and the first motion picture, even though writer D.C. Fontana's original drafts were far more original and compelling until Roddenberry began rewriting it, but the viewer's continued to watch.

There were a number of obvious difficulties in bringing *Star Trek* back to the small screen. First and foremost was the tremendous affinity and loyalty that fans had for the original cast. The new series intended to completely eschew Kirk & Company for an all-new crew of Starfleet officers, set nearly a century after the voyages of the first starship Enterprise.

Numerous ideas had been bandied back and forth during the early discussions between Roddenberry and the team he had brought together, largely veterans of the first series, including writers David Gerrold and D.C. Fontana, producer Robert Justman and Eddie Milkis and newcomers Herb Wright and Rick Berman. It was finally decided that the setting would be a new incarnation of the Enterprise with a cast which wouldn't include any vestiges of the original. Rather than attempt a retread of the first series, Roddenberry was intent on presenting all-new Starfleet officers.

"Gene had to create a new television show from 25 years of mythology that had grown up over an old one and he had to do it all out of whole cloth," says Berman of the creation of *Next*

Generation. "You have to understand what it's like to write a stylized 24th century script and know what words can be spoken and what words can't and how to go about all of the things we do to create this television show as opposed to if you were creating *MacGyver.* He also had a lot of people who felt they knew more about *Star Trek* than he did and he had to get pretty tough about it. We had a group of writers that came in and didn't have the benefit of someone as strong as Mike Piller. People had no idea what *Star Trek: The Next Generation* was going to be about. Gene felt the obsessive necessity to put his own print on everything to get the show going and I applaud him for that. By the time I was sort of in control of the series, in the second year, Gene had pretty much cemented his idea of what the show was going to be about and it was my job to continue, to keep it going and not to formulate it because he had done that."

After moving into spacious offices in the Hart Building on the Paramount lot [now occupied by Michael Piller and his baseball card collection], Roddenberry used his newfound stature to arrange for a non-stop unspooling of classic science-fiction movies to set the stage for what would be the fruitful discussions from which the new ensemble of *Trek* characters would spring. The producers decided early on that there would be no Vulcans onboard the new ship and late in the production Rick Berman and Herb Wright championed the addition of a Klingon officer. Roddenberry hated the idea. He wanted to stay clear of any characters from the first series, but was eventually swayed to include the character in a supporting role although the officer, Worf, as he was named, would grow in importance over the years to become a major part of the show.

Roddenberry directed his efforts towards refining the stories and the scripts for the series, leaving the massive logistics of keeping the show on schedule and on budget in the hands of producers Robert Justman and Rick Berman, who oversaw the day to day operations ranging from scheduling to color correction. Justman who shared Roddenberry's emotional reasons for returning to the show nearly twenty years after its cancellation, says, "When I left Star Trek in 1968, it was a disaster. It was a failure as far as the network was concerned and the industry. The only think that saved Star Trek two years in a row were the people who cared about it. By the time the third season rolled around, the handwriting was on the wall and Gene and I both know that it was so. I had a need to return to prove that the show did have value and was successful and could be successful again, and that you can go home again and prove to the people who doubted you that there was value there all along; that this was a worthwhile, if you'll pardon the expression, enterprise."

Working with veteran casting director Junie Lowry, the producers embarked on a massive search to personify the characters created by the new Trek production team. A massive talent search led to the casting of English Shakespearean actor Patrick Stewart as the new Captain, Jean-Luc Picard, a Frenchman. The casting of Stewart was an audacious choice since the actor was not only an Englishman playing a French captain, but in his fifties and distinctly bald. Discovered by producer Robert Justman while performing at UCLA, casting Stewart was one of the series first coups.

Rounding out the ensemble were veteran actor LeVar Burton as the blind navigator, Geordi LaForge; acting coach and choreographer Gates McFadden as the new doctor, Beverly Crusher; second-in-command Riker was to be played by Jonathan Frakes, security chief Tasha Yar was portrayed by Denise Crosby, who left the show at the end of the first year; Michael Dorn could be found under heavy prosthetics as the Klingon officer, Worf; and Wil Wheaton, who had made a strong impression on movie audience's in Stand By Me, played precocious acting ensign Wesley Crusher, the doctor's young son. Another triumph in casting for the show was the hiring of Broadway actor Brent Spiner to personify the show's resident Spock-substitute, android Data, who, like Pinnochio, sought to become human.

Production Designer Herman Zimmerman suggests that the new ensemble is more faithful to Roddenberry's original hopes for Star

Trek before the casting of William Shatner and Leonard Nimoy turned the show into a star vehicle. "If you want to go back to Mr. Roddenberry's original ideas, he wanted to create an ensemble cast and he did, but because of the really strong ability of Bill Shatner and Leonard Nimoy and the romance of those characters and the relationships between each other and Dr. McCoy, it became more of a star cast than an ensemble cast. In Next Generation Gene achieved what he was really striving for in the first place. He has the strength of Picard in Patrick Stewart, but he has a very level competent cast all the way through. I think he was more pleased than he was the first time around with the casting of Next Generation."

"I was very involved with the original casting on Star Trek and if I could pride myself on any casting coup it had to do with Patrick Stewart," adds Berman. "Bob [Justman] discovered Patrick Stewart and brought him to the attention of Gene Roddenberry and Roddenberry said no. I met Patrick Stewart and said to Bob Justman, 'We have to convince Gene to use this guy,' and Bob said to me, 'We can't, it's a waste of time. When Gene makes up his mind it's a waste of time to try and change his mind'. But in my case, ignorance was bliss. I didn't believe that and I was the guy who basically bugged Gene into realizing that Patrick was the best Picard."

Roddenberry's first choice for the role of the Enterprise captain in The Next Generation was Cagney & Lacey's Stephen Macht. "As far as the other characters, they were far more the selection of Bob Justman and mine than they were of anybody else," says Berman. "Gene basically approved, like the studio did, the people that Bob and I chose, and he was not all that involved in it. He was very stubborn about who he wanted to be Picard and, in the case of Marina Sirtis and Denise Crosby we selected them for the opposite roles, and he said I want Crosby to play Tasha and I want Marina to play Troi and that was his idea. Frakes was my choice. He liked Frakes, but his first choice was Bill Campbell

[Rocketeer, Crime Story]. Gene liked him and we brought him into see John Pike and he said no. The next person we chose was Frakes. He felt very strongly about what he wanted Frakes to be but he was never very stubborn about the casting."

Unlike the original show where friction and tension between the ensemble typified its three years of production and only elevated during the making of the feature film's involving well-documented early feuds between Shatner and co-star Leonard Nimoy, the cast of The Next Generation is quite enamored with each other.

"One of the reasons this show didn't take the dive we all feared it would in the back of our minds in comparison to the old show," Jonathan Frakes points out, "is because the characters were so well thought out ahead of time. I don't know how they cast this so well. We go out to dinner after 14 hour days. They hired actors who like to act instead of hiring movie stars or models. For virtually all of us, this is the biggest job of our career and we're so happy about that. It's an ensemble and I think it's a good ensemble."

"We're landlocked on this planet Earth," says Herman Zimmerman, Next Generation's original production designer who was charged with remaining faithful to the original production design of the sixties show while updating the technology and aesthetics for a saavier television audience. "Whether we put them in costumes of the future and generate imaginative settings, we are still dealing with good and evil, love and hate relationships and all of the basic emotions and problems that human beings are running into daily. That's one of the things that makes Roddenberry's view of the future so believable. It's a republican view of the future, where life can be easy. You don't have to work at something you don't like. You can find the thing that allows you to contribute and that is what you can do for a living."

Star Trek's standing sets which span two huge soundstages on the Paramount lot are astounding in their level of detail and one could actually believe they're aboard a spaceship when they become lost in the maze of corridors that connect the various sets on Stage 9.

• • • •

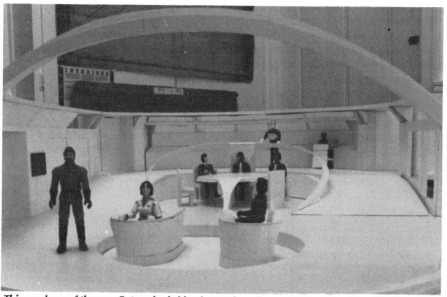

This mock-up of the new Enterprise bridge featured toy figures in the place of the ship's crew.

Nearby is Stage 16 which serves as the locale for various swing sets, planetary exteriors and locales. The level of craftsmanship which is involved in bringing a *Next Generation* episode to life is gargantuan and with a budget of nearly $1.5 million an episode, the show strives to achieve a feature film quality look while stretching the boundaries of a television budget.

"The new bridge design evolved, as did the exterior of the ship, from two basic concepts," says Herman Zimmerman. "One is it is unnecessary to have aerodynamics because space is a vacuum. It is, by the 24th century, in Mr. Roddenberry's mind, entirely possible that technology has reached such a state of proficiency that it has become an art form. Point two is that instead of a five year mission we have a 30 year mission with women, children and families aboard. We want to make the whole environment of the starship more comfortable. It never was a battleship. It's a far cry from an all gray militaristic starship. It's indeed a state of the art, comfortable machine that we're proud to call home."

Ultimately, the old adage that the more things change, the more they stay the same is borne out. *Star Trek* for all its newfound glitz and modern maturity, still harkens back to the essential elements which encompassed it in the '60s, and it is still wrestling with the same

issues which have intrigued audiences for the last twenty years.

"I think the content is much the same as it ever was," says former producer Robert Justman. "While our techniques may be a little slicker [and] the shows may have a better look, I think the show's content is much the same. Just because centuries have passed, we haven't dispensed of the Ten Commandments. They still work. I can't say I was ever satisfied. I'm pleased. I'm never satisfied. You can't turn out a Picasso every week. Supposedly we're dealing with some kind of art. It's not possible in a collaborative effort to turn out a work of genius once a week.

"Some people were afraid of the new *Star Trek* because the old people wouldn't be in it," recalls Justman. "It was a threat to them. But I don't think that lasted very long. You form new relationships all through life. Sometimes the old relationships are the best, sometimes they're not. But there's room in this world for diversity. People resist change for various reasons. It's just a natural reaction to put a show or an enterprise down out of hand, but it's not very science fictiony. The great thing about people interested in science fiction is that they have open minds. They're eager for new ideas. Otherwise, why do anything different? Let's do *Space Patrol*. It was on and people liked it."

The first 13 episodes were considered a disappointment. Indeed, the new Enterprise probably would have been mothballed by any of the trigger-happy networks, which favor terminating any expensive drama whose numbers don't justify their exorbitant license fees if they don't muster up to Nielsen standards early on. But Paramount, having anticipated a difficult start-up, side-stepped such dire and inevitable consequences by bartering the show into first run syndication, guaranteeing some well-needed breathing space to steer its wayward little starship that apparently couldn't back on course.

This proved no mean feat. Despite protestations that the new *Trek* would not replicate its progenitor, several of TNG's early episodes bore distinct similarities to those of the classic series, or dealt with Roddenberry's by-now familiar pet issues. including his perpetual God-fetish addressing judgmental alien beings, while at other times indulging his lust for exploring sexual issues in the basest of terms.

"First year of a series is a very exciting time to be aboard," says Herb Wright. "Its the riskiest, but also the most exciting. That's when you're making the rules. There's no one saying 'I've got the secret', because you're all trying to figure it out together. There's a sense of it becoming. On *Star Trek* you really had excitement, a new ship, a new cast and an opportunity to do shows that you couldn't have done 20 years ago with a much healthier effects budget and no more rubber monsters and cardboard walls. You walk on those sets and you think you can fly, but there was so much strife and turmoil the first year I couldn't deal with it anymore. First season, no one got protected. Everyone had a target drawn on their chest when they came in."

Recalls Wright of the infamous revolving door policy which typified the series in its first two years and saw myriad writers join the show only to be fired or leave several weeks—sometimes days— later . "It was like Vietnam, you didn't want to get close to them because you knew they wouldn't be there very long; Johnny Dawkins, Sandy Fries. They'd be given a script to write and direction and before they could learn what the show was about they'd be torn apart by the staff and thrown to the wolves or Gene would just say I hate them and they'd be out the door. It was very strange. I remember Sandy Fries thought he was king of the mountain for five minutes. He went home and had champagne and a big party and Monday morning he walked in and he was fired."

In fact, it is because of *Star Trek*'s idealistic and utopian view of the future that Berman suggests *Trek* has had such extraordinary turnover on its writing staff throughout the years. "We have to manufacture our conflict from other than interpersonal conflict among our characters and that does make it very difficult to write. The language has to be stylized, we don't know how people are going to speak in the 24th century and so we have them speak in a sort of stylized generic fashion. It's not 24th century, it's not contemporary and on the other hand its not medieval either. We have to deal with science fiction and a lot of people don't understand what SF is and a lot of people are interested in dealing with fantasy and the writers have to deal with a lot of technical elements. Any dramatic television show has a set of rules that you've got to follow. If you're writing *St. Elsewhere*, you've got to know about medicine. If you're writing for *L.A. Law*, you've got to know about juris prudence in the state of California. On the other hand, with *Star Trek* you've got two sets of rules. A set of rules dealing with physics and astrophysics and astronomy that we follow or try to follow as accurately as we can and then you've got a set of rules that have to with *Star Trek* which are made up rules, they're not

Next Generation's *former co-executive producer Robert Justman walking past the model of the* *starship Enterprise.*

real. There's no such thing as a dilithium crystal or people transporting. There's no such thing as warp drive and Romulans and Ferengi and Klingons. These things don't exist and as a result it's fantasy but it's 25 years worth of established rules and they have to be followed. So you've got the rules of science and the rules of *Star Trek*. Writers have to be willing to follow both sets of rule and its difficult."

However, Berman is the first to admit that while he may be at the forefront of staying true to Roddenberry's vision of the future, it is not one he personally shares. "I believe that for the purposes of our show Gene's vision of the

24th century is dramatically correct and it works for us. I probably have less. I don't think we're going to be living in a *Blade Runner* society but I think we'll be living in a future which will be very similar to the world we're living in now. Then again, this show has nothing to do with my vision of the future, I have become an expert in Gene Roddenberry's future, it's like learning a language and I'm fluent in it now and I can protect it and police it and nurture it in the same way that Gene did."

CHAPTER SEVENTEEN
Season 1 Episode Guide

"Encounter at Farpoint"

"The Naked Now"

"Code of Honor"

"The Last Outpost"

"Where No One Has Gone Before"

"Lonely Among Us"

"Justice"

"The Battle"

"Hide & Q"

"Haven"

"The Big Goodbye"

"Datalore"

"Angel One"

"11001001"

"Too Short a Season"

"When the Bough Breaks"

"Home Soil"

"Coming of Age"

"Heart of Glory"

"The Arsenal of Freedom"

"Symbiosis"

"Skin of Evil"

"We'll Always Have Paris"

"Conspiracy"

"The Neutral Zone"

Episodes #1& 2:
"Encounter at Farpoint"
Original Airdate: 9/26/87
Written by D.C. Fontana &
Gene Roddenberry
Directed by Corey Allen
Guest Starring: John de Lancie (Q), Michael Bell (Groppler Zorn), Colm Meaney (Battle Bridge Conn), Cary Hiroyuki (Mandarin Bailiff), Timothy Dang (Main Bridge Security), David Erskine (Bandi Shopkeeper), Evelyn Guerrero (Young Female Ensign), Chuck Hicks (Military Officer), Jimmy Ortega (Torres), DeForest Kelley (Leonard McCoy, "The Admiral")

The maiden voyage of starship Enterprise NCC-1701-D, introduces us to the new crew that will begin the next "ongoing" mission. First out, Captain Jean Luc Picard is to investigate the mysterious and somewhat miraculous Farpoint Station, a staging planet deemed vital to the interests of the Federation.

Enroute, they are boarded by the all-powerful Q, who feels that mankind has ventured far enough into space and will not allow further contamination. To this end, he places Picard and his crew on trial for crimes against humanity. It is the captain's suggestion that Q allow them to prove the worthiness of their species by completing their mission at Farpoint Station. Intrigued, Q agrees and is shown just how far man has come as the truth behind Farpoint is revealed.

••••

"Encounter at Farpoint" writer Dorothy Fontana contributed some of the original STAR TREK's most popular episodes, including "This Side of Paradise," "Journey to Babel" and "Charlie X." Additionally, she was the associate producer of the 1973 animated spin-off, and penned one of that show's most enduring episodes, "Yesteryear." Bearing this in mind, it's not surprising that she was chosen to script "Encounter at Farpoint."

"Roddenberry wanted to do a story that took place on a staging planet at the edge of space with a new station," she explains. "We were working on the characters at that point. The preliminary outline really broke out the possibilities. It was not what you now see. The crea-

ture that first appears is a spaceship, but it is a space-going gun platform. That is the threat. Then we find out that it is a creature. It shows up as a gun platform, and it's being used because it was weakened and nearly dead from starvation, which is a characterization I carried on. Of course we do manage to break the creature out of its enslavement. That was the very beginning idea, and then Roddenberry wanted one with the creature down on the planet, because he liked the idea of a mate.

"When we originally discussed it, I thought it could be its child, or an old creature that is dying and is captured, and the creature that comes to rescue it does so out of respect for its elders," she adds. "You could go many ways. I didn't think the only way you could go was a mate."

"The first episode really felt like two stories forced together," says Jonathan Frakes (First Officer Riker). "I feel that the later episodes were better, if for no other reason than that the company was better and knew their characters better and were less worried finding out if the show would succeed. I think the look of the pilot had the quality of the original."

Offers Marina Sirtis (Counselor Deanna Troi), "I watched the pilot with my hands over my eyes. I didn't feel it was working. I got some really good feedback from people, but personally, knowing what I can do as an actress and what was up there, I wasn't really happy. I was really pleased to make changes. I personally thought that if I continued to play Troi that way, it would get really boring because if you're telepathic, a psychologist, who is hugely super intelligent and has that kind of background, she would be so understanding, so nice, so forgiving, so laid back and perfect that I'd be the Linda Evans of *Star Trek*. What I wanted more of was Alexis."

Director Corey Allen, who received an Emmy Award for an episode of *Hill Street Blues,* was highly enthusiastic about helming the show, particularly the "Q" plotline.

"The script turned me on immediately," he enthuses. "'Q' is what you're doing right now. You're 'Q' and I'm 'A.' Every one of us has a constant Q pounding on the back of our head, saying,

John de Lancie, the man who would be Q at one of his frequent Star Trek convention appearances. (Photo copyright © Karen Witkowski)

'What about that? How do you feel? Are you really worthy?' It's the question we pose ourselves; it's a constant looking at ourselves, a questioning of ourselves and a probing. Many times we'll manifest that probe by getting involved in outside circumstances, saying, 'I'm tired of asking myself all these questions in my head. I think I'll go to the theatre and let the actors on stage do it. Or go to the boxing match and let two gladiators do it. I'm tired. I need their help.' I think what Gene Roddenberry did was put two adversaries on the screen so they could effectively deal with those questions.

"The 'Q' is in all of us. It's a question of worth. For many people the attitude is, 'If I'm worth something, it's because of my purpose, because of my birth or my humanity, or because I'm alive.' People meet that question in different ways, but it's usually, 'What is my question of myself, however I couch it? What is the question I constantly pose myself?' Most of us probably ask, 'Should I be here?' That *should* is the human part of it. *Why* am I here? is a little more clinical. Do I have the right to be here, probing space, captaining a ship, leading people, taking responsibility, living? I really

••••

believe that my understanding of that human questioning is what I brought to the episode. It's something that I do understand very well, and I feel good about my compassion about that question and my universalization of it. Essentially I was sharing myself.

"[The Farpoint scenario] wasn't as important to me as the concepts we've been talking about. There had to be an issue for the Enterprise to face, and it was okay with me that that was the issue, but the best part for me was that at first we *failed* to see that there was sentience; that there are passionate beings other than those that resemble ourselves. I thought that was a very nice issue to raise. We don't always recognize other sentient beings, and it's analogous of the way we treat each other. No one feels as deeply as I do, I keep thinking, and naturally that's bullshit. So I like the point it made, although it could have been any issue there."

Opines former executive producer Maurice Hurley, "I thought the execution was herky-jerky, because it was the first show. Having, basically, God tell man you've come far enough; that everywhere you've come, everything you've touched, you've sullied. I love that. I thought that was just awesome. There were also a lot of little things in it that I loved. Beyond that, it has the problems of the first episode of any show."

Episode #3:
"The Naked Now"
Original Airdate: 10/3/87
Written by Michael Bingham
Story by John D.F. Black
Directed by Paul Lynch
Guest Starring: Brooke Bundy (Sarah MacDougal), Benjamin W.S. Lum (Jim Shimoda), Michael Rider (Transporter Chief), David Renan (Conn), Skip Stellrecht (Engineering Crewman), Kenny Koch (Kissing Crewman)

The Enterprise is sent to investigate the status of the S.S. Tsilkovsky, which was investigating a collapsing star when all communication was lost. Upon arrival in that sector of space, an Away Team investigation learns that the entire crew is dead and that they had been gripped by madness.

Unbeknownst to anyone,

Geordi LaForge is infected with the disease and brings it aboard the Enterprise. The virus spreads rapidly through the crew, having the effect of alcohol and freeing them of their inhibitions. It is Commander Riker's vague (and highly improbable) memory of a similar occurrence on Captain Kirk's Enterprise that leads them down the road to a cure before the starship is caught in the wake of the collapsing star.

Naturally things work out in the end, though not before practically everyone has gotten laid.

••••

Star Trek fans are well aware of the fact that "The Naked Now" was a remake of the original series' first season episode, "The Naked Time."

The science fiction genre is not an unfamiliar one to director Paul Lynch, whose credits include episodes of *Werewolf, Beauty and the Beast, War of the Worlds, The New Twilight Zone* and, of course, *The Next Generation* and *Deep Space Nine.*

While outsiders may see his being saddled with "The Naked Now" as an unfortunate roll of the dice, Lynch himself doesn't agree.

"The same basic story [of 'The Naked Time'] holds true," he explains, "in that the Enterprise contracts something from another ship and the crew begins to change. Because it's a new cast, they change accordingly. Everybody drops the way they are and lets their inhibitions come out. I'd say that 'The Naked Now' is slightly more adult and a lot more comic than the original. In that show, one of the guys [Sulu] picked up a sword and started running around with it. In this it's much more of a character change in the way of romance and strangeness leading towards humor. Everybody in the show is affected by it in different ways, but not that dissimilar. For instance, while one person might be affected by becoming amorous in a serious way, someone else becomes amorous in a lighter sense. It's all quite subtle compared to the original, because the original episode was quite heavy-handed, like most of the original episodes were.

"The main difference," he continues, "is that the production has

changed over the years. The production design of the ship and the costumes and all of that are so much more futuristic 'modern' than the old series. The original show always looked like it cost $1.98, with four walls painted blue. The engine room in the old ship was a painting. The new engine room looks like it belongs in a spaceship in reality. It's wonderful and quite stunning."

A moment of controversy in the episode was the liaison between a "fully functional" Data and a scantily clad Tasha Yar. "That was the one moment I remember the most," says the director. "It was risqué and it was something *Star Trek* never did. Everyone had a great deal of fun doing it and ever since I've gotten the feeling they would like to do something like that again."

Notes Maurice Hurley with a groan, "That, to me, represented, 'Don't we have a new idea?' I didn't like that show at all. It just wasn't very good. What it did show, though, was that the new ensemble could interact, and that there were relationships between them that worked. But doing it was terrible. It was a warmed over premise. Why do it?"

Episode #4:
"Code of Honor"
Original Airdate: 10/19/87
Written by Katharyn Powers and Michael Baron
Directed by Russ Mayberry
Guest Starring: Jessie Lawrence Ferguson (Lutan), Karole Selmon (Yarenna), James Louis Watkins (Hagon), Michael Rider (Transporter Chief)

The Enterprise is in the midst of negotiating an invaluable medical vaccine from the people of Ligon II, when that world's leader, Lutan, kidnaps Tasha Yar and decides that he wishes to keep her, as she has smitten him.

What eventually unfolds is a classic game of political manipulation, as Lutan sets events into motion in such a way that his wife, Yareena, challenges Tasha to a death battle. Picard is in the difficult position of having to protect one of his own while preserving the peace and obtaining the vaccine.

••••

"I bought my first television specifically so I could watch *Star Trek*,"

Denise Crosby, first Tasha Yar and then the Romulan Sela on Next Generation, *seen here in* The Eliminators.

reflects writer Katharyn Powers. "I was a starving actress in New York at the time—so that was like putting out blood—but I had to watch the show. I've been a *Star Trek* fan for years. When I finally became a professional writer, there was no *Star Trek* to write for. So, for me, doing this script was like an 'If only....' that came true....The inspiration for 'Code of Honor' was to combine interesting characters with interesting problems, juxtaposed with this wonderful new cast. And even though it's a new cast, they still wanted to have the same kinds of *Star Trek* stories, the same feeling of camaraderie and family. To prepare for the script, we watched many of the old episodes and the movies to immerse ourselves in 'space.'"

Adds co-writer Michael Baron, "'Code of Honor' underwent many changes, but the idea was to create an alien civilization with an interesting look and a central theme to it. We based them somewhat on the Samurai culture in Japan and made parallels, which was fun to do. I've always been fascinated by Japanese culture and history."

"An execution problem," states Maurice Hurley matter of factly. "A good idea, but the execution, to me, just fell apart. Again, if you take that script and if the actors had been told to give it a different twist, that show would have been different. But it became too baroque and fell apart. But the concept

of having a guy saying, 'I have to have somebody kill my wife and this is the person,' is a good idea."

Former creative consultant Tracy Torme notes, "I felt like it was a '40s tribal African view of blacks. I think it was kind of embarrassing. Not only was the ending like [original series episode] 'Amok Time,' but it came dangerously close to *Amost & Andy*."

Episode #5:
"The Last Outpost"
Original Airdate: 10/17/87
Written by Herbert Wright
Story by Richard Krzemien
Directed by Richard Colla
Guest Starring: Armin Shimerman (Lebek), Jake Dengel (Mordoc), Tracey Walker (Kayron), Darryl Henriques (The Portal), Mike Gomez (Daimon Taar)

The Enterprise is in pursuit of a Ferengi vessel which has stolen the T-9 energy converter from a Federation outpost. The chase leads to the orbit of a planet in the T'Kon Empire, where both vessels suddenly find themselves held in stasis, all power rapidly draining. Each blames the other, but evidence soon points to the planet below as the source of the power drain.

After a beam down, humans come upon Ferengi for the first time. Together, they encounter the Portal, guardian of the Empire who puts them to

a test. The species which passes this test will survive, while the other will be disposed of.

••••

"In the script they're confronting the Portal, who is something of a cloaked creature," says Richard Krzemien, the writer who supplied this episode's original story. "He represents the entrance to the T'Kon Empire. Originally, that Portal was a small guy named Dilo, who was the caretaker of this planet, and he was meant to be a light, upbeat kind of character who got caught in the fact that he was asleep when his entire group of planets died. This is where the interesting thing about successive drafts comes in. The concept of that still exists, but it's how Dilo is embodied that's changed."

Maurice Hurley recalls when he was working on a film location once when the crew had to pass through an orchard. In the garden was a watchdog who would wag his tail and jump around while the crew was walking through. When they left, the dog would start barking ferociously. "The owner would look and see the dog barking and people leaving and make the assumption the dog was doing a helluva job. Really, the dog was just as lonesome and friendly and sweet a dog as you'd ever meet and that was the kind of image we wanted to put on 'Last Outpost.' I thought it would be

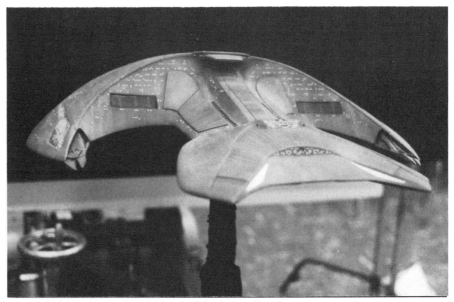

A model of the Ferengi ship, which would first be used in "The Last Outpost."

great, but it turned into this silliness with the Ferengi."

Director Richard Colla admits to having a difficult time evaluating the episode.

"My experience and relationship to a picture is that I start with a piece of material," Colla explains, "I read it and I am struck one way or the other on the positive side, and those are the highlights of the piece for me. Those areas that might have lapses in logical continuity are places that I need to fix, hopefully, in the story, because once we start to put it on the stage and start to make it, you're always compromising. You know you're going to compromise, but the struggle is to simply make a creative compromise so that you don't destroy the emotional essence of that moment of the story. In episodic television especially, the struggle is to try to maintain a level of quality of excellence at least to the point where you don't fall below an unacceptable level. You don't want to be in that terrible situation where you've just got to get it done. Given all of that, when you put it together, there are still going to be moments that don't work. Moments where you say, 'Gee, I really wish I had time to shoot a close-up over there,' and so on. When you're finally through the final phase, you're always fixing the mistakes. So the experience always is from the initial reading to the final, delivered product. It becomes a series of trying to solve problems, and the only thing that you really see are the problems. When you finally run the picture as an answer print, there's joy that it's done, but, boy, the real emotional experience for me is that I'm pissed I didn't fix the things that needed to be fixed. So I have no objectivity in the final analysis. I just have to do the best work that I can, finish it, put it behind me and let other people say whether or not they liked it."

Armin Shimerman, who portrays a Ferengi, has also portrayed a Newcomer in *Alien Nation*, and underground denizen Pascal in *Beauty and the Beast*. He is seen weekly as the Ferengi Quark in *Star Trek: Deep Space Nine.*.

Episode #6:
"Where No One Has Gone Before"
Original Airdate: 10/24/87
Written by Diane Duane and
Michael Reaves
Directed by Rob Bowman
Guest Starring: Eric Menyuk (the Traveler), Stanley Kamel (Kosinski), Herta Ware (Mother Picard), Biff Yeager (Argyle), Charles Dayton (Crewmember), Victoria Dillard (Ballerina)

A Federation propulsion expert named Kosinski and his alien assistant, the Traveler, come aboard the Enterprise to enhance the warp capabilities of the starship. Something goes horribly wrong, and after two warp accelerations, the Enterprise finds itself over 350 million light years from home. Returning to their own galaxy would take over three centuries!

Things go from bad to worse when, in this sector of space, reality breaks down, and the crew begins to hallucinate. The only way back is through the unexplained powers of the Traveler, who was actually the one responsible for this journey in the first place. The problem is that he is dying.

••••

The script for "Where No One Has Gone Before" read that the Enterprise has reached the end of the universe, "a concept that can't be described because it can't be understood," says Visual Effects Supervisor Rob Legato. "You sit there and scream that it can't be understood, but I've got to shoot it in three weeks. To them it's an eighth of a page and that's nothing. The trouble is that you come up with an idea and it's all in pieces until the final composite. You don't have any time to say, 'Okay, this is a good story point, let's add this or that.' It better be acceptable right off the bat. Then you have hours, not days, to embellish it."

"I did a page one rewrite of 'Where No One Has Gone Before,' and they absolutely hated it," smiles Maurice Hurley. "I think they wanted to fire me, and they would have if I didn't have a guaranteed contract. I said, 'Wait a minute, I'm used to writing from this point of view of vulnerability. I just write the most outrageous shit in the world and then we sit down and work it out. But don't attack it and don't attack me.' And

that's what happened, so I took it and started rewriting it some more, and it eventually turned out to be what you saw on the screen, and a show that I liked a lot. Everything about that episode worked. That's when everybody started to hit their stride a little bit. The casting was good, the Traveler was wonderful, the optical effects were excellently outstanding. You could feel things starting to come together."

"[Diane Duane and I] really lucked out," admits writer Michael Reaves. "It was our concept and everything, but we were massively rewritten. I will agree that it was the best episode [at that time]. Yes, they had an all-powerful alien, but at least he was not a cranky child. One of the things we liked about the show as aired is that there was some honest emotion involved, although not nearly as much as we had. I've only seen a few episodes of the show, but so far it seems very one-note to me. At least this alien had some problems; some things he wanted to accomplish that were viable within the STAR TREK universe. Also, one thing they did keep from our story is that this was a problem that was not solved by slowing something up, which I kind of liked. Production-wise it was wonderful, and the acting was all very good. It came together much better on the screen than we thought it would when we read the script. We were lucky, because it was out of our hands."

Director Rob Bowman recalls, "It was the fourth episode and the writers were really fresh, It was a very enlightening script, the likes of which you don't very often see on television. I felt very fortunate that it was such a great script but, personally, I was terrified because it was my first episode and I wanted to make a good impression. I worked on that show every day I had the script, which, including the shooting, was like 20 days for me. I used lots of storyboards, blocked the sets, walked around them for several weekends to get used to them, and thought out every possible angle. But for the first couple of days of shooting, it was pretty terrifying, mostly because of my being so new to the show, and also being so young I had to prove....it was a very good Hollywood crew, but there's always a couple of days of testing that you go through, especially when you're young. So there were the first two days where I was proving I had an idea of what I wanted to do. Once I felt the connection was made on the second day, we took off and I started to get lots of good input from the crew as well. Bob Justman and Rick Berman were very creative and very helpful. It was one of the tightest ships I've ever seen, and that was a real change."

Episode #7:
"Lonely Among Us"
Original Airdate: 10/31/87
Written by D.C. Fontana
Story by Michael Halperin
Directed by Cliff Bole
Guest Starring: John Durbin (Badar), Kavi Raz (Singh), Colm Meaney (Security)

In a plotline extremely similar to the original series' "Journey to Babel," the Enterprise is transporting Selay and Andican delegates to a peace conference on the planet Parliament. It's everything that Riker, Tasha and ship security staff can do to stop them from killing each other.

At the same time, the starship passes through a cloud which, unknown to anyone at first, consists of living entities. One of them is accidentally caught in the ship's computer and it moves from Worf, to Crusher and, finally, to Captain Picard, who, while under the alien influence, decides to have himself beamed into open space to rejoin the other cloud creatures.

••••

"In 'Lonely Among Us' I pulled from myself," says Dorothy Fontana, "some elements from 'Journey to Babel' in that the mission was to transport these diplomats from here to there. The flow was entirely different. They were a subplot to be, in point, a fun kind of thing as opposed to serious 'drama,' like in 'Babel.' So what I did was pull from myself and switch it around. I felt that was acceptable. A lot of people said, 'That's "Journey to Babel",' but, no, it's not. I wrote 'Journey to Babel' and I wrote this, too, and I feel there is a difference. There's a definite delineation and separation here, both in intent and content."

Offers director Cliff Bole, "I don't recall that being one of my better shows, but I worked as hard on that as I

worked on anything else. The subject matter affects the end product. There's some better written shows, obviously."

Episode #8:
"Justice"
Original Airdate: 11/7/87
Written by Worley Thorne
Story by Ralph Willis (John Black)
& Thorne
Directed by James L. Conway
Guest Starring: Brenda Bakke (Rivan), Jay Louden (Liator), Josh Clark (Conn), David Q. Combs and Richard Lavin (Mediators), Judith Jones (Edo Girl), Eric Matthews and David Michael Graves (Edo Boys), Brad Zerbst (Medical Officers)

The Enterprise deposits a colony on a planet in the Strnad system and then proceeds to Rubicum III for possible shore leave. The people there, the Edo, are extremely loving and sensual, and they make the crew welcome.

What the Away Team finds is that this is an idyllic world of paradise where everyone seems to have exactly what they need, and there is no crime whatsoever. Unfortunately what they learn as well is the reason for the lack of crime: all illegal actions, from the most minor to the most severe, are punishable in one way: death. This point is driven home when Wesley accidentally crushes some plants and is sentenced to die.

Picard must allow justice on this world to be carried out or ignore the Prime Directive and rescue Wesley. Complicating matters is a vessel in orbit around the planet claiming to be the god of Edo and demanding that the Enterprise leave this sector of space, and retrieve the colony it had so recently deposited on a nearby world.

••••

Although John D.F. Black, who wrote the original story for this episode, finds little redeeming about the final product, he does recall his initial thoughts on the idea's genesis.

"'Justice' is about the human answer to what you do when violence in the streets becomes rampant," he explains. "What do you do if you're a colony? What do you do, and how would it look to somebody else when you have responded in the only way you can?

"The story has to do with justice

Wil Wheaton (Wesley Crusher) parties down at a Star Trek convention appearance. (Photo copyright © Karen Witkowski)

for everybody, and how you deal with terrorism and anarchy. How do you stop it? And once you've stopped it, what happens next? Let's say that what we do is kill everybody who Is a terrorIst or suspected of being a terrorist. Now the people who have killed everybody, what do they do? We're talking about a society dealing with some aspect of itself. And this society [as originally conceived] is made up of Earth people who went out there to set up their own democratic society. It's what corrupted the Greek democracy."

"A great idea, though it got a little fanciful for me," says Maurice Hurley. "It was a part of the contemporary culture we're talking about here. If you want to start controlling crime, maybe the answer is, 'Listen, if you commit a crime at a certain level, it's the death penalty.' And where does that level start? Where does it stop? Why not any crime? Get rid of all the criminals, get rid of the criminal genes, let's whack them down and let's go. You can make that argument, and if a culture like our culture keeps going the way it's going, it's an argument that people may start pushing forward. There's a resurgence of people saying, 'We're not using the death penalty as much as we should be.' You hear that every day, and when you hear the arguments, it's hard at some level not to buy them. You say, 'Wait a minute, maybe there are some machines that are flawed at the factory and should be recalled.' Then you take it to its logical absurdity, and you can have a society like the one in 'Justice.' I thought the *idea* of that show was wonderful. It got too fanciful, sexual and there was an innocence that was missing. It got looney tunes for me. And I didn't like the machine-god idea at all."

Episode #9:
"The Battle"
Original Airdate: 11/14/87
Written by Herbert Wright
Story by Larry Forrester
Directed by Rob Bowman
Guest Starring: Frank Corsentino (DaiMon Bok), Doug Warhit (First Officer Kazago), Robert Towers (Second Officer Rata)

Ferengi Daimon Bok offers a gift to Picard: the somewhat battered Stargazer, which Picard had commanded years earlier. The ship's final mission had been the battle of Maxia, where, after being severely damaged but still managing to destroy its Ferengi opponent, it was set adrift. Unknown to Picard, Daimon Bok's son died at Maxia, and the Ferengi has held the captain accountable ever since.

To this end, he utilizes an alien mind-control device to get Picard back on board the Stargazer to relive the battle, only this time the Ferengi vessel has been replaced by the Enterprise.

••••

"'The Battle' was pretty good," comments Maurice Hurley, "because Patrick Stewart did such a good job. I thought he made that work. Originally I wasn't too hot about the episode, as I've seen it since. I think it's better than I originally thought. I still think the Ferengi were a waste of time. Goofy. No bushido involved; it was a joke. We had these arguments from the beginning. I was the lone voice screaming in the wilderness. If somebody's interested in gold, they're not much of an adversary. If we can make gold in our replicator—and we can—then it's like sand at the beach in Santa Monica. Who cares? Give 'em all the sand that they want. Get them out of here. They want gold? Here, take a truck

load and get out."

Rob Bowman smiles, "I love 'The Battle,' because there's so much to it. That was my second show and it was kind of a broad episode. The story seemed to have a lot of scope to it. I'm not sure why I felt that way, but it was a little bit intimidating when I first got the script. I was going to be dealing with Patrick Stewart, whose knowledge is unending, and I really wanted to tap that; I really wanted to get in there and make that man work. At the same time, I was concerned that I didn't have enough notches on my belt to bring the best out of him. I think what I ended up doing was making my own little version of that movie, while not letting Patrick do his version of it. The only thing I could be comfortable with was my version, so I'd say, 'This is what I want in this scene,' and Patrick just gave it to you. I think at that time, no other show had that look. We went dark in a lot of scenes and we did different angles and things the show hadn't done yet. For me, it was a real creative stretch and it felt great for the show. They loved how dark it went in some spots. Also, nobody ever used Steadicam on that show, and we used it on the Stargazer, which was actually a redress of the films' Bird of Prey bridge."

Episode #10:
"Hide & Q"
Original Airdate: 11/21/87
Written by C.J. Holland and Gene Roddenberry
Story by Holland
Directed by Cliff Bole
Guest Starring: John de Lancie (Q), Elaine Nalee (Survivor), William A. Wallace (Adult Wesley)

Intrigued by the Enterprise crew from the events of "Encounter at Farpoint," Q and those of his continuum want to study the species more closely. To this end, he decides to bestow a gift and chooses Riker as the recipient. As a result, the commander is given the same powers as Q, and must learn how to cope with them.

••••

"That was a turning point script, and now I'm talking about personalities," says Maurice Hurley, who used the pen name C.J. Holland. "I wrote that script

Jonathan Frakes (Commander William Riker) takes to the stage at a Star Trek convention. (Photo copyright © Karen Witkowski)

and Gene rewrote it, so I took my name off of it. That's where Gene and I had our little talk about the future. Mine was more action-oriented and less philosophical, if I can say that. It was more direct, a little more playful. I didn't think it was necessarily a better version, because that's a subjective choice. It was a matter of procedure of how the show was being done. It had nothing to do with who's right and who's wrong, because that's a subjective call. When you have people on a show who are your staff writers, you don't take work away from them. You get them to modify it to closer to what you want, rather than just do a rewrite."

"Nobody knew what these demons Q conjured up were going to look like until I walked onto the set with them because there was no time to show anyone the concept beforehand," says make-up supervisor Michael Westmore. "I didn't even know myself until I got it done."

Looking back, one can't help but note that the set construction looks extremely archaic compared to what they're doing on the show today.

"That was part of the shakedown," says director Cliff Bole. "We used a set that was similar to the look of the old show, and of course we didn't want to do it. One of the mistakes is that maybe we should have shot that at night, and not had it in day and showed the dimension of the set. But all that's changed. I think it had to do with the producers that were there. The more guys you have, the more stuff you have to spin off of them and things tumble when you do that. That problem doesn't exist now."

Episode #11:
"Haven"
Original Airdate: 11/28/87
Written by Tracy Torme
Story by Lan O'Kun
Directed by Richard Compton
Guest Starring: Majel Barrett (Lwaxana Troi), Rob Knepper (Wyatt Miller), Nan Martin (Victoria Miller), Robert Ellenstein (Mr. Miller), Danitza Kingsley (Ariana), Anna Katarina (Valeda Innis), Raye Birk (Wrenn), Michael Rider (Transporter Chief), Carel Struycken (Mr. Homn)

The Riker/Troi relationship is thrown into disarray when Troi's mother, Lwaxana, beams aboard to put into motion her daughter's pre-arranged wedding. This is as surprising to Deanna as it is to everyone else.

Shortly thereafter, her soon to be husband, Dr. Wyatt Miller, beams aboard and the two of them try to establish some kind of relationship before they take the plunge. Wyatt seems distant, however, due to the fact that for years he had a mental impression of a woman in his mind, and Deanna is not who he envisioned.

All things become clear when a Tarellian plague ship attempts to enter orbit around the planet Haven, despite the protests of the people on its surface, and one of the crew people is the woman of Wyatt's dreams.

••••

"'Haven' was originally called 'Love Beyond Time and Space,' and was written by a writer who I really don't think understood science fiction," says Tracy Torme, who happens to be the son of crooner Mel Torme. "When they offered it to me, there was good and bad. The bad was that I couldn't even get through the outline he had written, and the good was that I thought it was so unusable, that anything I did would be an improvement. It was kind of like a no-lose situation for me

in a way, so I basically told them that I thought the story would only work as a comedy. I think it was originally serious, and I wanted to do sort of a broad comedy about these two families who couldn't really stand each other, but wanted to go through with this wedding. My version was more caustic; the comedy had a sharper edge to it. 'Haven' was rewritten maybe 20 or 30 percent, and a lot of the comedy was softened and taken out of the original piece, so the net result was that I didn't particularly like the episode when it first aired. It's still one of my least favorite shows that I've been involved with. But for some reason, it's been pretty popular amongst fans. I'm grateful for that. When I see it again in repeats down the road, maybe I'll feel better about it than I do right now."

Episode #12:
"The Big Goodbye"
Original Airdate: 1/9/88
Written by Tracy Torme
Directed by Joseph Scanlan
Guest Starring: Lawrence Tierney (Cyrus Redblock), Harvey Jason (Felix Leach), William Boyett (Whelan), David Selburg (Lt. McNary), Gary Armagnal (Dan Hill), Mike Genovese (Desk Sergeant), Dick Miller (Vender), Carolyn Allport (Jessica Bradley), Rhonda Aldrich (Secretary), Eric Cord (Thug)

Captain Picard, driving himself to distraction in preparation for the Federation's first contact with the Jarada in 20 years, goes to the holodeck to relax. What he recreates is the fictional world of '40s detective Dixon Hill, but relaxation is out of the question as a malfunction alters this supposedly safe "game" of role-playing. Imagery and reality become one. Bullets are suddenly real...and so is death.

••••

"When I wrote the original treatment and draft of 'Haven,' the staff was really nice about it in their feedback," reflects Tracy Torme, who penned the Peabody Award-winning episode. "I think they were very pleased, and very quickly I knew they were going to offer me another one, which they did, and that became 'The Big Goodbye.'

"Gene wanted to utilize the holodeck and had thought of the idea of

doing a detective story there," he adds. "I have always been a big Raymond Chandler fan, and even more of a film noir fan. So I thought it would really be fun to do something like that. I'll just say that 'The Big Goodbye,' more than on any other script I've ever worked on for feature or TV, just fell into place almost magically for me. When I turned the first draft in, it's the closest I've ever been to being satisfied with a draft that I can remember. I just felt very relaxed about it, and felt that it was really going to work. Some scripts are a struggle and some scripts aren't. This one very definitely was not much of a struggle compared to some of the others, and so I have quite an affection for that show. I think everyone had fun making it. The actors, I believe, had a great time getting out of their uniforms. I was really very pleased with the way the technical people handled the show and a lot of the little touches they put in, and how they left the script alone. My only real complaint was about the Jarada aliens. They were much more interesting in the script, and because of budgetary reasons they ended up being sort of a plot point in the story as it is."

Smiles Maurice Hurley, "I thought it was just great. It was a use of the holodeck, it was a use of the cast, a use of the ensemble. I thought the acting in it was exceptional, the direction was wonderful and so was the lighting. It was like a breath of fresh air. It may not have been a breath of air for the audience, but it was for us. It was just fun to do. It's got humor and life to it. The thing is that Star Trek can't brood. If it broods, it gets self important and self-indulgent and preachy, like it has a tendency to do if it's not careful. But if it has some life to it, some humor, then it just jumps up and flies. It's different, but absolutely locked in the Star Trek format. Everything in there worked."

Director Joseph Scanlan found a variety of appealing aspects of "The Big Goodbye," thus making his entrance to the Star Trek realm an extremely satisfying one.

"The '40s setting was appealing, number one," he says. "It was a parody of The Maltese Falcon. We had a Sidney Greenstreet-type character, a Peter Lorre-type...they were all there. We had an office that was identical to the office that Bogie sat in in the 1940's. There was the same window, the same venetian blinds...just a great deal of fun."

One would nonetheless think it was difficult to combine the future with the past while maintaining the show's reality for the audience.

"Had you asked the question the other way...in other words, combining the past with the future world, I would say that it's a little difficult, and that is indeed what we had to do," Scanlan explains. "My problem, as I said to Gene, Rick and Bob, was that I'm not a fan of the show, so I'm bringing a different perspective. The holodeck was never, in my opinion, totally clear as to its function to the audience, and it's the first time that people, in effect, got trapped in it because of a malfunction of the equipment. They're trapped in the past, and yet it's not a time warp. It's very tough, I think (and, again, I'm a neophyte at this) to tell the audience that this is not a time warp when we are deeply involved with a subplot which really became the main plot in a holodeck image of San Francisco, where bullets start flying and somebody gets hit and starts to bleed. That's pretty tough not to consider a time warp, even though it was not. It was just an emotional and visual experience in the holodeck as equipment screwed up. I guess I'm answering the question, not directly, because I treated the two pieces as entirely different pieces. I, in actual fact, did all of the 1941 stuff as if Picard is indeed playing Philip Marlowe, or rather the name they gave him, Dixon Hill, and play that for all it was worth as a genuine thing. The only key, the only balance to keep the audience's memory of being on the ship is the dialogue that Tracy put in. There's a point when Captain Picard says to the doctor, 'We should be getting back to the Enterprise,' and she says, 'We're on the Enterprise.' He replies, 'Of course, it's becoming so real that I forgot.' That kind of thing."

Episode #13:
"Datalore"
Original Airdate: 1/16/88
Written by Robert Lewin & Gene

Roddenberry
Story by Bob Lewin and Maurice Hurley
Directed by Rob Bowman
Guest Starring: Biff Yeager (Argyle)

The Enterprise heads back to Data's home world to discover what happened to the colonists that had disappeared. There they find the remnants of what appears to be another version of Data, which they retrieve. Back on board, the science officer reactivates his "brother," Lore.

Apparently Lore is an exact duplicate of Data, with one notable exception: he is equipped with emotion.....as well as a twisted psyche, which threatens the entire crew of the Enterprise as he leads them to a trap involving a tremendous crystalline entity in space; the same entity responsible for the death of the colonists two decades earlier.

••••

"The sets, the design of it and the look of that show was brilliant," notes Maurice Hurley. "I thought that might have been the best looking show of the first season. There were some things back and forth in there that I didn't like in terms of the characterizations, but basically it was alright."

Recalls Rob Bowman, "The whole story behind 'Datalore' was that after 'Too Short a Season' [which would air later] I had no other *Star Treks* lined up. Bob Justman called me into his office at the end of that and said, 'We've got a script that you should really do,' and it was 'The Big Goodbye.' I read it and said, 'Hey, I'd like to stay and do this.' So we worked it out that I could. In the meantime, the next show that was going to start shooting after 'Too Short a Season' was going to be directed by Joe Scanlan, but the script they had was not in good shape. This was 'Datalore.' They got to a point in preproduction where they said they couldn't have the script ready in time and that we would have to switch scripts. So they switched 'Big Goodbye' with that, and I got 'Datalore.' Boy, was I ready to do 'The Big Goodbye.' It was going to have a different look and different texture, and was going to be a real different episode. But it was very well done by Joe, so the show didn't suffer.

"I took on 'Datalore' and said,

'Here's a show they don't think will work, and I'm going to make it work,'" he adds with a smile. "'I'm going to prove to these fuckers that they made a mistake with this show.' It got rewritten and there were some problems with the script, but it was a difficult one to write. Brent [Spiner] and I had a lot of discussions on it, because neither one of us was that thrilled about it. He was not very pleased, only because it has his character doing things that he didn't feel he would do or things he had developed in other ways. He didn't think it was completely in sync with his interpretation of what the character was. It was a learning experience, and we had lots of discussions with Rick Berman and Bob Justman. In a sense of working technique, there's lots of visual effects and split screens. It was a technically difficult show to do, and we had an extra day to shoot it because of that. I thought it was excellent. For me to tell somebody the plot, there's nothing unusual about it. It's the way that Brent played the character that made it unique. He did the one scene in his own office with Brent sitting down and Lore discussing what it's like to be human. He did one side, we shot through a double, then turned around, read it the other way and shot the other half of it. Those two characters in those scenes are different people, and that's three and a half pages. This is what I mean about these guys being open to new stuff. He really painted those characters differently. Lots of good communication with Brent on that show."

Episode #14:
"Angel One"
Original Airdate: 1/23/88
Written by Patrick Barry
Directed by Michael Rhodes
Guest Starring: Karen Montgomery (Beate), Sam Hennings (Ramsey), Patricia McPherson (Ariel), Leonard John Crofoot (Trent)

Searching for survivors of a freighter ship named the Odein, the Enterprise arrives at Angel One, a matriarchal society in which men are deemed a lower form of life. Riker leads an Away Team to the planet's surface, and finds that he must sleep his way to the top, so to speak, in order to discover the whereabouts of those he seeks.

••••

Meanwhile, the holodeck suffers yet another malfunction as Wesley Crusher catches an alien flu and spreads it swiftly throughout the Enterprise, leaving his mother, Beverly, the task of finding a cure before everyone on board dies.

••••

Comments from the crew regarding "Angel One" are rather succinct.

Says story editor Melinda Snodgrass, who wasn't aboard first season, "If the holodeck was really this untested, they would have shut down every one in the fleet!"

Notes Maurice Hurley, "Terrible. Just terrible. One of the ones you'd just as soon erase."

"'Angel One' was about a reverse role society," explains producer Herb Wright, "in which women ruled and men are subservient. It's been done a thousand times already, including Gene Roddenberry's *Planet Earth*. So the major issue that we wanted to make sure was straightened out was that I didn't want to do Amazon Women that are six feet tall with steel 'D' cups. My feeling was that the hit taken on this should be apartheid, so that the men are treated as though they are the blacks of South Africa. Make it political. Sexual overtones, yes, but political. Well, that didn't last very long. The sexual places it was dragged to were absurd."

Episode #15:
"11001001"
Original Airdate: 1/30/88
Written by Maurice Hurley and Robert Lewin
Directed by Paul Lynch
Guest Starring: Carolyn McCormick (Minuet), Gene Dynarski (Orvil Quinteros), Katy Boyer (One Zero), Alexandra Johnson (Zero One), Iva Lane (Zero Zero), Kelly Ann McNally (One One), Jack Sheldon (Piano Player), Abdul Alaam El Razzao (Bass Player), Ron Brown (Drummer)

The Enterprise stops off at a starbase for repairs, which are to be initiated by members of the computer-interdependent Binars, a race that functions as one. While these repairs are being implemented, much of the crew is granted shore leave. Picard and Riker head to the holodeck for some recreation, where Riker falls head over heels for a "woman"

named Minuet. Simultaneously, and unbeknownst to the captain or his first officer, the Binars have faked a containment shield breakdown, which results in the ship being evacuated. Once empty of all personnel (except our two heroes), the Enterprise is stolen out of spacedock and sent to the Binars' home planet, where it is hoped that the memory of the starship's computer will reactivate the main computer of that world, which has been damaged by sunspot activity.

••••

Says director Paul Lynch, "The Binars were great. Nobody seemed to know they were four very small girls we found. It was also interesting that they all talked in that kind of connective fashion. Carolyn, who played Minuet, was terrific, and she's in *Law & Order* now. A wonderful guy we dug up that they let me hire was a jazz pianist who was the leader of the group. He used to be the other guy on *The Merv Griffin Show* and he had this dry wit. We had him as the leader of the musicians and he was wonderful. It seemed to me at the time a very nice easy episode."

"Loved it," enthuses Maurice Hurley. "There were some things in there that came off so well. When they were sitting in the bar and talking about love, and how you fall in love with the image and the illusion....It just worked on that level, and then the Binars were just wonderful science fiction creations; that they dealt in this binary language and had their little buffers. [Make-up supervisor Michael] Westmore did some wonderful work on that. Jonathan was just great. He really did a terrific job and it may have been the first time he had been given a chance in the series to do something; to show who he is a little bit as a person and an actor. The holodeck worked great in that episode, and the episode was about when you realize your mate bears no resemblance to the illusion you fell in love with."

Smiles Jonathan Frakes, "A fabulous show. Those were the kind of chances we took first season that when they worked, they worked great. It was a very chancy show and I loved it. Those characters, the Binars, why haven't they returned? That was a very well conceived idea. They should have them as a regular

on the ship to fix the engines or whatever the hell they do."

Episode #16:
"Too Short a Season"
Original Airdate: 2/8/88
Written by Michael Michaelian and D.C. Fontana
Story by Michael Michaelian
Directed by Rob Bowman
Guest Starring: Clayton Rohner (Admiral Mark Jameson), Marsha Hunt (Anne Jameson), Michael Pataki (Karnas)

The Enterprise responds to a hostage situation on Mordan IV, where the lead terrorist, Karnas, demands that negotiations be handled by the 70-year-old Admiral Jameson. The admiral, it's revealed, had been on that world four decades earlier and negotiated another hostage situation, which ultimately resulted in decades of civil war on the planet.

Now, Karnas wants to extract revenge against Jameson, but fate may have beaten him to the punch. Jameson has taken a youth elixir which is rapidly de-aging him, though the side effects could be fatal. Now, the admiral has to face Karnas as well as his own wife, who feels betrayed in that by getting younger, he is stealing himself away from her.

••••

Explains Dorothy Fontana, "The high concept Michael Michaelian came in with was male menopause, which is a subject not often touched in television. Michael said, 'Well, I've been going through it lately, and I can really sympathize with the whole idea of wanting to go back to the man that he was and coming to grips with the man that he is and will be.' It was interesting, but he wanted to do it with reverse aging; someone seeking out that youth for a purpose. Of course using a science fiction gimmick, you can do it in a matter of days. Michael did a treatment and a first draft script, but the key element that always went a little wrong with it was the terrorist angle; why were we going to that planet? The Macguffin. A lot of what I put in at the end was also in Michael's story and drafts, but approached with a different emphasis. Also, instead of it truly being terrorists, it's all a trap, pulling Jameson to the planet. Those were pretty much the changes."

••••

"That was a show with a lot of dialogue," Rob Bowman recalls. "I considered it sit and tell, rather than show and tell, and I prefer to show the audience. I believe in the word, but one of your tools in making movies is visual aspects, and just as there is verbal dialogue there is visual dialogue. One without the other can get very monotonous. But the real treat for me was working with Clayton Rohner. He and I got together on weekends, and I think that's the most I ever spent with an actor off the clock, developing a character. We just decided to do it, and it was pretty much his episode, with all of them reacting to him. He was the saving grace of that episode, although he didn't really interact as well with the other characters as I would have liked. He really took it as his own episode. I remember all the other actors saying, 'This is not our show, it's Clayton's,' and I said, 'I know, but we can't change that now.' I think it was a solid episode, with lots of make-up challenges, special effects and a wheelchair that never worked. That thing became a joke. It is still a joke. People say, 'I hope this isn't going to be another wheelchair.' I think people may have lost their jobs over that thing. The prop people built it up and it was nothing. I had to shoot around it and couldn't move that guy anywhere, so it really was kind of a bummer."

Episode #17:
"When the Bough Breaks"
Original Airdate: 2/13/88
Written by Hannah Louise Shearer
Directed by Kim Manners
Guest Starring: Jerry Hardin (Radue), Brenda Strong (Rachella), Jandi Swanson (Duana), Paul Lambert (Lettian), Ivy Bethune (Katie), Derek Torsek (Dr. Bernard), Michele Marsh (Leda), Dan Mason (Accolan), Phillip N. Waller (Harry), Connie Danose (Toya), Jessica and Vanessa Bova (Alexandra)

As an act of desperation to continue their species, the people of Aldea (who are sterile) kidnap a variety of the Enterprise's most promising children, including Wesley Crusher. At first, they honestly believe that the starship will be willing to let them have the children for a price, but when Picard is unbending, they use their massive computer to hurl

the vessel three day's distance away. While Picard continues to try negotiations, Beverly does her best to discern the reason for the world's sterility, hoping that there will be a way to reverse the situation and get back the children.

••••

"I wasn't on staff yet when I pitched it, but I love writing about children," recalls writer Hannah Louise Shearer. "I thought it would be fascinating to deal with an aspect of the show that hadn't been dealt with which was all these families in space. It evolved in that way. Of course, it's my favorite episode. Gene [Roddenberry] and I talked about doing something contemporary [and] I think we managed to deal with a society that had lost its humanity in favor of technology. Wil Wheaton was just wonderful in that show. Alas, poor Wesley got the brunt of a lot of criticism, but he was really extraordinary with those kids and turned them into a little family on the set, and I think it really translated. He was a character growing up, and in any century that's a very difficult time, so why not use it?"

Maurice Hurley states, "That had a nice quality to it, sad and poignant at the same time. Again, it was done in seven days and you always say, 'God, we could have done this better, we could have done that better.' You've got to remember that these shows...this is a point that has to be made over and over and over again. You start thinking about the differences in these shows. It isn't another dope bust, another murder mystery, another lost kid. Each one of these shows is so completely different, one from the other, and yet they were executed in seven days on the stages. In the first year, for reasons I don't want to get in to, the show shut down for two days, but that had nothing to do with the show or anything else, but for two years the show virtually never had a shut down. In all of those shows that were turned out, they are so different one from the other, and it's astounding to me."

Episode #18:
"Home Soil"
Original Airdate: 2/20/88
Written by Robert Sabaroff
Story by Karl Guers, Ralph Sanchez &

Robert Sabaroff
Directed by Corey Allen
Guest Starring: Walter Gotell (Director Kurt Mandi), Elizabeth Lindsay (Luisa Kim), Gerard Prendergast (Bjorn Benson), Mario Roccuzzo (Arthur Malencon), Carolyne Barry (Female Engineer)

The Enterprise arrives to give medical exams to the terraforming scientists of Velara III, just as one of them is killed by an errant laser weapon, which almost dispatches Data as well. It turns out that the terraformers have disturbed a previously undiscovered life form which quickly takes control of the Enterprise, dismissing the humans as "ugly sacks of mostly water."

••••

"They just called me to do another, and I was happy to do so," says Corey Allen. "I think we struggled with that script for a very long time. The 'Q' in that one was, 'Do I recognize that there could be other life forms than the kind of life I'm used to?' To ask that question was okay, but I don't feel it was asked as strongly as it had been in 'Encounter at Farpoint.'"

Maurice Hurley adds, "An interesting idea, but the execution fell apart. I thought it was a wonderful idea. If you could think of all the problems you could possibly put together in one episode, we had it in that one. Casting, sets, location, time, the fact that the director was getting pages the day before we had to shoot....that was a real tough show to do."

Casting note: Water Gotell, who portrays the head terraformer, is perhaps best known as General Gogol in the James Bond films.

Episode #19:
"Coming of Age"
Original Airdate: 3/12/88
Written by Sandy Fries
Directed by Michael Vejar
Guest Starring: Ward Costello (Gregory Quinn), Robert Schenkkan (Dexter Remmick), John Putch (Mordok), Robert Ito (Tech Officer Chang), Stephen Gregory (Jake Curland), Tasia Valenza (T'Shalik), Estee Chandler (Ohana Mirren), Brendan McKane and Wyatt Knight (Technicians), Damel Riordan (Rondon)

••••

Wesley Crusher attempts entrance into Starfleet Academy by undergoing a series of written, psychological and behavioral examinations. Meanwhile, Picard is offered a position as the head of the Academy. Simultaneously, Admiral Quinn and his assistant, Lieutenant Commander Remmick, begin interrogating various crewmembers in their hopes of determining whether or not the good captain is a part of a conspiracy that Quinn feels is building within the Federation.

• • • •

"We left the ending open deliberately as to whether it was an external or internal Starfleet plot," says former story editor Hannah Louise Shearer, who did an uncredited script rewrite. "They already had an invasion story in mind."

"There were three stories in there that all came together in a wonderful way," opines Maurice Hurley. "I like that one a lot. It worked very well. Wesley was good, the kid who stole the spaceship was good, the whole testing program, how it worked, why he failed, why he didn't get into Starfleet Academy—that's the lesson. That's the kind of lesson you want to do when you're making a show like that. Not every show has a lesson, but there was some nice ones in that show about how to win and how to lose. What is winning? What is losing? What's important? What isn't?"

Episode #20:
"Heart of Glory"
Original Airdate: 3/19/88
Written by Maurice Hurley
Story by Michael Michaelian
Directed by Rob Bowman
Guest Starring: Vaughn Armstrong (Koras), Charles J. Hyman (Konmil), David Froman (Captain K'Nera), Robert Bauer (Kunivas), Brad Zerbst (Nurse), Dennis Madalone (Ramos)

A trio of Klingons are rescued from a damaged freighter within the Romulan Neutral Zone. One of them dies as a result of his injuries, but the other two, it turns out, are fugitives from the Klingon Empire. They try to convince Worf to abandon the humans around him, and help them capture the Enterprise. Admittedly, there are a few

brief moments of doubt as to what Worf will do.

• • • •

"I consider 'Heart of Glory' to be an information episode," explains actor Michael Dorn, who plays Worf, "because it gave you everything you wanted to know about what happened with the Klingons. Why did they become allies? Why is Worf there? How did he get there? That type of thing. It was very good, although I felt it could have been taken a little further. What I wanted was an epic battle in the end, but it was a good show for me, because it showed them that people are as interested in Worf as they are in the other characters."

Maurice Hurley, credited with writing the episode, states, "That's where I came as close to putting me on *Star Trek* as I possibly could in philosophy, point of view, position. I put my philosophies on paper, and it all worked together perfectly. That's where Rick Berman and I were hitting our stride; that's where we were locked at the hip in putting these shows together. When I had a problem, I could go in and we could sit there, close the door, yell and scream. I'd pace, he'd make suggestions. The two of us made stories work in that room that had to be shot within a couple of days. We were under enormous time pressure, and we were working hand in glove. We had a wonderful time, on that show especially."

Sighs Rob Bowman, "That was near the end of my season, and I was very, very tired. I was looking forward to time off. I was at a state of mental fatigue that I had never been in before. It was a very late script, Maurice wrote it in two days. I read it and said, 'Holy shit, this can be very good if you let me do this and let me do that.' That show was, I think, one of the easiest of my shows, because everything worked so well. Once I got the script, ideas on how things should look came very quickly. The final battle in engineering was supposed to be played on the first deck. Worf shoots [the Klingon] and he falls down. But nobody had shot in that chamber vertically, so we did some things in the end with the camera that hadn't been done before. Some ideas we tried worked very well. It was just a show where every hand we had was a 21. It just worked."

Michael Dorn (Worf) looking very un-Klingon like in this publicity shot.

Episode #21:
"The Arsenal of Freedom"
Original Airdate: 4/9/88
Written by Richard Manning and Hans Beimler
Story by Maurice Hurley and Robert Lewin
Directed by Les Landau
Guest Starring: Vincent Schiavelli (Salesman), Marco Rodriguez (Paul Rice), Vyto Ruginis (Logan), Julia Nickson (Lee Ann Su), Georges de la Pena (Solis), Marco Rodriguez, Vyto Ruginis, Julia Nickson

When the U.S.S. Drake disappears in orbit around the planet Minos, the Enterprise is sent to investigate. An Away Team reminiscent of the original *Star Trek* (Picard, Riker, Data and Dr. Crusher all take part) beam down and are immediately in trouble. They are attacked by various defensive weapons which view them as intruders, and in the midst of fleeing, Picard and Crusher fall in a pit, where Crusher is severely injured. Meanwhile, Geordi is in command of the Enterprise, which is coming up against orbital defensive weapons. A solution must be discovered before the Enterprise and her crew are destroyed.

• • • •

"In the original version, Picard fell and hurt himself," recalls director Les Landau. "In reading it, I suggested maybe

• • • •

Gates McFadden (Dr. Beverly Crusher) administers some behind-the-scenes gossip at a Star Trek convention. (Photo copyright © Karen Witkowski)

the doctor should be the one who gets hurt and Picard, being out of his element, should have the wherewithal to help her. That was a suggestion they took."

"It started out as a vastly different show," says writer and former *Next Generation* producer Robert Lewin. "It was originally going to be a love story in which Picard was dying and Beverly [Crusher] was going to reveal how she really felt about him. I tried to deal with that in a very sensitive and moving way, but it gradually changed because of Gene. He did not want to do a love story."

Maurice Hurley notes, "You look at that show and see that it's done in seven days, and it's unbelievable. If we'd had another couple of days, we could have made it even better. It was an attempt to look at a contemporary problem with a future perspective. We're kind of arm dealers to the world now. We make our F-14s and then we go over to the Persian Gulf and have to track the F-14s on radar because they're going to attack our own ships with our own missiles. There's some insanity going on here, and if you keep taking it to its ultimate conclusion.... We've got it boys; we've got the ultimate weapon here. It only kills people, leaves all the buildings.

It's better than a cobalt bomb. 'How do you know it works?' 'Well, come on, we'll give you a little demo.' Good night. Turn off the light. It's over."

Casting note: Julia Nickson, who plays one of the bridge personnel under Geordi's command, portrayed Sylvester Stallone's girlfriend in *Rambo: First Blood Part II.*

Episode #22:
"Symbiosis"
Original Airdate: 4/16/88
Written by Robert Lewin, Richard Manning and Hans Beimler
Story by Bob Lewin
Directed by Win Phelps
Guest Starring: Judson Scott (Sobi), Merritt Butrick (Captain Tejon), Richard Lineback (Romas), Kimberly Farr (Langor)

The Enterprise comes across a disabled Omaran ship and decides to provide aid, until they discover that a supposed plague cure being carried in canisters is actually a highly addictive drug that the Omarans have been supplying to neighboring Bracca for over two centuries. Picard abruptly finds himself embroiled in a battle between the drug suppliers and their clients, and he is torn between cutting off the supply and obeying the Prime Directive of non-interference. Ideally, he develops a unique approach that combines the two: by not providing the necessary repair equipment to the Omaran ship, the drug will not be delivered to Bracca and in a matter of time the people of that world will realize that their dependency is something that can be overcome.

••••

"It came about, coming off *Miami Vice*, as an interrupted drug bust," says Maurice Hurley, also a veteran of the once-popular cop show. "We came across a drug deal in progress and how does that play out? There were some nice *Star Trek*ian kind of problems that needed to be solved."

One problem that the vast majority of people felt could have been solved was not having Tasha Yar deliver a "just say no" speech to Wesley Crusher.

"That was Hurley who forced that one in there," the writer admits. "I take the blame for that. I jammed that in over everybody's objections. They were

screaming on the set, the actors were screaming, they were puking, they were yelling, 'We can't do this.' I said, 'No, there are kids out there. If we're going to make the message, let's make the message.' If it offends the adults or bothers some adults but it hits home with a couple of the kids, then, by God, we're going to do it. I'll take the heat on that one, but I'd probably do it again the same way for the same reasons."

Episode #23:
"Skin of Evil"
Written by Joseph Stefano and Hannah Louise Shearer
Story by Joseph Stefano
Directed by Joseph Scanlon
Guest Starring: Mart McChesney (Armus), Ron Gans (Voice of Armus), Walker Boone (Leland T. Lynch), Brad Zerbst (Nurse), Raymond Forchion (Ben Prieto)

A shuttlecraft containing Deanna Troi crashlands on a previously unexplored planet. An Away Team beams down to learn her fate, when they are confronted by what can only be described as an oil-slick, which is also a sentient being. This creature, which can rise from an oil puddle to a figure some six feet tall, is the personification of evil stripped off of the race that had once populated this world. Left behind, the creature has spent an eternity alone and now takes great pleasure in torturing anyone it comes into contact with. To this end, it kills Tasha Yar simply because it wants to. Now the crew has to figure out how it will rescue Troi while avoiding the creature's deadly touch.

••••

Writer Joseph Stefano, veteran of *The Outer Limits* and *Psycho*, says of "Skin of Evil": "I don't think I've ever said this before in response to a journalist. No comment."

"Infinite problems," groans Maurice Hurley. "Some of it worked, some of it didn't. I thought the funeral scene did. We just didn't have the opportunity to do that show correctly to make it what it could have been. I think the biggest problem was the slime creature. If he had been better, if we had been able to really do that, it would have taken three or six weeks. It just looked like what it was. It was too ambitious. When we try to do

••••

creatures, horror show stuff, it falls apart; just falls on its ass. You just can't make that stuff work in the time available. You can't do *Aliens* on *Star Trek*."

"I liked the idea," says Robert Lewin of Tasha's early and undramatic demise. "It was not my idea, it was actually an idea that came from the outside. It was from a person who was not on the staff and he suggested treating it that way and not having any real martyrdom. The attitude was that it's dangerous in space, that's what happens. Let's not get sentimental about it, we have a lot to do even though there was a slightly sentimental ending to it. I personally would not have done it that way. But when it was suggested, I saw it was a very good and clean way to do it."

Hannah Louise Shearer, who rewrote Joseph Stefano's original draft, explains, "Gene wanted an episode that dealt with sudden death. The other aspect was dealing with the character Stefano had created of pure evil. I have to admit I got sick when I rewrote the script, because it was very difficult to deal with a creature of pure evil. Gene and I had agreed that the crew of the Enterprise has no right to make judgments about other creatures out there and kill indiscriminately because of what they do. The job was to make the character of Armus believably evil and give it a basis for its horribleness that was understandable in a way. Not to destroy it, because we have no right to destroy life simply because we don't understand it, but to sentence it to a kind of karma that it deserves. I use the word karma, Gene didn't. I don't remember who came up with the idea of the hologram at the end of the show, but I ended up writing it. The act of writing it was a great catharsis and I felt also a wonderful opportunity to identify who these characters were. The most important thing was to get the emotions out of it. An opportunity to kill a main character in a series doesn't come along very often, and it was something I relished. What I wanted to deal with is how that affects those around her."

Jonathan Frakes cites "Skin of Evil" as one of his favorite episodes. "I think we took greater chances then than we do now. The shows may be better, the level of it, but 'Skin of Evil' was

absurd. We had Patrick sitting and talking into a black oil slick—but what was wrong with that? I suffered physically like a fool with Mikey, sure I'll get in that black fucking metamucil shit. That was absurd. That was a time first season when they took chances, some of them missed, but some were great. Like 'Naked Now,' the episode which we've never done anything quite like where everyone got drunk and horny. That was risky. All the early stuff with Brent as Sherlock Holmes. Bowman's work, that first Klingon show, those were all great."

Offers director Joseph Scanlan, "When you read the script, it has a wonderful intellectual quality to it, forgetting the complications of creating the creature. This entity had such an ironic quality. I thought his dialogue was extremely interesting and found his one on one with Picard to be the ultimate face off. I was very enthusiastic about doing it.

"When I was talking to the producers," he elaborates, "I said, 'If we don't make this monster believable, we are in deep water, because this could be a most wonderful concept, but he's a very sympathetic character.' It was important that we not have the audience feel sorry for him when it's over, but I would guess that if you and I took a poll, half the audience would feel great empathy for him. The poor guy is there in this little puddle and that's that. I think the producers really wanted him to be so evil that you'd say, 'Leave him there. Fuck him,' but of course it never happened that way. There was no way to avoid empathy for him, which led to the irony of the situation. He killed Tasha, he damn near killed Riker, and I still wasn't mad at him. Look at what his people had done. How could you not feel sorry for him?"

While this element plagued the director's mind throughout most of the episode's shooting, more problematic was the actual design of the creature.

"What the special effects department was going to do," he says, "was create an eight or ten inch scale model of the figure. They'd put him on a hot plate, shoot it and melt it, and then reverse print that so that when he stood up, he absorbed all of the blackness and there was nothing left on the ground. The downside is that any time you wanted to

Marina Sirtis (Counselor Deanna Troi) entertains the gathered audience of fans. (Photo copyright © Karen Witkowski)

shoot the figure, we would have to shoot this ten inch thing in whatever artificial set we could create. Very difficult to do, and tie in with the actors. I'm capsulizing here a bit, because I never had so many special effects meetings in my life. Does he have a head? Is there a clearly defined neck and shoulders, or does it all slope off? Is he drippy and gooey, as if the oil never ceases to run? There are a million possibilities.

"Anyway, we finally settled on building a ten foot pit in the studio floor. Ten feet deep by about six feet in length...about the size of a grave. One side of it went all the way down, and the other side had a hydraulic platform that went down about halfway so that the stunt guy could stand on it, full figure, on the surface of the planet, be reduced to about waist high and then, through his own ingenuity, submerge himself even further, either by crouching down or stepping off the platform and further into the abyss."

Despite all the preparation, he doesn't believe that the effect was pulled off successfully.

"If we had a four million dollar budget and were doing *Alien*, we had the potential for a very intelligent piece of work. But to do it in seven days is very tough. My first cut was just barely ade-

Former "Mama" Michelle Phillips portrayed Captain Picard's first Next Generation love interest in "We'll Always Have Paris."

quate and it took input from the producers to make it better. I had always wanted a Roddy McDowall-type of venomous evil coming out of the mouth of this guy, but the producers leaned more toward what you got, which was the throaty presence, but always somewhat ominous. The bottom line is that it became a caricature, I think, and as a result, as close as it came to being a good show, it was not a good show."

Episode #24:
"We'll Always Have Paris"
Original Airdate: 4/30/88
Written by Deborah Dean Davis and Hannah Louis Shearer
Directed by Robert Becker
Guest Starring: Michelle Phillips (Jenice Manheim), Rod Loomis (Dr. Paul Manheim), Isabel Lorca (Gabrielle), Dan Kern (Lt. Dean), Jean-Paul Vignon (Edourd), Kelly Ashmore (Francine), Lance Spellerberg (Transporter Chief)

Captain Picard is reunited with a former love (Michelle Phillips) when the Enterprise investigates the research outpost of Dr. Paul Manheim, whose experiments have resulted in a series of time distortions. If not corrected, the very fabric of time will be torn apart, destroying all reality.

••••

"A very good friend of mine suggested it and we needed a script in

five days," explains Hannah Louise Shearer. "It was an interesting experience based on that. We wanted something that was utterly romantic [and] that explored the character of Picard, [giving] some insight into why he was who he was. To me, unless you find out over the years who these people are, they're cardboard characters. I'm going to say something that's probably heresy: as much as we identify with the archetypes of the original *Star Trek* characters, I don't think we know very much about them. You know who the archetypes of Kirk and certainly Mr. Spock were, and when I was a kid I had a mad crush on him—all women did—but I didn't know who he was. I think the characters this time evolved much more quickly.

"Debra [Dean Davis] and I had a great time writing this show, because we were probably writing the most romantic episode in the world," she adds. "It was toned down 75% and it's very interesting, because women say it was their favorite episode, but men find it very uncomfortable. I think that was true on staff as well. The women in the office loved it, they loved the idea of Picard being in love and wanted him to make love to this woman, which was in our original draft. The men backed off from it very powerfully. So I think it was definitely a compromise episode which was successful in its own way. That romantic perception was mine and Debra's, not shared by Patrick, who had to play the role and who has a very clear vision of what his captain should be, so our perception in the original draft probably went too far and it was toned down to fit what his needs were and what his beliefs of the character were. I still think that men are more uncomfortable with it, but men are generally more uncomfortable in romantic situations than women. I think there is such an underlying sexism in everyone's viewpoint, it's very pervasive in our society. Debra and I had wanted to do something about a professor whose work wasn't appreciated and had to go off on his own. Maury wanted to do something about a time anomaly and dimensional changes, and we married the two elements which worked very well. It was not an easy show to write."

Casting note: Michelle Phillips,

of course, is late of the 1960's-70's band, The Mamas and the Papas.

Episode #25:
"Conspiracy"
Original Airdate: 5/7/88
Written by Tracy Torme
Story by Robert Sabaroff
Directed by Cliff Bole
Guest Starring: Henry Darrow (Admiral Savar), Ward Costello (Gregory Quinn), Robert Schenkkan (Dexter Remmick), Ray Reinhardt (Admiral Aaron), Jonathan Farwell (Walker Keel), Michael Berryman (Rixx), Ursaline Bryant (Tryla Scott)

The conspiracy hinted at in "Coming of Age" becomes reality when Picard is mysteriously summoned by several other starship captains, and informed of a plot to infiltrate and subvert Starfleet. The Enterprise proceeds to Earth to get some answers, where Picard and Riker and reunited with Admiral Quinn and Lieutenant Commander Remmick. In the tradition of *Invasion of the Body Snatchers*, they learn that key members of Starfleet have been taken over by members of an alien race hell-bent on ruling the galaxy.

••••

"It was alright, but I hated that horror show crap at the ending," says Maurice Hurley. "The thing is, and I've got to take the blame for this as much as anybody, I said, 'Let's do it, let's do it to a bust.' The problem is that *Star Trek* has to have, at the end, elevation. You have to feel an uplift at the end, somehow. And that show didn't even come close to giving you any feeling like that. There was no sense of feeling better about yourself. That's not a show that you would want to sit down and watch with your six year old kid. It was a mean show to me; just a mean little show."

Explains writer Tracy Torme, "The situation was similar to the one involving 'Haven' in that they had a show called 'The Assassins,' which had gone through a few drafts and was really not close to anything they wanted to do. It was sort of just sitting there. Again, I agreed to take it over, with the condition that I could really turn it upside down and basically create a new story. Originally it was a *Seven Days in May* kind of story about a coup inside of Starfleet, and various officers felt the Prime Directive was too restrictive and that the Federation was getting soft; that the peace with the Klingons had sort of made us complacent and somewhere down the line there would be a threat and we had better be prepared for it. The leaders of it were all friends of Picard. I really liked that story. It had nothing alien in it at all, and was really a paranoia story. Gene rejected it. Although he liked it, he didn't want to open that can of worms with the Federation. I was thinking 20th Century as opposed to 24th Century.

"I instantly knew that the story just had to change. Then what dawned on me was that this was the next to last show of the season and I really felt that although the show had improved a great deal, that we were still too comfortable and weren't pushing the limits of what we could do. I wrote 'Conspiracy' with the idea of doing something different; something with an unhappy ending, a harder edge, horror elements....I thought that if people hated it, it was only one *Star Trek* and we could always go back to what we always do next week. I wrote it intentionally to be different. I figured it would cause controversy, but I wanted it to be a different type of show. Thanks to Bob Justman and Rick Berman, especially, who really got behind it, it managed to keep 95% of the original hard edge. Because of that, it's a special show for me. I'm proud of *Star Trek* for being willing to take a chance. Die hard fans who want a nice, neat, comfortable universe at all times might be a little upset about it, but that's okay."

Executive Producer Bob Justman offers, "When I read the first version of 'Conspiracy,' I thought it was wonderful and it did things one would not have assumed that we would have done. It took some chances and I was just thrilled with what I read, and I was very happy that we were able to accomplish what we did. It was a grisly show, very chilling and very effective. It leaves you hanging. You know there's more to come. Those kind of things can work very, very well and in this case it did. It was strong and we couldn't have done what we did on network television."

"Maybe they were experimenting with a lot of stuff on the screen in motion pictures at the time," reflects director Cliff Bole. "I certainly felt the difference shooting it, but the way I looked at it was just another little test to see if the public would buy it."

Tracy Torme named the character of Ryan Sipe, one of those mentioned by Commander Tryla Scott (Ursaline Bryant) involved in the conspiracy, after his favorite football quarterback, Cleveland Browns Brian Sipe.

Episode #26:
"The Neutral Zone"
Original Airdate: 5/14/88
Written by Maurice Hurley
Story by Deborah McIntyre and
Mona Glee
Directed by James L. Conway
Guest Starring: Marc Alaimo (Commander T'Bok), Anthony James (Subcommander Thei), Leon Rippy (I.Q. Sonny Clemons), Gracie Harrison (Clare Raymond), Peter Mark Richman (Ralph Offenhouse)

Enterprise comes across a vessel containing a group of people in suspended animation, much as was the case with the original show's "Space Seed." Instead of finding genetically engineered supermen, the Enterprise awakens a yuppie stockbroker, a housewife and a country singer from the 20th Century who cause almost as much havoc as Ricardo Montalban's Khan did. This story serves as the backdrop for the first confrontation with the Romulans in over half a century, in which outposts are being destroyed along the Neutral Zone. As the Romulans make clear in the episode's final moments, "We're back."

••••

"A slambanger," laughs Maurice Hurley. "That was written in about a day and a half. That was the last show of the season and the strike deadline was on us. I think that script was written literally in a day and a half. The characterizations were good. I think there were some nice things in the casting and it was interesting, but it was pretty much a slapped together show. It was set up to be a three-pronged episode. The first prong was setting up this situation with the Romulans [and] these destroyed outposts, and this would lead to a little kind of alliance with the Romulans which ended up with us confronting the Borg. But we never had a chance to play that out. We set it up and it could have been fun. The Borg were a good concept. You've got to have the planning time to lay the foundation, but we didn't have the time second season [because of the Writer's strike]. That was disappointing since some of the stories we thought were going to work out and develop, we didn't and that was unfortunate. We couldn't do it because of the strike. An alright episode, but nothing great."

••••

CHAPTER EIGHTEEN
SEASON TWO

An Introduction

It's ironic that *Star Trek's* Writer's Guide is referred to as "The Bible" since Roddenberry's "thou shalt nots" abounded and those who violated his commandments were either struck down or left the show of their own volition.

"I think those people who have survived on the show are the people who are comfortable with the concept of what it's all about," says Rick Berman. "First season there were a group of writers who had friction with Gene, but it was not personal. It was over how people wrote the show. There were some personality conflicts, but no more than there are on most television series. It was all blown a little more out of proportion than I thought it deserved to be."

With Roddenberry's control of the show severely diminished after a variety of Writer's Guild problems during the first season and the departure of Robert Justman as Supervising Producer, due to health reasons late first year, Rick Berman took over as the "great bird" of the new galaxy class starship. Filling the void on the story side was Maurice Hurley, a veteran of *Miami Vice* and *The Equalizer*, who Roddenberry had brought aboard early first season. Despite botching a rewrite of "Where No One Had Gone Before", Hurley was allowed to stay aboard and quickly rose up the ladder to fill the power vacuum in Roddenberry's absence.

"Cop shows, lawyer shows and hard drama are my homefield," Hurley says. "I took *Star Trek* because of the challenge. It was something I had never done before."

By second season, Hurley was the head writer, having furiously completed rewrites first season to keep the teleplays coming in as filming on stage caught up with the material that was written. Complicating matters had been

the impending Writer's Strike forcing Hurley to dash off a script for "Neutral Zone", the first season capper, in a matter of days. By the time second season was ready to go before the cameras it was already late into the season due to the prolonged Writer's Strike forcing the staff to dust off an old script intended for *Trek's* 70's revival, "The Child". Substituting Troi for Ilia, they fine tuned the premise for *The Next Generation* and launched into the first couple of episodes.

"You don't look at the ensemble as characters on the show," says Hurley. "The ship is a character, the ensemble is a character. It's a strange way to look at it when you write the show. You don't, for instance, find one of the characters in violent verbal opposition to another character on what they're seeing or what they're doing. And you have to write it that way because that maintains the unity and integrity of the crew, which is critical. The show's been criticized by writers because there are no internal conflicts. Riker does not want Picard's seat, Geordi does not dislike Data because he has this advanced intellect, etc. Those conflicts and pettiness is not there, so you can't do *thirtysomething* in space. If you were to say, 'I think I can do better,' you probably can, but it's not *Star Trek*. If you're going to do *Star Trek* these are the rules you have to go by."

First year, lines were often being rewritten on stage and sometimes overdubbed in post-production to try and make sense of confusing storylines. Although second season was not as troubled, Hurley feels that the end of the first year was his best time on the show and that the Writer's Strike ruined the show's second season for him.

"The second half of the first season was great," says Hurley. "If we could have kept on that roll I might still be there. It was just rocking, too much fun to believe. There were problems, people yelling and screaming, but it didn't matter. We were all pulling on the oars and driving for the same goal. Everybody was busting their butt and it was great fun. If we had been able to kick in and keep going second season there would have been no telling.

"We had a lot of things we

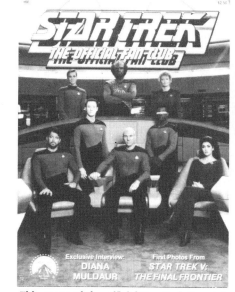

This cover of the official Star Trek *fan club magazine highlighted the show's second season, including Diana Muldaur as Dr. Pulaski.*

wanted to do," he says of the second season. "I like to move a character from one point at the beginning of the season to another at the end of the season, and one of the problems with *Star Trek* is the characters never change. If you look at the old series, they go through all these incredible adventures and they are still the same characters at the beginning that they are at the end. That's not the way life is. I wanted to arc the characters through the second season, but we didn't have the time to build the foundation. That was disappointing."

Hurley's strong arm tactics, however, were alienating a number of writers onboard, including Hannah Louise Shearer who ankled at the end of first season and Tracy Torme, the young writer who had earned critical kudos with his scripts for "Haven", "The Big Goodbye" and "Conspiracy". It was only with the help of Berman, Justman and Roddenberry himself that Torme was able to have his script 'Conspiracy' produced over the vocal objections of Hurley, who was opposed to the graphic violence and decidedly downbeat tone of the episode in which parasites invade the bodies of the leaders of the Federation on Earth, resulting in the Enterprise being brought home to combat the menace. Another producer who left the show

••••

claimed of Hurley, "He didn't want a fresh outlook and we carried out meaningless assignments dutifully."

Hurley also had many proponents, including Story Editor Melinda Snodgrass. "I learned a lot from him," says Snodgrass. "He was great because he always let me make my own changes. If he didn't like a scene he would tell me why and talk it over. But he always let me go away and fight with it. It was painful, but I really learned a lot about screenwriting in the crucible of a fast, hard apprenticeship."

Whoopi Goldberg was added to the cast as a recurring regular who would be the bartender at *Trek's* new interstellar bar & grill, the Ten Forward, built only a few soundstages away from Paramount's *Cheers* set. At the same time, Gates McFadden was unceremoniously fired and replaced by Diana Muldaur as Dr. Katherine Pulaski.

Despite the announcement that *Trek* would be honored with a Peabody Award for Excellence in Television for its episode "The Big Goodbye", a first season film noir set in the holodeck written by Torme, the second season was rife with turmoil. Shortly after the airing of "Elementary Dear Data", another holodeck adventure in which Data takes on the role of fictional detective Sherlock Holmes, the estate of Arthur Conan Doyle warned that they would sue the show if they used the Sherlock Holmes character again. The initial episodes were received poorly and the stunt casting of comedian Joe Piscopo as a stand-up comedian was eviscerated by fans. Gone were the Ferengi, who had been replaced at the end of the first season with the familiar *Trek* villains the Romulans. Disturbingly, whenever the new show faltered, it resorted to the original as a crutch. Unable to successfully create new villains, the Romulans began to serve as a primary source of conflict for the Federation despite Roddenberry's early vows that these alien antagonists would not be a part of his next generation. Likewise, the highly touted ensemble was reduced second season to a triumvirate clearly reminiscent of the first show. Picard, Riker and Data shared the spotlight as the gang of three that would dominate the stories throughout year two, while characters such as Worf, La Forge, Troi, Wesley and the newly added Muldaur were relegated to supporting status.

Muldaur was earning her share of disdain from fans who rejected the acerbic doctor who would continually admonish and torture the innocent android Data in much the way McCoy belittled Spock in the old show, but while Spock could easily defend himself and often got the last word with as little as a raised eyebrow concealing a sinister devilish Vulcan smirk, Data was like a child being abused by his foster parents.

Under Hurley's reign the show took on a darker tone, and although adhering to the strictures of Roddenberry's universe governing the interpersonal relationships of the characters, he was quick to point out that space was not always a happy and cheerful place to be. In the second episode of the season, "Where Silence Has Lease", the Enterprise is turned into a floating dissection laboratory by a curious alien creature who brutally kills the first red-shirted security guard of the new series on the bridge. If Roddenberry's stock and trade had been judgmental God-like beings, Hurley's take was slightly more malevolent. In "Loud As A Whisper" three ambassadors are killed, in "Matter of Honor" Riker finds himself unwelcome aboard a Klingon ship as part of a Federation exchange program, "Contagion" highlighted the dangers of technology when a computer virus results in the destruction of an entire starship, in "Time Squared" the Enterprise is faced with destruction when a Picard from the future warns of the ships impending destruction and, most importantly, Hurley devised the Borg, a race of omnipotent, cybernetic super foes who appeared invincible in the dark and threatening "Q Who."

Joining the show was Melinda Snodgrass, a popular fan writer whose "Tears of the Singers" had been a best-selling *Trek* novel for Pocket Books. Snodgrass' "The Measure of the Man", sold on spec to Hurley, was one of the standout episodes of the season. Opting out however was popular fan writer Tracy Torme, whose second season scripts "The Royale" and "Manhunt" had—according to the writer—been so mutilated by Hurley that he had to use a pseudonym on both works. Torme, who had served as a Creative Consultant in year two and had once been groomed to take over the reigns of the show, was not prepared to carry on the

meaningless assignments and suffer through the endless divisive rewrites that had characterized Hurley's tenure on the show, which had led such Producers as John Mason, Mike Grey, Burton Armus, Leonard Mlodinow and Scott Rubenstein to flee after as little as one episode's work.

"We didn't have the time we needed," Rick Berman says of the truncated season brought on by the Writer's Strike. "The quality of the first several episodes suffered in that we did not have the time that we would have liked to develop and polish the early scripts."

"I thought that the second year of the series, in general, was a year in which they had some real writing problems," offers third season writer Dennis Russell Bailey. "I think there were some really good episodes like Melinda Snodgrass who wrote what is probably the best episode of the series', "Measure of the Man", but in general I thought they had a real writing problem and they were going around forever blaming it on the Writer's Strike, which was nonsense. Every show on television had to deal with the writer's strike that year and it wasn't easy for anybody but they recovered."

But by mid-season, *The Next Generation* finally seemed to hit its stride. "We seemed to find a direction second season," says Melinda Snodgrass. "Once I came on board there suddenly seemed to be this climate of discussion among the writers about what we wanted to do with the show. My impression was that this was a new phenomenon. We were a little bit more on the same wavelength."

The season ended with a cost-cutting collection of clips episode, "Shades Of Grey" which did not bode well for the oncoming season. Hurley, who had grown tired of the infighting at the show, gave notice that he too would be leaving through the same revolving door he and Roddenberry purportedly had put in place. At the end of the second season, *TNG* was without a helmsman yet again.

"Two years was enough time in space for me," says Hurley who returned to Universal to develop shows and eventually landed at Warner Bros. producing the new *Kung Fu* for first run syndication. "I did some good, some bad, some mediocre, but it's not a show that I could continue to do. It's not where I come from."

• • • •

• • • •

CHAPTER NINETEEN
SEASON TWO

Episode Guide

"The Child"

"Where Silence Has Lease"

"Elementary, Dear Data"

"The Outrageous Okona"

"Loud as a Whisper"

"Unnatural Selection"

"A Matter of Honor"

"The Measure of a Man"

"The Schizoid Man"

"The Dauphin"

"Contagion"

"The Royale"

"Time Squared"

"The Icarus Factor"

"Pen Pals"

"Q Who?"

"Samaritan Snare"

"Up the Long Ladder"

"Manhunt"

"The Emissary"

"Peak Performance"

"Shades of Grey"

Episode #27:
"The Child"
Original Airdate: 11/19/88
Written by Jaron Summers, Jon Povill
and Maurice Hurley
Directed by Rob Bowman
Guest Starring: Seymour Cassel (Lt.
Commander Hester Dealt), R.J. William
(Ian), Colm Meaney (Transporter Chief),
Dawn Armenian (Miss Gladstone),
Zachary Benjamin (Young Ian), Dore
Keller (Crewman)

Deanna Troi is impregnated by
an alien presence, and comes to term
with the child in a matter of days. She
gives birth to what appears to be a normal child, but he ages rapidly from an
infant, to a toddler and then a ten year
old. The boy takes in everything around
him for analysis, and inadvertently affects
the growth of a deadly organism within
holding canisters, which threatens to
engulf the ship. Rather than put anyone
in danger, the child decides that it's better he join his own kind, and dies.

••••

With a writer's strike delaying
production on a second season,
Paramount dusted off this script which
Jon Povill and Jaron Summers had written
the series' aborted '70s revival with the
classic cast that led to *Star Trek: The
Motion Picture*. During a hurried rewrite,
Ilia became Troi. Additionally, Gates
McFadden was let go as Dr. Crusher,
with Diana Muldaur joining the cast as
Dr. Katherine Pulaski.

"'The Child' suffered from being
the first episode of the second season
more than anything else," says Maurice
Hurley. "I never even looked at the first
script. It was a premise that had been
written up for a series that was never
done, and I never even looked at it."

States Rob Bowman, "I know
that the idea of carrying the bug on board
in the containment grid came from the
movie *Sorcerer*, which came from a
French movie in which wet dynamite
had to be taken across the jungle. That
was our thread of jeopardy. As far as my
involvement, I think that being the first
episode of the second season, my thrust
was to make sure we gave the audience
something that would justify their wait
over the summer for the first episode.
Simply put, it was just that. Here's our

audience of loyal Trekkies who watch
our first season, and then have to sit
through summer reruns waiting for what
we are going to give them next season. I
said, 'We must give them a great first
episode to welcome them back, instead
of kind of resting on our laurels.' That
was the agreement between Rick Berman
and I, and we went a little bit extra on
quite a bit."

Episode #28:
"Where Silence Has Lease"
Original Airdate: 11/26/88
Written by Jack Sowards
Directed by Winrich Kolbe
Guest Starring: Earl Boen (Nagillum),
Charles Douglas (Haskell), Colm Meaney
(Transporter Chief)

The Enterprise is trapped in a
void that serves as a laboratory experiment for a super-powerful alien being.
Nagillum (Earl Boem) is intent on experimenting on the Enterprise and experienc-
ing the crew's emotions. When Picard
realizes that the creature will need to
destroy at least half of the crew's complement before attaining its desired results,
he threatens to self-destruct the ship. A
thinly veiled attack on animal research.

••••

"I love that show," says Maurice
Hurley. "You know where Nagillum's
name came from? We wanted to get
Richard Mulligan for the role, and if you
spell his name backwards, you've got
Nagillum. It looked terrible, just didn't
work at all, but the first two or three acts
of that show are just a humper.
Unfortunately, the ending didn't work at
all. But that's the whose sense of scientists out in the unknown, doing what they
really relish, what they want to do more
than anything else. What that show was
to me was our guys at three in the morning, they hear a noise in the attic. I put a
pillow over my head and go back to
sleep and hope it's nothing. They got up
to find out, 'Oh boy, what is it?' That's
what the show was. And then, again, I
hate to keep saying it, monsters and creatures just didn't work. One of things that
sometimes has to be remembered, and I
forgot it as much as anybody, was that
you forget these are scientists out there,
not soldiers. They're out there to learn, so
that sense of learning and investigation is

really important, more important than all
of the running and jumping, more important than the Ferengi, more important
than the Borg, more important than any
of that stuff is to deal with an idea or
something new."

Explains director Winrich
Kolbe, "I kind of like this one, but don't
ask me why. To me that episode was
kind of a baptism by fire, because I'd
never done any science fiction before.
Suddenly I come on to this script where I
go from the same bridge to the same
bridge to the same bridge to the same
bridge. We spent five days on the bridge.
One of the unique challenges of doing
Star Trek is that you're basically shooting
the same sets over and over again. It's
not like a cop show where there's a day
or a day and a half in the squad room
and the rest is out on location. So for me
'Where Silence Has Lease' was five days
on the bridge.

"The bridge is intriguing when
you step on it for the first time and you
look at it for about ten minutes," he continues. "Then it becomes an utter crashing bore, because it's nothing but tan
walls and a few twinkling lights. I did a
lot of choreography on that show. It's
probably the script that has the most
notes on where actors move—every step,
which I very rarely do. I usually like the
actors to drive themselves where they
have to go. On something like 'Where
Silence Has Lease' you have to keep the
camera constantly moving, and that was
a hell of a challenge. I spent a lot of time
on that bridge on my belly, hanging
down from the rafters and in any other
position to try and figure out what I
would do with the camera.

"As far as the idea of the alien
studying them, I kind of like it. It's a different perspective and basically every
story that we're telling, it doesn't matter if
it's book form or movies or TV, it's just a
matter of perspective. The problem with
this kind of story that I have is that I want
to make it a two-hour episode and really
push it. The different perspective is so
intriguing to me. We look at things in our
little universe and interpret people in a
certain way and they make sense of us or
they don't make sense of us. A foreigner,
for instance. The way he or she thinks or
sees things. You put that in outer space

••••

173

and have a totally different organization looking at us, now it seems to me that you want to push it further. You want that experiment to go further and us become almost like whatever they want us to be. Unfortunately it didn't go that far. That is probably my major beef. The problem is you only have 44 minutes and in those 44 minutes, unless you do story arcs, if you have to go out there and come back in 44 minutes you're kind of handicapped. You don't want to go out too far so you lose your audience and never catch them as you come back."

Episode #29:
"Elementary, Dear Data"
Original Airdate: 12/3/88
Written by Brian Alan Lane
Directed by Rob Bowman
Guest Starring: Daniel Davis (Professor James Moriarty), Alan Shearman (Inspector Lestrade), Biff Manard (Ruffian), Diz White (Prostitute), Anne Elizabeth Ramsey (Assistant Engineer Clancy), Richard Merson (Pie Man)

Realizing Data's familiarity with the canon of Arthur Conan Doyle hardly challenges Data's deductive capacities, Geordi attempts to create a worthwhile opponent in a Sherlock Holmes recreation within the holodeck. As a result, LaForge inadvertently gives life to a powerful, sentient Dr. Moriarty (Daniel Davis), who takes control of the Enterprise and kidnaps Dr. Pulaski.

••••

Reflects Maurice Hurley, "Wonderful episode. It was triggered off for Data by the experience of 'The Big Goodbye,' which was organic to the show. It wasn't a writer saying, 'Let's do this.' It was one of the people living on the Enterprise. And we did that show in seven days. We had carriages, old London, and I thought the guy who played Moriarty was just wonderful. I've never seen anybody play Moriarty better than that.

"By the way, there was an ending cut off of that show by Gene. We had a large fight about it. In that ending, Picard knew how to defeat Moriarty. He tricked him. He knew all along that Moriarty could leave the holodeck whenever he wanted to, and he knew because when Data came out and showed him a

drawing of the Enterprise, if that piece of paper could leave the holodeck, that means that the fail-safe had broken down. In turn, this means that the matter-energy converter which creates the holodeck, now allowed the matter to leave the holodeck, which was, up to that point, impossible. When he knew that paper had left the holodeck, he knew that Moriarty could as well, so he lied to him. The doctor says, 'How could you lie to Moriarty?' Picard basically says, 'Well, after all, dear doctor, it is Moriarty, and until we know whether he is saying what he's saying because that's how he really feels or if it's more of his guile and deceit, it's best to be very safe with this.' It was better than I'm saying, but that whole rationale was missing. Gene basically thought it made Picard look deceitful, dishonest and it hurt the character. I thought it made him look clever, and since you are dealing with maybe the most profound criminal mind in literature, you've got to be careful."

Director Rob Bowman remembers the episode extremely well. "That came about pre-season with Rick Berman," he details. "We got together and he told me some of the shows they would be doing, and if something sounded good I should stop him. He said they were doing a Sherlock Holmes episode, and before he could say Holmes I told him it was mine. I said, 'That will be my payback for 'The Big Goodbye.' So I kind of went with that with the vengeance that I would make it something great. It was a *huge* production. They built that whole street from the ground up on stage. Indoors. It's an awesome episode.

"The thing that became absolutely ludicrous about it as far as I'm concerned, was a poor decision on the part of those who made it. They went from an eight day schedule down to a seven day schedule for an enormous show. They made the shooting process one of the most unpleasant I've ever been through. I thought it almost killed the episode. The speed we had to shoot....it's like the script was an eight or nine day shoot. I don't mind doing a nine day shoot in eight days, as long as it's not a ludicrous schedule. But seven days is the least amount of time you can probably do an episode anyway that still looks

good. Of course you could do bottle shows, like I did on the season's last episode ['Shades of Gray'], where you just scramble for three days and shoot everything as fast as possible.

"Here was a show where we had all this great production value. Brent Spiner was about to do the best work I've ever seen him do. We had all these sets and they said seven days. I think that show is when I started to pull away from *Star Trek*, because I felt that it was a great opportunity to make a wonderful episode, and there was an arbitrary decision because the sets cost so much—I think $200,000—where they said, 'We'll save money by taking a day off the schedule.' It's like, 'Wait a minute, guys, first you have to take a day out of the script. You don't just take a day off the schedule to save $60,000.' As you can tell, I was pretty angry about it, and still have a little hostility towards what I went through on that show to make it happen.

"Certainly Brent Spiner came through with flying colors and everybody did. The original draft of that script was so eloquently written; absolutely beautiful, but it was probably a two hour episode at least and was written way, way down, but that was a wonderful script. We pulled the episode off."

Episode #30:
"The Outrageous Okona"
Original Airdate: 12/10/88
Written by Burton Armus
Story by Les Menchen, Lance Dickson and David Landsburg
Directed by Robert Becker
Guest Starring: William O. Campbell (Captain Okona), Douglas Rowe (Debin), Albert Stratton (Kushell), Rosalind Ingledew (Yanar), Kieran Mulroney (Benzan), Whoopi Goldberg (Guinan), Joe Piscopo (the Comic)

A space rogue named Okona (William O. Campbell) hitches a ride aboard the Enterprise, striking up a relationship with Wesley and a number of eligible female ensigns. Concurrently, two feuding races seek him for his crimes, accusing him of having impregnated the daughter of one, and having stolen a valuable national treasure from the other. Meanwhile, holodeck comedian Joe Piscopo and barmaid Guinan

Joe Piscopo attempted to teach Data a thing or two about humor in "The Outrageous Okona".

(Whoopi Goldberg) give Data a lesson in humor, as the android continues on his quest towards humanity.

Episode #31:
"Loud As a Whisper"
Original Airdate: 1/7/89
Written by Jacqueline Zambrano
Directed by Larry Shaw
Guest Starring: Howie Seago (Riva), Marnie Mosiman (Woman), Thomas Oglesby (Scholar), Leo Damian (Warrior/Adonis), Colm Meaney (Transporter Chief), Richard Lavin and Chip Heller (Warriors), John Garrett (Lieutenant)

A deaf mute negotiator, Riva (Howie Seago), who telepathically shares his thoughts through a chorus of interpreters, is sent to negotiate a peace on a feuding planet. When his chorus is killed during an ambush, he is forced to learn to communicate by using sign language. He is counseled by Troi, who helps him overcome his handicap and negotiate a successful peace.

••••

"Troi got to show her claws and she gives this guy a boost," says former story Melinda Snodgrass.

"An okay episode," muses Maurice Hurley. "I had higher expectations than the way it turned out. It should have been more effective."

Episode #32:
"The Schizoid Man"
Original Airdate: 1/21/89
Written by Tracy Torme
Story by Hans Beimler and Richard Manning
Directed by Les Landau
Guest Starring: W. Morgan Sheppard (Dr. Ira Graves), Barbara Alyn Woods (Kareen Brianon), Suzie Plakson (Lieutenant Selar)

Dr. Ira Graves (W. Morgan Sheppard), a dying, egomaniacal scientist, places his consciousness in Data's body to preserve his life. When the android begins acting strangely, the crew suspects that something is amiss. Joining the Away Team is Vulcan doctor Selar, the first appearance by Suzi Plakson on the show.

••••

"I had wanted to do a story about Data having hidden memories of the dead colonists from the planet he came from," reveals Tracy Torme. "A woman comes aboard who once had a triangular love affair with these two men from the colony. Their memories instantly come alive in Data whenever he sees her, and their personalities basically take him over. One was an Italian Don Juan-type, and the other was sort of an overzealous and very jealous kind of nerd, so Data would suddenly break into these personalities and become very jealous, possessive, amorous, or whatever, around this woman. I couldn't do it because Richard Manning and Hans Biemler already had a story they had sold, about genius Ira Graves and how he ends up transmitting his intellect into Data. So what we ended up doing, when Richard and Hans were not going to work on the show for whatever reason, was I combined the two stories. I used Ira Graves as a character and the setting on his planet, and put a lot of elements from my story into it. In their story, the scientist puts his intellect into Data and everyone knows about it ahead of time, so when he comes on board, it's not a secret that there's somebody else inside Data. That made the whole story play differently, so that was one of the major changes. A lot of the specifics from the show were taken from my original idea. It was a story I wanted to do, and I wanted to do it for Brent, who I admire a great

deal. This was really the only way I could do it."

Dismisses Maurice Hurley, "That was science fiction bullshit that didn't work for me, basically for one reason. We talk about Gene saying he didn't want Picard to be deceitful with Moriarty. My problem with 'Schizoid Man' is that once you take Data out of character and allow him to be somebody else, we really hurt the character. He was injured in that episode. To see him playing somebody else really damaged the character, for me. You can do that with a lot of characters, but Data is ingenuous, and this took some of that shine off of it. It's the little 14 year old girl and all of a sudden she's giving some guy a French kiss. Something's just a little bit off. There's that incredible innocence of Data that gets damaged."

Casting note: Suzie Plakson would reappear as Worf's love interest in "The Emissary" later in the season and has subsequently become a co-star of *Love & War*.

Episode #33:
"Unnatural Selection"
Original Airdate: 1/28/89
Written by John Mason and Michael Gray
Directed by Paul Lynch
Guest Starring: Patricia Smith (Dr. Sara Kingsley), Colm Meaney (Chief O'Brien), Patrick McNamara (Captain Taggart), Scott Trost (Transporter Ensign)

A genetic mutation on an experimental colony begins to rapidly age the colonists, and holding the clues to a cure is a genetically created being. Pulaski beams aboard a shuttlecraft to find an antidote, when she discovers that she too has been affected with the malady and is rapidly growing older.

••••

"I liked the episode a lot," says Colm Meaney, who plays Transporter Chief Miles O'Brien. "I thought it was really good. It held your interest, it was a marvelous sort of detective story in a way, while at the same time it was making a statement about the dangers of these wonderful scientific developments that can be used for great benefit. It also said something deeper about the dangers of them, and in a sense it begged

••••

Diana Muldaur (Dr. Katharine Pulaski) seen here with Richard Daysart on the set of L.A. Law.

the question should we really be trying to do this?"

Of working with Diana Maldaur in her short-lived stint as Doctor Katherine Pulaski, director Paul Lynch notes, "She was a lovely lady. She did have trouble remembering her lines, though. We solved it by putting them on cue cards for her."

Episode #34:
"A Matter of Honor"
Original Airdate: 2/4/89
Written by Burton Armus
Story by Wanda M. Haight, Gregory Amos and Burton Armus
Directed by Rob Bowman
Guest Starring: John Putch (Ensign Mendon), Christopher Collins (Captain Kargan), Brian Thompson (Lieutenant Klag), Colm Meaney (Chief O'Brien), Peter Parros (Tactics Officer), Laura Drake (Vekma)

As a part of a Federation exchange program, Riker transfers aboard a Klingon warship where he is challenged by the unaccepting warriors. Striking up a friendship with Lieutenant Klag (Brian Thompson), Riker slowly begins acclimating to their alien ways. But then the Klingons discover a structural breach they believe has been caused by the Enterprise. The captain, Kargan (Christopher Collins), attacks the starship

and demands Riker's allegiance to him, while the commander must attempt to save his former ship without betraying the oath he had taken upon joining the Klingon crew.

••••

"'A Matter of Honor' was just a good idea," Maurice Hurley smiles. "It dealt with a social problem. One of the things that the old *Star Trek* did that the new *Star Trek* can't do as well, was make comments on issues. Back then, opinions were changing, things were changing, times were changing and it was very volatile and dynamic. Now we're into a period where it's stagnant; there's no dynamic change happening. People have settled in to opinions on problems that have no clear cut solution. What's the solution to AIDS? How do you capsulate, in a word, the solution? There isn't any.

"Now you take a show like 'A Matter of Honor' and say, 'We're going to do a little culture swapping,' so we explore what it must be like to be the only black face in a room of 40 white people," he adds. "That must be kind of tough. That's what Worf, in a sense, is doing. He's the only Klingon on a basically human ship. So we said, 'Let's spin it. Let's put somebody on an all Klingon vessel and see how that works.' What's it like to be a fish out of water? What is it like to be the only white face in a meeting in Harlem? That's got to be a little funny, a little different, a little tense. That's how that show started, it was a way to look at a contemporary social problem and give it a spin. At the same time, when you watch that show, there are wonderful things in it. When Riker is sitting with the Klingons, the Klingon says he's surprised at Riker because he has a sense of humor. Riker looks at him and says, 'Son of a gun, I was thinking the same thing.' If Riker had said, 'I'm surprised you guys have a sense of humor,' it wouldn't have meant anything. But spin it, and all of a sudden it became the point of the whole show."

Recalls Rob Bowman with a smile, "Jonathan Frakes and I really got into that episode. That was a fun one to do. I think Jonathan was waiting to do something that was rough and had action, and it also had the bonding between he and Klaag. Every day was

Jonathan and I doing high-fives and trying to put forth on film all the energy and spirit and adventure that was in that script. It was great to do. I guess there's a spirit inherent in the Klingons that seems to push it forth in a certain direction with the characters and with the camera

"I was going through my divorce at that time, and was escaping into the world of space for some happiness. Probably helped me to concentrate a little better. I know I was very aggressive at that point, so we put that on screen. When we did the fight on the bridge, I wanted to be as rough as I could possible make it. We even had to pare it down a little bit, because what we had in mind was too much."

Episode #35:
"The Measure of a Man"
Original Airdate: 2/11/88
Written by Melinda Snodgrass
Directed by Robert Scheerer
Guest Starring: Amanda McBroom (Captain Philipa Louvois), Brian Brophy (Commander Bruce Maddox), Clyde Kusatsu (Admiral Nakamura), Colm Meaney (Chief O'Brien), Whoopi Goldberg (Guinan)

Commander Bruce Maddox (Brian Brophy), a gung-ho cybernetics expert, wants to disassemble Data in order to learn more about his inner-workings. Picard defends the android in court to establish his sentience, coming up against court appointed litigator Riker.

••••

"It's interesting about 'Measure of the Man,'" observes Melinda Snodgrass. "Everyone seems to view it as a Data script, but it's really a Picard script. Data is the catalyst, but the stress is all on Picard."

"Stunning," Maurice Hurley exclaims. "That's the kind of show you want to do. You get one of those shows done and you say, 'Okay, good, we got that one done.' You don't need too many of those to feel real good about a season. It just worked great, everything about it. And it dealt with an issue in a very interesting way. I thought Whoopi's place was good in that. She's a wonderful actress."

Enthuses director Robert Scheerer, "'Measure of a Man' is one of the greatest episodes we've done and it has nothing to do with me. It has to do with the content, what it had to say, how it deals with it, the depth that it goes and the way it's resolved. I love that show. It is indeed my favorite show. I guess you would have to say that what I enjoyed is the dilemma that they're put in to, especially Jonathan and Patrick having to deal with Brent not as a dear friend but as someone whose worth has to be resolved. And Jonathan had to take the other side. It was all just beautifully crafted. It was not typical episodic television and had a great deal to say about man, humanity, what our problems in the world are today and hopefully what we can do about it in the future."

Episode #36:
"The Dauphin"
Original Airdate: 2/18/89
Written by Scott Rubenstein and Leonard Mlodinow
Directed by Rob Bowman
Guest Starring: Paddi Edwards (Anya), Jamie Hubbard (Salia), Colm Meaney (Chief O'Brien), Peter Neptune (Aron), Madchen Amick (Teenage Girl), Cindy Sorenson (Furry Animal), Jennifer Barlow (Ensign Gibson), Whoopi Goldberg (Guinan)

Salia (Jamie Hubbard), an alien princess who beams aboard the Enterprise, must learn how to accept her responsibility as a mediator in a planetary dispute, and sacrifice a chance to live her own life. She is accompanied by her protector, Anya (Paddi Edwards), a shape-changing alien woman, who warns an infatuated Wesley to stay away from the girl, fearing she will be encouraged to stay aboard the Enterprise and relinquish her regal duties.

••••

Opines Rob Bowman, "Decent show about Wesley Crusher falling in love for the first time. In the first reading of the script, I felt that we had no show. I thought, 'Oh, shit, here's the one. This is where we all fall on our faces.' I just felt that there was no real conflict and the dialogue was more people talking *at* each other instead of *to* each other, just making statements back and forth. There really was no character evolve. It was basically you do that, I'll do that, you do that...and I just don't find that good char-

acter writing. I loved that girl. I was in love with her by the end of the episode. I enjoyed that shoot very much. The only thing I was embarrassed to shoot was the scene where the two monsters come together. I closed my eyes and photographed them, and when I saw it all with music, I thought it came out really nicely. And the end with Whoopi and Wil was a gem. But those costumes....When they showed me those costumes, I said 'You're going to save money, but you're going to make me photograph these?' I said, 'When the audience sees these, they're going to change the channel.' We cut them down so they were just seen on screen for blips—but geez!

"We did some neat effects, we were fortunate in the casting of the nanny. She came off great and Wil Wheaton, I thought, did a real fine job. I think it was just one of those episodes they wanted to make inexpensively, so it was just trying to make the best that we could out of a simple story."

Maurice Hurley is not a fan of the show either. "Again, we're dealing with a monster show, and we don't do well with monsters. The idea was good, but the execution didn't work. If we had more time, I think that show would have been better."

Freelance writer Marc Scott Zicree (season four's "First Contact") feels, "They really missed the boat with Wesley. In those early shows when Wesley was fifteen and going out and playing ball with the blonde aliens and falling in the bushes, they were writing him like he was five years old. He should be looking to get laid instead of playing ball. Then he falls in love with that girl and they share chocolate mousse—give me a break."

Episode #37:
"Contagion"
Original Airdate: 3/18/89
Written by Steve Gerber and Beth Woods
Directed by Joseph Scanlan
Guest Starring: Thalmus Rasulala (Captain Varley), Carolyn Seymour (Subcommander Toras), Dana Sparks (Weapons Officer), Colm Meaney (Chief O'Brien), Folkert Schmidt (Doctor)

A Federation starship, the

Yamato, is destroyed by a deadly computer virus which soon infects the Enterprise, while also threatening a Romulan warship. The clue to saving the ship lies on the legendary planet, Iconia, where Picard and Data beam down in hopes of unraveling the superior technology of a long dormant computer network of an ancient civilization.

••••

"One cannot escape the impact that this series and the whole *Star Trek* mythology continues to have," says Patrick Stewart. "I have been overwhelmed and made extraordinarily proud to continue to be associated with a program like this, because I have been reminded everyday of the continuing impact in all possible areas of what this show does."

Episode #38:
"The Royale"
Original Airdate: 3/25/89
Written by Keith Mills (Tracy Torme)
Directed by Cliff Bole
Guest Starring: Sam Anderson, Jill Jacobson, Leo Garcia, Noble Willingham

An Away Team beams down to a mysterious planet where a Las Vegas casino is vividly duplicated. Losing communication with the ship after passing through an antique revolving door, they explore the bizarre gambling establishment and discover the body of a long-dead American astronaut. What they also discern is that they are trapped in the plot of a pulp gangster novel called *The Hotel Royale*, created to entertain the lone survivor of the ancient Earth space expedition. Only by taking on the roles of the novel's characters—a group of foreign investors who purchase the hotel—and assuming their personas through the end of the book, can the Away Team escape being trapped in the alien simulation.

••••

There was quite a bit of behind-the-scenes dissent over this episode, particularly between Maurice Hurley and Tracy Torme, who was so disappointed with the former's rewrite that he used a pen name.

"I thought the script was weak in terms of the story premise," says Hurley. "I found out after we were in the middle of it that it was a take-off from the

••••

old series, about a society based on a book. 'A Piece of the Action.' There were gangsters in this one, gangsters in that one, and both based on a book. It seemed derivative to me, but I didn't know it was derivative until we were in the middle of it."

States Torme, "When I came in to pitch to Bob Lewin, he really liked that story which was at the time called 'The Blue Moon Hotel.' It was a story that I had always liked. There had been a lot of talk about doing it in the first year, but finally [second] year they gave me the green light and told me to go ahead and do it. It became 'The Royale,' and I wrote a draft which was, again, a bit of a departure for *Star Trek*. It was kind of a surrealistic piece, with a lot of comedy and a lot of sort of subtle satire in it.

"One of the executive producers and I had a severe disagreement about how the show should be done, and for reasons which I believe are personal rather than professional, I was informed that I was being removed from the script. At that point I immediately told them that I wanted my name off the script, because I knew the direction they were going to go in, and I just knew with all my heart that it was a bad choice. I've completely disowned the piece. I suppose skeletally it's my story, but when I started to reread the rewrite, I got ten pages through it and I got sort of a cold chill and had to put it down. An interesting thing is that the cast, the crew and even secretaries went out of their way to tell me how much they liked my draft, and they asked me in a totally puzzled manner, what on Earth had happened and why we had changed it. All I could do was shrug. Of course this is all my opinion, and you'd probably hear something different from the other side. Basically there's one person who had this disagreement with me and removed me. I felt like a lot of the comedy was taken out. A lot of the surrealism was taken out. I feel that it's very heavy-handed now, and it's gone from being a strange episode to being a stupid episode."

Admits director Cliff Bole, "I thought Tracy's original story was much better. Different strokes for different folks. Sometimes you get a story and there's no backup to go to. If you have two on hand, you might make the move to do another

one while you repair the first to make it better. Other times, time just crawls up your back and you have to shoot these every goddamned day. Once you start shooting, it goes straight through until you finish 26 of them. It's like a factory. Hollywood is a factory town, and every episodic show is like that. You can't shut down. 'The Royale' was one of those things that happen in television, where you have an idea and you have to get out there and shoot it because time is coming on you. It was a quickly put together show, but received well."

Episode #39:
"Time Squared"
Original Airdate: 4/1/89
Written by Maurice Hurley
Story by Burt Michael Bensmiller
Directed by Joseph Scanlan
Guest Starring: Colm Meaney (Chief O'Brien)

The Enterprise rescues a disabled shuttlecraft and finds an incoherent Captain Picard aboard. Reviewing the ship's logs, they discover the vessel was sent back in time to warn the crew of the Enterprise's impending demise in a deadly space anomaly. As the time of the ship's destruction nears, the Picard from the future begins to revive, while the Jean Luc of the present grows more and more uncertain for fear of endangering the vessel and repeating the steps his future self made, thus resulting in the ship's end.

••••

"Somebody else's idea," says Maurice Hurley, who wrote the script for the episode. "We've seen a lot of people do time backs and forths and jumps around. They're always coming back 500 years or 1,000 years. Nobody's ever really come back six hours. Six hours is what fascinated me. Also the idea that it was originally a prelude to the episode 'Q-Who?', but Gene didn't like it.

"Originally," he elaborates, "the events of the episode was put together by Q. He had manipulated all of them as a way to introduce himself. The way it was originally designed, is that three episodes later they're going through space. and all of a sudden Picard finds himself stuck in a shuttlecraft in a flash, and he sees the ship falling into the top of the vortex and exploding. He thinks he's lost his mind;

he doesn't know what's going on. Q appears and says, 'Hey, how ya doing?' Picard says, 'You caused that and all these other things?' Q says, 'Ah, well, surprised you didn't put it together earlier. Oh well, you *are* slow. Just a kind of calling card, something to do. Interesting, wasn't it?' And now he's into it. 'What do you want?' 'I want to join you.'

"So it was like the first one ended as a total, 'What the hell was that? It doesn't make any sense. I can't figure it out. Why would that happen? It would just be illogical as hell to have it happen.' But you go through an hour of being driven by this plot, and then you solve it, but you don't really solve it because you don't know what happened. Why would going forward be any different than going backward? Why would going into the center of it save you? It did, but why? It doesn't make any sense. But it does if Q is pulling the strings. Then the whole thing works. Those two were supposed to be tied together. It was a nothing ending, but if you realize at the ending that something happens where Picard says, 'This is a bullshit ending, everyone, it shouldn't have happened. What does it mean?' It means that there's something else here.

"The thing that I liked about it is that from the audience's point of view, since people follow the show so closely, the next time they see the vortex they say, 'Here we go again,' and they would connect those two shows instantly. And then to have Q jump in and have Picard make the conclusion at the same time the audience is making the conclusion, thought was a way to involve them at a level they hadn't been involved with the show before, where they're in a decision making process with Picard. It's a goofy way to do it, but it's different. Admittedly the ending of 'Time Squared' was confusing. The rationale behind it was gone."

Episode #40:
"The Icarus Factor"
Original Airdate: 4/22/89
Written by David Assael and Robert L McCullough
Directed by Robert Iscove
Guest Starring: Mitchell Ryan (Kyle Riker), Colm Meaney (Chief O'Brien) Lance Spellerberg (Ensign Herbert)

Riker is offered his own command, and the news is delivered by his estranged father, Kyle, a legend in the annals of Starfleet. Meanwhile, Worf begins acting strangely and must undergo the Klingon Age of Ascension. Both Riker and Worf achieve a personal catharsis with the first officer battling his father in a match of ambu-jetsu in the ship's gym, and the Klingon, accompanied by his human friends, in a recreation of the ritual aboard the ship's holodeck.

• • • •

"It was an emotional piece, a character piece between two people," points out director Robert Iscove. "The father has deserted Riker for 25 years, then he comes back and they have this confrontation. Well, according to Roddenberry, by the 24th Century we've all kind of resolved those feelings of anger. So it's very hard to play. If you're not going to serve the resentment and the anger, what happens once the two of them get together, you can't get into any real human drama. I did it because I'm a Trekkie and wanted to be involved. The original series was much more humanistic in its approach.

"The future *isn't* perfect," he adds. "But every time you push against it, the immediate people—Berman and all of them—agree with you, but then it goes to Roddenberry, the ultimate voice, who says you can't do that. I was supposed to do some more of them, but I said, 'Thank you very much, but I can't.' There's just no place to go with it. If you can't deal with the emotion, what's the point?"

Casting note: Action fans will recognize guest star Mitchell Ryan as the villain in Richard Donner's *Lethal Weapon*.

Episode #41:
"Pen Pals"
Original Airdate: 4/29/89
Written by Melinda Snodgrass
Story by Hannah Louise Shearer
Directed by Winrich Kolbe
Guest Starring: Nicholas Cascone (Davies), Nikki Cox (Sarjenka), Ann H. Gillespie (Hildebrant), Colm Meaney (Chief O'Brien), Whitney Rydbeck (Alans)

Data receives a distress call from an alien girl on a planet in the throes of geographic turmoil, and responds to her communiqué, thus violating the Prime Directive. Wesley, given his first command, in this case of a geographic survey team devoted to study the phenomena, must face the dilemma of whether to save the planet and restore its tectonic balance, or allow it to be destroyed.

• • • •

"In 'Pen Pals,'" says Melinda Snodgrass, "you can picture Data becoming entranced in answering [the] question, 'Is there anyone out there?' First, he's an android and if you ask him a question, you're going to get an answer. Secondly, the whole thing would be so charmingly intriguing to him, that he would do it. We kicked around who else to put in the role of the person communicating with the child and, finally, I said Data was the only one and everyone agreed with me. You never could picture any of the other characters doing that, but Data can make the mistake, and I don't mean that in a pejorative sense, and step out of his careful Starfleet training because he's really just growing up. He's more of a child than Wesley."

According to producer David Livingston, "Pen Pals" represented one of the first times that the series utilized a second unit to shoot ancillary footage for an episode. "We got to the point where we were going to do the walls disappearing," he recalls. "The midnight hour was rapidly approaching and I went up to Rob Legato and said, 'This is crazy, we can't do this.' He said, 'Right, let's do it second unit,' and I went up to [director Winrich] Kolbe and said, 'We're going to do this second unit,' and he said, 'Great.' That all became second unit, otherwise we'd still be shooting that episode."

Notes Maurice Hurley, "My second favorite premise, the first being 'The Last Outpost.' Somebody's out there, some little kid on some little planet sending out a CQ. Just like I did in my bedroom when I was ten years old with my little crystal sets, sending out CQs and never getting it back. But here somebody says, 'Anybody out there?' and a voice replies, 'Yes.' Wait a minute! Then the rest of it kind of got muddled around, mucked up and lost its purity, although it worked okay."

"An intriguing episode, though I'm not quite sure I did it justice," con-

cedes director Winrich Kolbe. "Something goes through my mind when I look at 'Pen Pals.' It seems to me that there was another script floating around then it got changed during the production, and I don't think it got changed for the better. It was one of those situations where I said, 'Come on, guys, let's push the damn thing. The relationship between this little girl and Data is something you want to explore. Data is a machine, how far can he go before he becomes a threat either to himself or the little girl or somebody else?' I don't think it ever came through and I don't consider it one of my better shows. I think we all did a damn good job, but it could have been better."

Episode #42:
"Q Who?"
Original Airdate: 5/6/89
Written by Maurice Hurley
Directed by Rob Bowman
Guest Starring: John de Lancie (Q), Lycia Naff (Ensign Sonya Gomez), Colm Meaney (Chief O'Brien), Whoopi Goldberg (Guinan)

Q returns, commandeering Picard in a shuttlecraft. Warning the captain of human complacency, the omnipotent superbeing transports the ship to the deepest recesses of the galaxy. There they encounter the unstoppable, cybernetic super race known as the Borg, who slowly begin to disassemble the vessel with their superior technology. Unable to defeat the collective race of hive creatures, Picard reluctantly tells Q that he's learned his lesson and asks him to transport the ship back home before it's obliterated.

• • • •

"It was thought we needed some kind of new threat, with the Klingons uncomfortable allies, that we could take seriously," says Melinda Snodgrass. "The Borg are in many ways Maurice Hurley's. It was his script and he was coping with creating this new villain. We kicked around a lot of different ideas and I realized that what we were really kind of describing was cyberpunk, so I talked a bit about that movement in science fiction, the idea of augmenting humanity. We felt we wanted to come up with a villain you just couldn't reason with."

• • • •

Maurice Hurley offers, "A good one. It was an attempt to create some new jeopardy, a new villain. You have to have an adversary that's worthy, so you made it impossible to defeat them. What we really wanted to do, but couldn't because of money, was insects. Insect mentality is great, because it is relentless. The Borg are a variation of an insect mentality. They don't care. They have no mercy, no feelings towards you. They have their own agenda and that's it. If all of them die getting   there, they don't care. If you want some bad assess, there you go!"

Offers Rob Bowman, "The avant garde tone I think we understood very well. We communicated a great deal. I think Maury knew better than anybody what we should do. The working relationships were essential. It was a very unusual show. We didn't know day to day if we were making a stinker or a winner. It was just too weird. When I saw the final answer print with the effects and the music, I thought, 'Wow, Maurice was right. It really is disturbing.' I don't know how he got it past Roddenberry. Maury was adamant about this. He championed this thing through with a fervor which couldn't be stopped and he was, basically, like a bull in a ring. Everybody got out of his way and a lot of people thought he was dead wrong. There were some angry arguments about this show. It was an incredibly difficult episode. Patrick even got a little bit hostile that the rest of us were not taking it seriously enough, we were a little bit too jokester and he was right.

"We wanted to make a great episode. The script was very unusual and the Borg were, we thought, really quite threatening and we wanted to get that across; the production value that was in the script. But time is always something you don't have enough of in television. The post production on that show is really what saves it. The matte shots, the stuff in engineering....we were able to do a pan with the phaser where Worf hits the guy and knocks it back. What we did in that shot, which has never been done before, is that we actually panned with the shot. They pulled it off and it looked great. I think that was a very abstract, almost avant garde episode with Q and

whatever the hell he was trying to prove with the Enterprise, telling Picard to be aware because there are some bad asses out there that you're not prepared for no matter what you think. This is just a lesson to you to keep your eyes and ears open, because there are things out there that you don't understand, and here's an example. For television, it's big stuff. But in order to make it big stuff, it's a lot of investment by everybody."

Episode #43:
"Samaritan Snare"
Original Airdate: 5/13/89
Written by Robert McCullough
Directed by Les Landau
Guest Starring: Christopher Collins (Grebnedlog), Leslie Morris (Reginod), Daniel Benzali (Surgeon), Lycia Naff (Sonya Gomez), Tzi Ma (Biomolecular Specialist)

The Pakleds, an apparently dimwitted race of beings, recruit Geordi's help to fix their malfunctioning drive unit and threaten him with violence unless he stays aboard to assist them with their technological incompetence. At the same time, Picard is escorted by Wesley via shuttle for a life-saving heart transplant. Enroute, he recounts his formative years, much to Mr. Crusher's great joy.

••••

"Very strange but nice," Maurice Hurley muses. "That was very different. It gave Geordi a nice turn, and the more you use LeVar, the happier the show will be, because LeVar is wonderful to work with."

Says Les Landau, "I dealt with a race of what appeared to be ugly and slow people. They have a need for things, which can be a reflection of our society. That's what *Star Trek* tries to do, take an almost unbelievable situation in an unbelievable time and somehow make all of us realize that's what's happening today, and what we can do to make the planet and the universe a better place. I think that is the essence of *Star Trek* and the tradition Roddenberry is trying to carry on."

Ironically, "Samaritan Snare" served as the impetus for writers Dennis Putnam Bailey, Lisa Wilke and David Bischoff to write third season's "Tin Man."

"The point at which we became

serious about trying to write a script for the show was about five minutes after watching 'Samaritan Snare,' which in my personal opinion was the most abysmal piece of *Star Trek* ever filmed," says Bailey. "My objections to it were that it always resorted to idiot plotting to make the story work, and that offended me a great deal worse than some of the awful shows which were done on the original series. I thought the way in which it was plotted and the way it was dealt with was an insult to the intelligence of the people who watched the show and the actors and characters in the show. None of the plot could have happened if all of the characters hadn't suddenly become morons that week.

"Someone must have been aware of how hokey it was, because they wrote obvious questions into the script which they chose not to answer," Bailey continues. "For instance, before Geordi beams over, Worf says explicitly to Riker, 'Do we have to send them our chief engineer because they have a little problem?' and it's never answered. If you don't want to answer it, don't bring it up. Another thing that is stupid is Deanna Troi comes on the bridge and says to Riker, 'I don't sense fear or confusion. Geordi is in danger. Bring him back,' and no one even responds to that. They simply act as if it wasn't said. On the trip over to the starbase, where Picard and Wesley have this long heart to heart talk, Wesley says why would anyone use a defective heart transplant. That's a minor point. A major piece of stupidity is they send him to a medical facility where it turned out that no one was qualified to handle the operation if it went at all wrong. I can't believe they expect viewers to be so stupid as to not ask about that. The fact that the routine was repeatedly said, throughout the show, to be an absolutely routine procedure and when it went wrong, it went wrong for no reason that was mentioned, except that it had to go wrong to have the climax. Then it turns out they have to call the Enterprise to bring Pulaski over to do the operation because she's more qualified and the people there weren't."

Casting note: Lycia Naff (the three-breasted mutant woman from *Total Recall*), returns as the bumbling ensign Sonya Gomez she first portrayed in "Q Who?"

••••

Episode #44:
"Up the Long Ladder"
Original Airdate: 5/20/89
Written by Melinda Snodgrass
Directed by Winrich Kolbe
Guest Starring: Barrie Ingham (Danilo O'Dell), Jon de Vries (Granger), Rasalyn Landor (Brenna O'Dell), Colm Meaney (Chief O'Brien)

Originally entitled "Send in the Clones" ("They didn't have the guts to stick with that title," says actor Jonathan Frakes), "Up the Long Ladder" has the Enterprise serve as a rescue ship transporting a primitive rural farming community away from their doomed planet, along with an advanced race of clones. The clones, realizing they are nearing their extinction due to the lack of sufficient genetically replicable material, plan to copy the DNA of Pulaski and Riker in hopes of restoring the race, this in spite of the duo's objections.

••••

"It was intended to be a commentary about immigration, because I hate the current American policy," says Melinda Snodgrass. "I wanted it to be something that says sometimes those outsiders you think are so smelly and wrong-colored, can bring enormous benefits to your society because they bring life and energy. That's what I was going for. Now my boss, at the time, was Maury Hurley, who is a major Irishman and leads the Saint Patrick Day's parade. When I was describing to him what I wanted to do, I was trying to come up with an analogy, and I said it was like a little village of Irish tinkerers, and he loved it so much he made me make them Irish tinkerers. I said okay, and that's how it came about.

"It is ironic, because I got enormous flack from the right to life coalition because they destroyed the clones," elaborates Snodgrass. "They thought I was condoning abortion. In fact, I did put a line in Riker's mouth that was very pro-choice and the right to life coalition went crazy. He says I told you that you can't clone me and you did it against my will, and I have the right to have control over my own body. That's my feeling and it was my soapbox, and it was one I got to get on. I was supported by Maurice all the way."

Episode #45:
"Manhunt"
Original Airdate: 6/17/89
Written by Terry Devereaux (Tracy Torme)
Directed by Rob Bowman
Guest Starring: Majel Barrett (Lwaxana Troi), Robert Costanzo (Slade Bender), Mick Fleetwood (Antedian Dignitary), Carel Struycken (Mr. Homn), Rod Arrants (Rox), Colm Meaney (Chief O'Brien), Rhonda Aldrich (Madeline), Robert O'Reilly (Thug), Wren T. Brown (Transport Pilot)

A sequel to "Haven" and "The Big Goodbye," in which a horny Ms. Troi (Majel Barrett) is on the prowl for a mate. She attempts to seduce Picard, who takes haven (no pun intended) in the holodeck as Dixon Hill to hide from her amorous advances. Also aboard are a band of alien delegates bent on sabotaging an upcoming diplomatic conference.

••••

As was the case with "The Royale," Tracy Torme was so disenchanted with the rewrite to "Manhunt" that he took his name off the script.

"The original concept was that it was a sequel to two of my shows from the first season. Two sequels in one," he smiles. "They had been talking to me for a long time about bringing Mrs. Troi back. Since 'Haven' wasn't one of my favorite episodes, I thought maybe somebody else could do a better job with the character, even though I had basically created it. Then I started thinking about it and realized that there was another element from another one of my shows that would fit in nicely, and it would be kind of fun to do two sequels in the one show. That really appealed to me, and Gene was very supportive.

"The problem is that some of the best writing I did on that show was for 'Manhunt' in the Dixon Hill segment," Torme continues. "I was determined to make different than 'The Big Goodbye' and to have part of the show on the holodeck where nothing goes wrong, nothing malfunctions. I love Raymond Chandler and I love *film noir*, so I wrote all of these very cynical, typical Chandleresque voiceovers for Picard to use and I had him program a specific Dixon Hill book, *The Long Dark Tunnel*.

Majel Barrett, perhaps best know as Lwaxana Troi, the Auntie Mame of the Galaxy, often entertains fans at conventions. (Photo copyright © Karen Witkowski)

The first one was based on *The Maltese Falcon*, this was *Farewell My Lovely* and a little bit of *Little Sister*. The Dixon Hill rewrite was as bad as 'The Royale.' I turned green when I saw it. They got on this kick where Picard kept saying it was based on this book he just read. He kept saying, 'That didn't happen in the book I read.' Not only was it like *Battlestar: Galactica*, but it was like 'The Royale,' where they had [said] everything was from a book. I was desperate, I went to Gene. It really got to me. 'The Royale' I just shrugged off, but they were just mutilating 'Manhunt' and, once again, I thought maybe with Gene stepping in he could save it. But he was out of the picture and everything would have to go through Maury [Hurley] and he didn't want to hear it. The Dixon Hill stuff was a complete turkey. The Troi stuff worked okay. I took my name off because I didn't want people thinking I wrote that."

"Ah, yes, the return of Dixon Hill," remembers Rob Bowman. "This one was to be Majel's episode, and she's a fascinating woman. I was asked to make sure that she does her best, so everyday that's what we worked on. There's really no story tie between her want, which is a mate, and Picard going to Dixon Hill. It was just a way for us to get to the old stuff. There's no reason for him to particularly go there. We had a great time doing the '40s stuff. I'd looked forward to that since 'The Big Goodbye.' It was a little disconnected, there was no reason for the *film noir*, but it was entertaining. I think I didn't have enough pace in the show, it was a little boring for me, but that may have just been the tone of the show. Torme had warned me ahead of time and said this is what's going to happen and it did. They changed it a great deal to accommodate Majel and sacrificed what Tracy and I thought were some of the *noir* nuances to the show. The emphasis was shifted from the *noir* to Majel. This is the boss' wife and she only does it once a year, so it should be accommodating for her and that's what you did."

Episode #46:
"The Emissary"
Original Airdate: 6/24/89
Written by Richard Manning and Hans Beimler
Based on Unpublished Story by Thomas H. Calder
Directed by Cliff Bole
Guest Starring: Suzie Plakson (K'Ehleyr), Lance LeGault (K'Temoc), Georgann Johnson (Admiral Gromek), Colm Meaney (Chief O'Brien), Anne Elizabeth Ramsey (Ensign Clancy), Dietrich Bader (Tactical Crewman)

A ship full of Klingons is being released from cryogenic freeze, believing that the Empire is still at war with the Federation. Only the Enterprise is within interception range of the ship, which will be in position to attack a system of Federation colonies if it is not stopped. A Klingon ambassador, K'Ehleyr (Suzi Plakson), the half-human/half-Klingon former lover of Worf, is shuttled aboard the ship to assist in a peaceful awakening of the Klingons in hopes of persuading the ship to return home without incident.

••••

Of "The Emissary," Maurice Hurley says, "Great idea and one that worked. Hard for that one not to work, but it worked well all the way through. With the Klingons you're dealing with emotion and passion. You've got somebody who can say something. You need that balance in the show sometimes. The show gets so intellectually smug and self-serving, and you need something like that to break it off; someone

willing to storm the barricades. The idea of the half-Klingon was fun."

Notes director Cliff Bole, "I liked the show and thought Michael Dorn did a real good job in it. I think I let [Suzi Plakson] get overboard a little bit. She was a little too broad, but she's a talented lady. I think the Klingon shows are fun to do, because you can go a little broad with them. Who the hell knows what a Klingon is anyway? Who knows how Klingons make love? In 'The Emissary' I came up with that thing where she digs into his hand and there's all that blood. I did that on the set. I was wondering what these people do, and I had the image of bones breaking and felt that's what they do when they get it on."

K'Ehleyr was played by Suzi Plakson, who had made an impression as the Vulcan Dr. Selar in Tracy Torme's "The Schizoid Man." Torme had wanted to develop a romance between Selar and Worf, an idea that was nixed by the producers because "The Emissary" was being planned. But Torme decried the show's premise as "obvious. Had it been a Vulcan, it would have been a lot more interesting."

Episode #47:
"Peak Performance"
Original Airdate: 7/8/89
Written by David Kemper
Directed by Robert Scheerer
Guest Starring: Roy Brocksmith (Sirna Kolrami), Armin Shimerman (Bractor), David L. Landers (Tactician), Leslie Neale (Ensign Nagel), Glenn Morshower (Ensign Burke)

As a result of his confrontation with the Borg, Picard consents to a war games drill in which Riker takes command of a Starfleet frigate. Riker makes use of a team of ancillary officers, including Worf and Wesley, to fend off the Enterprise in mock combat. During the engagement—which is being overseen by a master tactics strategist—the ship, with its weapon systems deactivated for the drill, is attacked by the Ferengi.

••••

"I loved that script," says Melinda Snodgrass. "When I came in, I thought it was a wonderful vehicle for Jonathan [Frakes] and I had a lot of fun doing the rewrite. I really enjoyed writing action, but we had a hard time selling it, because it costs a lot of money to have spaceships fight."

Notes Maurice Hurley, "A good idea that worked. The war games were fun, and the characters were good."

"A fun episode," says director Robert Scheerer. "And I love [guest star Roy] Brocksmith. He is just a wonderful comedic actor. I've used him two or three times on other shows."

Episode #48:
"Shades of Gray"
Original Airdate: 7/15/89
Written by Maurice Hurley, Hans Beimler & Richard Manning
Directed by Rob Bowman
Guest Starring: Colm Meaney (Chief O'Brien)

On an Away Team mission, Riker is disabled by a deadly virus and is put into stasis while Pulaski attempts to combat the disease before it kills him. In order to fight its spread, Riker must relive memories of previous missions, which segues into a series of clips from the first two seasons.

••••

"Piece of shit," states Maurice Hurley, who co-wrote the episode. "It was supposed to be a bottle show. Terrible, just terrible, and a way to save some money. I was on the way out the door. I wrote it, and Beimler and Manning did the rewrite."

Director Rob Bowman shares the consensus. "All we shot was three days of framework and they just stuck in flashback, and the only reason they do it is to save money. That's what it was about and all we did. I never saw a final cut. All I can say about the show is I shot it in three days...and it was a nice set. I told them it was going to take five days of shooting, not three, so they tried to pare it down. When they asked 'How can you do it in three?', I said, 'We can't change sets. If you want to get a maximum amount of filming done in three days, you can't move me all over the ship. Let's just stay in sickbay. I remember spending at least two full days in sickbay. I tried to be as interesting as I possibly could be with the camera, so it didn't seem like we just stole their money. It was Paramount saying, 'We gave you more money for 'Elementary, Dear Data' and for the Borg show. Now do us a favor and give us a three-day show.' So that's what you do. It's an accepted part of the medium."

•••••

CHAPTER TWENTY

SEASON THREE

An Introduction

Third season is widely considered the best season of *Star Trek: The Next Generation* ever produced, and signaled a dramatic change from the policies and dramatic tone of the first two seasons.

When Hurley announced he was leaving the show, Rick Berman brought aboard a science-fiction veteran, Michael Wagner, who had headed the writing staff on the short lived ABC series *Probe*. Wagner came aboard in hopes of charting a new, smoother course. But soon after joining the staff as an executive producer, he was off the show.

"I just don't think it was his [Wagner's] cup of tea as far as the way the show worked," opines director Cliff Bole, "and the way Rick and everybody knows the show so well that they all rely on each other. Input even comes in from the technical guys, who seem to have almost been in space. I just don't think it was the way he'd been operating in other places."

Wagner, who had toiled on the final frontier for only three weeks before departing, was replaced by Michael Piller, a former journalist, TV executive and censor who had worked briefly with Wagner on *Probe*, and who had also contributed to *Miami Vice*. Fresh from a four-year-stint on *Simon & Simon*, Piller arrived already a fan of TNG, and embraced the idea of reinvigorating the sputtering starship. It was Piller's conviction, in fact, that TNG already ranked as one of the best shows on television, comparing favorably with such critical darlings as *thirtysomething*, *Wiseguy* and even *L.A. Law*.

The classic *Star Trek* had not survived its third season. And Piller understood that its successor would have to last at least four for it to be profitably stripped in syndication. The writer/producer was therefore anxious to put his own imprimatur on the show.

Helped by old *Trek* hands Hans

Beimler and Richard Manning, who had worked on the show first season but had left over creative altercations with Hurley; and by Melinda Snodgrass, who had been honored with a Writer's Guild nomination for her "Measure of the Man" script, Piller began to craft some of the series' finest episodes.

With Hurley's exit, Berman also involved himself more with the writing, bringing Piller under his administrative and creative aegis. Unlike his predecessors, however, *Trek*'s new Caesar asserted his authority subtly, at first ordering costume changes and replacing several production crew-members. Berman was seeking a new and more distinct look. Piller, meanwhile, complemented Berman with his keen eye for strong spec material and although the two didn't always agree, they worked synergistically and continued to boldly take *Star Trek* where it had never been before.

The two producers inevitably directed their attentions to casting. Berman lured Gates McFadden back to reprise her role as Dr. Beverly Crusher, citing Muldaur's "lack of chemistry" with the rest of the cast. The fifty-something actress Muldaur soon found a role more suited for her personality on NBC's *L.A. Law*, where she was cast as the scheming and acerbic Rosalind Shayes.

Although under Piller and Berman *Trek*'s ratings improved, harmony did not always prevail behind the scenes, as the revolving door continued to swing. Story editor Richard Danus barely lasted a month and Trekkies Beimler, Manning and Snodgrass, responsible for some of third seasons' most distinguished episodes, quickly found themselves at odds with Piller, who had his own ideas about running a starship. By the end of the season, all were gone.

The performers, too, began to entertain notions about how to conduct business. Patrick Stewart, for instance, was unhappy with his role. On the original series, William Shatner had asserted the predominance of his character, excluding his supporting cast from most seminal dramatic scenes and episodes, but Stewart simply wanted a "piece of the action", pointing out that Riker and Data seemed to be receiving the most

Mark Lenard's portrayal of Sarek has spanned Star Trek's original series, animated spin-offs, film sequels and The Next Generation. (Photo copyright © Karen Witkowski)

attention. Distressed, Stewart felt Picard talked too much, he complained, but when anything happened, he was invariably left on the bridge while his subordinates got the call to action. "Watching Picard is like "visiting a social worker," concurred right-wing science fiction writer Ben Bova.

By mid-season, the new show was sufficiently secure with its place in the *Star Trek* pantheon to reintroduce Sarek (Mark Leonard), Spock's father from the original show and feature films. However, scandal erupted when guest star Michael Rappaport attempted suicide on the third day of shooting an episode, "The Most Toys" (He would successfully kill himself in a second suicide attempt several weeks later) which was hastily recast, forcing actor Saul Rubinek to step in to replace the actor.

The mood on the set had turned dour, and would infect the tired and weary cast for the rest of the season. Cast and crew were burned out by the prolonged shooting schedule necessitated by the Writers Guild Strike and anxious for summer hiatus.

"I've done television for 11 years and there is no show more difficult that I've ever been involved with than *Star Trek* on a number of levels," says third season writer/producer Ira Steven

••••

Behr, now a producer on *Deep Space Nine*. "It's just difficult because you're not just trying to tell a story that could work or not work, you're trying to tell a story that works within very special, limited parameters. The only thing I can compare an episode of *Star Trek* to is another episode of *Star Trek*," says Behr. "The rules are so clear and it's such a unique kind of thing that in the third season of *The Next Generation* I would come up with ideas that I would think would be really good and work that other people would say you can't do. Every writer whose ever had an ax to grind, and there are definitely axes to grind, has complained about that, but having been through that fire, that ordeal, I'm not quite at that same place."

Behr had first been approached by Maurice Hurley second season when he was working at Paramount on the NBC series *The Bronx Zoo*, but rebuffed his overtures to join the series when he went out to lunch with the former *Trek* producer. "He told me what it would entail to work on the show and I said 'goodbye, thank you'," notes Behr. "It was just very different than I was used to doing on series television."

Behr was eventually persuaded by Michael Piller to join the writing staff during the series' third season and left at the end of his first year after penning "Captain's Holiday" and "The Vengeance Factor" and contributing to numerous other rewrites.

"When I left *Next Generation* they had offered me a two year deal for the fourth and fifth season which, after going back and forth on, I decided not to take," recalls Behr. "The third season was such a demented time. It was so difficult for everyone involved, including Michael, to get it all together. The show had fallen way behind because of the things that happened in the beginning of the season and it was a long and unpleasant season. It was a time that the pressures of doing television were getting to everyone and they aren't a lot of fun to begin with. On the third season on this show it got ugly. I'm just talking about the pressures and I think we all reacted in ways that did not show anyone at their best. That's totally understandable and if it happened all over again, I'm sure no one would act any better. It was just a very difficult situation."

Tempers were not improved when in a lackluster third season episode co-written by Roddenberry's long-time secretary, Susan Sackett, the press latched onto a scene in which an ostensibly naked Troi and her mother share are stripped naked by the Ferengi according to their custom. In fact, actresses Sirtis and Roddenberry's wife, Majel Barrett, donned body stockings throughout.

By season's end, Piller, too, contemplated departing. Berman and Roddenberry persuaded him to stay on. The reinvigorated writer/producer contributed a season-ending cliffhanger, a critical and ratings smash in which he injected some of his own personal dilemmas about whether to leave the show or remain onboard. In this script, "The Best of Both Worlds," he used Riker as his fictional surrogate and shattered traditional *Trek* rules by employing extensive special effects and vicious character conflict.

By now, TNG was boldly on its way to where *Star Trek* had never gone before — a fourth season. It was already being stripped in many markets, delivering ample doses of *Trek* to *Trek*-hungry fans hitherto satiated only by reruns and infrequent feature films.

CHAPTER TWENTYONE
SEASON THREE

Episode Guide

"Evolution"

"The Ensigns of Command"

"The Survivors"

"Who Watches the Watchers?"

"The Bonding"

"Booby Trap"

"The Enemy"

"The Price"

"The Vengeance Factor"

"The Defector"

"The Hunted"

"The High Ground"

"Deja Q"

"A Matter of Perspective"

"Yesterday's Enterprise"

"The Offspring"

"Sins of the Father"

"Allegiance"

"Captain's Holiday"

"Tin Man"

"Hollow Pursuits"

"The Most Toys"

"Sarek"

"Menage a Troi"

"Transfigurations"

"The Best of Both Worlds, Part I"

Episode #49:
"Evolution"
Original Airdate: 9/23/89
Written by Michael Piller
Story by Michael Piller and
Michael Wagner
Directed by Winrich Kolbe
Guest Starring: Ken Jenkins (Dr. Paul Stubbs), Mary McCusker (Nurse), Randal Patrick (Crewman #1), Whoopi Goldberg (Guinan)

A science experiment of Wesley's goes awry when he accidentally releases intelligent micro-organisms, "nannites," into the ship's computer system. This accident jeopardizes the success of an important scientific mission under the auspices of Dr. Paul Stubbs (Ken Jenkins), an obsessed scientist who will stop at nothing to proceed with his career-saving experiment.

••••

Coming aboard to replace short-lived producer Michael Wagner was Michael Piller. Also beaming back aboard was Gates McFadden, who returned as Dr. Beverly Crusher after a brief hiatus. Departing was Diana Muldaur, who had not proved as appealing to fans of the show, but would soon go on to tremendous success as Rosalind Shayes in the once critically acclaimed NBC drama, *L.A. Laws.*

Of the episode, Piller explains, "I felt it was a real opportunity for some character growth for Wesley. I wasn't quite sure what that was when I started writing; I didn't know how everything quite fit together. I had this story about nannites. Once I got to know the scientist and realized who he was, I realized that the scientist is Wesley in forty years if he stays on the course of being the smart kid who is dedicated to his work and seems not to have much else going on in his life. I said, 'If I use that relationship to get it down to a more human level, I can help Wesley grow. I can help Wesley move into a relationship with a girl-friend.' There were ten minutes of romance between he and the little girl on the Enterprise that got cut out because the show was too long. But at the end, you saw him sitting down with her and the mother saying, 'That's what he ought to be doing.' That became the key ele-

ment to Beverly's re-entry into the series, which was, 'My son is not having a normal childhood.' We know a lot of kids like that. I saw that and had a sense that was needed.

"[Overall] I felt it was a B-episode. I thought it worked okay, but I didn't have an ending for it and neither did Mike [Wagner]. There are some character scenes I'm very proud of. I didn't dislike it. I was proud of the episode, but I thought it didn't quite come off."

States director Winrich Kolbe, "I didn't think that much of the show. It was basically Wesley Crusher's episode and that was intriguing in a way. But maybe I should just resign myself to the fact that in 44 minutes there are many interesting stories which cannot be told. I liked the fact that we had a scientist who tried to push an issue and then suddenly found out that there are ramifications he hadn't thought of, which is the lack of control of the nannites. So there was a certain amount of immaturity, cockiness or whatever. I liked that, but maybe due to the fact that it was Wesley and everyone considered it a child's show, even the writers, the issue wasn't dealt with properly. It's a very serious issue.

"Recently I was in Georgia," he continues, "and you can't avoid seeing the kudzu, a vine which was brought in from Japan for a variety of reasons. It's a very fast growing vine and it was supposed to be great for holding down enbankments. The only thing they didn't consider was that that vine in the more humid, warm climate of Georgia is taking off and devouring tracks of woodland. You can actually see it grow. We put a mark down where I wanted to put the camera and a day later we came in there and the mark was gone. Now that is something where somebody said, 'This would be very good.' The DNA cloning going on right now. Those are things that are the responsibility of the scientists that are very important. I think by making it a mother/son show and putting that element in there, that particular element of scientific responsibility got lost."

Episode #50:
"Ensigns of Command"
Original Airdate: 9/30/89
Written by Melinda Snodgrass

Directed by Cliff Bole
Guest Starring: Eileen Seeley (Ard'rian Mackenzie), Mark L. Taylor (Haritath), Richard Allen (Noe), Colm Meaney (Chief O'Brien), Mart McChesney (Sheliak)

Data is given his first command responsibility on a planet whose human colonists are in danger. The Sheliak, a violent alien race which stringently adheres to legal precedent, plans to colonize the world, which legally belongs to them. When the population refuses to evacuate, Data must improvise in order to persuade the populace to leave before the Sheliak reach the planet and destroy the colony. Aboard the Enterprise, Picard attempts to find a loophole in the Federation's treaty with the Sheliak to stall the attack.

••••

"I wish you could have seen my version," says Melinda Snodgrass. "I wanted to take Data one step further in his development as a human being. I wanted to stress him and have him face a situation where logic isn't enough, to show that in order to command you have to have charisma. You have to learn how to wave your dick and hope your dick is bigger than the other guy's."

Notes Cliff Bole, "That was one of those shows where we started off with these illusions of grandeur, and at the last minute we had to cut $200,000 out of it. It's the budget crunch."

Episode #51:
"The Survivors"
Original Airdate: 10/7/89
Written by Michael Wagner
Directed by Les Landau
Guest Starring: John Anderson (Kevin Uxbridge), Anne Haney (Rishan Uxbridge)

When the Enterprise finds only two survivors of an alien attack which destroyed the entire population of Rana 4, they are suspicious of the story told by Devin Uxbridge (John Anderson). Uxbridge maintains that he and his wife were the only ones to survive the raid, and that they are safe and should be left alone. Ultimately, Picard discovers that this seeming pacifist is actually a powerful shape-changing alien entity who assumed human guise to marry an earthling, and when she was killed by the invaders, he destroyed their attackers' entire species across the universe.

••••

"We were on location for a day," recalls Les Landau. "It made not only the audience but the crew happy. When you're tied to shooting indoors every day, it gets monotonous. We were lucky enough to go out to Malibu and we had a beautiful summer day. I think it was a unique story for *Star Trek* and one of my best works to date."

The episode was written by Michael Wagner, who warped out of the *Star Trek* offices as quickly as he warped in as executive producer, only to be replaced by Michael Piller.

Director Cliff Bole, who has helmed numerous *Next Generation* episodes, opines, "I just don't think it was his [Wagner's] cup of tea as far as the way the show worked, and the way Rick and everybody knows the show so well that they all rely on each other. Input even comes in from the technical guys, who have almost been in space. I just don't think it was the way he'd been operating in other places."

Episode #52:
"Who Watches the Watchers?"
Original Airdate: 10/14/89
Written by Richard Manning and Hans Beimler
Directed by Robert Wiemer
Guest Starring: Kathryn Leigh Scott (Nuria), Ray Wise (Liko), James Greene (Dr. Barron), John McLiam (Fento), Pamela Seagall (Oji), James McIntyre (Hali), Lois Hall (Dr. Warren)

When the Enterprise leads a rescue team to a Starfleet outpost that is studying a primitive culture, they inadvertently allow the atheist race a glimpse of their futuristic technology and are mistaken for gods. Wary of violating the Prime Directive, but needing to rescue a wounded Federation officer, Troi and Riker beam down in native garb. Although Riker escapes with the lost member of the science team, Troi is captured by the Nantokans, who have adapted Picard as their god.

••••

"We did *Henry VIII* in New York," says Jonathan Frakes of co-star Ray Wise (Liko), who is probably best known as psycho-daddy Leland Palmer

on *Twin Peaks*. "We went out to Vasquez Rocks where they used to shoot some of the old shows. Everybody feels better when we go out on location, even if it's only a day."

Casting note: Kathryn Leigh Scott portrayed Maggie Evans, the love of vampire Barnabas Collins in the horror soap opera, *Dark Shadows*.

Episode #53:
"The Bonding"
Original Airdate: 10/21/89
Written by Ronald D. Moore
Directed by Winrich Kolbe
Guest Starring: Susan Powell (Lieutenant Marla Aster), Gabriel Damon (Jeremy Aster), Colm Meaney (Chief O'Brien)

A shipboard story of a boy, Jeremy Aster (*Robocop II*'s Gabriel Damon), who must cope with the death of his mother, Marla (Susan Powell), who died while on an Away Team mission. Worf feels compelled to play surrogate father, since he led that mission, but everyone is shocked to find Marla alive and well aboard the ship. The crew learns that she is a re-creation, transported there by the guilt-ridden alien race which was responsible for the officer's death.

••••

Recalls Michael Piller, "I came in without any shows to shoot. There were no stories and no scripts in the works, which is the greatest nightmare you can imagine. There's nothing to fall back on and the appetite of any weekly show is voracious, because as soon as you've got a script done you have to have another one right behind it and it continues that way. I went through every scrap of paper to see what was here from past administrations that I could develop. The first thing that came to my attention, the first thing I saw that had any value, was a speculative script that had been sitting around called 'The Bonding.' It appealed to me enormously. It needed a little work and hadn't tied the alien story into the other story quite right. But I like that show a lot and am very proud of it. I think it struck the heart of *Star Trek*, exploring the human condition. This was a marvelous example of that."

Writer Ron Moore notes that the biggest change in his script was that when the boy first learns his mother had

Kathryn Leigh Scott, seen here as Maggie Evans on Dark Shadows, believed Picard to be a god in "Who Watches The Watchers?"

been killed, he recreates her on the holodeck. "The thing I was playing with is what are the dangers of the holodeck," says Moore. "A kid goes in and recreates his dead mother. What do you do in that situation? They felt that they didn't want to do another holodeck show at that point, that it moved the focus away from the aliens. What sparked the idea was that we have this shipload of a thousand people, and this time they've brought their families. It never seems the series has dealt head-on with some of the questions a family ship would inevitably bring up. I wanted to write a story about what happens when someone's mother dies, and what happens to that kid and our family on board the ship. That process naturally led to Worf, because he's an orphan as well."

"Interesting show," says Winrich Kolbe. "I'm a little bit ambiguous about the little boy who I used to call Clark Gable, Jr. because of his ears. Again, it was a cute episode and a good one for Michael, but again it's not something that intrigued me that much. It's just not as strong as some of the others."

Episode #54:
"Booby Trap"
Original Airdate: 10/28/89
Written by Ron Roman, Michael Piller

••••

and Richard Danus
Directed by Gabrielle Beaumont
Guest Starring: Susan Gibney (Dr. Leah Brahms), Colm Meaney (Chief O'Brien), Albert Hall (Galek Dar), Julie Warner (Christy), Whoopi Goldberg (Guinan)

When the Enterprise is trapped in a futuristic minefield which rapidly drains the ship's power, LaForge must devise a means to escape. He enlists the holographic aid of the ship's designer, Dr. Leah Brahms (Susan Gibney), by recreating her and the Enterprise design labs so that they can devise a means to navigate the ship to safety.

••••

"When we got the first draft of 'Booby Trap,' it was Picard talking to some woman in the back of the Enterprise, helping him to solve a problem," says Michael Piller. "It just said to me, 'Picard should be on the bridge, not chatting with some woman.' I said to myself, 'It should be Geordi, because Geordi is in love with the ship and this is a story about a guy in love with his '57 Chevy.' That played into Geordi's character, who's always been a fumbling guy around women, but if he could just marry his car, he'd live happily ever after. He gets to create the personification of the woman who created the engine he loves. It's sort of a relationship between he and his Pontiac."

"*Star Trek: The Next Generation* is what it is," says *Deep Space Nine* producer and *Next Generation* fifth season story editor Peter Alan Fields. "It's a science-fiction show. It doesn't mean illusion or fantasy. I think we need to do shows that you don't see on *thirtysomething* and I think the audience expects things with a science-fiction twist to them that doesn't make them less believable. I think the best kind of science-fiction is rooted in your own life, what can happen now and is a reasonable extension. To do a character story and blend it with science-fiction is that pinnacle we reach for and the one that comes to mind which I thought was a marvelous was 'Booby Trap.' You couldn't have seen it on *thirtysomething*. As science-fiction it worked and it was full of character, full of humanity and full of life."

Episode #55:
"The Enemy"
Original Airdate: 11/4/89
Written by David Kemper and Michael Piller
Directed by David Carson
Guest Starring: John Snyder (Centurion Bochra), Andreas Katsulas (Commander Tomalak), Colm Meaney (Chief O'Brien)

LaForge is lost on an Away Team mission to a hostile planet, where the Enterprise detected a downed Romulan shuttle. While being unable to communicate with the ship, Geordi encounters a wounded Romulan Centurion, Bochra (John Snyder), who takes him prisoner. Meanwhile, in sickbay, Crusher attempts to revive a dying Romulan and is led to Worf, who is the only person on board with the compatible blood type that can save him.

••••

Michael Piller was heavily involved in the rewriting of this episode. "I would say it ended up one of our furthest off scripts, and in a period of about seven days the staff and I turned it into what I think was one of the best shows of the season," he points out. "I would say that 'The Enemy' was about something, it helped Worf's character grow by a foot. When I originally made the suggestion that we let the Romulan die, there was a gasp in the room. Michael Dorn said to me, 'What are you doing to my character?' Of course after he realized what we were doing, and saw the reason for it, he fell in love with the idea. Rick Berman knew instantly it was the right thing to do. Once he was behind me, it was a race to the finish line. And it was absolutely the right thing to do. You knew the audience was waiting for Worf to come around, because they always do in television. But the character wouldn't do that and I think we made a really good decision. At first, though, it was quite a shock and a controversial decision. But you end up talking about survival and survival among enemies. I think it was just a natural character development. The character called for it."

Of his involvement in the episode, Michael Dorn explains, "I called the producers and said I didn't agree. I thought [giving blood] was the honorable thing to do. I thought people would look at

Andreas Katsulas, seen here in Someone to Watch Over Me, *portrayed the Romulan Commander Tomalak on several episodes.*

him [Worf] as a murderer. The producers felt that Worf was getting to be too human...just a guy with a big head. When the opportunity came for them to show that Worf was not human, that he is not bound by the same morals as we are, they felt it was a wonderful opportunity."

Now Dorn realizes they were right. "They had a great reason for doing it and that it made sense. I got into it. I think it's my favorite episode, even though I only have three scenes. It really showed three different sides of Worf. It was an exceptional show for that."

Episode #56:
"The Price"
Original Airdate: 11/11/89
Written by Hannah Louise Shearer
Directed by Robert Scheerer
Guest Starring: Matt McCoy (Devinoni Ral), Elizabeth Hoffman (Premier Bhavani), Castulo Guerra (Mendoza), Scott Thomson (DaiMon Goss), Kevin Peter Hall (Leyor), Dan Shor (Dr. Arridor), Colm Meaney (Chief O'Brien)

The Federation negotiates with the planet Crystalia for control of what is believed to be the first stable wormhole, when the Ferengi led by DaiMon Goss (Scott Thomson) intervene in the negotiations hoping to place their own bid. One of the negotiators, Deviononi Ral (Matt McCoy) becomes intimately involved with Troi, who learns he is half-Betazoid, giving him a special edge during the negotiating sessions against Riker.

••••

The pre-airing hype regarding a scene in which Troi beds alien ambassador Rol caused quite a stir among fans.

"It was never meant to be outrageous television," says Michael Piller. "We got quite a few letters from outraged people before it aired, but nobody wrote after it aired. I listen very carefully to those complaints."

Of the episode Piller adds, "One of the best scripts we had. I think if you listen to that show and don't watch it, you can really have fun with it. I really thought it was a disappointing episode. It just didn't make it and was not a great show. As far as servicing the character of Troi, it was quite a wonderful vehicle and she was marvelous."

Notes director Robert Scheerer, "The thing I remember most about that episode is working so closely with Marina, because I hadn't really worked with her that extensively. There was a very human quality to her and the show. Another show I thought she was wonderful in, which I didn't see, was 'The Loss.' Damn, she was wonderful in that. I was thunderstruck by that because it's not an easy thing to play."

Episode #57:
"The Vengeance Factor"
Original Airdate: 11/18/89
Written by Sam Rolfe
Directed by Timothy Bond
Guest Starring: Lisa Wilcox (Yuta), Joey Aresco (Brull), Nancy Parsons (Sovereign Marouk), Stephen Lee (Chorgon), Marc Lawrence (Volnath), Elkanah J. Burns (Temarek)

Picard mediates a dispute between a pirate band and the Sovereign (Nancy Parsons), the leader of their homeworld, in order to allow the renegades to return under a grant of amnesty. The murder of one of the band's clansman is perpetrated by Yuta (Lisa Wilcox of *Nightmare on Elm Street 4* and *5*), Riker's latest dalliance and the Sovereign's servant, who's seeking vengeance for the destruction of her clan.

••••

Timothy Bond, a veteran *TNG* director, helmed the installment. "If we had rehearsal it would be great, but we don't," says Jonathan Frakes about acting

in the show. "Everyone has come to realize that they're only so many ways to shoot the bridge, so let's get on with it. We all know the room and where we're going to go, and if you try to get too artsy-fartsy, you get yourself into what they affectionately refer to as the toilet."

The episode had a decidedly dark tone, particularly the teaser in which Riker leads an investigating Away Team that comes across numerous corpses.

"It was fun to do," laughs Timothy Bond. "The dialogue was of little consequence, and I think some of it was even cut. There's a tendency in television to say, 'I'm opening the door now.' Well, just open the door. It's not a radio show. So we were able to make that quite visual and the art department came up with this bizarre painted backdrop. They lit it with green light and there was smoke. That show also featured the best set I've ever had. We only had it up for two days and it was such a shame to tear it down."

The conclusion of the episode was somewhat controversial for two reasons: first, that Riker is forced to kill Yuta and, second, that Captain Picard has no reaction whatsoever to this action.

"They [the producers] *were* worried about the ending and the idea of Riker doing something like that," concurs Bond. "Regarding Picard, I'm afraid there is a reason for his lack of reaction: opticals. He couldn't move for that one period where she gets vaporized. In retrospect, maybe it was kind of a mistake of mine. I just had this idea that it would be really neat that when she's vaporized, Picard was there, in the shot. That meant putting several layers of elements into the shot and in order for it to work properly, Picard had to stay still. Not a good reason. When I saw it, I actually regretted the decision, but by then the ship had sailed. Believe me, Patrick noticed too. He even asked, 'I'm just supposed to sit here and do nothing?' The other problem is what *could* he do? We knew Riker had to kill the girl and we didn't want to get Picard shot by the phaser. In retrospect, what I should have done is what you usually do—don't have him in the shot. If he's not, then the audience doesn't think, 'Why doesn't Picard react?' We had a lot of rationales at the time, but we were wrong. Overall, though, I'm real

Nancy Parsons, co-manager of Motel Hell, was Marouk in "The Vengence Factor."

proud of the episode."
Episode #58:
"The Defector"
Original Airdate: 12/30/89
Written by Ronald D. Moore
Directed by Robert Scheerer
Guest Starring: James Stoyan (Admiral Jarok/Setal), Andreas Katsulas (Commander Tomalak), John Hancock (Admiral Haden), S.A. Templeton (John Bates)

Romulan Commander Tomalok (Andreas Katsulas), returns while chasing a Romulan defector. Sub-Commander Setal (James Stoyan) warns the Federation of a Romulan incursion in the Neutral Zone which will set the stage for a massive invasion. Picard, wary of the logistics clerk's story, discovers the officer is actually the legendary Admiral Jarok. As they charge into the Neutral Zone, Picard discovers no outpost and a fleet of Romulan ships waiting to take the Enterprise back to their homeworld for study.

••••

Ron Moore's second effort for the series was one he pitched to the producers after they bought his spec script, "The Bonding." On its strength, he was offered a staff job as story editor.

"They really liked the idea of having this sort of Cuban Missile Crisis at the Neutral Zone," says Moore. "I wrote the first draft and was involved in the rewrite. About two weeks later, after the show was put to bed, they had an opening on the staff. They called me up and said, 'We would like you to come

••••

aboard.' I said, 'Well, I don't know, maybe—I'm getting my shoes polished this week.' Meanwhile, I'd have stepped over my dead grandmother."

"Not an easy script to write," opines Michael Piller, "because the middle of it was very soft. It had a good ending and a good beginning. The first several drafts of that show had a lot of talking in the middle, questioning whether or not we trusted him. It was nice to come off of 'The Enemy' with a little bit of an echo. We don't do that a lot and I like when we can. Ultimately it was a combination of circumstances where a nice thing happened. One, we punctuated it with some little techno-babble stuff, detective work, messages from Starfleet and little pacing things that really helped the middle of that show. Second, we didn't know how to open the show. We wanted to open it with another Sherlock Holmes gag which probably would have been rather irrelevant. At the last moment, we got a phone call from the studio saying that we couldn't do Sherlock Holmes anymore because there's a lawsuit from some other show or movie...some other Paramount lawsuit involving the estate of Sherlock Holmes. Paramount didn't want another one, so Sherlock Holmes was out.

"We sat down a day or two before we started shooting to figure out what we were going to do. Someone suggested Shakespeare, so we went to Patrick, who's obviously our scholar, and said, 'What would be a good Shakespearean play that would echo the script?' Actually there was a Shakespearean play called 'The Defector,' but it was too unknown for our purposes. So he came back with *Henry V*, and he picked out the scene and section and we condensed it to use it as an echo. If you watch that episode, there's a scene where Picard and Data are talking about how the crew is holding up, and then Picard says a line or two that echoes the play. Then, in the confrontation with the Romulans, there are suggestions of *Henry V* in Picard's stance, bravery and decisions, and what the argument is about. If you are a musician, as I am, it is a trick that you throw into arrangements to echo other songs and play on a melody that reminds you of something else. I was very proud of that. I also liked

the tension, the decision making, lonely at the top. It almost became Picard's show as a result of adding King Henry to the mix. I was very pleased with it."

Offers Robert Scheerer, "There were a couple of extra scenes in that episode which had to be cut for time. I was sorry about that. There was a second interrogation scene that I just loved that, unfortunately, we couldn't use because of time problems."

An audience-pleasing moment of the episode is where it's believed Picard is outnumbered, when a group of Klingon warships decloak around the Romulans.

"You know, it's very frustrating at times on this show because, obviously, directorially one is on the stages and can only lead up to and away from those effects that make the show what it is. With Rob Legato and Dan Curry you just get the most magnificent effects, but I never see them before hand. I'll offer suggestions of what I think it should look like and Rick [Berman], of course, is deeply involved in that as is Michael Piller. First of all it's wonderful knowing you're going to get something terrific and always what thrills me is that there are always surprises, things I didn't expect were there which just absolutely knock me out. But it is a strange feeling leading up to something you don't know what it's going to be."

Episode #59:
"The Hunted"
Original Airdate: 1/6/90
Written by Robin Bernheim
Directed by Cliff Bole
Guest Starring: Jeff McCarthy (Roga Danar), James Cromwell (Prime Minister Nayrok), Colm Meaney (Chief O'Brien), J. Michael Flynn (Zayner), Andrew Bickell (Wagner)

Genetically altered veterans of a war on Angosia 3 have been consigned to exile on Lunar 7, a prison colony soldier Roga Danar (Jeff McCarthy) flees from before being captured by the Enterprise. Escaping from the brig, he attempts to lead his fellow officers in a coup against the government, which is petitioning to join the Federation. Troi learns that the soldiers which had once fought for Angosia, have now been banished and are pariahs from

their homeworld.

••••

Michael Piller admits to having mixed feelings about the episode. "I thought the story was thin and we filled it out with a good cat and mouse chase," he says. "I thought it played well on screen and was very action-oriented. 'Vengeance Factor,' 'The Hunted' and 'High Ground' were all shows which I developed, and was not really happy with any of them. I felt that they did touch on themes of importance and did ultimately deal nicely with those, and there's quite a bit of controversy about the ending [of 'The Hunted.']

"At first we were going to have a huge shoot out and have everyone wiped out in the end, but that didn't really make anybody a hero. Picard goes down there and we're caught in a stalemate. We've now created the character of this planet's society in such a way that Picard can make the statement at the end, 'This is not our affair. You guys are going to have to solve it. When you're ready, come back to the Federation and we'll reconsider your application.' I thought it worked. There are people on the staff to this day who think it doesn't. I think it's an important theme that you cannot explore enough, but I don't think we really got to the heart of it because the story was one-note, and it could have used a little more texture. Again, if we had a little more time....I give that about a B-. The whole theme of the show was let's look at how society treats its returning veterans. I thought from a conceptual level we handled that well, and we came up with good science fiction to make it interesting. There's some argument that the best soldier ever created bringing the Enterprise to its knees is a little hard to believe, and that might have been the weakness of the show. I enjoyed it, and was not ashamed of the show."

Offers director Cliff Bole, "I liked the story, because the premise was dealing with an issue in space that has happened and is happening in our present time. Originally, Danar was going to come back and there was going to be a big confrontation. That was cut due to budget and time. We simply did not have the time in seven days to do that. I thought the loss of that confrontation took away a little bit, making it slightly anti-climactic."

Episode #60:
"The High Ground"
Original Airdate: 1/27/90
Written by Melinda Snodgrass
Directed by Gabrielle Beaumont
Guest Starring: Kerrie Keane (Alexana Devos), Richard Cox (Kyril Finn), Marc Buckland (Waiter), Fred G. Smith (Policeman), Christopher Pettiet (Boy)

Dr. Crusher is kidnapped by a band of terrorists who are demanding independence for their territory, and believe the Federation has allied themselves with the government. They've created a method for instantaneous teleportation—which is slowly killing them—and transport aboard the Enterprise in hopes of destroying it. Meanwhile, Crusher attempts to save Kyril Finn (Richard Cox) and his fellows from the tissue degeneration which is destroying them.

••••

Says Michael Piller, "Another show that I wasn't particularly happy with. We set out to do a show about terrorists.. What was the statement we made about terrorism in this show? Was it the point where the boy puts down the gun and says, 'Maybe the end of terrorism is when the first child puts down his gun?' It was effective in the context of that show, but is certainly not a statement that provides any great revelation. You must be prepared to say something new about social issues. I would love to do a story about the environment. I would love to do a story about urban gangs, yet the dangers of starting a show with a concept that is socially motivated is that you better damn well find a personal story to tell and something new to say about that issue, otherwise you're not enlightening anybody. You're retreading old ground, and I think that's what we did in 'The High Ground.'"

Adds Melinda Snodgrass, "What I wanted to do was the American Revolution. They wouldn't let me, so we ended up doing Northern Ireland, which I felt made our people look incredibly stupid. I wanted it with Picard as Cornwallis and the Romulans would have been the French, who were in our revolution, trying to break this planet away. Suddenly Picard realized he's one

of the oppressors. Instead, we do 'Breakfast in Belfast,' where our people decide they're going to go off to Northern Ireland. That's what I was told to do."

Brannon Braga, fifth season story editor and an intern at the time of "The High Ground," relates, "Very rarely do we start thinking about an episode in terms of an issue. Let's do a show about AIDS, let's do a show about terrorism. We rarely think in those terms. We usually think in terms of neat science-fiction twists and that's what sends us in the direction of what's this story about and who's in it?"

"When we have started by saying let's do a show about terrorism, you get things like 'High Ground' which is an abomination," says Ron Moore. "It's our one terrorist show. We didn't have anything interesting to say about terrorism except that it's bad and Beverly gets kidnapped—ho hum. They take her down to the caves and we get to have nice, big preachy speeches about terrorism and freedom, fighting and security forces versus society. It's a very unsatisfying episode and the staff wasn't really happy with it. It's just an example of what happens when you start at the wrong place."

Adds Braga, "It's very on the nose, it's very obvious. It wasn't a *Star Trek*. The irony of the show is we can do anything. There's no reason for us to tell a mundane story. On *L.A. Law* you don't have a science-fiction element so you can't tell it any other way. But the frustrating thing about it was we desperately want science-fiction elements. It's hard to come up with those vital science-fiction twists."

Episode #61:
"Deja Q"
Original Airdate: 2/3/90
Written by Richard Danus
Directed by Les Landau
Guest Starring: John de Lancie (Q), Richard Cansino (Dr. Garin), Betty Muramoto (Scientist), Whoopi Goldberg (Guinan)

Q has been stripped of his powers (and his clothing) and deposited aboard the Enterprise for his indiscretions by his disenchanted peers in the Q continuum. Picard promptly places the powerless Q in the brig. Shortly thereafter, the Enterprise is pursued by a race of

aliens seeking revenge against Q for his vicious practical jokes against them, and he's saved by Data. Selflessly sacrificing himself to protect the Enterprise, Q's powers are restored by Q2 (Corbin Bernsen), and a joyous Q celebrates by materializing a Mexican salsa band on the bridge, along with a bevy of beauties and cigars for all.

••••

"I always think of Q as Lokki," says Melinda Snodgrass. "He's chaos. [Producer] Maury Hurley always thought Q was here to teach us a lesson, to guide and instruct us. I can understand that to some extent, but I really see him as a mischief maker. He really just wants to foul Picard's head."

Director Las Landau notes, "Needless to say, John de Lancie is a delight. He took a role, which granted was an exceptional part, and made more of it than was on the page. He made himself a recurring character. He's a dynamic personality and the character of Q is an unbelievably Trekkie, attractive character. The optical effects took a lot of time and effort on everyone's part. He arrives suspended in the air, he snaps his fingers and things happen. In order to make it happen right, aesthetically and creatively, it takes time. Q was always a fascinating character and very popular with the *Star Trek* audience. He kind of melds with Picard in a very unusual way in a battle of wits to see who will ultimately triumph. Although I think it's a standoff in its conclusion each time, Picard seems to always have the slight edge, which is as it should be."

"Wonderful show and a very difficult one to get on its feet," Michael Piller details, "but once it got there, we were very proud of it. Our first take on it was that Q lost his powers, came on board and we developed a whole story about how we were about to come into a war with the Klingons. It turns out that Q didn't really lose his powers after all, he was just playing with us and pulling our strings just so that he could make himself a hero, become an officer and prove his value. It wasn't a bad story, but ultimately we sat down with Gene and Rick Berman, and Gene said, 'If you're going to do a story—Godlike and brought down to Earth—then do it. Do a story

••••

about what it's like to lose everything that you are and have to discover your own humanity.' He kind of threw cold water on us and suggested we do it straight forward and that's what we did. We made it a comedy, we made it fun, but I think it has some extraordinary things to say about humanity."

Episode #62:
"A Matter of Perspective"
Original Airdate: 2/10/90
Written by Ed Zuckerman
Directed by Cliff Bole
Guest Starring: Craig Richard Nelson (Investigator Krag), Gina Hecht (Manua Apgar), Mark Margolis (Dr. Nel Apgar), Juli Donald (Tanya), Colm Meaney (Chief O'Brien)

Riker is accused of murdering an alien scientist, Dr. Apgar (Mark Margolis), and destroying a scientific space station. Picard arbitrates over a holodeck recreation of the events to establish whether or not there are sufficient grounds for his first officer to receive extradition to the planet, where the penalty for his alleged crimes is death.

••••

"Probably the hardest story to break," opines Michael Piller. "It was a technical nightmare for the director. I was very, very happy with the script and I thought the show was disappointing. I guess it didn't translate properly. It was very ambitious, but it got overly convoluted. The casting was off. If you had put Lana Turner in the role of the woman in that show, you would have understood it all—but I don't think it played as it was intended.

"That's about the best murder mystery I've been involved in developing in my career," he continues, "because every detail falls into place, every line comes together to explain how, what, when and where, and it really worked from a mystery standpoint. It's so complicated a mystery. In fact, it's like *The Big Sleep* in space. It's very complicated, yet if you take that script apart, nothing falls out of it. It ought to win an Edgar Allen Poe Award for best mystery of the year. I've been involved in a lot of crime caper shows, but this was a very proud script turned out. I just didn't

think it was great television. "

Cliff Bole admits that, directorially, "A Matter of Perspective" was not easy. "One of the toughest shows I've ever shot from the standpoint of keeping continuity and having to shoot something three different ways."

Episode #63:
"Yesterday's Enterprise"
Original Airdate: 2/17/90
Written by Ira Stephen Behr,
Richard Manning, Hans Beimler and Ronald Moore
Story by Trent Christopher Ganino and Eric A. Stillwell
Directed by David Carson
Guest Starring: Denise Crosby (Tasha Yar), Christopher McDonald (Lieutenant Richard Castillo), Tricia O'Neill (Captain Rachel Garrett), Whoopi Goldberg (Guinan)

During a conflict with the Romulans, the Enterprise NCC-1701-C is propelled forward in time through an anomaly and history is changed. Our crew is unknowingly thrust into an alternate universe in which the Federation is still engaged in a bloody war with the Klingon Empire. Only Guinan suspects something is wrong and urges Picard to return the Enterprise-C back in time where it will open the door for peace with the Klingons, or forever change history and thus doom the Federation against the superior forces of the triumphant Klingon Empire.

••••

Enthuses Michael Piller, "That was a classic episode. I never met Denise Crosby in person, but I am sure an admirer. She did a great job for us. That's just about as neat a show as we could do. It was as entertaining and unique a time travel show as you'll ever see. I don't know that there was a better episode third season. Hell, Picard sends 500 people back to their death on the word of the bartender. Come on, that's hard.

"I was very happy with it and, frankly, I give the credit to the director and the cast and the people who post-produced it," Piller elaborates. "The script was not one of the best scripts we wrote that season. Conceptually it was marvelous, coming out of the heads of some people here. I thought conceptually

it was the most exciting show we did. Because Christmas was coming, we had actor schedule problems, Whoopi was going off to do something after the first of the year, and so on. We had to rush that up in the schedule and gang-bang it out. There are little holes in the episode that we couldn't fix. It was such a complicated and fascinating premise, but it was ultimately the character material that really made everybody proud. It was a wonderfully produced show."

Two points posed to Piller is that the harder-edged Enterprise in the time altered future was much more reminiscent of the original series; and that as Enterprise-C went back through time, the audience should have seen the same time dissolve that took place in the episode's beginning.

"There are a lot of people who like that Enterprise a lot better," he laughs. "The 'blending' from one Enterprise to another was done as an after thought. After the show was cut and everybody looked at it....if you recall, the sequence of events, you're inside the Enterprise, you cut outside to see the ship coming through the hole, and then you see the crew blend into the time-altered Enterprise. Originally, you cut outside, and then match cut to a different Enterprise. Tasha is in place and everyone looks different. When people looked at it, they were saying, 'People are going to think we're cutting inside the other ship.' So we had to come up with an idea—which the guys in post-production did a marvelous job on—that showed the transition on camera, which was never scripted. Sometimes marvelous things happen because of emergency needs; a band-aid to cover up a mistake."

"To this day I do not understand 'Yesterday's Enterprise,'" confesses Jonathan Frakes. "I do not know what the fuck happened in that episode. I'm still trying to understand it—but I liked the look."

Co-writer Ron Moore explains, "I've heard from time to time, I wish you'd do some war stories, but this is the reality of war. It's not a pretty piece. But it was a lot of fun to watch that ship move, and see Picard biting Riker's head off. I wrote a couple of different story outlines on it. Somewhere during the course of that I came up with the idea that the alternate universe would really be nasty and awful and militaristic and that we're losing the war with the Klingons."

Note: The map Picard holds which displayed the Neutral Zone between the Romulan and Federation territories is identical to the map that appeared on the Enterprise viewscreen in classic *Trek*'s "Balance of Terror." This was due to the efforts of graphics wiz and unofficial *Trek* historian Michael Okuda.

Episode #64:
"The Offspring"
Original Airdate: 3/10/90
Written by Rene Escheverria
Directed by Jonathan Frakes
Guest Starring: Hallie Todd (Lal), Nicolas Coster (Admiral Haftel), Judyann Elder (Lt. Ballard), Diane Moser, Hayne Bayle, Maria Leone and James Becker (Ten Forward Crew)

Jonathan Frakes' first directorial effort in which Data creates a daughter for himself (Lal, played by Hallie Todd). Although hoping to tutor his new and improved cyborg in humanity, Data's plans are upset when Starfleet Admiral Haftel (Nicolas Coster) announces his plans to take Lal back with him for study. Picard is swayed to defend Data, who is reluctant to give his "daughter" up to her Federation foster parents.

••••

"The perfect show to follow 'Yesterday's Enterprise,' and a totally different kind of episode," points out Michael Piller. "The script and performances were great, and it was marvelously directed by Jonathan. My taste, it was as good a show as we had all year. When you have good character stuff, you've got my support. It's a very challenging concept. It was a concept I wanted to do, so we sat down with Gene and he came up with a number of suggestions and said this is what would make it fit into the *Star Trek* bible. Rick Berman added some crucial pieces to the puzzle. We are very determined to protect the uniqueness of Data as a character, but at the same time, it seemed to make perfect sense that one of the human traits that Data would have observed and perhaps covet, is procreation and parenting. He would also know that his value to

Starfleet was so great that if he were ever in an accident, he's too valuable to end with himself."

Melinda Snodgrass differs with the assessment. "I felt it was fairly obvious and tired and stupid and I didn't want to do it. I did a page one rewrite and Michael [Piller] did another rewrite. It had a lot to do with 'The Measure of a Man,' which I don't think we needed to do again so soon. It was a good show for Jonathan to start with. It was a nice bottle show and he didn't have to cope with alien cultures."

"I went to [Rick] Berman and said I'd like to do a show," recalls actor turned director Jonathan Frakes. "He said I'd have to go to school, and so I spent about 300 hours in the editing room and on the dubbing stage learning about that side of it. Editing was the side of things I felt weakest in. I naturally looked over the shoulders of all our regular directors and took some seminars, read textbooks and finally I didn't go away. Rick was kind enough to give me 'The Offspring' and I was thrilled, because I got a Data show and those always work. It was wonderfully satisfying and I'm very happy with that episode."

Chip Chalmers, who would subsequently become a director in his own right, served as assistant director of "Offspring."

"One of the more pleasant memories for me was 'The Offspring,' which was Jonathan Frakes' first directing job," reflects Chalmers. "Working with Jonathan, who is one of the funniest and kindest people that I know, was just a pleasure. To watch his eyes light up when he realized he could make his own vision happen was a real joy. It was really magical to watch him....play.

Episode #65:
"Sins of the Father"
Original Airdate: 3/17/90
Written by Ronald D. Moore and W. Reed Moran
Based on the Teleplay by Drew Deighan
Directed by Les Landau
Guest Starring: Tony Todd (Commander Kurn), Charles Cooper (K'mpec), Patrick Massett (Duras), Thelma Lee (Kahlest), Teddy Davis (Transporter Technician)

Worf returns to the Klingon

homeworld to defend his late father against charges of treason. He is prompted to do so by his younger brother, Kurn (Tony Todd), who is still alive and has transferred aboard the Enterprise as part of the Federation exchange program. Victimized by political infighting, Worf accepts excommunication from Klingon society to protect the council, which is rife with deceit. Council member Duras (Patrick Massett), plots to keep the truth of *his* father's dishonor and Worf's father's framing, in hopes of ascending to one day head the council.

••••

Michael Piller admits, "It was complicated, because we were combining characters and scripts, trying to put together a Worf story we liked. I think we came out of it fairly well, with a good show."

"I thought Tony Todd did a wonderful job as Worf's brother," says writer Ron Moore. "I was kind of worried, because there's always that hesitation when you're bringing in other family members no one else has ever seen. Half the audience is ready to throw things at the screen, and you're thinking, 'This better work.' I was there when he stepped on the stage and made it his own. I was in love with 'Sins of the Father' and I fought for it when there was some question about which way we were going to go with it. I really like the fact Worf took it on the chin that episode. It said he was willing to stand up and do the right thing for his people, even if they weren't going to do the right thing by him. Patrick and I were at the Saturn Awards together, and he made a really good suggestion. He felt that when Worf is asking Picard to be his chadich, Picard originally says a single Klingon word, but Patrick thought it would be nice if Picard knew the whole line of ritual. At that time there wasn't a formal ritual, and there wasn't one for Kurn either, so I went back and wrote a line for him to say in Klingon and I tied it into Picard."

Explains Michael Dorn, "There was a lot more involved in it than the writers realized. Things that have to do with Klingon loyalty and honor. They didn't give it its due. You look at Worf in a different light, and I've played him in a different light since that episode. This is now something they have come up with. I'm doing this on my own. Hey, it's their fault. They wrote it. So now, I'm going to carry on with it."

Director Les Landau enthuses, "Here was an opportunity to explore the Klingon world in depth from beginning to end. Meaning that Ron Moore came up with a wonderful story which Richard James, the art director, and Jim Meese, the set decorator, had to visualize in terms of set design and set decoration. Additionally, to which Marvin Rush, the cameraman, had to conceptually find a visual representation of what the Klingon world was all about. I think all three of those gentlemen accomplished that task totally. In fact, Richard and Jim went on to win Emmy Awards for that episode, which I'm very proud of. Marvin's work speaks for itself. It was visually one of the most dynamic episodes ever done. It looks like a feature film. There were long detailed conversations about how, conceptually, we should deal with them. Ultimately, Rick Berman gave the final approval for each and every one of the ideas and details, and we showed a world that was heretofore never seen before, and which the audience craves to see more of. I was never one of the original *Star Trek* fans, however. My attitude was, is and always will be to never see what has come before, but go where none have gone before and visualize what is in my thinking and mind as to what the visuals should be, which is dictated by the storyline. We must always come back to the words and what the story is, because without it, we have nothing to tell. After all, film and episodic television is nothing if not telling a story."

Episode #66:
"Allegiance"
Original Airdate: 3/24/90
Written by Hans Beimler and
Richard Manning
Directed by Winrich Kolbe
Guest Starring: Stephen Markle (Tholl), Reiner Schone (Esoqq), Joycelyn O'Brien (Haro), Jeff and Jerry Rector (Aliens)

Picard is abducted by aliens as part of a futuristic lab experiment, and replaced by a duplicate who acts in an atypical manner: seducing Dr. Crusher and singing drinking songs with the crew in Ten Forward. Meanwhile, Picard along with three other captured aliens attempt to escape from their containment, discovering that one of them is actually the lab-keeper.

••••

Michael Piller admits that the series needed a show to balance the budget of "Yesterday's Enterprise."

"'The Offspring' helped us a lot and so did 'Allegiance,'" he says. "I'm a great fan of intimate shows, and it was a simple show from a production point of view, because you needed one set. With trying to come up with good, solid stuff for Picard....we'd done a good job treating Picard as a captain, but he hadn't gotten to do the holodeck fantasies he likes to do, and he hadn't been able to have fun. We wanted to come up with some real fun for both Patrick the actor and Jean Luc the character, so we came up with this idea. It might have been two ideas put into one. One was Picard gets stuck in a no-exit situation, and a false Picard takes his place on the Enterprise. I loved the stuff on the Enterprise, wonderful character stuff and Patrick was wonderful. I thought it was a good, solid show and immediately following that was 'Captain's Holiday,' which, again, was borne out of the fact that we wanted to give the captain some characterization. Delightful episode."

"Picard does some things that had only been in the real Picard's mind," says Ron Moore. "Watching him sing in Ten Forward gave everyone a kick. And the scene with Beverly in his cabin was kind of fun. I like the fact we've taken him apart more and really are seeing what makes this guy tick."

This episode represents director Winrich Kolbe's favorite of the numerous he's directed. "I like it because we did something stylistically interesting in the lit room where the four people were incarcerated. It was Patrick's show and I always know when it's going to be Patrick's show it's going to be a good one because he's so damn good in everything that he does. If I had to choose a particular *Star Trek*, that would likely be it. I look the look of it and what Marvin Rush was able to do, and Richard James the set designer. What you have to consider in directing any kind of entertainment concept is time and money. We were so far behind after the first two days that basically the whole hierarchy of Paramount was camping out on my set. Then we went into the new set, the octagonal chamber and suddenly we were taking off. We came in under budget and under time. It was a set that was terrific to shoot in and I could put the camera anywhere I wanted to. I think the only thing I would change right now is I would get a steadicam in there so that we could have even more mobility than we had in that show. I really liked the episode."

Episode #67:
"Captain's Holiday"
Original Airdate: 3/31/90
Written by Stephen Behr
Directed by Chip Chalmers
Guest Starring: Jennifer Hetrick (Vash), Max Grodenchik (Sovak), Karen Landry (Ajur), Michael Champion (Boratis), Deirdre Imershein (Joval)

Picard is conned in to taking a vacation on Rycea, the Club Med of the cosmos, where the captain becomes an unwitting pawn of the unscrupulous Vash (Jennifer Hetrick). She is seeking the legendary tax-u-tat treasure and being trailed by former ally, Ferengi Sovak (Max Grodenchik), who hopes to retrieve it as well. Also searching for the powerful treasure are two Vorgon time travelers from the 27th Century, Ajor (Karen Landry) and Boratis (Michael Champion).

••••

Given the plot of "Captain's Holiday," it would appear that the experience of "Yesterday's Enterprise" uncorked the show's seeming fear of doing time travel stories.

"Time travel must be handled with delicacy," says Michael Piller. "I think it must be handled with a great deal of understanding, because there are so many problems. Rick Berman feels very strongly about that as well. The fascinating thing about 'Captain's Holiday' is that that really was the turning point in the script development. Ron Moore made a suggestion. Originally it was a *Maltese Falcon* kind of story where an old, rare thing had been lost and a bunch of people are looking for it on this island. The first draft of that had nothing to do with it. It was originally a good script, but it could have been *Magnum*. Ron was in

Corbin Bernsen (who had a bit part in "Deja Q") and Jennifer Hetrick (Vash in "Captain's Holiday") were married in L.A. Law.

here with the staff and said, 'Instead of it being from the past, couldn't it be from the future?' And I said, 'Which also means that the guys who are chasing it are from the future,' and that started putting a whole new spin on it. We actually came up with an extra tag that we cut out of the show. We never start a show off of the Enterprise, but we broke the format here. The guy shows up from the present and says, 'Is Jean Luc Picard here yet?' And they say, 'No, but he will be...' At the end of the show, we see these guys come back from the future again to replay the whole drama. We thought it was a little confusing and we cut it. It was sort of a *Twilight Zone* ending, and it didn't quite work."

"I really don't watch much television at all," says Jennifer Hetrick, who portrayed Vash in "Captain's Holiday" and returned in fourth season's "Q-Pid". "I had watched the original *Star Trek* when I was a kid on and off. I was never a Trekkie and was not really familiar with his show, but have since taken to it. I thought it was quite funny. It seemed like a *Romancing the Stone/Raiders of the Lost Ark*-type story. I did use that as an example, but not specifically for my character. I just used my own imagination and what I know of myself and found her very adventurous and conniv-

ing to a degree, but also vulnerable and committed. I loved the Ferengi, Sovak. I was spared the make-up fortunately. When I saw what everyone else had to go through, I was thrilled. Thank God, I was human."

"Captain's Holiday" represented Chip Chalmers directorial debut, a rare case of an assistant director taking control of an episode.

"'Captain's Holiday' is one of my favorites because it was the first," he enthuses. "This episode was also terrific because Patrick is such a wonderful actor. The other thing for me is that I got a wonderful actress, Jennifer Hetrick, and we had such a good time working on the show. What stands out for me is that I got very, very sick for a couple of days and during those two days we were shooting 'on' Rycea, actually stage 16, I was running a 102 degree temperature. These wonderful people put up a cot with lots of padding and a pillow right behind Rycea. We'd come out, rehearse, I'd muster up as much energy as I could while they were lighting, I would go lay down on my cot and pass out for 15 or 20 minutes while they set up. I'd go out, say action, shoot and we made it through those two days with everybody rallying around. I can look back at that show and smile for a lot of reasons, but certainly the happiest result is that we proved Patrick Stewart is extremely funny."

Episode #68:
"Tin Man"
Original Airdate: 4/29/90
Written by Dennis Putnam Bailey
and David Bischoff
Directed by Robert Scheerer
Guest Starring: Harry Groener (Tam Elbrun), Michael Cavanaugh (Captain DeSoto), Peter Vogt (Romulan Commander)
A telepathic Betazoid, narcissistic Tam Elbrun (Harry Groener), is assigned to the Enterprise to communicate with a new life form, a living space vessel dubbed "Tin Man." Complications arise with the intervention of two Romulan warships intent on keeping the life form from falling into Federation hands.

••••

"I was disappointed with 'Tin Man'," admits director Robert Scheerer. "It was an interesting show, but I don't

think that I pulled off the sense sufficiently of the living ship. God knows I tried. We struggled and struggled with it, but we ended up a little bit insufficiently fulfilled—I thought. An interesting show, but I don't think I did my best work in that show."

"I had gone to the sets a year before and Eric Stilwell told us 'Bottle shows, all they want is bottle shows,'" recalls uncredited co-writer Lisa Wilke. "'Don't go to another planet, make it as cheap as possible and maybe they'll buy it.'"

Dennis Putnam Bailey, who collaborated with his partner David Bischoff on the teleplay, says, "I wanted to demonstrate that we could turn in work they could use. The upshot of this was that they had reached a point third season where they really needed an extra show. Michael Piller and the rest of the staff were pulling stories out of nowhere and making them better than had been seen first and second year. Piller and the people he handpicked turned the show entirely around and they were up against the wall every week. They wrote 'Yesterday's Enterprise' in three days with five writers and it came out wonderfully.

"There came a point," he continues, "where we were told they wanted a script that was ready to shoot, so they could spend more time working on the scripts they thought had a lot of potential and needed rewriting. They had no expectations they could find a script out of nowhere. But Melinda Snodgrass read our script and brought it to Michael Piller and said, 'I think we can use it with very little rewriting.' Piller read it and decided they could use it. He passed it on to Rick Berman and, at this point, we wee told we were on Rick Berman's desk. It took about a week and I was running into walls. All I could think about was will they buy it? We got the call on a Monday night that they had bought the show and that they were going to start shooting it a week later. When we were doing 'First Contact' we went through the more normal process of developing story in script. It's a lot more stressful way to work than sitting in Maryland and mailing exactly the story you want to see and having them send you a check and say we'll film it next week."

••••

Some have criticized the story as bearing a striking resemblance to 1979's *Star Trek: The Motion Picture*, but as Bailey points out, "Tin Man" is based on a story written by him and David Bischoff in 1975.

"In 1975 Dave and I wrote and sold to *Amazing Science Fiction Stories*," the writer says. "It was a short story called the 'Tin Woodman' and we were nominated for a Nebula. It was a short story and the thrust was a deep space, interstellar exploring ship encounters a living organism space craft orbiting a star with which they cannot communicate. One of the characters in this story is an empathic woman who is a part of the bridge crew of this spacecraft and her job is to monitor the emotional states of the other crew members. They consider her useless for first contact because her abilities are so limited. They fall back to earth have this teenage telepath who can't shut off listening to other people's minds pulled out of a psycho-ward basically and put in a missile and sent out to them. He joins with the creature and goes off. We wrote this in '75 and when we wee developing stories for *The Next Generation*, I said to Dave we have a story that would fit into the series really well. We wrote it 20 years before with no intention of ever doing anything else with it."

Episode #69:
"Hollow Pursuits"
Original Airdate: 5/5/90
Written by Sally Caves
Directed by Cliff Bole
Guest Starring: Dwight Schultz (Lt. Barclay), Whoopi Goldberg (Guinan), Charley Lang (Duffy)

Barclay (Dwight Schultz), an introverted crewmember—introspective, shy and incompetent—retreats to the holodeck to spend his life in a fantasy world he creates for himself. This despite LaForge's persistent attempts to shape him into a superior officer. When Barclay misses an important staff meeting, Geordi invades his holodeck environs and discovers a recreation of *The Three Musketeers*, in which the characters are based on the command crew, including Troi as the goddess of empathy and Riker as a fearful knave.

••••

Laughs Jonathan Frakes, "That was a riot, and the goddess of empathy...."

Michael Piller agrees although he discounts the widely perceived view that the show was a jab at self-absorbed *Trek* fans who are so obsessed with the show that they are oblivious to reality.

"It was a wonderful hour of television," he says. "Splendid, original, fresh ideas. You can't get better than that. It really was not intended directly at *Star Trek* fans. It was certainly about fantasy life versus reality. More than any other character in the three years I have been at *Star Trek*, that character of Barclay was more like me than anybody else. My wife watched that show and saw what was going on, and said that's [me] because I'm constantly in my fantasy world. Fortunately, I make a living at it. I have an extraordinary fantasy life and use my imagination all the time. It's real life that I have the problems with. I was delightfully happy with the episode. That's the one I would like to have in my biography when they write it.

"Dwight Schultz had been a *Star Trek* fan for a long time," continues Piller. "He told Rick Berman, 'If you ever get something for me, I'd love to do the show.' Dwight had just done a feature with Paul Newman and was very hot, and we didn't think we'd get him. It was a marvelous character piece. It's a Geordi show, but Dwight is at the center of it. This was a script submitted by a speculative writer."

Director Cliff Bole also differs with the purported fan-inspired storyline "I didn't feel that, and I would have heard if it was intended. I certainly didn't approach it that way. Dwight Schultz was excellent. He really comes to work prepared and has a direction. He did a great job. The fantasy part of it was fun too. Technically, I had fun on that show. I also enjoyed the illusion within an illusion, like the Three Musketeers. I think the *Star Trek* fans respond to that more than they do to anything else. They like those little period fantasies."

Episode #70:
"The Most Toys"
Original Airdate: 5/12/90
Written by Shari Goodhartz

The A-Team's **Dwight Schultz** *and Mr. T prior to Schultz's occasional appearance on* **Next Generation** *as Barclay.*

Directed by Timothy Bond
Guest Starring: Saul Rubinek (Kivas Fajo), Jane Daly (Varria), Nehemiah Persoff (Toff)

Data is abducted by alien Saul Rubinek, who collects rare and valuable items and intends to turn Data into a museum piece, while the Enterprise crew is deceived into believing he has perished in a shuttlecraft explosion. Attempting to escape and warn the Enterprise, Data commandeers a shuttlecraft and, brandishing a phaser, realizes that sometimes it is indeed necessary to kill.

••••

Among the many mementos of Rubinek's collection were a Mickey Mantle baseball card and an otherworldly critter.

"The creature was a hand puppet that Michael Westmore created," reveals producer David Livingston. "It was this little creature that Saul Rubinek went up to and said 'bidi-bidi-bidi.' That was his call to the creature and that became a running gag. People on the set still say, 'bidi-bidi-bidi.'"

"[The late] David Rappaport was supposed to play a very key role," reflects Michael Piller, "and he attempted suicide during production. We had to recast and reshoot, and were lucky to get a good actor. I'm very pleased with the way the script came out. It was a rather sick character he's playing, but fascinating."

Reflects director Timothy Bond, "When I arrived, David [Rappaport] and I started talking about putting the show together and he seemed in good spirits. We did a couple of days shooting that went quite well and then, over the weekend, he tried to kill himself. Nobody quite knows why. He had been doing a wonderful job. Then on Sunday night at midnight I got a call from my assistant director who said, 'Our guest star is in intensive care and we don't know why. So we have to shoot around him tomorrow.' By the time I went in the next morning, there was a story going around that they had found him in his car with a tube running in from the exhaust. Obviously I had to replace him. The guy who ultimately played the part, Saul Rubinek, is somebody I went to school with. It just happened that he was passing through town as was just about to start *Bonfires of the Vanities*, the ill-fated film, and he's a Trekkie. He called me and asked if I could get him in to see the sets. I said I would try and would call him on Monday. So I called him and said, 'How much do you want to see these sets?' He never goes guest shots on television, but I persuaded him to do it.

"Recasting changed the character," he adds, "because David Rappaport was quite small. The requirement, dramatically, is that people had to be afraid of him. That was very trick for someone of David's size to pull off, and we had to do it through a different approach in the photography and the sense that he could always get a weapon and blow people away. David underplayed it, but I always had guys in the background who were pretty beefy. As a matter of fact, when I first started working on the episode, I had this idea—which I still think is brilliant, but they wouldn't let me do it—to build his spaceship to his scale, so the ceiling would be about four feet from the floor. When anybody got in, they would have to bend over. It would have made it a nightmare shoot, but I thought it would have been a powerful visual. When we lost David, thank God we didn't have the small sets.

"What I loved about the show was the hung jury at the end. Would

Data have killed him? Did Data try to kill him? And the final push in on Data when he gets to tell the guy that they've confiscated all his belongings. The guy says, 'You're enjoying this,' and Data says, 'No.' It was fun with Brent Spiner because he's such a good actor. He knows to show just enough for the audience to ask, 'Is he enjoying this?' It was fun to get that sort of feeling."

Episode #71:
"Sarek"
Original Airdate: 5/19/90
Written by Peter Beagle
Story by Marc Cushman and Jake Jacobs
Directed by Les Landau
Guest Starring: Mark Lenard (Sarek), Joanna Miles (Perrin), William Denis (Ki Mendrossen), Rocco Sisto (Sakkath)

An aged Sarek (Mark Lenard) is escorted aboard the Enterprise to a diplomatic conference, where it is discovered that his mind is gradually deteriorating with lapses into senility and illogic. Only his assistant, played by Rocco Sisto, can keep his emotions in check. When the tirade of emotions proves too much, Picard volunteers to mind-meld with Sarek to give him the time to successfully complete negotiations.

••••

"I think in some ways, it's even better than 'Journey to Babel,'" says writer Ron Moore. "Mark Lenard has a chance to do some solid acting. It's a character-driven show and that's different for us."

Opines Michael Piller, "The key to the whole season is in personal stakes and personal drama. The Sarek story touches a lot of people. The generation of this episode came from an idea that had been submitted to this show from outside. It was not an idea about Sarek, however. It was an idea about an ambassador who begins to have mental problems as he is being taken up on some mission. As we started talking about it in house on staff, we said what would really be interesting is if you took a very powerful member of either Starfleet Command or the Federation, and have them going through a time of their lives, like so many of our parents, where they're beginning to have problems with aging. From that point, it was two or three steps of some-

body saying, 'How can we turn it into a science fiction show?' Somebody said, 'If it were a Vulcan, you could have some real telepathic impact from some kind of disease,' and from that point it was really short-stepped to, 'What about Sarek?' Sarek is an extraordinarily honorable character who we felt obliged to protect and deal with in a very respectful manner. At the same time, this becomes an extraordinarily personal story. A real stunning show."

Notes director Les Landau, "There are some great moments in that show. When we first see Sarek listening to the concert and reacting to Data's beautiful playing of the violin and we, finally, see the tear fall from his eye....it reaches such a point within him that he can no longer take it and must leave the environs of the Enterprise theatre, which surprises the captain and Troi especially. There was just something about the way Mark Lenard played this moment and reacted that just made [it] extra special. The other moments that particularly come to mind in that episode is the mind meld between Picard and Sarek. Trying to come up with a way to conceptualize and shoot that became a frustrating point. I think, ultimately, when the two actors got to the set and showed me what they wanted to do, it just melded together and became a wonderful moment within the show. You always come to the set with a prepared framework for a particular scene, but you use that only as a schematic. When actors get to a set, all your planning can go out the window, and such was the case when Sarek finally says to Picard, 'Illogical, illogical,' to shed some kind of emotion. The dynamics between Picard and Sarek reach a level that I think is classic in Star Trek history. I think the most outstanding moment is when we finally see Picard sitting with Beverly, where he is the mind of Sarek thinking about his life that has come before, his former wife and the one and only reference to his son, Spock. If you watch what Patrick did in that scene, it is truly spectacular. I have had many great experiences on the show, but certainly that was one of the best. Patrick is so capable on so many different levels that one just let's him go. There is some discussion prior and after, but his ability is so right on, that one is reluctant to make any adjustment."

Episode #72:
"Menage A Trois"
Original Airdate: 5/19/90
Written by Fred Bronson and
Susan Sackett
Directed by Robert Legato
Guest Starring: Majel Barrett (Lwaxana Troi), Frank Corsentino (DaiMon Tog), Rudolph Willrich (Reittan Grax), Ethan Phillips (Dr. Farek), Peter Slutsker (Nibor), Carel Struycken (Mr. Homn)

Riker, Troi and her mother, Lwaxana, are kidnapped by a lovestruck Ferengi who not only wants the elder Troi for her body, but her brain—for its unique telepathic powers. Pursued by the Enterprise, the Ferengi captain is willing to release Troi and Riker in return for the hand of Misses Troi. Picard woos Lwaxana in an attempt to convince DaiMon Tog (Frank Corsentino), that he is truly in love with her. Meanwhile, Wesley makes a second attempt to gain entry to Starfleet Academy.

••••

"It's a comedy," says co-writer Susan Sackett. "It's not Shakespeare. We pitched a lot of stories and the last one was Mrs. Troi. At first, we were going to do O'Henry's "The Ransom of Red Chief' and it kind of evolved. We developed the story and the premise with Gene, and we would run things past him. His criticism helped make the characters believable. When we came up with something he thought would run, he said, 'Now take it to Michael Piller."

"I did a polish and the boys and I did another," adds Melinda Snodgrass of her re-write with former story editors Richard Manning and Hans Beimler. "I had asked to be let out four weeks after, because I had worked straight through a year and a half without a break and I wanted to come home to New Mexico."

Before the episode aired, a moment which aroused the ire of *Star Trek* fans was the alleged nude scene in which Troi and her mother are disrobed, according to Ferengi custom, while Riker looks on helplessly.

"We weren't nude, of course, at all!" Marina Sirtis, who along with Majel Barrett was garbed in a full body stocking, exclaims. "The Paramount publicity machine goes into action and they try

and find something different to draw the public's attention to that particular episode. It was the same thing with 'The Price.' There was this big ho-ha about Troi being in bed with somebody. For the first time ever in *Star Trek* you see two people in bed together—but when you actually saw it, it was pretty tame. But that's their job, publicity, and that's what they do."

For the record, those who want to see the busty Betazoid in the buff are advised to check out Michael Winner's dreadful version of *The Wicked Lady*, starring Faye Dunnaway, the same director's *Death Wish III* or the equally inane *Blind Date*, starring Kirstie Alley. No body stockings included.

Episode #73:
"Transfigurations"
Original Airdate: 6/19/90
Written by Rene Echevarria
Directed by Tom Benko
Guest Starring: Mark La Mura (John Doe), Charles Dennis (Sunad), Julie Warner (Christy)

An amnesiac alien being, dubbed John Doe (Mark Lamura), is saved from certain death by the Enterprise and Dr. Crusher discovers he is undergoing an evolutionary process. The doctor gains an affectionate attachment for the ailing alien, who helps Geordi find self-confidence with women after a talk about the book of love with Worf proves unsuccessful.

••••

"We wanted to do a show where we get to see 24th Century medicine up close and personal," offers Michael Piller. "Beverly Crusher uses all her skills to save an alien, reconstructing him and putting him back together and sort of falling in love with him. It's a very spiritual kind of show."

Episode #74:
"The Best of Both Worlds, Part I"
Original Airdate: 3/18/89
Written by Michael Piller
Directed by Cliff Bole
Guest Starring: Elizabeth Dennehy (Shelby), George Murdock (Admiral Hanson), Whoopi Goldberg (Guinan)

Ambitious Borg expert Shelby (Elizabeth Dennehy) hopes to become

first officer of the Enterprise, assuming the seat she believes Riker is vacating to take over the captaincy of his own ship. Then they discover the return of the Borg, which have destroyed Federation colony Jure 4. Confronting the Enterprise, the race of cybernetic beings kidnap Picard, and transform him into a spokesman by which they can announce their intentions to conquer the Earth. Leading a daring rescue attempt, Shelby, Data and Worf find that Picard has been turned into Locutus, the king of the Borg. Upon the Away Team's returning to the Enterprise, Riker prepares to unleash the force of the ship's main deflector dish in hopes of destroying the Borg vessel....and Captain Picard.

••••

"The conversations we had during the year about the Borg always seemed to come back to what ultimately did not come to pass," says Michael Piller. "We felt there had not been a worthy successor to the Klingons as adversaries in the new generation, and that was a very serious problem that a show like this has to wrestle with. Third season we spent a great deal of time developing the Romulans, and to a lesser degree the Ferengi, to be a continuing threat and a worthy adversary. But we also had always known that the Borg were there and that there had been a good response from the audience about them. But when the Borg came up, most of the people here felt they were boring because there was no personality you could put your teeth in to. The fact is because they were all one and there was no spokesman or star role, every time we talked about doing a Borg show, we said, 'Why don't we create a 'queen bee' that can be the spokesman for this group, and make her a character instead of just cold steel?'"

That idea did not sit well with Piller, who appreciated the unique quality of the Borg as villains and he was reluctant to conventionalize the alien menace.

"I really liked 'Q Who?', and so I resisted those suggestions," he says. "I never really came around to trying to do it, because to me there was something special and frightening about the Borg that their lack of character brought. For a show that dwells and specializes in character to be challenged and possibly destroyed by a characterless villain seemed, to me, to be a special kind of threat. But when we started talking about the cliffhanger and the Borg, we really did talk about who was going to be the queen bee."

And it was Piller who came up with the notion of a king bee: namely Jean Luc Picard—or Locutus, as he came to be known for a while.

"It all just fell into place," relates Piller. "I said, 'I've got it. Picard will be the queen bee.' There was actually an early draft of the story in which both Data and Picard were taken and combined as a Borg. Someone said why should they do this, and we didn't have a good answer so we dropped that idea."

But the challenge was what would happen on the Enterprise once Picard was abducted. Even with the extra money for space battles and sets, Piller was determined not to have "Best" turn into *Battlestar: Galactica*, but rather maintain the human drama which would serve as a backdrop to the epic drama he was weaving.

"We had no idea it was really a Riker story when we started out," Piller emphasizes. "I came up with the idea of having the Shelby character come onboard to challenge Riker. That seemed to play into the Riker emotions and the conflict over whether to take the other job or not, and that builds into the issue of whether or not he was big enough to fill the center chair. [This] led to the second part, which is the master versus pupil dynamic we set up, some of which was cut out of Part II for length, including a scene between Riker and Troi where Riker expresses is concerns and doubts about Picard. We lost a little character to justify all the action that had to go in there."

Admittedly, Piller has always found it easier to write character than *Trek-Speak*, that mystical science fiction language that *Next Generation* perfected. Writing about Riker's dilemma over whether to accept the captaincy of the USS Melbourne or remain with the Enterprise came easily, particularly in light of his own personal decision that he was wrestling with as to whether to remain on the show or move on himself.

Notes Piller, "Good writing usu-ally draws upon something that means something to the writer. At the end the third season, I had decided not to return to *Star Trek*. Rick and Gene asked me to come back because things were going very well, but I had so many other things I wanted to do. I wanted to write features and create my own shows. I had always told myself that I couldn't commit long term to anything, but as I was writing this script, I found myself in the position of Riker, who was trying to decide whether he was going to leave the ship or not. Much of what happened in Part One was about what was going on in my head."

In one scene taking place in Ten Forward, Riker confides to Troi that he might be afraid of "the big chair."

"Riker is talking to Troi about why he hasn't left," says Piller. "'What am I missing that I used to have? I don't seem to have that drive that I used to have,' and ultimately he comes to the realization that ambition isn't everything. If you're happy and comfortable and find the rewards of the people you work with, then it's something that counts for a great deal. We push ourselves and push ourselves, and sometimes it is good to do that—it has certainly been healthy for me and my career—but there are also times when you sit back and enjoy your successes, and being with the people you love. That was really me speaking through Riker."

Making production of the episode easier was the lesson taught by second season's "Q Who?"

"The set had been a problem," says David Livingston, "because we didn't have the money to build a complete one, and the Borgs had taken a long time. We made a lot of changes on them after they were first put together. The technical part of figuring out how to stick on all this tubing to these guys was a big deal. The R&D, so to speak, was really done on 'Q Who?' in the look of the Borg. When we got to 'Best of Both Worlds,' we knew what the problems were. We knew we had to build a different kind of set and it worked out really well."

After production wrapped, the Borg set lay idle on stage 16, collecting dust while cast and crew enjoyed their summer hiatus and fans pondered the second part of the saga, wondering what would happen after Riker ordered the Enterprise to fire on the Borg ship.

"When we finished the first half, we had no idea what the second half would be," admits Rick Berman. "Michael Piller, with a little help from me, resolved it. It was a lot of fun to be able to stretch the format and do something that was two hours as opposed to one."

Unlike fans who had spent the entire summer wondering how the Enterprise would defeat the Borg and rescue Picard, Michael Piller had waited considerably longer to start thinking about how he was going to write himself out of a seemingly impossible-to-solve cliffhanger.

"After my contract was signed," he laughs. "I never try to think of these things until I have to. I'm a very instinctive writer and the people I don't work with are the people who need all the answers laid out before they start writing. I find the discovery process is what the life of scripts is about. Yes, you need to have the broadstrokes and have a direction so you know where you're going, because television is too expensive and goes too quickly to run all the way down the road only to realize you don't have anything when you get to the end. But I do honestly believe that you let the characters take you and just listen to what the voices are saying when you write a script. Ultimately you'll find wonderful things. The danger, of course, is when you get a block, you can't figure out what the hell they're trying to say."

Guest star Elizabeth Dennehy recalls her experience on "Best of Both Worlds" quite well.

"The first part was the hardest," Elizabeth Dennehy, who portrayed Shelby, explains. "I didn't know anything about the show and I had to look like I knew, because I was in charge. I was a commander and the hardest thing in the world to do was making that dialogue sound like I spoke that way all the time. It was impossible. It's so easy to remember and memorize lines when they make logical sense or when you get blocked and you say when I move over here, I say this. But this was just memorizing timetables. It was just 2x2 is 4. I didn't know what a manipulation effect in the Borg ship's subspace meant. That's not

• • • •

English! It was like learning a foreign language by phonetics. It was just grueling and my first day was the hardest day of all. It was a scene in a big conference room where I'm talking to them about what the Borg do, and they're like tongue twisters. LeVar and Brent have the hardest stuff to learn. I don't know how they do it. You have to sit down and drill yourself, and that was the hardest thing. By the second show, I knew how to do it. On top of all the other things, you need to think about the person you're working with and the character and hitting your mark and don't block him there, and all those kind of things. But, geez, those lines. I yelled at Michael Piller when I first met him. The day he visited the set I had to say, 'Separate the saucer section, assign a skeleton crew,' and I asked him, 'Can you lay off on the alliteration a little, Michael....please.' He laughed. It was hard.

Remembers then assistant director Chip Chalmers, "'Best of Both Worlds' was definitely a get down and dirty show. I also remember the moment when Patrick, dressed in a Borg outfit, first walks up to the viewscreen and says, 'I am Locutus of Borg.' He came on to the set—everybody was wowed with what they had done to Patrick—and we got everyone settled down and did one rehearsal. All he had to do was walk up to the camera. He did so and towered over everyone. It was just so creepy and so spooky, and he said, 'I am Locutus of Borg. Have you considered buying a Pontiac?' And everyone was on the floor. That's the kind of thing that makes it wonderful to work on the show; those people have a wonderful sense of humor."

••••

CHAPTER TWENTY TWO
SEASON FOUR

An Introduction

In *Star Trek*'s fourth season, *Next Generation* faithfully continued to fulfill the mission of the starship Enterprise in boldly going where no man, woman or Andorian has gone before, while improving on the quality of its impressive third season voyages.

"Fourth season was the best season so far," said director Les Landau at the time. "The quality of the writing and the storylines have improved so much over the last four seasons, climaxing in what was delivered to the audience this year."

Michael Piller says, "I don't think there was one clinker in the whole group. Certainly third season we had some. Arguably you could say there were better shows third season, but week after week we maintained a much higher consistency of quality than we had or most shows ever achieve."

"The show has gotten better and better each year," agrees Rick Berman. "We all take it extremely seriously and that's the only way you can do it because its such hard work and the second you start getting sloppy the audience sees it instantly. The fact that we have kept up the quality and integrity of the show and simultaneously the audience has gotten bigger is a wonderful achievement. It's wonderfully good luck as well."

Surprisingly, third season—despite being widely regarded as a success for *Trek*—was also riddled with its share of problems which included an unhappy captain named Jean Luc-Picard.

"Patrick came to me in the middle of the season and said 'I'm bored, you haven't given me anything interesting to do' and he was very unhappy about it," reveals Piller. "He was upset with the way Picard was being treated and he had every right to be, but third season we basically were just trying to

keep our head above water because we didn't have anything in development. If you look back at [the fourth] season I don't think Patrick's had one complaint. He's got to die, been Borgified, all kinds of things."

Ron Moore, who returned to the show for a second year as the show's Executive Script Consultant, agrees that the shows improving quality was a result of more time spent refining the scripts. "We were able to get ahead on scripts fourth season," says Moore. "Last year time was short and we were off and just ahead of the gun. We had a better handle on it going into the fourth season so we never really got to that scary point where you're writing madly on the stage."

Upon reflection, fourth season was at times overthought, Piller offers. "One of the things that I would say about the first half of the season is that we had a few gimmick shows," he says. "They were really good adventures and had good hooks — things that are easily described in *TV Guide*. I think every series needs those and I look at the series as a whole and I would say the entertainment value of the first half of the season was very high, but I don't think there was much substance to it. The second half of the season I think was sterling television and we really reached the best television has to offer."

In prepping the fourth season in the summer of 1990, Berman, who had championed the series through stormy seas during its early shakedown period, did not have a detailed personal agenda for the show's new season.

"We did not really set a fourth season goal," says Berman. "We knew which characters we wanted to focus on and what kind of stories we wanted to do in very broad strokes. We knew Wesley was going to be leaving and, of course, we knew we had to start off with a show that finished up the Borg experience. Our ultimate goal was to do good episodes as opposed to working on a seasonal arc of some sort."

"There was no formal sit down," adds Ron Moore. "We had a lot of discussion with Michael and Rick about different stories. Right off the bat we were talking about the idea that we wanted to followup on 'Sins of the Father', the Borg shows

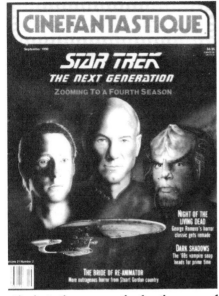

Cinefantastique covers the fourth season of Star Trek: The Next Generation.

and, at some point, do a 'Day In the Life' show. We also talked about doing something more with O'Brien and getting somebody married."

Jeri Taylor, who joined the show as a Supervising Producer after Producer Lee Sheldon left the show over the familiar "creative differences" which had sidelined so many of his predecessors, also had her own ideas regarding what she wanted to see happen on the Enterprise's latest treks.

"I didn't feel I needed to come in and fill any sort of vacuum," says Taylor. "My tastes are very much in synch with Michael Piller's and we really perceive the stories in very much the same way. If there's anything I wanted to do more of, it was developing the characters of Crusher and Troi because I thought they were underused and would like to flesh them out and make them more rounded and interesting people. There is a very small way in which I sometimes remind people about the role of women and sometimes they remind me. I'm not saying that this was a staff of men and I had to come in and show them the way, but maybe it was something a little more in the foreground with me than some of the others."

Taylor's perceptions of the role of females on *Star Trek* are shared by its main female protagonist, Marina Sirtis,

••••

who plays Counselor Deanna Troi.

"I don't think we've addressed feminism," says Sirtis. "The women on this show are very non-threatening and I don't think it's realistic, I don't think it's realistic in the 20th century so it's definitely not realistic in the 24th century. Ever since Denise left the show the two woman that are left are both doctors in the caring professions so we don't see women in power positions. We do see female admirals but I have to say the fans don't really care about our guest stars, they care about the regulars and what they want to see are the regular women having more power."

Sirtis felt that despite the continuing attention her character had received from the show's writers, Troi was still underutilized and underdeveloped. She refers to an original draft of the third season episode 'The Enemy' in which Geordi is stranded on a planet with a hostile Romulan soldier as an example.

"In the original draft which I happened to read which we're not allowed to see so we don't make conversations like this," Sirtis says, "it was Troi and Geordi stranded on the planet and because Geordi was blinded by the electromagnetics preventing his visor from working when we came across the Romulan it was actually Troi who incapacitated him. I felt very excited about this. I finally got to do something interesting and different and, of course, when the final script came not only was I not on the planet, but I had one line at the end of the show — and that was actually cut. That's the kind of thing that happens and I wish it wouldn't."

Michael Piller acknowledges that servicing the lesser-used members of the Trek ensemble was a consideration going into the fourth season.

"One of our goals from the beginning of fourth season was to find stories for each character, Troi among them," says Piller. "I think the last two years have seen her develop a great deal and that does not mean it's sufficient or there shouldn't be more done, but I believe that she used to be a character who looked at the screen and said 'I sense anger out there' and we've given her a chance to actually do therapy, to do some very serious stories and make

some critical contributions to the solutions or problems and really become a counselor in the best sense of the word. I don't really think that she's an underdeveloped character anymore. I feel very good about Troi. She's a really sexy lady who provides an enormous amount of emotional support to our other continuing characters."

Ironically, one of the main objectives fourth season was not only delving into Trek's future, but its past and the 1991-92 season boasted the return of a number of characters from Next Generation's first several years on the air. "We informally decided to go back into our own universe and bring back some of the more interesting characters that were created over the first three years," says Piller. "We created a whole universe here and we have a tendency to go onto the next new discovery, which is great. At the same time I think we have created some very interesting problems and characters which should be revisited. We're not serialized by any means, but we like the idea of doing revisits and that's why you saw so many of the characters from prior seasons make a comeback this year."

Not only were there the persistent references to the Daystrom Institute, the Tholian Wars and the like, but even to such obscurities as the nannites Piller introduced in his script to "Evolution" the previous year, and the ability of the main deflector dish to channel energy as established in "Best Of Both Worlds".

"I like continuity and those references," says Ron Moore. "The danger is you don't want to serialize the show. This isn't LA Law or something where you can carry stories over week to week. A first time viewer who sits down and watches 'Reunion' [Moore's sequel to 'Sins of the Father' in which Duras returns to assume the mantle of leadership of the Klingon Empire] will have to work and follow it pretty closely, but he can do it. I think you can watch that show and not have known what happened in 'Sins' because I don't think it's as important, it's just knowing that Worf has this problem. Of course, it's nice to know the backstory just as it's nice to know about his relationship with K'ehleyr, but all you need to know is something happened."

One of the most talked-about returns of the season was K'ehleyr, played by Suzi Plakson (who also starred as Dr. Solar in second season's "The Schizoid Man"). In "Reunion", Worf finds out he is a father and is reunited with his former love, K'ehyler introduced in second season's "The Emissary".

"All the comments were I loved the show, but why did you have to kill off K'ehlyr?" says Ron Moore, who co-wrote the episode. "That's usually the only comment I get. I loved it and I think it works just fine and if that wasn't there you'd be missing a big part of the story where Worf has to embrace his son in the end and finally getting to go after Duras."

Killing K'ehylr however was not the biggest risk the producers took fourth season, although few incidents on the show have engendered more outraged mail than her slaying. In fact, probably one of the points of contention which the creative team wrestled with early on in the season was the follow-up to Michael Piller's two part Borg epic, "Best Of Booth". Upon the second part's conclusion, a clearly shaken Picard trembles upon reflection on his seizure by the Borg.

"It was my intention to wrap up the two parter with the feeling that although everything is solved," Piller says, "life isn't so smooth and a man does not walk away from something like that and go back to work without having a little extra flashback nightmare. It's just that little uncertainty, the moment of discomfort that I wanted to leave the audience with."

Some of the staff were equally uncomfortable with the notion of Piller wanting to continue the story of Picard's abduction by the Borg into an unplanned third part. "The biggest decision of the hiatus was to extend the storyline of Picard's kidnapping into the third episode," says Piller. "That was very controversial and there were a lot of people who were very hesitant about doing a threesome and going down to earth. People felt it was not Star Trek and I have friends who are fans of the show who called and said I hope you never do that again. But I've got to tell you, for my money, 'Family' was one of the best pieces of film we did fourth season and it was also consistently the lowest rated in both the original and reruns. Maybe my friend was right — if you're not out in space, you're not hitting the audience where they want to be hit."

Director Winrich Kolbe who has been with the show since second season and contributed a number of episodes, weighs the challenges of helming a *Star Trek* adventure.

"There are certain advantages and pitfalls to doing this show," Kolbe says. "One thing I like about *Star Trek* is when I'm prepping an episode I go in at nine in the morning and I leave whenever I'm finished, but I stay basically in the studio and read the script. If I want to take a break I walk over to the stage and lay out my shots and take a walk back and read the script."

This is very different than most one hour dramatic series where Kolbe would spend a large amount of his time in the back of a van scouting locations for a show such as *Hunter*, for which he frequently directed. In the world of *Star Trek* where nearly everything is created within the confines of three soundstages on the lot, the need to drive around looking for locations to shoot is virtually eliminated."

"Television has grown up a lot," says Berman. "The cynical element of television. I think our show is a lot more believable than the old show and that's due in large part to the creator of the old show too because it was Roddenberry who was very vehement when we created *Star Trek: The Next Generation* that it had to be believable. That it would not deal with swords and sorcerers or be melodramatic. The old *Star Trek* had people who wore togas standing under arches and our *Star Trek* is much more contemporary and believable."

"They're still cardboard rocks," laughs producer David Livingston. "The creative people on this show are so talented that they're able to make cardboard rocks that are still all fake into a reality which I'm sometimes just blown away by. After all, as one of our coordinator's says, the Enterprise is just plastic on a stick. The only time you are ever disappointed is when you know that you've had to cut the money and, in our minds, we know that it could have been substantially better."

The budget for the year is deter-

Left-Right: NextGeneraton *writers Brannon Braga, Lolita Fatjo and Ron Moore.*

mined by the cost of the previous year's expenses. Livingston who is involved with the planning of the show's annual pattern budget elaborates.

"We do a cost analysis at the end of each season and find out what we spent and if we spent that amount of money last year then we budget the same amount for the next year," he says. "If Peter only spends $10,000 for opticals on a very simple show the money he saves I get to put into construction and vice versa. We have maintained the amount of money in all of our departments and increased them accordingly due to cost of living. It's not like there's any kind of contest going on about who gets the most money. We have tried to maintain— and have been successful in keeping— the money level at a sufficient level for our departments."

Larry Carroll, Co-Story Editor fourth season, was not too put off by the budget constraints, having had a history working in low-budget features which included the notoriously cheap Charles Band's Empire Pictures, the successor to the Roger Corman legacy of shooting on a shoestring.

"The average episode of *Star Trek* probably costs more than most of Charlie's pictures combined," jokes Carroll. "Michael Piller and Rick Berman really know what they can do and what they

can't do and they're masters at keeping the show within totally practical limits and then maximizing what they can do and squeezing every bit of production value out of it. It's really amazing."

"It's amazing because our budgets are still so tight," adds David Carren. "Whatever they do they really do it with such top quality that we're always struggling to keep it under budget anyway."

"We have what David and I have come to call the 'M' effect named after the Fritz Lang film, *M*, where he did everything off camera with Peter Lorre," says Carroll. "People come in here and pitch these stories with these fantastic things we could never begin to produce, and its simply because this show is so well produced and so well thought out that they don't miss those things and believe they're all part of *Star Trek*. They don't realize how incredibly sophisticated, lean and spare the storytelling is."

And even if the writers have visions of extraordinary space battles and vast planetscapes, those are ideas which are soon dismissed by Livingston upon his initial review of the first draft teleplay. "Scripts can always be cut," says Livingston. "Obviously Michael does not want to prevent the writers from having their imaginations flourish and if they think that they need 1000 people for something, they should write that, but it's going to come down to 10 people pretty quickly.

Generally, the writers have been very responsible in knowing how big the show is and what they can write to."

The bottom line demands of the show's budget often force the show to remain shipbound where standing sets already exist and do not require additional construction, thus resulting in an unofficial ratio of ship to planet shows even higher than the original series.

"We have to do ship shows for cost," Livingston says. "We try and balance that off and save enough money to do the big shows like our season finale, 'Redemption', in which we built the Great Hall again and had a couple of ships and a Klingon home. We try and keep the construction budget on par with the optical budget. They're not the same money but in terms of each year we try and allocate as much money to construction as we possibly can. To me the two most important parts of spending the money on the show are the opticals and construction. It does cost an awful lot of money to build those sets, but the goal is not to have the show take place on the ship all the time."

Often sets will be redressed and used in other episodes to help cut costs. "We use sets over and over again," says Livingston. "We can build a huge set and keep using it. We use sets over and over again and nobody in the audience has a clue, I hope. We are attempting not to have that quality of being a ship show. You would be surprised what we turn around and make happen. There was one set this year that we used three times in a row and I defy anyone to tell me that they were the same set because Richard James did such an amazing turnaround. It shows how well we're able to do it, Marvin Rush lights them differently and they're dressed differently by Jim Meese and they're shot differently. The money we get from Paramount is all up there on the screen."

The desire among the directors to continue to advance their craft and utilize the newest in advanced film technology often taxes the budget as well as the varied resources of *Trek*'s production team often bringing them into conflict with Livingston.

"The directors know coming in that we have a pretty good budget on this show," says Livingston. "They know that they are going to get a lot of goodies and if they're willing to fight for it, great. Let them come in and scream and pound on my desk, I want this set. When I shot my episode, I did. Sometimes though you just have to say no. Richard James will have designed something like the Taj Mahal and I use my red pencil, which is a cliché and a joke, and I start scratching it all up and saying we can't have this and this and out of that Richard sometimes comes up with something that's even more inspired. Budget limitations and schedule force everyone's creativity to go up one notch and they have to really figure out how to make this better. It's easy to spend tens of millions of dollars and, I think, we've seen enough feature films which have been horrible where they've just thrown caution to the wind and not really thought about what they're doing and spent a lot of money. We don't do that. Working on episodic television forces you to be more creative."

"They want a movie and they want it for $1.2 million," says director Kolbe. "Nothing ever goes smooth. They're very few shows where everything seems to come together. 'Identity Crisis' was going fine until we hit Stage 16 and then it was 17 hour days. I know that they were quite worried about us going over and it ended up going over by a half a day."

"He drives you a little crazy because his shots take a long time but he pushes it to the max and takes every second that we'll allow him to get and then probably more," Livingston says of Kolbe. "He's excellent with a camera and has a wonderful eye. He was a pointman in Vietnam and that's good training for a director. God bless him, he's technically a master and does his homework. He knows how to pull off that technical stuff."

Despite the turmoil which has shaken the writing staff over the years, the technical team has remained consistent except for some changes in crew made by Rick Berman at the beginning of third season. It is their devotion to bringing *Next Generation* to life that has been a truly unheralded triumph in reviving *Star Trek* for the small screen. "What we do is fake, it's not real," says Livingston. "Even though we work on a show that presents a positive image for the future and says there's hope for all of us, when you read the headlines that's reality. Gene's the idealist and I guess we'd all aspire to be that way, but unfortunately we're not. That's why a lot of people are on this show and stay here. It's uplifting and we have a good group of people. If this show was *Blade Runner* I don't think the people would last, they'd all be so depressed."

The fourth season in which the new characters have become firmly established in the minds of its viewers have provided a chance to break some of the rules which bound both the makers of the original series and the new. This new series equivalent of *Trek Classic*'s dreadful fare like "Turnabout Intruder" seems to be a thing of the past.

"I think it was a natural process of evolution," says fourth season Story Editor Larry Carroll. "Obviously, you say you're going to make a sequel to *Star Trek* and that's a pretty gutsy thing. You have a tremendous weight and there were a lot of brilliant decisions that were made in terms of the casting, the structure, the definition of the 24th century that when you look at them are amazing. They were not decisions people would normally go for. It was really gutsy getting a bald English actor to play the French captain of the Enterprise. It took a while for the show to come together and for it to really get up and get rolling but it's been a gradual process of evolution to find the stories that work right."

Carroll's writing partner, David Carren agrees. "There's one basic thing that never really changed and part of that evolution was the new *Star Trek* finding its way to being a family," he says. "The old show worked because it basically was a family. It was more like Kirk was a big brother than a father figure and everyone else was kind of his siblings and Spock was the wise Uncle. There were all kinds of interesting dynamics to their relationships. The family didn't really jell per se on this show until deep into the second season or even third where it really came together. I think Ten Forward was an important part of that, it was like that family milieu and all those elements fell into place and you saw there's Picard and he's the father and here's the rest of the members of his family."

"On the original series Roddenberry had that basic kernel of an idea which is that the Enterprise is one big happy family," says Marc Scott Zicree. "Harlan Ellison and he had all those enormous arguments because when Harlan wrote 'City on the Edge of Forever' he had drug dealers and all that on the Enterprise. Roddenberry took it all out and said 'No, these are the cream of the crop' and, in retrospect, you see Roddenberry was right and that's why you've got all these Trekkies dressing up in their uniforms and dreaming of being on the Enterprise. At least, he had the wisdom to realize there should be family spats because that's realistic, but by the time he got to the new show and he was pushing 70 I guess he wanted lukewarm farina and wanted there to be no conflict ever.

The *Star Trek* audience however is unique in the annals of television history and was more tolerant of the early flaws in the series' first two years and has endured through the early disasters and has been richly rewarded for their patience in the show's third and fourth season.

"I think is some respects the show has gotten better," says Marina Sirtis. "In other respects it's stayed the same. I'm going by what the fans say, because it's very hard to be objective when you're in the show. The fans tend to say that the writing and the storylines have gotten much better over the last four years, but I think that's possibly to do with the fact that now we have more or less a fixed writing staff. In the first couple of seasons the turnover was so immense that I don't think they could ever get a hook, they were here for ten minutes and then they were gone which wasn't really long enough to establish any kind of continuity or character development in their scripts. The writing has improved because we have a stable of writers that we've had for a while."

"When it clicks it's one of the best shows on television," says Zicree. "It's one of the few shows I watch and one of the few I want to write for. The episodes that really work are the ones that shake up the structure like Yesterday's Enterprise', which did this wonderful What If scenario. I like those kind of stories, but still the show has improved each year and the ratio of good episodes to bad has gotten better each year. In the first few years it was one good episode in every blue moon and if I saw another episode where superior aliens put them on trial..."

"I think we have to go back to the original idea and concept," says director Les Landau. "Gene created the model for what *Star Trek* is and will continue to be, and he has proven that it will exist on its own forever. I would hate to see the Enterprise lose Captain Picard, Number One, Data, Beverly, Troi or Geordi, but the idea, the universal concept of what *Star Trek* is about will endure because its a timeless story. What Gene created, Rick has followed up on and Michael puts down in words, will endure forever because we're dealing with universal themes about the human condition."

••••

CHAPTER TWENTY THREE
SEASON FOUR

Episode Guide

"The Best of Both Worlds, Part II"

"Family"

"Brothers"

"Suddenly Human"

"Remember Me"

"Legacy"

"The Reunion"

"Future Imperfect"

"Final Mission"

"The Loss"

"Data's Day"

"The Wounded"

"Devil's Due"

"Clues"

"First Contact"

"Galaxy's Child"

"Night Terrors"

"Identity Crisis"

"The Nth Degree"

"Q-Pid"

"The Drumhead"

"Half a Life"

"The Host"

"The Mind's Eye"

"In Theory"

"Redemption, Part I"

Elizabeth Dennehy, who portrayed Commander Shelby in both parts of "The Best of Both Worlds."

Episode #75:
"The Best of Both Worlds, Part II"
Original Airdate: 9/24/90
Written by Michael Piller
Directed by Cliff Bole
Guest Starring: Elizabeth Dennehy (Shelby), George Murdock (Admiral Hanson), Whoopi Goldberg (Guinan)

In the season premiere and conclusion of "The Best of Both Worlds," Riker's plan to use the Enterprise's deflector dish to disable the Borg ship fails. The alien vessel continues on its direct heading towards Earth, destroying a fleet of 48 starships. The Enterprise once again engages the Borg and rescue Picard/Locutus. Once aboard the Enterprise, Data accesses Picard's mind and plants a suggestion in the Borg collective consciousness that it is time for them to regenerate, resulting in the ship being put to sleep and the Borg self-destructing. Dr. Crusher successfully removes Picard's cybernetic implants, although memories of the abduction still haunt him.

••••

"I thought Part One was much better than Part Two," says writer and executive producer Michael Piller. "The reason was that Part Two had to deliver the goods promised by Part One, but they were not as interesting. If you look

at it as a two hour movie, it's really quite effective. As an episode by itself, I don't think Part Two really has a lot of character stuff. It has to have the battles and all the stuff I don't like writing. The one thing I will say about Part II, about which I was extremely pleased, was how I figured out to defeat the Borg, because, frankly, when I was writing it I had no idea. I basically discovered the solution at the same time the characters did. It just occurred to me that their strength was their interdependency, [so] why not make their weakness that same interdependency?"

"I actually had much less to do in the second one than the first," recalls actress Elizabeth Dennehy, who returned to the Paramount soundstages after a three month hiatus to pick up seconds after the first show ended. "I had the show on tape so I watched it quite a few times before we went back. The hard thing was remaining the same weight, because my weight goes up and down and those spacesuits are merciless. I'm sure I put on some weight between the first and the second one. The costumes are so awful, it's very hot on the Paramount lot. It's like you're on a frying pan and you walk around in this one piece outfit. They're dark and everyone walks around with them unzipped between takes. They have stirrups on the feet and big shoulder pads, so it's like you're being compressed and pulled by a rubber band together, and you just want to be put on a rack afterwards. It was so awful, I hated them. It's a rite of initiation that the whole cast will say, 'Elizabeth, say I hate my space suit,' and I said, 'I hate my spacesuit,' and they said, 'Okay, welcome.' It's a rite of passage there. And the fact you can't live like a human being, you can't eat and drink is probably good because it keeps you in shape, but it's a form of slavery which I'm not sure I could deal with knowing I could never go on a binge. I don't know how the girls do it all the time. And the wigs...I looked like Jane from *F-Troop* with that hairdo...and poor Michael Dorn and Brent. I don't know how they do it. I'd go insane. I was so lucky I played a human."

Notes director Cliff Bole, "I enjoyed doing those two shows more than anything I've ever done. They turned out really well. The Borg is like a

Klingon. You can do anything you want with them. They're fun and *real* expensive to play with. The two episodes do go together, and I wouldn't put it past Paramount to do that in the foreign markets. Part II's ending was a little bit of a cop out. We ran out of time. We only shoot 42 minutes. God, the old hours we used to deliver were like 51 or 52 minutes. There's just not a lot of time. You'd like to do a bigger ending. I don't have an answer for it, but it was just a real quick ending for such a big show. Paramount, at the beginning of the year, had pulled back a little bit budget-wise. It was also an attempt to do big and fast. They let us go a little bit on the first one because it was the first time we'd done a cliffhanger."

Episode #76:
"Family"
Original Airdate: 10/1/90
Written by Ronald Moore
Premise by Susanne Lambdin and Bryan Stewart
Directed by Les Landau
Guest Starring: Jeremy Kemp (Robert Picard), Samantha Eggar (Marie Picard), Theodore Bikel (Sergei Rozhenko), Georgia Brown (Helena Rozhenko), Whoopi Goldberg (Guinan), Dennis Creaghan (Louis), David Tristan Birken (Rene Picard), Doug Wert (Jack Crusher)

While the Enterprise is refurbished in spacedock, Worf's adopted human parents, Sergey and Helena (Theodore Bikel and Georgia Brown), visit the ship; Wesley is given a recording made for him by his late father, Jack (Doug Wert), and the captain returns to Earth to visit his jealous brother, Robert (Jeremy Kemp), in France. There, Picard undergoes a painful catharsis to purge the bitter memories of his Borg experience.

••••

"'Family' was really different for the series," agrees Ron Moore. "It was a very atypical show for the *Next Generation* and the original series too. I don't think they could have gotten away with a show like that either. Aside from the location work, conceptually it was very different for us. I think it's the only episode of *Star Trek*—old, new or movies—that never went to the bridge of the Enterprise once in the entire show.

["Family"] began with Michael Piller when he was doing 'Best.' He surfaced the idea early that it would not be quite fair to wrap everything up neat and tidy at the end of Part II—that we had made such a point of saying this is such a really horrendous thing that had happened to Captain Picard, that it was psychologically and physically raping the man and it wasn't fair to go on like nothing had happened. He thought here was an opportunity to do something we've never done before: we'll be at Earth, we can go home and do a story about the captain sort of finding himself again."

Offers Piller, "The normal objections were that we were not serialized. We try to tell stories that can be told in one hour and that's what we do very well. When I got to the end of Part II, we made the decision not to extend it and I called up Rick and said, 'Hey, listen. Next week Picard can be fine, but for a show that prides itself on its realistic approach to storytelling, how can you have a guy who's basically been raped be fine next week? There's a story in a man like Picard who's lost control. Delving into the psychological crisis that a man like that has to face, and what does he have to do?' Finally, I was persuasive enough to talk Gene and Rick into taking the chance, and I think everybody is glad we did."

Piller was able to champion "Family" without making some concessions to Rick Berman that would force it to conform to traditional *Star Trek* formula.

"When Rick said 'I'll let you take Picard to Earth,'" Piller reflects, "he told me 'I want a science fiction story going on aboard the ship at the same time.' So we struggled for weeks and weeks trying to come up with an interesting science fiction story that we could match with Picard going down to Earth. One version of it had a child stowaway that causes problems [but] we didn't like that, and then we came up with this idea that we went to Rick with. We said that while Picard's on Earth, up on the ship people are disappearing for no apparent reason and, ultimately, it's because of this wormhole, and he liked it, but said he didn't feel there was room for both stories. He said he thought we should do them as separate shows and come up

with something else. He decided we're not going to ruin the episode with Picard by trying to put some ridiculous scientific thing in, and we decided to do it the way it was originally conceived, and do it as a whole show about family."

Ron Moore recalls, "We decided as long as we were there at Earth, let's make it a show about people's families and do some other character's on the ship and explore their backgrounds. It became a very off-concept show, [looking] at the characters and how they got to be who and what they are."

One character, oft talked about but never personified, made his first appearance on *Trek*: Wesley's father, Jack Crusher (Doug Wert).

"Every fan and their cousin has written letters about Jack Crusher and wanting to see him," remarks Piller, who had suffered through reams of story proposals from prospective *Trek* writers "pitching" scripts about Beverly Crusher's late husband. "We had gotten a spec script about Jack Crusher in the holodeck, and Ron Moore came down and said maybe we should use it so we bought the premise from the people who wrote the script. We felt if we were going to do a story about family and really make that the theme of an episode, it was an element we really should explore and use as part of a script to sort of speak to the theme of family and how the reach and embrace of family can extend across even death. What Jack said in the scene about looking down at the newborn child Wesley, and seeing in his face all the people he had ever loved, was something I was feeling and going through at that time having just had a baby daughter. I think this particular season and, in general, my career and my work has always tried to reinforce family values, because to me as the world gets more technologically smart, we find more and more ways to separate us as family. It's a terribly important part of my life and my work."

Says director Les Landau "I think it was certainly one of my best episodes and one of the best episodes of *Star Trek* ever. 'Family' was the perfect follow-up to the Borg shows and the conclusion of that storyline. Picard was in a dilemma, what to do and what better place to do it than in the environs of

one's 'home.' After all, his home is the universe, but his specific home is La Barre, France. This was a story that was opened up. It was about Earth and a place that we could identify with human beings and no aliens. That opening moment where Picard walks into the vineyard and see his brother on his hands and knees picking grapes [and] his brother doesn't even acknowledge him, gives me chills just thinking about it.

"It was my first episode of the season, but it was the fourth episode to be filmed," recalls Landau. "Patrick ended the third season with the Borg show and then started the fourth season with a Borg show, and went on to two other shows that had relatively little to do with the result of the culmination of what had happened during the Borg incident, which was unbelievable. Patrick Steward had to adjust and say it's four months later, I have to go back to what did I feel, what I was going through, and relive all the events and make it believable that he had just come back from this incident and was going home. I think it was certainly one of my best episodes of *Star Trek* and one of the best *Next Generation* episodes ever. I'm not talking about my work, but the story, the acting, the production values. Everything about that show worked."

Episode #77:
"Brothers"
Original Airdate: 10/8/90
Written by Rick Berman
Directed by Rob Bowman
Guest Starring: Cory Danziger (Jake Potts), Brent Spiner (Lore & Dr. Noonian Soong), Adam Ryen (Willie)
   Data commandeers the Enterprise and beams down to a mysterious planet where we find he has been summoned by his creator, Dr. Soong (Brent Spiner), who intends to plant a chip in his electronic circuitry which will give him humanity. Then Lore (Spiner, again), Data's evil twin brother from season one's "Datalore," arrives.
   Lore, pretending to be Data, deceives Soong into planting the chip in him, depriving Data of his chance to be human. When the Away Team beams down they find Lore gone and Soong dying.

••••

"In fact, at one point it looked very hairy that we weren't going to be able to pull it off with Brent playing all three roles and we began a casting process of Chinese, elderly male actors," says Rick Berman, *Next Generation*'s guiding force, Executive producer and author of "Brothers," his first script for the show. "Keye Luke was one of the people we were thinking about, but we ended up finding a way production-wise we could do it. It would have been a lot less expensive to have done it with another actor, but we ended up doing it with Brent and that made it a little more fun. As for Lore, I would love to bring him back. We left him with a new chip in his head that was wrongly placed there, and so he is even more demented than before and he's off doing God knows what. I think we may hear from him again."

Adds Michael Piller, " Rick said, 'I'm writing this episode so Data can play every character,' and he stuck by his guns and we pulled it off. That's the only show where we had rehearsal. I said to Rob Bowman and Legato, 'You've got to rehearse this,' and they rehearsed for two or three days with Brent, figuring [it] out both for Brent as an actor and in terms of staging. They worked out some of the motion control shots and did a lot of preparation in terms of figuring out what to do, because that kind of preparatory time on the stage when everybody is standing around is not a good idea. What we did was we tape out the floor like in a stageplay, or a videotaped multi-camera show. We actually taped the floor and brought in steps and had props and pieces of furniture and they actually blocked it out and staged it. I'm glad we did, although we've never done that on this show before because it saved us a lot of time, if we hadn't it would have been really dicey.

"The story that Rick wrote did not have Lore in it," points out Piller. "We have a process that we call breaking a story where we put all the writing staff in a room and we look around and whatever the writer came in with serves as only a starting point. Everybody sits down and we go to a board and break it down into acts and scenes and we try and see how the show is going to lay out. I tell everyone that in this room it is a

safe environment and that they are to speak out with whatever ideas they have, even if it's stupid or wrong, because it may spark an idea in someone else that leads us to the solution of a particular problem in a script."

In the case of "Brothers," it was decided that the script needed an additional element of jeopardy. Enter: Lore, Data's twisted android brother introduced first season in "Datalore."

"Lore demanded to come back into that show," says Piller. "I'm very much into Zen writing and I believe these things. It was something that had to happen to make that show work and it was the right thing to do. And, of course, it made it a must-watch episode. We were standing around going through Rick's story and my feeling was that after reading his first draft that the idea of Data going back to see Dr. Sung and the story of the child who was hurt in the practical joke were not enough elements to hold up the episode. Once Data goes back to see Dr. Sung, it's basically a chat and without some jeopardy or another event to go on I was afraid it was going to be flat. We talked about what we could do and, ultimately, the obvious thing was that we bring Lore back. It wasn't said let's ring Lore back and do an episode with him, it was let's go see Sung and Lore. I knew from the moment we came up with it that Brent Spiner in three roles was going to make for an unforgettable episode and I think it was."

"Brothers" was so complex that director Rob Bowman and visual effects supervisor Rob Legato extensively rehearsed actor Brent Spiner prior to shooting the episode, thus requiring multiple exposure shots with motion control camera in which Spiner plays three different characters.

"That's the only show where we ever had rehearsal," says producer David Livingston. "I said to Rob Bowman and Legato you've got to rehearse this first. They rehearsed for two or three days with Brent figuring out both for Brent as an actor and in terms of staging how they would shoot the motion control shots. What we did was we taped out the floor like in a play or a multicamera show, and then actually blocked it out. I'm glad we did because it saved us a lot of time. If we hadn't, it would have been really dicey."

Sherman Howard (Captain Endar in "Suddenly Human") seen here as Lex Luthor in Superboy.

Episode #78:
"Suddenly Human"
Original Airdate: 10/15/90
Written by John Whelpley and Jeri Taylor
Story by Ralph Phillips
Directed by Gabrielle Beaumont
Guest Starring: Sherman Howard (Endar), Chad Allen (Jono/Jeremiah Rossa), Barbara Townsend (Admiral Rossa)

A human teenager, Jono (Chad Allen) is found aboard a damaged Tellerian ship and brought back to the Enterprise along with his comrades. Jono is responsive only to Picard's command authority. The captain tries to reacclamate him to human culture when his adopted father and commander of the Tellerian fleet, Endar (Sherman Howard), demands his return. If not, war will be declared against the Federation.

Jono, despite the desire of his grandmother—a Starfleet admiral—for him to return to Earth, rejects his heritage and rejoins Endar.

••••

A subplot involving Jono's injuries and the ambiguous manner in which they were attained, stirred some controversy on the show and generated some heated comments from viewers who perceived the episode as condoning child abuse.

"We got some pretty angry letters on that show," says Michael Piller.

"They said, 'How can you let an abused child go back to the people who are abusing him?' We really brought the child abuse issue up because it was the right and natural thing to bring up in the context of the story. There are real parallels to stories that go on in today's world about parents who fight over custody and one says there's been abuse. Who do you believe? But, mostly, it was a cultural clash story. It was a story of someone who was human who had been raised in a totally alien environment. Is he human any longer? That's really what that story was about."

Adds Rick Berman, "We wanted to make the point that the interpretation of broken bones was nothing more than normal childhood broken bones, and that these people were sort of prejudiced in this direction. It was in no way intended to be an episode that had anything to do with child abuse. It was the Wild Child. It had to do with a boy being brought from one culture to another and not fitting in with either, and the inevitable need for him to return back to the world in which he grew up."

"I thought we made it clear that he had a loving and protecting father in the alien," Michael Piller interjects. "We did have Picard make his own concerned confusion evident to the audience and I am a very great believer in grays and that there are not always answers to the tough and difficult questions. It was part of their culture and a normal loving thing that wasn't meant to imply child abuse. If we didn't say that, it's too bad. I think that episode was marvelously written by Jeri Taylor and it was strong enough to hire her on staff. I was disappointed by the show primarily because the aliens weren't alien enough. I felt there was some miscommunication on some level. The whole idea of that show was missed because these savage, different alien type creatures turned out to be very human."

Episode #79:
"Remember Me"
Original Airdate: 10/22/90
Written by Lee Sheldon
Directed by Cliff Bole
Guest Starring: Eric Menyuk (The Traveler), Bill Erwin (Dr. Dalen Quaice)
Dr. Crusher becomes trapped in a parallel universe in which the crew of the Enterprise is seemingly disappearing off the ship, while the real crew desperately tries to rescue her. The fear is that one of Wesley's warp bubble experiment might turn deadly, trapping Crusher in the alternate universe.

Once the entire crew has disappeared, the doctor races against time to escape from inside the warp bubble. Only with the help of the Traveler does she succeed.

••••

"That was a very interesting high concept episode," says Rick Berman. "I thought it was possibly a little bit overly confusing. You're fooling the audience a little and I don't like to do that. They were looking at one world when, in fact, we were dealing with parallel universes and that was potentially confusing."

Making a return visit to *The Next Generation* to serve as a deus ex machina to get Beverly back for next week's episode, was "Where No One Has Gone Before" fan fave, the Traveler (Eric Menyuk). "I think that was an afterthought," admits Berman. "That was a question of finding a way to resolve the story."

Interjects Cliff Bole, "They added the character of the Traveler at the last minute. They added him because he's big at the conventions. He was just a walk-on. They were searching for some way to patch up the ending, so the Traveler came in."

The first two drafts did not have the Traveler in it," explains Michael Piller. "The first draft ended with the realization of what had happened turning out to be a dream episode. We didn't find that satisfying, so we decided at the end of act three to pull everything from the first 60 pages into the first three acts and tell the audience what's going on on the other side of the warp bubble and how they're trying to get Beverly back. We spend the next two acts deciding how to get her back. At the beginning of the year we said that we wanted to bring the Traveler back for something, so why not use him in this episode to help Beverly back."

Episode #80:
"Legacy"
Original Airdate: 10/29/90
Written by Joe Menosky
Directed by Robert Scheerer
Guest Starring: Beth Toussaint (Ishara Yar), Don Mirrault (Hayne)
The legacy of Tasha Yar continues to haunt the Enterprise crew when they come upon her sister, Ishara (Beth Toussaint) on the late Tasha's warring homeworld, where a Federation ship's emergency shuttle has crashed.

Offering to assist the Away Team in rescuing their stranded comrades, Ishara hides a secret agenda which will allow her to disable the defenses of her clan's enemies and lead an offensive strike against them. As she prepares to disable the generator during the rescue mission, Riker stuns her with a phaser before she can betray them all.

••••

"It was a good episode because of the performance of the girl and the relationship between her and Data," says Michael Piller. "There's nothing as poignant as seeing the betrayal of an innocent, as Data is. I was very happy with this show, but it doesn't stay with me. It's a show that has great entertainment value, but it doesn't stick as one that I'll always remember."

"'Legacy' was fun to do," says director Robert Scheerer. "First of all, I had Beth Toussaint, who prior to that episode I had used on an episode of *Matlock*. She was quite wonderful, very attractive, sexy and a good actress. We were having trouble finding someone for the role and I mentioned Beth and showed the tape. Everyone said she was wonderful and she came in and did it. A great pleasure to have her be accepted and the fact that she was good.

"Obviously," he continues, "I had to go back and watch those first season episodes featuring the Tasha Yar character because I didn't know anything about her. That kind of research was interesting."

Episode #81:
"Reunion"
Original Airdate: 11/5/90
Written by Thomas Perry, Jo Perry, Ronald D. Moore and Brannon Braga

••••
210

Story by Drew Deighan, Thomas Perry and Jo Perry
Directed by Jonathan Frakes
Guest Starring: Suzie Plakson (K'Ehleyr), Charles Cooper (K'Mpec), Patrick Massett (Duras), Robert O'Reilly (Gowron), Jon Steuer (Alexander)

K'Ehleyr (Suzie Plakson from second season's "The Emissary") returns to the Enterprise, surprising Worf by bringing his illegitimate son (first Kirk, now Worf—didn't they ever hear of condoms in the 24th Century?) aboard. At the same time, K'Mpec (*Star Trek V's* Charles Cooper), the head of the Klingon High Council, confides in Picard that he has been poisoned and that the fate of the Klingon/Federation alliance rests with Picard, who must decide whether the treacherous Duras (Patrick Massett) or Gowron (Robert O'Reilly) will rule the Klingon Empire.

Jockeying for power, Duras discovers K'Ehyler's attempts to investigate events which imply that his father betrayed the Klingons to the Romulans (not Worf's as the character stated in "Sins of the Father") and murders her. Seeking vengeance, Worf slays Duras aboard his ship and Gowron prepares to ascend to rule the High Council.

••••

"Rick's been throwing me nice episodes," says director/actor Jonathan Frakes. "Three people got killed, there was murder and revenge. I've been lucky. Suzi [Plakson] was great. A lot of people are sorry she's dead. It's a character that people really loved or hated because she was so big and shameless in her performance. I loved it."

"We love Suzie and that character, but it worked because you cared about her and we made an effort not to do it capriciously and for no reason, just to get her off the show so Worf wouldn't have to deal with her," says Ron Moore. "I have pals that like the show and they were upset. It took Worf's character in a different direction; which is sort of what we did with 'Sins.' Anybody who watches that episode is moved and outraged by the killing of K'Ehleyr. You're mad and you have that same need for vengeance that Worf does. If we've tapped into those feelings so when Worf goes back to his quarters and grabs that sword and the

audience is screaming for Duras' head, then you've done it. You really had to do that scene in the Captain's Ready Room where Picard calls Worf onto the carpet for what he did and puts it to him."

"I killed K'Ehleyr," says Michael Piller proudly. "The original idea was about Worf's kid and bringing K'Ehleyr back, who was having a relationship with Duras. But when we started talking about how to make the story work, I'm the one who said she should die. Finally it was clearly what seemed to want to happen in the story, that she should be trying to find out what Duras was up to and he kills her. Worf, enraged, kills Duras. You wanted to get to a place where Worf was going to take Duras apart, and there's no real good reason for him to do it unless she dies....he had it coming."

Episode #82:
"Future Imperfect"
Original Airdate: 11/12/90
Written by J. Larry Carroll and David Bennett Carren
Directed by Les Landau
Guest Starring: Andreas Katsulas (Tomalak), Chris Demetral (Jean-Luc/Ethan/Barash)

After beaming down to a mysterious planet, Riker awakens in sickbay and finds that 16 years have apparently passed. He has a son, and peace negotiations are continuing in earnest with the Romulans. Riker's fears that this could be a Romulan plot to discover the secret location of Outpost 23 actually turns out to be the fantasy of a lonely little boy.

••••

"It was an opportunity for Jonathan to take charge of an episode and it just shows the dynamic quality of Riker to have to deal with not only having aged fifteen years, but to discover that you have a son and have been married and [are] captain of the Enterprise," says director Les Landau. "Can you imagine waking up one day and finding out that you've skipped fifteen years on your CD? There were lots of tricks and false leads, and yet there was something universal about the theme of this alien at the end which was the embodiment of this little boy. The final moment where Riker sees this alien being in the caverns of this other world and says I will take you with

me and you will always be a part of me, goes back to the basics of what *Star Trek* is all about. It's that caring for the human condition, love for the universal being. It sounds very esoteric and snobbish to talk this way, but that's when *Star Trek* is at its best."

"We've had some amazing pitches, but the most notable we ever heard was in 'Future Imperfect,' where the team came in and said we have a story where Riker wakes up from an accident 15 years in the future," recalls Brannon Braga. "It's 15 years in the future, Riker has a son, is the captain of the Enterprise and has no idea what happened. Mike Piller said, 'Stop, we'll buy it.'"

Adds Michael Piller, "We got for months without hearing good ideas. Larry and David came in on one hot week and brought a couple of ideas. The first thing out of their mouth was Riker wakes up and it's 15 years in the future and he has a son. I said sold and they did it and did a real good job on it. The Romulan gag of it being a double switch was added by accident. The first draft was a little flat after we got into the story, just like 'Remember Me.' You had a situation where you are into it and something strange is happening and yet it can't just turn out to be a dream at the end of the show because it's not satisfying. What you do is you get to the third act and you need to do something that moves the action forward. This is one of the best examples of the notion that you shouldn't censor yourself. I just talked and David Carren said, 'You mean that he thinks it's a real Romulan plot for an act?' and I said, 'That's not what I mean at all'— then I said, 'Stop, wait a minute, what if that's exactly what we do and play it out as a Romulan gag for an act.' That's what I think made that show work."

"We pitched the major story elements," says David Carren. "The only major element that came up was that it was a Romulan plot and you find out it's a fantasy within a fantasy. Originally it basically went through five acts and then you found out that it was the little boy's fantasy."

Notes Piller, "Ideas just come in waves. For some reason, everyone seemed to be coming in with an amnesia story and you saw three of them on the air this year on our show and one of them we saved for next year. 'Future Imperfect' was one of our better amnesia stories. For a while everyone seemed to be coming in with stories about children and we had more children in the first 12 episodes than ever before. The only thing they didn't come in with was amnesiac children stories. It became a great gag around here."

Guest star Andreas Katsulas, playing Romulan Centurion Tamalok for the last time, says, "I felt much more comfortable when he was an incredible giant on the screen, just a face. Suddenly when I had to account for everything else, I didn't feel support and nothing was supporting what I was doing. I was happy not to recur unless it would have gone back to a screen character."

Episode #83:
"Final Mission"
Original Airdate: 11/19/90
Written by Kasey Arnold-Ince
and Jeri Taylor
Story by Kasey Arnold-Ince
Directed by Corey Allen
Guest Starring: Nick Tate (Dirgo),
Kim Hamilton (Sonji)

Wil Wheaton's swan song to *Star Trek*, in which a shuttlecraft carrying Picard and Wesley to a negotiating conference crashes on a desert planet. When they attempt to gather water from a shielded fountain, Picard is critically wounded and Wesley must take charge.

The shuttle captain, Dirgo, persists in his attempts to raid the water spring and is killed by the system's defensive mechanism. Wesley must rely on his wits to figure out a way to obtain some water before Picard dies.

••••

"The idea had originally been to have Wesley and Picard crash together on a planet and do a role reversal, but it had been an ice planet," reveals writer Jeri Taylor. "The nature of the planet changed because we felt we could make it a much more realistic dry planet than ice planet. It would look hokey and fake and we don't like to do that. That's the episode I probably put more work on than any all year long, because it was a combination of a very delicate kind of interpersonal story, and the dreaded technical story which is the garbage

scow in space. So I had this supertechnical thing going on at the same time as this delicate kind of interpersonal story."

Michael Piller relates, "There had been a lot of very bad feeling around here about the way Tasha Yar was sent off. So we were determined to give Wesley a send-off that had real value and something that stayed with us. We finally decided that he would go to the Academy, which I think was Gene's idea [and] the most reasonable and easiest idea, which also keeps him alive for future episodes. I think Jeri did a wonderful job on the script and Corey Allen, who is one of my favorite directors, gave you the best pieces of film you can get. If it gets an A- instead of an A, it's only because the story itself, of two guys trapped on a planet and how do we get off, in general is not very original, and the story of the garbage scow was no great shakes either. But I think we handled it pretty well."

"The only thing I said they couldn't do was they waned to go back outside again, and I said we had to do it inside," explains David Livingston. "They wanted to do the fountain outside, but we ended up doing the rest on Stage 16. It was Rick's idea to change it from ice and that was a great, great idea, [and] very critical to the episode's success. The crane shot in the beginning is great. I could hear Maurice Jarre's score in the background."

Says Rick Berman, "It was a little more expensive because we went on location and the opticals. We had huge optical problems with the fountain. It was a nightmare. It was something we built and it didn't work. Then we were going to do it optically and that didn't work. So we had a lot of technical problems. That's one of my favorite episodes. I think it was very poignant and the acting on the part of our guest cast, Nick Tate, Patrick's work and Wil's, was just excellent. I thought it was just a terrific piece of drama."

Episode #84:
"The Loss"
Original Airdate: 12/21/90
Written by Hilary J. Bader, Alan J. Adler
and Vanessa Greene
Story by Hilary J. Bader

Directed by Chip Chalmers
Guest Starring: Kim Braden (Janet Brooks), Whoopi Goldberg (Guinan)

Troi loses her empathic powers due to a cloud consisting of two-dimensional creatures which are leading the Enterprise into a deadly cosmic string fragment.

Faced with being human, Troi announces her desire to resign as ship's counselor and, despite the sympathy of the crew, turns curt and hostile as she drowns in her own self-pity. It is only when the creatures are freed from the ship's perimeter that Troi regains her powers and asks to resume her regular duties.

••••

"I pushed for this episode a lot," says Rick Berman. "It was fascinating to me that someone would lose one of their senses and be unable to explain it to others because they didn't have it in the first place. If you were the only sighted person in a colony of blind people and suddenly you lost your vision and they all said 'So what?'...that's what this was. I think Marina did a really good job. We create conflict by infecting people with weird space anomalies and alien microbes and making people act differently, so when people are off character, they can have a little bit more conflict. In this case, it came out of her losing one of her senses."

States Michael Piller, "It was a very difficult story to get right. I felt the script was adequate, it's not one of my favorites. The problem in conception was that you have a phenomenon that nobody can identify with. We said this is our blind show, but we can't do a blind show like other shows. This basic idea has been pitched to us every season, with Troi losing her sense of empathy. Finally, because we needed a Troi show, we said let's do it here."

A B-story, which is a term used to describe an additional story paralleling the main plotline, involves two-dimensional creatures which have caught the Enterprise in its field. This was incorporated into the Troi story.

"We had gotten the 'B' story from our intern, Hilary Bader," Piller says. "I said let's match this to the Troi story, and it was difficult to satisfy all of us, because everybody said she's going to get her sight back, or rather her insight back, by the end of the episode. We toyed briefly about not giving it back to her, but the bottom line for me was that these shows work because the journey is interesting and that what she learns and what she goes through has to be interesting and involving and, ultimately, educational in that we are showing off the stages of someone who has a serious disability, and what they go through when they are suffering this."

"The handicapped people came up and thanked me," Sirtis smiles. "That's exactly the way they feel, it's the way I expressed their emotions. 'The Loss' was very, very popular."

Chip Chalmers enthuses, "An episode with some character conflict. There was that scene where Deanna went storming into sickbay and really got it on with Beverly, 'If I were you, I wouldn't have sat on my butt and would have been trying to do something about this,' and she goes storming out. People who saw that scene loved it. Whoopi Goldberg was also in that episode and, of course, she's a gem. She came after the show and said she wanted to do it. Obviously they immediately said, 'You've got it.' She *makes* the time. Whoopi's got a feature film opening every three months it seems, and she makes the time to do *Star Trek*. When she was a little girl, she saw the original show and a world where different races got along. A black woman could be sitting at the communication controls of a spaceship. That's not only okay, it's great. I think that was impressed on her at kind of an early age and she's always had a tremendous amount of admiration for the concept."

Episode #85:
"Data's Day"
Original Airdate: 1/7/91
Written by Harold Apter and
Ronald D. Moore
Directed by Robert Wiemer
Guest Starring: Rosalind Chao (Keiko), Sierra Pecheur (T'Pel), Alan Scarfe (Mendak)

A day-in-the-life episode which follows Data around the ship as he prepares for Chief O'Brien's (Colm Meaney) upcoming wedding nuptials, that prepa-ration beginning with Dr. Crusher teaching him to tap (the scene was choreographed by Gates McFadden herself, who, among other accomplishments, choreographed *Dreamchild* and *Labyrinth* for the late, great Jim Henson).

Meanwhile, a Vulcan ambassador beams aboard to lead secret negotiations with the Romulans. When it appears that she has been killed in a transporter accident, Picard discovers that she is actually a Romulan spy coming out from the cold.

••••

"'Data's Day' was a show I had supported us doing for quite a long time," says Executive Script Consultant Ron Moore. "The idea of doing a day in the life is a fairly common television convention that you kind of get around to doing. To do it on this show was very challenging and we've never done a show even remotely like it. Harold Apter pitched that in the third season and we've been trying to get it off the ground ever since. At one point, it was going to be a Picard day-in-the-life, then a day-in-the life of the ship and it went through a lot of changes until we came to the decision that Data was the perfect vehicle to do that with, because he's the only one who's up 24 hours a day."

"We've had more people come in with the average day-in-the-life of the Enterprise story," notes Rick Berman. "It's a story that never works. Then we decided to do it all from the point of view of Data with logs and I was skeptical about it, but the writers were interested and pursued it. I ended up being pleasantly surprised, but it was an off-episode."

One of the early considerations had been to replace Wesley after "Final Mission" with a female conn officer who would get romantically entangled with Transporter Chief Miles O'Brien, an idea which was ultimately rejected.

"I was against that because I felt that O'Brien was too good a character and potential benefit to the show to make him another star's supporting character," says Piller. "I felt he would always sort of be a sounding board for someone else to talk to and I didn't want to waste him on that. So we never did get around to replacing Wesley and O'Brien emerged on his own."

Surprisingly, rather than create a new female conn officer who would marry O'Brien, the chief was married off to a new supporting player, Keiko, ship's botanist who was played by Rosalind Chao.

"It all grew out of doing a day in the life story," says Ron Moore. "When you're talking about doing that, you sort of say what are the things that happen behind the scenes? What happens during a day on the Enterprise? Some of the things that come up are a baby gets born, maybe somebody dies—maybe not. Then somebody said what if someone gets married and that sparked. We obviously didn't want any of the regulars getting married, because that's a big thing and we didn't want it to be a faceless nobody. Everybody was delighted with the work Colm Meaney had been doing for us and we did want to do more with him as the series was going on. So we said this is a neat idea—we'll marry O'Brien."

The marriage to O'Brien was not the only problem in the story for "A Day in the Life of the Enterprise," which would ultimately become "Data's Day." In addition, there was the question of what else would happen to keep audiences glued to their television screens.

"We thought we needed to provide a frame," says Ron Moore, who rewrote Harold Apter's original script. "Otherwise you'd be left with a lot of little vignettes and there's no common threads to take you through the day. We needed an over-arcing story going on that we could refer to every once in a while, and also that gave us the opportunity to show that although the viewer at home gets to watch the entire episode, how it would be different from just Data's point of view where they would get just a little bit of information here and another briefing here. Obviously Picard knows everything and suddenly there's all this jeopardy happening, but Data hasn't been in on the whole thing all the time."

"Rick believed that you cannot have a show that has no jeopardy or drama on *Star Trek*," Michael Piller says. "I agreed with him, otherwise all you're doing is a scrapbook. It was a story that we kept over from last year and nobody could really figure out what to do. The story went through the various permutations a day in the life story always goes through. Are we going to do everybody? Are we going to do Picard? Ultimately we decided that Data would give us the most unique perspective of life on the Enterprise and it also gave us insight into Data. My feeling was if you take a show like 'The Defector' from last season and instead of showing the audience everything that everybody sees, you only take it from Data's point of view and he only gets to see the tail end of scenes and certain things that he's exposed to....What if there is actually a major story playing out and Data's only on the fringe of it? To me, that's a fascinating concept."

Episode #86:
"The Wounded"
Original Airdate: 1/28/91
Written by Jeri Taylor
Story by Stuart Charno, Sara Charno and Cy Chermak
Directed by Chip Chalmers
Guest Starring: Bob Gunton (Captain Ben Maxwell), Rosalind Chao (Keiko), Marc Alaimo (Gul Macet), Tim Winters (Glen Daro), John Hancock (Admiral Haden), Marco Rodriguez (Glen Telle)

A dark, fatalistic episode for *Trek*. A rogue starship captain launches a one-man war against an alien race with which the Federation has recently negotiated a peace treaty.

Attacking the alien Cardassians, the captain (Bob Gunton), whose wife had been brutally killed, is talked out of his path of vengeance by a former member of his crew, Chief O'Brien. Picard warns the Cardassian leader that he realizes they have been rearming and that Captain Maxwell was right. He intones ominously that the Federation "will be watching."

••••

"It was sort of *Heart of Darkness* with the rogue captain out of control," says producer/writer Jeri Taylor. "It started with the idea that if you had been at war with a country and now you are not at war with them anymore, you can't just immediately become friends. If you're trained to look at people as the enemy, it's hard to now be their friends. While in the 24th century people have a much more expansive view of the galaxy and are able to do

it a little better, we planted the idea that some people had just a little more residual problem with that sort of thing, and harbored some resentment. [It's] a very provocative kind of area to get into. The material was somewhat epic in nature, which is always fun to do, and yet at its core was this very personal story between him and Picard, where two strong and able people tee off against each other. And there is the wonderful device of the song at the end of the episode, in which Colm Meaney really came into his own and did a wonderful job. When he and Maxwell sing that song at the end, I really just loved that moment."

"That was a wonderful English hymn that was used in *The Man Who Would Be King*," says Rick Berman. "I always loved it and we worked it in where O'Brien and Gunton's character sing it together. It's another episode that's constantly pitched to every television show where you've got to bring back the guy who's lost it, but we dealt with prejudice in that episode. Some people felt Gunton [as Captain Maxwell] played it very soft, but I thought he did a great job."

David Livingston comments, "I thought that was the best makeup for an alien race that Michael had done. They looked so realistic and unique and powerful. He astounds me, he does all of his own sculpting. He's a real sculptor and he designs all these things and gets a piece of clay and sits there with his little knife. Two hours later, he's up in the office showing us his head. He makes a mold and they pour the mold right from his sculpting to the pieces. The best contribution I made to this show was hiring Michael Westmore. That's my one coup. My best coup. He's hung in here because he gets to do so many different things—it's not like *Rocky*, where he kept making noses for Sylvester Stallone. After a while, how many noses can you make? Michael is a true artist and he loves his work and just blows me away."

Points out director Chip Chalmers, "This episode aired during the Gulf War and was about Picard doing everything he could to prevent a war, happening during a time when the United States of America was doing everything it could to *start* a war. I thought it was a real interesting

dichotomy of ideas. That was one of the best written shows that I've seen in a while. We also had to deal with the Cardassians, which meant new ships, new aliens and we introduced a new enemy that's finally able to speak on the level of Picard. They're not grunting, they're not giggling, they're not mutes or all-knowing entities. Here are the Cardassians who also graduated first in their class and they're able to carry on highly intelligent conversations with Picard, but they're sinister as hell. It was fun to introduce a whole new alien race."

Episode #87:
"Devil's Due"
Original Airdate: 2/4/91
Written by Philip Lazebnik
Story by Philip Lazebnik and William Douglas Lansford
Directed by Tom Benko
Guest Starring: Marta DuBois (Ardra), Marcelo Tubert (Acost Jared), Paul Lambert (Dr. Howard Clarke)

Reworked from an original premise for the aborted *Trek* '70s TV revival, "Devil's Due" plays like a 1966 Enterprise voyage in which Kirk, er, Picard, must argue in court that a woman, Arda (Marta Dubois), claiming to be the devil, is really a charlatan. His goal is to prove this in order to nullify a contract she has on that world and the Enterprise.

Picard challenges the validity of her claim. Data serves as arbitrator in a contest of wills which could cost Picard his soul...or something equally valuable, his self-esteem.

••••

Ironically, this traditional *Trek* was, at the time, the highest rated show of the series since "Encounter at Farpoint," and whether that's due to the show's special effects-laden trailer, a sultry female protagonist (in early drafts, a male) or, as David Livingston speculates, "the fact there was no basketball game on that night," we can only guess. Even more than the usual litany of writers had a hand in crafting a rewrite of this decade old teleplay: Philip Labebnik (*Wings*) William Douglas Lansford, Lee Sheldon, Melinda Snodgrass, Larry Carroll, Dave Carren and Michael Piller.

••••

"It was a very difficult story because it's such an atypical story," explains Larry Carroll, "and it was a very hard story to get a handle on, but Michael really believed in it. It seems like every other writer in the Writer's Guild worked on this episode."

"It was like an old *Star Trek*," says Jonathan Frakes. "It's ironic that it was an old *Star Trek* story, because it's really a Kirk story. It was so 60's."

Says Michael Piller, "'Devil's Due' was a story that had been put into development third season when we had no stories and no scripts in development. We owned a script from the failed attempt to bring *Star Trek* back. Basically, because I had no product, I told Melinda Snodgrass to go out and get that script, which I had been told was a decent script, and rewrite it, [sticking] our characters' names in. That didn't work at all, and we started talking about how we could change it to better suit our show. We never succeeded in breaking it last season and, during the hiatus, I gave it to Philip Laezbnik, who is a writer for Paramount on *Wings* and a real *Trek* fan. He turned it inside out and made it a delightful show. It was too funny, though, and the people felt it was playing it all for laughs. I loved that draft of the script, but not everybody did. It was put into rewrite by approximately 15 people between Phil's script and the final draft, which I took, changing the male devil into a female devil for fun. [I] put back as much of Phil's original script as I could, and the bottom line was I felt the script was very funny and satisfying. It was very off for our show, and I thought it's origins showed, but ultimately it was a funny little show and a nice part of our mix."

David Livingston states, "That went through a lot of revisions and they changed it to a woman, which was a great fix. We brought her in for a lot of sessions and never found the right part for her. She came in and just blew us all away. Like, how do you do better? Let's just start shooting. Where's her wardrobe? We want more of that. I'm always pushing for more humor on this show. I think we get a little too serious sometimes. It's nice to be a little lighter. We talk about it and get a lot of sour looks. Certainly Brent offers a lot of

comic possibilities and we're exploring them more and more."

Episode #88:
"Clues"
Original Airdate: 11/11/91
Written by Bruce D. Arthurs
and Joe Menosky
Story by Bruce D. Arthurs
Directed by Les Landau

The crew of the Enterprise gradually discovers that they have "lost" 24 hours since encountering a mysterious wormhole in space. Data begins to exhibit suspicious signs pointing to a cover-up.

Following the clues, Picard learns that the Enterprise crew's memories were erased by a xenophobic race intent on preserving their solitude. The ship returns, and the aliens threaten to destroy the Enterprise unless they can assure them of success in erasing all knowledge of their existence.

• • • •

"It was a very difficult episode to do," says director Les Landau. "It's a story that repeats itself three or four times. How do we make it interesting and still tell the story? As it unfolds, we find that we are repeating ourselves in time, and, again, it's for the benefit of another species. Directorially, it was the most difficult assignment I've had on *Star Trek* and probably one of the most rewarding. In order to show different points in time and flashbacks within flashbacks was very difficult. I tried to create a style that was very fluid and singular in its point of view, until the very end when we came back to normal time [and] the camera work and editing became very cutty.

"There was a fluidity to all of the earlier sequences and a rhythm that, as the show developed before our eyes, became more tempoed to show that we were getting closer and closer to real time. There are long takes early on and longer camera moves in the first flashback. In the second one they're less fluid and long. Finally, when we come back to real time in act five, there are static shots where there's hardly any movement and a great deal of editorial cutting to show that we are back in real time.

"You try and fine a thread in every episode that you can use to tell the

story. It was shot in such a way that it demonstrates what the story's all about, but there are always a shot or two or three that I fall in love with that I put in my cut, that don't make it to the screen. It's like playing golf. When you play golf, you remember every shot you hit. Filming an episode is exactly the same thing. You remember every shot you hit, and when it's missing from your scorecard at the very end, you know you've either bogeyed, parred or birdied your round. It's a perfect analogy."

Michael Piller enthuses, "I really loved that show. It's one of my favorites of the year. It was a perfectly realized classic mystery put together into a *Star Trek* format, which came together into a very satisfying episode. It was written by a writer we hired off a spec script, who is a mailman in the Phoenix area. He gave us a very good story, [but] the script needed some work. Mostly restructuring caused by the departure of Wil Wheaton and a major dialogue polish. Joe Menosky came in during the hiatus and did the polish. [He] did such a good job, that I thought he deserved to be on staff.

Episode #89:
"First Contact"
Original Airdate: 2/18/91
Written by David Russell Bailey, David Bischoff, Joe Menosky, Ronald D. Moore and Michael Piller
Story by Marc Scott Zicree
Directed by Cliff Bole
Guest Starring: George Coe (Chancellor Durkin), Carolyn Seymour (Mirasta Yale), Michael Ensign (Krola), George Hearn (Berel), Steven Anderson (Nilrem), Sachi Parker (Tava), Bebe Neuwirth (Lanel)

The Enterprise must make "first contact" with an alien world on the verge of attaining warp technology. When Riker is injured on the planet, Picard must accelerate his plans to retrieve his wounded first officer or risk violating the Prime Directive.

Ultimately, the minister of the planet rejects the Federation's overture, realizing that by embracing other cultures in the galaxy, he will jeopardize his homeworld where the citizenry is not ready to accept that they are not the center of the universe.

• • • •

••••

"That had a different bent because it was a story about the guest and the point of view is from another culture," muses Jonathan Frakes. "I'm not sure that the writing in that episode was as good as it could have been. I really liked the story idea, [but] it had loopholes. It was loaded with great actors; George Coe and George Herr and Bebe, who was a delight. What a funny woman. I loved that scene. Cliff Bole directed that one, and he had me do it a lot of ways, some of which were really not good. I was thankful that they chose the takes that worked."

Reflects Cliff Bole, "Originally, when I read it, my challenge was how to handle all the talking, because it was a very talky show. Real talky, and sometimes between only two people. I think we came out alright with it. I'd like to do one that gets into a nice big conflict. I think that's a story idea that can deal with an issue. They make contact and really step into it. Picard actually made reference to that in the dialogue [of 'First Contact']. He said something about that happening with the Klingons, that the first contact with them resulted in a hundred year war."

"First Contact" began with writer Marc Scott Zicree, who was one of the first freelancers to propose story ideas to the fledgling *Next Generation* in 1986.

"It's very hard to sell to *Star Trek*," explains Zicree. "They've gone months without buying any stories. I had done up something like 50 or 60 stories in pitching to the show. Usually I sell on the first or second story. I must have run fifteen stories by them before we hit 'First Contact.' Piller liked the stuff so he kept saying keep going. At one point Ira Behr was joking and said this guy is an idea machine, we should just lock him in a room and have him slip paper out from under the door. It was the day before Thanksgiving in 1989, and the meeting was at 5:00 in the morning. Everyone was sick of being there and wanted to go home, and it was a hard pitch for a while."

And with Zicree's pitch for "First Contact," Piller was hooked. It was an irresistible concept that had never been done in the *Star Trek* mythos and seemed so obvious—the Enterprise

makes first contact with a planet to arrange its entry into the Federation.

"It may be the most important episode of the season," enthuses Piller. "I can't tell you if it's the best or not. It was pitched by a very good writer, but he just couldn't find the right tone of the show. We gave it to the writers who did 'Tin Man' for us, and the way they wrote the show it didn't work either. The story was something we had around from last year, which nobody could quite solve. Eventually I said I have the vision of this show in my mind. I sat down and, ultimately, it was my version that made it to the air."

Michael Piller concedes that the difficulty of the episode was not the idea itself, but rather the rules of writing *Star Trek*.

"Our rules told us we never have open shows, and we wrote the first two drafts from our point of view and I realized it wasn't working," says Piller. "The thing that was holding us back was a rule, and I'm very much a supporter of the rules of Gene's universe, but I also love to break them if they're in the interest of the show. I went to Rick [Berman] and said that even though I know he doesn't like to break format, this could be a special show if he would let me write it from the alien point of view. He did, as long as I let everyone know that we weren't going to ever break this rule again. No other show in the history of *Star Trek* has taken the alien perspective of our characters, and I think that makes it very special and very unique. I was very pleased with the way it turned out, and I think it's thought provoking and a fresh and original idea."

Adds Marina Sirtis, "I thought it was one of the most interesting episodes of the season. It was something so obvious that we hadn't addressed, and an issue that hadn't been brought up in 150 episodes of *Star Trek*. Of course there are going to be people who are going to get warp power and are going out into space. How do we deal with this? I thought it was a really good episode and Patrick agreed that we were exactly the right two people to go down to the planet and say hi."

Most people involved concur with the notion that "First Contact" is lit-

tle more than *The Day the Earth Stood Still* transplanted to the 24th century with the Enterprise crew as the aliens landing in Washington.

"That was really the concept that I always saw," says Piller. "I said it was a '50s space movie except we're the aliens and that's really the way I tried to write it."

David Livingston, the show's producer responsible for bringing the alien world to the screen, agrees that "First Contact" is indeed a 24th century take on the aliens landing, with better special effects than any 1950's movie ever had.

"It's the first episode where we really broke the mold," he opines. "From a visual standpoint, we tried to create sets, wardrobe and medical instruments that looked evocative of our culture today, but were different, and add enough that they didn't say we just rented a gurney from Central Props. We took a lot of pains in terms of talking about the props and the set dressing, so that it looked a little bit odd. I think we were pretty successful. It was very hard, but I think the audience identified with these people. It was how I would feel at first contact."

Episode #90:
"Galaxy's Child"
Original Airdate: 3/11/91
Written by Maurice Hurley
Story by Thomas Kartozian
Directed by Winrich Kolbe
Guest Starring: Susan Gibney (Dr. Leah Brahms), Whoopi Goldberg (Guinan)

Maurice Hurley, former *Next Generation* executive producer, returned to contribute a teleplay in which the Enterprise accidentally kills a pregnant space creature, whose offspring attaches itself to the Enterprise hull. Also returning is Leah Brahms (Susan Gibney), first introduced in season three's "Booby Trap" as a hologram who helps Geordi navigate the ship from a minefield. Now the real McCoy (pun definitely intended) beams aboard the Enterprise in the flesh. Geordi courts her, only to discover that the fetching scientist is married. Together they nonetheless save the space baby.

••••

"They're two great stories," says Rick Berman. "First, that of the fantasy woman Geordi thinks he's met, but didn't, and now he actually has to meet her; and the simultaneous story of the space baby latching onto the ship. They were two very nice stories that worked well together. A lot of the baby effects, especially once it latched on to the ship and went swimming out with its friends at the end, was all computer animation, which is something we rarely use because it's not usually all that believable, but it's wonderful in this show."

"I always felt that the idea of having reality versus fantasy was an interesting theme to explore and the Leah Brahms character allowed us to do that in this episode," details Michael Piller. "This to me was one of the best concepts we had all year. *Star Trek* is a show of ideas and although we've had good shows the first half of the season, the second half had some really great ideas and this was one of them. The writer who brought it in and pitched it, couldn't really make the story work, so we needed somebody else to go to work on it. Maury [Hurley] had expressed an interest in writing a script or two for us this year, and we were delighted to have the opportunity to work together again. I sent it over to him and said, 'Can you make this work?', and he did. I just thought the idea of an alien creature adopting the Enterprise as its mother is something you can't do on any other show."

A scene that consistently elicits guffaws among the cast is the inevitable shaking of the ship caused by phaser fire and other space hazards. "I've got that down now," laughs Marina Sirtis. "It was kind of embarrassing in the beginning, but maybe I've become more Americanized. Americans are much looser than English people and you have to just relax and let go, which is actually easier said than done for an English person because we're so reserved."

For director Winrich Kolbe, the production problems created by shaking are far more significant than the embarrassment felt by the actors.

"In 'Galaxy's Child' Marvin Rush designed a special head which had a strong set of springs and you really could rattle the head out of the camera. The only problem was that in the style we have in dramatic television, which is

single camera, you shoot a master or a master that movies and various close-ups, and you've got to make sure all those moves synchronize at the same strength or you're going to end up with Picard shaking like crazy and Worf right above him barely moving."

Episode #91:
"Night Terrors"
Original Airdate: 3/18/91
Written by Pamela Douglas and
Jeri Taylor
Story by Shari Goodhartz
Directed by Les Landau
Guest Starring: Rosalind Chao (Keiko),
John Vickery (Hagan), Duke Moosekian
(Gillespie)

The Enterprise crew, trapped in Tykin's Rift, is affected by sleep deprivation and starts imagining their worst nightmares. Through a series of eerie dreams and communications with a comatose Betazoid survivor of a ship whose crew went insane from the same malady, Troi discovers and contacts an alien ship also trapped in the rift. Together, they work to escape before it's too late.

••••

"That was a yawner, wasn't it?" muses Jonathan Frakes rhetorically. "That was a shitty piece of special effects work when Troi was flying with those cloud around her. That was below our standard."

"A great deal of all that work was done second unit in post production in that Rob Legato had a great deal to add to those sequences," explains Les Landau. "We designed all these wonderful flying sequences where Troi would come in and out of the clouds, and see something off in the distance. It was Rob's ability and artistic wherewithal to lay in the various layers of what she was going through and what she was seeing and, yes, it was time consuming. Fortunately, the production decided that this was something we should do second unit without the main crew since there was very little sound work to be done and it was one of the rare instances where we had a full blown second unit. The cameraman who shot that was Tom De Nivi. It was like doing another day's work on *Star Trek* with a totally different crew. 'Night Terrors' was a seven day

shoot with one day of second unit.

"You want to create an illusion, and the scene that comes to mind is the scene where Beverly is examining all the bodies in the morgue, and suddenly is it real or is it fantasy? What has her lack of dreams and sleep done to her mind? Again, I think that sequence is very effective in what happens to an individual under such circumstances. I think that sequence really worked and made the point. There were other little moments that each character tried to find in order to show that dilemma."

Muses write Jeri Taylor, "This was a real tough episode. It was convoluted, it was a little mysterious, technical, quasi-supernatural. It was all over the map and there were a lot of different episodes to try and make cohesive. I rewrote and rewrote it, and I never thought that we were ever going to put that one to bed. It was strange. Troi's dream sequences are not something you get to see every week."

"Sleep disorder stories are the most commonly pitched stories we have here," says Rick Berman. "The sleep disorder was that our people were not getting enough REM sleep [and] they were all going mad which, in fact, is what would happen. It was all medically accurate, but it was kind of hard to follow and got convoluted. I don't think there was anything very terrifying in it."

Michael Piller states, "It deals with dream deprivation, which I think is an interesting phenomena to explore, but it was the first show right after Christmas hiatus and I don't think everybody was quite back on their feet yet. As a result, the energy level was way down and the timing was off and the nature of the problem made everybody start reading slowly. When the film was finished, it was nine minutes too long [*Trek* episodes must clock in at 43 minutes] and we had to cut huge pieces out of it in order to make it fit into an hour. The bottom line was that it was no longer a script because they were dream deprived. They were all talking slowly and after a while that gets pretty boring, and the middle of that show sagged and was slow, boring and disappointing."

••••

Episode #92:
"Identity Crisis"
Original Airdate: 3/25/91
Written by Brannon Braga
Story by Timothy De Haaf
Directed by Winrich Kolbe
Guest Starring: Maryann Plunkett
(Commander Susanna Leitjen)

The crew of an Away Team mission Geordi was on five years earlier while serving on the USS Victory, are all disappearing. He finds out his friend and colleague, Susanna Leitjen (Maryann Plunkett) is metamorphosizing into an alien creature, and that he's next.

As Geordi begins to unravel the mystery via a holodeck recreation of the mission, he begins his startling transformation. It's only with the help of Leitjen that the Away Team is able to return him to the ship before his transformation is complete.

••••

"It was a very tough script to solve," admits Michael Piller. "The script was originally bought as a spec script submitted by a fan. It was very heavy on point of view and [contained] stylistic devices we didn't want to do. The original script had two non-*Star Trek* characters going through what Geordi and this woman eventually went through. It was a very complicated, complex production that the director did a terrific job on. It had scenes within scenes and I was very happy with the show. It may not have been one of the best scripts we wrote, but it's a great example of how those guys in production can really turn out a helluva product."

Utilized in the filming of the episode was a state-of-the-art ultra-violet lighting system.

"We were talking about how we're going to make these guys glow and Peter Lauritson said to me, 'Why don't we try ultra violet?'" recalls David Livingston. "I said because we had done a test the year before. I almost dismissed it, but then pulled out the tape and looked at it and said this stuff is great. [I] went to Michael Westmore and Bob Blackman and said we want to do this, and they designed these suits and we painted them with u/v and put these contact lenses in to this woman's eyes that glowed. It was fabulous and we got Mark

and Brian [the LA radio deejays who were given their own short-lived series on NBC] to walk around in these suits. LeVar looked fabulous.'

"We used heavy blue light for the set lighting, and it's different lighting than you see elsewhere, because all the source coming from behind the camera is blue light. That's a decision we made and it should look harsh, and unrealistic and not well lit because it's not lit from one single blue source. It's basically a beacon shining out. It looked different than anything else and that was intentional. What I was surprised at was how powerful the u/v reflected back, and MTV is using it a lot now. I liked our use because it was integrated into the story. We used it to make it work dramatically rather than doing it as an effect. To me, that was a major accomplishment. We didn't do it to just be glitzy, we did it because it tied in dramatically with the story."

States director Winrich Kolbe, "That was an interesting show and a lot of. First of all, LeVar Burton is a hell of an actor and it's a lot of fun working with him, even though I'm sure there was a lot of pain and agony on his part going into that suit. Technically speaking we didn't make things any easier for him because we had to light everything with black light. So we're kind of restricted camera-wise to do what we wanted to do because of all of those tremendous black light units. It was a hell of a set, but a technical nightmare. But everybody seems to be happy about it."

Episode #93:
"The Nth Degree"
Original Airdate: 4/1/91
Written by Joe Menosky
Directed by Robert Legato
Guest Starring: Dwight Schultz
(Barclay), Saxon Trainor (Larson), Jim Norton (Einstein)

Barclay from "Hollow Pursuits" returns and has his intellect enhanced by beings attempting to bring the Enterprise to the center of the universe to say hi.

Engaging in discussions with a holodeck recreation of Albert Einstein and hooking himself in to the ship's computers, Barclay propels the ship into the center of the galaxy.

••••

"We had sort of put in our laundry list of things we wanted to bring back fourth season," says Michael Piller. "'Hollow Pursuits' was a wonderful episode last year, and [Barclay] is a very interesting character and a great actor. We were having trouble finding something that would make it worthwhile to bring him back. Joe had this concept of somebody who became super intelligent and said, 'Maybe this could be our Barclay show,' and we weren't sure what we were going to do with our premise at first, but we finally got a story together and I was really pleased with the way it turned out. Joe Menosky has said he was really proud to have his name on that show, more so than any other show. That's Rob Legato's second episode and Rob did a masterful job in terms of interpreting the story. I think Rick came up with the idea of doing Cyrano. It was kind of a con on the audience. I think the most interesting thing in that was the room where he attached himself to the computer. We've used laser beams in post production for firing things and lighting effects, and we've had several meetings where we've wanted to use them in production but have never done it. Rob suggested it on this episode and it was a wonderful idea—all those beams coming down and hitting his head are all laser beams and mirrors. It's all live, it's another effect we want to use more of. It's the first time on stage that we've done it. It's really weird and it allows you to move the camera. If it was laid in in post, you wouldn't be able to. It has a real immediacy and in terms of technical stuff that was a real advancement in terms of using lasers on stage.

"Rob came up with that thing too. Part of it was shot at eight frames per second, and part at six frames. Then we harmonized the voice down to that speed so that the voices work within that eight frames. It was a wild effect. It was a great episode for him to do so he could draw on all of his tricks."

Says Brannon Braga, "We struggled for a year with how to have Barclay come back. We didn't want him to play the nervous chap in the holodeck again and Joe Menosky came up with the science-fiction notion of a probe which is

••••

218

essentially a ship in a bottle. It was a good twist on that particular character which you could only get to with a science-fiction gag."

Rob Legato utilized live laser effects on the stage in "The Nth Degree."

"We've used laser beams in post production for firing things and lighting effects," says David Livingston. "We've had several meetings where we've wanted to use them in production but have never done it. Rob suggested it on this episode and it was a wonderful idea. All those beams coming down and hitting his head are all laser beams and mirrors. It's all live and done on the stage. It's really weird and allows you to move the camera. If it were laid down in post-production, you wouldn't be able to. It has a real immediacy and in terms of technical stuff was a real advancement for us in the use of lasers on stage."

Episode #94:
"Q-Pid"
Original Airdate: 4/22/91
Written by Ira Steven Behr
Story by Randee Russell and
Ira Steven Behr
Directed by Cliff Bole
Guest Starring: John de Lancie (Q), Jennifer Hetrick (Vash), Clive Revill (Sir Guy)

Vash (Jennifer Hetrick from "Captain's Holiday") joins an archaeological conference aboard the Enterprise and is reunited with Picard. Meanwhile, Q returns as a matchmaker who puts the two lovebirds and the crew of the Enterprise in a recreation of Robin Hood to teach Picard a lesson about love.

Picard storms Sir Guy's castle, where he and the Away Team rescue Vash's Maid Marian from Guy's evil clutches. Q essays the role of the Sheriff of Nottingham.

••••

"It had everything that I liked as a director," says Cliff Bole. "It had Q, who's a very entertaining guy and character. What more would I love to do than *Robin Hood: The Movie*? Here I was able to do that. I stepped back in time, there was sword fighting, some boisterous 12th century characters and also the spaceship. What more can you get? That's the ultimate as a director. Some guys like to do the man in the gray flannel suit, and I

like to do fantasy.

"It was a show where Picard falls out of character a little bit," he emphasizes. "He's not as stoic as he usually is and falls for a beautiful woman, who was raised to do that. I got a few letters about 'Q-Pid' that the women who wrote asked why weren't the ladies involved in a more modern way with the fighting. It was my feeling that we went back to the 12th century and we wee doing the 12th century, and I can't change history."

"Marina and I have always laughed about the fact that both of us can do fencing and that sort of thing," says Gates McFadden. "We're the ones who bash pots over warriors' heads, instead of doing karate or whatever. I personally love going on the Away Team missions and would love to do more of them."

"Everytime it's in *TV Guide* this episode gets a Close-Up," laughs Michael Piller. "I'm not sure why. I just think we came up with the idea of a love triangle between Q, Picard and Vash, and to bring her and Q together, which I thought was a great premise, but we couldn't lick it. It came together in a meeting with Ira Behr, who had created Vash, and we said why doesn't he do it. While we were trying to break it, someone said if we want to do a love triangle, let's throw these characters into one of the classic love stories. King Arthur was discussed with Guenivere, and then Robin Hood. Brannon [Braga] said something about wanting to do Robin Hood and Robin Hood was about to be released by about 15 motion picture companies. We said why don't we steal all their thunder? It just seemed to be that Ron Hood and his band of merry men was a very nice group to put our guys into, and then we just played it for fun. That was what was so great about the fourth season and wasn't so great about the fifth season. Each week you were never quite sure what was going to come on."

Episode #95:
"The Drumhead"
Original Airdate: 4/29/91
Written by Jeri Taylor
Directed Jonathan Frakes
Guest Starring: Jean Simmons (Admiral Satie), Bruce French (Sabin), Spencer Garrett (Simon Tarses), Earl Billings

Jean Simmons, seen here as Elizabeth Collins-Stoddard on the revival of Dark Shadows, played a futuristic Joe McCarthy in "The Drumhead."

(Admiral Henry), Henry Woronicz (J'Ddan), Ann Shea (Nellen)

A Klingon is caught on board the Enterprise spying for the Romulans, resulting in Admiral Satie coming on board to get to the heart of a suspected espionage ring. What develops is a witch hunt for his collaborator; a witch hunt that eventually leads all the way to Picard.

••••

Ironically, "The Drumhead," one of *Next Generation*'s most provocative episodes, originated as a money-saving installment. The same monetary considerations that gave us the dismal "Shades of Grey" resulted in this timely and passionate (and inexpensive) story.

"We saved $250,000 on this episode," smiles actor/director Jonathan Frakes. "It was the lowest budget of the season, but the risk is that shows like this are too chatty and people like a little action. But if you like dialogue and acting, this is certainly the episode. It's the McCarthy trials, a real guilty until proven innocent approach that Satie takes and she [Jean Simmons] was brilliant. She's an enormous Trekkie and watches the show every week, and then gets on the phone with her friends and they talk about the episode. The people who are fans of this show never cease to amaze me."

Writer Jeri Taylor, who essentially started from scratch on an episode

David Ogden Stiers, with M*A*S*H co-stars Alan Alda and Mike Farrell, portrayed Dr. Timicin in "Half a Life."

Ron Moore had proposed called "It Can't Happen Here," notes, "It's basically a witch-hunt with the idea it's taking the McCarthy era and the Salem witch hunts that can happen even in our enlightened 24th Century, and how these individual personal liberties can be stepped on. If you do that ever so lightly, even in the name of freedom, liberty and the preservation of the Federation, that becomes disastrous. It's a very provocative story and one which is a little darker than some of the others. It's nothing but talk and it was a real challenge as a writer to make that work."

"That should have been a 'Shades of Grey,'" Michael Piller adds pointedly. "The studio asked us for one. They wanted a clip show to help them out with financial problems and to make sure we balanced our budget, since we spent a lot of money on some of our shows. Rick [Berman] and I discussed it and we both hate, *hate,* clip shows. We think they're insulting to the audience. They tune in and then you create this false jeopardy and then flashback as their memory goes to the wonderful time they had before they got trapped in the elevator, and that bullshit. We just absolutely said if there's anyway to avoid this, can we come up with an episode that will cost the same but at least will be a story with integrity because clip shows don't have any integrity. The studio finally

agreed to let us try, and we came up with 'The Drumhead,' which is obviously a very inexpensive episode without any special effects. But it gave us a chance to tell a very important story."

Episode #96:
"Half a Life"
Original Airdate: 5/6/91
Written by Peter Allen Fields
Directed by Les Landau
Guest Starring: Majel Barrett (Lwaxana Troi), David Ogden Stiers (Dr. Timicin), Michelle Forbes (Dara), Terence McNally (B'Tardat), Carel Struycken (Mr. Homn)

Mrs. Troi falls in love with an alien scientist, Timicin (David Ogden Stiers), who is supposed to kill himself on his 60th birthday in accordance with the rules and rituals of his planet's culture.

••••

"It's a much different type of Mrs. Troi episode," says actress Marina Sirtis. "It's not quite as flippant or light as they tend to be. It starts off quite light, but then it has a real message with a little morality play, which is something I like to do. I didn't have much to do, which is good since I don't want it to be a given that every time mom comes aboard, I have to deal with her. I think it's more interesting that when she does come back, other characters have to deal with her."

Offers director Les Landau, "It showed a whole new side to Majel Barrett as an actress and the character of Mrs. Troi. She's usually this flimsy, whimsical Auntie Mame of the universe, but in this episode she's a very sensitive, warm and caring individual. It deals with the whole issue of growing old and how society deals with the elderly and, in my mind, it was one of the most pertinent storylines I have done. The opportunity to work with Majel and David Ogden Stiers was great. He was totally supported in casting by Rick and Michael, and this episode probably has less to do with our regular characters than any other episode in the history of the show. It goes back to the 'Family' situation, which is the beauty of dealing with people like Michael Piller and Rick Berman in that they are open to exploring, not only the universe, but new ideas within the confines of that universe. That is the beauty of what *Star*

Trek is and what Gene Roddenberry created, which is a commentary on the current issues of our time. I think it has become Rick Berman's mandate to continue that theory and put forward the best possible entertainment with a subtext of something that is relevant to today's society. Again, I'll refer to 'Half a Life,' which brings back to us the character of Mrs. Troi and the fact that she—for the first time—falls for another being from another planet, who at the age of 60 is destined by his society to be put away because when one reaches the age of 60, one is put to sleep. That's an issue which is very current in how do we deal with, and what do we do with, our elders. They may have reached an age where by numbers they are old, but mentally, physically, emotionally, sexually, professionally, they are, if not at their peak, certainly have a lot to contribute. That was a very poignant episode, which goes back to dealing with issues at hand, like 'Sarek,' which deals with senility and diseases of the mind."

Writer Peter Allan Fields, later promoted to co-producer of *Deep Space Nine*, did a crash course in Lwaxana lore to prepare himself for writing "Half a Life."

"I saw both 'Haven' and 'Menage a Troi' quite a while before I even began writing and I didn't refer to them at all when I was writing my first Lwaxana Troi story except to find out her title was 'holder of the chalice...', and all of that sort of thing," says Fields. "I went through the script for 'Haven' to find out who the hell I was writing about and that wasn't difficult to accomplish. I couldn't figure out at first how much rank and privilege she had and then I realized you give her as much as they'll let her have. She takes it."

Episode #97:
"The Host"
Original Airdate: 5/13/91
Written by Michael Horvath
Directed by Marvin V. Rush
Guest Starring: Franc Luz (Odan), Barbara Tarbuck (Leka), William Newman (Kalin Trose), Nicole Orth-Pallavicini (Kareel)

Dr. Crusher falls in love with a Federation ambassador, Odan (Franc Luz), who is being ferried aboard the

Enterprise to negotiate a planetary dispute. When Odan is injured, the crew discovers a parasitic creature inside his body which is the real ambassador.

••••

"The Host" was directed by series Director of Photography Marvin Rush, who negotiated his camera around the ever expanding stomach of the pregnant Gates McFadden.

"The episode had to be shot in such a way that we couldn't see her stomach," says Jonathan Frakes. "They would not address the fact that the actress was pregnant. It was an interesting problem. You really found yourself more concerned with hiding her with furniture or with your body, or shooting from her boobs up. That was very restrictive."

"It's one of the most outstanding stories we've ever done," says story editor Brannon Braga. "Being in love with someone is not very fresh. Having the parasite as the real intelligence and the body as the host is. It was not originally pitched as a love story, it was pitched as a squirmy worm who's really the intelligence. What's ironic is that the most repulsive story ever pitched to us ended up being the most touching love story and that's why this show is so unique."

Elaborates Ron Moore, "The addition of Beverly to that story is the vital component. A lot of freelancers would take that premise and say this is a show about the ambassador and the struggles of the parasitic creature and the war negotiations. No one really cares about that. But when it becomes a Beverly problem, who's in the position with the problem, and to some extent Riker, that's how it became a *Star Trek* story."

Ultimately 'The Host' has become one of the most popular *Trek* episodes in light of its non-polemic, but effective, advocacy of tolerance and acceptance.

"I had no advance knowledge of the story I was going to direct and I don't believe the company does a great deal of that," says Marvin Rush. "I'm sure they have in mind who might be good for a particular episode, but sometimes directors who have planned for an episode don't get the episode they wee going to be given because they're not ready and there are rewrites and revi-

sions. There are things that affect those choices. I believed, in my case, I was given a ship show that involved something that was a challenge that the cameraman would be good at. That one thing was that Gates, who played the romantic lead opposite Odan, was seven months pregnant and the one trick you need is someone who can figure out how to photograph that and not give away the fact the leading lady is in fact pregnant. That may or may not have been a factor to them. I suspect that it was a consideration. I think it was ready, the script was ready to go."

Although many questioned Dr. Crusher's rejection of Odan, once transplanted into a female body, as homophobic, Rush disagrees vehemently.

"Most of the people that I have talked to thought the show worked pretty well and were entertained. Some comment was that they were unhappy with the ending because it was left a question. There was, or could have been, a sort of homosexual aspect to is and we chose not to go that route with it. I felt that it was more about the nature of love, why we love and what prevents us from loving. To me the best analogy is if your beloved turned into a cockroach, could you love a cockroach? It's the same person, if the person is the personality and core within, but can you get past the outside? We as humans are affected by the whole package, including the outside shell, and Gates in her last scene talks about maybe someday our ability to love won't be so limited. She says mankind may one day be able to deal with this, but I can't. To me that is about the nature of love and I think it's an interesting, worthy discussion. Rather than deal with the fact it was because of any homosexual bent per se, it's just that in our culture and our society people who are heterosexual who want the companionship of a male because they are a female, wouldn't be able to deal with that opposite situation."

Episode #98:
"The Mind's Eye"
Original Airdate: 5/27/91
Written by Rene Echevarria
Story by Ken Schafer and
Rene Echevarria

Directed by David Livingston
Guest Starring: Larry Dobkin (Ambassador Kell), Edward Wiley (Governor Vagh), John Fleck (Commander Taibak)
In this 24th Century retelling of *The Manchurian Candidate*, Geordi is cast in the role of Laurence Harvey and—who would have thought?—Data is Frank Sinatra in a story that has LaForge brainwashed by the Romulans to assassinate a Klingon governor. The objective is to undermine the alliance between the Federation and the Empire.

••••

"The Mind's Eye" is notable for introducing Tasha Yar's daughter as the silhouetted sub-commander quietly observing Geordi's torture, played by an uncredited Denise Crosby.

Enthuses David Livingston, "I couldn't ask for a better episode to do as my first directorial assignment, since it didn't have scenes with eleven people in the observation lounge talking for ten pages. Every scene had something going on, some action. They were all short scenes and I could do some weird stuff and was thrilled. I'm kind of hyper and nervous and uptight, and I had always been afraid of directing, but I finally said, 'David, if you're going to have the opportunity, it's on this show, so go for it.' I had the best professional time of my life on that episode. I got to make all the decisions and you get to do what you want within the constraints of the budget."

Keeping an eye on the bottom line, and filling in as producer while Livingston played with his new toy, was Merri Howard. "She acted as line producer and ran a tight ship," Livingston says. "She challenged me at all the right places and we had our battles, just like I have with the directors, but we worked everything out amicably. But you sure get a different perspective on the production people. I used to say that directors have the conscience of rattlesnakes, but I've now added to that—at least they have [a] conscience, unlike production people...and I'm one of those people."

Donning his director's hat, Livingston is quick to point out that there's little graphic violence, only psychological violence as opposed to such episodes as "Yesterday's Enterprise" and "Conspiracy."

••••

"In Theory" had Ensign D'Sora (Michelle Scarabelli, seen here as Susan Francisco in Alien Nation) fall in love with Data.

"I saw the gashes on the set of 'Yesterday's Enterprise,' and I said I don't know if I should let Westmore do it," Livingston recalls. "I knew I was going to hear from Rick in dailies, but he loved it. I was afraid it was a little too grotesque. In 'Conspiracy,' Dan [Curry] really pushed it there when he blew the head up. We have to be a little prudent about violence, and I don't think we would do something that strong again. The violence in 'Mind's Eye' is all psychological. It's like *Manchurian Candidate* in that respect. I rented the movie before I shot this episode. I love it. I screened the film on two successive weekends, and took notes and studied it. [*Candidate* director Frankenheimer] shot everything in oners on that movie. He has some others that go on for four or five minutes. I think it's John Frankenheimer's best movie, Frank Sinatra's best movie, Laurence Harvey's best movie and Angela Lansbury's best movie. But, of course, it's not Janet Leigh's best film...she did something in a shower once."

Episode #99:
"In Theory"
Original Airdate: 5/27/91
Written by Joe Menosky and Ronald D. Moore
Directed by Patrick Stewart

Guest Starring: Michele Scarabelli (Jenna), Rosalind Chao (Keiko), Whoopi Goldberg (Guinan)

The long-anticipated Data love story is finally consummated by the show's two executive story editors (writers Ron Moore and Joe Menosky), in which an Enterprise cadet, Jenna (Michele Scarabelli of *Alien Nation*), on the rebound from a bad relationship, falls for the didactic Data, the stoic android devoid of emotion.

••••

Ironically, it was the captain who turned to his first officer for advice when he took the helm of an episode for the first time.

"We had a couple of conversations," admits three-time director Jonathan Frakes of Stewart's directorial debut. "He was fabulous and took to it beautifully. He's a very sensitive man and he did a great job. He was also lucky that he got a Data show as his first. Brent really is an incredible actor with unbelievable range and technique, and certainly the most popular character, so it's a real plus to get that combination."

Episode #100:
"Redemption, Part I"
Original Airdate: 6/17/91
Written by Ron Moore
Directed by Cliff Bole
Guest Starring: Robert O'Reilly (Gowron), Tony Todd (Kurn), Whoopi Goldberg (Guinan), Barbara March (Lursa), Gwynth Walsh (B'Etor), Ben Slack (K'Tal), Nicholas Kepros (Movar), J.D. Cullum (Toral), Denise Crosby (Romulan Commander)

The conclusion to the triumvirate arc dealing with Worf's Klingon dishonor, which began with "Sins of the Father" and continued with "Reunion." The Enterprise returns to the Klingon homeworld so that Picard can fulfill his role as arbiter of the Rite of Succession and allow Gowron (Robert O'Reilly) to accede to the role of ruler of the High Council. Meanwhile, Worf attempts to clear his family name.

••••

Returning for an encore performance was the new Klingon super-starship first designed for "Reunion." Since 1979, *Trek* has been recycling stock footage of the battle cruisers that got KO'ed by V'ger in *Star Trek: The Motion Picture*, and the Bird of Prey cruiser from *Star Trek III*. During fourth season, money was finally budgeted to give the Klingons a new ship.

"It's a great model," says David Livingston. "We've used a lot of stock footage from the features, but at some point it just gets old. Peter came in and said we have to do something, and we finally did. Discussions had been going on for a while and we decided we just needed something larger and more menacing. In 'Redemption,' it looms very large in the legend. The problem is it's not just building the model, it's also having to shoot all the new motion control shots with them, so it's a big deal. But we put money into each season to do refurbishing and do the new ship shots. Peter uses the money to develop those things, and what we got out of fourth season was the new cruiser."

••••

•••••

CHAPTER TWENTYFOUR

SEASON FIVE

An Introduction

Ironically, what was perceived by many as one of *Next Generation*'s finest seasons did not materialize easily. Starting in 1991, after part one of the season finale's cliffhanger "Redemption" aired, the writing staff was already scrambling for new ideas after having exhausted their supply of teleplays at the end of fourth season.

"We all just looked at this empty script status reports and said how the hell are we going to come up with 26 stories?" says staff writer Brannon Braga, who was promoted to Story Editor for the show's sixth season. "We had some real gems come from freelancers and a lot of gems came from the staff. They didn't come easy, but they did come."

"There are some series where it's easier to develop ideas like a contemporary show," says Supervising Producer Jeri Taylor. "*Simon & Simon* or *Murder She Wrote* where you can just devise a location and say I think we'll have it take place at the ballet and you set a murder mystery there. We don't have that option, we don't have a ballet or a rodeo. Every story needs to be unique with a science-fiction phenomenon and have an emotional base and all those kinds of things. When you've done as many as we have, they get harder and harder to scratch for. It's true of any series, you can never stay ahead of it because production is like this giant maw that just eats scripts. We fantasize that during the summer hiatus we'll get ten scripts done but they're treated with tender loving care that you can't just churn them out. Each one is molded carefully and scrutinized line by line and it's just such a careful effort that the time it takes doesn't allow you to accumulate a trunkload of scripts ready to go."

Facing the task of completing work on another season's worth of Treks, considering the paucity of good material, is a daunting prospect for the Supervising Producer who was promoted to Co-Executive Producer for the show's sixth season.

"It is the single most difficult challenge that we face," explains Taylor. "Even now I wake up at three in the morning saying 'Twenty six stories! Twenty six stories? Where are they going to come from?' We take pitches constantly, we have a completely open script submission policy, the staff brainstorms and we ask for help from the outside. We knock ourselves out. We do whatever we can to scratch around and somehow there have always been 26 stories, most of which are quite wonderful, some of which are extremely special and some of which are not quite as terrific as they might have been. Looking at the mix the fifth year, it's a very solid and respectable effort, but it's real, real tough."

A number of scripts and stories have been purchased by the staff as a result of their open script submission policy, which requires a signed Paramount release form with any submissions and does not require teleplays to be submitted by an agent. This has resulted in Script Coordinator Eric Stillwell being deluged with over 3,000 spec scripts a year from fans, the large majority from starstruck Trekkies who have little idea of how to craft a legitimate screenplay.

Jeri Taylor confesses to being extremely happy with the quality of the show in its fifth season. "I'm very pleased," she says. "None of them is ever easy to mount and complete and there have been any number of points along the way where all of us say 'Gulp, are we going to have any ideas?'. Ideas are the hardest thing to come by for this series. We started into this season about this time last year with only a few things in the works and never had a big, comfortable kind of reservoir of scripts and stories. We always felt like we were scrambling during the season but that's kind of par for the course. There were anxieties along the way, but I look back at the season now and think 'We really did some good stuff' and I'm very proud of it and would hold it up against any of the other years. I think the last four or five shows of the season are some of our strongest efforts and they may

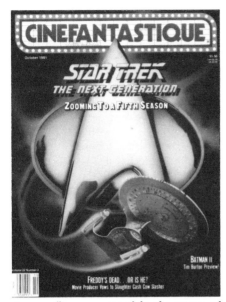

Season five as covered in the pages of Cinefantastique magazine.

even become classics, although the fans will determine that."

Through the years, the difficult challenge in adhering to the strict *Star Trek* formula has seen many writers arrive and depart quickly on the show. Few have been able to adhere to the stringent parameters set by Producers Rick Berman and Michael Piller based on the guidelines drafted during the show's genesis by Gene Roddenberry.

"It's so easy for these scripts not to be believable and to make them contrived and make them fantasy like, to make these scripts hokey and illogical and muddled," states Executive Producer Rick Berman, who has completely overseen the production of the show since its second season. "The writing of the show at every level; the story level, the structural level, the dialogue and the polishing, is so tricky. It's so difficult for writers to write dialogue that's not contemporary and also not sword and sorcery. Gene in the first year was incredibly particular to the point where the writers hated it. Today, I am as particular as is Michael. We have to be, we've learned."

"There was a lot of turmoil in the first year as all television shows have and a lot of turmoil came out of the writing staff," recalls Berman. "Gene's [Roddenberry] perfectionist attitude towards first season scripts was such

•••••

that it was very difficult for the writers and a lot of them left either willingly or not. I now, all these years later, totally understand and so does Mike Piller what Gene was after. This is a very difficult show to write and we have to work so carefully with new writers and we have to work very hard in making these scripts work unlike many other shows and it's very difficult."

Ironically, it was a first season writer, Herb Wright, who segued from *Trek* to Paramount's *War of the Worlds* five years ago, who Berman recruited back to the show fifth season to juice up the science-fiction content of *Next Generation*. Wright departed several months later over creative differences in the show's direction with Executive Producer Michael Piller.

When Wright returned to the show in 1991, he found things had changed dramatically, both on-screen and off. "Fifth season was no comparison," he states. "People were so much happier and calmer and quieter and really helping each other. It was a kinder, gentler place to be. The first year I was the kinder, gentler guy and the fifth year I came back and I was suddenly the hawk. In story meetings people would say 'In this scene let's kiss the baby and I'll say, 'Bullshit, let's kill the baby' and everybody would look at me and say what's wrong with him?"

Wright recalls meetings during the first season in which Roddenberry's attorney would be involved in story conferences. "It was so bizarre," Wright says. "Gene was bringing his attorney to staff meetings and he was giving us notes on scripts and secretly rewriting them at night and taking people's names off and putting other people's names on. He would call up writers at home, freelancers, ask them what was going on, how they were doing. It was horrible, one of the principle reasons I left. And [first/second season Producer Maurice] Hurley was the last straw for me. He was basically playing drinking buddies with Gene. Meanwhile, Robert Lewin had fallen all the way upstairs to the small office Brannon is now in.

"I was the kid on staff then," he adds. "I came back and all of a sudden I was the old man. It's radically different, not only in content, but in the make-up of the staff and the way it's put together. They're such pros, I can't tell you how difficult it is to turn out a *Star Trek* each week and keep it the kind of quality they get."

"The first year was very chaotic," agrees Berman. "But the second year Gene stepped away and Maurice Hurley and I took the reigns and there was additional shakedown but things smoothed out a little bit and in the third year Piller came and it was shaky at first and then started to stabilize and it has been very stable ever since. It's stable on all fronts. The post production people, the editors, the visual effects specialist who do such wonderful things for the show. It's a well oiled machine and it gets better and more consistent and the key is that everybody continues to be as demanding upon themselves and take it as seriously as they have taken it.

"To produce a show that is this complex you have to be an incredible stickler for detail and you have to be very hard on yourself to continue to take it that frighteningly seriously and everybody still does and that is true from the top right down to the production assistants," elaborates Rick Berman. "We've got some writers in Jeri Taylor, Ron Moore, Joe Menosky, Brannon Braga and now Peter Fields who are really starting to get a feel for the show. They've gone through a very long process in learning, but they are all learning it now and we're all pretty much in agreement about what the show is and what makes it work and what doesn't work and what is contrived and what is not good science-fiction and that's a key part of the ingredient too. It's really not a question of if the show has gotten better or that it's a different show, it's just a little bit more mature. The people who are doing it have gotten a little bit better at it. The thing that I'm most proud of is the general sense of consistency. We've gone through a number of regimes and the show has not necessarily gotten any better, but been more consistently good. I think since the beginning we've turned out some wonderful episodes; there are some wonderful episodes in the first season, in the second but, on the other hand, I think we do more wonderful episodes now. That comes out of the process of experience. I think more so than any show in this town we have had very little fall off of key personnel; we pretty much have the same people working on the show that we've had working for two, three and sometimes five years."

"It is a different process," says Brent Spiner, who portrays the unemotional android Data, of the show's evolution from first to fifth season. "There's less experimentation now. I think there's less stretching of the envelope than we did in the first few years. We were looking to find the show in the first two years and what worked and what didn't and what seemed to be appealing and what wasn't and the powers that be seemed to make their decision about the format and what worked and what didn't work and kind of went with that for the last three years. I'm not sure that's as exciting to work on in a creative aspect. To me it doesn't feel like a particularly creative process as much as a recreative process at this point. That's not to put down the efforts of our writers and producers, because I think they've done a miraculous job and it's very, very difficult to turn out 26 quality episodes every year. I do think they have managed to get a high number of quality episodes on the air in a very short amount of time, which I think is difficult. But for an actor I think the fun is exploration. Particularly for me. I've always enjoyed when I've done plays' rehearsal more than performance because I think discovery is the fun and the playing of it is the job. It's a large ensemble, but I have no real huge complaints. It's been a very rewarding piece of work and I never before have done a job for this long. When I've done Broadway I've always taken three month contracts, because the fun for me is the rehearsal and the performance becomes routine. I grow tired of the routine after a few months and I never imagined I could do a show for six years and play the same character. The good thing is that I get to play a different show every week and that keeps it interesting. There's always the hope that the next episode is going to be a great, great episode and that kinds of keeps us going."

However, even among the staff there is not universal accord over the fifth season's Enterprise missions. Michael Piller has mixed feelings when assessing the success of the shows broadcast during that period, but attributes this largely to the order in which the shows were broadcast. High concept episodes like "The Game" and "Disaster" aired back to back as did the personal dramas of "New Ground" and "Hero Worship", and the politically charged "Redemption" and "Unification" were only separated by a few installments.

"It's no secret that I've had mixed feelings about fifth season," says Piller. "If you were to look at the season week by week, I think that every week we delivered an entertaining hour of television and reliable, fun viewing and I'm not sorry we did any episode. What I'm not happy about as I look back is the mix. There were too many political shows in one block, too many personal dramas in one block, we were light on science fiction in the first half of the year and then I think around the last ten shows we really hit our stride. If you were to take those last ten shows and spread them out through the season, mix up the other ones and hold two or three to next year, it would have been a delightful season. I had a real sort of melancholy in the middle of the season saying, 'Darn, I felt like a championship basketball team that couldn't get its fast break together.' We did a lot of very good shows, but I didn't feel like we were really scoring the big wins. Then I think we put together probably five at the end of the season which could almost be considered up there with our best work."

Piller is the first to admit however that he judges *Trek* by the highest of standards and his doubts shouldn't necessarily negatively reflect on what is unquestionably one of the best shows on television. "I think I'm particularly hard on us all," says Piller. "I think it's better to be hard on yourself than content with what you're turning out and as long as it inspires and doesn't frustrate the people work here. I hope that's the case. I think the staff came through marvelously towards the end of the season. The staff has grown to be extraordinarily self sufficient. There have been times when I have felt unneeded and I think that the things that I provide in terms of conceptual help—general direction—will be as present as ever. In the case of emergencies I will be here, but I've spent a great deal of this season allowing the staff to work out its own problems and to get through to the end. In prior seasons if there was an emergency I would jump in and fix it, but this season I've only done that maybe four or five times on certain scripts that I had a vision on that nobody really seemed to appreciate or get. The rest of the scripts the staff handled themselves. I was involved with the structure and maybe certain elements, but they really finished them and Jeri finished them and I have full faith in these people. I think what I can provide is not nearly what I needed to provide in season three. I think it will work out just fine."

• • • •

CHAPTER TWENTYFIVE
SEASON FIVE

Episode Guide
"Redemption II"

"Darmok"

"Ensign Ro"

"Silicon Avatar"

"Disaster"

"The Game"

"Unification, Part I"

"Unification, Part II"

"A Matter of Time"

"New Ground"

"Hero Worship"

"Violations"

"The Masterpiece Society"

"Conundrum"

"Power Play"

"Ethics"

"The Outcast"

"Cause and Effect"

"The First Duty"

"Cost of Living"

"The Perfect Mate"

"Imaginary Friend"

"I, Borg"

"The Next Phase"

"The Inner Light"

"Time's Arrow"

Episode #101:
"Redemption II"
Original Airdate: 9/23/91
Written by Ronald D. Moore
Directed by David Carson
Guest Starring: Denise Crosby (Sela), Tony Todd (Kurn), Barbara March (Lursa), Gwynyth Walsh (B'Etor), J.D. Cullum (Toral), Robert O'Reilly (Gowron), Michael G. Hagerty (Larg), Fran Bennett (Admiral), Nicholas Kepros (Movar), Colm Meaney (O'Brien), Timothy Carhart (Hobson), Jordan Lund (Kulge), Stephen James Carver (Helmsman), Clifton Jones (Ensign Craig)

Picard discovers the Romulans are secretly providing aid to the Duras family, which is plotting to take over the Klingon Empire. Meanwhile, Worf joins his brother, Kurn (Tony Todd) as they try to keep the empire together under the leadership of Gowron (Robert O'Reilly).

••••

For director David Carson, it was not very difficult following the first part of a story which was directed by someone else.

"I do think I did my episode quite a bit differently in style from the way Cliff Bole did it," explains Carson. "I prefer to use very long lenses on the camera and I tend to make the picture very grainy, exciting, interesting and I like to throw the background a little out of focus, just to keep an element of mystery. I like to use as much mystery as I can, given the gritty nature of the story. So I like to use images, smoke, darkness, shafts of light. I find that very dramatic and I went for that as much as I could on 'Redemption.' Maybe more so than was done on the first part. But when you're doing a part two, one has to always look at the first part to see where the story's going and how it's been approached. You can't just depart from it completely because both parts have to go together.

"I find the more gritty stories fascinating," adds the director of such episodes as "The Enemy" and "Yesterday's Enterprise." "Not only do I enjoy the stories and the suspense of storytelling, but I also like the pictures that some stories produce. I think the Enterprise represents some of the 'cleaner' aspects of *Star Trek*, given this amazing, futuristic ship. Obviously the feeling is more gritty on the Klingon ships.

"I particularly enjoyed the Klingon warrior bar in 'Redemption,' because we've never seen one before. Rick Berman encouraged me to invent new ways of behaving, which is why they banged their heads together as a game; or arm wrestling with pointed daggers attached to their wrists. It was totally Klingon and it's an interesting world to work in. When you have the good fortune to have an episode like 'Redemption,' you are able to make this wonderful contrast between the clean, optimistic world of the Enterprise, and the down and dirty world of the Klingons. That's just great for a storyteller."

"I thought it was a good opportunity for me," says actor Michael Dorn. "But they also packed a lot of things into one episode...a lot of things. It was too much. I thought the Data story should have been a whole episode; it was an interesting story in which he encounters prejudice and that's a really strong point that needed more time, but they chose not to. There was also the story of how I get back to the Enterprise and the whole thing about Denise Crosby. That's three big stories for one episode, but they're the people who write it and are in charge."

"Some fans wrote and said they thought Data was really emotional in 'Redemption'," reflects Brent Spiner. "I didn't think so at all. What I was playing was a character who was in a command situation for the first time and the only model he had was the man he served under, Captain Picard. So when he yelled 'Do it!', it wasn't because he was emotional but because he thought it would engender a response because that's what Picard would have done."

Recalls writer Ron Moore, "I had more fun writing Part II than I. We knew there were a lot of stories to tell but I didn't want to lose any of those threads, and the Data thing was the most fun of all of them. I wish there were a couple more minutes because you watch it and it blazes along, [but] it was a little constrictive. The parallels to the coup in the Soviet Union was very ironic. It was something that resonated around in my mind. Part II had a little more life than part I. The problem is explaining the

Sela/Tasha backstory. It was tough to write and I knew it would be confusing and that, in essence, is the difficulty with doing continuity on the show. It's fun and gives us the sense of being a real place, but you have to explain it to people who haven't seen all those other episodes. It was not an easy explanation—that all came from Denise. She came up with the concept, which I rolled my eyes at the first time I heard. But as we started to get into story on 'Redemption Part II,' I needed some sort of Romulan thing to actually happen this time since we kept saying they're doing this stuff. It just seemed natural. It fit and we did it."

Says Co-Executive Producer Michael Piller of Denise Crosby's unorthodox encore, "Sela was not created to be a new regular character on the show. I would disagree that her return was botched. I found it quite effective, I found Sela's backstory to be quite emotionally touching. The only objection that I had to the show was that in the critical moment of the fifth act, exposure of the Romulans charge, we missed one important shot that didn't sell the remarkable nature of what Data had accomplished. Otherwise, I rather liked the opening episode of the season."

"It was a terrific episode," adds Executive Producer Rick Berman. "We've played out our Klingon political trilogy to a point where we can take a rest for a while. But I thought it was delightful and [director] David [Carson] did a marvelous job."

"I think it was the bigger of the two episodes," says Co-Producer David Livingston, responsible for the physical production of the series. "It was a more ambitious show. We didn't have the Klingon bar [in the first part] and that was a tough set to light and very cramped. It looked great, we added atmosphere on the set. The other sets were repeats. Because of money, we weren't able to build the whole Klingon Hall, which was kind of unfortunate. Richard James also wanted to make some modifications to the hall, so it was kind of tough for both Cliff on Part One and David on Part II to cover it because they literally didn't have half the set. They had to turn people around and shoot it into the other

Damnation Alley's *Paul Winfield* was the alien captain Dathon in "Darmok", a highlight episode of season five.

walls. We changed the tapestry on the back wall and things like that. We did a lot of cheats."

Episode #102:
"Darmok"
Original Airdate: 9/30/91
Written by Joe Menosky
Directed by Winrich Kolbe
Guest Starring: Paul Winfield (Tamarian Captain)

Picard is transported to an unknown world, where he encounters an alien captain played by *Star Trek II*'s Paul Winfield, who communicates through metaphors. Unable to understand the captain, Picard doesn't know if his intentions are hostile or not.

••••

"I just think 'Darmok' is the prototype of what *Star Trek* should be," says Co-Executive Producer Michael Piller. "It dealt with a very challenging premise and many of our best shows are scripts that have been around a long time. 'Darmok' had been around for two years. It was a script that was curious and interesting, and one which Rick hated and wanted to abandon. I said 'No, I want to make it work' and finally I gave it to Joe [Menosky] and asked him if he had any ideas on it, because he's a very bright and intellectual kind of guy. He came back with a memo

that had a stunning piece of philosophy about language and communication. He created a whole language for that episode and it's just astonishing. The episode worked on every level; it had the philosophy dealing with language and what it does for us; two: great acting performances, it had a monster and a space battle—it had everything."

Offers Director of Photography Marvin Rush, "I thought 'Darmok' was pretty challenging, primarily because night was done on soundstage and it has a very believable, beautiful look to it from my point of view. It doesn't look it but because Paul Winfield walked all the way around the fire and appeared to be lit from within the fire, that was a real tricky shot. I had two or three of those shots in the sequence. You only see parts of them in the edit but we did them as complete circles so that any one take would stand on its own. It was a very complicated bit of floating flags and dimming lights up and others down, and when the torch was tossed we had lights that dimmed up on cues. It was a very complicated show and it was all done on really long lenses."

Admits director Winrich Kolbe, "I have mixed feelings about that episode. I like it as a story. I feel that I was hampered as a director in many areas because of the many obstacles, especially when we finally went down to the planet and went into the battle. The battle is something rather physical and you want to be there with your camera where it belongs. If you have to pan, you have to pan. The moment you go into opticals that's over. First of all, it was kind of a downer. Even somebody who knows what's supposed to happen will look at the dailies and say, 'Wait a minute, what is this thing?' I finally said, 'Guys, let me just stage the thing the way I see it, and then let me explain to you what I want to do, because you can't write out every shot and I can't shoot the shots the way you write them anyway because there's always one element missing—which is the monster.' So everything had to be shot in certain angles and you had weird set-ups in there. You had half a head looking up and unless you knew that was a shot that goes into that particular area with the monster coming down. The editor freaked out and said, 'I don't know what to

do with this stuff.' I said, 'Just relax, when I'm finished you and I will sit down and put this episode together because I know the staging.' Then, because of the expense of opticals, I had to edit in the camera with the understanding that the editors would never know what the other side of the editorial process was, the monster.

"Storywise, it was a hell of a story. It was almost flawless. It tangled a very interesting subject and a very complicated subject as well, and I think it did it well. The other difficult thing for me was....can you imagine not speaking Russian and, in your case, having to write an article in Russian? It makes it kind of difficult. Even though I had a translation of the dialogue, it wasn't quite there and for me it was like directing a Russian movie without speaking the language, but you work your way through it. So that was an additional challenge. The episode seems to have struck a chord. It's a show we can all be proud of."

Episode #103:
"Ensign Ro"
Original Airdate: 10/7/91
Written by Rick Berman and
Michael Piller
Directed by Les Landau
Guest Starring: Michelle Forbes (Ensign Ro), Ken Thorley (Barber Mot), Cliff Potts (Admiral Kennelly)

The Enterprise is sent to negotiate a peace between the Cardassians and the militant rebel leader of the Bajorans, Orta, after the rebels are suspected of having attacked a Federation colony. Meanwhile, Starfleet Admiral Kennelly secretly plots with the Cardassians to destroy the Bajoran leaders.

••••

"What was in the back of our mind was the need for a character, and we thought we needed another woman on the show," says Michael Piller about creating the enigmatic Ensign Ro. "When we talked about what kind of woman we would want, we thought it would be nice to have someone who had a little backstory and somebody we could use to create some conflict. So Rick and I worked on the concept of Ro and it was a show I was very satisfied with."

Introducing a new character into the *Trek* ensemble was not the easiest of tasks, particularly in light of the drubbing the introduction of Sela took from the fans.

"It's a terribly difficult thing," offers Piller. "It's one of the season's greatest accomplishments. Not just by Rick and I, but by the acting of Michelle, who is just a wonderful performer. You don't just throw in new people because this audience is really particular about who they're going to make part of the family, but I've heard almost no resistance to Ensign Ro."

Piller feels that by having Ro embraced my Guinan in her freshman outing, viewers immediately were prepared to accept the new character regardless of what the crew of the Enterprise perceived as her myriad flaws. "I think Guinan embraces Ro in a very personal way. She basically took Ro by the hand and said she deserves your attention and deserves to be embraced by you. When she took Ro to Picard for that very reason, in essence, she was doing that to our audience. It was not a very easy show to write; it was not until we found that relationship between Ro and Guinan that I was personally satisfied that we really had done something magnificent."

"Mike and I felt very seriously that we wanted a character to be introduced to our mix that had a little bit of an edge and had a backstory that wasn't Starfleet Academy sweetness and light, red, white and blue," says Rick Berman. "We wanted a character whose life had enough conflict in it that they could have a little bit of an attitude but fit within the structure of Roddenberry's dictum that these characters are developed in such a way that they don't have attitudes. So we created this character and gave her a backstory and a good introductory story in 'Ensign Ro' that I think established her rather quickly."

Says Supervising Producer Jeri Taylor, "It's so nice to have someone with some edges and a dark side and some conflict. We've gotten a lot out of her. Ensign Ro was really conceived just to be a new character to give us somebody at the con and we may develop somebody for that position on the bridge now that's she moving to *Deep Space Nine*. There's nothing broken about *Star*

Trek, but it's important to inject fresh life to juice it. We've talked about some kind of startling character changes for the regulars. I don't know if those are going to happen, but we are at least discussing the kind of things that can freshen character arcs after six years. We're not going to radically change anyone, but there *are* twists and turns and maybe we'll bring in someone new to replace Ro."

"I've become very attached to *Star Trek*," says the energetic and slender Forbes, who is prone to breaking out into laughter at the slightest provocation. "I love everyone who works on the show. The stories are very interesting. It's a wonderful place where imagination just runs wild. That's rare and a lot of fun. On all levels, in writing, acting, sets, it's a wonderful place to be and be around."

Episode #104
"Silicon Avatar"
Original Airdate: 10/14/91
Story by Lawrence V. Conley
Teleplay by Jeri Taylor
Directed by Cliff Bole
Guest Starring: Ellen Geer (Dr. Marr), Susan Diol (Carmen)

The Crystalline Entity returns from "Datalore" and destroys a fledgling Federation colony. The Enterprise pursues the entity and attempts to communicate with it, while a Federation expert on this destructive force, Dr. Marr, whose son was killed on Omicron Theta, Data's planet of origin, is intent on destroying it.

••••

Director Cliff Bole does not necessarily agree with the notion that attempting to communicate with the entity after all it had done was a ludicrous extreme of an optimistic future.

"It's not, if you can control the fact that it won't happen again, and I think Picard made it clear that he wouldn't destroy anything until it was explored. And it did finally show that it had another side, and I think that's what he was saying," Bole opines. "It can be characterized with modern society's attitude, 'Let's make sure we're not making any mistakes,' knowing full well they can handle it if they were wrong.

"I'm pretty satisfied with it," he adds. "If I could go back and shoot it again, I'd make some changes. A little bit

of character change. I think I would have made Marr stronger in places and in the ending I thought we were weak. Then again, she was over the edge. You know, when you've only got 40 minutes of picture, it's tough to take a character and go all the way through the change and what happens to somebody. We're doing short stories here. Why does she do what she does? Sometimes you just don't have the film time to explore it properly. We're selling nine minutes less than the old show. You can do a lot of character development in those nine minutes.

"But you stand on what you've done and it's like theater in the round. It's not like a feature where you look at the footage and say, 'I'm going to change this and reshoot it.' You don't have that time. It's theater in the round, it's impromptu and we do good work with the resources we have available."

"I didn't think it was a very good episode," confesses Brent Spiner. "If this was to really conclude the story of the crystalline entity, I don't think it was really the way to go. Apparently, they were having problems getting the next episode ready for production and this script was ready to go, but it wasn't very remarkable."

"It was a great premise," adds Michael Piller. "The idea of the crystalline entity as Moby Dick really appealed to me. I don't think the show was as effective as I wish it could have been."

"I enjoyed working on it a lot," says Supervising Producer Jeri Taylor, who wrote the episode's teleplay. "The crystalline entity was no one's favorite optical or bad entity, and there were doubts as to whether we should even resurrect it. Along came this story from a very young, inexperienced writer, Lawrence Conley, and he tapped into something that made us say, 'This works, this is a story that really has to be done.' I wanted to do it because I felt—being a mother and a woman—I could identify with what would have to be the worst kind of loss anyone could ever suffer, which would be the death of a child. I was really able to tap into those feelings and tell a story about a woman whose vendetta over the loss of her son ruined her."

Episode #105:
"Disaster"
Original Airdate: 10/21/91
Story by Ron Jarvis and Philip A. Scorza
Teleplay by Ronald D. Moore
Directed by Gabrielle Beaumont
Guest Starring: Erika Flores (Marissa), John Christian Graas (Jay Gordon), Max Supera (Patterson), Colm Meaney (O'Brien), Rosalind Chao (Keiko), Michelle Forbes (Ensign Ro), Cameron Arnett (Ensign Mandel), Jana Marie Hupp (Ensign Monroe)

The Enterprise is struck by a deadly natural phenomena which disables the ship, trapping members of the crew throughout the vessel while the magnetic field containing the anti-matter in the engine room faces imminent collapse.

••••

"'Disaster' was pitched by a couple of outside writers and it's something we had never done before," says Jeri Taylor. "I believe in variety. I think that it freshens a series. If you see the same story week after week it becomes deadly dull. We have things on the air which hardened fans would say is not a *Star Trek* and I say, 'Who says?' It may not fall in the mold of what people call a traditional *Star Trek* or fit some formula. I'm very much for breaking formula, changing something and doing a different kind of story. It was let's do something different—stop them dead in space and give them lots of problems. I thought some fans thumbed their nose at it, but in a mix of varied stories it was a good infusion of life."

"I thought let's just have fun with it," says episode writer Ron Moore. "We put our people in interesting and fun situations. It was nice to put Troi in the captain's chair and Picard in the elevator shaft. It was very episodic, and I remember the best moment was when we were breaking the story. Michael left the room and we were looking at different elements—Data and Riker in the powertube, in particular—and somebody said 'What if Riker takes Data's head off?' Michael came back in and we said, 'You're going to hate this, but what if we took his head off?', and he laughed and rolled his eyes and said 'Do it. No one will let us do it, but go ahead, it'll be fun'. I wrote it and Rick [Berman] never

said a word. It's amazing that we got away with it."

Says Piller, "I think 'Disaster' was a fun show, it achieved everything that we set out to do. Ron wrote a nice script, I loved the stuff with Data's head disembodied. It had a real pace and rhythm. It didn't reach the upper echelon of episodes for me because it didn't really have a mystery or science fiction base to it. I think we made a mistake in that show with Ensign Ro. We gave her the role of the disbeliever who had no where to go but lose in the end because she didn't believe Troi. I think, as I wrote in a memo, it would have been much better if she'd been around a year with some victories before we threw her right in to that situation to look rather foolish. And I didn't like the moment where she had to come back and say, which was almost the same arc as that character in the opening who apologized to Data, 'Gee, you were right, Counselor and I was wrong, and I respect you.' To me, after Troi made the right decision in a crisis, Ro's character, and I'm not sure if anybody would agree with me on this, would have said, 'You still could have killed him and I still think I was right and you're just lucky it came out this way.' That's the way I would have ended it with her. The bridge sequence was my least favorite part of the show because it seemed very predictable to me. Everything else I thought was really quite wonderful."

Episode #106:
"The Game"
Original Airdate: 10/28/91
Story by Susan Sackett and Fred Bronson and Brannon Braga
Written by Brannon Braga
Directed by Corey Allen
Guest Starring: Wil Wheaton (Wesley Crusher), Ashley Judd (Robin Lefler), Colm Meaney (O'Brien), Katherine Moffat (Etana), Diane M. Hurley (Woman)

While on shore leave, Riker is given an addictive electronic mind game that rewards the player with an orgasmic-like physical sensation. He begins to distribute the device aboard the Enterprise, making the crew pawns of the alien race who have created "the game."

••••

"'The Game' kicked around for quite a while and went through lots of permutations," recalls Ron Moore. "They turned it upside down and Brannon struggled with that for quite a while and they landed on this concept. Like 'Darmok,' it was long in development with different approaches."

"'The Game' was not one where we said let's do high concept," says Jeri Taylor. "It had been in development for two seasons and we had many, many approaches and writers taking cracks at it. It had a very long development history. Through an evolutionary process—without really intending to ape that movie [*Invasion of the Body Snatchers*]—this insidious spread of a game had its origins in kids being addicted to video games now, and what happens to them. That was the original intent and that's what drove the final story and script. That insight followed the development."

"We were going for fun and high concept," says writer Brannon Braga. "It's an atypical show in some ways and a lot of people had trouble believing Picard would become addicted and all these people would get hooked, but that's the story. Either you tell it or you don't. Not that we didn't give a lot of thought to how the characters became addicted. The characters only become addicted because they were getting the game from people they trusted, which is exemplified in the notorious chocolate scene, which had a very mixed reaction, but I had a lot of fun writing it. We were going for a fun show and thought it would be the perfect one to bring Wesley back in. It's ironic to have the adolescent come back to find all the adults are addicted to a game which is something you'd expect the other way around. And it was an opportunity to give Wesley a girlfriend. When I was writing the teleplay, I tried to relax him a little bit and took the opportunity to make him a more relaxed character with some personality and some spunk. He's more savvy because he was at the Academy and has gone through some changes and he'll pick up on Robin Leffler."

"I thought that was a great episode," says Michael Piller. "That was an episode that dealt with my fascination

in watching my two sons with their obsession for video games and doing a show that dealt with a non-world shattering issue but people's obsession, almost addiction, to certain types of games. There's another show that was abandoned. It had been around for a year and we had actually had two drafts of it written and I said this cannot be fixed. The tables were reversed [when] Rick [Berman] said that I kept saying we didn't have any science-fiction premises and I was groaning and kvetching. He said what about that 'Game' story, and I said I can't make that work, we abandoned it. He said 'Why don't you give it to that kid, Brannon?' He'd been interning and staff writing. He delivered that script and did some wonderful things. He wrote scenes that didn't depend on action but went straight to character; and a two minute scene with Troi and a chocolate sundae which was wonderfully written. He has an extraordinary talent to find the moments in script where you can throw in character development and spend the time doing that for the sheer delight of getting to know that character better—and *not* interrupting the flow. He grew up this season into a full-fledged professional writer and I'm delighted that he'll be coming back next year with a credit."

"That's a fun episode," adds Jonathan Frakes. "A friend of mine asked me if I still had the game. He wanted it as a present. It was like O.D.'ing on Nintendo. They told me it was going to be this incredible graphic, and all it was a tuba on a checkerboard."

Episode #107:
"Unification, Part I"
Original Airdate: 11/4/91
Story by Rick Berman and Michael Piller
Teleplay by Jeri Taylor
Directed by Les Landau
Guest Starring: Graham Jarvis (Dokachin), Erick Avari (B'ljik), Joanna Miles (Perrin), Mark Lenard (Sarek), Stephen D. Root (K'Vada), Malachi Throne (Pardek), Daniel Roebuck (Romulan #1), Norman Large (Neral), Mimi Cozzens (Soup Woman), Leonard Nimoy (Spock), Karen Hensel (Admiral), Majel Barrett (Computer Voice)
When the Federation suspects the legendary Ambassador Spock

(Leonard Nimoy) has defected to the Romulans, Picard and Data are sent to Romulus to ascertain his true motives.

•••••

"Originally it came out of Frank Mancuso, the chairman of Paramount at the time, who said to Leonard when they were planning *Star Trek VI*, why don't you figure out some way to pass the baton," says Rick Berman of Spock's visit to *The Next Generation*. "Maybe you could make some elements of *Star Trek VI* that reflect on *Next Generation*, and work with Berman to make *Next Generation* reflect *Star Trek VI* to have some backpacking. I sat down with Leonard and Nick Meyer, and we discussed elements of our show. Nick looked at at least a dozen episodes and we tried to find a way to join the two in certain respects. That was done in subtle ways in *Trek VI*. And then we sat down with Leonard and we said we'd like you to do an episode or two. We needed to do something in the 24th century that reflected something that happened in the 23rd century without giving away any elements of the movie, because our episode was going to run before the movie came out. We talked about it and went away. Mike and I spent a lot of time kicking things around and finally we came back to Leonard with an idea he didn't particularly like. We made a big change while we were talking in the room and he loved it. He was very kind to agree to do it and did it for a very reasonable sum of money, considering the kind of money he demands.

"We sat down and wrote the two episodes. I think the fix had to do with the idea that unification of Vulcan and Romulan societies was something that Spock realized was happening and had been happening for centuries, and that it had to be nurtured along. The idea of him staying behind to continue that process and that the Romulans were in fact—unbeknownst to themselves—going through the same evolutionary early metamorphosis in their culture that the Vulcans had those many centuries ago. He had to be there to help them work with it. It became more of a show that dealt with a peaceable as opposed to a warlike element, and Leonard felt very strongly about that. We futzed with it

here and there based on Leonard's notes and, mostly, our own."

Adds Berman, "These were the two highest rated episodes we've ever done since the pilot and I think they were quite good. I was happy with both of them. Surprisingly, I felt Part 1 worked out a little better than Part 2. Understandably, Part 2 was pretty talky, but Leonard did a great job. It was a bitch to shoot Leonard's scenes since we had to have him do it all in 5 days—his part in two episodes. Granted he only had one scene in Part One, but it was difficult and we put in long hours. But we did it."

One pre-occupation that didn't concern Berman was how to acknowledge the show's progenitor, "*Classic Trek*", during Spock's foray into the 24th century. "I don't have any great belief in paying homage to the original show. The Spock we were dealing with in those two episodes was much more the Spock from the movies than from the original series. I certainly feel very strongly about being accurate. The fans of *Star Trek* would be let down if we were not to do our very best to be true to the nomenclature and rules of the two series. We have to treat it with respect. We were dealing with a character that was based on 25 years worth of development and, specifically, on what this character and his world was doing in *Star Trek VI*."

Opines Ron Moore, "I think the Sarek scene in Part One is great, and I was really happy that they did it and had the courage to kill the character and send him out that way."

Differs Jonathan Frakes, "I thought it was a real cheat. You expected Spock to be in the first part and he doesn't show up until the end. It was deceptive, but it was nice to see some sense of continuity between the two universes. To me, the highlight of the two episodes was the scene where Picard was trying to sleep and Data stood by watching him. That was funny. Leonard's a classy guy. I thought it was very nice of him to do our show. He didn't have to, and he exhibited great class when he was here."

"I was really gratified when Michael asked me to write one of the episodes," says "Unification Part One"

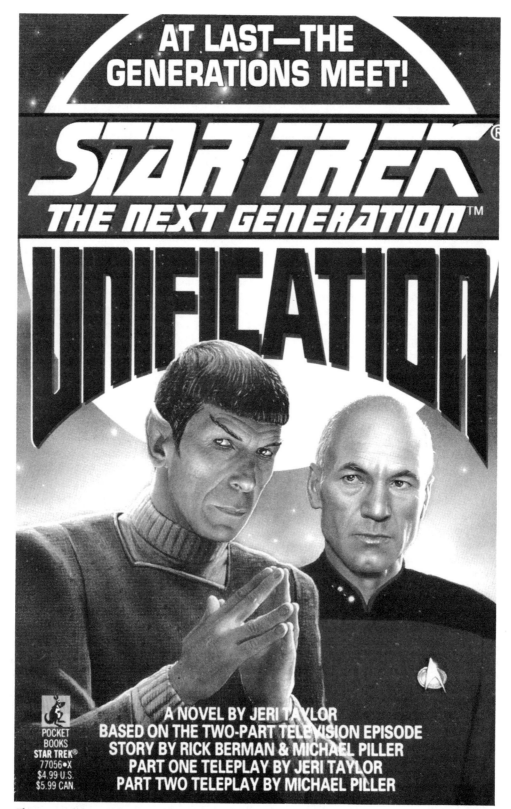

The cover of the novelization of "Unification," the two-part episode of Next Generation that allowed Mr. Spock to meet Captain Picard.

writer Jeri Taylor. "He had set out to write them both, but they were back to back and it was overwhelming. He turned to me and I felt very complimented that that project, which was so important, was entrusted to me. He and Rick had worked out the story for both episodes and I fleshed it out in our script breaking process. He had come in with a lot of the philosophical, political discussions and what I got of course was the prolonged tease to Spock's appearance. He came on at the very end and the challenge was to tap dance well enough to sustain interest, even though this highly anticipated character was not there. I was really pleased with how the episode turned out. Once you have Spock and Picard and Spock and Data, you have gold, so the challenge was are we going to be able to keep the balls in the air enough to make that first episode work? I thought it was exciting, the mystery worked and it was a well-realized episode in its own right—almost to everyone's surprise, since it was felt this is the one we have to do to get to the good stuff. But it held its own in very equal terms with the second part."

Episode #108:
"Unification, Part II"
Original Airdate: 11/11/91
Story by Rick Berman and Michael Piller
Teleplay by Michael Piller
Directed by Cliff Bole
Guest Starring: Leonard Nimoy (Spock), Denise Crosby (Sela), Stephen D. Root (K'Vada), Malachi Throne (Pardek), William Bastiani (Omag), Daniel Roebuck (Romulan #1), Susan Falldender (Romulan #2), Vidal Peterson (D'Tan), Norman Large (Neral), Harriet Leider (Amarie)

Picard, who has found Spock on Romulus, learns that the Vulcan has come to the Romulan homeworld on a secret mission to reunite the Romulans with their progenitors on Vulcan, but quickly learns that he is a pawn in Sela's plans to invade Vulcan.

• • • •

"Les Landau did part one, but I did part two first," explains director Cliff Bole. "We shot out of order due to availabilities. If this is an education for the people who watch television, sometimes

you have to do crazy things. We shot two first, which was the conclusion, and then said, 'Okay, now we've got to come up with number one.' It takes a lot of talent to do that writing wise. This was only because we had a certain amount of availability with Leonard that we had to deal with.

"I admit that I have some disappointment with the story," he adds, acknowledging the fact that episode writer Michael Piller is highly critical of his own script, "but I think Michael is being a little hard on himself. We were dealt a hand and we had to deal with it. We had a certain amount of time and I think Michael did a real good job with it. Again, he's being real self-critical and we do that. We could have done better. But we had an assignment and had to do it, and I think we filled that gap real well. I'll defend that to the end.

"The strengths of the episode, are probably the things that don't show on the screen," Bole continues. "We pulled it together with the limited availability to an actor and we knew damn well that people were going to watch this show. The things that stand out in my mind are that it was a joy to work with Leonard. I don't find a lot of weaknesses with the show. I really don't. A lot of people thought it was a little slow in places, but Leonard's been playing this character for 30 years and he has a delivery. That's Spock. By the way, he was 100 years older in this episode than in anything we've seen. Negatively speaking, that show we should have opened up. We should have gone out. We should have put some air in that show. We shouldn't have been in a cave so long, we should have gone out and had a little more action."

"It's no secret I was disappointed more by my own work on it than anything else," says "Unification II" writer Michael Piller. "I thought it was a historic opportunity and I don't think we delivered what the potential of it was. I remember watching it for the first time cut together and saying, 'This is dark, it's flat, who cares, it's talky.' I'm a writer who depends a great deal on his instincts and they almost always lead me in a good direction. This time I don't think they did. If I had it to do over, I would do

a science-fiction mystery with weird stuff and get Spock involved in some form or fashion. It was unfortunate that we chose to do another political story so close to the stuff we had just done on the Klingon Empire. It was a politically heavy opening of the season. It came out of lofty goals, and goals that were very true to the nature of the show.

"It was our feeling that if you're going to bring Spock out of retirement, it should be something of cosmic significance. The unification of the Romulans and the Vulcans really struck me as the appropriate story to tell, because we're really telling the story of the unification of the original series and *Next Generation*, symbolically closing the gap that had always been in the fans' minds, if no one else's, between the two shows. I said what a great way of having this metaphor and building the series around this reunification. I thought that was marvelous, so we built the story and we had to make a decision whether we were going to do two parts or one, and we made a decision to do two parts. Right or wrong, we would have never been able to produce—for our budget—that story for an hour, though it would have made a much better hour show than two hour show. I was very pleased with Part One, oddly enough. I know a lot of people were very angry that they didn't get to see Spock until the last beat of the last scene, but I thought there were more interesting elements in Part One than there were in Part Two. I liked the stuff with Sarek, I thought it was very moving."

"We all broke the story together and we sat around and gave notes and discussed different things about Spock," says *Classic Trek* fan and *Next Generation* Producer Ron Moore. "My only real involvement was that I was a little bit more steeped in the old *Star Trek* than most people. I gave Mike [Piller] little insights, nothing really heavy, but little questions about Vulcans and I talked to Jeri about the relationship between Sarek and Spock. I was happy to see mention made of the original show. I didn't push and didn't mention anything because I wanted them to just do it. When we did work on 'Sarek' third season, there were a couple of little references that I asked for to the old show which I got. Now and again I slip in something as a reference."

"I thought the mystery we set up was interesting, the character we met with Riker and the scene between Data and Picard on the Klingon ship is perhaps the single best relationship scene that this series has ever done," says Michael Piller. "I think that was classic. To me it was a good roadshow. My plan for Part Two with Rick—and I'm trying to take the blame, not the credit—was I wanted to tell a story about the maturity of one of drama's great characters. What happens to a Spock in the 85 years between then and now? How has logic and emotion played a part in his life? What is the growth of the man beyond logic? What was the conflict between he and his father and the death and passing of generations? I thought they were meaningful pieces of business to explore the man. I did not want a lot of plot to get in the way of the examination of the man and I felt that the show would be carried by the conflict between Spock and Picard, with Picard ironically representing the father through the mind meld. In fact, it was Picard who represented the original philosophy of *Star Trek* and Spock who was moving onto the future, so when the two came together it was sort of a reversal. It was all great stuff and it sounded wonderful in my mind and on paper, but the bottom line for me was that the relationship between Picard and Spock didn't have the chemistry. I don't think it was in the script and I don't think it came out on screen. There was not enough plot to pick up the slack when that didn't work. Throwing Sela into the mix didn't help. I thought it would be nice to have her as the archenemy, but it didn't really work out. It was talky without action, and it had some good scenes."

Says Brannon Braga, "I felt overall it was a little bit talky. Personally, I don't have a predilection to political stories. I find them inherently dry and the political elements of 'Unification Part One' I found somewhat dull overall. I thought it succeeded with some wonderful scenes in both episodes, mainly character scenes like between Data and Picard where he [Picard] is trying to

sleep; and there's a great scene between Spock and Data that everyone was waiting for. On the whole, I didn't care for the plot and the fan response was mixed. I know Michael was disappointed. It's hard to say any of our shows are bad, because if nothing else, they look great. I thought Part One was good. The death scene was very moving, the final scene between Spock and Picard was very moving and that arc I would have rather seen explored rather than the political stuff with Sela. I would have liked to have seen that Romulan subplot taken backseat and wish that Leonard Nimoy would have played the role less old. Mike wrote it much more lively. It should have had some of the feel of the original series where he's the guy whose onto everything and super alert. He seemed a little zoned out."

Episode #109:
"A Matter of Time"
Original Airdate: 11/18/91
Written by Rick Berman
Directed by Paul Lynch
Guest Starring: Matt Frewer (Berlingoff Rasmussen), Stefan Gierasch (Hail Moseley), Sheila Franklin (Ensign), Shay Garner (Female Scientist)

A mysterious visitor, historian Berlingoff Rasmussen, who has materialized from the future in a time pod, says he is observing the Enterprise crew on a critical mission to save an asteroid devastated planet from environmental destruction.

••••

"I am fascinated by all the episodes that have dealt with the implausibility of time travel," confesses Rick Berman. "I have always had in my head the idea of an episode that had someone who was capable of time travel and professes he is from the future, and we find out he is actually from the past. It's part of that Mark Twain feeling of what Leonardo Da Vinci could have done with a calculator or Alexander the Great with a shotgun. I developed the show with Robin Williams in mind for the role. He had said he wanted to do the show, but when it got finished his wife was 8 1/2 months pregnant and he had just finished *Hook*, and was starting something else. He couldn't do it, but I was very pleased with the direction it went in and very pleased with Paul Lynch, who

Matt Frewer, best known as Max Headroom, was Berlingoff Rasmussen in "A Matter of Time."

we hadn't used as a director since the second season."

"Nobody ever just hands in a script—not me, not even Rick," says Michael Piller. "It was a delightful change of pace and tone from the grimness and darkness of the Spock episode. It was just at the right time. Rick and I and the staff worked long and hard with him on the script and he had a lot of challenges to overcome. That fourth act where Picard and Rasmussen have a one scene act is wonderful and I enjoyed that a lot.

"In 'A Matter of Time' I was dealing with a B story that involved a world that had a series of volcanic problems, and the need for the Enterprise to come and do something that would hopefully fix it but would eventually screw it up. The solution Data comes up with will hopefully fix it, but could eventually destroy the planet," says Berman. "To sit with the scene guys and research and develop it and to try and come up with something that would work, you get lost in the technical elements of it. You need other people to come and hit you over the head and pull it back. Sometimes we succeed with that and sometimes we don't."

"It was more of a comedy than a drama," says director Paul Lynch. "Matt Frewer [who played the role originally written for Robin Williams] was wonderful as a space con man. He's an actor who left Canada to study in Britain and had been part of the theatre scene there. He got the reputation of being large for his comedy roles, but he was a consummate actor and he found the level of comedy and realism of the character which is what makes him such a good character. He was never schticky."

Episode #110:
"New Ground"
Original Airdate: 1/6/92
Story by Sarah Charno and
Stuart Charno
Teleplay by Grant Rosenberg
Directed by Robert Scheerer
Guest Starring: Brian Bonsall (Alexander),
Georgia Brown (Helena), Sheila Franklin
(Ensign), Richard McGonagle (Dr. Ja'Dar),
Jennifer Edwards (Lowry)

Worf's mother brings his son, Alexander, back to the Enterprise when she realizes that she and her husband can no longer give the youngster the attention he needs. Meanwhile, an experiment with a new warp field soloton wave goes awry, jeopardizing the ship.

••••

Enthuses director Robert Scheerer, "I love that show and I love working with Michael. Michael and I have a fun relationship. I was so proud of him in this episode and I'm very impressed with the kid, Brian Bonsall. Brian was very nervous the first day, but he loved the make-up and he's a very bright boy. The first day both of us were kind of feeling our way, seeking a common ground, and from the second day on it was just a joy. And Michael just grows by leaps and bounds on the show every year. It's a joy to watch an actor grow like that."

And what does he think of the Soliton Wave aspect of the storyline? "I've gotten to the point after doing so much episodic material that I find it hard to take one total anything and judge it. What I tend to look for more and more are moments and pieces and successes dealing with a part of an episode, or a character or character relationships. Otherwise it gets so damn depressing because you so rarely get something that comes all together. I suppose the wave

wasn't a powerhouse, but the relationship between father and son was so strong for me, that that was the joy of that show."

"I think it was something we had been thinking about since we saw him last year," Michael Piller says of the introduction of Alexander, Worf's son, as a member of the ensemble. "We thought it would be a lot of fun to have a young Klingon and to see what Worf would be like as a father, and to use Alexander to see different parts of the ship. I think Brian Bonsall did a wonderful job acting in the role. It's been an interesting addition."

"I was involved quite a bit with that script," says Ron Moore. "We had talked about leaving Alexander on the ship in 'Reunion,' but it was one more plot element we didn't want to have to deal with. The idea of bringing him back was something we kept in the back of our mind and we just decided to do it. I thought it was a good decision for the character of Worf. The idea is to keep in mind who these people are. Worf is more Klingon than the Klingons are. He doesn't seem to have a real good sense of humor, he doesn't laugh a lot. The Klingons are these boisterous Vikings in space, and his whole relationship with his son is geared towards making him the perfect little warrior. The fact that Alexander's mother didn't share any of those ideas immediately puts the two in conflict, which was good because that's the essence of drama and it's built in stories of the two of them knocking heads."

"We got a lot of negative response to the episode," recalls Brannon Braga. "Ron did as good a job as anyone could have done. I liked the relationship that was developed between father and son and I think that's an episode where you could complain it's getting to be like a soap opera on the ship. Perhaps because the B-story was just that, a B-story, with the soloton wave. There's a feeling that you need that jeopardy story and it's something Mike Piller advocates, and I think he's right. You need something to drive the story forward, but our best episodes successfully integrate the two; 'Darmok' had an A-B story, but they were vital to one another. Not only were they vital in terms of plot, but in themes as well, which is why that show worked

so well. A show where it didn't work was 'In Theory.' I just wanted to see more of the Data arc. I didn't want to see that other story at all. It was interesting with that woman through the floor, nice imagery, but that's it. You really want to go back to the other thing. Then there are shows with only one plot."

Offers Rick Berman, "I thought it was well done, but it doesn't stand out for me. Our greatest desire is to have shows where either the A-B story stands so well alone that they can be intermingled the way two plots on *LA Law* are, or the A-B story have a reason to intermingle with each other. Then there's the other event where a show is strong enough to have one story with the science fiction and character drama. The shows that I find the most disappointing are the shows where we have a wonderful character piece and a weak science fiction story. It's a wonderful character development piece of drama and some parasite, or some dripping goo or some asteroid disaster that's looming has to be forced into the story. We do our best to avoid those, but sometimes they happen."

Enthuses Michael Dorn, "I've been very lucky. Worf has been busy. He had a mate, lost her, has a son, adoptive parents and real parents that were killed, and he was paralyzed for a while. I've been very fortunate where they have touched on a lot of Worf's character."

"New Ground" was written by *Time Trax* executive producer and co-creator Grant Rosenberg.

"The good thing about *Star Trek* is I'm good friends with Rick Berman and I've known Mike Piller for years as well as Jeri Taylor," says Rosenberg. "They're so smart and so good at what they do that it was just a delight working with them. The contributions they all made were very good. But it's a lot easier being on this side of the desk. I was a writer/producer under contract at Paramount and I was writing *MacGyver* and various other shows. Rick Berman called me and said, 'We need a *Star Trek*, would you like to write one?' and I said, 'I'd love to.' They said do not come in with ideas. The chances of you coming in with a fresh idea that we haven't heard or rejected or done is slim. So they gave me an idea which had been developed by a writing team which never went from idea to script and they handed me a story and we stripped it down to its bear bones. The idea dealt with Worf's son and we built back up from there."

Episode #111:
"Hero Worship"
Original Airdate: 1/27/92
Story by Hilary J. Bader
Teleplay by Joe Menosky
Directed by Patrick Stewart
Guest Starring: Joshua Harris (Timothy), Steven Einspahr (Teacher), Sheila Franklin (Ensign), Harley Venton (Transporter Chief)

The Enterprise discovers the sole survivor of a destroyed research vessel, the Vico: a boy whose parents have been killed when the ship was exploring a Black Cluster. The youth, in attempting to cope with his pain, begins to emulate Data.

••••

"I like 'Hero Worship' the best of all the kid shows because it's the most interesting," says Brannon Braga. "Good performances and an intriguing mystery, thinking that aliens had destroyed the ship. It's an offbeat premise in which an emotion recluse tries to emulate Data's personality. It's always nice when you have a new twist, and this twist is Data confronting someone who wants to be an android as opposed to him wanting to be human. Picard's saying, 'Make him the best android he can be,' and the scene where Data confesses to wishing he knew what the taste of malted was like, is very touching."

"I thought it was a great premise," enthuses Michael Piller. "It wasn't a memorable show, but I thought it was very entertaining. What made this interesting was Data has always been emulating human behavior, and here a human is emulating android behavior. One of the goals of the script was for Data to appreciate more of what he is and who he is, and that there's something to learn from and appreciate. I think 'Hero Worship' and, as a whole, this has been a very good season for Deanna Troi. We have used her as a counselor as well as she has ever been used. She has certainly had more time on screen and what I think has come out of it is proof that she is really a wonderful actress and has levels of credibility

and truth on the screen. I'm a big fan of hers and she really rose to the challenge this year."

"On 'New Ground' we had a fire on Stage 16 and on Patrick's show we did go over to the other ship where the kid had to be rescued," says David Livingston. "Deceptively, even though the rest of the shows take place on ship, those scenes we shot on 16 take up a lot of time and add production value to the show. Very rarely do we ever just do a bottle show. There's always some kind of element that will be visually interesting. "

Episode #112:
"Violations"
Original Airdate: 2/3/92
Story by Shari Goodhartz & T. Michael and Pamela Gray
Teleplay by Pamela Gray and Jeri Taylor
Directed by Robert Weimer
Guest Starring: David Sage (Tarmin), Ben Lemon (Jev), Rosalind Chao (Keiko), Eve Brenner (Inad), Craig Benton (Crewman Davis), Rick Fitts (Dr. Martin), Doug Wert (Jack Crusher), Majel Barrett (Computer Voice)

A telepathic alien race, the Ullians, who have the unique gift of probing humans' long-forgotten memories, are being ferried aboard the Enterprise when members of the crew begin to fall into unexplained comas.

••••

"It's true that every one of these scripts goes through a very protracted and difficult development process," says Jeri Taylor. "Nothing you ever see on the air started that way. We have a very free flowing exchange of ideas in the staff, people don't agree with each other, which is extremely healthy. We hash it out, we fight, we argue, we rend our hair. It becomes very passionate and I think that's a healthy thing to happen. 'Violations' was very dear to my heart, because it was a rape story and we felt we wanted to avoid the classic rape story, which is someone gets raped and then we do the emotional aftermath. That's a story that's been told and told and told and told. We felt we had nothing fresh to offer. This was one of the first of the episodes that made us go on a course we will be going on next season in terms of the feeling and the style of the

story material. It was spooky, weird, alien, unusual. It worked so well we said maybe we need more of that and maybe the science fiction aspect of *Star Trek* is not getting all the play that it needs. Sometimes we get political, we get emotional, but are we really going with the weirdness of the Roddenberry universe? Are we seeing aliens that are truly alien? There were other writers involved, many different approaches. We ultimately came to the show that was on the air, and it was miles from where it started."

"'Violations' was a story we had in development for quite a while," says Ron Moore. "It always hinged on trying to find a way to tell what is in essence a rape story from a science-fiction standpoint. Then it became an issue of what are those little dream sequences going to be and how are we going to present the antagonist and the victims, and what are they saying about the characters and what are going to be the things that are intimate and personal to them? With Riker it was a decision to be more action-oriented, and you didn't want the guy to have such a keen insight into everybody that he'd know what the most personal moment would be. We just wanted them to all look a little different."

"We knew that about Beverly and Troi, but where did Riker rushing people out of engineering come from?" asks Jonathan Frakes. "That's a no-brainer. Riker would just say, 'That's the way it is. People die, shit happens. His worst fear is *not* rushing people out of engineering. That didn't come out of character. Bob Weimer really had a field day, though. He got to use all these science-fiction techniques, 60mm lenses and everything, and that let him give it the look that it had."

"You have to make sure you don't misinterpret what this guy was doing," says Michael Piller of the nightmare hallucinations precipitated by Ben Lemon as Jev. "He was basically going into your memories and playing in them for his own amusement, pleasure and fulfillment. He was not going in and exploring any character's greatest fear. He might go in and feel that today he wants to see Troi's sexual secrets and tomorrow he may want to see Riker's unhappiest memory and see him suffer. I don't think it's something Riker carries with him as a burden for the rest of his life. It's a memory that's part of his life, just like Tasha's first death would be for him."

Adds Brannon Braga, "I would have rather seen Geordi in the burning house memory. His flashback wasn't as powerful, but it's a great science-fiction show and I'm a big fan of surreal imagery. The show's picking up speed now and this episode is *Star Trek* at its best. It started with the premise and then the rape analogy started to come into play. This is the best kind of *Star Trek* development which is in story. We had a good story—mind rape, mental violation of memories—and it becomes an oblique science-fiction metaphor for a compelling issue of today. Beautifully directed; stylistically, the most daring show we've done."

"'Violations' was a very interesting concept," Rick Berman states. "It was one that I was a little bit critical of at first until it started to wend its way into a script. I thought it worked out quite nicely and Bob Weimer did a lovely job. It was his ability to get quite abstract in filmic techniques. I'm a great believer in *Star Trek* not using filmic techniques that call attention to themselves. *Star Trek* has enough 'gee, wow' to it just by the nature of its story elements and the nature of its visual effects. On the other hand, on an episode like this where we had to do abstract memory sequences, we let Bob go hogwild. As a result, I think we had a wonderful episode with some great acting. It was very mystical and very interesting."

Episode #113:
"The Masterpiece Society"
Original Airdate: 2/10/92
Story by James Kahn & Adam Belanoff
Teleplay by Adam Belanoff and
Michael Piller
Directed by Winrich Kolbe
Guest Starring: John Snyder (Aaron Conor), Dey Young (Hannah Bates), Ron Canada (Marcus Benbeck), Sheila Franklin (Ensign)
A genetically altered society living in a biosphere is threatened by the approach of a stellar core fragment while Troi falls for the planet's leader, Arron Connor.

••••

"This was the beginning of me feeling better about the season," confesses Michael Piller. "It was another one of these shows that had been around for a while and a lot of writers had taken a shot at. It dealt with genetic engineering and abortions and interesting things for Geordi to do, and the relationship between Troi and the leader of the society. I think it's a real classic tragedy, because everybody was trying to do the right thing in that episode and it ended up in destruction. Aside from some disappointment in casting, I was rather pleased with that. I think a lot of people were rather pleased they liked it as much as they did."

"It's a very philosophical issue that we felt seriously about, and a show that I thought was disappointing and didn't turn out as well as I had hoped," admits Rick Berman. "It was slow and talky and we had casting problems. As for the abortion issue, that's nonsense. It was totally unintended. I think that there are a very few people on our writing staff who would be involved with something that would be a non-choice outlook."

Jeri Taylor agrees. "Michael and I are at odds about it. It was an idea I didn't like from the beginning. I didn't like the concept. I wasn't wild about the script. I thought it was one of our weakest episodes of the season."

Says Ron Moore, "This is another example of a show that doesn't really work too well. We sort of show up at a genetically perfect colony—which in and of itself is starting to bore me—and when we get there, it's 'Gee, Troi falls in love with one of the people.' You can't wait to get up and get a beer."

Visualizing the biosphere was a challenging task for the production team, which utilized blue screen to create the unusual environment. "Rick wanted to make sure we could see the effects outside the window," says David Livingston. "He didn't want to do what we normally do on stage, which was something tangible and real. That presented some challenges to the director, because the blue screen was right in the middle of the set, but he shot around it a little bit and I think it worked out successfully."

Admits director Winrich Kolbe, "The people were too damn perfect, and

I don't think perfection makes for good drama. I wasn't too intrigued with the lead actor either and that turned out to be kind of a flat episode for me."

Episode #114:
"Conundrum"
Original Airdate: 2/17/92
Story by Paul Schiffer
Teleplay by Barry M. Schkolnick and
Joe Menosky
Directed by Les Landau
Guest Starring: Michelle Forbes (Ensign Ro), Liz Vassey (Kristin), Erich Anderson (MacDuff), Erick Weiss (Crewman), Majel Barrett (Computer Voice)
The crew suffers a collective cause of amnesia after they are scanned by an alien ship and are led to believe they are at war with the Lysians, a technologically inferior race who, they are told by Executive Officer Keiran MacDuff, they are supposed to destroy.

••••

"I think what made that episode worthwhile to me as a creative person was if you strip away everything that our memories give us about ourselves, then we're stripped of inhibition and parts of us that we might use to define ourselves in social interaction. How would we see ourselves?" suggests Michael Piller. "There's a psychology that says you have an outer self and an inner self, and if the outer self is stripped away and the inner self is all that's left, you're dealing in a very raw way in seeking your place in this strange and extraordinary universe. When you have Riker and Ro suddenly engage in a romantic relationship, that's sort of their raw inner selves coming out and that made it fun."

"It was fun working with Frakes," ponders Michelle Forbes. "It's an interesting problem for a character, because you have a very defined character that leans one way. When you have amnesia you wonder if that brings out a side of you that's always wanted to come out. Would you really be comfortable with that? It's an interesting thing. I had a really good time with that episode."

Opines Brannon Braga, "It was a leftover from last season, since we had already done two amnesia stories ['Future Imperfect' and 'Clues']. It was a tough show to lick and Joe Menosky

••••

237

finally made it work. The stuff about the character triangle is great, and it was well directed. The one problem I felt that could have kept the story moving was the mystery of the Number One who wasn't Number One. For some reason his character didn't work. I wish it would have been stronger, because this would have been a classic. We always want to explore characters in some capacity. I hope that's why people tune in. Certainly we'd like to come up with more conundrums and situations. I'd like to find more challenges which feature a science-fiction confrontation like in 'Conundrum.'"

"The most interesting thing to me was the whole Riker/Troi/Ro triangle that was going on," says Ron Moore. "It was interesting to see Ro with the tension gone and to see that she was in fact attractive to Riker and vice versa. The two of them, if they were different people, would have had a great relationship. There was a lot of fun there. I liked the last scene with Riker and Troi and Ro. That was the most interesting element of the show to me. It was a bottle show, we couldn't go very many places, but watching the actors do different takes on their characters was interesting. It's always been a question of this is our show and we want to remain true to what our vision of *Star Trek was*, and try and tell good drama. Sometimes we get a little too serious ourselves. There are times to tell other types of stories. I think we could loosen up a little bit. It's not a comedy, but we can have more humor."

"'Conundrum' was around for a couple of years," says Jeri Taylor. "It was a tough show to do. Everyone took a shot at writing that and what it gave us was some marvelous character development with Ro, Riker and Troi. It invigorated the relationships and showed another side of Ro in that she plays comedy very nicely."

"A high concept idea where everyone wakes up," says Rick Berman. "It's a thought provoking episode, I thought. Not one of the greats. It's based on that whole concept of what if? If you have nine people who don't know who or what they are, will they find themselves? Will they find the pecking order? Will the captain become the captain?"

Episode #115:
"Power Play"
Original Airdate: 2/24/92
Story by Paul Ruben and Maurice Hurley
Teleplay by Rene Balcer and Herbert J.
Wright & Brannon Braga
Directed by David Livingston
Guest Starring: Rosalind Chao (Keiko), Colm Meaney (O'Brien), Michelle Forbes (Ensign Ro), Ryan Reid (Transporter Technician), Majel Barrett (Computer Voice)

Troi, Data and Riker investigate the disappearance of the starship Essex two centuries before via shuttlecraft, but a fierce storm forces the ship to crashland. O'Brien transports through to rescue the others but as they beam out, the spirits of the planet's exiled prisoners which inhabit the ionosphere possess Data, Troi and O'Brien.

••••

"There were two challenges in filming 'Power Play,'" says producer and episode director David Livingston. "I told other people that the best two things about it were that it was an action show, which we don't have a lot of. You just can't do 26 of those a year, they're too expensive. The other great thing was taking three of our continuing characters and having them play something entirely different. It was a chance to work with them and create totally new characters, and that was a lot of fun. We came up with names for them on the set. Marina was Slash, Data was Buzz and Colm was Slugger. It was fun working our way through that and they were all great. That script went through a lot. The writers are conscious of how difficult it is for the director once we're actually shooting, especially with an action piece, to keep changing. The two times I've directed I've done most of my prep over the weekends. I just need quiet and to sit on the stage all by myself and draw stick figures. I need to draw out each show and how it connects editorially for me to be able to have a picture of how the whole scene is going to fit together. In doing that, I will be, hopefully, open-minded enough to adjust once I see what the actors bring to it in terms of staging. But I have to have some kind of plan. And I had a lot of time to prepare—my show fell over the Thanksgiving Holiday and I

had four days there and two other weekends involved during prep. So I had a lot of time and the script was pretty well together by the time we started prep. But, boy, I think there were seven writers involved over the period of a year."

"The first time I wrote it, I thought bottle show: Ten-Forward, Picard and Troi talk," recalls Brannon Braga. "Mike Piller said don't be afraid to write seven or eight page scenes with Picard and Troi. I said, 'Okay, Mike, I won't.' Jesus! Seven or eight pages? I had a tough time writing that and when I turned it in, Piller said he felt that we'd taken it as far as it could go and we shouldn't produce it. If it had been produced as I had written it, the episode would have been a little too familiar as a hostage show. So what happened was Herb Wright had just come in and Mike said we need some new blood, and gave it to Herb. Together we came up with the twist of them claiming to be the ghosts and that's what I think brought the show level up and gave it a dimension of mystery and twists that it really needed. In the end it turned into a really great action show. To me, it was a breath of fresh air. It had no pretensions. Instead of exploring some theme or idea, it was just action and phaser blasts. What are you going to do, deny that and say it's not fun?"

For the episode's early scenes in which Troi, Riker, Data and O'Brien crash in the shuttlecraft, Livingston braved the treacherous terrain of Stage 16.

"It was tough because we had atmosphere and wind and lightning," he says. "One of those elements is hard enough. Just being on Stage 16 is hard enough. But we had all of those elements and eventually all the actors had to lie down in them. The stage floor had a sandy surface, so when you have the wind blowing, the sand starts blowing around and I was real concerned about it getting into people's eyes. In fact, Marina's make-up became so messed up that she had to have a complete redo before we could continue shooting that day. We had to go over to Stage 9 and wait for her make-up to be done. Not through any fault of hers, just the fact that she wasn't presentable on screen, because the sand had sandblasted her and she looked like a house after the guys come through with their hoses. But 16 allows you to do stuff with a camera that you can't do anyplace else. Certainly you don't get to do it on the bridge. You get to use toys, as we call them. On that show, we used the python crane arm, which allows you to reach deep into the set and then crane back and not reveal the tracks, so you can do shots that are expansive, interesting and challenging. If you're going to direct, no one just wants to show people just sitting across a desk for four pages."

Once onboard the Enterprise, the majority of the action took place in Ten-Forward. "It was real hard," says Livingston. "We had to do a lot in there and that's where everyone was held hostage. It's like shooting on an aircraft carrier, it's a big empty room. I tried to keep it active and I look at the show now and it gets pretty static at times. I wish I had figured out a way to move people around a little bit more later on in the show. Structurally, from a writing standpoint, it's really great all the way through. Act two is really good. It's all action and then after that it settles down a little bit. You kind of wish it could have been that way all the way through for a teaser and five acts, but you just can't sustain that on episodic television."

"'Power Play' had the distinction of being one of the best directed episodes of the season, but only made me angry because it was empty," says a disturbed Michael Piller. "We need to do bottle shows on this series in order to pay the piper. We need to do contained non-optical direct shows and this was always intended to be one of them. It was meant to be a show that was dark and brooding, and the shows I've always used as prototype were 'Key Largo' and 'The Petrified Forest.' Very contained situations. We had a hard time making that work and making it interesting for five acts. It's not a difficult premise, it's been done on a lot of shows, a lot of times and television has found a way to make those premises kind of work. Brannon and Herb came in with a twist that I liked about making them seem like ghosts from a past ship, which gave us a spin on it. Ultimately it became a major action show and instead of helping us get even, knocked us into the stratosphere. I wasn't very fond of that

show, but very fond of David's direction. If that show had any merit at all, it was because he directed it with an extraordinary sense of style. The three actors who were given the job of being the aliens carried it with wonderful performances. The script came together very late, and I don't think the actors got the script until the day before and they were unhappy about it. They had a right to be. Brent, Marina and Colm really put together interesting performances, but I was not happy with the script."

Points out Brent Spiner, "I always love to play another type of character. The challenge here was to make sure my character didn't sound or act like Lore, and I don't think he did. It's really fun to get those curves, because so much of Data is already defined. When you get to play someone else and let loose like Leonard Nimoy occasionally got to do in the old show, it's really rewarding."

Episode #116:
"Ethics"
Original Airdate: 3/2/92
Story by Sara Charno & Stuart Charno
Teleplay by Ronald D. Moore
Directed by Chip Chalmers
Guest Starring: Caroline Kava (Dr. Russell), Patti Yasutake (Nurse Ogawa), Brian Bonsall (Alexander)

Worf is paralyzed when a support beam breaks in the cargo bay and a container falls on him. Despite the assistance of a renowned neuro-geneticist, Dr. Russell (*Born on the Fourth of July*'s Caroline Kava), Worf insists on committing ritual suicide rather than accept living his life as a cripple.

• • • •

Notes director Chip Chalmers, "The interesting thing about 'Ethics' is that for the first time that I can remember, there have been some *serious* inter-personal conflicts on the ship. That's one of the rules, nobody gets in each other's face. We had some pretty serious conflicts, and I think that was of huge redeeming value to that particular episode, because for the first time people saw Riker and Worf yelling at each other. We also saw real tears and real emotions.

"As a matter of fact," he adds, "they decided at the last minute that we'd gone a little too far at one point.

Riker says, 'Do you remember all the people that died in the line of duty? At least they died trying. Here you are lying on your hospital bed,' and he circles around the bed and he's nose to nose to Worf and literally yelling, 'Why don't you just get off your ass and take the challenge!' And Worf screams, 'Enough, enough!' Then Riker backs off a little bit. The general thought was that it had just gone a little too far and it was cut."

"I wanted to show two sides of a difficult debate," explains Ron Moore. "There's been a lot of criticism of this show and I've heard feedback from people who thought we were advocating euthanasia. Other people thought we were saying bad things about the disabled and the value of people with a disability. Other people would say, of course, Dr. Russell was absolutely wrong, she was as bad as Dr. Mengele and others would say how dare Beverly get in the way of Worf's right to die. The balancing act was to make sure both sides of the argument had validity, were compelling and real positions. It was not my favorite show to work on and I found it very difficult. The medical stuff is not what I'm drawn to and it's hard to make interesting."

"I love grays," muses Michael Piller. "I don't love black and whites. I don't like answering questions so easily for the audience. That was one of the things that I liked so much about 'Masterpiece Society.' The answers were not so easy to come by, and with 'Ethics,' again, we went out of our way not to make it easy for the audience to know what the right thing to do was. I think we succeeded pretty well with that one. We wanted to explore the issue and it's only fair to explore it if you give both voices the equal fairness that they're voice and opinions deliver. Now if you're on your toes, you'll say what about the voices of prejudice in sexual orientation in 'The Outcast?' My answer is I don't think there is another side that's easily supportable. I think that bigotry is bigotry, prejudice is prejudice, and it can be said with all the fervor and belief, but it still comes out as prejudice. I don't know how to make an intolerant person attractive."

"It was basically the doctor show," says former *Trek* producer Herb

Wright. "I think Ron did a good job on it within the parameters he was given, but one of the things I thought we should do was something more grotesque. My suggestion was that instead of doing a whole new spine, they had to release little creatures into his bloodstream which would eat away what was wrong with him and see that happen. You can take a turn in the road, but they wanted to stay with something that's a more traditional doctor show than science-fiction."

Visualizing 24th century medicine at work was the daunting task faced by David Livingston. "The medical operating room was pretty elaborate. That was a pretty big set on 16, and Chip did that wonderful wide angle shot at the beginning of the operation where you really saw it. There were a lot of inserts because of doing an operation. The cargo bay scene was pretty big where we had all the bodies and patients laid out, but from a production standpoint I didn't have a lot to do with that show because I was shooting 'Power play' while that was prepping."

Episode #117:
"The Outcast"
Original Airdate: 3/16/92
Written by Jeri Taylor
Directed by Robert Scheerer
Guest Starring: Melinda Culea (Soren),
Callan White (Krite), Megan Cole (Noor)

While working with Soren, a member of an androgynous alien race known as the J'naii, Riker and Soren begin to fall in love despite a prohibition by the planet's leaders which forbids relationships with other races that have gender. Violation of this law has dire consequences for the perpetrator.

••••

"Fascinating show," comments director Robert Scheerer. "It kind of broke the mold of other *Star Treks* in that it's two people—only. Yes, other people were there momentarily, but I had never done an episode where two people were so totally in the show throughout. They were in every scene with the rarest exception. It was one moment after another with them and watching this relationship grow, and then the kicker at the end when she is 'treated.' God, that show was exciting to do. Again, treating

the whole sexuality in a wonderful almost comedic way, I thought, in many instances was delicious. I guess it was one of the most commented on shows they ever had."

"I really wanted to write this episode," says Supervising Producer Jeri Taylor. "It came out of staff discussion. We had wanted to do a gay rights story and had not been able to figure out how to do it in an interesting science-fiction, *Star Trek*-ian way. It came up with the idea of turning it on its ear and I really wanted to do it because, partly, it would be controversial and I welcome that. The idea of any drama is to touch people's feelings and engage them, whether you make them laugh, cry, angry. As long as you stir something in them, then you've been successful and I knew this would touch a lot of buttons in a lot of people. I am not a gay person, but as a woman I do consider myself in a particular minority; I know what it feels like to be disenfranchised—not in that precise way—and I felt like I had a touchstone to some of the feelings that must be involved. On a personal level I wanted to write it. It's the episode of the whole two years I'm the most proud of and the most glad that I could be associated with. We've gotten every range of response, but largely positive."

"I didn't think they were gutsy enough to take it where they should have," says Jonathan Frakes. "Soren should have been more obviously male. We've gotten a lot of mail on this episode, but I'm not sure it was as good as it could have been—*if* they were trying to do what they call a gay episode."

Counters Rick Berman, "It was very interesting figuring out what to do. We were either going to cast with non masculine men, non feminine females or females who could play an androgynous character. Obviously you wouldn't pick a 6'4" muscle-bound man nor a voluptuous woman. We knew we had to go one way or another, so we read both men and women for the roles and decided to go with women. It might have been interesting to go with men, but it was a choice that we made."

"I'm delighted to hear Jonathan say that," remarks Brannon Braga. "If it would have been a man playing the role, would he have kissed him? I think

Jonathan *would* have because he's a gutsy guy. I think they would have preferred some more androgynous looking actors—they looked like women and the actress who played it did so unemotionally. While Jeri's script was rich with humor and the character had banter and spark and wit, the actress, although she did a fine job, played it a little too unemotionally as if androgyny meant emotionless as well. Why should it?

"A very special episode. I think that there are no subjects taboo for this show and what's so risky about making the statement that intolerance is bad? What's so risky about that? Some people reacted to the show in a way that I didn't understand. They thought we were advocating a particular sexual preference. I don't think that's true at all. I think we were advocating tolerance, I think the show could have been in a completely different arena. We could have used a show that dealt with racism rather than sexual preference and it could still be an interracial relationship. But that didn't seem to have the cutting edge or the science-fiction feel of an androgynous race. The risks were what Jeri did with the gems of the episode, like talking about sexual organs on the shuttlecraft. I felt they could have gone further [and] Picard could have been less passive. Riker's a big boy and he sparks conflicts in ethics among the characters. To get someone in there whose a catalyst for conflicts among our characters is a rare thing."

"I was very happy with 'The Outcast,'" says Michael Piller. "I thought Jeri [Taylor] did a marvelous job on the script and to me this was the turning point of the season and this was where I thought we started doing excellent television again. We had been the target of a concerted organized movement by gay activists to put a gay character in the show. What it came down to was Roddenberry had been barraged by letters and had discussed with us before his death the possibility of having two men hold hands in some scene, which was totally irrelevant to the issue of homosexuality. I didn't think, nor did Rick, that was an appropriate way to do a story that addressed the issues of sexual intolerance, which I felt was really what the broader issue was about. And so that's what we decided to do, and we decided to tell a story that was about sexual intolerance. The twist, I thought, turned out very well."

Berman concurs, "We'd been spending a lot of time wrestling with all the elements of the requests of the gay community for us to involve a gay character on the show. It got a lot of publicity both good and bad. We wrestled with a lot of different stories, and came up with a very obvious metaphor for the gay community and the intolerance they receive on this planet. It's very difficult to show people being tolerant—it's much easier to show people being intolerant—and to have people relate to them. In this instance we felt it better to draw the parallel, and the story that came in was wonderful. The acting was very well done. I think we dealt with well meaning people and their intolerance and our people in the 24th century's absolute lack of acceptance of their intolerance and the frustration of fighting it. It did not satisfy certain remnants of the gay and lesbian community because it was not what they were asking for, which was to introduce a gay or lesbian character in a normal and acceptable way as one of the members of the crew. But I think it did deal with the issue of intolerance towards sexual orientation and it met that objective well."

"Mail has been very split on this episode," says Ron Moore. "We have people across the spectrum; people who salute us for doing it, then there are people that say we didn't go far enough—that it was too subtle, it was too oblique and wanted it to be more upfront, blunt and obvious. Other people were just freaked out that it was an assault on values and that they hated it and how dare we do something like this and they'll never watch the show again. It was the best of the ways we'd like to do these shows. You have an interesting issue, a good science fiction premise, conflict and its an exploration of our characters in different ways."

Episode #118:
"Cause and Effect"
Original Airdate: 3/23/92
Written by Brannon Braga

Directed by Jonathan Frakes
Guest Starring: Michelle Forbes (Ensign Ro), Patti Yautake (Nurse Ogawa), Kelsey Grammer (Captain Bateman)

The Enterprise becomes trapped in a time warp in which the crew is forced to endlessly repeat the same experience in which the ship faces inevitable destruction after a collision with another starship from the past.

••••

"I was supposed to be prepping 'Cause' at the same time I was shooting 'The Outcast'," recalls director/actor Jonathan Frakes. "But I was in every scene of it so I didn't follow an ordinary pre-production process, but I got the script, took it home and broke down how I wanted to shoot it. I had no casting to do since we offered the part to Kelsey [Grammer], who accepted. It was just a matter of deciding how I wanted to shoot it and finding a different way to shoot each scene. In a conversation with [DP] Marvin Rush, we came up with the famous Waverly Smothers bungee cord camera, bungi-flex. It was just working at home at night and finding ways to make each scene look different in spite of the fact the words were the same. The problem was, of course, that it could become monotonous showing the same thing several times."

Says writer Brannon Braga, "I love time travel stories and I don't know who doesn't. We wanted to do a time travel story that had never been done before. Being trapped in a time loop is one I've never seen before. It was a high concept show that, frankly, when I wrote it didn't have all the elements in place. I didn't know how to get out of it. I didn't have the poker scene and Joe Menosky told me half-jokingly, 'Man, you're in trouble'. I said 'You really think so?' and he answered, 'Man, you're in big trouble.' When I did a preliminary beat sheet, I came up with the idea of the poker game and a message in the poker scene. I didn't know what the message was. The break session lasted two full days, but it was fruitful and gratifying because we came out of there with a structure that was working. I came up with the poker game while I was eating pancakes and pouring syrup. I had no idea how it happened—because it was before the sugar rush. I

knew then that the poker game would somehow be utilized for once, and lay it in so the viewer thinks it's just a poker game and it turns out to be the key to saving their entire existence. Three didn't really come into play yet. I didn't want the numbers to come up later and Riker was going to win the hand with three Aces, which was going to be an additional indicator that Riker's the one.... it's his suggestion. Eventually that was dropped because Rick felt Data could program in three but not give Riker three aces, and he's right and that was dropped."

Finding the catalyst for getting the Enterprise out of the time loop was Braga's biggest problem. "I didn't know what the message was," he says. "But it was the most fun to write of all the episodes I did this season. In a way, doing the same scenes over was comforting; it was fun to come up with different takes and to think how I could get that glass to break each time. It wasn't until I got to the final draft that I thought to have the glass break over the intercom on that final loop through. So it was finding those little nuggets and pathways and weave through as we were structuring it. That was a terrific challenge. It was fun to watch."

"You will never beat that teaser," enthuses Ron Moore of the episode's opening in which the Enterprise explodes. "That's the definitive one. I like it, it's a neat episode. I was talking to Brannon when he was writing it and to see the ship blow up and then Captain's log, it's really fun. We knew the structure of the show was going to be kind of monotonous, and the challenge was always going to be for the writer to find a different way in and to make it the same but different. Also a big challenge for the director, which I think Jonathan really rose to. Each time through the loop has a different feel, a different nuance, a different look. I think he did a wonderful job on making it an interesting show. Brannon laid different clues and feelings through the episodes. The poker games for a while was the cliché padding. If the show was short, it was to time to write a poker game. Because we had written it so much, we stayed away from it and now it got used for a reason. It actually had a function."

••••

241

Herb Wright agrees, " We had a lot of fun running through the room on that one. It's a helluva challenge because when the audience has seen it once and you show it to them the second time, the temptation for them is to jam the button on the remote. The challenge is how do you keep them excited, motivated and involved and wondering what the fuck is going on. And in the teaser you're starting off and you've destroyed the ship so if that isn't going to get you to tune back in, I don't know what will."

"It was dangerously repetitive by definition and I thought it could be misinterpreted like a clip show," says Rick Berman. "That's why I made it very clear to Jonathan that he couldn't use any footage again and that everything had to be photographed again and done in a slightly different way. I think it was a popular episode and worked well."

Says David Livingston of Frakes' efforts on the episode, "Jonathan had to shoot each of those repeated actions in an entirely different way. That was the challenge and what he did to that show was masterful. He was able to visually interpret each of those events each time so it didn't seem repetitive and he pulled it off. From a directing standpoint, it was a difficult show to do. Once you get past that, from a production end it wasn't that tough in terms of having to build stuff. What was tough was the post on the show and the second unit that went on to blow up the ship. Rob Legato had Stage 10 and we built large scale mock-ups of the Enterprise and of the other ship, or at least the nacelle on the other ship and we kept blowing up stuff on Stage 8. getting these tremendous explosions which we can hopefully use in the future. But Rob and Dick Brownfield were in heaven. They were like kids in a candy store. Nothing better than just being able to blow up something. Everything there was newly created just for that episode. We had a bunch of Enterprises, they didn't have all the detail but they had enough that when you cut to them you believed them."

Episode #119:
"The First Duty"
Original Airdate: 3/30/92
Written by Ronald D. Moore and
Naren Shankar

Directed by Paul Lynch
Guest Starring: Wil Wheaton (Wesley Crusher), Ray Walston (Boothby), Robert Duncan McNeill (Nicholas Locarno), Ed Lauter (Lt. Commander Albert), Jacqueline Brookes (Admiral Brand), Richard Fancy (Captain Satelk), Walker Brandt (Hajar), Shannon Fill (Sito), Richard Rothenberg (Cadet)

At the behest of his squadron leader at Starfleet Academy, Wesley agrees to cover-up the true facts behind an accident in which one of his fellow flight team members was killed when his shuttle collided while attempting to practice a prohibited maneuver for the Academy commencement activities.

••••

"It was very difficult and ultimately we knew we were taking a big risk," says Jeri Taylor of the moral quagmire Wesley wrestles with in "The First Duty". "There were arguments pro and con. We didn't start out developing the story that way. Through an evolutionary process there were many different endings and approaches which were discussed and all of them somewhat inflammatory. We knew it was a gamble, but we have to keep pushing at the edges and stretching ourselves and I felt this episode humanized Wesley in a way that he never has been and maybe now would allow fans to actually like him. He wore this awful mantle of the genius child who always saved the ship and in that sense seemed remote from a real person. He was the perfect Wesley, and that was hard for people to identify with. He made a mistake, a bad mistake; he's flawed. People are and I think in enriches him as a character, it gives him texture, maturity. It gives him something he now has to work through. That makes you a finer person in the end instead of just being a plastic perfect teenager."

"I like what we did with Wesley in 'First Duty' a lot," says Ron Moore. "I was strongly in favor of what we did with the character in that show and I was glad it was supported by Rick and Michael. We took that character in a really interesting direction and I think it helps him grow as a character a lot and makes him more accessible and human. I'm just really happy with what the episode became. It's probably my favorite

episode of the year. It had a lot of meaty stuff; the Picard/Wesley scene is powerful. When he looks up from behind the desk and gets up you think he's going to slug him. Picard just had a real heartfelt anger in his face."

"It's interesting when you don't feel you're obliged to do a show around a character and you find an idea that just seems to work for him. It seems like sometimes the most natural thing in the world," adds Michael Piller. "This is a great show and we almost didn't do it. When we pitched it to Rick, he said, it's not a *Star Trek. Star Trek* is about going off into space and exploring new planets. It's not about going back to earth. He's right, of course, and no one's going to argue that he's not, but I looked at him and said 'Look, to me we have the opportunity to do something special. We have the chance to explore an issue that is extra meaningful to a lot of young people. If you're involved in drugs or teenage misbehavior or crime, and you may know that it's the wrong thing and you have the choice of being loyal to your friends or doing what is honest—that is a great issue for us to explore. And I said to Rick it gives us a chance to go to Starfleet Academy for the first time and, I got to tell you, with a show that desperately seeks good ideas, I don't think we can afford to pass on this one. And he said 'Sold, as long as you only have three sets.'

"I remember the most interesting part of that script was when Nareen and Ron were here elaborating on what they wanted to do and Ron said Wesley can't turn in his friends. I said 'Ron, this is about truth and doing the right thing.' Ron is a very good young writer and he was right in the place that he needed to be in order to explore the other side of that issue. We had a long argument about whether it was the right thing to do and basically Ron felt that we were assassinating Wesley's character and no one would ever forgive him for turning in his friends. We went through a lot of elaboration about what was really important and what was the message we wanted to give to our audience. It was not a question of loading the dice; you want to make the other side as strong as you possibly can. Ultimately you have to make a decision to dramatically resolve the conflict with your character. Ron reluctantly agreed to go forward with this ending in mind—that the truth is the most important thing—which is what I want my kids to believe. Ron hasn't had any kids so he doesn't know that yet. What is most interesting is he got into the script and the issue of protecting the friendship was the hardest for him to get right, that for whatever he started, I'd say remember the way you argued that he shouldn't turn in his friends? I need that in the script to balance it. I need that sentiment to be in there, and strong and its got to be sold. Ultimately he got there. Great script, and very well cast and very well directed.

"It's interesting that one of the things that was late coming into that story was Picard's sin," says Piller. "We had to have scenes with Boothby and Picard and we had scenes where they talked about the case, they talked about things, but the scenes weren't clicking and they were the weakest parts of the show. We started talking about maybe he helped Picard out with a problem and maybe he got into trouble, and we tried to figure out what it was. Rick said it doesn't matter what Picard's trouble was. We keep that part of our character a mystery, which we like to do every once in a while. That was a great decision and what it did for us was put in perspective in a life cycle sort of way that if you make a mistake when you're young and its found out, you have to pay a price for it. It doesn't mean your life is ruined. It means you can still become Jean Luc Picard. It gave a much broader perspective to the story. It's interesting of course that in the very first scene Picard's being called to the principal's office and that was just a gag, a throwaway Ron had come up with. It wasn't until much later that we said, you know, it's already set up in that first scene that he was in trouble. Why don't we use it? It's very interesting the way some things just seem to fall into place. It was like it was waiting to be discovered."

"I made a real pain of an ass of myself with the writers on this one," admits Rick Berman. "If I recall, in the early stages, they wanted Wesley's crime to be a little more heinous, the cover-up more obvious and Wesley's punishment to be more severe. I found that unacceptable. Wesley is Wesley. He is one of our characters and heroes and he's capable of lapses in judgement, capable of making decisions on an emotional basis as opposed to thinking them out, but not capable of some of the more severe things that were suggested. And not capable of overt cover-up, lying to Starfleet Academy officials. So we basically tempered it down, still keeping it believable and the crime that was serious and would result in a punishment. But it was very difficult dealing with the relationship between Wesley and Picard. If Picard says to Wesley you're going to tell what happened, and if you don't I will. That puts Wesley in a very weak position dramatically. *If* he tells, he does because he was forced to and if he doesn't, Picard will. There was a lot of fine tuning to keep it from becoming too contrived. I think the direction by Paul Lynch was excellent and the casting was great. Getting Ray Walston to play Boothby was fortuitous and the casting of the three other Starfleet kids was successful. It was not a typical episode, it was not science fiction in nature, it was earthbound and it was a very dramatic character piece and courtroom drama. As filmmaking and one hour dramatic television, I thought it was riveting. It was a terrific episode and by dealing with some of the hi-tech abilities to detect what they were doing, we got elements of science-fiction in there as well."

"The thorny issue was does he lie or does he just admit to tell the truth," says Herb Wright. "Is it a lie of omission or is it an open running lie and the story waffles back and forth because the danger was that somehow we were going to paint this guy as a liar and never be able to redeem him again. To be able to balance the peer pressure that one would face in a situation like that, an adolescent show-off maneuver that ends up in tragedy, to say hey aren't we better than every one else and that Wesley was in on it....it was a tough show to figure out how to do that and not diminish and harm the character forever. It was a very heated discussion. He was young and he had certain frailties and he had mixed loyalties. This would be something he'll have to learn, that we're not all perfect—even in the 24th century—and we would have to go through some bumps and grinds to become the perfect people we are."

Reflects director Paul Lynch, "I thought Wil Wheaton rose to great heights in his performance. He worked great for me as did the other boy Robert McNeill, who I had worked with on *The New Twilight Zone*. He and Wesley played very well off of each other. It was a good, intriguing story, and a mystery that dealt with futuristic things. I had a great time with it, although I don't usually like doing trials just because of the amount of time you have to spend on a trial to do it well. You have to cover the audience and everybody in the audience listening as everything goes through in order to make it play. I think, although I'm not sure if it still holds true, that at the time it was the most film they'd ever used on an episode of *Star Trek*. If an average episode used 35,000 feet, I used 75,000 feet. That was mostly because of the coverage, because when I shoot a trial I shoot the people listening to everything that's said. I don't just take reactions. I used an awful lot of film, but the show turned out well. When I was doing it they were a little upset because I was using so much film.

"Mostly, though, the episode came out well because of Wil Wheaton, who really showed his stuff. It's nice to see because he was a good young kid actor when we first started *Next Generation*, and now he's matured into a good first-rate actor. It's nice to see the difference over the years."

Episode #120:
"Cost of Living"
Original Airdate: 4/20/92
Written by Peter Allan Fields
Directed by Winrich Kolbe
Guest Starring: Majel Barrett (Lwaxana Troi), Brian Bonsall (Alexander), Tony Jay (Campio), Carel Struycken (Mr. Homm), David Oliver (Young Man), Albie Selznick (Juggler), Patrick Cronin (Erko), Tracey D'Arcy (Young Woman), George Edie (Poet), Christopher Halste (First Learner)

Mrs. Troi returns to the Enterprise in order to marry Campio (Tony Jay), a visiting dignitary she's never met, while a cloud of parasitic particles

Tony Jay, shown here with Ron Perlman on the set of Beauty and the Beast, *was Campio in "Cost of Living."*

released from a destroyed asteroid in the Pelloris Field begins to wreak havoc aboard the starship.

••••

"I think it was something one needed to have there rather than something that was an intrinsic part of the show," says writer Peter Allan Fields of the science-fiction B-story. "I'd be lying if I said that didn't bother me somewhat. I'm sure it bothered Michael and Rick Berman as well at first, but once we got into it, the story seemed to work all right. It's true thought that the so-called dreaded B-story was, in this case, something that almost didn't belong. Because we wanted to develop the personal story as much as we could rather than flesh out a convenient jeopardy story, we felt in this particular instance even though the B story was valid and researched just as carefully as the others, the personal story should take precedence. We don't want to do them all like that. This is a science-fiction show and the science is fun, but in this case it was the personal story that was most important."

Rick Berman admits to an initial wariness over the show's atypical premise.

"I had a lot of trepidation about it," says Berman. "I was extremely pleased by the way it turned out. The first draft of the script was absolutely

wonderful and Peter injected charm and heart and humor into the characters and wonderful dialogue. As we revised the script, I felt it wasn't getting any better, the revision process was hurting it in terms of some of the wonderful dialogue. But we had other problems within the story we had to deal with . I had some problems, some costuming and make-up things that troubled me, but by the time we put it together and added some wonderful visual effects to the show, I found it utterly charming. It had heart and warmth. This is a show that was premised as Auntie Mame arriving aboard and taking Worf's son under her wing to bring him out of his shell in her own flamboyant way, and its delightful, funny and wonderful.

"Dorn gives a funny, great performance," continues Berman. "There are problems that exist with Worf. We turned him into a dad and a character who has to deal with the frustration of a sometimes troublesome son which is not really *Star Trek*. It has its good points and its bad points, but the relationship between the little boy and Majel, Troi and her mother and between Worf and his son, are delightful here. Michael wasn't even guaranteed all episodes in the first season and I feel that Michael as an actor and the character of Worf have both grown more than any other one of our characters or actors. and I'm delighted with the direction Michael's acting has gone. It's a shoe-in character. What's more delightful than a Klingon onboard the Enterprise? And the writers have been taking advantage of it and Michael has been running with it."

Creating the environs of Mrs. Troi's holodeck Disneyland meant a lot of research and development for the production team to build a mudbath and visualize the menagerie of alien entertainers. "It's a kid's fantasy world and Richard [James] just kind of went for it," says David Livingston. "We went for it in terms of costume and make-up, a lot of wild hairdos and this set which included a mudbath which took a lot of R&D, but Dick Brownfield pulled it off. Majel and others were concerned that it wasn't going to be warm enough, but it was warm and toasty and everyone loved getting in to it. It was very goopy, but it

wasn't real mud. It was a special solution that we're allowed to use in the movies which wouldn't be harmful to anybody and it was an approved solution they could be in. They all got kind of a kick out of it and it was fun seeing all those actors sloshing around in it."

Winrich Kolbe points out, "That was fluff, but nice fluff. It was a comedy written for Majel and I think she did a hell of a job in there. I wouldn't consider it a *Star Trek* episode *par excellence*. It fulfilled a certain function, but it was not *Star Trek* at its best.

Episode #121:
"The Perfect Mate"
Original Airdate: 4/27/92
Story by Rene Echevarria &
Reuben Leder
Teleplay by Reuben Leder &
Michael Piller
Directed by Cliff Bole
Guest Starring: Famke Janssen (Kamala), Tim O'Connor (Briam), Max Grodenchik (Par Lenor), Mickey Cottrell (Alrik), Michael Snyder (QOL), David Paul Needles (Miner #1), Roger Rignack (Miner #2), April Grace (Transporter Officer), Charles Gunning (Miner #3)

A beautiful empathic mesomorph, Kamala, who is intended to serve as a peace offering to end a centuries-old war, is freed from stasis by a Ferengi and

Tim O'Connor, Briam of "The Perfect Mate," seen here in the television version of Buck Rogers.

seduces Picard.

••••

"On a positive note, I think, like the Borg show, it showed that Picard has a flaw, you can cut into his character," offers Cliff Bole. "When I say that's positive, that means you can continue to make that character work. I think this is a real case for Picard, because he normally wouldn't have allowed himself to be so vulnerable."

"What was interesting was I was writing myself out of this funk," says Michael Piller. "I had started feeling good about stuff with 'Masterpiece Society' and I think the staff was following and feeling the same way with the material they were starting to turn out. Jeri was starting to turn out some wonderful material with 'The Outcast.' We were stuck and this ["Perfect Mate"] was a script a lot of people had put a hand to, and it wasn't working very well. The relationship between Picard and this woman wasn't working. She is an empathic metamorph and has the ability to be whatever a man wants her to be. For all those people who thought we were so sexually open-minded with the other shows, they're going to start sending in their letters and saying what's wrong with you guys on this one? This is the adolescent male fantasy of all time. But I think there's room for all kinds of shows and, essentially, if you come up with a character and throw her into a situation, you see how it works. I think the challenge of the show is if Picard is confronted with his perfect mate, could he resist her? The fun is to see him resist and he's doing all these things to try and resist and does he resist? You have to decide. The thing is complicated by the fact that he knows she just does it for him and for him the idea is, 'How do I deal with that when I find that there's something about her that I'm attracted to?' In a long memo to Rene Echeverria, I said this show does not work if the audience, at least the men, do not fall in love with this woman too. She must be fully rounded, bright, engaging, with a great personality and the audience should say, 'I see the problem for Picard.' If there's no magnetic electricity between the two of them and it

doesn't happen for me as a man watching her, then the audience will not accept for one second that Picard would even give her a second thought."

"I'm very pleased with it," says Rick Berman. "The actress is about as beautiful as any woman any of us have ever seen and she gave a delightful performance. It's an episode which, during the final stages of writing by Michael, went through a lot of changes with a lot of heated discussions that went on, and a lot of different things that could have happened to this woman. We shot two different endings and there were two more we didn't shoot. None of us will ever know which of the four would have been best."

A disappointed Michael Piller explains, "The trick ending which no one liked but me and Patrick, may have been the product of a writer who was trying too hard, but I was overruled. I felt at the end of the show Picard has to deliver this woman into the hands of her arranged mate. By this time in the picture he has become very close to her and I wanted to do an ending which, in fact, had three endings. I wanted to do an ending where he stopped the ceremony and said, 'No, she's staying with me.' The way that it was written was Par Lenor delivers her, Picard cringes as she kisses this man who she doesn't love. The second ending was he interrupts and says, 'I'm sorry, I can't allow this to continue,' and so while they're walking down the aisle and it seems each time it's the end of the show, we in fact cut back to them walking down the aisle so it's continuing and we understand these are things happening in Picard's mind. Finally he gets to the end, and the third ending is she interrupts and tells both of them she isn't staying for either one of them. She says through Picard's influence she's been enlightened and is going off in search of adventure, leaving both men standing there. I was overruled. I think that those who overruled me would say that her leaving was not justified by anything else in the script, but I would argue with that."

Episode #122:
"Imaginary Friend"
Original Airdate: 5/4/92
Story by Ronald Wilderson & Jean

Matthias & Richard Fliegel
Teleplay by Edithe Swensen &
Brannon Braga
Directed by Gabrielle Beaumont
Guest Starring: Brian Bonsall (Alexander),
Noley Thornton (Clara), Shay Astar
(Isabella), Jeff Allin (Daniel Sutter),
Patti Yasutake (Nurse Ogawa),
Sheila Franklin (Ensign)

The imaginary friend of one of the crew's young daughter, Clara Sutter, becomes a frightening reality when she threatens to destroy the ship.

••••

"I was always very turned on by the idea," says Rick Berman. "Where else but in science-fiction could you do an idea about an imaginary friend who turns out not to be imaginary? It's a story about an alien who takes the form of a little girl's imaginary friend and begins to perceive our world through the eyes of a child. I think it turned out quite nicely, and we got two great performances. It's very difficult to work with kids because they're not as experienced and you only get them for a few hours a day, but in the case of this episode we got two very nice performances. I would not rank this as one of my favorites for the season, but it was a lot of fun."

Less generous in his praise is former producer Herb Wright. "It's not a show that dealt with our regulars and not a show that needed to be on *Star Trek*," he asserts. "I think Michael [Piller] was trying to do *E.T.*, but what made that film work is hard to do on *Star Trek* aboard the Enterprise. E.T. was an alien in a suburban neighborhood trying to get home. It was like the lost pet that turns out to be a genius alien. But 'Invisible Friend's' problem was how do you have, in effect, an adolescent alien? I think the problem is that when you narrow your focus to what kind of show you want to do to the point where you're doing 90 percent personal stories and you're trying to do them in outer space on a 24th century starship, you're going to run into a brick wall and there's only so many times you can do that."

"I did the final rewrite on it and 'Invisible Friend' was the most gratifying script I wrote this season," recalls Brannon Braga. "It wasn't quite working in its original guise and Jeri Taylor and Pete Fields and I broke the story and tried to make the imaginary friend more of the bad seed. Before, it was more like Puff the Magic Dragon and it was that the alien was simply curious and didn't have an evil intent. It just kind of laid there and was playful fluff. We decided to make the alien malevolent, where it's mean to the kid. I've taken to calling it Romper Room: The Next Generation. Kid stories appeal by their very nature. There's an innocence to kids and kids can have conflict. The funny thing about kid shows in the *Star Trek* universe is you can get conflict with kids because they're not developed yet like our perfect adults. In a strange kind of way, kids can have more problems and conflict than our regulars. They can still be imperfect. It is a fun episode and hopefully people won't be so sick of seeing children on the show."

Episode #123:
"I, Borg"
Original Airdate: 5/18/92
Written by Rene Echevarria
Directed by Robert Lederman
Guest Starring: Jonathan Del Arco (Hugh Borg)

A wounded young Borg is taken aboard the Enterprise and taught humanity by the ship's crew. Meanwhile, Picard and Guinan confront their own personal demons relating to the cybernetic, super race.

••••

"The minute I saw the story I fell in love with it," says Rick Berman. "The dramatic relationships are so vivid. Guinan, who comes from a people that were destroyed by the Borg, Picard who was brutalized and violated by the Borg—both are put in the position of being prejudiced. Geordi and Dr. Crusher are in the position of being open-minded and eventually sympathetic to this young man and the end result is a wonderful series of relationships and wonderful scenes between Guinan and the Borg. There's another arc that deals with Geordi and the Borg, Geordi and Picard, and Picard and the Borg, and they are all wonderfully strong, small two-character scenes. The writing was wonderful and the acting great. It was directed by Bob Lederman making his directorial debut, and I'm very pleased with it."

Uncredited co-writer Jeri Taylor agrees, "I think it will become a classic. I think it's a wonderful concept and it's just real special. It's *Edward Scissorhands* in a sense. The Borg will never be the same again."

Michael Piller, whose "Best of Both Worlds" was the Borg's first return visit and widely regarded as one of the new *Trek*'s finest hours, agrees that "I, Borg" was a satisfying follow-up. "I think it's just a great premise which forces both Guinan and Picard to confront their own prejudices," says Piller. "And you would think these are two characters who have none, but when it comes to the Borg the old issue is 'know your enemy.' It's a lot harder to hate them if you know them and it deals with the issue of what happens to these communal Borgs which cannot be treated as anything else but parts of the whole when one is separated and becomes an individual. How do you treat him when he is an individual? I feel that if you take the unstoppable villain, the stereotype and you turn it inside out, that's great dramatic storytelling. Because you don't allow the audience to ever get comfortable with what they expect the Borg show to be. 'You think you know what the Borg are, well you've got the prejudices too, pal.' You think they're unstoppable villains and now you're going to look one in the eye and decide whether you're going to kill him or not."

"I think this is a real good way to bring the Borg back, because they're very limiting in the way they are," says Ron Moore. "They're this huge collective with no voice to communicate to and you can't relate to these guys. We keep saying they're unstoppable and if we keep stopping them it undercuts how unstoppable they truly are. They're very mindless, they don't have personality, they're hard to deal with dramatically. In 'Best of Both Worlds' you take Picard and make him Locutus and you've got something. This was a chance to take him out of that and make him a person. What are your responsibilities with that person? One of the analogies we used were the experiments where they were teaching chimps sign language and then the experiment is over and what do you have? Someone who's sort of on the cusp of intelligence or communication skills,

but what do you do? You've taken this animal and broadened it to something else, but you can't just throw it back into the jungle. We tossed that around. I thought it was a real good show to do."

Episode #124:
"The Next Phase"
Original Airdate: 5/11/92
Written by Ronald D. Moore
Directed by David Carson
Guest Starring: Thomas Kopache (Mirok), Susanna Thompson (Varel), Kenneth Meseroll (Ensign McDowell), Michelle Forbes (Ensign Ro), Shelby Leverington (Brossmer), Brian Cousins (Parem)

Ro and Geordi are apparently killed in an explosion aboard a disabled Romulan warbird, but are actually "phased" into another dimension where they encounter an evil Romulan Centurion. The duo have to convince the Enterprise crew that they're not dead before the ship is destroyed by a Romulan trap.

••••

Admits director David Carson, "This was an extremely difficult episode to do, because it dealt with special effects of a type people were familiar with from *Ghost*, which *Star Trek* had never attempted before. It was one of the most difficult technical episodes they'd ever done just by the nature of having people walk through people and an environment where people exist in different phases. I thought the story hung together quite well, and it turned out in quite a good way."

"I hate that title, but I'm very pleased with the episode," says Rick Berman. "It's a wonderful high concept story. The story really pumps along and there's great Romulan mystique and some wonderful things with people running through walls and the audience gets to see two different realities. It was very difficult to shoot in blue screen with people putting their hands through consoles and walls. It looked relatively easy on paper, but took a lot of time to make the visual effects work. It's a great piece of science fiction."

Michael Piller was also pleased with the final result, despite initial trepidation. "I get a little tired of Romulans and I was a little reluctant to make this a

Romulan show," he says. "It's Ron [Moore's] script's attempt to do a bottle show, but it turned out to be a high budget special effects intensive show. It had been pitched as actually similar stories by two people. We bought the ideas and combined them into one and Ro developed the story and wrote it. I think it's terribly important to give credit to Ron Moore for the work he did this season. Last year I said Ron Moore was the best Klingon writer I had on staff, but, god forbid, he should ever work on a show that had human beings. This season Ron has put it all together. He is a complete writer now and certainly one of the strongest elements of any staff you could possibly hope for. It's been a pleasure watching him grow."

"It was fun," offers Brannon Braga about the Ensign Ro vehicle which was originally written for Geordi and Troi. "Troi's had enough running and jumping this year. We felt why not give Ro something and I'm glad she did, because she kicks a Romulan in the chest and does a kick worthy of Bruce Lee. She's some sort of acrobat. That scene in my opinion makes the whole show."

"We all just love Michelle Forbes," says Jeri Taylor. "Her performance has really brought so much to the show. She's a real character and not just a catalyst for conflict. She's less conflicted because she's likable and at heart a good person who's starting to get along with the crew. Even if she was staying on the ship, she wouldn't have remained the fireball she was at first. As far as a character that has that kind of feisty fire, there are no plans to bring a new character in."

Episode #125:
"The Inner Light"
Original Airdate: 6/1/92
Story by Morgan Gendel
Teleplay by Morgan Gendel &
Peter Fields
Directed by Peter Lauritson
Guest Starring: Margot Rose (Eline), Richard Riehle (Batal), Scott Jaeck (Administrator), Jennifer Nash (Meribor), Patti Yasutake (Nurse Ogawa), Daniel Stewart (Young Batal)

A mysterious space probe disables Picard and sending his unconscious body to the deck of the bridge. When he awakens, he seems to be somebody entirely different and experiences a lifetime of memories in a matter of twenty-five minutes.

••••

"This episode allows us to bring Picard and a wonderful group of guest actors together and create a world," enthuses Rick Berman. "We see Picard at half a dozen different ages involving wonderful prosthetics and a man's lifetime in the course of an hour. It's quite dramatic and well written and [Peter] Lauritson did a lovely job directing it."

Opines Michael Piller, "It's a great premise about a man who lives 45 years of his life in 25 minutes. Patrick gives a remarkable performance. He gets to be six or seven different ages and it works. As we were breaking the story with the writers, I remember putting all the lines on the board and with each one creating the blocks to have connections and relationships grow in this other life for Picard, so that by the end of the show when they die or they are lost, there is an emotional impact that the audience should absolutely be heartbroken that he's lost these other people he loved and spent his life with. I actually had tears in my eyes when we were breaking this story and I hope we were on the money."

For Patti Yatsuke, who plays Nurse Ogawa, assisting Dr. Crusher on the bridge was a novel experience. "My big game on this show was that all I did was work in sickbay. I had one scene where I finally got to see another part of the ship. I told them I was so excited about this one because I'm actually on the bridge now. That's been kind of my game, seeing how many rooms of the ship I can get into. I can't wait to be transported."

The big-budget "Light" came as a surprise to producer David Livingston, who was hoping to end the season with some budget-savers. "It put me into kind of shock because we had all these big shows at the end, but what happened was we didn't have other scripts that were in the pipeline. Fortunately we had the money to be able to do it. We had to make some substantial changes, especially on the last show. We made a lot of changes and adjustments to be able to pull it off

in terms of the time and the money."

As "Inner Light" demonstrated, Patrick Stewart had become a much more active participant in the show's fourth and fifth seasons than he had been in the first three.

"I've been seriously hurting people for about two years now, and that's given me deep satisfaction," says Stewart. "Also, they addressed the romantic, the real romantic side of Picard. Perhaps, if there's one area which I would personally enjoy because it gives me a lot of pleasure and they haven't had much of it in the past, is the humorous, ironic, wittier side of our good captain. Two or three seasons ago I might have been complaining about being too much of a desk captain, a briefcase captain. My body count has risen dramatically in the last few episodes."

Executive Script Consultant Peter Allan Fields explains, "Someone named Morgan Kandell wrote the story and the first draft as well when I started to work the premise and structure from the story and made up my own sort of relationships. It was an opportunity to give Captain Picard an entire lifetime which is the antithesis of the kind of life he had always lived aboard the Enterprise. I understand Patrick enjoyed playing it very much, and it was a delight to be able to write it. Picard doesn't change, even though he's not the captain his personality doesn't change. But now he has a life he's never had; he has love, a home, marriage, a family and things that are not burdens; things he never thought he needed before. He not only has them but he loves them and is used to them and loses them. We cover a period of 30 years all in the space of 25 minutes of time of supposed unconsciousness. I think it turned out pretty darned well."

Episode #126:
"Time's Arrow"
Original Airdate: 6/15/92
Story by Joe Menosky
Teleplay by Joe Menosky &
Michael Piller
Directed by Les Landau
Guest Starring: Jerry Hardin (Samuel Clemens), Michael Aron (Bellboy), Barry Kivel (Doorman), Ken Thorley (Seaman), Sheldon Peters Wolfchild (Indian), John

M. Murdock (Beggar), Marc Alaimo (Gambler), Milt Tarver (Scientist), Michael Hungerford (Roughneck)

Data's head is discovered in a cave on earth, which prompts the Enterprise to lead an investigation into earth's past where they discover aliens abducting humans from the 19th century to the future. Additionally, they discover Guinan!

••••

"We didn't intend to do a cliffhanger this year," explains Michael Piller, "but once *Deep Space Nine* was announced, there were rumors that *Next Generation* was being canceled, that it was being downgraded in importance. There were letters of protest saying pay attention to the show that matters. Rick and I started talking and we both agreed this was not the time to not do a cliffhanger after two years. The next season is going to be the best season we've ever had, and I wanted to have the momentum of having a cliffhanger. I wanted people talking.

"We decided it was going to be a time travel story," he elaborates, "and we were trying to do a show all season long about Data trying to pass himself off as human. We had come up with a scenario about going to a humanoid planet that was very awkward and we couldn't figure out why the Enterprise was not coming back. And somebody said the way to do this story was to have Data come back to Hollywood and walk down Melrose Avenue. We started talking in those terms. That would have been okay, and we kept searching for the era. Do we want to do the 50's, well *Back to the Future* did the 50s. The 60's? Well, maybe everyone does the 60's. And then we had a running gag that Data goes back to save JFK and two weeks after the script was done somebody actually submitted a spec script, totally by coincidence, where the Enterprise goes back in time to save JFK. I don't think this year Gene would have been ready to jump on that bandwagon and then we said the 70's, but we said what is there to go back to see? And then they said the 80's, maybe. We even went to the 90's and we didn't like that. Then we said the near future and Rick Berman finally said what about the 19th century? Why don't we

Michael Westmore has Data's head in hand as he prepares it for "Time's Arrow." *(Photo copyright © David Ian Salter)*

do Marc Twain?

"We sat down and started doing that story and it was going to be fine. I brought everybody in on Sunday to do the break, because it was really late and it came together late in the season. Joe said something about Guinan and I said we need her in the show, I dictated that and Joe said she'd be alive back then and started going on to other things. I said if she was alive, what if that's where she met everybody and what if that's where the relationship with the *Star Trek* group started and she met Picard. Ultimately that's where Picard helped her out of trouble back then and she came back to find him before he met her, knowing she was going to be on the Enterprise to complete the circle. I called up David Livingston and said can we have Guinan for two days; once in the present, once in the past and this became yes, no, yes, no and Joe was writing one story and then another. Finally, when she heard the story idea, she fell in love with it and committed to do both the current show, which she's already done, and the next show in an expanded role."

"We very much wanted to do an episode that dealt with Data time traveling back to contemporary earth and walking down the street where Beaver Cleaver lives," recalls Rick Berman. "As

we got into the story, I found something very contrived and overly coincidental about people coming back to our exact time. It's not believable for me, and we started thinking about other decades. Every decade we thought about had been done or wasn't worth doing. Every decade reflected on something else. It didn't make any sense unless it was something that we could take advantage of living in 20th century America. Contemporary was not working, and I think it was me who came up with a story where Data ran into Mark Twain, which put us into turn of the century California, which was not as easy to do. It became a costume piece, it became a piece where we had to seek out locations."

"'Time's Arrow' is a particularly fun episode," offers Brent Spiner. "I have no plans over the hiatus, so I'm going to spend that time in anticipation about what happens to Data at the end of the cliffhanger."

The difficulties in recreating turn of the century America was a production nightmare for David Livingston and production designer Richard James.

"The last episode is the toughest and an expensive one, but it ended up being that way because it has so many different elements," says Livingston. "We went on location for

••••

two days in two different places. Both location days were period pieces involving a lot of extras in period wardrobe. There was a lot of set dressing and the art department worked to create the proper milieu of San Francisco in the 1890's. So those two locations were big. We had to shoot in this Pasadena mansion for this ballroom set and they have time restrictions, so you're limited in the amount of time you can be there. Anytime you shoot on location in Los Angeles, it's tough. But when we start doing period stuff, you can't come in there and shoot it and leave like shooting a cop show in downtown LA. You have to dress it and make it look right."

Shooting the eerie time travel sequences on Stage 16 were equally challenging, he explains. "The time travel portions of this thing where we see these aliens that time travel and we go meet them on Stage 16 was very difficult shooting. The aliens were blue screened in because they glow. In order to photograph them with our people, it's a three-stage process. We shoot our people on the set, we have to shoot plates and then we have to shoot the aliens. Then Rob Legato has to matte all that stuff together, and the process of shooting something sometimes takes two or three times longer to do than it normally would, because there are so many layers to the process. Everything about the show is big and ambitious, but Michael and Rick said this is our cliffhanger and we want a show that's going to give the audience a lot of stuff. So we gave them a lot of stuff in an unbelievable episode, and I think it's been the hardest of all seasons."

"Rick and Mike both love time travel, but most time travel stories just don't work," says Brannon Braga. "They're hokey or push the boundaries of credibility. We've done three this season. I think it's just because most time travel

stories are back in history to that pivotal event, or don't change the timeline. That stuff is cliché and we don't want people to try and develop time travel stories, because it needs to be in house. 'A Matter of Time' was a lot of fun. It was different because it was the story of the man who came to dinner, and 'Cause and Effect' is a story Rick loved, because he had never seen it before. 'Time's Arrow' is a period piece which we haven't done."

Concludes Berman, "It was on earth and by adding Mark Twain and other historical characters who will not become known until the second part which will open up the sixth season, it ended up being quite delightful. But all our attempts to hold the cost down, which was a very important job, to some degree failed. Everything took a little bit longer than we thought. We bit off a little more than we could chew and we went a few days over schedule. But it's very big and very colorful and very exciting. If we can come up with a way to finish it, we'll give you the other half next year."

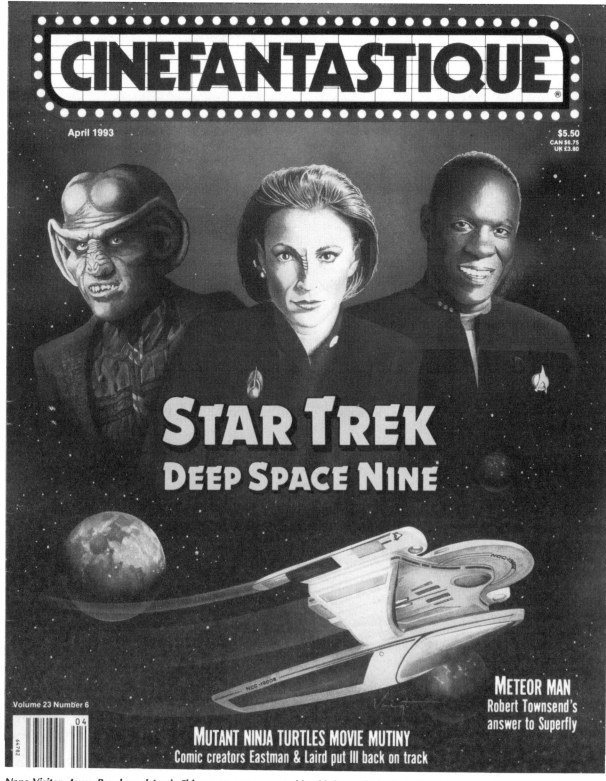

Nana Visitor, Avery Brooks and Armin Shimerman as represented by this issue of Cinefantastique devoted to Deep Space Nine.

••••

CHAPTER TWENTYSIX

STAR TREK
Deep Space Nine

"I think one of the things they're striving for is to look at the people in the 24th century who are not as much at peace with themselves as the crew of the Enterprise is in *Star Trek: The Next Generation*," explains director David Carson, who helmed the 2-hour premiere episode of the latest *Star Trek* spin-off, *Deep Space Nine*. "In *The Next Generation*, it's always been a big thing when a character goes through an emotional or personal crisis. The stories usually end at peace with hope, not only hope in society but hope in the behavior of people, who most of the time behave in an exemplary manner.

"I have a feeling that the darker, grittier tone is one of the reasons they wanted me to direct the pilot," continues Carson, who has helmed such *Next Gen* episodes as "The Enemy," "Yesterday's Enterprise" and "Redemption." "They wanted my experience with grit in *Star Trek*. It is true that this will be a much grittier environment than the Enterprise, which is part of the attraction. And it's my feeling that that part of the grittiness of *Deep Space Nine* is not only the setting, but the attempt to access the slightly weaker side of human nature, while still telling extremely powerful and insightful stories. Perhaps the most striking thing about *Deep Space Nine* is the immense strength of the two-hour movie's storyline, which has a universality that is quite striking."

Star Trek: Deep Space Nine, created by *Next Gen*'s executive producers Rick Berman and Michael Piller, debuted in January 1993 with a two-hour premiere to be followed by 18 one-hour episodes. The big question in the beginning, of course, was would it fly or would it prove to live up to any of the monikers that had been labeled to it, such as *Deep Space Nine From Outer Space, Deep Space:1999* or what Jonathan Frakes jokingly referred to as *Deep Throat Nine*?

Boasting the same substantial budget as *Star Trek: The Next Generation* and state of the art special effects, Berman and Piller have attempted to give the series its own distinct identity in much the same way *Next Generation* has consciously steered clear of comparisons with *Trek Classic*. It remains to be seen if *Star Trek* will work as well as a brand name as it has a phenomenon, though early indications are that it will.

The idea for a new *Star Trek* series has its genesis in a lunchtime conversation between Piller and Berman.

"About a year ago," says Berman, "give or take a month or two, Michael and I started talking about the possibility of doing another series, a spin-off, a sequel, another show set within the *Star Trek* universe and we spent a number of lunches tossing it around. We had a number of ideas which were both *Star Trek* in nature and those that were non-*Star Trek* in nature. Michael and I discussed it with Gene when we were still in the early stages, but never anything conceptual. Then I got a call for Brandon Tartikoff who was the new chairman of Paramount Pictures [subsequently replaced by Sherry Lansing]. He asked me to come in and talk to him and he said we'd like to have you do another series for us. Not necessarily another *Star Trek* series, but another dramatic series. A series that could be brought to you 'from the people who give you *Star Trek: The Next Generation*.' I told him the best way to do that was to couch it in the structure of another series set within the umbrella of *Star Trek*."

One person not involved with the show was the late Gene Roddenberry, who was already very ill by the time Berman and Piller had completed their brainstorming about the series.

"We never got a chance to discuss it with Gene," says Berman. "By the time we had it to the point that it was discussable, he was in pretty bad shape and not really in the kind of condition that it would have been wise to discuss it with him. On two specific occasions I was with him at his house and we tried to bring to up, but it wasn't really appropriate."

Roddenberry had said on several occasions that only he could successfully create and cast a *Star Trek* series, which was the argument he used to defeat Harve Bennett's *Starfleet Academy* prequel idea. Berman is not worried about the faction of fandom that would agree with Roddenberry and consider Berman and Piller's attempt to co-opt the mythos as heresy.

"I'm not concerned about it," says Berman. "Before Gene died we worked together for close to five years and within the first of those five years I had his total confidence. I learned his language and his religion and his outlook. It's not necessarily my religion, my language and my outlook, but I learned it and I have been obsessively true to it through the second season, the third, the fourth, the fifth. Gene's involvement in the *Next Generation* has been minimal since the first year of the show and this new series—and any other *Star Trek* venture that I am involved with—will be absolutely true to that vision for the simple reason, that's what this show is.

"This show has been very successful because it's a show that rests on Gene's idea of the future. That will not change and I'm totally confident I can maintain Gene's ideals for the television series in terms of philosophy, in terms of attitudes, in terms of his feelings regarding fiction versus science fiction, fact vs. fantasy, believability. Things that were very important to Gene have been important to me for enough years that it's very easy for me to continue what. I have been doing. It will be no different for the new show. As for people who might say this was not created with Gene Roddenberry as part of the process, I hope we satisfy them."

Piller believes that *Deep Space Nine* continues to carry forth the same philosophy of *Star Trek* that *Next Generation* has rigidly adhered to over five seasons.

"The philosophy of Gene Roddenberry guides us. He didn't have any exposure to the specifics of this series, but he's with us in anything that we have to do with *Star Trek*. We have learned from him and from experience that stories that combine science fiction with a philosophy with an optimism with

••••

The cast of Star Trek: Deep Space Nine. (Photo copyright © Celebrity Photo Agency)

a comment on social issues and an exploration of human values, are the stories that work for *Star Trek*. Those are the stories that will work for us."

Logistically, running two series simultaneously will be a difficult task for Berman who intends to continue overseeing *Star Trek: The Next Generation* while producing *Deep Space Nine*. Other members of the *Trek* production team will be serving double duty on the new series, including make-up supervisor Michael Westmore.

"We have a remarkable group of people," says Berman. "There are 150 odd people who work on this television show and they all now have five years of experience doing it. We are able to borrow talents of our own people for the new series. In some cases people will split responsibility and in some cases secondary people for a number of years will move up within *Next Generation* or move over to the new series. A great many of the creative responsibility on the show will come from people who are involved with the series already."

In September of 1993 when *Next Generation* will go into its seventh season, as Berman predicts, *Deep Space Nine* will begin its first full season of 26 episodes, thus promising 52 episodes of *Star Trek* for the 1993-94 season. So for Berman, there's no time to sit back and contemplate the excitement of fashioning

his own universe.

"There's really no time to say this is nice," notes Berman. "I was involved with *Star Trek: The Next Generation*; from literally day one, before Gene had any idea what he was going to do with the show, and I was probably, with the exception of [Robert] Justman, the closest to him in terms of that creative process. To some degree, Bob Justman was my equal in that sense, but as the year moved on Gene tended to embrace me more as Bob started to step away. I have nothing but incredible things to say about Bob Justman, he was one of the single most important elements in the success of this series, but it was just as exciting then as it's going to be now. I don't think there's a feeling of wow, this one's ours."

Like the creation of *The Next Generation*, determining what the show would be was an important consideration during the conceptual stages.

"We realized that if we were going to do another *Star Trek* series that was going to overlap *Next Generation* by a couple of years, it would be foolish to bring another Enterprise or the like into it," says Berman. "We had an opportunity to have five years of experience on the *Next Generation*. For me five, Michael three, and when you do a television show for that period of time there's all sorts of things you wish for that you don't

have. An analogy that I've used is if you build a house and it's one of your first houses and you start living in it, you find yourselves saying we should have moved the kitchen door over here. It would have been more practical if we had made the steps one step higher. We could have gotten that in there if we had put the family room off the kitchen instead of off the living room. We are in that wonderful position of now being able to build that second house and taking advantage of all the wish we could ofs."

Although there will be more conflict in the new show, Berman quickly points out that early press reports that *Deep Space Nine* would be a darker show in tone are incorrect.

"There's no intention of making this darker," says Berman. "These people are in a more uncomfortable and alien environment and dealing with people who are not as peaceful and loving and family-like as the cast of characters onboard the Enterprise. But the fundamental core of these characters will still be the same noble, honorable and heroic qualities that a Picard or Kirk has given the audience in the original two series."

The series premiere was written by Michael Piller and based on a story by Berman and Piller. During the last three years that Piller has been on the show, Berman and he have cultivated a growing friendship and mutual respect.

"Michael and I are pretty much on the same wavelength," says Berman. "We have our own little fights and squabbles like any people trying to create something like what will be 46 hours of television next year, but philosophically and creatively we're remarkably in synch. There's never been any argument in terms of the direction the series will go or the direction any of the characters will go. It's something we've been in synch about since we started talking about it."

Says Michael Piller, "This is something that I've been looking forward to for a long time and something Rick and I have been talking about for years. We asked the studio to allow us to develop something a couple of years ago and we had Gene's blessing and the studio said, 'No, we're never going to do a *Star Trek* spin-off' and Brandon Tartikoff came and a month later there was a call saying we're going to do a *Star Trek* spin off. It's very exciting, its very intimidating. We understand that the critical reception of this will be from the harshest judges there are in television because the standards set by the two *Star Trek* series and the legacy that Gene has given us is an extraordinary challenge. We will not fill Gene's boots, but we will certainly put on a very good television show that is in the spirit that Gene would have wanted."

Piller agrees that finding new avenues for conflict was an important priority in fashioning the new series.

"We have learned that the most difficult part of writing *Star Trek: The Next Generation* is when you're dealing with the kind of characters we have who love each other, who are good people and all top of the line Starfleet officers. It's hard to have conflict between those people," says Piller. "We have to find ways of getting new conflicts, which has been a wonderful challenge. I think as a writer I've grown because I haven't been able to rely on traditional tricks that writers would like to be able to use to find conflict between characters. In the development of this new series we felt we had the opportunity to create an environment that by its very nature brought people into conflict again.

"Instead of the state of the art Enterprise which is the most comfortable spaceship in the imagination, you have a bunch of Starfleet officers onboard an alien space station that doesn't work all that well, that isn't built up to Federation or Starfleet specs, and is the most uncomfortable environment. We put them next to the planet Bajor, which is where Ensign Ro originated from, which we have created as an extraordinary spiritual, mystic planet which could not be more different than the humanist 24th century man that we have evolved into in *Star Trek*. These are friends and they think that things that occur in the universe are divine intervention. We're dealing with logic and this is another source of conflict. We are not on a Starfleet facility, we're sort of the Federation administration on this Bajoran space station which is called Deep Space Nine, and on this station you have aliens of all shapes and sizes who are coming through for various reasons, all with their own agendas, and we

have to deal with that."

Director David Carson doesn't see this potentially static setting to be a problem. "I think the space station has been designed in such a way that is completely different from the ship, so it does have a different feeling to it. It's sort of like a town, I suppose, in a funny kind of way. A town in terms of its social set-up. I suppose a good analogy would be on the Enterprise we very rarely leave the officers or people who are driving the ship and that side of things, but there are hundreds of other people on board the Enterprise doing whatever it is they do. I think one of the things *Deep Space Nine* does is expand its frame of reference from not just the officers that deal with the space station, but also involves the other people who we rarely see. That's what I mean by a town-like setting."

Adds director Winrich Kolbe, "*Deep Space Nine* is *Gunsmoke*. It's the town that everybody comes to. Get the characters in there. That's actually the selling point and because of its setting, it will become more of a character show. We get the people in there who represent the different opinions. We don't have to schlep through some deserted canyon in order to get there, they have to come to us."

One question regarding the show is the amount of synergy between *Next Generation* and *Deep Space*.

"The two writing staffs are not going to collaborate in the very business affairs sense," says Piller. "I am not hiring one great big staff to work on two shows. I think that would require that I pay everybody to work on two shows and I don't think that's possible. But I've made it very clear in the very earliest discussions that I see no reason why they should not be interested, thinking creatively, even writing for one staff or for the other and vice versa. I hope that occurs. There's a lot of time pressure and focus that has to come with it ,but this may freshen up some of us jaded folks. I hope it does. I do not see these two staffs as being competitive, I want them to support each other. I want them to be in the same building. Everything we can possibly do to make this a team effort."

Says Berman, "We're hoping there will be seven or eight people who'll be involved with both of the shows. The

writing staffs will be in either one building or two, hopefully in one. It's a question of office space. The production staffs will be in one building, hopefully post production will be in one building. There will be some degree of synergy, certainly with the visual effects people and costuming people and make-up people whose expertise will be spread across both shows."

Joining the staff of the new show under Piller is former *Next Generation* Executive Script Consultant Peter Allan Fields, who is Story Editor on the new series. He has very simple goals for the new show.

"I like to write good characters, but so does every writer," says Fields. "That's what we shoot for . I'd like to write interesting, bright drama. Something that is fun, but isn't necessarily funny, and fun to watch, and commiserate with and identify with. It took me so damn long to learn how to write the *Next Generation* characters and now I have to start all over again, but the other side of that is I'll be helping to form the way these characters do speak and their characters and the way they look at life. Of course that carries its responsibilities as well as its privileges, because I'm the one who'll be drummed out of town if I don't do it well. But I do look forward to that. *Deep Space Nine* excites me very much because it's untried territory. It's not going to be an extension of *Star Trek: The Next Generation*. I think people out there are afraid it might be, but it won't be at all. The characterizations and the outlook is different. There's a wonderful place for *Star Trek: The Next Generation*, but there's as much room for another kind of a series as there is space out there. If we do it right, we can have ourselves a wonderful time."

Being free of the constraints of *Next Generation* is both rewarding and limiting at the same time, says Fields. "The five years of stories that have been written are part and parcel of the restraints. Data has always wanted to be human and it would be easy for us to do a story where Data could have been human for a minute, but then what would have happened? That would have broken a layer and we would have had to do it again and the whole thing from

• • • •

Avery Brooks (Hawk) and Robert Urich (Spencer) working together on ABC's **Spencer: For Hire.**

The New Cast & Characters

Star Trek: Deep Space Nine introduces a new ensemble of characters and actors who, like those of previous *Treks*, is anchored by a leader along the lines of Captains James T. Kirk and Jean Luc Picard. In this case his name is Commander Benjamin Sisko, and he brings with him quite a package of emotional quandaries to be conquered.

"Our commander is somebody who's lived a life of tragedy," explains Michael Piller, "in essence because when Picard was with the Borg and led the Borg on their attack, he was a commander on one of the ships destroyed by Picard's leadership of the Borg. He lost his wife and now he's raising his son by himself and he hasn't really been able to go on with his life since he lost her. One of the arcs of the first story is some conflicts with Picard and how he gets by some of those things."

Adds director David Carson, "I think when you have somebody like that, who leads the story, he has to come to terms with what has happened to him, otherwise he spends his entire time in a bitter rage, which he doesn't. This is a buried part of his psyche, but it's nevertheless there."

Nonetheless, believes director Winrich Kolbe, this aspect of Sisko's character paves the way for something emotionally explosive down the line.

"Anybody who saw the pilot has to be aware of the fact that we had an unwilling leader of the group in Sisko," he points out. "Now *that* is intriguing. If he was unwilling once, even though at the end he said he's going to fulfill his obligations, there is a time bomb in that character. He's not the character anymore who says, 'I'm loyalty above all and I'm going down with the ship.' There is a possibility that he might do something totally different, totally unexpected."

David Carson believes that Sisko was the most difficult part to cast, because "that character is taking over the traditional role of Captain Kirk and Jean Luc Picard. Whoever plays that part is going to be the sort of standard-bearer for the next several years, because I don't

---

then on would have been worth nothing. *Deep Space Nine* will build a set of its own constraints. It's much freer now because it's not as formed and any show that's just getting started moves more than just people watching it. The more familiar the characters become, the more that improves the writers and the more idiosyncrasies they get and the more likes and dislikes they have, the more it begins to build up its own history."

"It'll be interesting to see how it develops," says Producer Ron Moore, who remains onboard *The Next Generation*. "It's anticipated that the two writing staffs will be fairly closely knit and there will be ideas thrown back and forth. It'll help that stories that won't work for us will be able to go to *Deep Space Nine* and vice versa. Hopefully there will be a larger body of ideas to draw from and different formats. The nuances and types of stories they have to tell may not be what it's like in a year. It's a long road, and the effects back and forth will be interesting to watch."

"There will be millions of people who watch the first few episodes of *Deep Space Nine* with a bit of cynicism," says Peter Fields. "To them, it's just *Star Trek: The Next Generation* makes money so they want to make more money and they're going to put out a pale imitation—which is not the case at all. Rick and Mike want this show to have its own

identity and indeed it will for better or worse. This show needn't be like the other two. It's going to be science-fiction, and there will be one or two characters crossing over, but this will be a whole new different show.

"*Deep Space Nine* gives my own imagination a little more room to roam because there aren't that many rules set down yet," continues Fields. "They don't have on-camera histories yet. It's a little bit scary, but I wake up in the morning rarin' to do it. I've never really experienced it before to this extent. Ever since I started working on *Star Trek: The Next Generation*, I get up in the morning and can't wait to get to work."

Prior to the shooting of the *Deep Space Nine* pilot, director David Carson enthused, "It's immensely exciting to be involved at the outset, because you attempt to shape the perspective of how the series will be seen, for the pilot may shape what happens in the series. It's tremendous to be part of the set off, particularly with such a big budget and such a push from Paramount. When you walk on to the set, as I did yesterday, you walk into the construction of the sets. The art department is teeming with people and drawings, and everyone is inventing this new world. You can feel this sense of immense confidence, excitement and optimism."

think anybody doubts that this series is going to run as long as the others did."

Ultimately the role went to Avery Brooks, a black actor perhaps best known as Hawk in the television series *Spencer: For Hire* and *Hawk*. The casting of Brooks as Sisko was heralded in *Newsweek* as a "revolutionary" move.

"We decided that the role could be played either by a white man or a black man, or as in the case of Picard by an American or Englishman, or Belgian or German," Carson, who was deeply involved in the casting of the series, details. "In fact, we did interview a Belgian actor and a German actor who came over from England. What race or creed he was was very important, but it was never a question of whether or not there were opportunities for everyone, every type of person to play the role. In the end, even though you would expect us to say this, I think all of us can quite truthfully say that we were able to come down to what we considered to be the best actor for the job. I think that Avery Brooks is a phenomenal actor. I've rarely come across an actor with a combination of his incredible depth of ability to portray emotions and feelings, but also his extraordinary technical skill in front of the camera and an amazing strength of performing with the lens. He's a real joy to work with. And the way he senses out a character.....He has developed his character beyond "The Emissary" into a very subtle blend of types of feeling and the way he handles himself in different situations. He's extraordinarily deft and constantly interesting, and I think the character gives him much more ability to have these differences in his psychological make-up than Picard, who's a much more straight-forward character you can probably predict will react in what way in different situations. It's very difficult to do with Sisko, and Avery plays with delight those opportunities."

For Brooks, finding himself confined within three soundstages on the Paramount lot is a far cry from the location shooting in Boston and Washington, D.C. he had done on *Spencer* and *Hawk*, respectively. "Of course when you're moving around and on location you work 14-16 hours a day," says Brooks. "It's a different kind of rhythm. Working

inside requires that you not lose your energy and your focus and your concentration, because it's easy after 12 or 13 hours to realize you've been working that long and your body says, 'I want to go home.' This pilot was particularly difficult. Of course, now I can't blame my performance on the weather."

When Stewart and Shatner were cast, both, despite an impressive array of supporting credits, were not as well known as Avery Brooks. Brooks had created a very recognizable visual icon during his three years playing Hawk, slowly but malevolently enunciating, "S-p-e-n-c-e-r" to Robert Urich week after week. Executive Producer Rick Berman didn't feel his lack of anonymity was a liability in casting him as Sisko.

"He played the second role on a show and it did not last a long time," says Berman. "There are actors I tend to stay away from because I feel they have overly familiar faces. But to me a good actor is somebody you don't think about how familiar they are. If they're right, they're right."

Despite early rumors, denied by Michael Piller, that Richard Dean Anderson of *MacGyver* was a front-runner for the coveted role of Sisko, Brooks was chosen days before the beginning of principal photography on the pilot. Ironically, Brooks played his best known role bald and the question remained, in light of Patrick Stewart's well-noted baldness, would Brooks continue the tradition?

"We think he looks best with hair," says Producer David Livingston. "In fact, we looked at several variations of hair and we felt the one we chose was the most appealing and the way he looked best. It was simply a cosmetic decision and had no bearing on Patrick Stewart."

"It happened very quickly for me," recalls Brooks on his casting. "I was in the Caribbean and I talked to my agent and he asked me if I was a fan of *Star Trek*. I said, 'Well, I watch it, of course.' He said, 'I have a script you might want to read.' I read it and I was thrilled. The writing was extraordinary, the story very compelling. And so I pursued it. And then, I was on my way to lay down something on tape in New York and my car started to slip out of gear. I called my wife and said, 'I don't think I can make

A somewhat more casual moment for Quark (Armin Shimerman) between takes of Deep Space Nine. *(Photo copyright © Jeff Jacobson)*

it.' I called the people frantically and said I don't think I can make it in, but they let me do it again. But I was out of town. They said, 'We need you to come to California now,' so I flew out from Atlanta and it happened very, very fast and I'm thrilled."

Like Stewart, Brooks commands an instant respect on the set from his fellow actors and will no doubt prove to be not only a role model for people of all races, but write a new chapter for the advancement and depiction of blacks on television. "I think you can see that quality when you meet him," states Michael Piller. "When we walked into the room, we knew we had found our Sisko. We had been looking for a quality that continued with the heroic leadership potential, but we knew that very big boots had to be filled. We had two great stars in the leadership role of captains and commanders in the past, and it was very difficult to find someone who really impressed everybody in the room with the same presence of command that Avery did."

Adds Rick Berman, "I think the key word is presence. We needed someone who could match, or hopefully exceed, the sense of presence that Patrick Stewart exudes on a pretty regular basis as Captain Picard. We didn't want to go backwards, we wanted to go forwards. We

Nana Visitor in costume as Major Kira Nerys, the former Bajoran terrorist, on the set of Deep Space Nine. (Photo copyright © Celebrity Photo Agency)

were looking for a good actor, but more than anything we were looking for someone with that sense of commanding presence which this guy seems to give us."

For Brooks, *Deep Space's* allegorical approach to addressing contemporary issues is a refreshing change from the mundane fare offered on network television. This is reflected in the fact that he portrays a single parent, which he feels illustrates the show's topicality in addressing 90's concerns within the framework of future society.

"We're dealing with a single parent and single parenting," says Brooks. "In the last twenty years there's a very different notion in our society and, indeed, our world about what that means, so of course in an allegorical way this show is very 90's. We're on the verge of the 21st century and then it will be very teens. Teens in the 21st century."

Although new to STAR TREK, Brooks' admits to an instant affinity for the material. "I'm new to it," said Brooks. "Of course, I was familiar with it because I grew up watching television, but I am definitely a fan now. Science fiction appeals to the child in all adults and when you tease the mind as well, the people are going to come in flocks."

A key factor in the success of the original *Star Trek* bridge crew, was the inclusion of Mr. Spock, an alien who could provide a unique perspective on humanity. That same function was fulfilled on *Next Generation* by Data and, now, on *Deep Space Nine* by station security chief Odo.

Explains Michael Piller, "He was the security chief that the Bajorans assigned to the space station when the Cardassians were there. We inherit him because he's very savvy about the goings on of this Promenade. But he's a guy who has his own way of doing things and he'll take the law into his own hands to make things the way he wants to. He also happens to be a shape shifter and he has a very interesting back story. He doesn't know where he came from. He showed up one day in a space ship. He's the only one of his kind and he's searching for who he is. It's part of what his drive is. He's found his place in society as a man of the law, but his way of doing things is not all the way our main commander's way of doing things is, and they have an interesting conflict."

Director Winrich Kolbe finds the character of Odo an intriguing one. "I did a show where Odo is trying to discover where he came from, but he unfortunately winds up with somebody he doesn't believe," says Kolbe. "He doesn't believe anybody to begin with, but this guy he *really* doesn't believe. When this guy suddenly begins to tune in on Odo's shape-shifting capability, he says, 'Maybe I know something that might be intriguing to you.' And then Odo's character says, 'Forget it, you're a liar and a thief and I can't trust you,' but then follows him anyway. It's intriguing because there is a person who's very, very distrustful, which makes the perfect sheriff. He pushes the envelope of what the police should be. The police should be trusting nobody, and Odo's philosophy of arrest first, ask questions later is an intriguing aspect of his profession which obviously puts him into conflict with Sisko. We're talking about issues about society. We're talking about death penalty, the Napoleonic code versus the Anglo-Saxon code. Are we guilty until proven innocent or innocent until proven guilty? That is something intriguing, and Rene

Auberjonois is such a fascinating actor."

Although viewers may best remember Rene Auberjonois as Clayton Endicott III on the hit ABC series *Benson*, it would be difficult to recognize him underneath the prosthetic Michael Westmore has designed for him to transform the Emmy and Tony Award winning actor into Odo.

Points out David Carson, "Like Avery Brooks, Rene has this extraordinary classical background. He, like Avery, is a classically trained stage actor. Both of them have come out of this tradition of performance. So to have the luxury of someone like Rene Auberjonois playing a shape-shifter is quite extraordinary, because he isn't really first and foremost a TV actor who comes out of *Benson*. He has turned this character into somebody absolutely fascinating. And the fact that he is classically trained makes him particularly able to work with the mask-like thing that's on his face. He's an actor who's learned how to work with and through a mask because he's trained with masks and, I think, trained other people to act with masks. You get much more richness and depth out of somebody like him than somebody who doesn't have that depth of experience."

"Odo, in terms of the kind of person he is and his incredible dignity and sense of justice, is very appealing to me," says Auberjonois. "He's sort of a curmudgeon and he's a very rigid man. He's uptight but he's also got a wonderful deadpan kind of humor. Beyond that he's got a very human kind of pain because he doesn't know who or what he is, so there's this kind of existential struggle going on inside of him because he's really just a liquid form. He takes the shape of a humanoid but it's only so he can exist in this world."

As a shape shifter who metamorphsizes into numerous shapes and sizes every episode, the actor is the focus of many of the series' state-of-the art visual effects. Since the work is often done in post production, it requires a special discipline to imagine a world of creatures and illusions that doesn't exist until Rob Legato's fertile imagination gets to incorporate them.

"It's the nature of being an actor," Auberjonois explains. "For people who are not professional actors, the easiest thing to do is just to remember what it's like to play house. I remember as a kid there was a place in the attic where my brother and I used to go to pretend to be scientists. It's just this willing suspension of disbelief. There's something wonderful about Odo because I turn into all these different things. We shoot things where I just sort of stand there and I know that I've just turned back from being a rat and it's magical for me to see that."

Portraying Odo is not Auberjonois' first foray into the *Star Trek* universe, the actor having played the nefarious Colonel West at the request of personal friend and director Nicholas Meyer, in a sub-plot that had been cut from *Star Trek VI*'s theatrical release, but restored for its subsequent video edition. In these scenes, the Colonel plots with Klingon conspirators and the Romulan ambassador Nanclus to prevent a peace treaty from being signed between the Klingons and the Federation. Ultimately, Colonel West is revealed as the man under the Klingon make-up attempting to assassinate the Federation president at the Khitomer Peace Conference.

"I wasn't in *Star Trek VI* because the character was cut out," says Auberjonois, who admits to often being cast as a villain. "I have not seen it. I did it because Nick Meyer is a personal friend and asked me to. I was in Scotland hiking with my wife and rushed back to get the make-up all done. I've played a lot of different kind of parts and I usually play villains and I love them. I remember when my son was much younger and I was doing *Richard III* at the same time I was doing *Benson*. He asked why do you always play the bad guy and I said it's because they're usually the best part to play."

However, Auberjonois' Odo is certainly a hero of the series and he's thrilled to be probing the limits of the final frontier, both literally and figuratively. Odo is the focus of one of the series' earliest episodes, directed by Paul Lynch, "A Man Alone", which addresses prejudice and discrimination. It reflects an evolution for the character that pleases Auberjonois, although even he is not sure what the writers have in store for the mysterious shape-changer in the future.

"It's evolving and there are certain things that I know about him that are clear from the scripts that we've done so far and the bible," points out the actor. "The writers know a lot more about where it's going than I do. I like not knowing and opening the script each week and seeing a new facet of the character for me to consider. I like that challenge each week and it keeps it fresh for me which is very important when you're doing a week in and week out schedule and watching the character develop like this. When you're doing a series, the characters always develop to a degree, but I think in this kind of situation, more than a sitcom where the characters really are cast and you know what's going to happen, there's a certain wisdom revealed in the character. He has an incredible intelligence and in another there's a weakness in his character that's revealed, a rigidity he has to work through, a human quality which is very interesting."

Auberjonois hopes that Odo is as well-accepted as Spock and Data, and is pleased to have been cast in the role.

"It's certainly a good gig, there's no question about that," says Auberjonois. "I guess it would be less than candid for me to say that when I first approached it that it was in a very mercenary sense that I'm an actor with two kids in college and I wanted to get this job and it was a good part. My main intention was to go out as an actor and be practicing my craft and get the job. I was never a big Trekker. I've seen my share of *Star Trek* and *The Next Generation* and always admired them and thought it was something I felt would be appropriate for me to do. I have a lot of classical training and my background is in the theater, so all of those things motivated me to think it's a good job to get involved with. As I've been absorbed into this world and read all the bibles and backstories and done my homework, I have been more and more impressed by the depth of the subjects that it deals with in a general sense. On a personal level, my character, Odo, is wonderful."

Also pleasing to the actor are the interrelationships developing with the other characters on the show. "There's something specific with every other character," he notes. "My relationship with Nana Visitor who plays Major Kira Nerys is a very interesting one, because she is above me in rank and yet she comes to me for a certain kind of wisdom. I'm very interested in seeing how that develops. For me, the mystery of who he is is going to be the thing that keeps me plugged into the character and, in a way, I hope it takes a long, long time to figure out who

The relationship between Odo (Rene Auberjonois) and Quark (Armin Shimerman) is one that the writers have latched on to in a big way. (Photo copyright © Jeff Jacobson)

A lighter than usual moment between Odo (Rene Auberjonois) and Quark (Armin Shimerman). (Photo copyright © Jeff Jacobson)

he is. I don't mean to be pollyanish about it but I'm just so happy with the character and the stories that we've had to do. Ask me that question in a couple of years, maybe I'll be a jerk, but right now I'm just in here plugging and loving every minute of it."

Following in the steps of Dr. Leonard "Dammit Jim" McCoy and Dr. Beverly Crusher is no easy task, but that's exactly what Julian Bashir is attempting as chief medical officer of Deep Space Nine. Notes Michael Piller wryly, "Julian Bashir is a young, ambitious, wet behind the ears, thinks he knows it all, young man who just graduated from Starfleet Medical, and came out here because this is where heroes are made and this is where the adventure is and this is the wilderness. He's got a lot to learn."

Cast in the role of Bashir is 26 year old Londoner, Siddig El Fadil, who has starred on stage in productions of *Brother Eichmann* and *Sinbad, the Sailor*. He probably made his greatest impression as King Keisal in the PBS prequel to *Lawrence of Arabia*, *A Dangerous Man*. That was the role that caught the interest of *Deep Space Nine* executive producer Rick Berman.

"The one casting credit I feel I can take and am very proud of is Siddig," says Berman. "I had seen Siddig on public television and I sought him out and

had the Paramount people in London find him. He read for us in London and he's someone no one would have ever considered. He is, as time will tell, an extraordinary actor."

Enthuses director David Carson, "What a wonderful actor he is, freshly minted from British drama school. A very wonderful candor and openness of feeling about him. And for such a young actor, very experienced with the lens. Very good at turning his hand to all the tricks of the emotions the writers have asked of him so far. He's, again, a wonderful addition to the team."

It's a testament to *Star Trek*'s ability to transcend ethnic and racial boundaries that an actor like Siddig could be cast in a role patterned in such a distinctly Michael J. Fox vein. "I read in London with about 30 people," recalls Siddig. "I think they auditioned all over Europe. And then I did one for the big cheeses here. It was bizarre, one day I did the test in London and two days later they asked me to fly to Hollywood where I had never been and, on the same day, they gave me the job, which was great."

Everyone on the show has high expectations for the actor. "Bashir is one of my favorite characters," says producer/writer Ira Steven Behr. "I think the Siddig is going to go through the roof. He's good looking, fun and he's got ener-

gy. I think the key to the show is that people have a lot of energy."

Siddig found he didn't need to do much preparation for the role. "I read through the whole medical encyclopedia," he laughs. "No, actually I didn't do a thing because I'm incredibly lazy. What's state-of-the art medical now is completely irrelevant in the future. It's nice to know about genealogy or genetics or whatever, which I can pick up from my education, which I just finished recently, but I haven't gone into it because the words have their own life regardless of what's written in the manuals. I just want to sound like I know what I'm doing. When they mention a word in the scripts that I don't know, you sometimes have to look it up because the only way it will make sense is if you know what it actually means. You just stick that funny looking thing in someone's neck and pray to god that it's the right place."

Unfortunately, as the doctor onboard Deep Space Nine, El Fadil has found himself wrestling with the longtime *Trek* dilemma of technobabble, the mystical *Trek* mumbo science that passes for scientific accuracy in depicting a 24th century civilization.

"They have a sadistic love of it," laughs El Fadil. "But I actually quite enjoy it. It's the nearest thing to Shakespeare. Stretching the mind to get your tongue around it and make sense of it when you talk. I actually quite enjoy trying to see if I can make something of it without making it sound flat. That's part of the lie of trying to make it sound like I'm actually a doctor or a science officer. Data on the *Next Generation* is an unbelievable robot because he does it flawlessly."

The actor quickly points out that he's not fearful of comparisons with the previous *Star Trek* doctors since his character is so dramatically different than either of the roles which have preceded him. "I've seen the other shows, but they're such different people than I am," he says. "They've gone for someone younger and he's more naive and he's not burdened with anything except for the novelty of everything he sees and how best to negotiate it. It completely mirrors my experience, jumping around and being overenthusiastic comes very naturally to me."

"The most difficult role to cast is always a beautiful girl," claims Executive Producer Rick Berman. "Beautiful women are few and far between and to find one who can act and who doesn't want to bypass television to go into the movies is very difficult since there are very few of them. Fortunately, we finally found Terri."

Finally is the operative word for Berman, since the role of Science Officer Dax was the last one to be cast several weeks after production began on the pilot, complicating an already arduous casting process. The search for Dax makes casting Vivien Leigh in *Gone With the Wind* look like child's play.

"It's so overwhelming," says Farrell. "I'm so glad it's over. It's so incredible getting *Star Trek* anyway because it's such a legend. In August when I first got it, it was like a roller-coaster ride that I couldn't get off of, and you don't know what's going to happen."

Rick Berman admits that part of the difficulty of casting the role was the problems they had in explaining the part to those auditioning. "It was very difficult to say you're a beautiful woman and a 400 year old androgynous character at the same time."

Recalls Co-Executive Producer and Co-Creator Michael Piller, "We were already in production when we cast Terry and part of the reason that it's so difficult to cast is because it's a character that's a little harder to define. I could write a book about Trills now but what does that mean in the day to day existence of these people? How do we make it different from Terry Farrell? How do you make it something alien and yet accessible? It's a very interesting mix of qualities that I think the studio wanted. Rick and I felt that we wanted a woman who was attractive and yet a superior actress. We saw a lot of very talented young women, but they just didn't get it. Some would change their voices, to make it sound like a man's voice coming out of a woman. It was hard. The casting people will tell you that the roles of people 25-35, attractive and brainy are the hardest roles to cast in television. It's hard to find the next Meryl Streep. It's hard to find the next Glenn Close."

Fortunately, Terry Farrell, who had recently finished work on the Tony Hicox film *Hellraiser III*, was called in by casting director Junie Lowry-Johnson to audition. "Terry came in the last day or two of casting for this show and we had her back a couple of times," says Piller. "We had two or three others that we were very interested in, but truth is Terry was the only actress who came in to read where Rick and I looked at each other and agreed that she had hit the scenes that she was reading. We had finally gotten to the place where we had to cast somebody and Terry did not have the experience of some of the others, and we knew, and she knows that there was a great challenge of acting and performance ahead of her. So far it's amazing to watch her because you can see a much stronger performance. She's starting to grow more and find this role."

Farrell agrees and says the key to her audition was playing the role with an amused detachment as opposed to attempting to personify a woman with a "short, fat snake inside."

"I think she has fun with people," says Farrell. "In the scene I had to audition in I said I used to be an old man and Avery expects to see him in that context. He had never seen me before as a woman so how else do you play that other than to have fun with somebody? It would be fun if you dressed up in make-up and the other person doesn't know you're fooling them and they're trying to believe you're who they say you are, but you don't look anything like you did last week. Just having fun with it was the key for me."

Recalls David Carson, "Most of the time with Terry was struggling to see what in fact a Trill should look like. Together with the fact that she was cast very late, we had all these problems of what should be stuck on her face. There were countless tests and some people didn't like this, some people didn't like that, until eventually she came out with spots. I don't know if you know this, but Trills have an established look which is a sort of lumpy prosthetic look on their faces. As you'll notice, she in fact doesn't have any. When we first started shooting her, she had these old prosthetic lumps on her face. But frankly they did not add to her undeniable attractiveness, so everybody decided that her face should be left alone and spots should be added which went under the collar of her costume, thereby being suggestive of where else the spots might be. Not that anybody will *ever* know."

Preparation Farrell didn't make for the role was boning up on her science. "In biology I did really well, I got straight A's, but this is different," she explains. "I'm not the doctor! You just open the writer's guide and I call and ask them and ask Michael Piller—who's really nice if you have a question—about the technical jargon. Sometimes they write a question mark where the 'tech' should be and you wonder what's going to be the word there. Cough it up! I know they're going to freak me out and then I end up getting something like 'The ionic L-band emission patterns don't match'. I'm supposed to know this by heart? Tech with a question mark? I'm getting more used to it now. That's what really upset me during the pilot because I didn't even know where to start. What am I talking about? I'd try to relate it to a car and it wasn't working."

As for the future, Farrell, admits she does have some concerns about the inevitable stardom that comes from being a part of the *Star Trek* mythos — although typecasting isn't one of them.

"I get real worried about it and become private and inwards," says Farrell. "I don't know if I'm ready for Spago's. On my way to work at four in the morning, I worry about it. You forget when you're doing an interview like this when I'm saying it to you it doesn't feel like I'm saying it to 9 million people. You don't realize the impact of it. When I did *Paper Dolls* I got a lot of attention and I had the Andy Warhol 15 minutes of fame and I couldn't go to the mall anymore. Then I stopped for a while and I could go back to the mall again. Now if I can't...it's okay, because I don't like the mall anyway."

Cirroc Lofton makes his television debut as the 14-year old son of commander Benjamin Sisko. Having lived on four different starships and been stationed on two planets, Jake yearns to return to earth rather than be forced to live aboard Deep Space Nine.

Unlike the usually venal reaction engendered by children on most science-fiction series, the character of Jake Sisko is dissimilar to the infamous Boxey of *Battlestar: Galactica* or Wesley Crusher who earned the derision of fans of *The Next Generation* for saving the ship. Jake is simply a young teenager who has been forced by his father's job to pick up roots and move yet again. It's a dilemma that many member's of the audience can relate to and a role that Michael Piller hopes will explore the real issues facing single fathers and their off-spring. "This has nothing to do with the Wil Wheaton character which was a super genius who seemed to save the ship every week," says Piller. "This is a kid who is growing up in his life with his dad. The two of them struggle as fathers and sons do everyday in our lives. This kid does not have any great technical skills, he's not going to save the ship. He's a kid. And we will see other parts of the station through his eyes. The bottom line is that this hero, this leader, our star, had to be different. He couldn't be Picard, he couldn't be Kirk. He had to be Sisko. And to me, and to Rick, we felt giving him a son as an added burden enriched his character and the opportunities to see him on a personal level that we rarely got to see Kirk and Picard on."

Equally important to the creators of the series was addressing the contemporary issue of single fatherhood. Avery Brooks' Sisko is very much a man of the 90's in the way that Picard has been representative of the 80's and Kirk, the 60's.

"Frankly, I think that anything you could do to provide a role model for kids and parents is a good thing," says Piller of Jake's relationship with his father. "Family values has become a curse word this year, but I think it's important that we, as writers and creators, continue to provide strong role models on television for parents and for television."

Of Lofton, David Carson opines, "A very, very talented young man. He had minimal drama training, according to his mother, and for a boy who's had so little training, he's really quite good. He was way and above the best actor that we saw for the role, and we saw many, many actors. I think he has a refinement of manner and a refine-ment of feature as well, which makes him just that little bit set apart, which I think is very good for Sisko's son. His family comes from Ethiopia and I suppose his background has had some effect on him, his bearing and how he looks. But I think he's very bright and has a big future. The thing about Cirroc, though, is that he's growing so fast now that we're doing the series. We're not quite sure when he's going to overtake Avery."

Perhaps if one is looking for a deeper subtext to the show, it is only through inclusion and the creation of an extended family of characters that the re-building of Deep Space Nine is achieved. Ultimately, *Trek* is about a family, an ensemble of characters that work together for the common good bringing together people of different races, ethnic persuasions and even species. If *Star Trek* is indeed preaching, if only maybe to the converted, it tells us that only by becoming a global family, an extension of Sisko's immediate family through which he has undergone catharsis, can we aspire to achieve even greater good and the utopian ethos of Roddenberry's universe that man strives to attain.

Colm Meaney has served aboard the Enterprise since it's first encounter at Farpoint, although most fans won't remember it since he was a nameless face on the battle bridge. Since then, through sheer charisma, the actor has elevated himself from an anonymous transporter chief to the only married recurring character on *The Next Generation* and now as a co-star aboard *Deep Space Nine*.

"My favorite on *Star Trek* since the beginning has been Colm Meaney," says Rick Berman of the actor who personifies Miles O'Brien, a name which was finally revealed during the series' fourth year. "I adore Colm's work."

Sharing Berman's enthusiasm is director David Carson. "I've worked with him before on *Next Generation*, and he's tremendous. Very wonderful, warm, interesting varied actor, and I think it's an interesting choice to have him come over from *Next Generation*. He wasn't particularly prominent over there and to suddenly reveal him is a good way of linking the two series without doing it heavy-handedly. I think that's a really good choice."

"I was in New York for a year with *Breaking the Code* and that was the year of the writer's strike, so *Star Trek* didn't get going again until September or October," recalls Meaney of his return to *Next Generation* after having shot the pilot. "When I came back, they brought me on as Chief O'Brien. For the first five or six shows that I did, he just kept cropping up and I was Transporter Chief. Then, a script arrived and suddenly he had a name."

Meaney has kept busy on the silver screen as well as the small screen starring for Alan Parker in *The Commitments* as a reverent fan of Elvis; and in Ron Howard's *Far & Away*. During his treks away from the decks of the Enterprise, the actor has also appeared as the ill-fated captain of a 747 in *Die Hard II: Die Harder*, a cop in *Dick Tracy*, Dennis Quaid's brother in Alan Parker's *Come See the Paradise* and most recently the malevolent terrorist who menaces Steven Seagal in *Under Siege*. Surprisingly, Meaney agreed to join the cast of *Deep Space Nine* when he was approached by Producers Rick Berman and Michael Piller to become a regular on the new series.

"We knew we wanted to do something with O'Brien, who we brought over to the show," says writer/producer Ira Behr. "Colm is a really fine actor and he's had limited chances on *The Next Generation*. This year he's a lead and we're trying to find different and new things to do with him. One of those things is to team him up with Bashir in a certain way. Bashir sees O'Brien as kind of the old pro from Dover, the guy who's done it all. The way I see is O'Brien is as the working man's hero and so does Bashir. Bashir wants to be like him and wants to know him and emulate him. O'Brien looks at this young kid from the Academy with that English, upper class accent and it's like, 'Go away kid, you bother me.' It could be fun because you don't usually see that. We shot a scene where Bashir is talking, talking, talking and he turns to O'Brien and says something to O'Brien and he just gives Bashir a look, with not one line of dialogue, that's like 'Get the fuck away from me kid. It's funny, it's good and it's character."

Meaney agrees that O'Brien has sort of become the everyman of *Star Trek*. "O'Brien is somebody who is more human," says Meaney. "He obviously likes his job, but he also has other aspects to his personality. He doesn't have the element of being a fearless super human. There are situations they get into which, because of their Starfleet training, they react to as if it's normal, with steely nerves and all that, but I think O'Brien doesn't like that stuff too much."

Armin Shimerman is no stranger to Ferengi. Having pioneered the weasley role of a Ferengi in the first season *Next Generation* episode introducing the race, "The Last Outpost", Shimerman was a natural choice for the role of Quark, the bar-keep of Deep Space Nine.

A veteran of such series as *Brooklyn Bridge, Beauty and the Beast* and *Alien Nation*, Shimerman has also appeared in the films *Blind Date, Like Father, Like Son* and *Death Warrant*. The actor is quick to contrast his new character of Quark with previous Ferengi incarnations, who many fans dismissed as an incpt attempt by *Trek* to find a new adversary for the Federation during its early evolution. "The Ferengi have always, in the past couple of years, seemed to be very broad and on the verge of slapstick," says Shimerman. "I would like to reel that in a little. On the other hand, that is what they've established, so I must include that as well. I don't know what was in their heads about the comic values of myself, but what I think they found in the early episodes is the great comic potential between Odo and Quark. There's this sort of Mutt and Jeff relationship that both Rene and I are savoring a great deal. I think that's where a lot of the humor is going to come from. Quark is still libidinous, Quark is still avaricious and he's still ambitious and Quark's still short...but I think the humor will come from all those things and his relationships with the humans and the shape shifter."

Writer/producer Ira Behr shared Shimerman's enthusiasm for the developing relationship between Quark and Odo. "I think Michael and Rick both realized that this is a learning process of finding out together who these people are. Then, of course, you cast the god-

damn thing and the actors make it who they are and you sit back and say 'Okay, maybe that's not what I had in mind exactly', but it works and so all the best laid plans of all these things go out the window the second the camera's roll. What I found interesting and fun about this show is not so much each individual character but how the characters began to interact on the show. Making Odo and Quark this kind of twosome is just going to have juice for ages because Odo is this kind of repressed, haunted figure. Rene's really playing the makeup to a certain extent, which is that he's a man alone, which you don't see a lot in the 24th century, and Quark is a Ferengi. He's not your typical cringing Ferengi, he's a Ferengi with a little edge to him too and their comic relationship I find is something that's going to be a lot of fun."

Shimerman attributes his casting to his previous outings as a Ferengi on the series and felt he could best personify the new Ferengi character they had created for *Deep Space*.

"They remembered me from five years ago as one of the first Ferengi," says Shimerman. "I think what Rick said to me was they remembered how strong a Ferengi I was because they wanted that for Quark. He also has to be able to play chess with Sisko. They wanted that quality. I did not have to audition as many

times for a series regular as I would if they had not seen my work. The first time that I had a callback, and usually there are a number of actors sitting there, it was only me and Max Grodenchik. He's played a Ferengi before because we had done the most Ferengi [episodes] At the final audition it was just me and they gave me the impression after I was cast that they had indeed written the part with me in mind."

Offers David Carson, "Armin and I worked together on another science fiction show called *Alien Nation*. Armin is terrific. Like Rene, he has taken to the mask completely and is developing the character wonderfully. Unlike most of the Ferengi characters there have been, Quark is not quite so silly. He has a much more malevolent presence, which I think is very good because it adds to the drama. He's, again, delightful to work with, extremely able technically and in all other ways. He's also a very patient man. Everybody knows when they guy into this show that's what's it's going to be; that you're going to spend hours in a make-up chair. But such is the enthusiasm for the show that everybody buys into it completely. I mean, Michael Dorn's been doing it for several years now."

Shimerman does, however, admit to a degree of frustration about working under the huge prosthetic appli-

A final touch of make-up is added to Rene Auberjonois' mask that is utilized in his portayal of Odo. (Photo copyright © Jeff Jacobson)

• • • •

ance that covers his face, but laughed that, unlike LeVar Burton, at least he can use his eyes. "I think every actor would prefer if all of his face was shown," says Shimerman. "I would be a fool to say otherwise, but I think the mask works really well and the combination of the mask and whatever inflections I can give to my voice and my eyes I think comes across quite well. It means working a little harder and being a little bit bigger. I'm used to playing roles where its very low-key and underplayed and I've been trying to teach myself to do that for years. Now all of the sudden I'm being asked to overplay a little. It's just a new challenge."

As originally conceived, first officer of Deep Space Nine would have been *Next Generation*'s Ensign Ro, but those plans were scrapped when actress Michelle Forbes decided that she would rather pursue a film career than get tied down to a series for five years or more.

"Michelle Forbes is a wonderful actress and her character of Ensign Ro created the entire canvas for this new series," says Michael Piller. "It had always been assumed that she would be one of the people spun off and moved over to the new series. [But] she wants to be a feature actress."

Fortunately, Forbes' departure from these plans came at the same time Piller was working on a rewrite of the pilot to strengthen the first act, which meant changing the character of Ro to another Bajoran with a new and different backstory. This, he soon discovered, proved an advantage rather than a disadvantage for the new series.

"I found there was a great deal more conflict in having the Bajoran not be Starfleet," explains Piller. "Immediately you have different priorities and agendas, and the two people immediately have a conflict with each other the moment they step onto the station. The one between Sisko and Ro would have been a much different one because ultimately she's Starfleet and has to do what the boss says. Kira can do things which are not appropriate Starfleet behavior. We created this character and it was really a matter of rewriting two or three scenes that defined where she was from and a couple of speeches in other scenes which were mostly

action type scenes."

One of the moments that episode director Winrich Kolbe remembers upon viewing the pilot is a confrontation between Sisko and Major Kira Nerys (the Ro replacement), in which Sisko warns her that if she ever goes over his head again, he'll serve it on a silver platter.

"I love that," smiles Kolbe. "That to me is more human, it is more contemporary—and I'm talking about 1993. Sometimes we have to work together with people with whom we occasionally disagree with and have differences of opinion with, yet despite that they are capable of fulfilling their job. In the pilot, I think Sisko said, 'I want you because you're Bajoran.' He could have had any one of a million Bajorans, somebody who would say, 'Yes, sir, whatever you want.' He wanted somebody who comes from the background of Kira, who was in the underground against the Cardassians. A nationalist, so to speak. It intrigues me because I feel that, yes, we are changing, but we are not necessarily becoming more advanced. There's nationalism 2,000 years from now and it will always be there because it's something genetically inside us. Like racism, which is something that's always coming out. We only seemingly live in a better social society if we are able to combat it, but the moment we let our guard down, bingo, there's the conflict. I like that in DS9 when it comes down to the Kira/Sisko conflict. It's politics, but it's the politics of Starfleet, of the larger unit which says, 'We want to expand our influence,' and the small unit which is the planet Bajor which says, 'Hey, it's all very nice but you're taking over. We don't want you either.' Talking about metaphors. The Americans in Somalia. Who's interest are we really representing?"

David Carson admits that the casting of Kira was difficult. "Though no more so than when you're setting up something completely new, because on these television things everything is done by committee. So you're juggling three million opinions at the same time. It's sort of a different world from the one that I'm used to in that sense. You feel as though you're walking through a minefield as you struggle towards the final choice in television, it seems to

me, because there are a whole mixture of opinions to be taken into account, some informed, and some uninformed. Sometimes, as we all know, terrible mistakes happen in casting. I think, though, we were extremely lucky this time and everybody had the necessary patience to not say yes because we had to start shooting. In fact, some of the roles weren't cast until we were three weeks into it. We had to change the schedule around to accommodate it. With a show like this, getting a good cast is really so important."

Nana Visitor, a veteran of a number of television shows including the short-lived *Working Girl*, based on the hit motion picture, cast as the former Bajoran terrorist and second-in-command of *Deep Space Nine*, confesses to not being an avid *Star Trek* fan when she joined the new series. "I watched *Star Trek* when it was in re-runs," she says. "I think I know them all from cooking dinner in my brownstone in New York. I was a fan of the quality of the show, but I was not a Trekkie."

Ironically, Visitor didn't even realize *Deep Space Nine* was a *Star Trek* spin-off when she read for the role. "I didn't get it and I didn't understand that this was *Star Trek* when I auditioned," says Visitor. "I did not understand what I was getting into. I didn't even know I was wearing a nose and I talked to Rick Berman and he said 'At least the prosthetic is one of the least we have' and I said 'What prosthetic?' and he said 'It's nothing, it's just a small elephant nose that you wear' and he had me going for five seconds. But I didn't know, I had no idea. I just knew I wanted to play this woman very badly."

"The cast and company is so lucky to have her," enthuses David Carson. "She's one of these rare chameleon kind of actors who is able to assimilate herself into a character and transform it into something you don't expect. She's also very beautiful and she obviously delights in playing this role. I was very pleased when she walked into the room and I think that once she did, she was the only Kira that we thought could play the role. Of course we weren't going to tell anybody that until we'd signed a deal with her. She was and

• • • •

is extraordinary. She's also delightful to work with and she's able to tune her emotions to the camera. She also has this specific, tangible relationship with the lens, which is delightful for a director to work with."

Visitor's hopes for the character reflect the inner passions felt by Kira, whose loyalty to her people and home world motivate her actions.

"My hope is that Kira may change from this course of being someone who isn't necessarily always right and who has a button pushing relationship with Sisko," Visitor offers. "They just set each other off in a certain way, but she's growing and changing. In our second episode, she opens up to Odo and asks for help with her problems. I get to do it all. I hope it stays this way. I love the physical stuff and that she's running a ship and waging war."

The one aspect of the production that Visitor, who recently had a baby, finds warying, is the long hours required to shoot the show. "They're long days," she says. "And that's something we're all finding our sea legs with, 16 hour days. I have a six month old baby and I'm just figuring out how to see him and do this. It's not impossible, but you have to be more creative. My husband brings him at lunch sometimes and I feed him Gerber and then it's kind of interesting to go and yell at Sisko and then come back and say 'Come on, it's apricots and tapioca'."

For Visitor, *Deep Space* is a region of the universe she hopes to be exploring for a long time. "*Star Trek* has got so much strength and age behind it and it's cutting edge television," she notes. "We're doing things I've never done or seen on television, and there's this kind of care and the kind of scripts I've never seen. Once in a while I'll have someone I haven't heard from in a year say 'Wow, I hear you're on *Deep Space Nine*, I'm such a Trekkie,' and then I'll say, 'Gee, this is new and different.' I feel that in those very faraway moments on the telephone but in the day to day it doesn't mean a thing except they have the power to allow us to do what we do and they give us wonderful material to do it with."

The Pilot

"EMISSARY"
Original Airdate: Week of 1/4/93
Teleplay by Michael Piller
Story by Rick Berman and Michael Piller
Directed by David Carson

Star Trek: Deep Space Nine premiered the week of January 4th with its two-hour season opener, "Emissary." Like *Next Generation*'s "Farpoint" pilot, the segment had the added responsibility of introducing viewers to an entirely new ensemble of actors and characters.

In the episode, Commander Benjamin Sisko (Avery Brooks) is placed in command of the Deep Space Nine space station, in orbit of the planet Bajor. DS9, as it's more commonly referred to, has recently been vacated by the Cardassians' occupying forces. Upon his arrival, Sisko's new command team is only first being assembled when he learns that the mystical prophet of Bajor, Kai Opaka, has the last in a series of mysterious orbs, all believed to have been confiscated by the Cardassians.

Investigating the mysterious power of the orb, Sisko is plunged into the first known stable wormhole, wherein lies the alien prophets who fear humanity and cannot understand the nature of linear existence. While Sisko professes the basic goodness of humanity, Kira Nerys and the rest of DS9 are placed in a battle situation with a Cardassian warship.

"I thought it was an interesting parallel," says "Emissary" director David Carson. "Inevitably you have people who want to see more action than philosophy going on. But it seems to me that the first two-hour story is about a man (Sisko) coming to grips with a loss, a terrible loss in his life. That's the main story and it's set against the Federation taking over a space station outside Bajor and then the Cardassians. The two stories are joined by the spiritual elements of the Orbs, where they actually lead Sisko to discover himself. In fact, I think that the two stories join together. In a way it's good that it isn't a linear development. In many of the great stories of the world, like for example *War and Peace*, you have two entirely different chunks going along at different paces. I rather enjoyed the fact that you were in one

area where Sisko is desperately telling these people that he's dealing with something that was violent to himself but was also telling them that we are not a threat to you; we as a linear people value life more than anything else. Then in the other storyline you've got people beating the shit out of each other, which completed negated what he was saying. It's true. We have an idea of ourselves as humans that we value life more than anything else but we don't practice it. So that was the idea of that parallel imagery going on in that story."

"When you create a premise pilot, which is what we did, you create a two hour show where you have to set up an entire world and an entire group of characters and what brings them together and at the same time tell an entertaining and meaningful story," says Rick Berman. "You have a big job cut out for you. Mike and I started creating the premise for this show, the backstories for the characters and the relationships these characters were going to have, and what sort of story would unfold. What 'Farpoint' and five and a half years of *Star Trek* did was allow me to know what was possible and what wasn't. What our visual effects guys could give us and what they couldn't. What sets we could expect and how much we could expect to get done, and what was pie in the sky."

Michael Piller, who looked at the *Next Generation* pilot written by Gene Roddenberry and D.C. Fontana before writing "Emissary", found it helpful in breaking his own story. "There's a great deal about this structure that's similar to 'Encounter At Farpoint'," says Piller. "One of the tricks I learned from watching 'Farpoint' again was that they didn't introduce Riker and Geordi and Beverly until two or three acts in. I said to Rick [Berman] when we were structuring this, let's hold off the arrival of two of our regulars late enough that I can do something with the other characters. My first suggestion was everyone was there and they're working and it wasn't as effective."

Ironically, one of "Encounter At Farpoint's" strongest plot elements, the arrival of the menacing Q, was added by Roddenberry to pad out D.C. Fontana's

• • • •

263

script when he relented to studio demands that the opener clock in at two hours as opposed to the 90 minute premiere he lobbied for.

"I think the Q thing did come out of a time requirement, but there isn't any question in my mind that the best thing in that show is the Q story," says Piller. "If it had been only that other story it would have been a disappointment. The other thing that comes out of 'Farpoint' is a vision of Roddenberry's where we have Picard arguing for the future of mankind representing the advocate of humanity to this Q who puts humanity on trial. That's an extraordinarily philosophically ambitious idea and it really helps to define why *Star Trek* is what it is. Without that it would have been spaceships and monsters and special effects."

Incorporating a strong philosophical point of view into *Deep Space Nine* was of essential importance to Piller.

"Rick said the first day we sat down to meet about this that somehow this story must have the philosophical ambition that the 'Encounter at Farpoint' script had and that *Star Trek* represents," recalls Piller. "Ultimately, what we created was this interaction and confrontation between alien and human that is not so different from 'Encounter at Farpoint', but, of course, on a weekly basis we are exploring issues and philosophies through encounters with aliens. What we have in the pilot is aliens who have no knowledge of a linear existence and what does that mean for Sisko, who is trying to deal with the context of his own personal crisis as it comes out through this philosophical explanation of here's why you don't need to fear me. We are not a threat to you. We're different and differences can be good', he says, echoing the same theme that humanity has overcome and we can co-exist in the universe."

In terms of making the pilot more spiritual than one would have expected, David Carson says that it was among the creators' numerous ambitions. "I think there was a deliberate attempt," he says, "to make those differences and to let emotions and mysticism and spirituality and those sorts of words which are never normally attached to *Star Trek*, and probably people would deny they're

there, but they are definitely within this show. There was an effort made to let them blossom whereas under normal circumstances in *The Next Generation* they would not have been allowed to see the light of day. From that level down to basic things like O'Brien kicking the transporter panel. You don't see *that* in *Next Generation*."

The pilot's theme of co-existence was amplified by Piller in his second draft when the Los Angeles riots magnified the problem of the divisiveness that existed in our contemporary society, providing a new impetus for revising a teleplay he felt was too dull.

"What happened was I had written the first draft of the script which we had not sent to the studio yet. Rick read it and a lot of people liked it," says Piller. "But something was really bothering me and I couldn't figure out what the devil it was. What it turned out to be was the first hour wasn't good enough. Through the introduction to Sisko we saw things on the station. and it scared the hell out of me. When I looked at the second hour of 'Unification,' because I'll always consider that a character study of Spock, I realized it was talking and nothing goes on. It was fascinating talk but nothing was happening and I was very unhappy with that. When I looked at this, I was really troubled because I was not falling in love with my own dialogue and my own characters and I was extremely critical. Rick will tell you that throughout this process he has said to me things like it must be terrible waking up every morning and being as negative as you are, but I felt very strongly—and Rick will agree that I dragged him into this rewrite kicking and screaming—that the first hour was flat and that nothing happened and that it was basically dealing out the characters for everyone to see."

Ultimately, what Piller realized was that the characters existed without purpose in his original draft and by the riots providing a metaphorical iconography for the rewrite, Piller was able to inject new life into the stalled script.

"I said, 'Sisko's not a hero,'" Piller recalls. "Sisko's got to come in and have something to do and have a problem that he has to deal with as a hero. While our mystery is unfolding, which

will ultimately blossom in the second hour, Sisko must take this by the hand. In the first draft of the script our guys essentially come to the Beverly Center [a Los Angeles mall] and he decides to stay. I said that's great and the studio said we want to open with a shot of the Promenade and people gambling. So I wrote it that way and I realized it didn't work. Sadly, though, while I was going through this agonizing process, we had the riots in Los Angeles and both of us— Rick was the first to verbalize it—wanted to somehow say that there is something to be said in our show about humanity co-existing and coming together. We wanted to build this into the alien interaction that we have in the second hour of the script."

Quickly thereafter, the hi-tech DS9 station had been transformed by Piller's pen into a ruined and cannibalized wreck. In Piller's rewrite of the teleplay which is clearly influenced by the devastation he was witnessing on TV news reports about Los Angeles, his opening description of the station's Promenade reads, "Our first look at this extraordinary setting is a shock. The striking Cardassian/Bajoran architecture is mysterious and impressive...and we can see how exciting a locale this could once have been. But now it's almost deserted...and it has been ravaged by vandals...storefronts have been broken out...trash and broken stock from the stores litter the thoroughfare...phaser blasts have burned scars on the walls..."

"I had started thinking that it was not a dramatic situation for a man to come to the Beverly Center," says Piller. "It's not very dramatic for someone to go to their favorite mall and decide to stay, but for a man who decides to go to South Central Los Angeles in ruins and stays, *that's* dramatic. In order to bring drama to the first hour I argued with Rick that we should come to a space station that's in ruins and that Sisko must begin the rebuilding process in the first hour in order to be driving the story."

Interestingly, what developed out of Piller's new approach to the material was the relationship between Quark and Odo that many of the writers subsequently have glommed onto as the best character dynamic since the bickering between McCoy and Spock in the original *Star Trek*. "We had always had a shape shifting gag for Odo in the end of Act I and we had always had a Ferengi boy, Nog, that would become a friend of Sisko's son," says Piller. "In the rewrite, using all the elements that we had that were waiting to be thrown in, I put Nog at the scene of the crime and put him in trouble. I realized that when Sisko arrives at the scene where Odo is shape shifting and they meet at the end of Act I, there is this situation where the Ferengi kid is going to jail for being an accomplice to a crime that has been committed. Sisko, who has come to this ruined Promenade, sees the Ferengi guys packing up their gear who used to run the bar and the gambling facilities ready to leave, and decides he's going to use this to his advantage."

Sisko, threatens to incarcerate Quark, the Ferengi barkeep, unless he stays aboard the station and helps in the re-building process as a "community leader". Despite being repulsed by the idea, Quark is reluctantly forced to stay at Sisko's urging. "In that scene where Odo is watching Sisko in action and Sisko is doing this number on Quark, I suddenly found myself writing these asides between Odo and Quark," says Piller. "Quark is saying, 'What do you want me to stay for?' and Odo says 'I'm a little mystified myself commander, the man is a gambler and a thief' and Quark comes back and says 'I am not a thief' and Odo says 'Yes, you are. You're a thief.' Suddenly, these guys are going at each other and I realized there's a magic there. There is a relationship there. These two guys have been arch-enemies that have been at each other's throats for the last several years — and they love it. They get off on this trying to one-up each other and there's a love that comes within for one another between the good guy and the bad guy that we really explore in the first episode. That's the discovery of character and interaction Rick and I wanted so much to have. It's a conflict that's fun and restores to *Star Trek* something that hasn't really been in evidence since the original show."

One scene that came easier for the writer is the show's sensational opening teaser which offers a glimpse into *Star Trek* history by depicting the Borg battle at Wolf 239, whose aftermath is only glimpsed in "Best of Both Worlds, Part II". "It's a great backstory for our hero and it's a piece of action that our audience has heard about on the sound monitors and never seen," says Piller. "It was, of course for me, who wrote the original Borg two-parter, a great opportunity. To go back and do some more was just too irresistible. You want to desperately open your show with a bang and what could be a better way to open the show than to have Jean-Luc Picard as Locutus on screen saying, 'You will surrender, resistance is futile.'"

States David Carson, "I think we made tremendous efforts in the two-hour movie to put a lot of production value on the screen to make it seem not like a TV movie, but a really big, thunderous movie that you would sit in the movie house and see. And to give it a feeling of scale and complexity in the way that we shot it and the way that I directed the actors. It gives the audience the feeling that they're not just watching some other TV sequel, but that they're watching a movie. It's my feeling that TV needs to try and harness a lot more of the qualities of movies because they're up against so many on cable TV and everywhere else. That's what we strove to do during that time.

"It was intended to have as large a scale as we could in the beginning so that you were propelled into the film with a lot of interest and a lot of information to assimilate and absorb, and let it unravel from there. We were also conscious that since the opening is such a terrific whiz-bang affair and because the show is quite complex, we didn't want to hurtle all the acting and dialogue along at the usual television speed, which is sort of like 90 miles per hour, but to give it some consideration and let the characters develop and expand. And allow the thing to have a little more cinematic time rather than wall-to-wall dialogue. In fact, when we finished shooting it we discovered that the whole thing was twenty minutes too long and we had to take twenty minutes out of it."

Although Michael Piller's teleplay was completed weeks before production began, shooting the pilot was also an incredibly arduous affair compli-cated by delays in casting and set construction which made it an even more difficult shoot than "Farpoint" six years earlier. "I had the same anxieties and hesitations about even wanting to do it because I knew what a struggle it was going to be and the pilot was hard," says producer David Livingston, a veteran of the *Next Generation*. "Fortunately I didn't have to deal with the day to day minutia of a production manager and I could sort of sit back a little bit. Bob DellaSantina is the wonderful production manager I hired to do this job and he just took care of everything for me. It was tough and I told everyone it was going to be tough. It wasn't like doing another episode or a double episode. It's doing a whole new thing again, plus it was a pilot. We had all forgotten what that was like. We've had the Life of Riley here for five years and it's all going to change. It was very difficult because there are so many dynamics working; building all these new sets and a whole new cast and new wardrobe. Michael Westmore had to create a bunch of new make-ups, including Odo's, which was very difficult. All of those dynamics made it very, very tough."

Although most of the cast was lined up before production began, late casting of the roles of Sisko and Dax, one week into shooting on the pilot, made it an extremely difficult shoot for the department heads.

"They cast early, but we couldn't get them until one week before the show started shooting," says costume director Bob Blackman. "The principals arrived pretty much at the same time, but for an episode where there was a lot for them to do and a lot of multiples costumes, it was difficult. Sisko had six or seven outfits to wear in the pilot. As we get a board with a shooting schedule saying the first week you'll be shooting this and the second you'll be shooting this and the third and so on, that's how we build, in that kind of order since everything is made to order. We had a lot of the background costumes started, but the shooting schedule started changing when they didn't have Dax cast and the more they would pull stuff up from the fifth week of shooting and stick it into the first week, the more you're com-

• • • •

265

pletely unprepared. It was amazing, but we pulled it off."

For David Carson, one of the most appealing aspects of "Emissary" and, indeed, *Star Trek* itself, is the use of the various scripts as allegories.

"I think if you can draw parallels to things, it's absolutely wonderful," he opines, "because people make the inferences for themselves without you hitting them over the head. I think that so often people turn off their TVs because everything is being preached to them. But, again, if you give audiences an allegory or parable and let them draw their own inferences, if they want to see Bosnia in it, then good for them because it's done its work for them on that level. If they don't, then equally good for them because it does its work on another level. I think if you can entertain first but include all sorts of different messages to people in different ways, that's wonderful. To many people it ['Emissary'] must have meant a great deal on its base, emotional level about grief and leaving grief behind. How you deal with that sort of thing. The number of people who watched it who have been in that situation—most of us have lost a loved one—and to watch it spelled out in that way, gives you a chance to relate to it in a way you can't if you're listening to a psychiatrist or some guy on a chat show telling you what you really ought to be doing or feeling. You're able to step back and observe it. It's like having a song sung to you or a poem read to you, where you

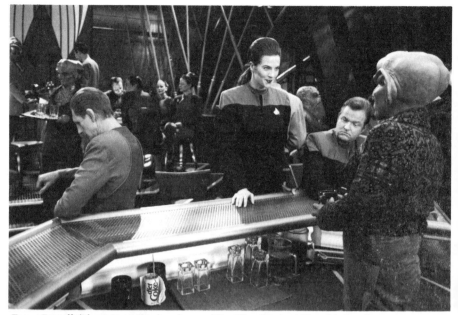

Terry Farrell (Lieutenant Dax) enjoys a bit of laughter at Quark's bar between set-ups. (Photo copyright © Jeff Jacobson)

can relate to the imagery with whatever perceptions you as a viewer bring to it, which is the same as looking at a painting. I don't mean to be pompous about it, but I think it has a lot of interesting elements inside it which is what makes it good and a cut beyond much of what is seen on TV."

••••

CHAPTER TWENTYSEVEN
Conclusion

It's hard to believe that *Star Trek* has been with us now for over a quarter century. More than that, *Trek* continues to thrive.

Star Trek: The Next Generation's sixth year was arguably its best ever. Beginning with several lackluster episodes—including "Realm of Fear" in which Barclay is trapped with monsters in the transporter beam; "Rascals", which turned Picard, Guinan, Keiko and Ensign Ro into children; and "Schisms" where invaders from subspace begin abducting the crew of the Enterprise—the season improved considerably soon afterwards. The producers seemed intent on carrying through with a mandate to return to science-fiction plots after being evicerated by fans for having relied too heavily on soap opera-type contrivances in the previous year. Unfortunately, the hokey sci-fi of year six didn't resonate as well as the science-fiction stories which worked fifth season such as "Violations".

However, by mid-year, *Star Trek* had hit its stride, producing some of the best *Next Generation* installments produced. For instance, Ron Moore brought Scotty back to the Enterprise in grand style in "Relics", which featured a holodeck recreation of the original Enterprise bridge. Yet the true turning point in the season was the "Chain of Command" two parter, which introduced *Robocop*'s Ronny Cox as a disagreeable Starfleet captain. For those who wanted to see conflict on the show, they got it in spades in this exciting, action-packed two-parter, which included a harrowing interrogation of Captain Picard by David Warner as a malevolent Cardassian. The film's torture scenes were terrifingly accurate, thanks to the input of Amnesty International.

Other terrific voyages included "Face of the Enemy" in which Troi is transformed into a Romulan on an espionage mission; and "Tapestry", one of *Star Trek*'s finest hours, in which Picard dies and Q proves to the stoic captain that it truly has been "a wonderful life". Breaking with tradition, yet again, *Next Generation* embarked on another mid-season two parter, "Birthright" in which the Enterprise visits Deep Space Nine.

Meanwhile, *that* fledgling series featuring the station on the fringes of the galaxy, was faring less well. Although *Deep Space Nine* boasted stellar ratings and a handful of standout episodes, including "Captive Pursuit" and "Q-less", fans quickly seemed to be growing disenchanted with its derivitive plots often wrapped up with a less than healthy dose of technobabble. By mid-season, *Next Generation* was back ontop of the ratings charts while *Deep Space*'s orbit had started to decay. However, it would be wise to remember, that *Next Generation*'s first season was lackluster as well, and with the exciting ensemble of characters that have been assembled and the talented creative team behind the *DS9* voyages, the future still looks bright.

Meanwhile, the original cast has apparently finally been put out to pasture with reports indicating that Rick Berman will captain a *Star Trek: The Next Generation* movie in 1994 when the series sails to the silver screen, leaving *Deep Space Nine* to continue to soar on the small one. The *Trek* principals, however, are not content to accept retirement, with

William Shatner taking the helm of a new sci-fi franchise, *Tek-War*, for Universal, based on his series of books. Meanwhile, Walter Koenig is developing several comic book and literary properties, and George Takei will be starring in an upcoming low-budget martial arts film. It wouldn't suprise anyone to see Leonard Nimoy, who is friendly with Berman, play an integral part in the *Next Generation* movies both behind-the-camera and, perhaps, in front of it as well.

One thing is clear, the Enterprise is continuing to go where it has never gone before. Now more than ever, *Star Trek Lives*. Sometime in the 24th Century, Captain Picard and Commander Benjamin Sisko are continuing to write the captain's logs for all the new treks that lay ahead.

In the immortal words of Captain Jean-Luc Picard (or as Q would have it, John Luck Pickard), "Make it so!"

••••

••••

APPENDIX
Lost Episodes of The Next Generation

"FERENGI GOLD"
Written by Gene Roddenberry

Gene Roddenberry began what was his last effort for *Star Trek* with a bit of background, explaining that the intent of "Ferengi Gold" was to comment on the fact that the Enterprise has risen above 20th century greed. "*Star Trek*'s people value personal challenge and satisfaction above materiality," he said, "and our story comments on the difference between them and the super-capitalistic little Ferengi aliens. Plus, we also hope to tap the 'Wheel of Fortune' fascination of our television audience, i.e. its affection for prizes and displays of valuables....Last but not least, this is also about *sex*. Our story is about sex *and* gold."

As though this were something new to *Star Trek*, the bridge crew of the Enterprise is abuzz with the rumor that this particular star cluster they're in contains a world that has developed on a parallel course to earth. The vessel approaches Lerta-117. Dr. Kate Pulaski (this story was obviously written for season two) comes to the bridge, establishing herself as something of a historian who has never seen a parallel world before. According to Data, a populated area on Lerta bears many similarities to Boston in the 1770's. Picard wishes that it mirrored France at that time, for it would have been earth's first experience with political freedom. Pulaski counters that North America was first and considerably more interesting. Data quells the debate by noting that so-called parallel worlds are only similar to each other rather than identical.

Enterprise draws closer, and more accurate readings reveal that the culture mirrors North America in the 18th century. Riker wants to lead an Away Team but Picard is reluctant to possibly interfere. Worf abruptly announces that a Ferengi cargo ship is locked in a lower orbit and has not yet detected Enterprise. Picard has the starship put in a parking orbit on the opposite side so that the planet will lie between the two ships.

Due to the presence of the Ferengi, Picard authorizes Riker to take an Away Team down to the surface. Riker, Troi and Geordi (wouldn't his visor draw unwanted attention?) beam down in the appropriate clothing. They're able to blend in, though two things come to mind as they observe this world: "The female members of this planet are unusually lovely—tall, fair-skinned beauties." Also, the people wear a great amount of gold jewelry. At least now they can understand why the Ferengi are so interested in this world.

To question the natives, Riker has a tricorder beamed down. Pretending to be a stage actor and magician, he "does an excellent job of double-talking about 'lights and shadow and images,'" but ultimately it turns out that the locals don't recognize either the Ferengi or their cargo vessel. It's suggested that Riker perform his magic for their spiritual leader, the Reverend Mathis Fergreson. The Away Team is led to a *motorbus* (highlighting one of the differences between this world and earth of this era), which takes them away.

They arrive at the Commons Church and meet Reverend Fergreson. Roddenberry noted, "Religion here is similar with differences from Christian religon...As for Fergreson, think of Jerry Falwell but in a situation of far more power and respect than Falwell is permitted." Riker shows him the tricorder images and Fegreson responds that "it's the Angels of Beotane (God)," and these people must be holy ones to hold such images. The Reverend had been told by the "angels" not to mention them except to the most trusted leaders. These angels, he adds, are far to the west.

Noting the Reverend's gold bracelet, Riker asks if the angels are interested in the substance. "Of course," is the response. "It is Holy metal, beloved of Beotane and His Angels. From it they receive their strength and purity."

Picard has the Away Team beamed back aboard. In the transporter room, he explains that sensors indicate gold is about as abundant here as it was on earth, but it is found in rich vein concentrates, making it quite simple to mine. It is the captain's determination that the Ferengi, their greed be damned, not interfere with the evolution of this world. This parallel society could potentially be important for Federation scholars, but contamination must be minimized. The best move would probably be to send the Away Team to the location of Ferengi transporter activity. Riker starts to assemble his people when Picard (in a silly, childish and out of character moment) "bribes" Pulaski into agreeing with him that Riker is fatigued and, due to regulations, must stay aboard. Riker objects but is effectively overrruled. Ultimately Picard, Pulaski, Troi and Data beam down.

They appear in the vicinity of a mining location and immediately notice several "tattered" natives who exhausitvely work the mine. On one of the native's wrists is an odd-looking bracelet. One Ferengi with an electronic whip weapon (as seen in "The Last Outpost") watches over them. Lots of gold is in evidence. At that moment, the Away Team is ambushed and rendered unconscious.

In the mine it becomes apparent that the natives being brought in are females, and the Ferengi are delighted that they captured two more (Pulaski and Troi). According to the treatment, "They bring Troi and Pulaski back to consciousness first—followed by not a little lascivious pinching and prodding, expressions of delight at their firm bodies. What we're seeing is a side of the Ferengi only hinted at previously....Like Earth's 'robber barons' of long ago, the Ferengi relate to females as *objects*, mindless possessions, and treat them accordingly....Gold is only part of their interest on this simple little world. To these big-eared little aliens, females are something to be controlled by waving shiny baubles under their noses or by easily deceiving them with promises. Sexual equality is considered ridiculous."

When they awaken, Picard and Data are wearing the bracelets they noticed earlier, which are actually agony devices activated whenever the Ferengi are displeased with them (shades of "Gamesters of Tiskellion"). We alternate

••••

between threats to the Away Team and an ongoing discussion of how horny the Ferengis are and how this planet represents a true paradise to them beyond just gold.

At first Pulaski and Troi and totally uncooperative with their Ferengi "hosts," but change their attitude when they are told they will be beamed aboard the cargo vessel for distribution at the ship's next stop. Meanwhile, Picard and Data are forced to stack gold ingots but their identity is revealed when Picard's hidden communicator falls to the ground. Realizing that it's up to them, "Troi and Pulaski come on to the Ferengi with every trick they've learned in their space travels....[They] know how to be super-seductive." Their intent is to delay the Ferengi from killing Picard and Data while silmutaneously convincing the Ferengi to drop their guard, which gives the duo the opportunity to gain the upper hand. Troi and Pulaski free Picard and Data and the four of them beam back to the Enterprise.

Picard is described as being angrier than we've ever seen him because of the Ferengi plan to utilize the world below them as a forced labor slave-camp as well as their treatement of the native women. Picard considers it the equivalent of rape. He develops a plan which will cause the Ferengi to have to abandon their hope of kidnapping native women because, if all works out, "they won't have the room." He then gives the order for Enterprise to be revealed to the

cargo ship. Phasers and photon torpe-does are armed. "Surprised by the unex-pected appearance of a Federation heavy cruiser, shocked by its menacing readi-ness, the Ferengi captain is only to happy to accept Picard's invitation to beam aboard for a meeting."

During that meeting, Picard notes that the Ferengi have as much right to be here as the Federation, but since this world holds such a historical interest to the Federation, the hope is that it would be allowed to evolve naturally. To this end, he claims, the Federation will purchase any rights that the Ferengi may have. As a result, Picard has ton after ton of gold patterned from energy by the Enterprise transporters beamed over to the cargo ship. The vessel departs with every available inch loaded with the gold. On the planet there is confirmation that the prisoners have been released.

"For those who may not under-stand the mechanics of a 'robber baron' society," Roddenberry noted, "Picard

points out that what they've done is to seriously disrupt the Ferengi economy. The value of gold to them was based on its scarcity." Even if this bullion doesn't flood the market, it will probably cause the government to ban visits to planets whee gold can be found so readily. Data comments on the more positive aspects of gold, and Picard responds that if the Ferengi can learn from this treasure to appreciate the artistic loveliness of gold, "this might accomplish more than even wrecking their economy."

STAR TREK *THE NEXT GENERATION* TECHNICAL MANUAL
Written by Rick Sternbach and Michael Okuda, the
technical advisors to STAR TREK: THE NEXT GENERATION.
Full of diagrams, technical schematics and ship's plans: the
one book that examines the full spectrum of technology
behind the STAR TREK: THE NEXT GENERATION universe.

ISBN: 1 85283 340 8   £12.99

814 0   834 5   824 8   829 9

The STAR WRECK Adventures
A PARODY. Positively unauthorised, unendorsed, unofficial and unintelligent.
The most out-of-this-world spoofs ever of the immortal TV series. Boldly go
where nobody ever wanted to go before!

ISBN: 1 85283 814 0 / 824 8 / 829 9 / 834 5   £2.99

And coming soon . . .

EXPLORING DEEP SPACE AND BEYOND
The first comprehensive unofficial guide to the sf genre of
deep space settlement. Includes an in-depth analysis of
Paramount's hit TV show – **Deep Space 9,** CBS's **Space
Rangers,** and Pen Densham's **Babylon 5.**

ISBN: 1 85283 571 0   £6.99